DISCARD

EYEWITNESS HISTORY

The American Revolution
Updated Edition

David F. Burg

☑️Facts On File
An imprint of Infobase Publishing

*In memory of Richard William Burg
and Rollin Henry Rendlesham*

The American Revolution, Updated Edition

Copyright © 2007, 2001 by David F. Burg
Maps on pages 427–439, copyright © 2007, 2001 by Infobase Publishing

Facts On File, Inc.
An imprint of Infobase Publishing
132 West 31st Street
New York NY 10001

Library of Congress Cataloging-in-Publication Data
Burg, David F.
    The American Revolution / David F. Burg—Updated ed.
        p. cm.—(Eyewitness history)
    Includes bibliographical references and index.
    ISBN-10: 0-8160-6482-2 ISBN-13: 978-0-8160-6482-3 (alk. paper)
    1. United States—History—Revolution, 1775–1783—Personal narratives. 2. United States—History—Revolution, 1775–1783—Sources. I. Title.
E275.A2B87 2007
973.3—dc22   2006033096

Text design by Joan M. McEvoy
Cover design by Cathy Rincon
Maps by Sholto Ainslie

Printed in the United States of America

VB JM 10 9 8 7 6 5 4 3 2 1

This book is printed on acid-free paper.

CONTENTS

ACKNOWLEDGMENTS

The plethora of materials available on the era of the American Revolution forces a certain happy dependence on the work of many others in preparing a book such as this one, and so I would like to offer a broad thanks to the historians of the era. I wish to thank the University of Kentucky Libraries and also the J. Douglas Gay, Jr., Library at Transylvania University for the use of their collections and facilities. My special thanks to Robert W. Kenny, Jr., military researcher, and Peter Harrington, curator of the Anne S. K. Brown Military Collection at Brown University Library, for their kind help in providing photographs and illustrations. For their assistance with photographs, I also thank the staffs of the Library of Congress and the National Archives and Records Administration and Martha King of the National Gallery of Canada. And I thank as well Gary Berton, president of the Thomas Paine National Historical Association Museum, for permission to quote from Paine's works. Finally, once more, I thank my wife, Helen Rendlesham Burg, for her patience and support and her friendly ear.

PREFACE

As we know to our discomfort, we live in a time when ignorance of the past is widespread in the United States. Recent studies indicate that even graduates of top-tier colleges and universities cannot accurately answer even the most rudimentary questions about American history, let alone the history of Europe or other continents. In fairness, perhaps it has always been the case that Americans by preference tend to focus most intently on the present and the future and that the Internet and other recent technologies, augmented by extensive television viewing, have merely increased this tendency and promoted the view that the past is irrelevant. Perhaps even, without acknowledging it, we accept the validity of Henry Ford's judgment: "History is bunk." And perhaps much of history—or, rather, much of historiography, at least—is bunk. If it seems so, then the fault probably lies largely with historians for presenting the past as indigestible food—narrowly conceived, pedantically presented, tiresomely written, insufficiently seasoned.

The Eyewitness History series, I like to think, provides one of the better antidotes to this mistaken view of history and our ignoring of the past. Admittedly, a book in this series lacks the visual and aural impact of television and film, but it can certainly offer plenty of plot, personal experience, compelling characters, and engaging action. The book's large canvas—constructed of narrative, chronicle, quotation, and biography—appeals to the eye, the mind, and the imagination. The viewer can enter the canvas at whatever point seems most attractive and can reenter repeatedly, finding something new on each visit. Through this process, or so we hope, the viewer will be inspired to go beyond the canvas, desiring to learn more about some event, person, or statement and therefore seeking out added information with the help of the book's bibliography.

The reader should of course keep in mind that this book affords only an overview of the American Revolution. To experience the full story, you must search out other books. The most exhaustive study I am familiar with on the subject is Mark Mayo Boatner III's *Encyclopedia of the American Revolution*—a 1,251-page tome that is indispensable to the historian but likely forbidding to the student or general reader. Perhaps the most inclusive narrative history is Page Smith's very engaging *A New Age Now Begins: A People's History of the American Revolution,* published for the 1976 bicentennial, although its two volumes totaling 1,838 pages (not including the index) may exceed many readers' interest in the subject. Even Robert Middlekauff's outstanding and highly readable *The Glorious Cause: The American Revolution, 1763–1789* comprises 687 pages, but it serves the reader well. These three works should at least suggest to the inquiring reader that solid individual histories and ample material exist to reward any search. And with the experience of reading this Eyewitness History as a starting point, you can pursue these other sources knowledgeably.

Many teachers, myself included, like to believe that students should regard knowledge as its own reward. Certainly the acquisition of knowledge through books should provide an enduring reward that can be recalled with pleasure, satisfaction, and insight in future years. For that to occur, however, the reader must bring to the reading an attitude of engagement, interaction, imagination, and inquiry. As that great sage Ralph Waldo Emerson declared in "The American Scholar," "One must be an inventor to read well." Books are meant to inspire, he said, when well used, but using them well requires "creative reading." To learn from books, then, is to invent, to create, and to grow. Creative reading is an active sport that strength-trains the mind. The trophy for creatively reading history is increased understanding of the past as a continuing event that creates the context for your own life today. You cannot hope to understand the influences that created that context that created you and that frame the events of your contemporary world without some solid understanding of past events. You cannot truly know who you are, and hence you cannot grow, without a knowledge of history. Cicero, the renowned Roman orator, philosopher, and defender of the Republic, stated this truth well: "Not to know what has been transacted in former times is to be always a child." Read history, then, or risk stunting your growth.

PREFACE TO THE UPDATED EDITION

This enhanced and updated edition features much new material. All of the narrative sections have been expanded, with inclusion of extended discussion of the arts and new entries concerning the roles of American Indians, blacks, Jews, and women in the Revolution. More than two-dozen pages of extracts from personal journals kept by junior officers, soldiers, and noncombatants have been added to the Eyewitness Testimony sections of every chapter. The biographical section includes a dozen additional entries. Fifteen new illustrations appear throughout the work. More than 40 new titles may be found in the bibliography.

The first chapter on the years 1756–74 contains additional information on the population of the colonies and on such cultural figures as Phillis Wheatley, John Trumbull, and Charles Wilson Peale, as well as added material on architecture, theater, and music. In chapter 2 (1775) appears an augmented discussion of George Washington's assumption of command as well as added material on both slaves and smallpox. An analysis of the inherent conflict between the American system of slavery and the revolutionaries' quest for liberty casts some new light on the meaning of the Declaration of Independence central to the third chapter's content on the year 1776. Chapter 4 (1777) contains added information on women's contributions to the war effort. A new discussion in chapter 5 (1778) focuses on difficulties in providing supplies for both men and horses and on the role theater played during the terrible winter at Valley Forge, which reveals some insights into both Washington and his soldiers during that crisis. Additional discussion of both the struggles of American Indians and the roles of blacks and women fleshes out the sixth chapter (1779). In chapter 7 (1780), there is additional information on Sir Henry Clinton's expedition to and siege of Charleston and on Benedict Arnold's treason. Chapter 8 (1781) contains an expanded description of the British surrender at Yorktown and a discussion of the roles Robert Morris and Haym Salomon played in Continental finances. The final chapter covering the years 1782–83 provides more information on the experiences of women and blacks as well as a look at the fate of rebel veterans upon their return home from war. This new edition also contains a section of notes and several additional maps.

INTRODUCTION

Even at the time, the advent of the War of the American Revolution in April 1775 may have seemed almost accidental. If the American Patriots had been allowed to disperse peacefully at Lexington Green, as they appeared to be doing, and no blood had been spilled on that grassy site, reconciliation between the colonists and the "mother country" would at least have remained a possibility. But the bloodshed there generated the resistance at Concord Bridge, where outraged minutemen "fired the shot heard round the world," and as the British troops fell back toward Boston, beleaguered by Patriot snipers, news of the slaughter at Lexington spread throughout Massachusetts and to the colonies beyond—time, chance, and death forced the turning of a historic corner. The battles at Breed's Hill and Bunker Hill, where the British eventually won but after suffering unexpected and demoralizing losses, confirmed that the distance could not be retraced nor the hostility retracted. As some already perceived at that moment, unless soundly defeated and subjugated, the American colonies were destined for independence from Great Britain.

Others on both sides of the Atlantic sustained the hope that a reconciliation could still be effected. But if the war already proceeding in North America was not yet in itself irreversible, then the unrelenting policies of King George III and his government, headed by Lord North, sealed the ultimate fate of the conflict. Their adamant insistence, against the entreaties of the Whig opposition, that the Americans must, in effect, bow to the will of Parliament ensured continuing American resistance. Aroused delegates to the Second Continental Congress that convened in Philadelphia a few weeks following Lexington and Concord made two fateful decisions—assuming control of the Patriot army and choosing George Washington as the army's commander in chief. Although driven from the heights around Boston, the new Continental army under Washington effectively surrounded the city, bottling up the British army that had come under the command of Gen. William Howe. The Patriots expanded the war effort by launching a daring but unsuccessful expedition into Canada.

Entering 1776, American artillery captured at Fort Ticonderoga rendered the British occupation of Boston untenable, and Howe withdrew from the city. Washington moved the Continental army to New York City, intent on engaging the British there. The impetus toward independence came to dominate the deliberations of the Continental Congress, and on July 4, 1776, the delegates approved a final draft of the Declaration of Independence, largely the work of Thomas Jefferson. The engagement in New York City that Washington had anticipated occurred in October but proved disastrous for the American cause, and by the end of the year, the British held control of the city and most of New Jersey. Tempted by despair, the Patriots revived their hopes after Washington crossed the Delaware River on Christmas night and achieved a stunning victory at Trenton.

Washington followed up with a victory at Princeton in January 1777 and then pushed the British out of most of New Jersey before sequestering the Continental army in winter quarters at Morristown. Adopting a new strategy, the British government sent an expeditionary force under Gen. John Burgoyne to Quebec with orders to march southward and drive the Patriots from upper New York, to secure Albany, and to help sever the northern and New England colonies from the middle and southern colonies. Howe's army sailed out of New York Harbor to invade the Chesapeake Bay. After inconclusive battles at Germantown and Brandywine, he captured Philadelphia, forcing the Continental Congress to withdraw to York (where the delegates adopted the Articles of Confederation) and then to Lancaster. Although Burgoyne recaptured Ticonderoga and other sites, fortunately for the American cause Horatio Gates's army soundly defeated him at Saratoga and forced the surrender of his army—a victory that decided the French government to officially recognize the United States. With his army exhausted, Washington moved into winter headquarters at Valley Forge.

In February 1778, the French signed treaties of alliance and commerce with the United States, signaling their entry into the war on the American side. Changing tactics again, the British government replaced Howe with Gen. Sir Henry Clinton and determined to focus on the South, where the Loyalists were believed to be in the majority. Concerned over French involvement, the North ministry in London also dispatched the Carlisle Commission to North America to negotiate a reconciliation—a doomed effort, as the Americans insisted on independence. As Clinton evacuated Philadelphia and moved his troops overland toward New York City, Washington led his army, reorganized and retrained with the help of a Prussian general, Baron Friedrich von Steuben, into battle at Monmouth Court House, New Jersey. The battle ended indecisively, but the British force was nearly decimated before retreating to New York City. On the western frontier, George Rogers Clark captured Kaskaskia, Cahokia, and Vincennes from the British. The year ended with the British pushing their southern strategy, as General Augustine Prévost captured Savannah.

As the war in the North stagnated in 1779, the British rampaged in the South, capturing Augusta and other sites in Georgia, attacking Portsmouth and Norfolk in Virginia, and advancing on Charleston in South Carolina. Although an American army under Gen. Benjamin Lincoln laid siege to Savannah, the effort aborted when the assisting French fleet and troops commanded by Adm. Comte Charles d'Estaing sailed off. Clinton did dispatch troops to capture West Point, New York, but Gen. Anthony Wayne's astonishing victory at Stony Point stymied the effort, and Clinton's troops simply returned to hunkering down in New York City. In addition, Washington sent Gen. John Sullivan on a punitive expedition against the Six Nations that left the Iroquois devastated. Certainly the most enthralling story of the year occurred in September, when John Paul Jones's *Bonhomme Richard* engaged the British ship *Serapis* in ferocious battle to win a stunning victory.

The year 1780 opened with a mutiny among Washington's hungry, poorly clothed, and unpaid troops in winter quarters at Morristown, but fighting in the North effectively ceased, except for periodic skirmishes. Although Comte de Rochambeau landed safely with 6,000 French troops at Newport, Rhode Island, Washington's army was too weakened to join the French in a campaign.

Sir Henry Clinton moved south to pursue the strategy devised the previous year, and the British entrapped Gen. Benjamin Lincoln's army at Charleston, forcing Lincoln's surrender. The Loyalist British Legion led by Sir Banastre Tarleton swept to repeated victories over the rebels in the Carolinas and Georgia. The British gained near total control of South Carolina and Georgia, securing their position with a crushing victory at Camden against an army commanded by Horatio Gates, who actually fled the scene of the battle. Further demoralizing the Patriots, news of Benedict Arnold's treason raced through the states in October. A glimmer of hope arose in the same month, however, when western Patriots defeated Loyalists at King's Mountain, South Carolina, and Washington named Gen. Nathanael Greene to replace Gates as commander in the South.

The final year of actual warfare, 1781, opened as 1780 had, with a mutiny in Washington's army—this time a more serious manifestation among the Pennsylvania troops, which Gen. Anthony Wayne helped to defuse. Developments in the South, however, showed promise. Gen. Daniel Morgan effectively annihilated Tarleton's British Legion at the Battle of Cowpens. And, although repeatedly defeated by Charles, Lord Cornwallis's, army, Gen. Nathanael Greene exacted such heavy casualties against Cornwallis and Francis, Lord Rawdon, especially at Guilford Courthouse and Eutaw Springs, that the British ability to sustain warfare in the South suffered irreparable impairment. Troops sent by Washington under command of the marquis de Lafayette helped to squeeze Cornwallis in Virginia. Finally, learning that a French fleet commanded by Adm. François de Grasse was en route from the West Indies to the Chesapeake Bay, Washington gambled and raced his and Rochambeau's armies to Virginia to trap Cornwallis at Yorktown. Cut off from a sea rescue by de Grasse's fleet and surrounded by besieging American and French troops on land, Cornwallis surrendered on October 19. Cornwallis's defeat effectively ended the War of the Revolution, leaving the final outcome of the conflict to the peace negotiators in Paris.

The Revolutionary War evokes diverse images. Some may think immediately of Emanuel Leutze's immense, fanciful painting *Washington Crossing the Delaware.* To others may come images of George Washington's cold, hungry, barefoot soldiers at Valley Forge. Yet others may call to mind the American triumph at Yorktown that decided the war's outcome, perhaps as depicted in John Trumbull's painting *Surrender of Lord Cornwallis at Yorktown,* with the commanding figure of Washington astride his horse as its central focus. Whatever the image, the likelihood is that George Washington forms part of it. And for good reason.

Washington towers over his compeers as the greatest American of his time. Yes, he had his faults—among them periodic anger, hesitancy, and dejection—but his nobility of character rendered these insignificant. Neither a superior tactician nor general, he never achieved an incisive victory in a full-scale battle with the British, as a few of the officers he commanded did, but he nevertheless finally won the war—an achievement none of his officers could have attained. He achieved final victory through perseverance, resoluteness, determination, dedication, commitment—qualities of character, not learned capabilities. Firmness of character defined the measure of Washington's exceptional stature. In consequence, it is no exaggeration to aver that, without George Washington, the American Revolution would have foundered, and the United States would not have secured its existence as a new nation. Images of events shift or fade over the centuries; Washington's stature endures.

1

Prelude to Revolt
1756–1774

THE SEVEN YEARS' WAR

As with any momentous historic experience, the American Revolution did not erupt suddenly. Its cumulative causes extended through several major events of the preceding years, especially the Seven Years' War of 1756–63 and its own causes and results. That war, which effectively decided the future of North America, was a global conflict involving Europe, Asia, North America, and the Atlantic Ocean and Mediterranean Sea. But it actually began in the spring of 1754 on the wilderness frontier of the Pennsylvania colony with a skirmish between a large troop of French soldiers and 150 colonial soldiers led by George Washington, a surveyor then 21 years old. The Americans lost.[1]

By May 1756, France and Great Britain officially declared a state of war, acknowledging the hostilities that had existed in North America since that skirmish. In August, King Frederick the Great of Prussia, Great Britain's only ally on the European continent, commenced battle against the coalition of Austrian, French, and Russian forces that opposed him. Receiving only financial support from Britain, Frederick struggled resolutely and ruthlessly to withstand his enemies. Frederick succeeded, partly because of ineptitude among the coalition's generals; partly because the French, fighting both in Europe and overseas, had to divide their forces; and finally because Empress Elizabeth of Russia died in January 1762 and was succeeded by Peter III, who greatly admired Frederick and immediately switched allegiances, placing Russia's forces at Frederick's disposal. Frederick achieved a peace settlement in early 1763.[2]

BRITISH-FRENCH STRUGGLE

In the meantime, Great Britain and France pursued the war in Europe, in the Mediterranean, in India, and in North America. In Europe, Britain early capitulated to France, allowing for French occupation of the Electorate of Hanover, the original homeland of Britain's royal House of Hanover dynasty, represented by the nation's current king, George II. In the Mediterranean, the British also fared badly, with a disastrous loss to the French of the important base Minorca in the

1

Balearic Islands. Misfortune also plagued the British in India. In June 1756, the nawab of Bengal, a French ally, imprisoned 146 Britons in a small room with only two windows, where all but 23 perished of suffocation—the infamous "Black Hole" of Calcutta. The tide began to turn for Great Britain, however, when William Pitt became prime minister in 1757.

Pitt's war ministry (1757–61) committed British resources wholeheartedly to prosecution of the war. The government incurred huge budget deficits, as the ministry funded the war effort through government loans placed through Pitt's business and personal connections with the City, the nation's financial center in London. After repudiating the capitulation of Hanover, Pitt came to Frederick the Great's aid, sending increased funds to the Prussian king and dispatching English troops to Hanover to fight under Prussian command. Pitt also replaced British commanders who had bungled the early war effort. The alarmed French planned a cross-channel invasion of England, a plan that became known to the British government but never achieved fruition. Instead, in 1759, the Royal Navy soundly defeated squadrons of the French fleet stationed in both the Atlantic and the Mediterranean. The British thereafter punished the nawab of Bengal and captured French posts in India and North Africa. And in 1762, British forces took control of the Philippines and Cuba from France's new ally, Spain, while also capturing France's sugar islands in the West Indies.[3]

This portrait of George Washington was painted by Charles Wilson Peale in 1772. *(Courtesy of Anne S. K. Brown Military Collection, Brown Library)*

THE FRENCH AND INDIAN WAR

In North America, the conflict emerged from preoccupation over whether the British or the French would control the Upper Ohio Valley, and it came to be known as the French and Indian War. Here also, the British would reverse their losses—with the support of the British colonists. On this front, the early years of the war had been a disaster for the British as a consequence of the ineptitude of their commanders and superior French forces. Gen. Edward Braddock, who had been placed in command of British troops in Virginia, led 1,400 redcoats and some colonials against Fort Duquesne in June 1755. In the ensuing battle with the French and their Indian allies, Braddock and most of his force lost their lives; only 500 survivors were able to return to Virginia, under the leadership of Col. George Washington, who had served as Braddock's aide-de-camp. Subsequently, Indians allied with and armed by the French staged brutal raids against defenseless British colonial outposts on the frontier.

Elsewhere, the conflict had unfolded similarly. In August 1756, French troops commanded by Gen. Louis-Joseph de Montcalm-Gozon, marquis de Montcalm de Saint-Véran, captured Fort Oswego in north-central New York, destroyed the fort, and returned to Montreal. Montcalm triumphed again in August 1757, taking Fort

William Henry at the southern tip of Lake George in New York, and in July 1758, French troops, again led by Montcalm, successfully defended Ticonderoga at the northern tip of Lake George against British forces. But the course of the war began to turn the same year as Pitt, aware of the great potential significance of North America, committed large naval and land forces to the effort.

Near the end of July 1758, British forces led by Gen. Jeffrey Amherst and Adm. Edward Boscawen defeated the French at Louisbourg, Nova Scotia. In August, British troops commanded by Gen. John Bradstreet captured Fort Frontenac (now Kingston, Ontario), and in November, the British finally succeeded in driving the French from Fort Duquesne, which they renamed Fort Pitt (Pittsburgh) in honor of the prime minister.

The turning point of the war in North America occurred in late July 1759, as Amherst's force captured Fort Ticonderoga to take control of Lake Champlain, while at the same time another British army captured Fort Niagara. The decisive victory followed when troops commanded by Gen. James Wolfe sailed up the St. Lawrence River and prepared an attack against Quebec, which Montcalm had heavily fortified. There, in pitched battle on the Plains of Abraham on September 13, 1759, the British achieved victory, but both Wolfe and Montcalm died from wounds suffered in the fighting. These British victories and a further triumph at

The Battle of the Plains of Abraham decided the outcome of the French and Indian War. (The Death of General Wolfe *by Benjamin West, 1770, courtesy National Gallery of Canada, Ottawa*)

Detroit, which the French surrendered to American Maj. Robert Rogers and his so-called Rogers's Rangers militia in late November 1760, sealed the outcome of the war in North America. New France—all of Canada and the French frontier below the border—now lay effectively in British control.[4]

THE TREATY OF PARIS

The Seven Years' War and its North American counterpart officially concluded in February 1763 with the signing of the Treaty of Paris. Although Pitt's policies had won the war for the British, he had been forced from office in October 1761 by the opposition of King George III, who had inherited the crown a year earlier. Thus Pitt's successors, a government headed by John Stuart, Lord Bute, determined the moderate terms of the peace treaty. By those terms, the British returned control of Guadaloupe and Martinique in the West Indies to the French, along with their former possessions in Africa and India that the British had captured, although the British now had clear ascendancy in India. In accepting the treaty, the French relinquished all claims to North America, except for two islands in the St. Lawrence River. Great Britain thus assumed control of Canada and all the territory within the eastern Mississippi River and Ohio River valleys. In addition, by the treaty's terms, Great Britain returned control of the Philippines and Cuba to Spain, which had belatedly allied with France in 1762; in exchange, Spain ceded the Floridas to Great Britain.

As a result of the Treaty of Paris, North America's future now appeared to rest squarely in the hands of the British government. Great Britain also had effective control of the seas. France and Spain would continue as colonial powers but with diminished aspirations. The subsequent Treaty of Hubertusburg, signed on February 15, 1763, awarded Silesia to Frederick the Great, raising Prussia to great-power status in Europe—and creating a strong future rival to France, Spain, Austria, and Russia on the Continent.[5]

AMERICAN CONSEQUENCES

The outcome of the war seemed entirely positive for the British; yet, its ultimate consequences would cost them control of their American colonies south of Canada. The war and its aftermath substantially changed the relationship between Great Britain and its American colonists. For one thing, the war experience had generated some contempt among British commanders and troops for their American militia allies—a generally undisciplined lot who resisted fighting far from home, welcomed combat only for highly prized and easily achieved objectives, and mostly contented themselves with letting the British army do the fighting and the British government pay for the costs.

Paying the bill—a crushing debt of £140 million for the worldwide struggle—would become a major cause of contention. Initially, however, the colonists ended the war generally devoted and committed to their "mother country" and filled with esteem and affection for their king. Their loyalty to both was unquestioned. Though lacking unity among themselves, the colonies shared a mostly English culture in language, social values, religion, and politics. Yet, tensions would soon arise between them and Great Britain over westward expansion, revenue policies, and governance of the colonies—all to be exacerbated by unimaginative and inept leadership in Parliament, the rigidity of George III and his ministers, and prevalent English condescension toward the colonists.[6]

WESTWARD EXPANSION

One of the first measures destined to create ire was the government's decision in 1763 to station a standing army in the colonies, ostensibly to protect the colonists from marauding Indians but also to consolidate British control in the newly won territories. The government, through the Board of Trade, also tried to restrict westward expansion, especially pressed by the Virginians (prominently George Washington), and to reserve the western lands for the Indians as a means of limiting future hostilities between whites and Indians. But the Indians perceived increasing white encroachment and responded in May 1763 with Pontiac's Rebellion—a series of attacks orchestrated by Chief Pontiac of the Ottawa on frontier settlements in Maryland, Virginia, and Pennsylvania and on military posts west of Fort Pitt.

In October 1763, the British ministry responded with a proclamation banning white occupation in the West between the Appalachians and the Mississippi River and creating three new colonies—Quebec, East Florida, and West Florida. By the end of 1764, countermeasures by the British army and American militias ended Pontiac's Rebellion. The Proclamation of 1763, however, failed to end white movement westward, as did British troops' efforts at enforcement, which simply generated animosity.[7]

THE TAX ISSUE

The major issue leading to revolution, however, centered on efforts of the British government to raise revenues, primarily through taxes, to pay the war debt and to offset expenses of the British military serving in the colonies. In fact, concern over the debt influenced nearly every policy of the British government from 1763 until 1776. Residents of Great Britain largely accepted increased taxes as customary, but the British government had never before imposed direct taxes on the American colonists on the principle that it would be a violation of their rights since the colonists lacked representation in Parliament. In addition, British attempts at collecting customs duties had failed through colonists' crafty evasions, bribing of corrupt officials, and persistent smuggling.

Now, in February 1764, the ministry of George Grenville hit the colonists with the Revenue Act of 1764. Popularly labeled the Sugar Act, it actually reduced the customs tax on imported molasses (used to make rum) from six pence to three pence per gallon. However, the act promised genuine enforcement of the new tax in place of what Americans had been accustomed to: smuggling molasses from the French or Dutch West Indies by bribing customs officials at only one-and-a-half pence per gallon. In addition, the act also imposed tariffs on coffee, wine, iron, and other products and enumerated colonial products, such as lumber, that could now be exported only to Great Britain.

The Sugar Act also provided for new enforcement measures to eliminate smuggling and corruption through proper ship manifests, inspections, and prosecution of violators in vice-admiralty courts rather than colonial courts whose juries took a lenient view of smuggling. This new tax measure thus represented a departure from the previous policy of simply regulating trade within the British Empire and a shift to raising revenue directly from the colonies. In effect, Parliament now assumed, for the first time, the power to levy taxes on the Americans.

Americans reacted swiftly and irately, in part because the colonies were mired in economic depression following the war. Such outspoken opponents as James Otis of Massachusetts, supported by Samuel Adams and the Boston Town Meeting, denounced the Sugar Act as a violation of American colonists' political rights because it imposed a tax without their consent or their representation in Parliament. Most protestors, however, focused on the ecomomic consequences of the act—a tack that merchants throughout the colonies took, emphasizing the act's potentially negative effect on commerce. For the most part, the protesters comprised the economically ascendant and their supporters in the colonial legislatures. But the response represented a portent, as future protests would involve ever-widening segments of the entire public.[8]

THE STAMP ACT CRISIS

In March 1765, Parliament approved a new measure proposed by the Grenville ministry—the Stamp Act. The act required American colonists to purchase an official stamped paper as a tax on nearly every type of document, including legal forms, licenses, newspapers and other printed materials, diplomas, and even playing cards. Although Americans would serve as tax masters (collectors), violators of the act would be tried in admiralty courts rather than by juries of their peers. Grenville anticipated that the act would raise £60,000 per year to defray the costs of defending the colonies. What he failed to anticipate—despite the warnings and remonstrances personally delivered by American agents of several colonial legislatures, including Benjamin Franklin, representing Pennsylvania—was the colonists' reaction.

Because the act affected nearly everyone, protesters represented most of American society, with organized resistance in every colony. Adding to the colonists' disaffection, the provisions of the Quartering Act had taken effect in March, requiring the colonies to house and feed British troops, although not in private homes. Two responses with long-term repercussions emerged from Virginia and Massachusetts. In late May, with the majority of its members already returning to their homes, a rump session of the Virginia House of Burgesses, inspired by Patrick Henry's rhetoric, approved five resolutions—the Virginia Resolves. One of these declared that only the Virginia assembly, not Parliament, had the right to impose taxes on Virginians—a principle that received widespread approval as copies of the resolves circulated throughout the colonies. And, in June, the Massachusetts legislature engaged the tax controversy by issuing an appeal to all the colonies to send representatives to a Stamp Act Congress.

Attacks on property took place in some cities in reaction to the Stamp Act. In August, protesters in Boston, spurred on by the Sons of Liberty, attacked and sacked the homes of the lieutenant governor and the stamp master and hanged the latter in effigy from a tree, later to be named the Liberty Tree. Similar rioting and effigy hangings occurred in Newport, Rhode Island, and in several Connecticut towns. The intimidation inherent in such protests persuaded tax masters in most of the colonies to abandon their appointments and duties.[9]

THE STAMP ACT CONGRESS

The Stamp Act Congress proposed by Massachusetts convened in New York through most of October, with 27 delegates attending. Georgia, North Carolina, and Virginia, whose royal governors had prohibited their legislatures from choosing delegates, had no representation, nor did New Hampshire, which had confirmed its agreement with the congress's decisions in advance. The congress approved petitions and resolutions to be sent to the king and Parliament. In these, the congress recognized the right of king and Parliament to govern the American colonies and to regulate their commerce but asserted that taxes could be imposed on the colonists only with their consent. Although moderate, these resolutions and the congress itself set a precedent for united action among the previously fractious colonies.

Adding to the pressures on the British government, nearly a thousand American merchants signed nonimportation agreements to boycott British goods. As a result, British merchants suffered financial losses, and they began to petition the government to repeal the Stamp Act. Grenville had been set on adamant enforcement of the act, but his ministry was forced out in July 1765, months before the act's provisions were to take effect, so that the door was open to amelioration. Recognizing that the act could not be enforced, and influenced by British merchants' appeals, Charles Watson-Wentworth, Lord Rockingham, the new prime minister who succeeded Grenville, obtained Parliamentary and royal approval to repeal the Stamp Act in March 1766.

News of the repeal reached America in early May. Jubilation and an end to the nonimportation policy followed. But at the very same time Parliament had approved repeal, it had also passed the Declaratory Act, which stated that the colonies were "subordinate" and that Parliament had the right to enact any law it desired "to bind the colonies and people of *America*." Thus the principle of taxation without representation or consent evoked by the Americans remained an issue destined to provoke future conflict.[10]

THE TOWNSHEND ACTS

In June 1767, Chancellor of the Exchequer Charles Townshend proposed to Parliament a series of acts that reignited the conflict. The Rockingham ministry had been eased out of office in July 1766 and was succeeded by a ministry headed by Pitt, but as Pitt was ill, Townshend had assumed leadership of the ministry. The Townshend Acts comprised the chancellor's program for America.

Although rejecting as absurd the Americans' distinctions—propounded by Franklin in London—between direct taxes and indirect taxes, or internal taxes and external taxes (duties on imports), Townshend nevertheless chose to set new duties on American imports of

Bostonians pay the excisemen.
(Courtesy of the National Archives and Records Administration)

such popular British goods as paints, glass, lead, paper, and tea. The receipts were to be used to pay royal officials' salaries. This time, the colonists initially reacted moderately. They simply pushed to restore the nonimportation policy to boycott British goods and encouraged colonial manufacturers to produce the needed items. As a result, by the end of 1769, imports of British products would decline by nearly half.

In addition to the new taxes, Townshend proposed suspending the New York assembly and negating its legislative initiatives for its refusal to comply with the Quartering Act. He also suggested creating a Board of Customs Commissioners to be headquartered in the colonies. (Boston was chosen as the headquarters site.) By the end of June 1767, the new taxes and these additional proposals had all been approved. Townshend also had new vice-admiralty courts set up in Halifax, Boston, Philadelphia, and Charleston to process violators of the new customs taxes. The customs commissioners proved overbearing and their agents rapacious, in effect harassing American merchants (John Hancock of Boston prominent among them), often in hopes of obtaining unfavorable judgments and thus securing their share of forfeitures (one-third the value of each ship and its cargo). The new courts, operating without juries, provided an unsympathetic venue for defendants. Ironically, Townshend would not be among those harvesting the sour fruits of his policies—he died suddenly on September 4, 1767.[11]

MASSACHUSETTS RESPONDS

One widely distributed response to the Townshend Acts appeared in John Dickinson's *Letters from an American Farmer,* in which he argued, among other points, that the Townshend duties violated Americans' constitutional rights as British citizens. Dickinson wrote from Pennsylvania, and his prudently worded views were well received throughout the colonies. His letters were published in England at the behest of Benjamin Franklin.[12]

Characteristically less prudent, Massachusetts radicals plotted a more active opposition. Initially, however, their response took the judicious form of influencing the House of the Massachusetts General Court (legislature) to send a request in January 1768 to the earl of Shelburne, secretary of state for the southern department with the authority to recommend colonial policy, that the Townshend Acts be repealed. Then, in February, James Otis and Samuel Adams persuaded the Massachusetts House to approve a circular letter drafted by Adams, to be sent to each of the other colonial legislatures, advocating that the legislatures "harmonize with each other"—a politic plea for unity and cooperation. The letter also reiterated the colonists' constitutional rights, asserted the impossibility of attaining colonial representation in Parliament, and, although conceding Parliament's supreme legislative authority, pointed out that Parliament nevertheless derived its authority from the British constitution and was therefore subject to constitutional restrictions in passing legislation. In March, the Virginia House of Burgesses reacted strongly to the letter, approving forceful protests to the king and Parliament that insisted on the House of Burgesses' equality with Parliament. In May, it issued a harshly worded circular letter of its own, advocating joint measures by the colonies against any British policy that tended to "enslave them."

Ensuing events in Boston and London hurtled the controversy toward violence. In Boston, the new customs commissioners determined to enforce customs procedures rigidly and to squelch smuggling. After a failed confrontation with John Hancock over his having customs officials forcibly ejected from his brig *Lydia*—the attorney general supported the legality of the ejection—the commissioners decided to make a lesson of Hancock and in June had the British man-of-war *Romney* seize his sloop *Liberty*. A Sons of Liberty mob assembled at the wharf to oppose the seizure but were unsuccessful, so the mob attacked and beat the comptroller and a customs collector supervising confiscation of the *Liberty* and then hunted down and beat other customs officials. The following day, the terrified customs commissioners and their families fled to the *Romney*. Governor Francis Bernard's efforts to manage the situation failed utterly, and within a week the Sons of Liberty controlled Boston. Under orders of his recalcitrant superiors, Bernard demanded that the Massachusetts House rescind the circular letter. When the demand was rejected—by a 92 to 17 vote—he dissolved the legislature.[13]

Meanwhile, in London, outraged by the circular letter despite its moderate wording, the government had decided to send troops to Boston for quartering as a standing army. The ships carrying the troops arrived in Boston at the end of September, and, on October 1, the 14th and 29th Regiments disembarked to establish quarters in the city. Responses to the Boston events evolved slowly in the other colonies, solidifying American opposition to the Townshend Acts and support for the circular letter. And the harshness of the British troops' occupation of Boston—including the affront of rapes, assaults, robberies, and public beatings and executions of attempted army deserters on Boston Common—as a violation of personal liberties would generate a smoldering fire of resentment among the citizens.[14]

THE BOSTON MASSACRE

On the first day of August 1769, Governor Bernard, admitting that the situation in Boston was hopeless, set sail for England, leaving Thomas Hutchinson, the American-born lieutenant governor, in charge. The lieutenant governor soon had a precedent for things to come in the city. Troops had been stationed in New York City since 1766, following the colony's opposition to the Quartering Act, and they had collided continually in riots and brawls with mobs organized by the

British troops fire on a riotous mob, killing or wounding 13 men during the Boston Massacre. *(Boston Massacre, courtesy of Anne S. K. Brown Military Collection, Brown University Library)*

local Sons of Liberty. In mid-January 1770, after some soldiers chopped down the city's liberty pole as a taunt to the Sons of Liberty, an ensuing battle ended with one American dead and many others wounded.

Soon after, in early March, brawls erupted from soldier-citizen confrontations in Boston. On the snowy night of March 5, these confrontations culminated in a fatal riot as a mob menaced Pvt. Hugh White, the sentry on guard at the customs house on King Street. At the nearby main guard station, Capt. Thomas Preston watched anxiously as the mob grew, some armed with clubs and swords, and tempers rose. Preston decided to march to White's assistance with a force of six privates and one corporal. Once aligned with White, they found themselves surrounded by surly rioters who hurled snowballs, ice, and shouts of "Kill them!" Preston ordered his men to load their muskets.

Suddenly, a hurled piece of ice hit one of the privates, causing him to slip and fall to the icy ground; regaining his footing, he fired his musket into the crowd. The other soldiers paused momentarily and then fired their muskets. Eight men in the crowd fell wounded; three others died instantly, among them African-American freeman Crispus Attucks; another succumbed a few hours afterward; and a fifth man died several days later from his wounds. The next day, disorder prevailed as an angry mob of a thousand roamed the streets. Hutchinson had Preston and the other soldiers involved confined to jail, diffusing some of the anger. On the following day, accepting the inevitable, he ordered the 14th and 29th Regiments withdrawn from the city to Castle William in Boston Harbor.

Surprisingly, in the days and weeks that followed the Boston Massacre (as Americans quickly dubbed the shooting), the mood in the city grew calm. Local leaders turned their attention to securing trials of Preston and his men, but for the sake of fairness and in the hope that tempers would further cool, judges postponed the trials until the fall. Preston, defended by John Adams, and the other soldiers were judged innocent, except two who were convicted of manslaughter but released. Although quiet prevailed throughout the colonies in subsequent months, the Boston Massacre provided a focus and underpinning for Americans' continuing anger and propelled them toward the conclusion that further appeals and petitions to the British government for redress of their grievances would prove futile. If so, they must now begin to ask, then what were the alternatives?[15]

A LULL IN THE STORM

Finally giving in to the Americans' protests, Parliament repealed the Townshend Duties in April 1770—all the duties, that is, except the one imposed on tea. American Patriots grumbled and boycotted British tea, but many accepted the duty and consumed legal tea, and the merchants' nonimportation movement quickly dissipated. The new British ministry that had come to power in March 1770, headed by Frederick, Lord North, tended to ignore the colonies, and no serious confrontations or challenges to the British government's authority occurred for nearly three years.[16]

Two events in 1772, however, suggested that the quiet would not endure. British authorities had continued their efforts to suppress smuggling, the routine American way of commerce, and to enhance these efforts, the Royal Navy had dispatched the schooner *Gaspee,* commanded by Lt. William Dudingston, to the waters of Narragansett Bay, where numerous inlets provided an ideal habitat for smuggling to thrive. The *Gaspee* had succeeded in its task for several months, but on June 9, it ran aground while chasing a suspected smuggler. During the night, locals boarded the ship, shot and wounded Dudingston, and burned the ship to the waterline. The local sheriff thereafter arrested Dudingston and freed him only after his admiral paid his fine. A royal commission appointed months later to investigate failed to identify the culprits in this crime, but, quite ominously, its mandate included the power to send suspects to England for trial.

In November 1772, Samuel Adams, disturbed by the prevailing quiet, decided to roil the pot. Agitated by the fact that royal officials were now paid from proceeds of the import duties rather than by legislatures, as was formerly the case (giving the legislatures some control over the officials), Adams asked now Governor Hutchinson to convene the Massachusetts General Court (legislature) to consider this issue. Hutchinson refused. In response, Adams easily persuaded the Town Meeting to create a Committee of Correspondence to propound the colonists' rights and grievances and to exchange communications with the other colonies.[17]

THE TEA ACT CRISIS

The popular commodity tea now inspired the confrontation that eventuated in open rebellion. During the entire colonial period, the British East India Company enjoyed a monopoly on all trade between India and the rest of the British Empire. The company had thereby reaped enormous profits for many years, but military expenses and the cumulative effects of corruption and inefficiency had recently jeopardized its finances. At that point, the company had 17 million pounds of tea stored in English warehouses as a result of American merchants' nonimportation boycotts and smuggling of cheaper Dutch tea.

To alleviate the East India Company's financial problems, the North ministry, in May 1773, passed an act, the Tea Act of 1773, that would allow the company to export its warehoused tea directly to the American colonies instead of distributing it through the standard practice of selling goods to English wholesalers who then resold them to American wholesalers for distribution to American retail merchants. The tea would also be exempted from the regular export duties and assessed only the reduced tax remaining on tea from the Townshend Duties (to sustain Parliament's right to tax the colonies), so that it would be cheaper even than the smuggled Dutch tea but still return a huge profit to the company. In addition, only American merchants of proven loyalty to the Crown would be entitled to sell the tea. This blatant act of favoritism enraged American radicals and merchants, especially those supplied through smuggling operations. The opponents realized that the act ultimately signified that Parliament could grant control of any segment of American commerce to any company it chose.

The East India Company selected its consignees in various American ports and set about shipping 1,700 chests of tea to them. Captains of American ships in London refused to transport the tea, so it was loaded aboard English ships. Threatened by radicals led by the Sons of Liberty, consignee merchants in Charleston, New York, and Philadelphia relinquished their control of the tea. Local authorities in Charleston had the tea unloaded and stored unsold, and those in the other two ports had the ships bearing the tea returned to England unloaded.

But, surprisingly, the Boston consignees resisted the radicals' pressures, and so the company dispatched three ships laden with tea chests that would arrive in Boston Harbor in late November and early December.[18]

THE BOSTON TEA PARTY

Because the Sons of Liberty could not intimidate the Boston consignees, Sam Adams reverted to the tactic of mob pressure. On November 28 the tea-bearing ship *Dartmouth* arrived in harbor. Aroused by Adams's harangues, crowds roamed the city's streets, determined to prevent the tea from being unloaded. Governor Hutchinson insisted the tea would be unloaded, the taxes collected, and the law enforced. But the *Dartmouth* remained moored in the harbor unloaded, soon joined by two other tea ships, while all waited for the 20-day limit during which the duty must be paid on the *Dartmouth*'s cargo to expire on December 16.

During the final days of November, Adams drew mass meetings of 5,000 to the Old South Meeting House that drafted resolutions and sent them to the consignees, demanding that the tea be returned to England. Backed by the governor, the consignees rejected the demands. The Boston Committee of Correspondence turned to garnering support from committees in nearby towns and throughout New England. Another mass meeting held on December 14 sent a demand to the *Dartmouth*'s owner, Francis Rotch, to request clearance for the ship's return to England. Rotch, accompanied by 10 men sent by the meeting, toured the customs offices, seeking clearance. The customs collector denied the request, and on the 16th, Governor Hutchinson, noting that Rotch lacked clearance, refused him a pass for the *Dartmouth* to sail past Castle William. Hutchinson planned to seize the tea for nonpayment of the duty.

Rotch appeared at an evening meeting at Old South Meeting House to report his failure, and Sam Adams announced that nothing more could be done—apparently a signal to action, for the crowd responded with war whoops and raced from the building to the wharf. There, about 50 men, faces darkened and costumed as Indians, boarded all three of the tea ships, hoisted the tea chests on deck, smashed open the chests, and hurled them into the harbor's waters as

Patriots hurl East India Company tea into Boston Harbor. *(The Boston Tea Party, courtesy of Anne S. K. Brown Military Collection, Brown University Library)*

the assembled crowd cheered their support. The "Indians" claimed to be "making saltwater tea." Their plot completed, the raiders slipped away, leaving the ships themselves unharmed. But the Boston Tea Party had concocted an expensive brew.[19]

OUTRAGE AND REPRISAL

Governor Hutchinson's official report on the Boston Tea Party, preceded by news of the event a week earlier, reached London on January 27, 1774. Thereafter witnesses, including Francis Rotch, arrived for government interrogations. The full story of the Boston Tea Party evoked indignation, outrage, and fury among both politicians and populace. They saw the destruction of the tea as a clear challenge to the supremacy of the king and Parliament in colonial affairs. George III declared of the Americans, "We must master them or totally leave them to themselves." Parliament decided to master them.

First, however, the North ministry chose humiliation. The king's Privy Council summoned Benjamin Franklin, agent for Massachusetts, to appear on January 29 for a hearing ostensibly to consider a Massachusetts petition requesting that Hutchinson and Lieutenant Governor Andrew Oliver be removed from office. Franklin stood impassively in the councillors' presence as Solicitor General Alexander Wedderburn heaped revilement on him for over an hour. Franklin left without responding. No one had mentioned the petition. But the message seemed abundantly clear, and even former friends of the colonies in Parliament now refused to offer any support.

The urgent question, as Lord North defined it, was simply whether the British government had "any authority" in America. In answer, Parliament decided

The Tea-Tax Tempest, an engraving of 1778, depicts the origins of the American Revolution. *(Library of Congress)*

Benjamin Franklin attends the Court of St. James. *(Courtesy of the National Archives and Records Administration)*

that the Americans must be subjugated, obligating the North ministry to propose the necessary policies and legislation to achieve this end. Lord North announced his program on March 14. Heading the ministry's agenda was closing the port of Boston and moving the headquarters of the province's government to a quieter locale.[20]

THE INTOLERABLE ACTS

Parliament proceeded to enact a series of laws the colonists named the Intolerable Acts. Three Coercive Acts initiated the series. The first of these, the Boston Port Act, to take effect June 15, closed Boston Harbor to all commerce until the city's citizenry provided payment to the East India Company for the tea destroyed in the Tea Party; some coastal ships bearing foods and fuels would be allowed to enter the harbor, but no oceangoing vessels. The Massachusetts Regulatory Act (or Massachusetts Government Act) changed the colony's royal charter—an unprecedented action—increasing the powers of the royal governor, who could now appoint or remove most of the civil officials; banning town meetings; allowing the House of the legislature to be elected still but the Council to be appointed by the Crown; and empowering sheriffs, not freeholders, to select juries. And the Impartial Administration of Justice Act stipulated that any royal official who was accused of a capital crime would be sent either to England or to another colony for trial.

In addition, in June, Parliament passed two more acts guaranteed to anger the colonists. A new Quartering Act essentially revised the acts of 1765 and 1766 to permit the billeting of troops with private families. Finally, the Quebec Act, although meant to conciliate Quebec's French residents and unrelated to the four punitive acts, became viewed by the American colonists as one of the Intolerable Acts. It expanded the boundaries of the province of Quebec to include all the inland territory extending to the Ohio and Mississippi Rivers, thereby eliminating colonial land claims in the West. It also accepted French as an official language of the province along with English, restored French civil law, permitted Roman Catholics to hold offices, and officially recognized the Roman Catholic faith—this last considered an especial affront by American Protestants.

As if to reinforce the British intent to subjugate the colonists, at least in Massachusetts, Gen. Thomas Gage arrived in Boston in mid-May to assume the post of governor. Nevertheless, many colonists accepted his appointment and even the Intolerable Acts. A group of Boston merchants, for example, offered to pay

This cartoon entitled "The Able Doctor," engraved by Paul Revere for the *Royal American Magazine* in June 1774, depicts America "swallowing the bitter draught." *(Courtesy of the National Archives and Records Administration)*

the East India Company for the destroyed tea and thus satisfy the demand of the Boston Port Act. But the Boston radicals mobilized the Town Meeting to reject payment for the tea and called on the other colonies to cease all trade with Great Britain. The other colonies, with Rhode Island taking the lead in May, proposed holding a meeting of representatives from all the colonies and began to select their delegates.[21]

THE FIRST CONTINENTAL CONGRESS

The Continental Congress convened in Philadelphia on September 5, 1774. Only Georgia, where the residents were fearful of being denied the protection of troops during a continuing Creek Indian uprising, had decided not to send delegates. Those attending from the 12 other colonies represented a wide spectrum of political views. Although few had met previously and many voiced disagreements, the delegates generally admired one another and completed their meeting with a strong sense of achievement. Samuel Adams and his cousin John Adams attended as representatives from Massachusetts; George Washington, Peyton Randolph, and Richard Henry Lee, from Virginia; Silas Deane, from Connecticut; John Jay, from New York; John Dickinson and Joseph Galloway, from Pennsylvania; Christopher Gadsden, Edward Rutledge, and John Rutledge, from South Carolina.

The delegates chose Peyton Randolph as the Continental Congress's president, decided each colony would have one vote, and began their debates. The most crucial issue focusing their debates concerned the definition of Americans' rights. The delegates reached a final agreement that these rights derived from nature, from the British constitution, and from the various colonial charters. They also decided that all importation of goods manufactured in Britain or Ireland should cease effective December 1, 1774. But they managed to sidestep responding to the Suffolk Resolves, which requested the Continental Congress's support for Massachusetts and were delivered to the Congress by Paul Revere on October 6.[22]

RESOLVES AND THE ASSOCIATION

The two noteworthy achievements of the Continental Congress arose out of their areas of agreement. On October 14, the delegates approved a Declaration of Resolves of the Continental Congress. The declaration stressed that the law of nature, the British constitution, and the colonial charters constituted the foundation of the American colonists' rights. It outlined some of these rights, including the unlawfulness of taxation and the imposition of standing armies without the colonists' consent, and it condemned the Intolerable Acts.

The Continental Congress also agreed on a policy of nonimportation of British goods into the colonies and nonexportation of American goods to Great Britain and created the Continental Association to effect this purpose. To enforce the association, the Continental Congress specified that committees should be elected "in every county, city, and town" and should be empowered with such tactics as inspections, public disclosure of offenders, ostracism, and other forms of peer pressure. Fearful of the economic consequences for their farmers, Virginia and South Carolina engineered an extension of the date for the beginning of nonexportation until September 10, 1775, so that Virginia farmers could sell their tobacco crops and South Carolina's farmers their rice. The ban on importing East India Company tea would begin immediately, and that on all other British goods on December 1, 1774. Members of the Continental Congress signed the association on October 20.

On following days, the Continental Congress drafted petitions and addresses to King George III and to the people of Great Britain, America, and Quebec. The delegates rejected petitioning Parliament on the grounds that the petition could be construed as an American admission of Parliament's authority. Their labors completed, the delegates dissolved the First Continental Congress on October 26, with the understanding that if events made it necessary, Congress would reconvene on May 10, 1775. The delegates traveled homeward, respectful of one another and garnering adulation from most Americans for their accomplishments.

On this eve of revolution, the population of the 13 American colonies numbered about 2.5 million—a tenfold increase over the population of 1700. Notably, blacks comprised 500,000 of this total—that is, approximately 20 percent—almost entirely slaves; although the vast majority lived in the South (over half, in fact, in Virginia and Maryland), about 4,000 slaves and a few hundred free blacks lived in Philadelphia, New York, and Boston. Philadelphia, the largest American city, now had 40,000 residents; New York, 21,000; Boston, 17,000; Charleston, 12,000; Newport, R.I., 11,000. By contrast, the population of London alone was approaching 1 million; the total population of England and Wales exceeded 8.5 million. In addition, Great Britain boasted the world's largest navy and an army second to none. An observer devoted to literature might have characterized the impending conflict as the Lilliputians attempting to menace Gulliver.[23]

As a harbinger of things to come, while the Continental Congress had been completing its work, General Gage preemptively adjourned the Massachusetts legislature, motivating the representatives and additional delegates spontaneously selected to convene as the Provincial Congress. This surrogate legislature established the Committee of Safety, headed by John Hancock, and voted to recruit a militia of 12,000 men and to purchase guns and ammunition to arm them. As 1774 ended, prospects for peace and reconciliation between the American colonists and their mother country appeared increasingly bleak.[24]

BEYOND POLITICS

Life continued in other venues despite war and rebellion, of course. Quite significantly and perhaps also ironically, the Enlightenment formed the backdrop for the Seven Years' War and the political events leading to the American Revolution. Whatever their politics or professions, the men involved in these events, both Britons and colonists, ingested the principles embedded in John Locke's *Two Treatises of Government* and *Essay Concerning Human Understanding* and Sir Isaac Newton's *Principia Mathematica* with their implications of orderliness, even precise mechanisms governing both nature and society. Contemporaries also most likely knew something of Carolus Linnaeus's advancements in biological taxonomy and perhaps even of Antoine Lavoisier's promising work in chemistry, and on both sides of the Atlantic, they admired Benjamin Franklin's experiments with electricity.

Such scientific advancements inspired a counterpart in David Hume's extreme philosophic empiricism questioning the validity of reason and the certainty of any form of knowledge, thereby placing himself outside the mainstream of Enlightenment thinking and severely limiting his audience. But in France, Denis Diderot fostered rationalistic inquiry through his massive *Encyclopédie,* which defined the mechanistic views of the *philosophes,* while his contemporary and colleague Jean-Jacques Rousseau philosophized about human equality, the social contract, and the innateness of the educational process. Voltaire produced works—some incisively satiric and cynical—in history, philosophy, and literature that readers in England and America may well have read in French, then regarded as the international language.[25]

Although a lesser era in English letters compared with earlier ages, the decades of the 1750s through the 1770s nevertheless provided a few significant and popular authors. Prominent among the poets stood Thomas Gray. Oliver Goldsmith attained popularity as both poet and novelist, perhaps especially with his 1766 novel *The Vicar of Wakefield.* But the biographer, poet, critic, and compiler of the acclaimed *Dictionary of the English Language,* Samuel Johnson, held preeminence among British writers. Probably the only contemporary American writer whose prose found readers on both sides of the Atlantic was Benjamin Franklin, but, with the possible exception of the long-deceased Anne Bradstreet, the colonies were yet to produce a poet or novelist the English would deem worthy of note. Nonetheless, Philip Freneau at least gained a wide American audience for his poems reflecting the Patriots' revolutionary zeal. His compatriot in this effort, Phillis Wheatley, a former slave whose poetry had gained wide recognition before the war, also composed poems extolling the Patriots' cause.[26]

In art, however, Americans fared better. Bostonian John Singleton Copley's accomplishments in portraiture already revealed him as an artist of exceptional talent. He had produced several renowned works by the early 1770s, including a portrait of poet Mercy Otis Warren, sister of James Otis and close friend of Abigail Adams, and a portrait of the gifted silversmith Paul Revere. As conflict between Massachusetts and Great Britain increased, Copley's opportunities to paint portraits dried up. So he acceded to the urgings of artists in England and in June 1774 sailed for London, leaving as his principal successor the most accomplished Philadelphia portrait painter, Charles Willson Peale.

In London, Copley would become an associate of his exact contemporary, Pennsylvanian Benjamin West, who had taught Peale during the years 1767 to 1769. The most celebrated American artist in history, West now ranked among the leading painters in Great Britain and was George III's favorite artist. Exemplifying the neoclassicism of the time, West's great works included *The Death of General Wolfe,* an enormously popular historical painting, completed in 1770. Among other painter colleagues of Copley in England, Sir Joshua Reynolds and Thomas Gainsborough shone brightest. Unfortunately for the future of native American art, neither Copley nor West would ever return to his home country.[27]

Charles Willson Peale also experienced the good fortune of studying with West, for more than two years in 1767–69, but then returned home to Philadelphia—a fortunate outcome for American art. Following Copley's departure in 1774, Peale became the leading portrait painter in the thirteen colonies. As the Revolutionary War approached its end in 1781, he added an exhibition gallery to his Philadelphia studio and launched the ambitious undertaking of painting not only the major American military and civil leaders of the war but also leading foreign diplomats and ambassadors to the fledgling republic. These portraits comprise Peale's greatest enduring legacy, and they have enjoyed consistent attention and admiration to the present time.

Probably less accomplished as an artist than Peale, John Trumbull followed Peale's and Copley's lead, traveling to London in 1780 after ending his military career in order to study with Benjamin West. Unlike his predecessor Peale, who adopted West's emphasis on portraiture, Trumbull chose to pursue West's other great interest, historic narrative painting. As Peale undertook to produce portraits of leading revolutionary figures in the war's aftermath, so Trumbull chose to paint canvases depicting many of the war's main events, although in his preliminary preparations for these works he also made portrait miniatures of George Washington and others. Most familiar of Trumbull's works to the majority of Americans are the vast murals he painted for the Capitol rotunda in Washington. Trumbull's contemporary Gilbert Stuart, later renowned for his portraits of George Washington, also sailed for London, arriving at age 19 in 1775, to remain as a student in West's studio for the duration of the Revolutionary War.[28]

Although Christopher Wren had left a compelling architectural legacy in England, with other professionals such as the brothers James and Robert Adams following in his wake, the American colonies had not a single trained architect. Both private and public buildings replicated the Georgian style popular in England, with master builders or gentleman-amateurs deriving designs from such popular carpenter handbooks as Batty Langley's *The City and Country Builder's and Workman's Treasury of Designs* (London, 1745) and such profusely illustrated architectural studies as *A Book of Architecture* (London, 1745) by James Gibbs, a devotee of Wren. George Washington, for example, used Langley's book in preparing designs for many features of Mount Vernon, including the Palladian window on the mansion's north end. The more talented amateur Thomas Jefferson employed mathematical principals and his own talents as well as such sourcebooks in designing the features of Monticello. Other amateurs, including physicians and carpenters, helped design many of the Georgian-style private and public buildings in or near Williamsburg, Charleston, Philadelphia, and Boston. The prominent lawyer Andrew Hamilton, for example, served as the primary designer of the State House in Philadelphia, subsequently known as Independence Hall, constructed during the years 1732–47 and probably the most important building in the colonies. As the Revolution impended, Philadelphia contained more than 4,700 brick structures. And, foreshadowing its much later role in the architectural avant garde, New York City by 1777 already boasted 6,000 buildings constructed of brick and tile, some as tall as six stories.[29]

POPULAR ARTS

Among more popular art forms, burgeoning theater—then only British plays and actors—and music evidenced some expanding cultural interest among the colonists. Following the French and Indian War, new theater buildings arose in New York, Annapolis, Baltimore, Williamsburg, and Philadelphia. George Washington himself greatly enjoyed attending plays, frequenting theaters in Philadelphia, Williamsburg, Annapolis, and Alexandria. Not surprisingly, William Shakespeare's works enjoyed frequent performance, but among the most popular plays of the time was Joseph Addison's *Tragedy of Cato,* a favorite with Washington. Other popular plays of the period included George Farquhar's *The Beaux Stratagem* and John Gay's *The Beggar's Opera,* still somewhat familiar to today's audiences, since Kurt Weill and Bertolt Brecht transposed them into *The Three Penny Opera* in the 20th century. At least one play rendered distinctly American themes, as Robert Rogers's *Ponteach* (1766) portrayed the great Chief Pontiac and the mendacity of white settlers' dealings with American Indians. Mercy Otis Warren wrote a two-act farce entitled *The Group,* published anonymously in 1775; and Hugh Henry Brackenridge penned the play *The Death of General Montgomery, in Storming the City of Quebec* in 1777. An early American theater tradition might have resulted from such beginnings. But as the Revolution ensued, clerical opposition—an earlier emphasis in both the Puritan and Quaker traditions—and then that of the Continental Congress (for both patriotic and economic reasons) brought darkness to all the theaters for the duration of the war.

Neither clerics nor Congress would find music objectionable, especially as among the prominent works of the time, *The New England Psalm Singer,* published in 1770 and the first book of strictly American songs, evidenced a clearly religious tone. Bostonian William Billings wrote the text for the book. He also composed hundreds of songs; but, as English law frustrated his efforts to obtain copyright for them and gain any resultant royalties, he redirected his anger over this failure toward aiding the Patriot cause, hauling supplies for the Continental army and writing songs excoriating the enemy. The great, enduring song of the revolutionary effort was "Yankee Doodle Dandy," a folk song originally intended to deride the Patriots but instead transformed by them into their own fighting ballad; they added scores of verses to the original, many of them ribald, to be played by their fifers and drummers. Fife and drum corps would lead both sides into battle and also convey orders through their tunes.[30]

Although it may seem unlikely, the philosophic, scientific, and artistic achievements of the Enlightenment in England and Europe influenced the courses of both American patriots and the British government as their conflict festered. For one thing, George III and other monarchs latched onto the concept of "enlightened despotism," whereby they could portray themselves as champions of reason and progress while upholding their hereditary right to power and their authority as interpreters of natural laws—an underpinning, perhaps, of George III's stubbornness.

In the opposite camp, both friendly politicians in England and patriots in America grounded their political principles in the writings of Locke and Newton, as the Declaration of Independence would attest for the patriots. (Later, the United States Constitution would reflect the thinking not only of Newton and Locke but also of the French philosophes, most especially their progenitor Charles-Louis de Secondat, baron de La Brède et de Montesquieu.) Finally, even art may advance nationalistic sentiments, as *The Death of General Wolfe* doubtless suggests, and thereby influence the course of events. All of these diverse factors contributed in some way toward making the ensuing American Revolution apparently inevitable.

CHRONICLE OF EVENTS

1756

February 3: Responding to a French threat to invade England because of English seizure of French ships and subsequent imprisoning of French sailors, the Newcastle ministry issues a proclamation that instructs residents of the southern counties of England to drive their cattle inland in the event of a French landing.

April 19: A French naval force invades British-controlled Minorca.

May 20: A British fleet under the command of Adm. John Byng, sent to rescue Minorca and reinforce the Fort St. Philip garrison, still held by British soldiers, engages the French fleet there in battle. But Byng's tactics prove ineffectual, and the French fleet escapes after crippling several of Byng's 14 ships. Byng refuses to give chase.

May 24: Having made no attempt to communicate with Fort St. Philip, Byng decides to retreat without landing on Minorca, thereby leaving the fort and Minorca to their fate—certain French control. He sets sail for Gibraltar.

August 14: French troops commanded by Gen. Louis-Joseph de Montcalm-Gozon capture Fort Oswego in north-central New York. They neutralize the fort's military capabilities and return to Montreal.

August 29: Frederick the Great of Prussia launches a preemptive invasion of Saxony, heading for Dresden, capital of Saxony.

September 10: Frederick enters Dresden.

October 1: Prussian and Saxon forces engage in battle at Lobositz.

October 14: The Saxon army surrenders to the Prussians at Lobositz. The Saxon elector Frederick Augustus II, also king of Poland, retires to Poland, and Frederick the Great absorbs most of the Saxon army into his own.

November: William Pitt becomes prime minister of Great Britain.

November 24: Elected a member of the Royal Society on April 29, Benjamin Franklin personally attends a meeting and is formally inducted as a fellow of the society.

1757

March 14: Admiral Byng, who was brought home, court-martialed, and condemned to death because of ministerial and public anger over his failure at Minorca, is executed at Portsmouth.

May 6: Prussian forces commanded by Frederick the Great defeat the Austrian army near Prague; the Austrians retreat into Prague, and the Prussians begin to lay siege to the city.

June 18: An Austrian force commanded by Count Leopold von Daun and sent to relieve Prague defeats Frederick's army at Kolin, forcing the Prussians to abandon the siege of Prague and retreat from Bohemia.

June 26: French troops led by Gen. Louis-Charles Le Teller, duke d'Estrées, defeat the British at Hastenbeck, opening Hanover and Brunswick to French occupation.

August 9: General Montcalm's forces capture Fort William Henry at the southern tip of Lake George in New York.

August 10: Indians serving with Montcalm massacre the British troops captured at Fort William Henry.

August 30: A Russian army defeats a Prussian force at Gross-Jägersdorf but then surprisingly retreats.

November 5: Troops of Frederick the Great, spearheaded by cavalry commanded by Gen. Friedrich Seydlitz, achieve victory over an Allied (Austrian, French, and Russian) army at Rossbach.

December 5: Although greatly outnumbered, Frederick's army surprises and overwhelms the Austrians to achieve a stunning victory at Leuthen.

1758

January 10: With Frederick occupied elsewhere, a force sent by Empress Elizabeth of Russia invades East Prussia with the intention of annexing the province.

April 29: A British fleet commanded by Adm. Sir George Pocock engages a French fleet commanded by Count Anne-Antoine d'Aché in the Bay of Bengal but with no decisive outcome.

July 8: The French force under Montcalm, defending Fort Ticonderoga at the northern end of Lake George, defeats an attacking force of 17,000 British and colonial troops, inflicting 2,000 casualties.

July 26: Following a 48-day siege, the French garrison at Louisbourg, Nova Scotia, surrenders to British forces commanded by Adm. Edward Boscawen and Gen. Jeffrey Amherst. The British capture 6,000 prisoners and raze the Louisbourg fortress.

August 1: Admiral Pocock's fleet again engages the French in the Bay of Bengal, again with an indecisive outcome, except that the French commander, d'Aché, decides to sail for the islands of the Indian Ocean.

August 25: Frederick's troops engage the invading Russian army at Zorndorf in a ferocious battle that ends only with the fall of darkness. Both sides sustain horrendous casualties—the Prussians more than 37 percent of their 36,000-man force and the Russians 50 percent of their 21,000 troops. During the night, the Russians begin to fall back toward Landsberg and Königsberg.

August 27: A British force led by Col. John Bradstreet captures Fort Frontenac (near present-day Kingston, Ontario).

September 8: Admiral d'Aché's fleet, having returned to the Bay of Bengal, once more engages in an indecisive battle. The French commander will, however, decide that the state of his ships obliges him to abandon the effort, leaving the British in control of the bay.

September 12: After a forced march from Zorndorf, Frederick's army arrives near Dresden, frightening off an Allied force, led by Count Leopold von Daun, that had threatened to destroy a British army commanded by Prince Henry.

September 14: French troops at Fort Duquesne, Pennsylvania, crush a small British force of 850 men, led by Maj. James Grant, whom Brig. Gen. John Forbes has sent to reconnoiter the fort. Grant has made a tactical error in dividing his force, and the French inflict a heavy toll—killing 270, wounding 40, and taking many prisoners, including Grant.

October 14: The Austrian force of 90,000 men led by Daun defeats Frederick's army of 37,000 at Hochkirch; the Prussians withdraw, unpursued by the shaken Austrians.

November 20: Frederick reoccupies Dresden following a siege by Daun's army, which has withdrawn to Prina on the news of Frederick's approach.

November 24: Learning that General Forbes's army has advanced to within 15 miles of Fort Duquesne, French troops blow up some of the fort's breastworks, set fire to the buildings, and embark on boats to retreat down the Ohio River.

November 25: British troops occupy Fort Duquesne. The British immediately build a stockade and rename the site Fort Pitt (present-day Pittsburgh) in honor of William Pitt.

1759

February 12: The University of St. Andrews in Scotland awards an honorary doctor of laws degree to Benjamin Franklin.

May 31: The Pennsylvania assembly enacts a law forbidding play performances, designating a fine of £500.

July 26: Under threat of a siege by General Amherst's army, the French abandon Fort Ticonderoga and withdraw to Crown Point, New York.

August 1: A Prussian and British force of 45,000, commanded by Prince Ferdinand, defeats a superior French force of 60,000 at Minden, sending the French into retreat toward the Rhine, with Ferdinand in pursuit.

August 12: Having crossed the Oder River the previous day, Frederick's army of 50,000 becomes lost and divided in thick woods, engages an army of 90,000 Austrian and Russian troops at Kunersdorf, and suffers disastrous defeat. Frederick loses nearly half of his army.

September 4: Deprived of any aid from Frederick following his disastrous defeat at Kunersdorf, Dresden once again falls to the Austrians.

September 13: A British army commanded by Gen. James Wolfe defeats French troops commanded by General Montcalm in battle on the Plains of Abraham near Quebec. The British win control of the city, but both commanders die during the combat.

November 20: In the Quiberon Bay off of Brittany, a British fleet, commanded by Adm. Sir Edward Hawke, engages a French fleet under Hubert de Brienne, count de Conflans, in a battle fought in the dark, off a rocky coast, during a severe gale, and on a lee shore—a unique battle in naval history. Two British ships wreck upon the rocks, but they manage to capture or destroy five of the French ships, including Conflans's flagship (the French commander washes ashore on a spar). The British victory leaves the French navy unable to mount offensive actions for virtually the remainder of the war. It also puts to rest a plan hatched by the ministry of King Louis XV of France to invade England.

December 13: In Philadelphia, Michael Hillegas opens the first music shop in America.

1760

April 12: Pennsylvania-born artist Benjamin West, age 21, sets sail from Gloucester, Massachusetts, aboard the *Betty Sally,* bound for Italy to pursue his career as a painter.

July 12: Frederick the Great's army begins to lay siege to Dresden.

July 29: Threatened by a large force commanded by Daun, Frederick abandons the siege of Dresden and withdraws toward Meissen.

August 1: Frederick begins a march into Silesia, summoning a force led by Prince Henry to join him.

August 7: As Colonel Montgomery's expedition, sent to relieve Fort Loudon, Tennessee, has been defeated by the Indians and forced to return to South Carolina, a force of Cherokee captures the fort. Captain Demere surrenders his troops under condition that they be allowed to withdraw freely.

August 10: Cherokee kill Demere's troops as they are retreating toward Fort Prince George in South Carolina.

August 17: Frederick reaches Breslau following a harrowing march to Liegnitz, his and Prince Henry's combined force having been virtually surrounded en route by superior Austrian and Russian armies and having successfully engaged the Austrians as he marched. Frederick has duped the Russians into believing that he

King George III ascended to the throne in 1760. *(From* The Pictorial Field Book of the Revolution, *2 vols., by B. J. Lossing. New York: Harper Brothers, 1851 and 1852.)*

inflicted total defeat on the Austrians, so the Russians begin a withdrawal from the area.

October 9: A combined force of Cossacks, Austrians, and segments of the Empire Army captures Berlin.

October 11: Learning that Frederick's army is approaching Berlin, the occupiers abandon the city.

October 25: King George II dies in London. He is succeeded by his grandson George III.

November 3: Following an especially bloody engagement that rages into the darkness of night, Frederick forces the Austrians to withdraw from positions around Torgau, but at terrible cost—30 percent of his force. Both sides are left so depleted that they will be incapable of confronting each other in any meaningful engagement for many months.

November 29: An American militia force commanded by Maj. Robert Rogers occupies Detroit, accepting the surrender of the French commander Beletre.

1761

February 24: Speaking before the Massachusetts Supreme Court, James Otis delivers a strong political statement opposing English rule in America—the first such public statement of its kind in the colonies.

August: Louis XV of France and Charles III of Spain enter into a "family compact" obligating Spain to declare war on Great Britain if France has not obtained a peace settlement by May 1, 1762.

September 30: The Moro Castle citadel, Cuba, besieged by troops and ships commanded by Adm. Sir George Pocock, surrenders to the British.

October 5: Opposed by George III and dismayed by the government's refusal to declare war on Spain, William Pitt resigns.

October 10: Havana surrenders to the British.

1762

January 5: Empress Elizabeth, the czarina of Russia, dies. The throne passes to Peter III, who immediately proposes bringing the war with Prussia to a peaceful conclusion.

March 16: Prussian and Russian officials sign an armistice agreement.

April 30: Oxford University confers an honorary doctor of civil law degree on Benjamin Franklin; his son William receives a master of arts degree during the same ceremony.

July 9: Totally alienated from her husband, Czar Peter III, and assisted by her lover, Gen. Grigory Orlov, Catherine II (the Great) proclaims herself empress of Russia and acquiesces in her husband's assassination.

October 29: Prince Henry, with the support of Major General Seydlitz's cavalry, wins victory over the Empire Army at Freiberg.

November 1: Benjamin Franklin arrives in Philadelphia from England.

November 2: Representatives of the warring nations meeting in Paris sign a preliminary draft of a peace agreement.

1763

February 10: Negotiators meeting in Paris, France, complete the Treaty of Paris, concluding the Seven Years' War (French and Indian War). By the terms of the treaty, France cedes her territories in North America to Great Britain. By a separate treaty, Spain receives control of New Orleans and lands west of the Mississippi, with Great Britain acquiring control of the Floridas from Spain in exchange for restoring control of Cuba and the Philippine Islands to Spain. France is allowed to retain stations in India and on the slave coast of Africa, and the islands of Guadeloupe and Martinique in the West Indies are returned to her. But because France is not allowed to fortify its stations in India, Britain gains the ascendancy on the subcontinent.

April 27: At a meeting of representatives from the Algonquian tribes near Detroit, Pontiac—chief of the Ottawa and leader of the loose confederation among the Ottawa, Ojibway, and Potawatomi—outlines his plans to stage simultaneous attacks on the British frontier forts during May. Pontiac's cohorts abhor English encroachments on Indian lands and exclusion of Indians from English forts. This is contrary to French practice; and French traders and hunters have encouraged the uprising.

May 7: Pontiac leads Ottawa and other Indians in an attack on the fort at Detroit. Failing to take the fort, the Indians begin to lay siege to it. The raid marks the beginning of Pontiac's Rebellion (also known as Pontiac's War or, in England, as Pontiac's Conspiracy).

May 16: The Wyandot (Huron) in Pontiac's Rebellion capture Fort Sandusky (now Sandusky, Ohio).

May 25: The Indians capture Fort St. Joseph (now Niles, Michigan).

May 27: The Indians capture Fort Miami (later Fort Wayne).

June 2: Two huge teams of Indians stage a game of lacrosse outside Fort Michilimackinak in Michigan—a subterfuge that draws British soldiers out of the fort to watch. Suddenly, the Indians arm themselves with weapons they had concealed. They massacre the soldiers, slaughter the fort's occupants, and raze the fort.

June 22: Indians involved in Pontiac's Rebellion unsuccessfully attack Fort Pitt.

July 27: Indians begin a siege of Fort Pitt.

July 31: At the Battle of Bloody Run, Pontiac achieves victory over a British force that is attempting to lift the siege of Fort Pitt.

August 5: British troops, commanded by Col. Henry Bouquet, defeat an Indian force at the Battle of Bushy Run, freeing Bouquet to march to the relief of Fort Pitt (now Pittsburgh).

August 21: American artist Benjamin West arrives in London.

October 7: Concerned over Pontiac's Rebellion, continuing Indian attacks, and land speculators demanding grants on the trans-Appalachian frontier, George III signs the Proclamation of 1763, which forbids settlers from crossing the Appalachian divide, a western boundary of the thirteen colonies defined by the proclamation, and also outlaws land purchases west of the divide. The proclamation also establishes three new colonies—Quebec, East Florida, and West Florida—in an effort to placate the settlers. Many settlers, however, denounce these measures for preventing their access to the West.

October 12: Leaders of Pontiac's allies, the Potawatomi, Ojibway, and Wyandot (Huron), discouraged by the unaccustomed tactic of siege warfare, make peace with the British.

October 30: Having learned that he can expect no assistance from the French, Pontiac abandons the siege of Fort Pitt and withdraws with his Ottawa warriors to the Miami River.

December 2: British officials instruct governors of the frontier colonies that they must obtain approval of any land grants that might include Indian areas—an effort to deter colonists from encroaching on the Indian territories.

1764

February 14: James Davenport receives a patent for spinning and carding machinery he has invented and founds the Globe Mills in Philadelphia.

April 5: Parliament enacts the Revenue Act of 1764, known in the American colonies as the Sugar Act. The law imposes tariffs on sugar, wines, coffee, and numerous other products imported into America in large quantities. Its intent is to raise revenues to reduce the huge debt incurred during the Seven Years' War and also to pay the costs of maintaining an army on the western frontier (estimated at £200,000 per year). The act also doubles taxes on European products imported via Great Britain and reduces to three pence the six-pence-per-gallon tax on foreign molasses, originally enacted in 1733. To ensure compliance and reduce smuggling and corruption, the law also creates new enforcement measures.

1765

March 22: Parliament enacts the Stamp Act, which imposes a tax on all legal documents, licenses, newspapers, almanacs, pamphlets, playing cards, and dice, requiring that they bear stamps to prove the tax has been paid. The act's purpose is to raise revenues to pay the costs of defending the colonies; its provisions are to take effect on November 1.

March 24: Provisions of the Quartering Act take effect. The act stipulates that whenever army barracks are unavailable or filled, British troops must be accommodated in inns and taverns or, if necessary, in vacant homes or barns, at the expense of the colonists. It also requires that colonists provide troops with wagons and drivers, firewood, beer, candles, salt, vinegar, and other items at fixed rates.

May 3: Dr. John Morgan and Dr. William Shippen, Jr., establish the first medical school in the colonies at the College of Philadelphia.

May 29: Patrick Henry introduces five Resolves in the House of Burgesses meeting in Williamsburg, Virginia, that attack provisions of the Stamp Act and the concept of taxation without representation. In supporting the Resolves, he asserts that only the legislatures in the individual colonies have the right to impose taxes within their colonies. During his speech, opponents interrupt him with shouts of "Treason!" Henry responds, "If this be treason, make the most of it." The House passes the Resolves.

May 30: After Henry and other delegates have left town, remaining members of the Virginia House of Burgesses rescind the provision in the Resolves, propounding that only the Virginia assembly can impose taxes on Virginians. But the Newport, Rhode Island,

Mercury publishes the full original version of the Virginia Resolves, thus making possible their dissemination throughout the thirteen colonies.

June: The General Court of Massachusetts issues a Circular Letter to all other colonial assemblies that invites them to elect delegates to attend a congress to discuss organizing a formal resistance to the Stamp Act's provisions.

July 10: George Grenville, head of the treasury and first minister since the spring of 1763, having become personally unacceptable to George III, is forced to resign, leaving Charles Watson-Wentworth, Lord Rockingham, to form a government.

August 14: In Boston, mob violence, generated by the Sons of Liberty, targets Andrew Oliver, who has agreed to assume the post of stamp master. The rioters hang Oliver in effigy from a limb of a Newbury Street tree that becomes known as the Liberty Tree. At dusk they take down the effigy, march to a building purportedly intended to become the stamp office, and raze it. They move on to the home of Oliver, who has fled with his family. The mob beheads the effigy of Oliver, breaks windows in his house, and then drags the effigy to Fort Hill, where it is burned. Some rioters return thereafter to Oliver's house, where they smash in the doors and destroy some of the furnishings. They stone and drive off Lt. Gov. Thomas Hutchinson, who has arrived at the house to try to persuade the mob to disperse. Royal Governor Francis Bernard, alarmed by these events, takes refuge in Castle William, a fortress in Boston Harbor.

August 15: A delegation of Boston citizens visits Oliver and persuades him to resign as stamp master.

August 26: During the night, Boston rioters attack and vandalize the homes of William Story, prominent Tory and deputy register of the admiralty, and Benjamin Hallowell, comptroller of customs. Then they proceed to Lieutenant Governor Hutchinson's empty house and wreak havoc with both the structure and its furnishings.

October 7–25: Twenty-seven delegates representing nine colonies meet in New York City as the Stamp Act Congress. The delegates approve 13 resolutions, the first three of which review the rights of Englishmen, prominently the right not to be taxed without Parliamentary representation; the fourth stresses the impossibility of the colonies' being effectively represented in Parliament. The eighth resolution protests the Stamp Act duties as both a subversion of the colonists' rights and an excessive burden. The final resolves call for repeal of the Stamp Act while reaffirming the rights of British subjects to petition the Parliament. The Stamp Act Congress sets a strong precedent for future collective action. In addition, the congress's petition to the king, drafted by John Dickinson, evokes Great Britain's vested economic interest in the colonies, declaring, "By this Protection, she will forever secure to herself the Advantage of conveying to all Europe the Merchandizes which America furnishes, and of supplying thro' the same Channel whatever is wanted from thence. Here opens a boundless Source of Wealth, and Naval Strength; yet these immense Advantages . . . are in Danger of being forever lost . . . by the late Acts of Parliament, imposing duties and taxes on these Colonies. . . ."

November 1: As Guy Fawkes Day approaches and coincident with the date when the Stamp Act is supposed to take effect, a Stamp Act riot erupts in New York City. The rioters execute and bury a symbolic "Liberty," burn the colony's governor in effigy, throw stones through windows, and vandalize the homes of officials before the riot is quelled.

1766

February 22: Responding to American colonists' protests, opposition voiced in Parliament, and declining trade resulting from American merchants' boycotts, the House of Commons votes 276 to 168 to repeal the Stamp Act.

March 4: The House of Commons approves the Declaratory Act, which asserts that the American colonies are subordinate to both the king and Parliament and that Parliament has the power to enact laws that are binding on the colonies "in all cases whatsoever," making clear Parliament's authority not only to impose taxes but to legislate all matters affecting the colonies.

March 17: The House of Lords approves the Commons' repeal of the Stamp Act.

March 18: King George III approves repeal of the Stamp Act, effective May 1. At the same time, the House of Lords approves the Declaratory Act.

July 25: Unable to arouse continuing Indian rebellion and finally convinced that the British have the upper hand, Pontiac concludes a peace treaty with Sir William Johnson, superintendent of Indian affairs, at Oswego, New York.

October: On South Street in Philadelphia, David Douglass, owner and manager of the American Com-

pany of Comedians, builds the Southwark Theater, the first permanent theater in the American colonies.

November 10: Under the auspices of the Dutch Reform Church, Queen's College (later Rutgers) is chartered at New Brunswick, New Jersey.

1767

April 24: A production of Thomas Godfrey's *The Prince of Parthia* opens at the Southwark Theater.

June 29: Parliament approves the Revenue Act proposed by Charles Townshend, chancellor of the exchequer. The act imposes taxes—known as the Townshend Duties—on some English manufactures imported into the colonies, including lead, glass, painter's colors, paper, and tea, to pay the salaries of royal colonial officials whose salaries have heretofore been provided by the colonial assemblies.

September 4: Charles Townshend dies suddenly.

October 1: Terms of the Suspending Act, approved by Parliament in June, take effect. As a punishment of the New York assembly for refusing to comply with the Quartering Act, the Suspending Act deprives the assembly of the right to pass legislation and declares null and void in advance any acts the assembly may approve in defiance of this act.

October 28: Boston Patriots call a town meeting that approves a resolution encouraging a boycott of English goods and expansion of local manufacturing.

December 2: The first of John Dickinson's *Letters from a Farmer in Pennsylvania to the Inhabitants of the British Colonies* is published in the *Pennsylvania Chronicle and Universal Advertiser.*

1768

February 11: In the House of the Massachusetts General Court, a radical faction led by Samuel Adams and James Otis, having previously failed due to Royal Governor Francis Bernard's opposition, now succeeds in gaining the assembly's approval of a Circular Letter. The letter, to be sent to speakers of the assemblies of the other colonies, urges support of a united stand against the Townshend Acts.

March: Responding to the Massachusetts Circular Letter, the Virginia House of Burgesses moves beyond the letter's intent and approves sending protests to the king and Parliament against the Suspending Act and the Townshend Duties; their petition concedes that Parliament has jurisdiction over regulating imperial trade, while insisting that the House of Burgesses has equal rank with Parliament as a legislature.

March 18: A rowdy crowd of all ages and both sexes parades through the streets of Boston celebrating the anniversary of the Stamp Act's repeal.

April: Boston merchant John Hancock has two minor customs officials forcibly removed from his brig *Lydia* when they go below decks without authorization or a writ of assistance. The royal customs commissioners have the Massachusetts attorney general file criminal charges against Hancock, but following an investigation, the attorney general drops the charges on the grounds that the customs officials have exceeded their authority and Hancock has acted legally in having them removed from the *Lydia.*

May 8: In London, Benjamin Franklin publishes a British edition of John Dickinson's *Letters from a Farmer in Pennsylvania,* which he has edited. The collection of letters is enormously popular and successful in the American colonies, generating the work's publication not only in this British edition but also in a French edition.

May 16: The Virginia House of Burgesses issues its own Circular Letter, advocating that the colonies take joint measures against any British policies that "have an immediate tendency to enslave them" and expressing hopes for a "hearty union" of the colonies.

June 10: Still disgruntled over the *Lydia* affair, Boston customs commissioners order the seizure of another of John Hancock's ships, the *Liberty,* on trumped-up charges based on narrow technicalities. Comptroller Benjamin Hallowell and Collector Joseph Harrison seize the *Liberty* and signal the man-of-war *Romney* to have it towed away from Hancock's wharf. A mob organized by the Sons of Liberty unsuccessfully attempts to thwart the seizure and then attacks and beats Hallowell and Harrison. As the night proceeds, the mob increases, attacking the houses of officials and beating customs officials.

June 21: Under orders from Lord Hillsborough, secretary of state for the American colonies, Governor Bernard in Boston, where the Sons of Liberty are now in control, sends Hillsborough's order to the Massachusetts General Court that it must rescind its Circular Letter.

June 30: By a vote of 92 to 17, the Massachusetts General Court refuses to rescind the Circular Letter; in response, Governor Bernard follows Hillsborough's orders and dissolves the legislature.

August 15: Merchants in Boston agree on a policy of nonimportation of English goods. James Otis and Sam Adams stage a celebration of the anniversary of the Oliver riot that includes cannon fire, a parade, songs, and 14 toasts, ending with one to the "Glorious Ninety-two," the legislators who voted against rescinding the Circular Letter.

August 25: Following Boston's lead, the merchants of New York adopt an agreement not to import English goods.

August 27: Governor Bernard receives word that British troops have been dispatched to Boston.

September 22: The convention of Massachusetts towns meets in Boston, with 70 representatives of 66 towns and several districts—30 additional towns will be represented before the convention concludes. The first order of business is to petition Governor Bernard to recall the legislature into session—a petition Bernard refuses to accept, while also urging the convention to disband.

September 27: With issuance of a "Result of Convention" that petitions the king and calls again for reconvening the Massachusetts legislature, the convention of cities ends with no exhortations to militancy against the landing of troops in Boston.

October 1: Two regiments of British troops—the 14th West Yorks and the 29th Worcesters—disembark from ships that have recently arrived in Boston Harbor from Halifax and establish living quarters in the city, the 14th in Faneuil Hall and the 29th in tents pitched on Boston Common. As winter approaches, they will occupy warehouses and other buildings rented from private citizens.

October 31: Somewhat horrified by the severity of punishments used in disciplining British troops, Bostonians now witness the ultimate punishment on the common, where Pvt. Richard Ames, convicted of desertion, is executed by firing squad.

1769

March: After Parliament fails to respond to the Pennsylvania legislature's petition for relief from the Townshend Duties, Philadelphia merchants adopt a policy of nonimportation of British goods.

May: Virginia adopts nonimportation of British goods.

June: Maryland joins other colonies in refusing to import British goods.

June 7: Daniel Boone and his party of hunters reach the terminus of the Cumberland Gap and see for the first time the land that will become Kentucky.

July: South Carolina joins the nonimportation movement.

August 1: Governor Bernard sets sail out of Boston Harbor, bound for England, as residents raucously celebrate his departure.

September: Georgia adopts nonimportation.

November: North Carolina joins the other colonies in refusing to import British goods.

1770

January 16: British soldiers chop down the Liberty Pole in New York City, saw it into segments, and leave the pile in front of a tavern the Sons of Liberty use as their headquarters.

January 17: In New York City, the Sons of Liberty, in the presence of 3,000 supporters, erect a new Liberty Pole. British soldiers let loose a broadside that menaces the crowd. A skirmish results, followed by a full battle on Golden Hill.

January 18: The conflict in New York ends with one dead and many wounded.

February 23: In Boston's North End, a Patriot crowd besieges the importing shop of Theophilus Lily, a Tory who refused to sign the Nonimportation Agreement. His fellow Tory and neighbor Ebenezer Richardson attempts to help Lily, but the crowd forces Richardson's withdrawal into his home; the Patriots smash in his door and hurl a rock that hits his wife. Goaded to violence, Richardson fires on the crowd from a second-story window, mortally wounding 11-year-old Christopher Snider. The mob nearly lynches Richardson on the spot. Snider dies at 9:00 P.M.

March 5: Wrangling civilians urged on by radical leaders and beleaguered troops in Boston spark a fatal encounter under the evening moonlight. Capt. Thomas Preston conducts a group of soldiers to the rescue of the customhouse sentry, who was threatened by a hostile crowd. The crowd, some shouting "kill them," pelts the soldiers with snowballs and ice. One soldier loses his footing, regains it, and fires his rifle. Others then fire sporadically. Eleven men in the mob fall wounded; three die instantly—including one of the leaders, a free black named Crispus Attucks—and two receive mortal wounds. The mob swells and roams through the streets, demanding vengeance. The Boston Massacre, as it is quickly dubbed,

provides martyrs and a rallying issue for the American Patriots.

April 12: Obliged to concede that the Townshend Duties are a failure—the costs of maintaining troops in Boston exceed the tax revenues, also greatly reduced by the Americans' nonimportation tactic—Parliament repeals the Townshend Acts. But in deference to Prime Minister Frederick, Lord North, and to sustain the principle that Parliament has the power to tax without the colonies' consent, members also vote to retain one of the duties—the tax on tea. In response, the colonies, with the exception of Boston merchants, will revoke their nonimportation agreements on all goods except tea.

October 24–30: Captain Preston, the British officer held responsible for the Boston Massacre, is brought to trial in Boston. Defended by John Adams and Josiah Quincy, Jr., he is acquitted.

November 27–December 5: The eight other soldiers arraigned with Capt. Preston are tried, defended by Adams and Quincy; six are acquitted, and two are found guilty of manslaughter.

1771

August: At the home of Bishop Jonathan Shapley, Benjamin Franklin begins to write his *Autobiography.*

1772

June 9–10: Trade between Great Britain and the American colonies has greatly increased since repeal of the Townshend Duties, but American smuggling has remained commonplace as colonial merchants and shipmasters try to evade British customs tariffs. The Narrangansett Bay coastline, with its numerous inlets, affords a primary area for smuggling operations that bring goods into Rhode Island for transport inland. In an effort to interdict these operations and to support the customs service, the Royal Navy in March has sent the schooner *Gaspee,* commanded by Lt. William Dudingston, to patrol the Narrangansett waters. Over the months, Dudingston has seized several trading vessels, and the local sheriff has threatened his arrest. On June 9, Dudingston runs the Gaspee aground while pursuing a suspected smuggler and is unable to free the ship. During the night, locals board and take the ship by force, shoot and wound Dudingston, and torch the ship, which burns to the waterline. The local sheriff then arrests Dudingston and refuses to release him until his commanding admiral pays the lieutenant's fine.

The lieutenant will be sent back to England to face a court-martial, while authorities unsuccessfully attempt to bring the perpetrators to justice.

November: Sam Adams is distressed by the political quiescence in the colonies resulting from repeal of the Townshend Duties and angered over the payment of royal officials' salaries from proceeds of the tax on tea, which he argues places the officials beyond the influence of the colonial legislatures. He moves the Boston Town Meeting to ask Governor Thomas Hutchinson to convene the Massachusetts General Court to consider the issue of paying officials with tea tax funds. Hutchinson refuses, reminding the town of his authority over the legislature and the town's limited rights. In response, Adams persuades the Town Meeting to create a Committee of Correspondence to circulate protests. The committee immediately goes to work and by the end of November issues *Votes and Proceedings . . . of Boston,* known throughout the colony and beyond as the Boston Pamphlet. The widely read tract outlines Great Britain's perceived plot to enslave America through taxation without representation, the recent depredations of British troops in Boston, depriving colonials of trial by jury through use of admiralty courts and commissions, and the threat to religions' practices posed by the plan to send Anglican bishops to America. It also stresses the colonists' rights as British subjects, declaring them to be "absolute Rights."

1773

January: A commission appointed by the British government to investigate the *Gaspee* affair is unable to ascertain guilt. But its report, issued later in the summer, will reveal a condition the colonists find menacing—namely, that the commission was empowered to send to England for trial anyone it accused, a violation of the ancient right to a trial by one's peers. This revelation provides yet another issue for those advocating independence.

January 12: The colonies' first officially established museum is founded in Charleston.

February 27: Construction of Christ Church (Anglican), where George Washington's family worships, is completed in Alexandria, Virginia.

March: Alarmed by the revelation of the *Gaspee* commission's power to revoke trial by jury in the colonies, influential members of the Virginia House of Burgesses—among them Patrick Henry, Thomas Jefferson, and Richard Henry Lee—create a Committee of

Correspondence to communicate with other colonies while also gathering information about British actions. The House of Burgesses encourages other colonies to do the same. Within a year, all the colonies but Pennsylvania will have followed Virginia's lead.

May 10: Parliament approves the Tea Act of 1773. An effort by Lord North's government to rescue the financially distressed British East India Company, the Tea Act awards the company a monopoly on the tea trade with the colonies, allowing the company to ship surplus Indian tea directly to the colonies. The act also retains the three-pence duty on tea imposed by the Townshend Acts, while forgiving regular export duties, so that the company will be able to sell tea in America for less than the cost of smuggled tea. Tory merchants will reap the advantage of being privileged to sell the monopoly tea.

July 14: The first annual conference of American Methodists convenes at St. George's Church in Philadelphia.

October 16: In Philadelphia, a mass meeting adopts resolutions declaring that anyone importing British East India Company tea is "an enemy to his country" and appoints a committee to pressure local tea consignees to give up their commissions. By December, all of the consignees, mostly wealthy Quaker merchants, will have done so. New York City follows a similar path.

November 5: The Boston Town Meeting adopts the resolution approved in Philadelphia and pressures local tea consignees to relinquish their commissions.

November 30–31: The *Dartmouth,* first of the East India Company ships carrying a tea cargo, having arrived in Boston Harbor two days earlier, Samuel Adams and other Sons of Liberty hold mass meetings at Old South Meeting Hall to demand that the tea be sent back to England. The duties must be paid on the tea by December 16.

December 16: Two other ships with tea cargos, the *Eleanor* and the *Beaver,* have joined the *Dartmouth* at Griffin's Wharf. The *Dartmouth* has not been cleared by customs, and Governor Hutchinson has denied it clearance to sail, so the Patriots meeting at Old South fear the owner will attempt to have the tea unloaded. When Samuel Adams announces that nothing more can be done, the crowd whoops and hastens from the meetinghouse, bound for the waterfront. About 50 men, thinly disguised as Mohawk, break away from the crowd and board the three ships at Griffin's Wharf. They hoist the casks of tea on deck, break them open, and hurl the tea into the harbor's waters. Some 90,000 pounds of East India Company tea is destroyed, as the 342 casks that had stored the tea float with the tide, bobbing in the seawater as far out as Dorchester Neck. The defiance expressed in the Boston Tea Party is certain to elicit a response from the North ministry.

1774

January: The first magazine in the colonies to include frequent illustrations, *Royal American Magazine,* is founded.

January 27: Although informal news of the event has already arrived in England on January 19, the official report on the Boston Tea Party prepared by Governor Thomas Hutchinson now reaches the ministry in London. Concern grows among the ministry that something must be done to assert the supremacy of the king and the Parliament in the colonies.

January 29: In London, the Privy Council holds a hearing on a petition from Massachusetts requesting that Hutchinson and Oliver be removed from office. As the agent for Massachusetts, Benjamin Franklin has been ordered to appear before the council, where he is subjected to more than an hour of vituperation and calumny, delivered by Solicitor General Alexander Wedderburn in an effort to totally discredit him. Franklin listens impassively and then leaves. The petition is never mentioned. The North cabinet decides that some action must be taken to impose dependency on the American colonies.

March 14: The North ministry, after weeks of discussion, publicly announces the actions it plans to take in Massachusetts—closing the port of Boston and moving the provincial government to another town.

March 18: North introduces the Boston Port Bill in the Commons. The bill mandates closing the port of Boston to all ocean-borne trade, with the exception of some coastal vessels bearing food and fuel. The port is to remain closed until the king permits its reopening, but only after the East India Company has received compensation for the destroyed tea.

March 31: Parliament approves the Boston Port Act; it is the first of a series of laws that become known as the Intolerable Acts, or the Coercive Acts, whose purpose is to force the rebellious Bostonians into submission and to intimidate merchants and recalcitrants in other cities who have supported the boycott of East India Company tea. The effort will backfire, however, as sympathizers in the other colonies send food and

money to sustain the Bostonians. Royal governors in several colonies will be forced to dissolve legislatures to prevent their passing laws in support of Boston.

May 13: Gen. Thomas Gage, commander of the British army in the colonies, arrives in Boston with a royal commission as governor of the province—in effect a declaration of martial law in Massachusetts. Gage's orders are to establish as strong a military garrison in Boston as he deems necessary.

May 17: Rhode Island issues a call for convening a congress of the colonies. Philadelphia and New York respond favorably, and approval of the idea soon emanates from most of the colonies.

May 20: Parliament approves the second of the so-called Intolerable Acts, the Massachusetts Government Act, which alters the charter of Massachusetts, placing the colony entirely under royal authority—the Crown will appoint council members, the royal governor will appoint officials of the colony, and town meetings are forbidden except with the governor's approval. Parliament also approves the Administration of Justice Act, which stipulates that any royal official accused of a capital crime must be sent to England or to another colony for trial. The king signs both acts.

June 2: Parliament approves the last of the Intolerable Acts, a new Quartering Act that empowers British commanders to billet troops anywhere in Boston they deem suitable, now including private homes; the act also requires Massachusetts residents to pay the costs of housing and feeding the troops.

June 10: The Massachusetts General Court, meeting in Salem, approves the convening of a congress of the colonies. In response, Gen. Thomas Gage, in control of the colony in the absence of Governor Hutchinson, dissolves the assembly. An unrelated event, the artist John Singleton Copley sets sail for England.

June 17: Sam Adams and other radicals manage to convene the Boston Town Meeting, which votes against paying for the tea destroyed during the Boston Tea Party.

June 22: Parliament approves the Quebec Act, which establishes a permanent government in Quebec and extends the boundaries of British Canada to the Ohio and Mississippi Rivers, effectively eliminating the lower colonies' land claims in the West. The act further alienates the Americans by extending religious rights to Roman Catholics in Quebec. Protestants in the lower colonies regard this recognition of "popery" as a threat; many consider it yet another Intolerable Act.

June 27: The Boston Town Meeting endorses the Solemn League and Covenant, sponsored by the Committee of Correspondence, which pledges its signers to cease all trade with Great Britain by refusing to buy any British goods imported after August 31 and boycotting any merchant who refuses to sign the covenant.

July 10: John Singleton Copley arrives in London.

September 1: About 260 British troops stationed at Boston embark at the Long Wharf and cross over to Charlestown, where they seize and cart off what remains of the gunpowder stored at the powder house for use of nearby towns and the province. News of the raid spreads quickly, along with a false rumor that the soldiers fired on local patriots resisting the seizure and killed six. As the rumor spreads into Connecticut, it expands with the added rumor that British ships in the harbor shelled Boston.

September 4: Thousands of aroused patriots marching toward Cambridge disperse after learning that the rumors about Charlestown and Boston are false.

September 5: General Gage orders the erection of fortifications at the Neck, which connects Boston to the mainland. With troops stationed here, the city is effectively both cut off from the rest of Massachusetts and under siege.

The First Continental Congress convenes in Philadelphia at Carpenter's Hall. Sam Adams and his cousin John Adams are among those representing Massachusetts; George Washington, Patrick Henry, Peyton Randolph, and Richard Henry Lee, Virginia; Silas Deane, Connecticut; Caesar Rodney, Delaware; John Jay, New York; John Dickinson and Joseph Galloway, Pennsylvania; Christopher Gadsden, Edward Rutledge, and John Rutledge, South Carolina. The delegates elect Peyton Randolph president of the congress and choose a committee to begin formal discussions focused on the twin issues of defining Americans' rights and determining exactly how to defend those rights.

September 6: After a day of debate, members of the congressional committee agree that Americans' rights derive from the laws of nature, the British constitution, and the various colonial charters. A subcommittee will pursue drafting a declaration of the rights based on these principles, while the committee as a whole turns its attention to the issue of how to defend Americans' rights.

September 9: Massachusetts's Suffolk County adopts the Suffolk Resolves, written by the Boston Patriot Dr. Joseph Warren. The resolves denounce the Intolerable Acts and advocate that residents of Massachusetts withhold payment of taxes to the Crown until the acts are rescinded; that they cease all trade with Great Britain, Ireland, and the West Indies; and that they make preparations for war with Britain.

October: The Massachusetts General Court, meeting illegally in Concord and reconstituting itself as the Provincial Congress, with John Hancock as president, establishes the Committee of Safety, headed by Hancock, with authority to call up the militia, and votes to purchase 20 field pieces, four mortars, and 5,000 muskets and bayonets.

October 6: Paul Revere rides into Philadelphia and delivers a copy of the Suffolk Resolves, already commended by the congress, and a letter from the Boston Committee of Correspondence to the Continental Congress. The letter requests the congress's counsel on how the citizens of Boston might appropriately respond to British militarization of the city and suspension of the legislature. The congress will approve the Suffolk Resolves but hedge on the issue of advising Boston's citizenry.

John Hancock was president of the Continental Congress. *(From The Pictorial Field Book of the Revolution, 2 vols. by B. J. Lossing. New York: Harper Brothers, 1851 and 1852.)*

October 14: The Continental Congress approves a Declaration of Rights and Grievances. The declaration affirms the initially agreed-upon concept that Americans' rights derive from the laws of nature, the British constitution, and the colonial charters. It also asserts the colonies' right to generate their own laws and taxes because of lack of representation in Parliament, accepts the Crown's right to regulate the colonies' external commerce, affirms allegiance to the Crown, rejects acts of Parliament that violate colonists' rights, and lists "infringements and violations" committed by Parliament.

October 20: Delegates to the Continental Congress sign the "Association," which commits the colonies to an immediate boycott of East India Company tea, a ban on imports from Great Britain effective on December 1, and, if it proves necessary, a prohibition of exports to Great Britain effective September 10, 1775. The congress provides for enforcement of these agreements through creation of elected local committees that will inspect customs-house books, publish the names of offenders, and otherwise apply peer pressure.

October 26: Following adoption of a petition to the king and addresses to the people of Great Britain, America, and Quebec, the Continental Congress dissolves, with the understanding that it will reconvene on May 10, 1775, if necessary.

November 17: Twenty-six Philadelphia patriots found the Philadelphia Troop of Light Horse, one of the first military units in the colonies.

December 13: The text of the Suffolk Resolves arrives in London; the outraged attorney general declares it treason.

EYEWITNESS TESTIMONY

1756

There is no Virtue, the Honour whereof gets a Man more Envy, than that of *Justice*, because it procures great Authority among the common People; they only revere the Valiant, and admire the Wise, while they truly love Just Men; for in these they have entire Trust and confidence, but of the former, they always fear one, and mistrust the other. They look on Valour as a certain natural Ferment of the Mind, and Wisdom as the effect of a Fine Constitution, or a happy Education; but a Man has it in his own Power to be just; and that is the Reason it is so dishonourable to be otherwise. . . .

. . . . .

Love your Enemies, for they tell you your Faults. He that has a Trade, has an Office of Profit and Honour.
Benjamin Franklin, from Poor Richard improved: Being an Almanack and Ephemeris . . . for the Year of our Lord 1756, *in Leonard W. Labaree, ed.,* The Papers of Benjamin Franklin, *vol. 6, pp. 319 and 321.*

You mention your frequent Wish that you were a Chaplain to an American Army. I sometimes wish, that you and I were jointly employ'd by the Crown to settle a Colony on the Ohio. I imagine we could do it effectually, and without putting the Nation to much Expence. But I fear we shall never be call'd upon for such a Service. What a glorious Thing it would be, to settle in that fine Country a large Strong Body of Religious and Industrious People! What a Security to the other Colonies; and Advantage to Britain, by Increasing her People, Territory, Strength and Commerce. Might it not greatly facilitate the Introduction of pure Religion among the Heathen, if we could, by such a Colony, show them a better Sample of Christians than they commonly see in our Indian Traders, the most vicious and abandoned Wretches of our Nation? . . .
Benjamin Franklin, from a letter to Calvinistic Anglican priest George Whitefield, July 2, 1756, in Leonard W. Labaree, ed., The Papers of Benjamin Franklin, *vol. 6, pp. 468–469.*

Your Information of my being chosen a Member of the Royal Society, was extremely agreeable, and the more, as I had not the least Expectation of ever arriving at that Honour. . . . I must request the Favour of you to present my humble Thanks to the Society, whose truly noble Designs I wish I may be able in any Degree to promote. . . .
Benjamin Franklin, from a letter to Peter Collinson, November 5, 1756, in Leonard W. Labaree, ed., The Papers of Benjamin Franklin, *vol. 7, p. 11.*

I am just return'd from the Forks of the Delaware, where I with some others attended the Governor, at a Conference with the Indians. They complain of Injuries from the Proprietors [Thomas and Richard Penn]. I hope he will give timely Orders to redress them when they come down next Spring. It is said by many here, that the Delawares were grosly abus'd in the Walking Purchase; that they have frequently complain'd, and their Complaints were suppress'd or conceal'd, and the 6 Nations set on their Backs to make them quiet. That they have remember'd these Things, and now, by the Connivance of the 6 Nations, as 'tis thought, and supported by the French, they have taken Revenge. Much has the Province suffer'd by this War; some hundreds of Lives lost, many Farms destroy'd, and near £100,000 spent, yet the Proprietor [Thomas Penn] refuses to be taxed, except for the trifling Part of his Estate. . . .
Benjamin Franklin, from a letter written at Philadelphia to Peter Collinson, November 22, 1756, in Leonard W. Labaree, ed., The Papers of Benjamin Franklin, *vol. 7, pp. 23–24.*

1757

He that would rise at Court, must begin by
   Creeping.
Many a Man's own Tongue gives Evidence against
   his Understanding. Nothing dries sooner than a
   Tear.

. . . . .

As these huge tremendous Bodies travel thro' our System, they seem fitted to produce great Changes in it. Mr. Whiston has gone a good Way towards proving that the Comet of 1668, was, in one, of its Revolutions, the Cause of the Deluge, by coming so near this Earth as to raise a vast Tide in the Abyss. . . . The same Comet Sir Isaac Newton has calculated, when in its Perihelion December the 8th, was heated by its Nearness to the Sun to a Degree 2000 times more hot than red hot

Iron, and would require 50,000 Years to cool again. This same Comet, Dr. Halley observed Nov.11, was not above a Semidiameter of the Earth from the Earth's Way; so that had the Earth at that time been in that Part of its Orbit, something very extraordinary might have happened either by Water or Fire.

Benjamin Franklin, from Poor Richard improved: Being an Almanack. . . , *1757, in Leonard W. Labaree, ed.,* The Papers of Benjamin Franklin, *vol. 7, pp. 76 and 90–91.*

It was not until it was too late, we discovered that the French were on the Ohio; or rather, that we could be persuaded they came there with a design to invade his Majesty's dominions. Nay, after I was sent out in December, 1753, and brought undoubted testimony even from themselves of their avowed design, it was yet thought a fiction, and a scheme to promote the interest of a private company, even by some who had a share in the government. These unfavorable surmises caused great delay in raising the first men and money, and gave the active enemy time to take possession of the Fork of Ohio (which they now call Duquesne), before we were in sufficient strength to advance thither, which has been the chief source of all our past and present misfortunes. For by this means, (the French getting between us and our Indian allies), they fixed those in their interests, who were wavering, and obliged the others to neutrality, 'till the unhappy defeat of his (late) Excellency General Braddock.

George Washington, from a letter to the earl of Loudoun, January 1757, in John C. Fitzpatrick, ed., The Writings of George Washington, *vol. 2, pp. 6–7 and 17–18.*

I leave some Enemies in Pensilvania, who will take every Opportunity of injuring me in my Absence. However, as they are my Enemies, not on my own private Account but on that of the Publick, I seem to have some Right to ask the Care of my Friends, to watch 'em and guard my Reputation and Interest as much as may be from the Effects of their Malevolence. I chearfully leave my dearest Concerns ynder that Care, having no reason to doubt the Continuance of the Friendships I have so long experienc'd.

Benjamin Franklin, from a letter written in New York to Joseph Galloway, April 11, 1757, in Leonard W. Labaree, ed., The Papers of Benjamin Franklin, *vol. 7, p. 179.*

Hon'ble Sir: Since closing my packet for your Honor of this date, I have received by Express, from Fort Cumberland the agreeable news of Lt. Bakers return to that place with 5 Scalps &c. one french officer, prisoner. Two other Officers were also made prisoners; but one of them being wounded and unable to march, the Indians killed; and the other they served in the same manner soon after: and bot contrary to the intreaties of Mr. Baker. In this they took revenge for the death of the truly brave Swallow-Warrior, who was killed in the Skirmish, and for the *wound* received by his son; whom they brought from the head of Turtle-creek, where the Engagement happened (about 100 miles beyond Fort Cumberland) on their Shoulders, without eating a morsel the whole distance. The name of the Officer commanding the french troops on the Ohio, together with the names of the two who were killed, and the other taken prisoner, are given in by the latter, as enclosed. The party they engaged, consisted of 10 french, 3 of whom were Officers; who had parted only the day before with fifty odd Shawnese, returning from war. Our people wou'd have taken the whole party, had it not been for the unfortunate loss of the indian chief, which put a stop to his mens pursuing. If this party was to meet with a reward for their Scalps and Services, with no more difficulty, than Warhatchie did in Maryland; it wou'd be attended with happy consequences. If they do not, discontent and murmuring will ensue.

George Washington, from a letter to Robert Dinwiddie, governor of Virginia, June 12, 1757, in John C. Fitzpatrick, ed., The Writings of George Washington, *vol. 2, pp. 57–58.*

No man I conceive was ever more plagued than I have been with the Draughts that were sent from the several counties in this Government, to complete its Regiment: out of 400 that were received at Fredericksburgh, and at this place [Fort Loudoun], 114 have deserted, notwithstanding every precaution, except absolute confinement has been used to prevent this infamous practice. I have used the vigorous measures to apprehend those fellows who escaped from hence (which amounted to about 30) and have succeeded so well that they are taken with the loss of one of their men, and a Soldier wounded. I have a Gallows near 40 feet high erected (which has terrified the *rest* exceedingly), and I am determined if I can be justified in the proceeding, to hang two or three on it, as an example to others.

George Washington, from a letter to Col. John Stanwix, July 15, 1757, in John C. Fitzpatrick, ed., The Writings of George Washington, vol. 2, pp. 97–98.

. . . No troops in the universe can guard against the cunning and wiles of Indians. No one can tell where they will fall, till the mischief is done, and then 't is vain to pursue. The inhabitants see, and are convinced of this, which makes each family afraid of standing in the gap of danger; and by retreating, one behind another, they depopulate the country, and leave it to the enemy, who subsist upon the plunder. This, Sir, is a matter of fact which you may depend on from me; and further, if we pursue a defensive plan next campaign, there will not, by autumn, be one soul living on this side of the BlueRidge, except the soldiers in garrison, and such of the inhabitants as may seek shelter therein. This, Sir, I know to be the immovable determination of the people; and, believe me, when I tell you, that I have been at great pains, before I could prevail on them to wait the consultations of this winter, and the event of spring.

I do not know on whom those miserable, undone people are to rely for redress. If the Assembly are to give it to them, it is time that measures at least were concerting, and not when they should be going into execution, as has always been the case. If they are to seek it from the Commander-in-chief, it is time our grievances were made known to him; for I cannot forbear repeating again, that while we pursue defensive measures we pursue inevitable ruin, the loss of the country being the inevitable and fatal consequence. There will be no end to our troubles, while we follow this plan, and every year will increase our expense. . . .

George Washington, from a letter written at Fort Loudoun to John Robinson, Speaker of the Virginia House of Burgesses, October 25, 1757, in John C. Fitzpatrick, ed., The Writings of George Washington, vol. 2, pp. 154–155.

1758

Get what you can, and what you get hold;
  'Tis the Stone that will turn all your Lead into
    Gold,
as Poor Richard says. . . .

This Doctrine, my Friends, is *Reason* and *Wisdom;* but after all, do not depend too much upon your own

Industry, and *Frugality,* and *Prudence,* though excellent Things, for they may be blasted without the Blessing of Heaven; and therefore ask that Blessing humbly, and be not uncharitable to those that at present seem to want it, but comfort and help them. Remember Job suffered, and was afterwards prosperous.

And now to conclude, *Experience keeps a dear School, but Fools will learn in no other, and scarce in that;* for it is true, *we may give Advice, but we cannot give Conduct,* as Poor Richard says: However, remember this, *They that won't be counseled, can't be helped,* as Poor Richard says: And farther, That *if you will not hear Reason, she'll surely rap your Knuckles.*

Benjamin Franklin, from Poor Richard Improved, *1758, in Leonard W. Labaree, ed.,* The Papers of Benjamin Franklin, *vol. 7, p. 349.*

. . . At present few or none give their Negro Children any Schooling, partly from a Prejudice that Reading and Knowledge in a Slave are both useless and dangerous; and partly from an Unwillingness in the Masters and Mistresses of common Schools to take black Scholars, lest the Parents of white Children should be disgusted and take them away, not choosing to have their Children mix'd with Slaves in Education, Play, &c. But a separate School for Blacks, under the Care of One, of whom People should have an Opinion that he would be careful to imbue the Minds of their young Slaves with good Principles, might probably have a Number of Blacks sent to it; and if on Experience it should be found useful, and not attended with the ill Consequences commonly apprehended, the Example might be followed in the other Colonies, and encouraged by the Inhabitants in general. . .

Benjamin Franklin, from a letter written in London to John Waring in Philadelphia, January 3, 1758, in Leonard W. Labaree, ed., The Papers of Benjamin Franklin, *vol. 7, p. 356.*

I have no Prospect of Returning till next Spring, so you will not expect me. But pray remember to make me as happy as you can, by sending some Pippins for my self and Friends, some of your small Hams, and some Cranberries. Billy [their son] is of the Middle Temple, and will be call'd to the Bar either this Term or the next. I write this in answer to your particular Enquiry.

. . . . .

I think I have now gone thro' your Letters, which always give me great Pleasure to receive and read, since I cannot be with you in Person. Distribute my Compliments, Respects, and Love, among my Friends, and believe me ever my dear Debby Your affectionate Husband.

Benjamin Franklin, from a letter written in London to his wife, Deborah, June 10, 1758, in Leonard W. Labaree, ed., The Papers of Benjamin Franklin, *vol. 8, pp. 92, 93, 94, and 95.*

In a former letter I mentioned the experiment for cooling bodies by evaporation, and that I had, by repeatedly wetting the thermometer with common spirits, brought the mercury down five or six degrees. Being lately at Cambridge, and mentioning this in conversation with Dr. Hadley, professor of chemistry there, he proposed repeating the experiments with ether, instead of common spirits, as the ether is much quicker in evaporation. We accordingly went to his chamber, where he had both ether and a thermometer. By dipping first the ball of the thermometer into ether, it appeared that the ether was precisely of the same temperament with the thermometer, which stood then at 65 . . . But when the thermometer was taken out of the ether, and the ether . . . began to evaporate, the mercury sank several degrees. The wetting was then repeated by a feather that had been dipped into the ether, when the mercury sunk still lower. We continued this operation, one of us wetting the ball, and another of the company blowing on it with the bellows, to quicken the evaporation, the mercury sinking all the time, till it came down to 7, which is 25 degrees below the freezing point, when we left off. . . . From this experiment one may see the possibility of freezing a man to death on a warm summer's day, if he were to stand in a passage thro' which the wind blew briskly, and to be wet frequently with ether, a spirit that is more inflammable than brandy, or common spirits of wine.

Benjamin Franklin, from a letter written in London to John Lining, June 17, 1758, in Leonard W. Labaree, ed., The Papers of Benjamin Franklin, *vol. 8, pp. 108–109.*

There's three Parties gone from hence towards the Enemy's Country within these few days. The largest of them, (consisting of an Officer and 18 Cherokees,) March'd 3 days ago. I always send out *some* white people with the Indians, and will to day or tomorrow, send an Officer and some alert white men, with another Party of Cherokees as you desire it; tho' I must confess, that I think these Scalping Parties of Indians we send out, will more effectually harass the Enemy (by keeping them under continual Alarms) than any Parties of white People can do; because small parties of ours are not equal to the undertaking, (not being so dexterous at skulking as Indians;) and large ones will be discover'd by their spies early enough to give the Enemy time to repell them by a superior Force; and at all events, there is a great probability of loosing many of our best men, and fatiguing others before the most essential Services are enter'd upon and am afraid not answer the propos'd end.

. . . . .

The malbehaviour [stealing goods] of the Indians with you, gives me great concern; if they were hearty in our Interest their Services wou'd be infinitely valuable, as I cannot conceive *the best* white Men to be equal to them in the Woods; but I fear they are too sensible of their high Importance to us, to render us any very acceptable Service.

George Washington, from a letter written at Fort Cumberland to Col. Henry Bouquet, July 16, 1758, in John C. Fitzpatrick, ed., The Writings of George Washington, *vol. 2, pp. 237–238.*

We have begun our march for the Ohio. A courier is starting for Williamsburg, and I embrace the opportunity to send a few words to one whose life is now inseparable from mine. Since that happy hour when we made our pledges to each other, my thoughts have been continually going to you as another Self. That an all-powerful Providence may keep us both in safety is the prayer of your ever faithful and affectionate friend.

George Washington, a letter to Mrs. Martha Custis, July 20, 1758, in John C. Fitzpatrick, ed., The Writings of George Washington, *vol. 2, p. 242.*

We are still Incamp'd here, very sickly; and quite dispirited at the prospect before Us. That appearance of Glory once in view, that hope, that laudible Ambition of serving Our Country, and meriting its applause, is now no more! Tis dwindled into ease; Sloth, and fatal inactivity, and in a Word, All is lost, if the ways of Men in power, like the ways of Providence are not Inscrutable; and, why [are] they not? For we who view the Action's of great Men at so vast a distance can only form conjectures agreeable to the small extant of our knowledge and ignorant of the comprehensive Schemes intended; mistake, plaguily, in judging by the Lump; this may be, and yet every F—l will have his Notions; prattle and talk away, and pray why may not I?

. . . . .

See therefore how our time has been misspent; behold the golden opportunity lost; and perhaps never regain'd. . . . Rather let a full Representation of the matter go to His Majecty. Let him know how grossly his Hon'r and the Publick money have been prostituted. I wish I was sent immediately home as an Aide to some other on this Errand. I think without vanity I cou'd set the Conduct of this Expedition in its true colours, having taken some pains, perhaps more than any other to dive into the bottom of it . . .

George Washington, from a letter written at Fort Cumberland to John Robinson, Speaker of the Virginia House of Burgesses, September 1, 1758, in John C. Fitzpatrick, ed., The Writings of George Washington, *vol. 2, pp. 276–278.*

If you allow that any honor can be derived from my opposition to our present system of management, you destroy the merit entirely in me by attributing my anxiety to the animating prospect of possessing Mrs. Custis, when—I need not tell you, guess yourself. Should not my own Honor and country's welfare be the excitement? 'Tis true, I profess myself a votary of love. I acknowledge that a lady is in the case, and further confess that this lady is known to you. Yes, Madame, as well as she is to one who is too sensible of her charms to deny the Power whose influence he feels and must ever submit to. I feel the force of her amiable beauties in the recollection of a thousand tender passages that I could wish to obliterate, till I am bid to revive them. But experience, alas! sadly reminds me how impossible this is, and evinces an opinion which I have long entertained, that there is a Destiny which has the control of our actions, not to be resisted by the strongest efforts of Human Nature.

George Washington, from a letter written at Fort Cumberland to Mrs. George William Fairfax, September 12, 1758, in John C. Fitzpatrick, ed., The Writings of George Washington, *vol. 2, pp. 287–288.*

I have the pleasure to inform you, that Fort Duquesne, or the ground rather on which it stood, was possessed by his Majesty's troops on the 25th instant. The enemy, after letting us get within a day's march of the place, burned the fort, and ran away (by the light of it,) at night, going down the Ohio by water, to the number of about five hundred men, from our best information. The possession of this fort has been a matter of great surprise to the whole army, and we cannot attribute it to more probable causes, than those of weakness, want of provisions, and desertion of their Indians. Of these circumstances we were luckily informed by three prisoners, who providentially fell into our hands at Loyal Hannan . . . the information caused us to march on without tents or baggage, and with a light train of artillery only, with which we have happily succeeded . . .

. . . . .

This fortunate, and, indeed unexpected success of our arms will be attended with happy effects. The Delawares are suing for peace, and I doubt not that other tribes on the Ohio will follow their example. A trade, free, open, and upon equitable terms, is what they seem to stickle for, and I do not know so effectual a way of riveting them to our interest, as sending our goods immediately to this place for that purpose. It will, at the same time, be a means of supplying the garrison with such necessaries as may be wanted; and, I think, those colonies, which are as greatly interested in the support of this place as Virginia is, should neglect no means in their power to establish and support a strong garrison here. Our business, (wanting this) will be but half finished; while, on the other hand, we obtain a firm and lasting peace, if this end is once accomplished.

George Washington, from a letter written at Fort Duquesne to Francis Fauquier, lieutenant governor of Virginia, November 28, 1758, in John C. Fitzpatrick, ed., The Writings of George Washington, *vol. 2, pp. 308–309 and 310.*

1759

I rejoice to hear of the Establishment of Peace with the Indians, and the Repose now enjoy'd by our Frontiers. . . . But I fear, if the present Expedition against Canada, should, as most Expeditions do, fail of Success, the French will return to the Ohio, and debauch the Indians again from our Friendship, if they are not retain'd in that Friendship, and the French discourag'd from the Attempt, by our keeping Possession of Fort Duquesne and the other Forts erected to secure our Communication with it.... I hope, therefore, Pittsburg will not be abandon'd. But by establishing a Trade with the Indians on the fairest Terms, giving them the strongest Assurances that no Encroachment shall be made on their Lands; no Settlements attempted without fair Purchase, and those only in a small Compass round the Forts just to supply them Provisions; the Indians may be thoroughly reconcil'd to our abiding there.

Benjamin Franklin, from a letter written in London to Joseph Galloway, April 7, 1759, in Leonard W. Labaree, ed., The Papers of Benjamin Franklin, *vol. 8, p. 312.*

Gentln. The Inclos'd is the Ministers Certificate of my Marriage with Mrs. Martha Custis, properly as I am told, Authenticated, You will therefore for the future please to address all your Letters which relate to the Affairs of the late Danl. Parke Custis Esqr. to me, as by Marriage I am entitled to a third part of that Estate, and Invested likewise with the care of the other two thirds by a Decree of our Genl. Court which I obtain'd in order to strengthen the Power I beforef had in consequence of my Wifes Administration.

· · · · ·

On the otherside is an Invoice of some Goods which I beg of you to send me by the first Ship bound either to Potomack or Rappahannock, as I am in immediate want of them. Let them be Insur'd, and in case of Accident reshipp'd witht. Delay; direct for me at Mount Vernon Potomack River Virginia....

INVOICE OF SUNDRY GOODS TO BE SHIP'D BY ROBT. CARY, ESQ., AND COMPANY FOR THE USE OF GEORGE WASHINGTON—VIZ: May, 1759

1 Tester Bedstead 7 1/2 feet pitch, with fashionable bleu or bleu and White Curtains to suit a Room lind w't the Ireld. paper.—
Window Curtains of the same for two Windows; with either Papier Mache Cornish to them, or Cornish cover'd with the Cloth.

1 fine Bed Coverlid to match the Curtains. 4 Chair bottoms of the same; that is, as much Covring suited to the above furniture ... to make the whole furniture of this Room uniformly handsome and genteel.
1 Fashionable Sett of Desert Glasses, and Stands for Sweet Meats Jellys &ca. Together with Wash Glasses and a proper Stand for these also.—
2 Setts of Chamber, or Bed Carpets—Wilton.
4 Fashionable China Branches, & Stands, for Candles.
2 Neat fire Screens
50 lbs Spirma Citi Candles
6 Carving knives and Forks—handles of Stain'd Ivory and bound with Silver.
A pretty large Assortment of Grass Seeds ...
1 Large, neat, and easy Couch for a Passage.
50 yards of best Floor Matting.—
2 pair of fashionable mix'd, or Marble Cold. Silk Hose.
6 pr. Of finest Cotton Ditto.
6 pr. Of finest thread Ditto.
6 pr. Of midling Do. To cost abt. 5/.
6 pr. Worsted Do of ye best sorted—2 pr. Of w'ch, to be White. N.B. All the above Stockings to be long, and tolerably large.
1 piece of finest and most fashionable Stock Tape.
1 Suit of Cloaths of the finest Cloth, & fashionable colour made by the Inclos'd measure.—
The newest, and most approv'd Treatise of Agriculture—besides this, send me a small piece in Octavo—call'd a New System of Agriculture, or a Speedy Way to grow Rich.
Longley's Book of Gardening.—
Gibson, upon Horses the latest Edition in Quarto—
Half a dozn. Pair of Men's neatest Shoes and Pumps ...
6 pr. Mens riding Gloves rather large than the middle size.
One neat Pocket Book, capable of receiving Memorandoms & small Cash Accts. To be made of Ivory, or any thing else that will admit of cleaning.—
Fine Soft Calf Skin for a pair of Boots—
Ben leathr. for Soles.
Six Bottles of Greenhows Tincture.

Order from the best House in Madeira a Pipe of the best Old Wine, and let it be Secur'd from Pilferers.

George Washington, from a letter written at Williamsburg to Robert Cary & Company, Merchants, London, May 1, 1759, in John C. Fitzpatrick, ed., The Writings of George Washington, *vol. 2, pp. 319–321.*

We are extremely anxious here to know the Event of the Expedition against Ticonderoga and Quebeck, particularly the latter, which has been represented by those who are no Friends of Mr. Pitt's Measures as impracticable on Account of the Navigation. For my Part, I think there is nothing in that Objection, and that if any Thing prevents General Wolfe's Success it must be the Want of a sufficient Number of Men. If that should be the Case, whoever directed the carrying on an Expedition to Niagara, and another to Venango, at the same Time as the two grand Expeditions were on foot, will incur a great deal of Censure. It will be ask'd, If the Taking of Quebec would not render all the others unnecessary? And if so, Should not the chief part of our Forces have been directed to that Quarter? . . .

William Franklin, son of Benjamin, from a letter written in London to Peter Schuyler, June 19, 1759, in Leonard W. Labaree, ed., The Papers of Benjamin Franklin, *vol. 8, p. 408.*

1760

January. Tuesday. 1. Visited my Plantations and receiv'd an Instance of Mr. French's great love of Money in disappointing me of some Pork, because the price had risen to 22/6, after he had engaged to let me have it at 20/. Call'd at Mr. Possey's in my way home and desir'd him to engage me 100 Bar'ls. of Corn upon the best terms he coud in Maryland. And found Mrs. Washington upon my arrival broke out with the Meazles.

. . . . .

Thursday, 3d. The Weather continuing Bad & ye same causes subsisting I confind my self to the House. Morris [an overseer] who went to work yesterday caught cold, and was laid up bad again, and several of the family were taken with Measles, but no bad Symptoms seemed to attend any of them. Hauled the Sein and got some fish, but was near being disappointd. of my Boat by means of

an Oyster Man who had lain at my Landing and plagud me a good deal by his disorderly behavior.

George Washington, diary entries, January 1760, in John C. Fitzpatrick, ed., The Writings of George Washington, *vol. 2, pp. 340–341.*

No one can rejoice more sincerely than I do on the Reduction of Canada; and this, not merely as I am a Colonist, but as I am a Briton. I have long been of Opinion, that the Foundations of the future Grandeur and Stability of the British Empire, lie in America; and tho', like other Foundations, they are low and little seen, they are nevertheless, broad and Strong enough to support the greatest Political Structure Human Wisdom ever yet erected. I am therefore by no means for restoring Canada. If we keep it, all the Country from St. Laurence to Missisipi, will in another Century be fill'd with British People; Britain itself will become vastly more populous by the immense Increase of its Commerce; the Atlantic Sea will be cover'd with your Trading Ships; and your naval Power thence continually increasing, will extend your Influence round the whole Globe, and awe the World! If the French remain in Canada, they will continually harass our Colonies by the Indians, impede if not prevent their Growth; your Progress to Greatness will at best be slow, and give room for many Accidents that may for ever prevent it. . . .

Benjamin Franklin, from a letter written in London to Scottish judge and author Henry Home, Lord Kames, January 3, 1760, in Leonard W. Labaree, ed., The Papers of Benjamin Franklin, *vol. 9, pp. 6–7.*

I received a Letter or two from you, in which I perceive you have misunderstood and taken unkindly something I said to you in a former jocular one of mine concerning CHARITY. I forget what it was exactly, but I am sure I neither express nor meant any personal Censure on you or any body. If anything, it was a general Reflection on our Sect; we zealous Presbyterians being too apt to think ourselves alone in the right, and that besides all the Heathens, Mahometans and Papists, whom we give to Satan in a Lump, other Sects of Christian Protestants that do not agree with us, will hardly escape Perdition. And I might recommend it to you to be more charitable in that respect than many others are. . . .

Benjamin Franklin, from a letter written in London to his sister Jane Mecom, January 9, 1760, in Leonard W. Labaree, ed., The Papers of Benjamin Franklin, *vol. 9, pp. 17–18.*

... Is it because you have left your native land at the risk of your lives and fortunes to toil for your mother country, to load her with wealth, that you are to be rewarded with a loss of your privileges? Are you not of the same stock? Was the blood of your ancestors polluted by a change of soil? Were they freemen in *England* and did they become slaves by a six-weeks' voyage to *America?* Does not the sun shine as bright, our blood run as warm? Is not our honor and virtue as pure, our liberty as valuable, our property as dear, our lives as precious here as in *England?* Are we not subjects of the same King, and bound by the same laws, and have we not the same God for our protector?

What, then, can you think of those abject *Americans,* those slaves by principle, those traitors to their own and posterity's happiness, who, plunging the dagger into the vitals of their own liberty, do not blush at declaring that you are not *entitled to the same security of property, the same rights and privileges of the freeborn subjects of* England? Let me ask those enemies to your welfare, how much thereof are you entiled to? Who will measure out and distribute your poor pittance, your short allowance? Is a tenth, an hundredth, or a thousandth part to be the portion of your liberty? Abject, detestable thought! The poor *African,* who is taken captive in war and dragged an involuntary slave to *Jamaica* calls for your humanity and compassion; but the voluntary wretch that works out his own and posterity's slavish condition for the sake of a little present lucre, promotion, or power is an object deserving your deepest resentment, your highest indignation.

> *Joseph Galloway (probably), from* A Letter to the People of Pennsylvania, &c., *Philadelphia, 1760, in Bernard Bailyn, ed.,* Pamphlets of the American Revolution, 1750–1776, *vol. 1, pp. 270–271.*

... The discouraging Sales I have generally got for all Tobos. [tobaccos] Shipped of my own growth, has induced me to dispose of my last year's Crop in the Country, the price being good and certain, but this may not always happen, and while I can Ship without loss I shall always be glad to have it in my power of consigning you a part....

The French are so well Drubd, and seem so much humbled in America, that I apprehend our Generals will find it no difficult matter to reduce Canada to our Obedience this Summer, but what may be Montgomery's Fate in the Cherokee Country I wont so readily determine.

It seems he has made a prosperous beginning having penetrated into the Heart of the Country, and is now advancing his Troops in high health and Spirits to the relief of Fort Loudoun. But let him be wary, he has a crafty, Subtil Enemy to deal with that may give him most trouble when he least expects it. We are in pain here for the King of Prussia, and wish Hanover safe, these being Events in which we are much Interested.

> *George Washington, from a letter written at Mount Vernon to London merchant Richard Washington, August 10, 1760, in John C. Fitzpatrick, ed.,* The Writings of George Washington, *vol. 2, pp. 344–345.*

I am not a little pleas'd to hear of your Change of Sentiments in some particulars relating to America; because I think it of Importance to our general Welfare that the People of this Nation should have right Notions of us, and I know no one that has it more in his Power to rectify their Notions, than Mr. Hume. I have lately read with great Pleasure, as I do every thing of yours, the excellent Essay on the *Jealousy of Commerce.* I think it cannot but have a good Effect in promoting a certain Interest too little thought of by selfish Man; ... I mean the *Interest of Humanity,* or common Good of Mankind: But I hope particularly from that Essay, an Abatement of the Jealousy that reigns here of the Commerce of the Colonies....

> *Benjamin Franklin, from a letter written in Coventry, England to David Hume, September 27, 1760, in Leonard W. Labaree, ed.,* The Papers of Benjamin Franklin, *vol. 9, p. 229.*

1761

Dear Sir: Since my last of 14th July I have in appearance been very near my last gasp; the Indisposition then spoken of Increased upon me and I fell into a very low and dangerous State. I once thought the grim King would certainly master my utmost efforts and that I must sink in spite of a noble struggle but thank God I have now got the better of the disorder and shall soon be restord I hope to perfect health again.

I dont know that I can Muster up one title of News to communicate, in short the occurrances of this part of the World are at present scarce worth reciting for as we live in a state of peaceful tranquility ourselves, so we are at very little trouble to enquire after the operations against the Cherokees who are the only People that disturbs the repose of this great Continent and who I believe woud gladly accommodate Differences upon almost any Terms not I conceive from any Apprehensions they are under on account of Our Arms but because they want the Supplys which we, and we only, can furnish them with. We catch the reports of Peace with gaping Mouths, and every Person seems anxious for a confirmation of that desirable Event provided it comes, as no doubt it will, upon honorable terms.

George Washington, from a letter written at Mount Vernon to Richard Washington, October 20, 1761, in John C. Fitzpatrick, ed., The Writings of George Washington, *vol. 2, p. 371.*

1762

In Compliance with my Lord Marishall's [George Keith, Earl Marischal] Request, communicated to me by you when I last had the Pleasure of seeing you, I now send you what at present appears to me to be the shortest and simplest Method of securing Buildings, &c. from the Mischiefs of Lightning.

Prepare a Steel Rod 5 or 6 Feet long, half an Inch thick at its biggest End, and tapering to a sharp Point, which Point should be gilt to prevent its rusting. Let the big End of the Rod have a strong Eye or Ring of half an Inch Diameter: Fix this Rod upright to the Chimney or highest part of the Building, by means of Staples, so as it may be kept steady. Let the pointed End be upwards, and rise three or four Feet above the Chimney or Building that the Rod is fix'd to. Drive into the Ground an Iron Rod about an Inch Diameter, and ten or twelve feet long, that has also an Eye or Ring, in its upper End. . . .

A Building thus guarded, will not be damaged by Lightning, nor any Person or Thing therein kill'd, hurt or set on fire . . .

Benjamin Franklin, from a letter written in London to David Hume, January 21, 1762, in Leonard W. Labaree, ed., The Papers of Benjamin Franklin, *vol. 10, pp. 17–18.*

I have sent off your Letter to Lord Marischal, who . . . is at present very much employd in settling the Controversy about the Eternity of Hell-Torments, which has set the little Republic of Neuf-chatel in Combustion. I have ventur'd to recommend to his Lordship the abridging these Torments as much as possible, and have usd the Freedom to employ your name, as well as my own, in this Request: I have told him,

that, as we have taken so much Pains to preserve him and his Subjects from the Fires of Heaven, they cannot do less than guard us from the Fires of Hell. My Lord told me . . . that the King of Prussia could not at first be brought to regard this theological Controversy as a Matter of any Moment, but soon found . . . that these were not matters to be slighted. But surely, never was a Synod of Divines more ridiculous, than to be worrying one another, under the Arbitration of the King of Prussia and Lord Marischal, who will make an Object of Derision of every thing, that appears to these holy Men so deserving of Zeal, Passion, and Animosity.

David Hume, from a letter written at Edinburgh to Benjamin Franklin, May 10, 1762, in Leonard W. Labaree, ed., The Papers of Benjamin Franklin, *vol. 10, p. 81.*

Dear Sir: Soon after the Appraisement of the Decd. Colo. Custis's Estate it seemed to be a matter of doubt whether Davy (a boy) who was appraised among his Negroes belonged to him, or Mr. Dandridge your Father. Your Bro: then having, as I have understood, the Administration of his Affairs, conceived him to be the property of the latter and offered the boy to Mrs. Washington at the Appraisement price, which She agreed to, and I thought the thing had been concluded upon, but as it appeared to be a matter liable to dispute I intended to take the Courts direction's upon it . . . until mentioning the Affair again to your Bro:, he told me that he now had nothing to do in it, and that I must speak to you about it. . . . I therefore take this method of knowing if it is agreable to you for me to take the boy at the Appraisd price, provided the Court shall adjudge the Right to him to lye in your Father . . . and as Mrs. Washington relinquished her right to a Childs part of the whole Estate, and seems desirous of making a Gardner of this boy, I imagine you will not be against it. . . .

George Washington, from a letter written at Mount Vernon to Captain William Dandridge, May 20, 1762, in John C. Fitzpatrick, ed., The Writings of George Washington, *vol. 2. pp. 375–376.*

Dear Sir: I am sorry to be the Messenger of ill news, but it is incumbent upon me to inform you of the Death of the Mare you committed to my care; how she died, I am able to give you but a very unsatisfactory acct., for on the 3d. Instt. I set out for Frederick and left her to all appearance as well as a Creature could be . . . and on my return in 8 days time, I got the News of her death. She discovered no visible Signs of ailment as I am told in the morning of the 7th. when let out of the Stable, but before Night was swelled to a monstrous size and died in a few hours. . . . She had no Foal in her, which assures me that she never woud Breed. As I am convinced she had a competent share of Ariel's performances; not content with which, She was often catched in amorious moods with a young horse of mine not withstanding my utmost endeavours to keep them asunder.

You will feel the loss of this accident more sensibly, but cannot be more concerned at the acct. than I was, for I had pleased myself with the thoughts of delivering her to you in fine order when you returned to Belvoir.

George Washington, from a letter written at Mount Vernon to George William Fairfax, October 30, 1762, in John C. Fitzpatrick, ed., The Writings of George Washington, *vol. 2, pp. 385–386.*

1763

. . . The Preliminaries of Peace, on which I congratulate you, are since come to hand, and are universally approved of in these Parts. While we retain our Superiority at Sea, and are suffer'd to grow numerous and strong in North America, I cannot but look on the Places left or restor'd to our Enemies on this Side the Ocean, as so many Pledges for their good Behaviour. Those Places will hereafter be so much in our Power, that the more valuable they are to the Possessors, the more cautious will they naturally be of giving us Offence. So that I think this peace has all the Appearance of being a durable one.

Benjamin Franklin, from a letter written in Philadelphia to Richard Jackson, March 8, 1763, in Leonard W. Labaree, ed., The Papers of Benjamin Franklin, *vol. 10, p. 208.*

Tis no small pleasure to me, to hear of the great proficioncy you have made in the French tongue, A Tongue Sweet, and harmonious, a Tongue, useful to Merchants, to Statesmen; to Divines, and especially to Lawyers and Travellers; . . . for . . . the French language is pretty much now, what I have heard the Latin formerly was, a universal tongue.

By the favor of my Father I have had the pleasure of seeing your Copy of Mrs. Wheelwrights Letter, to her Nephew, and having some small acquaintance with the French tongue, have attempted a translation of it, which I here send, for your perusal and correction.

I am sensible that I am but ill qualified for such an undertaking, it being a maxim with me that no one can translate an author well, who cannot write like the original, and I find by Experience that tis more difficult to translate well, than to write well.

Abigail Smith, future Mrs. John Adams, from a letter written at Weymouth, Massachusetts, to her cousin Isaac Smith, Jr., March 16, 1763, in L. H. Butterfield, ed., Adams Family Correspondence, *vol. 1, pp. 3–4.*

This upon my Soul is a genuine Acct. of my Affairs in England, here they are a little better because I am not much in debt. I doubt not but you will be surprized at the badness of their condition unless you will consider under what terrible management and disadvantages I found my Estate when I retired from the Publick Service of this Colony; and that besides some purchases of Lands and Negroes I was necessitated to make adjoining me (in order to support the Expences of a large Family), I had Provision's of all kinds to buy for the first two or three years; and my Plantation to stock in short with every thing; Buildings to make, and other matters, which swallowed up before I well knew where I was, all the money I got by Marriage nay more, brought me in Debt, and I believe I may appeal to your own knowledge of my Circumstances before.

George Washington, from a letter to Robert Stewart, April 27, 1763, in John C. Fitzpatrick, ed., The Writings of George Washington, *vol. 2, p. 397.*

Our Wheat in this part of the Country is in great measure destroyed by the Rust, and other defect in the ear; and our Crops of Indian Corn and Tobacco in a manner lost in Weeds and Grass, occassioned by continual and excessive Rains, that has not only forced these out in very uncommon abundance, but prevented all sorts of tillage where our Lands lay flat. . . .

George Washington, from a letter written at Mount Vernon to Burwell Bassett, July 5, 1763, in John C. Fitzpatrick, ed., The Writings of George Washington, *vol. 2, p. 401.*

You have seen, in general, by the public papers, what a Cry is raised against the peace, and how unpopular it has rendered Lord Bute. I wish I cou'd say, that making this peace was Lord B's only fault, for I agree with you in thinking it a very good one. But I am sorry to tell you, that my Countryman has shewn himself altogether unequal to his high Station. Never did a Ministry, in our Memory, discover so much Weakness. They seem to have neither Spirit, Courage, Sense, nor Activity, and are a Rope of Sand. . . . From all of this you may easily conceive, we are in a very unaccountable and untoward Situation. Here is a Young, virtuous, *British* King, who can have no Interest separate from that of his People, and who, tho' not possessed of any striking Talents, or any great Degree of Sagacity, yet having much Good Nature, and a Disposition to please, rendered, in the beginning of his Reign, singularly unpopular; and a Minister [Bute], hating Corruption, abhorring Hypocrisy, and having the Prosperity of his Country really at heart, the Object of universal Disgust. . . .

William Strahan, from a letter written at Bath, England, to his intimate friend Benjamin Franklin, August 18, 1763, in Leonard W. Labaree, ed., The Papers of Benjamin Franklin, *vol. 10, pp. 324–325.*

The present Indian War, made upon our Western Posts and Settlements by the Chippaways and Ottawaws, French Indians, with whom we never before the Conquest of Canada had any Correspondence, was undoubtedly stirr'd up by the French Commandant in the Illinois Country, who sent Belts among them last Fall, before the Peace. They prevail'd on the Delawares to join them, who are grown fond of Plunder since the last War. But I think when the Indians see us in Possession of the Illinois Posts, . . . this War will cease. I hope however that they will be well chastis'd, particularly the Delawares, before we talk of Peace to them. Or they will be continually breaking with us.

Benjamin Franklin, from a letter written in Boston to Richard Jackson, September 22, 1763, in Leonard W. Labaree, ed., The Papers of Benjamin Franklin, *vol. 10, p. 342.*

1764

I do not suppose, Sir, that you look upon the present inhabitants of Virginia as a people conquered by the British arms. If indeed we are to be considered only as the savage ABORIGINES of this part of America, we cannot pretend to the rights of English subjects; but if we are the descendants of Englishmen, who by their own consent and at the expense of their own blood and treasure undertook to settle this new region for the benefit and aggrandizement of the parent kingdom, the native privileges our progenitors enjoyed must be derived to us from them, as they could not be forfeited by their migration to America.

. . . . .

Under an English government all men are born free, are only subject to laws made with their own consent, and cannot be deprived of the benefit of these laws without a transgression of them. To assert this is sufficient; to demonstrate it to an Englishman is useless. He not only KNOWS, but . . . FEELS it as a vital principle in the constitution, which places him in a situation without the reach of the highest EXECUTIVE POWER in the state, if he lives in an obedience to its laws.

If then the people of this colony are freeborn and have a right to the liberties and privileges of English subjects, they must necessarily have a legal constitution, that is, a legislature composed in part of the representatives of the people who may enact laws for INTERNAL government of the colony and suitable to its various circumstances and occasions; and without such a representative, I am bold enough to say, no law can be made.

Richard Bland, from The Colonel Dismounted, *Williamsburg, 1764, in Bernard Bailyn, ed.,* Pamphlets of the American Revolution, 1750–1776, *vol. 1, pp. 319–320.*

If these internal taxations take place, and the principles upon which they must be founded are adopted and carried into execution, the colonies will have no more than a show of legislation left, nor the King's subjects in them any more than the shadow of true English liberty; for the same principles which will justify such a tax of a penny will warrant a tax of a pound, an hundred, or a thousand pounds, and so on without limitation; and if they will warrant a tax on one article, they will support one on as many particulars as shall be thought necessary to raise any sum proposed. And all such subjections, burdens, and deprivations, if they take place with respect to the King's subjects abroad, will be without their consent, without their having opportunity to be represented or to show their ability, disability, or circumstances. They will no longer enjoy that fundamental privilege of Englishmen whereby, in special, they are denominated a free people. The legislative authority of the colonies will in part be actually cut off. . . . Nay, may it not be truly said in this case that the Assemblies in the colonies will have left no power or authority, and the people no other freedom, estates, or privileges than what may be called a tenancy at will; that they have exchanged, or rather lost, those privileges and rights which, according to the national constitution, were their birthright and inheritance, for such a disagreeable tenancy? . . . May it not, upon the whole, be concluded that charging stamp duties or other internal duties by authority of Parliament . . . will be such an infringement of the rights, privileges, and authorities of the colonies that it may be humbly and firmly trusted and even relied upon that the supreme guardians of the liberties of the subjects will not suffer the same to be done, and will not only protect them in the enjoyment of their just rights but treat them with great tenderness, indulgence, and favor?

Thomas Fitch, et al., from Reasons Why the British Colonies in America Should Not Be Charged with Internal Taxes, *New Haven, 1764, in Bernard Bailyn, ed.,* Pamphlets of the American Revolution, 1750–1776, *vol. 1, pp. 393–394.*

The colonists are by the law of nature freeborn, as indeed all men are, white or black. No better reasons can be given for enslaving those of any color than such as Baron Montesquieu has humorously given as the foundation of that cruel slavery exercised over the poor Ethiopians, which threatens one day to reduce both Europe and America to the ignorance and barbarity of the darkest ages. Does it follow that 'tis right to enslave a man because he is black? Will short curled hair like wool instead of Christian hair, as 'tis called by those whose hearts are as hard as the nether millstone, help the argument? Can any logical inference in favor of slavery be drawn from a flat nose, a long or a short face? Nothing better can be said in favor of a trade that is the most shocking violation of the law of nature, has a direct tendency to diminish the idea of the inestimable value of liberty, and makes every dealer in it a tyrant, from the director of an African company to the petty chapman in needles and pins on the unhappy coast. It is a clear truth that those who every day barter away other men's liberty will soon care little for their own. To this cause must be imputed that ferocity, cruelty, and brutal barbarity that has long marked the general character of the sugar islanders. They can in general form no idea of government but

that which in person or by an overseer . . . is exercised over ten thousand of their fellow men, born with the same right to freedom and the sweet enjoyments of liberty and life as their unrelenting taskmasters, the overseers and planters.

. . . . .

I can see no reason to doubt but that the imposition of taxes, whether on trade, or on land, or houses, or ships, on real or personal, fixed or floating property, in the colonies is absolutely irreconcilable with the rights of the colonists as British subjects and as men. I say men, for in a state of nature no man can take my property from me without my consent: if he does, he deprives me of my liberty and makes me a slave. If such a proceeding is a breach of the law of nature, no law of society can make it just. The very act of taxing exercised over those who are not represented appears to me to be depriving them of one of their most essential rights as freemen, and if continued seems to be in effect an entire disfranchisement of every civil right. For what one civil right is worth a rush after a man's property is subject to be taken from him at pleasure without his consent? If a man is not his *own assessor* in person or by deputy, his liberty is gone or lays entirely at the mercy of others.

James Otis, from The Rights of the British Colonies Asserted and Proved, *Boston, 1764, in Bernard Bailyn, ed.,* Pamphlets of the American Revolution, 1750–1776, *vol. 1, pp. 439–440 and 447.*

The reason given for this extraordinary taxation, namely, that this war was undertaken for the security of the colonies, and that they ought therefore to be taxed to pay the charge thereby incurred, it is humbly apprehended is without foundation. For—

(1) It was of no less consequence to Great Britain than it was to the colonies that these should not be overrun and conquered by the French. . . . Put the case that the town of *Portsmouth* or any other seaport had been besieged and the like sums expended in its defense, could any have thought that town ought to be charged with the expense?

(2) The colonies contributed their full proportion to those conquests which adorn and dignify the late and present reign. One of them in particular raised in one year seven thousand men to be commanded by His Majesty's general. . . . All of them . . . have

incurred heavy debts, which it will take them many years to pay.

(3) The colonies are no particular gainers by these acquisitions. None of the conquered territory is annexed to them. All are acquisitions accruing to the crown. . . .

(4) Great Britain gaineth immensely by these acquisitions. The command of the whole American fur trade and the increased demand for their woolen manufactures from their numerous new subjects in a country too cold to keep sheep. . . .

Oxenbridge Thatcher, from The Sentiments of a British American, *Boston, 1764, in Bernard Bailyn, ed.,* Pamphlets of the American Revolution, 1750–1776, *vol. 1, pp. 491–492.*

How do you now? For my part, I feel much easier than I did an hour ago, My Unkle haveing given me a more particuliar, and favorable account of the Small pox, or rather the operation of the preparation [inoculation], than I have had before. He speaks greatly in favor of Dr. Perkins who has not, as he has heard lost one patient. . . .

I hope you will have reason to be well satisfied with the Dr., and advise you to follow his prescriptions as nigh as you find your Health will permit. . . .

Abigail Smith, from a letter written at Weymouth, Massachusetts, to her fiancé, John Adams, April 7, 1764, in L. H. Butterfield, ed., Adams Family Correspondence, *vol. 1, p. 15.*

My dear Diana

For many Years past, I have not felt more serenely than I do this Evening. My Head is clear, and my Heart is at ease. Business of every Kind, I have banished from my Thoughts. My Room is prepared for a Seven Days' Retirement, and my Plan is digested for 4 or 5 Weeks. My Brother retreats with me, to our preparatory Hospital, and is determined to keep me Company, through the Small Pox [that is, inoculation and its aftermath]. Your Unkle . . . especially by the Favour he left me from you [her letter of April 7], has contributed very much to the Felicity of my present Frame of Mind. For, I assure you Sincerely, that, (as Nothing which I before expected from the Distemper [small pox] gave me more Concern, than the Thought of a six Weeks Separation from my Diana) my Departure from your House this Morning made an Impression upon me that was severely painfull. I thought I left you, in Tears and

Anxiety—And was very glad to hear by your Letter, that your Tears were abated. . . .

John Adams, from a letter to his fiancée, Abigail Smith, April 7, 1764, in L. H. Butterfield, ed., Adams Family Correspondence, *vol. 1, p. 16.*

I long to come once more to Weymouth before I go to Boston. I could, well enough. I am as well as ever, and better too. Why should not I come? Shall I come and keep fast with you? Or will you come and see me? I shall be glad to see you in this House, but there is another [now John Quincy Adams Birthplace] very near it, where I should rejoice much more to see you, and to live with you till we shall have lived enough to ourselves, to Glory, Virtue and Mankind, and till both of us shall be desirous of Translation to a wiser, fairer, better World.

I am, and till then, and forever after will be your Admirer and Friend, and Lover,

John Adams, from a letter written at Braintree, Massachusetts, to his fiancée, Abigail Smith, April 11, 1764, in L. H. Butterfield, ed., Adams Family Correspondence, *vol. 1, p. 23.*

I have one Request to make, which is that you would be very careful in making Tom, Smoke all the Letters from me, very faithfully, before you, or any of the Family reads them. For, altho I shall never fail to smoke them myself before sealing, Yet I fear the Air of this House will be too much infected, soon, to be absolutely without Danger, and I would not you should take the Distemper [small pox], by Letter from me, for Millions. I write at a Desk far removed from any sick Room, and shall use all Care I can, but too much cannot be used.

John Adams, from a letter written at Boston to his fiancée, Abigail Smith, April 13, 1764, in L. H. Butterfield, ed., Adams Family Correspondence, *vol. 1, p. 29.*

1765

It is notorious that smuggling, which an eminent writer calls a crime against the law of nature, had well nigh become established in some of the colonies. Acts of Parliament had been uniformly dispensed with by those whose duty it was to execute them; corruption, raised upon the ruins of duty and virtue, had almost grown into a system; courts of admiralty, confined within small territorial jurisdictions, became subject to mercantile influence, and the King's revenue shamefully sacrificed to the venality and perfidiousness of courts and officers. If, my friend, customs are due to the crown; if illicit commerce is to be put an end to as ruinous to the welfare of the nation; if by reason of the interested views of traders and the connivance of courts and customhouse officers, these ends could not be compassed or obtained in the common and ordinary way, tell me, what could the government do but to apply a remedy desperate as the disease? There is, I own, a severity in the method of prosecution in the new established court of admiralty . . . here; but it is a severity we have brought upon ourselves, When every mild expedient to stop the atrocious and infamous practice of smuggling has been tried in vain, the government is justifiable in making laws against it, even like those of Draco, which were written in blood. The new instituted court of admiralty and the power given to the seizor are doubtless intended to make us more circumspect in our trade, and to confine the merchant, from motives of fear and dread, within the limits of fair commerce. . . .

> *Martin Howard, Jr., from* A Letter from a Gentleman at Halifax, *Newport, 1765, in Bernard Bailyn, ed.,* Pamphlets of the American Revolution, 1750– 1776, *vol. 1, p. 541.*

I should be glad to know how the gentleman [Martin Howard, Jr. at Halifax] came by his assurance that "a stamp duty is confessedly the most reasonable and equitable that can be devised" (*ibid.*). Some few may be of this opinion, and there never was a new invented tax or excise but its favorers and partisans would highly extol as the most just and equitable device imaginable. This is a trite game "at ways and means." But old assertions will not pass for clear proofs with "philosophically inquisitive minds.". . .

. . . . .

. . . Where does the gentleman find it decreed that the British "*coloniae* have no right of bearing honors in Great Britain"? Has not the King's Majesty, the fountain of honor, an undoubted right by his prerogative to confer any rank he may be graciously pleased to bestow on his American subjects, as well as on those in Great Britain? Cannot the word of a King as easily make even a Halifaxian Letter Writer or his Rhode Island friend a knight of the garter or thistle as if either of them had

been dropped and drawn their first breath in one of the three kingdoms?

The gentleman may in his anger wish for the laws of "Draco to be enforced on America," and in his fierce anger, for the "iron rod of a Spanish inquisitor." These may be sudden gusts of passion, without malice pretense, that only hurt his cause. . . . But hard, very hard must his heart be who could employ all his stock of learning in a deliberate attempt to reduce the rights of the colonists to the narrow bound of a bare permission to "use the English laws and religion without a suffrage in things sacred or civil and without a right to bear honors in Great Britain," "except that of being shot at for six pence a day in her armies at home as well as abroad.". . . If he is an American by birth, what does he deserve of his country for attempting to realize to this and to all future generations the dreary prospect of confinement to the use of the laws and religion of a region 3000 miles beyond sea, in framing which laws and in forming the modes of which religion they shall have no voice nor suffrage, nor shall they have any preferment in church or state, though they shall be taxed without their consent to the support of both?

> *James Otis, from* A VINDICATION *of the British Colonies, against the Aspersions of the Halifax Gentleman, in His Letter to a Rhode Island Friend, Boston, 1765, in Bernard Bailyn, ed.,* Pamphlets of the American Revolution, 1750–1776, *vol. 1, pp. 569 and 570–571.*

. . . I should be obliged to you for sending me one of the Rotheram (or Patent Plows). If the construction of them are not thoroughly understood in Liverpool you woud do me a singular favour in getting it from a place of that name in Yorkshire (where I suppose they were first Invented and now are made) for none but the true sort will answer the end of my sending for it and I had rather be at the expence of the Carriage from thence than not have the right kind or be disappointed. You will please order it to be made exceeding light as our Lands are not so stiff as your's nor our Horses so strong. . . .

> *George Washington, from a letter written at Mount Vernon to Crosbies & Trafford, March 6, 1765, in John C. Fitzpatrick, ed.,* The Writings of George Washington, *vol. 2, p. 421.*

At present few things are under notice of my observation that can afford you any amusement in the recital.

The Stamp Act Imposed on the Colonies by the Parliament of Great Britain engrosses the conversation of the Speculative part of the Colonists, who look upon this unconstitutional method of Taxation as a direful attack upon their Liberties, and loudly exclaim against the Violation; what may be the result of this and some other (I think I may add) ill judgd Measures, I will not undertake to determine; but this I may venture to affirm, that the advantage accrueing to the Mother country will fall greatly short of the expectations of the Ministry; for certain it is, our whole Substance does already in a manner flow to Great Britain and that whatsoever contributes to lessen our Importation's must be hurtful to their Manufacturers. And the Eyes of our People, already beginning to open, will perceive, that many Luxuries which we lavish our substance to Great Britain for, can well be dispensd with whilst the necessaries of Life are (mostly) to be had within ourselves. This consequently will introduce frugality, and be a necessary stimulation to Industry. If Great Britain therefore Loads her Manufactures with heavy Taxes, will it not facilitate these Measures? they will not compel us I think to give our Money for their exports, whether we will or no, and certain I am none of their Traders will part from them without a valuable consideration. Where then is the Utility of these Restrictions?

As to the Stamp Act, taken in a single view, one, and the first bad consequences attending it I take to be this. Our Courts of Judicature must inevitably be shut up; for it is impossible (or next of kin to it) under our present Circumstances that the Act of Parliam't can be complyd with were we ever so willing to enforce the execution; for not to say, which alone would be sufficient, that we have not Money to pay the Stamps, there are many Cogent Reasons to prevent it; and if a stop be put to our judicial proceedings I fancy the Merchants of G. Britain trading to the Colonies will not be among the last to wish for a Repeal of it.

George Washington, from a letter written at Mount Vernon to Francis Dandridge, September 20, 1765, in John C. Fitzpatrick, ed., The Writings of George Washington, vol. 2, pp. 425–426.

Friends and Countrymen.

The critical Time has now come, when you are reduced to the Necessity of forming a Resolution, upon a Point of the most alarming Importance that can engage the Attention of Men. Your Conduct *at this Period* must decide the *future* Fortunes of your-

selves, and of your Posterity—must decide, whether *Pennsylvanians,* from henceforward, shall be Freemen or Slaves. . . .

We have seen the Day on which an Act of Parliament, imposing Stamp Duties on the *British* Colonies in *America,* was appointed to take Effect . . . that strikes the Axe into the Root of the Tree, and lays the hitherto flourishing Branches of *American* Freedom, with all its precious Fruits, low in the Dust.—

. . . . .

If you comply with the Act, by using Stamped Papers, you fix, you rivet perpetual Chains upon your unhappy Country. You unnecessarily, voluntarily establish the detestable Precedent, which those who have forged your Fetters ardently wish for, to varnish the future Exercise of this new claimed authority. . . .

. . . . .

Your Compliance with this Act, will save future Ministers the Trouble of reasoning on this Head, and your Tameness will free them from any Kind of Moderation, when they shall hereafter meditate any other Taxation upon you.

They will have a Precedent furnished by yourselves, and a Demonstration that the Spirit of *Americans,* after great Clamour and Bluster, is *a most submissive servile Spirit.* . . .

The Stamp Act, therefore, is to be regarded only as an EXPERIMENT OF YOUR DISPOSITION. If you quietly bend your Necks to that Yoke, you prove yourselves ready to receive any Bondage to which your *Lords* and *Masters* shall please to subject you. . . .

John Dickinson, from An Address to "Friends and Countrymen" on the Stamp Act, November 1765, in Paul Leicester Ford, ed., The Political Writings of John Dickinson, 1764–1774, pp. 201, 202, and 203.

What would *France* give for such *extensive* dominions? Would she refuse the empire of *North America,* unless the inhabitants would submit to any taxes she should please to impose? Or would she not rather afford them her utmost protection . . .? In short, the amazing increase of the wealth and strength of this kingdom, since the reign of queen *Elizabeth* . . . appears to be sufficient proof of their importance: And therefore I think it may justly be said, that THE FOUNDATIONS OF THE POWER AND GLORY OF GREAT BRITAIN ARE LAID IN AMERICA.

When the advantages derived by the mother country from her colonies are so *important* and *evident,* it is amazing, that any persons should venture to assert, "that she poured out her wealth and blood in the late war, *only for their defence and benefit;* and that she cannot be recompensed for this espence and loss, *but by taxing them.*"

If any man who does not chuse to spend much time in considering this subject, would only read the speeches from the throne during that period, with the addresses in answer to them, he will soon be convinced *for whose benefit Great-Britain* thought she was exerting herself. For my part, I should not be surprized, if those who maintain the abovementioned assertions, should contend, that *Great-Britain* ought to tax *Portugal.* For was not that kingdom "defended by the troops and treasure of *Great-Britain?*" And how can she be "otherwise recompensed for this espence and loss?" If the protection of *Portugal,* though no taxes are received from thence, was beneficial to *Great-Britain,* infinitely more so was the protection of the colonies.

John Dickinson, from The Late Regulations Respecting the British Colonies on the Continent of America Considered, *December 7, 1765, in Paul Leicester Ford, ed.,* The Political Writings of John Dickinson, 1764–1774, *pp. 239–240.*

1766

Whereas several of the Houses of Representatives in his Majesty's Colonies and Plantations in *America* have of late, AGAINST LAW, claimed to themselves, or to the general Assemblies of the same, the SOLE and EXCLUSIVE right of imposing Duties and TAXES upon his Majesty's SUBJECTS IN THE SAID COLONIES AND PLANTATIONS; and have in pursuance of such claim, passed certain votes, resolutions, and orders, DEROGATORY TO THE LEGISLATIVE AUTHORITY OF PARLIAMENT, and inconsistent with the dependency of the said Colonies and Plantations, &c. therefore be it declared, &c. that the said Colonies and Plantations in *America* have been, are, and of right ought to be subordinate unto, and dependent upon the imperial Crown and Parliament of *Great Britain,* and that the King's Majesty by and with the advise and consent of the Lord's spiritual and temporal and Commons of *Great Britain,* in Parliament assembled, had, HATH, and OF RIGHT OUGHT TO HAVE,

full power and authority to make laws and statutes, of sufficient force and validity to BIND the Colonies and People of America, Subjects of the Crown of *Great Britain,* IN ALL CASES WHATSOEVER.

The Declaratory Act, March 4, 1766, quoted in Paul Leicester Ford, ed., The Political Writings of John Dickinson, 1764–1774, *pp. 481–482.*

As to *Great-Britain,* I glory in my relation to her. Every drop of blood in my heart is *British;* and that heart is animated with as warm wishes for her prosperity, as her truest sons can form. As long as this globe continues moving, may she reign over its navigable part; and may she resemble the ocean she commands, which recruits without wasting, and receives without exhausting, its kindred streams in every climate. Are these the sentiments of disloyalty or disaffection? Do these sentiments point at independency? Can you believe it? Will you assert it? I detest the thought with inexpressible abhorrence, for these reasons; first, because it would be undutiful to our sovereign; secondly, because it would be unjust to our mother-country; and thirdly, because it would be destructive both to her and to us.

John Dickinson, from An Address to the Committee of Correspondence in Barbados, *1766, in Paul Leicester Ford, ed.,* The Political Writings of John Dickinson, 1764–1774, *p. 267.*

Sir: Your Bills of Loading for my Tobacco are come to hand, by which it would appear that the Tobacco was Shipd in good order, whereas I am informed (and by mere chance too) that some of the Tobo. Was entirely ruind and the whole much damaged. I have in consequence sent the bearer Mr. Lund Washington to examine into a state of it, and to have the damages settled upon an equitable footing; or, if this cannot be done that you will then take the whole upon yourself and pay me the Currt. Cash price which Tobacco was then, or is now, selling at it [*sic*] in the Country. One of these I must insist upon being determined not to Submit to the loss I shoud otherwise sustain by the damage I am told the Tobo. Met with.

George Washington, from a letter written at Mount Vernon to Captain Joshua Pollard, August 22, 1766, in John C. Fitzpatrick, ed., The Writings of George Washington, *vol. 2, p. 441.*

. . . methinks your S[ale]m acquaintance have a very odd kind of politeness. By what I have heard of them, they have well learnd the lesson of Iago, to Rodorigo, "put money in thy purse." It is the Character of the whole people I find, get what you can, and keep what you have got. My advice to you is among the Romans, do as the romans do. This is a selfish world you know. Interest governs it, there are but very few, who are moved by any other Spring. They are Generous, Benevolent and Friendly when it is for their interest, when any thing is to be got by it, but touch that tender part, their Interest, and you will immediately find the reverse, the greater half the World are mere Janases.

Abigail Adams, from a letter written at Braintree, Massachusetts, to her sister Mary Smith Cranch, October 6, 1766, in L. H. Butterfield, ed., Adams Family Correspondence, *vol. 1, pp. 55–56.*

1767

. . . Do you not know that the year before last I even attempted to make but very little Tobacco, and last year none: How then am I to make remittances for Goods to Cloath a numerous Family, supply a House in various necessaries, and support it in all its various expences? Have I any hidden resources do you imagine, that will enable me to do this? or do you not think it more feaziable, that from the product of my Grain (Wheat and Corn) the means must be raised? Will the Merchts. send me these Goods without remittances? if they do, I must not expect to pay advanced prices for them? As Merchts. answer me. After keepg. my Corrispondts. in Engld., Madeira, or elsewhere out of the promised remittances from this, or that Genl. Court wd. they be satisfied do you think with my writg. thus, Messrs. Carlyle and Adam who bought my Wheat and was to pay me upon delivery thereof, has done it but in part, and therefore you are disappointed; would they I ask be content with this excuse? or do you conceive it reasonable that, I shoud deny myself these conveniences, indeed for the most part absolute Necessaries because it may be attended with some difficulty to you to make the payment according to Contract, or more beneficial perhaps, to apply the money to some other purpose? . . .

George Washington, from a letter written at Williamsburg to Carlyle & Adam, February 15, 1767, in John C. Fitzpatrick, ed., The Writings of George Washington, *vol. 2, pp. 445–446.*

By this time it may be easy for you to discover, that my Plan is to secure a good deal of Land, You will conse-

quently come in for a very handsome quantity and as you will obtain it without any Costs or expences I am in hopes you will be encouragd to begin the search in time. I woud choose if it were practicable to get pretty large Tracts together, and it might be desirable to have them as near your Settlement, or Fort Pitt, as we coud get them good; but not to neglect others at a greater distance if fine and bodies of it lye in a place. . . . For my own part I shoud have no objection to a Grant of Land upon the Ohio a good way below Pittsburg but woud willingly secure some good Tracts nearer hand first.

I woud recommend it to you to keep this whole matter a profound Secret . . . and this advice proceeds from several very good Reasons and in the first place because I might be censurd for the opinion I have given in respect to the King's Proclamation and then if the Scheme I am now proposing to you was known it might give the alarm to others and by putting them upon a Plan of the same nature (before we coud lay a proper foundation for success ourselves) set the different Interests a clashing and probably in the end overturn the whole all which may be avoided by a Silent management and the [operation] snugly carried on by you under the pretence of hunting other Game . . . and if there appears but a bear possibility of succeeding any time hence I will have the Lands immediately Surveyed to keep others off and leave the rest to time and my own Assiduity to Accomplish.

George Washington, from a letter written at Mount Vernon to frontiersman and surveyor William Crawford, September 21, 1767, in John C. Fitzpatrick, ed., The Writings of George Washington, *vol. 2, pp. 470–471.*

1768

. . . [Parliament's suspension of the New York legislature for failing to comply fully with the Quartering Act] is a parliamentary assertion of the *supreme authority* of the *British* legislature over these colonies, in *the point of taxation,* and is intended to COMPEL. *New-York* into a submission to that authority. It seems therefore to me as much a violation of the liberty of the people of that province, and consequently of all these colonies, as if the parliament had sent a number of regiments to be quartered upon them till they should comply. . . . It is indeed probable, that the sight of red coats, and the hearing of drums, would have been most alarming; because people are generally more influenced by their eyes and ears, than by their reason. But whoever seriously considers the matter, must perceive that a dreadful stroke is aimed at the liberty of these colonies. I say, of these colonies; for the cause of *one* is the cause of *all*. If the parliament may lawfully deprive *New-York* of any of *her* rights, it deprive any, or all the other colonies of *their* rights; and nothing can possibly so much encourage such attempts, as a mutual inattention to the interests of each other. *To divide, and thus to destroy, is the first political maxim in attacking those, who are powerful by their union.* . . .

John Dickinson, from Letter I of Letters from a Farmer in Pennsylvania . . . , *1768, in Paul Leicester Ford, ed.,* The Political Writings of John Dickinson, 1764–1774, *pp. 310–311.*

Upon the whole, the single question is, whether the parliament can legally impose duties to be paid *by the people of these colonies only,* FOR THE SOLE PURPOSE OF RAISING A REVENUE, *on commodities which she obliges us to take from her alone,* or, in other words, whether the parliament can legally take money out of our pockets, without our consent. If they can, our boasted liberty is but

Vox et praeterea nihil.
A sound and nothing else.
A FARMER

John Dickinson, from Letter II of Letters from a Farmer in Pennsylvania . . . , *1768, in Paul Leicester Ford, ed.,* The Political Writings of John Dickinson, 1764–1774, *pp. 321–322.*

We have an excellent prince, in whose good dispositions towards us we may confide. We have a generous, sensible and humane nation, to whom we may apply. They may be deceived. They may, by artful men, be provoked to anger against us. I cannot believe they will be cruel or unjust; or that their anger will be implacable. Let us behave like dutiful children, who have received unmerited blows from a beloved parent. Let us complain to our parent; but let our complaints speak at the same time the language of affliction and veneration.

If, however, it shall happen, by an unfortunate course of affairs, that our applications to his Majesty and the parliament for redress, prove ineffectual, let us THEN take *another step,* by withholding from *Great-Britain* all the advantages she has been used to receive from us. THEN let us try, if our ingenuity,

industry, and frugality, will not give weight to our remonstrances. . . .

John Dickinson, from Letter III of Letters from a Farmer in Pennsylvania . . . , *1768, in Paul Leicester Ford, ed.,* The Political Writings of John Dickinson, 1764–1774, *pp. 327–328.*

The *nature* of any impositions laid by parliament on these colonies, must determine the *design* in laying them. It may not be easy in every instance to discover that design. Wherever it is doubtful, I think submission cannot be dangerous; nay, it must be right; for, in my opinion, there is no privilege these colonies claim, which they ought in *duty* and *prudence* more earnestly to maintain and defend, than the authority of the *British* parliament to regulate the trade of all her dominions. Without this authority, the benefits she enjoys from our commerce, must be lost to her: The blessings we enjoy from our dependence upon her, must be lost to us. Her strength must decay; her glory vanish; and she cannot suffer without our partaking in her misfortune. *Let us therefore cherish her interests as our own, and give her every thing, that it becomes* FREEMEN *to give or to receive.*

John Dickinson, from Letter VI of Letters from a Farmer in Pennsylvania . . . , *1768, in Paul Leicester Ford, ed.,* The Political Writings of John Dickinson, 1764–1774, *pp. 348–349.*

May *George,* belov'd by all the nations round,
Live with heav'ns choicest constant blessings
  crown'd!
Great God, direct, and guard him from on high,
And from his head let ev'ry evil fly!
And may each clime with equal gladness see
A monarch's smile can set his subjects free!

Phillis Wheatley, slave and poet, from her poem "To the KING's *Most Excellent Majesty. 1768," in her* Poems on Various Subjects, Religious and Moral, *published in London in 1773, in William H. Robinson,* Phillis Wheatley and Her Writings, *p. 159.*

. . . In short, if they [Parliament] have a right to levy a tax of *one penny* upon us, they have a right to levy a *million* upon us: For where does their right stop? At any given number of Pence, Shillings or Pounds? To attempt to limit their right, after granting it to exist at all, is as contrary to reason—as granting it to exist at all, is contrary to justice. If *they* have any right to tax us—then, whether *our own money* shall continue in *our own pockets* or not, depends no longer on *us,* but on *them.* "There is nothing which" we can call our own; or, to use the words of Mr. *Locke*—"WHAT PROPERTY HAVE WE IN THAT, WHICH ANOTHER MAY, BY RIGHT, TAKE, WHEN HE PLEASES, TO HIMSELF?"

These duties, which will inevitably be levied upon us—which are now levying upon us—are *expressly* laid FOR THE SOLE PURPOSES OF TAKING MONEY. This is the true definition of *"taxes."* They are therefore *taxes.* This money is to be taken from *us. We* are therefore *taxed. Those* who are *taxed* without their own consent, expressed by themselves or their representatives, are *slaves. We are taxed* without our own consent, expressed by ourselves or our representatives. *We* are therefore—SLAVES.

John Dickinson, from Letter VII of Letters from a Farmer in Pennsylvania . . . , *1768, in Paul Leicester Ford, ed.,* The Political Writings of John Dickinson, 1764–1774, *pp. 356–357.*

. . . Is it possible to form an idea of a slavery more *compleat,* more *miserable,* more *disgraceful,* than that of a people, where *justice is administered, government exercised,* and a *standing army maintained,* AT THE EXPENCE OF THE PEOPLE, and yet WITHOUT THE LEAST DEPENDENCE UPON THEM? . . .

John Dickinson, from Letter IX of Letters from a Farmer in Pennsylvania . . . , *1768, in Paul Leicester Ford, ed.,* The Political Writings of John Dickinson, 1764–1774, *p. 372.*

Two reasons induce me to desire, that this spirit of apprehension may be always kept up among us, in its utmost vigilance. The first is this—that as the happiness of these provinces indubitably consists in their connection with *Great-Britain,* any separation between them is less likely to be occasioned by civil discords, if every disgusting measure is opposed *singly,* and *while it is new:* For in this manner of proceeding, every measure is most likely to be rectified. On the other hand, oppressions and dissatisfactions being permitted to accumulate—*if ever* the governed throw off the load, *they will do more.* A people does not reform with moderation. The rights of the subject therefore cannot be *too often* considered, explained or asserted: And whoever attempts to do this, shews himself, whatever may be the rash and peevish reflections of pretended wisdom, and pretended duty, a friend to *those who*

injudiciously exercise their power, as well as *them* over whom it is so exercised.

John Dickinson, from Letter XI of Letters from a Farmer in Pennsylvania . . . , *1768, in Paul Leicester Ford, ed.,* The Political Writings of John Dickinson, 1764–1774, *pp. 386–387.*

Gentn: My old Chariot havg. Run its race, and gone through as many stages as I could conveniently make it travel, is now renderd incapable of any further Service; The intent of this Letter therefore is to desire you will bespeak me a New one. . . .

As these are kind of Articles, that last with care agst. Number of years, I woud willingly have the Chariot you may now send me made in the newest taste, handsome, genteel and light; yet not slight and consequently unserviceable. To be made of the best Seasond Wood, and by a celebrated Workman. The last Importation which I have seen, besides the customary steel springs have others that play in a Brass barrel, and contribute at one and the same time to the ease and Ornament of the Carriage; One of this kind therefore would be my choice; and Green being a color little apt, as I apprehend to fade, and grateful to the Eye, I woud give it the preference, unless any other color more in vogue and equally lasting is entitled to precedency, in that case I would be governd by fashion. A light gulding on the mouldings that is, round the Pannels) and any other Ornaments that may not have a heavy and tawdry look (together with my Arms agreeable to the Impression here sent) might be added by way of decoration. A lining of a handsome, lively cold. leather of good quality, I sh'd also prefer; such as green, blew, or &ca., as may best suit the col'r of the outside, Let the box that slips under Seat, be as large as it conveniently can be made . . . and to have a Pole (not Shafts) for the Wheel Horses to draw by; together with a handsome sett of Harness for four middle sized Horses. . . . On the Harness let my Crest be engravd.

If such a Chariot as I have here describd cd. be got at 2d. hand little or nothg. the worse of wear, but at the same time a good deal under the first cost of a new one . . . it wd. be very desirable; but if I obligd to go near to the origl. Cost I wd. even have one made . . . not of Copper however, for these do not stand the powerful heat of our sun.

George Washington, from a letter written at Mount Vernon to Robert Cary & Company, June 6, 1768, in John C. Fitzpatrick, ed., The Writings of George Washington, *vol. 2, pp. 488–489.*

1769

Having once or twice of late hear you Speak highly in praise of the Jersey College, as if you had a desire of sending your Son William there . . . I shou'd be glad, if you have no other objection to it than what may arise from the expense, if you would send him there as soon as it is convenient and depend on me for Twenty five pounds this Currency a year for his support so long as it may be necessary for the completion of his Education. If I live to see the accomplishment of this term, the sum here stipulated shall be annually paid, and if I die in the mean while, this letter shall be obligatory upon my Heirs or Executors. . . . No other return is expected, or wished for this offer, than that you will accept it with the same freedom and good will with which it is made, and that you may not even consider it in the light of an obligation, or mention it as such; for be assur'd that from me it will never be known. . . .

George Washington, from a letter written at Mount Vernon to his friend William Ramsay, January 29, 1769, in John C. Fitzpatrick, ed., The Writings of George Washington, *vol. 2, pp. 499–500.*

. . . I always was of opinion that the placing a youth to study with an attorney was rather a prejudice than a help. We are all too apt by shifting on them our business, to incroach on that time which should be devoted to their studies. The only help a youth wants is to be directed what books to read, and in what order to read them. . . .

Thomas Jefferson, from a letter written at Shadwell, Virginia, to Thomas Turpin, February 5, 1769, in Julian P. Boyd, ed., The Papers of Thomas Jefferson, *vol. 1, p. 24.*

At a time when our lordly Masters in Great Britain will be satisfied with nothing less than the deprication of American freedom, it seems highly necessary that some thing shou'd be done to avert the stroke and maintain the liberty which we have derived from our Ancestors; but the manner of doing it to answer the purpose effectually is the point in question.

That no man shou'd scruple, or hesitate a moment to use a-ms in defence of so valuable a blessing, on which all the good and evil of life depends; is clearly my opinion; yet A-ms I wou'd beg leave to add, should be the last resource. . . . Addresses to the Throne and remonstrances to parliament, we have already, it is said, proved the inefficacy of; how far then their attention to our rights and priviledges is to be awakened or alarmed by starving their Trade and manufactures, remains to be tryed.

The northern Colonies, it appears, are endeavoring to adopt this scheme. In my opinion, it is a good one. . . . That there will be difficulties attending the execution of it every where, from clashing interests, and selfish designing men (ever attentive to their own gain . . . in preference to any other consideration) cannot be denied; but in the Tobacco Colonies . . . these difficulties are certainly enhanced, but I think not insurmountably increased, if the Gentlemen in their several Counties wou'd be at some pains to explain matters to the people, and stimulate them to a cordial agreement to purchase none but certain innumerated Articles out of any of the Stores after such a period, not import or purchase any themselves. . . .

George Washington, from a letter written at Mount Vernon to George Mason, April 5, 1769, in John C. Fitzpatrick, ed., The Writings of George Washington, *vol. 2, pp. 500–501.*

Gentn: Inclosd you will receive Invoices of Goods wanted for myself and Master Custis for this place and our Plantations on York River, as also for Miss Custis. . . . But if there are any Articles containd in either of the respective Invoices (Paper only excepted) which are Tax'd by Act of Parliament for the purpose of Raising a Revenue in America, it is my express desire and request, that they may not be sent, as I have very heartly enterd into an Association . . . not to Import any Article which now is or hereafter shall be Taxed for this purpose until the said Act or Acts are repeal'd. I am therefore particular in mentioning this matter as I am fully determined to adhere religiously to it, and may perhaps have wrote for some things unwittingly which may be under these Circumstances.

George Washington, from a letter written at Mount Vernon to Robert Cary & Company, July 25, 1769, in John C. Fitzpatrick, ed., The Writings of George Washington, *vol. 2, pp. 512–513.*

Run away from the subscriber in *Albemarle,* a Mulatto slave called *Sandy,* about 35 years of age, his stature is rather low, inclining to corpulence, and his complexion light; he is a shoemaker by trade, in which he uses his left hand principally, can do coarse carpenters work, and is something of a horse jockey; he is greatly addicted to drink, and when drunk is insolent and disorderly, in his conversation he swears much, and his behaviour is artful and knavish. He took with him a white horse, much scarred with traces, of which it is expected he will endeavour to dispose; he also carried his shoemakers tools, and will probably endeavour to get employment that way. Whoever conveys the said slave to me in *Albemarle,* shall have 40s. reward, if taken up withing the county, 4 1. if elsewhere within the colony, and 10 1. if in any other colony, from THOMAS JEFFERSON.

Thomas Jefferson, advertisement for a runaway slave printed in the Virginia Gazette, *September 7, in Julian P. Boyd, ed.,* The Papers of Thomas Jefferson, *vol. 1, p. 33.*

1770

Upon the whole, as you are situated in a good place for seeing many of the Officers at different times, I should be glad if you woud (in a joking way, rather than in earnest, at first) see what value they seem to set upon their Lands; and if you can buy any of the Rights of those who continued in the Service till after the Cherokee Expedition, at the Rate of about five, Six, or Seven pounds a thousand acres I shall be obliged to you, and will pay the money upon demand....

If you should make any purchases, let it be done in your own name, for reason's I shall give you when we meet; take Bonds in large Penalties to convey all their Rights under the Kings Proclamation to you; and they shoud be obligd to suffer their names to be made use of to obtain the Land, as the Kings Proclamation requires a Personal application to the Govnr. And Council in order to entitle them to receive the Respective quantities granted....

George Washington, from a letter written at Mount Vernon to Charles Washington, January 31, 1770, in John C. Fitzpatrick, ed., The Writings of George Washington, *vol. 3, pp. 2–3.*

In vain he flies, by Justice Swiftly chaced
With unexpected infamy disgraced
Be Richardson for ever banished here

. . . . .

Snider behold with what Majestic Love
The Illustrious retinue begins to move

With Secret rage fair freedoms foes beneath
See in thy corse ev'n Majesty in Death.

Phillis Wheatley, slave and poet, from her poem "On the Death of Mr Snider Murder'd by Richardson," an occurrence of February 23, 1770; Wheatley refers to Snider as "the first martyr for the cause," in William H. Robinson, Phillis Wheatley and Her Writings, *pp. 139–140.*

HIS EXCELLENCY
The Right Honourable Norborne Baron de Botetourt, his Majesty's Lieutenant and Governor General of the Colony and Dominion of Virginia, and Vice Admiral of the same.
To Thomas Jefferson Esquire
By Virtue of the Power and Authority to me given as his Majesty's Lieutenant and General of this his Colony and Dominion, I, reposing special Trust and Confidence in your Loyalty, Courage and Conduct, do hereby constitute and appoint you the said Thomas Jefferson to be Lieutenant of the County of Albemarle and Chief Commander of al his Majesty's Militia, Horse and Foot, in the said County of Albemarle....

From the commission of Thomas Jefferson, June 9, 1770, in Julian P. Boyd, ed., The Papers of Thomas Jefferson, *vol. 1, p. 42.*

The time of Life he [John Parke Custis] is now advancing into requires the most friendly aid and Council (especially in such a place as Annapolis); otherwise, the warmth of his own Passions, assisted by the bad example of other Youth, may prompt him to actions derogatory of Virtue, & that Innocence of Manners which one coud wish to preserve him in: For wch reason I beg leave to request, that he may not be suffered to sleep from under your Roof, unless it be at such places as you are sure he can have no bad examples set him; nor allow him to be rambling about of Nights in Company with those, who do not care how debauched and viceous his Conduct may be.

George Washington, from a letter written at Mount Vernon to Reverend Jonathan Boucher, December 16, 1770, in John C. Fitzpatrick, ed., The Writings of George Washington, *vol. 3, pp. 35–36.*

1771

The apprehensions of a war, the delay of Commerce, the distress of individuals, and the liberal expences of public treasure have at length ended in this—after a negociation of four months—that the object in dispute, Port Egmont [Falkland Islands], shall be restored to the Crown; with this proviso, however, to remain a bone of contention for the future. . . . Nothing, it is said, prevented the Spaniards from coming to an open rupture, but the great aversion of the french King to War. Indeed the present state of his kingdom gives him very good reason to be indisposed to foreign hostility. He has lately ventured on an exploit, that may probably involve him [in] a very considerable dilemma—the exile of his prime minister, and of the whole (or at least, of most of the members of the) parliament of Paris.—America is not to become an object of parliamentary attention during the present session. Both Houses are extremely cautious, with regard to making their debates public. . . . I find that the mercantile part of Boston have lost sight of principle, as well as of resolution. The large orders, which are sent here for *Tea,* perplex the mind of every friend to our interest or reputation, and give credit to the high reflections, which had before been made on our political falsehood and hypocrisy.

Isaac Smith, Jr., cousin of Abigail Adams, from a letter written at London to John Adams, February 21, 1771, in L. H. Butterfield, ed., Adams Family Correspondence, *vol. 1, pp. 71–72.*

Women you know Sir are considerd as Domestick Beings, and alto they inherit an Eaquel Share of curiosity with the other Sex, yet but few are hardy eno' to venture abroad, and explore the amaizing variety of distant Lands. The Natural tenderness and Delicacy of our Constitutions, added to the many Dangers we are subject too from your Sex, renders it almost impossible for a Single Lady to travel without injury to her character. And those who have a protecter in an Husband, have generally speaking obstacles sufficient to prevent their Roving, and instead of visiting other Countries; are obliged to content themselves with seeing but a very small part of their own. To your Sex we are most of us indebted for all the knowledg we acquire of Distant lands. As to a Knowledg of Humane Nature, I believe it may as easily be obtained in this Country, as in England, France or Spain. Tis natural I believe for every person to have a partiality for their own Country. Dont you think this little Spot of ours better calculated for happiness than any other you have yet seen or read of? Would you exchange it for England, France, Spain or Ittally? Are not the people here more upon an Eaquality in

point of knowledg and of circumstances—there being none so immensely rich as to Lord it over us, neither any so abjectly poor as to suffer for the necessaries of life provided they will use the means. . . . Shall we ever wish to change Countries; to change conditions with the Affricans and the Laplanders for sure it were better never to have known the blessings of Liberty than to have enjoyed it, and then have it ravished from us.

Abigail Adams, from a letter written at Braintree, Massachusetts, to her cousin Isaac Smith, Jr., in London, April 20, 1771, in L. H. Butterfield, ed., Adams Family Correspondence, *vol. 1, pp. 76–77.*

These are the Insults that I have exposed myself to, by a very small and feeble Exertion for S. Adams to be Register of Deeds. Thus are the Friends of the People after such dangerous Efforts, and such successfull ones too left in the Lurch even by the People themselves. I have acted my sentiments, with the Utmost Frankness, at Hazard of all, and the certain Loss of ten times more than it is in the Power of the People to give me, for the sake of the People, and now I reap nothing but Insult, Ridicule and Contempt for it, even from many of the People themselves. However, I have not hitherto regarded Consequences to myself. I have very chearfully sacrificed my Interest, and my Health and Ease and Pleasure in the service of the People. . . . But, I have learn'd Wisdom by Experience. I shall certainly become more retired, and cautious. I shall certainly mind my own Farm, and my own Office.

John Adams, from diary entry of May 2, 1771, in L. H. Butterfield, ed., Diary and Autobiography of John Adams, *pp. 10–11.*

Thus I find Discontents in all Men. The Black thinks his Merit rewarded with Ingratitude, and so does the white. The Black estimates his own Worth, and the Merit of his Services higher than any Body else. So does the White. This flattering, fond Opinion of himself, is found in every Man.

John Adams, from diary entry of June 17, 1771, in Butterfield, ed., Diary and Autobiography of John Adams, *p. 36.*

I must request the favour of you to be particular in directing the Scythe Maker to furnish me Scyhtes exactly agreeable to my Order, otherwise they will be of very little use to me; As, in the first Instt. I have given the Size that suits our business best, in the next, as they are intended to fix to Cradles for cutting Wheat and other grain, if one Scythe gives way in the throng time of Harvest another can be put to the same Cradle immediately, without loss of time; Whereas a Scythe differing in length or shape, requires a Cradle proportionate and takes more time to make than we have to spare at that busy Season. . . .

George Washington, from a letter written at Mount Vernon to Robert Cary & Company, July 20, 1771, in John C. Fitzpatrick, ed., The Writings of George Washington, *vol. 3, p. 60.*

The public affairs of France are infinitely more embarrass'd than those of England. . . .

A prime minister exiled—another substituted in his room, the object of public odium—parliaments one after the other dissolved and banished—and the princes of the blood (one only excepted) thrown into disgrace! . . .

To so sensible a nation as the french, it must be a most mortifying circumstance, that the revolutions of their government are often dependent on the amours of their monarch. This is notorious in the late change of their administration. The history of the present *Sultana* of their Court [Madame du Barry] is curious. It seems that she is the natural daughter of a monk, and was a domestic in a family at Paris. A particular nobleman is struck with her beauty. As he had either already formed such a connection, or was afraid of degrading his dignity too far, he persuades his brother to marry her. In course of time, to serve the political purposes of a family, she is recommended to the King, who is particularly fond of bestowing his caresses on a married lady. To make herself appear in more respectable light at Court, she claims an affinity with an ancient family of Ireland, the present possessor of whose title, Lord Barrymore, a nobleman equally distinguished for his conjugal fidelity in London, as *Madame la Comtesse de Barre* for her unspotted virtue in Paris, is so very condescending as to own the relation; and she is now treated with as much respect, as if she owed her connection with the monarch to birth instead of fortune. I had not an opportunity, tho I spent a day at the Palace of Versailles, of admiring the charms of this celebrated Lady.

Isaac Smith, Jr., cousin of Abigail Adams, from a letter written at London to John Adams, September 3, 1771, in L. H. Butterfield, ed., Adams Family Correspondence, *vol. 1, pp. 78–79.*

Dear Sir: Your claim to a share of the 200,000 Acres of Land under Governor Dinwiddie's [1754] Proclamation has been entered, and the Governor and Council have settled the proportion's which shall fall to each Man's Lott (according to the Rank he enterd the Service with) by which each Field Officer is allowed 15,000 Acres, each Captain 9,000, each Subaltern 6,000; each Cadet 2,500. A Sergeant 600, a Corporal 500, and each private Soldier 400 Acres a piece.

George Washington, from a letter written at Mount Vernon to Robert Stobo, November 22, 1771, in John C. Fitzpatrick, The Writings of George Washington, *vol. 3, p. 73.*

1772

Government is nothing more than the combined Force of Society, of the united Power of the Multitude, for the Peace, Order, Safety, Good and Happiness of the People, who compose the Society. There is no King or Queen Bee distinguished from all others, by Size or Figure, or beauty and Variety of Colours, in the human Hive. No Man has yet produced any Revelation from Heaven in his favour, any divine Communication to govern his fellow Men. Nature throws us all into the World equall and alike.

Nor has any Form of Government the Honour of a divine original or Appointment. The Author of Nature has left it wholly in the Choice of the People, to make what mutual Covenants, to erect what Kind of Governments, and to exalt what Persons they please to power and dignities, for their own Ease, Convenience and Happiness.

. . . . .

The Preservation of Liberty depends upon the intellectual and moral Character of the People. As long as Knowledge and Virtue are diffused generally among the Body of a Nation, it is impossible they should be enslaved. This can be brought to pass only by debasing their Understandings, or by corrupting their Hearts.

John Adams, from notes for an oration at Braintree, Massachusetts, diary entry of February 10, 1772, in L. H. Butterfield, ed., Diary and Autobiography of John Adams, *pp. 57–58.*

Dr. Sir: Inclination having yielded to Importunity, I am now contrary to all expectations under the hands of Mr. [Charles Wilson] Peale; but in so grave—so sullen a mood—and now and then under the influence of Morpheus, when some critical strokes are making, that I fancy the skill of this Gentleman's Pencil, will be put to it, in describing to the World what manner of man I am. . . .

George Washington, from a letter written at Mount Vernon to Reverend Jonathan Boucher, May 21, 1772, in John C. Fitzpatrick, ed., The Writings of George Washington, *vol. 3, pp. 83–84.*

It has been my Fate, to be acquainted, in the Way of my Business, with a Number of very rich Men— Gardiner, Bowdoin, Pitts, Hancock, Rowe, Lee, Sargeant, Hooper, Doane. Hooper, Gardiner, Rowe, Lee, and Doane, have all acquired their Wealth by their own Industry. Bowdoin and Hancock received theirs by Succession, Descent or Devise. Pitts by Marriage. But there is not one of these, who derives more Pleasure from his Property that I do from mine. My little Farm, and Stock, and Cash, affords me as much Satisfaction, as all their immense Tracts, extensive Navigation, sumptuous Buildings, their vast Sums at Interest, and Stocks in Trade yield to them. The Pleasures of Property, arise from Acquis[it]ion more than Possession, from what is to come rather than from what is. These Men feel their Fortunes. They feel the Strength and Importance, which their Riches give them in the World. Their Courage and Spirits are buoyed up, their Imaginations are inflated by them. The rich are seldom remarkable for Modesty, Ingenuity, or Humanity. Their Wealth has rather a Tendency to make them penurious and selfish.

John Adams, from diary entry of June 30, 1772, in L. H. Butterfield, ed., Diary and Autobiography of John Adams, *pp. 61–62.*

The Money arising from the Sales I would have laid out in Negroes, if choice ones can be had under Forty pounds Sterl; if not, then in Rum and Sugar from Barbadoes, or any of the Windward Islands; and Sugar and Molasses if the Flour sh'd be sold in Jam'a.

If the Return's are in Slaves let there be two thirds of them Males, the other third Females. The former not exceeding (at any rate) 20 y'rs of age, the latter 16. All of them to be strait Limb'd, and in every respect strong and likely, with good Teeth, and good Countenances, to be sufficiently provided with Cloaths.

George Washington, from a letter written at Mount Vernon to Daniel Jenifer Adams, July 20, 1772, in John C. Fitzpatrick, ed., The Writings of George Washington, *vol. 3, p. 98.*

Spent this Evening with Mr. Samuel Adams at his House. Had much Conversation, about the State of Affairs—Cushing, Hancock, Phillips, Hawley, Gerry, Hutchinson, Sewall, Quincy, &c. &c. Adams was more cool, genteel and agreeable than common—concealed, and restrained his Passions—&c. He affects to despise Riches, and not to dread Poverty. But no Man is more ambitious of entertaining his Friends handsomely, or of making a decent, an elegant Appearance than he. He has lately new covered and glased his House and painted it, very neatly, and has new papered, painted and furnished his Rooms. So that you visit at a very genteel House and are very politely received and entertained.

Mr. Adams corresponds with Hawley, Gerry and others. He corresponds in England and in several of

John Adams became a member of the Continental Congress. *(Courtesy of the National Archives and Records Administration)*

the other Provinces. His Time is all employed in the public Service.

John Adams, diary entry of December 30, 1772, in L. H. Butterfield, ed., The Diary and Autobiography of John Adams, *p. 74.*

1773

Mr. Simpson: As the Negro Fellow I bought In Alexandria will by no means consent to leave this Neighbourhood and as you did not seem Inclind to take him without I have sent a young Fellow which I bought last Spring in his room. In coming from Boston here he got Frost Bit and lost part of his Toes which prevents his Walk'g with as much activity as he otherwise would but as they are quite well, and he a good temper'd quiet Fellow I dare say he will answer the purpose very well. I also send you a fine, healthy, likely young Girl which in a year or two will be fit for any business, her principal employment hitherto has been House Work but is able, or soon will be to do any thing else.

George Washington, from a letter written at Mount Vernon to Gilbert Simpson, February 23, 1773, in John C. Fitzpatrick, ed., The Writings of George Washington, *vol. 3, p. 117.*

I have often thought it a Misfortune, or rather a Fault in the Friends of American Independence and Freedom, their not taking Care to open every Channel of Communication. The Colonies are all embarkd in the same bottom. The Liberties of all are alike invaded by the same haughty Power: The Conspirators against their common Rights have indeed exerted their brutal Force ... differently in the several Colonies, as they thought would best serve their Purpose of Oppression and Tyranny. How necessary then is it; that *All* should be early acquainted with the particular Circumstances of *Each,* in order that the Wisdom & Strength of the whole may be employd upon every proper Occasion....

Samuel Adams, from a letter written in Boston, April 10, 1773, to Arthur Lee, in Harry Alonzo Cushing, ed., The Writings of Samuel Adams, *vol. 3, pp. 25–26.*

We now rise a bank of considerable height, which runs nearly parallel to the coast through Carolina and Georgia ... above the level of the ocean, may be two or three hundred feet (and these are called the sand-hills), when we find ourselves on the entrance of a vast plain, generally level, which extends west sixty or seventy miles.... This plain is mostly a forest of the great long-leaved pine (*P. palustris* Linn.) the earth covered with grass, interspersed with an infinite variety of herbaceous plants and embellished with extensive savannas, always green, sparkling with ponds of water, and ornamented with clumps of evergreen, and other trees and shrubs, as *Magnolia grandiflora, Magnolia glauca, Gordonia, Ilex aquifolium, Quercus,* various species, *Laurus Borbonia, Chionanthus, Hopea tinctoria, Cyrilla,* ...

William Bartram, English botanist, recording his observations of a scene near Augusta, Georgia, in May 1773, from his Travels through North & South Carolina, Georgia, East & West Florida, *first published in Philadelphia in 1791, in Mark Van Doren, ed.,* Travels of William Bartram, *pp. 51–52.*

I hear a Buz among my Neighbours, that the *East-India Company's* Tea is to be guarded by Men of War, and landed by a Military Force; that the Reason, why the General did not come to review the Troops in your City, was, lest in his Absence the Tea should arrive in *New York,* and his Presence might be necessary to land and protect it. Though I have no Doubt but this Company, hackneyed as they are in murders, Rapine and Cruelty, would sacrifice the Lives of Thousands to preserve their Trash, and enforce their measures; yet I can hardly persuade myself that the Ministry are so mad, as to give Orders, at the Hazard of losing the Affection of the *Americans,* to preserve that, which, considering the Time it has already lain in the *East-India Company's* Ware-houses, must already be in a perishing State.

But should that be the Case, let us disappoint their Malice. We have yet a command of our Persons. Our Houses, Stores and Wharves are at our own Disposal. Resolve, therefore, nobly resolve and publish to the World your Resolutions, that no Man will receive the Tea, no Man will let his Stores, nor suffer the Vessel, that brings it, to moor at his Wharf, and that if any Person assists in unlading, landing or storing it, he shall ever after be deemed an Enemy to his Country, and never be employed by his Fellow Citizens. I am sure, from what I have formerly known of our PORTERS, there is not a Man among them, that will lend a Hand; and I question, whether among the whole Class of *Labourers* that ply about the Wharves, there will be found One, who would not rather go without his Dinner than, for double Wages, touch the accursed Trash. Believe me, my Friend, there is a Spirit of Liberty and a love of their Country among every Class of Men among us, which Experience will evince, and which shew them worthy the Character of free-born *Americans*. . . .

> *John Dickinson, from "A Letter from the Country to a Gentleman in Philadelphia," November 27, 1773, in Paul Leicester Ford, ed.,* The Political Writings of John Dickinson, 1764–1774, *pp. 461–462.*

The Tea that bainfull weed is arrived. Great and I hope Effectual opposition has been made to the landing of it. To the publick papers I must refer you for perticuliars. You will there find that the proceedings of our Citizens have been United, Spirited and firm. The flame is kindled and like Lightning it catches from Soul to Soul. Great will be the devastation if not timely quenched or allayed by some more Lenient Measures.

Altho the mind is shocked at the Thought of sheding Humane Blood, more Especially the Blood of our Countrymen, and a civil War is of all Wars, the most dreadfull Such is the present Spirit that prevails, that if once they are made desperate Many, very Many of our Heroes will spend their lives in the cause, With the Speach of Cato in their Mouths, "What a pitty it is, that we can dye but once to save our Country."

. . . . .

Such is the present Situation of affairs that I tremble when I think what may be the direfull consequences—and in this Town must the Scene of action lay. My heart beats at every Whistle I hear, and I dare not openly express half my fears.—Eternal Reproach and Ignominy be the portion of all those who have been instrumental in bringing these fears upon me. There was a Report prevaild that to morrow there will be an attempt to Land this weed of Slavery. . . .

> *Abigail Adams, from a letter written at Boston to Mercy Otis Warren, poet and sister of patriot James Otis, at Plymouth, December 5, 1773, in L. H. Butterfield, ed.,* Adams Family Correspondence, *vol. 1, pp. 88–89.*

Last Night 3 Cargoes of Bohea Tea were emptied into the Sea. This Morning a Man of War sails.

This is the most magnificent Movement of all. There is a Dignity, a Majesty, a Sublimity, in this last Effort of the Patriots, that I greatly admire. The People should never rise, without doing something to be remembered—something notable And striking. This Destruction of the Tea is so bold, so daring, so firm, intrepid and inflexible, and it must have so important

Consequences, and so lasting, that I cant but consider it as an Epocha in History.

This is however but an Attack upon Property. Another similar Exertion of popular Power, may produce the destruction of Lives. Many Persons wish, that as many dead Carcasses were floating in the Harbour, as there are Chests of Tea:—a much less Number of Lives however would remove the Causes of all our Calamities.

The malicious Pleasure with which Hutchinson the Governor, the Consignees of the Tea, and the officers of the Customs, have stood and looked upon the distress of the People, and their Struggles to get the Tea back to London, and at last the destruction of it, is amazing. Tis hard to believe Persons so hardened and abandoned.

. . . . .

The Question is whether the Destruction of this Tea was necessary? I apprehend it was absolutely and indispensably so. . . .

> *John Adams, from diary entry of December 17, 1773, in L. H. Butterfield, ed.,* The Diary and Autobiography of John Adams, *pp. 85–86.*

1774

. . . in every human Breast, God has implanted a Principle, which we call Love of Freedom; it is impatient of oppression, and pants for Deliverance—and by the Leave of our modern Egyptians [slave owners] I will assert that the same principle lives in us [blacks]. God grant Deliverance in his own Way and Time, and get him honour upon all those whose Avarice impels them to countenance and help forward the Calamities of their fellow Creatures. This I desire not for their Hurt, but to convince them of the strange Absurdity of their Conduct whose Words and Actions are so diametrically opposite. How well the Cry for Liberty, and the reverse Disposition for the exercise of oppressive power over others agree I humbly think it does not require the penetration of a Philosopher to determine.

> *Phillis Wheatley, poet manumitted four months earlier, from a letter of February 11, 1774, to Reverend Samson Occom, excoriating the hypocrisy of slave-holding Christian ministers, subsequently published in New England newspapers, in William H. Robinson,* Phillis Wheatley and Her Writings, *p. 332.*

Again and again, revert to your old principles; seek peace and ensue it; leave America, if she has taxable matter in her, to tax herself. I am not here going into the distinctions of rights. . . . Leave the Americans as they anciently stood, and these distinctions, born of our unhappy contest, will die along with it. They and we, and their and our ancestors, have been happy under that system. . . . Be content to bind America by laws of trade; you have always done it. Let this be your reason for binding their trade. Do not burden them by taxes; you were not used to do so from the beginning. Let this be your reason for not taxing. . . . But if, intemperately, unwisely, fatally, you sophisticate and poison the very source of government by urging subtle deductions and consequences odious to those you govern from the unlimited and illimitable nature of supreme sovereignty, you will teach them by these means to call that sovereignty itself in question. When you drive him hard, the boar will surely turn upon the hunters. If that sovereignty and their freedom cannot be reconciled, which will they take? They will cast your sovereignty in your face. Nobody will be argued into slavery. . . tell me what one character of liberty the Americans have and what one brand of slavery they are free from, if they are bound in their property and industry by all the restraints you can imagine on commerce, and at the same time are made packhorses of every tax you choose to impose, without the least share in granting them. When they bear the burdens of unlimited monopoly, will you bring them to bear the burdens of unlimited revenue too? The Englishman in America will feel that this is slavery, that it is *legal* slavery will be no compensation either to his feelings or his understanding.

Edmund Burke, from a "Speech on American Taxation"
in Parliament, April 19, 1774, in Burke, Selected
Writings and Speeches on America, *pp. 110–111.*

We live my dear Soul, in an Age of Tryal. What will be the Consequence I know not. The Town of Boston, for ought I can see, must suffer Martyrdom: It must expire: And our principal Consolation is, that it dies in a noble Cause. The Cause of Truth, of Virtue, of Liberty and of Humanity: and that it will probably have a glorious Reformation, to greater Wealth, Splendor and Power than ever.

John Adams, from a letter written at Boston to Abigail
Adams, May 12, 1774, in L. H. Butterfield, ed.,
Adams Family Correspondence, *vol. 1, p. 107.*

Brethren, It is not my design to travel through all the ministerial manaeouvers respecting us, since the com-

mencement of this Reign. It is not necessary. Sufficient, I trust, it will prove, to lay before you such a series of correspondent facts, as will thoroughly convince you,—that a plan has been deliberately framed, and pertinaciously adhered to, unchanged even by frequent changes of Ministers, unchecked by any intervening gleam of humanity, to sacrifice to a passion for arbitrary dominion the universal property, liberty, safety, honor, happiness and prosperity of us unoffending, yet devoted Americans—And that every man of us is deeply interested in the fate of our brethren of *Boston.*

If such a series is not laid before you, the combined force of which shall tear up by the roots, and throw out of your bosoms, every lurking doubt, centure me as an enthusiast too violently warmed by a sence of the injustice practised against my beloved country.

John Dickinson, beginning of Letter II, from Letters to
the Inhabitants of the British Colonies, *May 1774,*
in Paul Leicester Ford, ed., The Political Writings
of John Dickinson, 1764–1774, *pp. 473–474.*

This town has received the Copy of an Act of the British Parliament, wherein it appears that we have been tried and condemned, and are to be punished, by the shutting up of the harbor and other marks of revenge, until we shall disgrace ourselves by servilely yielding up, in effect, the just and righteous claims of America. If the Parliament had a Right to pass such an *edict,* does it not discover the want of every moral principle to proceed to the destruction of a community, without even the accusation of any crime committed by such community? . . . There is no crime alleged in the Act, as committed by the Town of Boston. . . .

Samuel Adams, from a letter written in Boston, May 14,
1774, to James Warren, Massachusetts legislator, Patriot,
and husband of Mercy Otis, in Harry Alonzo Cushing,
ed., The Writings of Samuel Adams,
vol. 3, pp. 111–112.

Pretences and reasons are totally different. The provocations, said to be given to our sister colony [Massachusetts], are but the PRETENCES for the exorbitant severity exercised against her. The REASONS, are these—the policy, despicable and detestable as it is, of suppressing the freedom of *America* by a military force, to be supported by money taken out of our own pockets, and the supposed convenience of opportunity for attaining this end. . . . The people in that kingdom [Great Britain] have been with great cunning and labor, inflamed *against the Colonies in general*. They are deluded into a belief, that we are in a state of rebellion and aiming directly at a state of independency; though the first is a noxious weed that never grew in our climates; and the latter is universally regarded with the deepest execration by us—a poison we never can be compelled to touch, but as an antidote to a worse, if a worse can be—a tree of forbidden and accursed fruit, which, if any Colony on this continent should be so mad as to attempt reaching, the rest would have virtue and wisdom enough to draw their swords and hew the traitors into submission, if not into loyalty. It would be their interest and their duty, thus to guaranty the public peace.

The Minister addressing the House of Commons, uses several expressions relating to *all the Colonies,* and calls the stoppage of the port of *Boston* "a punishment inflicted on those, *who have disobeyed your Authority.*" Is it not extremely remarkable, after such a variety of charges affecting *all* the Colonies, that the statutes of vengeance should be leveled against a *single* Colony?. . . Because Administration and Parliament do us *Americans* the honor to think, we are such very edeots that we

Samuel Adams led the Patriot opposition in Massachusetts. *(From The Pictorial Field Book of the Revolution, 2 vols., by B. J. Lossing. New York: Harper Brothers, 1851 and 1852.)*

shall not believe ourselves interested in the fate of *Boston,* but that one Colony may be attacked and humbled after another. . . .

. . . . .

. . . Surely you cannot doubt at this time, my countrymen, but that the people of *Massachusetts-Bay* are suffering in a cause common to us all; and therefore, that we ought immediately to concert the most prudent measures for their relief and our own safety.

. . . . .

In the last place I beg leave to offer some observations concerning the measures that may be most expedient in the present emergency. Other nations have contended in blood for their liberty, and have judged the jewel worth the price that was paid for it. These colonies are not reduced to the dreadful necessity. So dependent is *Great-Britain* on us for supplies, that Heaven seems to have placed in our hands means of an effectual, yet peaceable resistance, if we have sense and integrity to make a proper use of them. A general agreement between these colonies on non-importation and non-exportation faithfully observed would certainly be attended with success. Let us consider that we are contending with our ancient venerable and beloved parent-country. Let us treat her with all possible respect and reverence . . . so as to convince our brethren in *Great-Britain* of the importance of a connexion and harmony between them and us, and of the danger of driving us into despair. Their true interests and our own are the same; nor should we admit any notion of a distinction, till we *know* their *resolutions* to be UNALTERABLY HOSTILE.—

John Dickinson, from Letter IV, Letters to the Inhabitants of the British Colonies, *May 1774, in Paul Leicester Ford, ed.,* The Political Writings of John Dickinson, 1764–1774, *pp. 491–492, 493–494, and 499–500.*

Our Assembly met at this place the 4th. Ulto. according to Prorogation, and was dissolved the 26th. for entering into a resolve of which the Inclosd is a Copy, and which the Govr. thought reflected too much upon his Majesty, and the British Parliament to pass over unnoticed. . . . [I]n short the Ministry may rely on it that Americans will never be tax'd without their own consent that the cause of Boston the despotick Measures in respect to it I mean now is and ever will be considered as the cause of America (not that we approve their conduct in destroyg, the Tea) and that we shall not suffer ourselves to be sacrificed by piece meals though god only knows what is to become of us. . . .

George Washington, from a letter written at Williamsburg to George William Fairfax, June 10, 1774, in John C. Fitzpatrick, ed., The Writings of George Washington, *vol. 3, pp. 223–224.*

Mr. [Samuel] Winthrop has been just making some Observations, which I think worth sending to you. Upon Reading an Observation in the Farmers [John Dickinson] fourth Letter, that some of our, (the Massachusetts) Resolves and Publications had better have been suppressed, Mr. Winthrop said, that many Things in our News Papers ought to have been suppressed. For example, Whenever there was the least popular Commotion, or Disturbance, it was instantly put in all the News Papers, in this Province. But in all the other Provinces they took Care to conceal and suppress every such Thing.

Another Thing He says, We ought to avoid all Paragraphs in our Papers about our own Manufactures—especially all vapouring puffing Advertisements about them, because such Paragraphs only tend to provoke the Ministry, Merchants and Manufacturers in England, to confine and restrain or prohibit our Manufactures.

But our Presses, in Boston, Salem, and Newbury Port are under no Regulation, nor any judicious prudent Care. Therefore it seems impracticable to keep out such Imprudences.

The Printers are hot, indiscreet Men, and they are under the Influence of others as hot, rash and injudicious as themselves, very often.

For my own Part it has long been my Resolution to avoid being concerned in councilling, or aiding or abetting any Tumult or Disorder, to avoid all exceptionable Scribbling in the Newspaper, of every Kind, to avoid all Passion and personal Altercation or Reflections. I have found it difficult, to keep these Resolutions exactly, all but the last however I have religiously and punctiliously, observed, these six Years.

John Adams, from a letter written at Pattens at Arundell to Abigail Adams, July 4, 1774, in L. H. Butterfield, ed., Adams Family Correspondence, *vol. 1, pp. 122–123.*

As to your political sentiments, I would heartily join you in them, so far as relates to a humble and dutiful petition to the throne, provided there was the most distant hope of success. But have we not tried this already? Have we not addressed the Lords, and remonstrated to the Commons? And to what end? Did they deign to look at our petitions? Does it not appear . . . that there is a regular, systematic plan formed to fix the right and practice of taxation upon us? Do not all the debates . . . in the House of Commons on the side of the government, expressly declare that America must be taxed in aid of the British funds, and that she has no longer resources within herself? Is there any thing to be expected from petitioning after this? Is not the attack upon the liberty and property of the people of Boston, before restitution of the loss of the India Company was demanded, a plain and self-evident proof of what they are aiming at? Do not the subsequent bills (now I dare say acts), for depriving the Massachusetts Bay of its charter, and for transporting offenders into other colonies or to Great Britain for trial, where it is impossible from the nature of the thing that justice can be obtained, convince us that the administration is determined to stick at nothing to carry its point? Ought we not, then, to put our virtue and fortitude to the severest test?

George Washington, from a letter written at Mount Vernon to Bryan Fairfax, July 4, 1774, in John C. Fitzpatrick, ed., The Writings of George Washington, *vol. 3, pp. 228–229.*

. . . On the eleventh instant, a party of men from the Roxbury Camp went to Long Island, in Boston Harbor, and brought off fifteen of the regulars prisoners, between twenty and thirty horned cattle, and about one hundred sheep. The prisoners were sent from the head-quarters yesterday, to Concord. The same account says that General Gage's troops are much dispirited; that they are very sickly, and are heartily disposed to leave off dancing any more to the tune of Yankee Doodle, and that General Gage has sent many reputable housekeepers in Boston, to prison, for refusing to work day's work on board the men of war, and the fortifications.

Christopher Marshall, Philadelphia merchant, official, and Quaker, from diary entry of July 24, 1774, in Marshall, Extracts from the Diary of Christopher Marshall, *pp. 32–33.*

I think the appointment of the new counsel is the last comic scene we shall see Exhibite'd in the state Farce which has for several years been playing off. I fear the

Tragic part of the Drama will hastely Ensue, and that Nothing but the Blood of the Virtuous Citizens Can repurchase the Rights of Nature, unjustly torn from us by the united arms of treachery and Violence. Every Circumstance Contributes to Lead this people to Look with more impatient Expectation for the result of the approaching Congress. The persons Deputed to that purpose have an important part to act, a part on which depends in a great measure the Future Freedom and Happiness of a Wide Extended Empire. Mr. Adams has justly Compared them to the Amphyctiones of Grece, and as their work is not less arduous, may they acquit themselves in such manner as that their Names may stand as high on the Records of Fame as those of any of that Respected Body. May they be Endowd with Virtue and judgment, Wisely to deliberate and Resolve, and Fortitude and Vigour to Execute whatever may be thought Necessary to Reestablish the Welfare and Tranquility of their much injured Country.

Mercy Otis Warren, from a letter written at Plymouth to Abigail Adams, August 9, 1774, in L. H. Butterfield, ed., Adams Family Correspondence, *vol. 1, p. 138.*

He [a white trader] is at this time unhappy in his connexions with his beautiful savage. It is but a few years since he came here . . . and by his industry, honesty, and engaging manners, had gained the affections of the Indians, and soon made a little fortune by traffic with the Siminoles: when unfortunately meeting with this little charmer, they were married in the Indian manner. He loves her sincerely, as she possesses every perfection in her person to render a man happy. Her features are beautiful, and manners engaging. Innocence, modesty, and love, appear to a stranger in every action and movement; and these powerful graces she has so artfully played upon her beguiled and vanquished lover, and unhappy slave, as to have already drained him of all his possessions, which she dishonestly distributes among her savage relations. . . .

. . . My reasons for mentioning this affair, so foreign to my business, was to exhibit an instance of the power of beauty in a savage. . . . It is, however, but doing justice to the virtue and moral conduct of the Siminoles, and American aborigines in general, to observe, that the character of this woman is condemned and detested by her people of both sexes. . . .

. . . it is from the most delicate sense of the honour and reputation of their tribes and families, that their laws and customs receive their force and energy. This is the divine principle which influences their moral conduct, and solely preserves their constitution and civil government in that purity in which they are found to prevail amongst them.

William Bartram, English botanist, commenting on American Indians encountered on a large island in Lake George on the St. Juan (St. Johns) River in Florida, summer 1774, from his Travels through North & South Carolina, Georgia, East & West Florida, *first published in Philadelphia in 1791, in Mark Van Doren, ed.,* Travels of William Bartram, *pp. 110–111.*

With all the Opulence and Splendor of this City [New York], there is very little good Breeding to be found. We have been treated with an assiduous Respect. But I have not seen one real Gentleman, one well bred Man since I came to Town. At their Entertainments there is no Conversation that is agreeable. There is no Modesty—No Attention to one another. They talk very loud, very fast, and altogether. If they ask you a Question, before you can utter 3 Words of your Answer, they will break out upon you, again—and talk away.

John Adams, from diary entry of August 23, 1774, in L. H. Butterfield, ed., Diary and Autobiography of John Adams, *p. 109.*

Came to town, Hon. Thomas Cushing, Samuel Adams, Robert Treat Paine, and John Adams, delegates from the Province of Massachusetts Bay, with whom came in company, from New York, John Rutledge, delegate from South Carolina, who took his passage to New York.

Christopher Marshall, Philadelphia merchant, official, and Quaker, noting the arrival of delegates to the Continental Congress in his diary, August 29, 1774, in Marshall, Extracts from the Diary of Christopher Marshall, *p. 9.*

At Ten, The Delegates all met at the City Tavern, and walked to the Carpenters Hall, where they took a View of the Room, and of the Chamber where is an excellent Library. . . . The General Cry was, that this was a good Room, and the Question was put, whether We were satisfyed with this Room, and it passed in the Affirmative. A very few were for the Negative and they were chiefly from Pennsylvania and New York.

Then Mr. Lynch arose, and said there was a Gentleman present who had presided with great Dignity over a very respectable Society, greatly to the Advantage of America, and he therefore proposed that the Hon. Peytoun Randolph Esqr., one of the Delegates from Virginia, and the late Speaker of their House of Burgesses, should be appointed Chairman and he doubted not it would be unanimous.—The Question was put and he was unanimously chosen.

· · · · ·

This is a Question of great Importance.—If We vote by Colonies, this Method will be liable to great Inequality and Injustice, for 5 small Colonies, with 100,000 People in each may outvote 4 large ones, each of which has 500,000 Inhabitants. If We vote by the Poll, some Colonies have more than their Proportion of Members, and others have less. If We vote by Interests, it will be attended with insuperable Difficulties, to ascertain the true Importance of each Colony.—Is the Weight of a Colony to be ascertained by the Number of Inhabitants merely—or by the Amount of their Trade, the Quantity of their Exports and Imports, or by any compound Ratio of both. This will lead us into such a Field of Controversy as will greatly perplex us. Besides I question whether it is possible to ascertain, at this Time, the Numbers of our People or the Value of our Trade. It will not do in such a Case, to take each other's Words. It ought to be ascertained by authentic Evidence, from Records.

John Adams, from diary entry of September 5, 1774, in L. H. Butterfield, ed., Diary and Autobiography of John Adams, *pp. 122–124.*

I hope future Ages will quote our Proceedings with Applause. It is one of the great Duties of the democratical Part of the Constitution to keep itself pure. It is known in my Province, that some other Colonies are not so numerous or rich as they are. I am for giving all the Satisfaction in my Power.

The Distinctions between Virginians, Pennsylvanians, New Yorkers and New Englanders, are no more.

I am not a Virginian, but an American.

Slaves are to be thrown out of the Question, and if the freemen can be represented according to their Numbers I am satisfied.

John Adams, notes on a statement by Patrick Henry during a debate in the Continental Congress, September 6, 1774, in L. H. Butterfield, ed., Diary and Autobiography of John Adams, *p. 125.*

We are all well here. I think I enjoy better Health than I have done these 2 years. I have not been to Town since I parted with you there. The Governor [Hutchinson] is making all kinds of warlike preparations such as mounting cannon upon Beacon Hill, diging entrenchments upon the Neck, placeing cannon there, encamping a regiment there, throwing up Brest Works &c. &c. The people are much alarmed, and the Selectmen have waited upon him in concequence of it. The county congress have also sent a committee. . . . In consequence of the powders being taken from Charlstown, a general alarm spread thro many Towns and was caught pretty soon here [Braintree] . . . and about 8 o clock a Sunday Evening there pass[ed] by here about 200 Men, preceeded by a horse cart, and marched down to the powder house from whence they took the powder and carried [it] into the other parish and there secreeted it. I opened the window upon there return. They pass'd without any Noise, not a word among them till they came against this house, when some of them perceiveing me, askd me if I wanted any powder. I replied not since it was in so good hands. The reason they gave for taking it, was that we had so many Tories here they dare not trust us with it. . . .

Abigail Adams, from a letter written at Braintree, Massachusetts, to John Adams, September 14, 1774, in L. H. Butterfield, ed., Adams Family Correspondence, *vol. 1, pp. 151–152.*

Dined with Mr. Chew, Chief Justice of the Province, with all the Gentlemen from Virginia, Dr. Shippen, Mr. Tilghman and many others. We were shewn into a grand Entry and Stair Case, and into an elegant and most magnificent Chamber, untill Dinner. About four O Clock We were called down to Dinner. The Furniture was all rich.—Turttle, and every other Thing—Flummery, Jellies, Sweetmeats of 20 sorts, Trifles, Whip'd Syllabubs, floating Islands, fools—&c., and then a Desert of Fruits, Raisins, Almonds, Pears, Peaches—Wines most excellent and admirable. I drank Madeira at a great Rate and found no Inconvenience in it.

John Adams, from diary entry of September 22, 1774, in L. H. Butterfield, ed., Diary and Autobiography of John Adams, *p. 136.*

The Congress will, to all present Appearance be well united and in such Measures, I hope will give Satisfaction to the Friends of our Country.

A Tory here is the most despicable Animal in the Creation. Spiders, Toads, Snakes, are their only proper Emblems. The Massachusetts Councillors, and Addressers are held in curious Esteem here, as you will see.

The Spirit, the Firmness, the Prudence of our Province are vastly applauded, and We are universally acknowledged the Saviours and Defenders of American Liberty.

The Designs, and Plans of the Congress, must not be communicated, until compleated, and We shall move with great Deliberation.

John Adams, from a letter written at Philadelphia to Abigail Adams, September 14, 1774, in L. H. Butterfield, ed., Adams Family Correspondence, *vol. 1, p. 155.*

. . . I will not despair, but will believe that our cause being good we shall finally prevail. The Maxim in time of peace prepair for war, (if this may be call'd a time of peace) resounds throughout the Country. Next tuesday they are warned at Braintree all above 15 and under 60 to attend with their arms, and to train once a fortnight from that time, is a Scheme which lays much at heart with many.

. . . There has been in Town a conspiracy of the Negroes. At present it is kept pretty private and was discoverd by one who endeavourd to diswaid them from it—he being threatned with his life, applied to Justice [Edmund] Quincy for protection. They conducted in this way—got an Irishman to draw up a petition to the Govener telling him they would fight for him provided he would arm them and engage to liberate them if he conquerd, and it is said that he attended so much to it as to consult Pircy [Hugh, Earl Percy] upon it. . . . I wish most sincerely there was not a Slave in the province. It allways appeard a most iniquitious Scheme to me—fight ourselfs for what we are daily robbing and plundering from those who have as good a right to freedom as we have. You know my mind upon this Subject.

Abigail Adams, from a letter written at Boston to John Adams, September 22, 1774, in L. H. Butterfield, ed., Adams Family Correspondence, *vol. 1, pp. 161–162.*

. . . I was involuntarily led into a short discussion of this subject by your remarks on the conduct of the Boston people, and your opinion of their wishes to set up for independency. I am as well satisfied as I can be of my existence that no such thing is desired by any thinking man in all North America; on the contrary, that it is the ardent wish of the warmest advocates for liberty, that peace and tranquility, upon constitutional grounds, may be restored, and the horrors of civil discord prevented.

George Washington, from a letter written at Philadelphia to Capt. Robert MacKenzie, October 9, 1774, in John C. Fitzpatrick, ed., The Writings of George Washington, *vol. 3, pp. 246–247.*

Phyladelphia with all its Trade, and Wealth, and Regularity is not Boston. The Morals of our People are much better, their Manners are more polite, and agreeable—they are purer English. Our Language is better, our Persons are handsomer, our Spirit is greater, our Laws are wiser, our Religion is superiour, our Education is better. We exceed them in every Thing, but in a Market, and in charitable public foundations.

John Adams, from diary entry of October 9, 1774, in L. H. Butterfield, ed., Diary and Autobiography of John Adams, *p. 150.*

In Congress, nibbling and quibbling—as usual.

There is no greater Mortification than to sit with half a dozen Witts, deliberating upon a Petition, Address, or Memorial. These great Witts, these subtle Criticks, these refined Genius's, these learned Lawyers, these wise Statesmen, are so fond of shewing their Parts and Powers, as to make their Consultations very tedius.

Young Ned Rutledge is a perfect Bob o'Lincoln— a Swallow—a Sparrow—a Peacock—excessively vain, excessively weak, and excessively variable and unsteady—jejune, inane, and puerile.

Mr. Dickinson is very modest, delicate, and timid.

John Adams, from diary entry of October 24, 1774, in L. H. Butterfield, ed., Diary and Autobiography of John Adams, *pp. 156–157.*

2

Shots Heard Round the World

1775

APPROACH TO WAR

To the casual observer the storm that threatened as 1774 closed probably appeared to have quieted as 1775 opened because no overtly hostile acts occurred in the early months of the year. But beneath appearances the storm raged on—most certainly in Massachusetts, and in England as well. The adamant rhetoric voiced by the king and in Parliament revealed unwillingness to compromise. In February, William Pitt and Edmund Burke futilely appealed once more in Parliament for ameliorative policies toward the Americans, Burke made a final eloquent but ineffectual appeal in late March. As King George III and his ministers now saw it, the colonists must either submit or rebel and face Britain's overwhelming armed might. The Massachusetts radicals deemed only one of these options agreeable. And so London and Boston determined the course of events.

At the end of January, George III fatefully authorized Gen. Thomas Gage to use military force in maintaining royal authority in Massachusetts. Although Gage would not receive the king's order until April, he had already amassed in Boston a force of about 4,000 troops, plus artillery and also ships in the harbor armed with heavy cannons. As February began, the illegal Second Massachusetts Provincial Congress, with John Hancock serving as president, convened across the river in Cambridge. The delegates intended to formulate a policy response to the augmenting of the Boston garrison and to the Fishery Act, which prohibited the New England colonists from trading with any nations but Great Britain, Ireland, and the West Indies and from using the Newfoundland banks fisheries, a shattering blow to Massachusetts's economy and its dependence on cod and whale fishing. Later in February the Provincial Congress adjourned to reconvene in Concord, where delegates approved creating a commissary to store arms and ordnance, soliciting militia support from adjacent colonies, and otherwise preparing for armed conflict. In late March, the Virginia assembly voiced support for the Massachusetts rebels through the powerful advocacy of Patrick Henry, whose ringing phrase "give me liberty or give me death" succinctly defined the paramount issue for many Americans.

And then came April. General Gage had decided on a show of strength as March ended. He sent a brigade of troops commanded by Col. Hugh Percy on a practice march through Cambridge and Watertown. The Provincial Congress, meeting in Concord, viewed the march as a hostile act that indicated that Gage was determined to fulfill his royal mandate and impose Parliament's disagreeable policies on Massachusetts by force. Consequently, on April 5 the delegates adopted 53 articles of war—a clear challenge to Gage. The preamble to the articles professed the colonists' innocence of rebellion, treason, and sedition and invoked the legacy of the Pilgrims' struggle for civil and religious rights as just cause for the colonists to prepare for war.[1]

THE BATTLE OF LEXINGTON

On April 14, Gage received a letter from William Legge, the earl of Dartmouth, secretary of state for the American colonies. Dartmouth reproached Gage for his inaction and ordered him to move circumspectly and arrest the leaders of the Provincial Congress. Although concerned that he lacked sufficient troops because his request for 20,000 reinforcements had been rejected, Gage decided to take advantage of the discretion Dartmouth's letter granted him. He detached about 700 men, grenadiers and light infantry, from their regiments for special assignments. His plan was not to arrest leaders of the Provincial Congress, as Dartmouth had ordered, but instead to send the detachment to Concord and Worcester to seize militia caches of arms and ammunition. The Provincial Congress adjourned, with its members dispersing. In Boston rumor and conjecture laced the discussions at the Green Dragon, the Bunch of Grapes, and other taverns.

And on April 16, Dr. Joseph Warren sent Paul Revere to Lexington to warn John Hancock and Samuel Adams that Gage might be planning to arrest them; they relayed the warning to Patriots in Concord, who began moving their store of arms and ammunition to Worcester. While returning to Boston, Revere arranged with cohorts in Charlestown to expect lanterns shining in the steeple of Old North Church as a warning signal that British troops were on the march—two lanterns if the British set out by water, one lantern if they departed by land over Boston Neck. Informed by the signal, his henchmen were to send warnings on to Concord, as Revere expected he would be unable to leave Boston.[2]

Gage's efforts to maintain secrecy failed, as Dr. Warren learned on April 18 that the British detachment would march on Concord early the following morning and summoned Revere and William Dawes to ride out ahead of the troops' departure with a warning for Patriots in Lexington and Concord. Arriving first, Dawes immediately rode off across Boston Neck toward Lexington to warn John Hancock and Sam Adams. Before rowing across the Charles River to Charlestown, Revere dispatched Capt. John Pulling to display two lanterns from Old North to signal that the British would set out by water rather than land. Dawes raced freely toward Lexington, but Revere encountered British officers, hastily fled on an altered course, and spread the alarm in Medford and Menotomy. Reaching Lexington before Dawes, Revere brought the news to Adams and Hancock at Parson Clark's home in time to allow their escape. He waited for Dawes, and the two set off for Concord, joined by Dr. Samuel Prescott. Halted by four British officers with drawn pistols, the couriers took flight—Dawes fleeing back to Lexington, Prescott leaping a stone wall, and Revere seeking refuge in a woods. Trapped by hidden British officers, Revere reported that 500 militiamen were assembling at Lexington. The officers took him to Lexington and

released him without his horse. He found Adams and Hancock still at Parson Clark's home and fled with them in a chaise.[3]

At about 5:00 A.M. on April 19, the unit of the British detachment commanded by Maj. John Pitcairn traversed the road to Concord and entered Lexington, where 130 minutemen, only 70 of them bearing arms, waited on the village green under the leadership of Capt. John Parker. Pitcairn rode forward and ordered the minutemen to disperse. Accepting the futility of their position, they began to do so without surrendering their arms, when a shot rang out, and a British officer ordered his men to fire. Seven minutemen fell dead on Lexington Green, and a British soldier bayoneted the wounded Jonas Parker, John's

Paul Revere completes his famous ride. *(Courtesy of the National Archives and Records Administration)*

This image depicts the Battle of Lexington. *(Courtesy of Anne S. K. Brown Military Collection, Brown University Library)*

aged cousin, as he sprawled on the grass attempting to reload his musket. With the brief Battle of Lexington ended, Pitcairn and his officers managed to reform their frenzied men and, joined by Lt. Col. Francis Smith's troops, marched on toward Concord. News of the carnage at Lexington swept through the countryside, and armed Patriots hastened to join the resistance.[4]

THE BATTLE OF CONCORD

Dr. Prescott had reached Concord at 11:00 A.M. with his warning; alarm bells had summoned the militiamen. Reuben Brown rode to Lexington, heard the gunfire, and returned with the news of battle there. About 150 minutemen gathered to confront the approaching British troops. They dispersed when the troops came into sight and reassembled at Punkatasset Hill north of the Concord River. As the British troops took stations at Concord's North Bridge, searched Col. John Barrett's house for arms, or refreshed themselves in the local taverns, Patriot reinforcements arrived from nearby villages. The militiamen descended from Punkatasset Hill to a ridge near the North Bridge. Alarmed to see that the British had set fire to Concord's courthouse and a blacksmith shop—although the soldiers quickly doused the flames—Barrett's adjutant roused the Patriots to defend the town. Led by Barrett, Maj. John Buttrick, and Lt. Col. John Robinson of Westford, the Patriots advanced as two fifers played "The White Cockade."

In command of the British troops at the North Bridge, Capt. Walter Laurie withdrew his men to the east end of the bridge and sent a messenger to Colonel Smith for reinforcements as the minutemen gathered at the bridge's east end. Laurie's troops opened fire, wounding an American. A second British volley killed two and wounded two among the Patriots; return fire killed three redcoats and wounded several others, including officers, causing the British to fall back in disarray to Concord. Lacking the discipline to mount an offensive, the Patriots allowed the entire British company to reform and to begin marching back to Boston at

Troops meet for the Battle of Concord at the North Bridge. *(Courtesy of the Anne S. K. Brown Military Collection, Brown University Library)*

noon. But as they proceeded the British suffered repeated musket barrages from patriots racing before them to fire from behind trees, stone walls, and houses.[5]

At Meriam's Corner the British fired a warning volley at Meriam's house, and the unexpected return fire killed two soldiers and wounded others. As the retreating soldiers crowded onto a bridge, rebel shots felled many of them. For 16 miles the minutemen harassed their enemy, sending the redcoats into a panicky retreat. Near Lexington the rebel firing wounded Colonel Smith and caused Major Pitcairn's horse to bolt. As the frazzled redcoats staggered onto Lexington Green, expecting the worst, a force commanded by Lord Percy arrived from Boston to their rescue. The troops struggled back through Cambridge, constantly harried by the Patriots. Enraged by the sniping, the redcoats attacked homes, killed the males they found, and looted and burned. They finally reached safety at Bunker Hill and Breed's Hill in Charlestown, protected by the guns of the British fleet. In the Battle of Concord and the British retreat, the Patriots lost 49 men, with another 46 wounded; the British had 72 dead and 201 wounded. The final toll perhaps seemed comparatively light, but the shots fired during and after the battles of Lexington and Concord would echo for years as the opening volleys of the American Revolution.[6]

BOSTON AND TICONDEROGA

The Massachusetts Provincial Congress reconvened at Concord and voted to call up 13,600 Massachusetts militia immediately, with Gen. Artemas Ward as their commander, and to request militia recruits from the other New England colonies to raise the total force to 30,000. Militiamen from New Hampshire, Connecticut, and Rhode Island joined the Massachusetts militia and local patriots in surrounding Boston, with Ward as their commander in chief. With his beleaguered garrison pinned down in Boston, General Gage expected the rebels to launch a massive attack at any moment.[7]

Ethan Allen confronts Captain De la Place while capturing Fort Ticonderoga. *(The Capture of Ticonderoga, Ethan Allen and Captain De la Place, courtesy of the National Archives and Records Administration)*

Convinced of the strategic value of Fort Ticonderoga, Benedict Arnold received a commission as a colonel, recruited troops, and headed for Lake Champlain. Learning of a rival expedition of about 100 Green Mountain Boys, an irregular militia from the New Hampshire Grants area commanded by Ethan Allen, Arnold reluctantly joined forces with Allen in early May about two miles below the fort. With 83 men in two barges, they rowed across the lake, landing at daybreak. Scrambling over the fort's crumbled south wall, they encountered a lone sentry, who fled after his gun misfired. After wounding one of Allen's men with a bayonet, a second sentry, chastened by a blow to the head with the flat of Allen's sword, led Allen and Arnold to the officers' quarters. Rudely surprised, the fort's commander, Capt. William De la Place, surrendered. Without firing a shot, Arnold and Allen obtained possession of Fort Ticonderoga, taking 50 prisoners, various supplies, and about 100 cannons. A party of Allen's men under command of Lt. Col. Seth Warner also captured Crown Point on Lake Champlain without encountering resistance; and Arnold led a successful raid on the British fort at St. John's in Quebec, capturing some boats and supplies to bring back to Ticonderoga. For the time being at least, New England seemed secure against a British invasion from Canada, and hopes were raised that sympathetic Canadians might come to the American rebels' support.[8]

THE SECOND CONTINENTAL CONGRESS

As Arnold and Allen effected their conquests in upper New York, the Second Continental Congress convened in Philadelphia on May 10. Peyton Randolph again filled the role of president, but before the month ended he returned to serve in the Virginia assembly. Thomas Jefferson replaced Randolph as a delegate from Virginia, and the congress elected John Hancock president. Among the delegates were many returnees from the First Continental Congress but also some new faces, including Hancock; Pennsylvania's Benjamin Franklin, who had only just returned from England the week before; and New York's George Clinton, Robert R. Livingston, and Philip Schuyler. Although remaining officially unrepresented, Georgia, missing from the first congress, now had at least one delegate, Lyman Hall from St. John's Parish.

The Second Continental Congress's early initiatives included sending a public appeal, drafted by John Jay, that invited the Canadians' support and expressed hope of the two regions' uniting "in the defense of our common liberty." The delegates also confronted two issues defined by the Massachusetts Provincial Congress, which asked the Continental Congress to decide whether Massachusetts should assume control of its civil government and whether the Continental Congress should assume control of the militia forces besieging Boston. In answering the second question, the Continental Congress voted to raise militia companies from Maryland, Pennsylvania, and Virginia and appointed a committee to draft rules for administrating the Continental army. And on June 15, the delegates unanimously chose George Washington of Virginia as commander in chief of the Continental army.[9]

THE BATTLE OF BREED'S HILL AND BUNKER HILL

As Washington assumed command and the Continental Congress approved an organizational plan for the Continental army, including appointment of Artemas Ward of Massachusetts and Charles Lee of Virginia as major generals, Ward

General Israel Putnam leaves his plow for the defense of his country. *(Courtesy of the National Archives and Records Administration)*

Washington takes command of the army at Cambridge. *(Courtesy of the National Archives and Records Administration)*

moved to tighten the noose at Boston. He sent 1,000 men commanded by Col. William Prescott to fortify Bunker Hill. Brig. Gen. Israel Putnam met Prescott at the neck of the Charlestown peninsula with wagonloads of dirt and brushwood to build the fortifications. Ignoring Ward's orders, the two officers decided to fortify Breed's Hill, nearer to Boston Harbor, and their men worked through the night to dig trenches and erect walls.

When the Sun rose on June 17, observers aboard British ships in Boston Harbor detected the new fortifications on Breed's Hill. The ships and a British battery on Copp's Hill opened fire, but the rebels continued building fortifications. At Putnam's urging, Prescott weakened his position by sending troops to fortify Bunker Hill as well, after John Stark and James Reed had arrived with two regiments of reinforcements from New Hampshire. Strong earthworks protected the American line along the rise of Breed's Hill, but these diminished to little more than rail fencing stuffed with grass on the left toward the Mystic River, where Stark's men gathered. At midday, British troops commanded by Gen. William Howe crossed the Charles River on barges, disembarked at Breed's Hill, formed in ranks, and prepared a frontal bayonet attack.

Protecting the Americans' left, Stark ordered his men to hold their fire until the Royal Welch Fusiliers moved within yards of their defensive line and they could "see the whites of their eyes." His men's concentrated volley decimated the approaching fusiliers, sending them into retreat, as their comrades fell back before similar barrages of accurate musket fire. Howe rallied his troops for another attack. Their third attack succeeded, as Prescott's men had exhausted their ammunition, and the British poured over the wall to bayonet or shoot at close range the scurrying rebels. Under covering fire from Stark's men, Prescott's troops retreated to Bunker Hill, where Putnam's troops joined them in an orderly withdrawal from the peninsula. Although the British now controlled Charlestown peninsula, they had endured appalling losses, with 226 dead and 828 wounded—nearly 48 percent of their attacking force—while the Americans' casualties numbered 140 dead and 271 wounded. Among the dead was Major John Pitcairn, felled

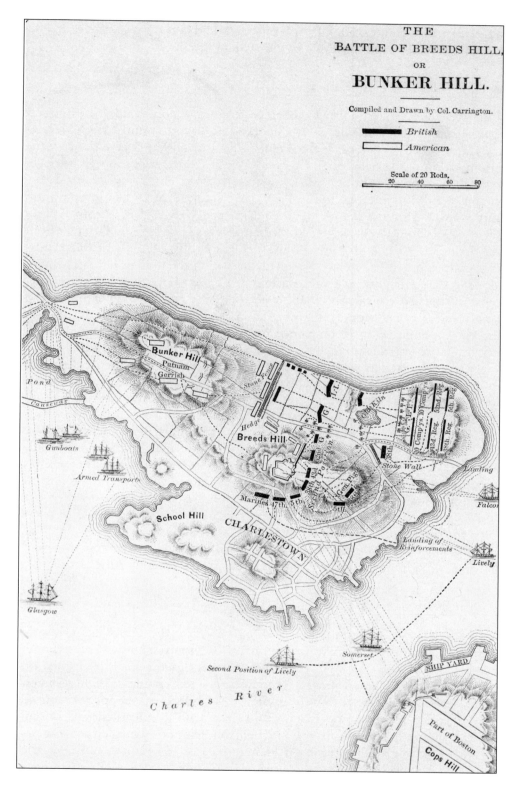

This map provides an outline of the battles of Breed's Hill and Bunker Hill. *(Courtesy of the Anne S. K. Brown Military Collection, Brown University Library)*

by several musket balls, including one fired by Peter Salem, a black freed from servitude to enlist in the militia, who had been among the major's opponents at Concord. Though defeated, the Americans discovered weaknesses in the British juggernaut; though victorious, British officers found in the Battle of Breed's Hill and Bunker Hill a cautionary tale of dismaying portent.[10]

WASHINGTON TAKES COMMAND

When Washington arrived at Cambridge to assume command, his profound concerns about his decision to accept the duty found confirmation. He had not commanded troops since the French and Indian War. The Massachusetts terrain, although he had visited Boston some 20 years earlier, appeared totally unfamiliar, as did the prospect of laying siege to a city. His "army," hardly qualifying as a fighting force, comprised a "rabble in arms," in British general John Burgoyne's derisive view. All New Englanders—perhaps 1,500 from Rhode Island, 5,000 from Connecticut, 1,000 from New Hampshire, and 10,000 from Massachusetts—struck the new commander as a scruffy lot, filthy, dissolute, profane, undisciplined. They were mostly farmers, saddlers, shoemakers, carpenters, coopers, wheelwrights, and other artisans. Among these men, all recuperating from the trials of Bunker Hill, could also be found a number of African Americans—not a welcome sight for a Virginia slaveholder, although Washington himself was continually accompanied on horseback or otherwise by his body servant, the slave William ("Billy") Lee, through the entirety of the war.

In the commanders already on site, Washington at least found some dedicated leaders: General Nathanael Greene with his New Hampshire "Army of Observation," General Israel Putnam and his Connecticut contingent, John Stark with his New Hampshire regiment, and Colonel John Glover from Marblehead, Massachusetts. They faced formidable obstacles in forming their units into an effective army, however, as suggested by the fact that few of the men wore uniforms and all shouldered disparate types of arms and carried only enough powder to fire nine shots each. Always impeccably uniformed and commanding in deportment, Washington set about trying to effect discipline among this motley array of men—they had a clear example to follow in the soldierly aspects of Greene's troops. And to overcome his ignorance of the terrain, Washington directed the artist John Trumbull, son of Connecticut governor Jonathan Trumbull (the Elder), to prepare maps and drawings of both the local geographic features and the British fortifications.[11]

CONGRESSIONAL DECLARATIONS AND DECISIONS

With the prospect of continuing war confirmed by the tolls of casualties at Breed's Hill and Bunker Hill, the Continental Congress presented its orders to General Washington and escorted him as he took leave from Philadelphia on June 23 to travel to New York and on to Boston. The Continental Congress also committed itself to funding the war effort with bills of credit (paper money), authorizing an initial appropriation of no more than 2 million Spanish milled dollars "for the defense of America." Then the delegates struggled with drafting and redrafting a Declaration on Taking up Arms. Adopted in early July, the declaration defined the colonies' reasons for resorting to arms while advocating reconciliation and denying the colonies intended to seek independence, but it also asserted that Great Britain was the aggressor.

Perhaps the prickliest issue facing the Continental Congress as the summer progressed was the subject of union. Benjamin Franklin drafted a tentative

"Articles of Confederation and Perpetual Union," approved by Jefferson and presented for the Continental Congress's consideration. But the delegates decided to postpone consideration of the document as well as the issue of opening up American ports to trade. They agreed on creating a post office department, with Franklin as postmaster general, to facilitate communication among the colonies; on a means of redeeming currency that obligated each colony to pay its share; and on appointing commissioners to council with the Indians in an effort to ensure their remaining peaceable. With an official delegation from Georgia added to its ranks in September, the Continental Congress bolstered the war effort by appointing the Naval Committee, creating a small navy, and appointing Esek Hopkins as the new navy's commander in chief.[12]

THE INVASION OF CANADA

In anticipation of an offensive, the Continental Congress in June appointed as commander of the Northern Department Gen. Philip Schuyler. Schuyler was assigned by Washington to occupy posts on Lake Champlain and Lake George and authorized by Congress to organize an invasion of Canada. Schuyler arrived at Ticonderoga in the second half of July. He sent a scouting party under Maj. John Brown to reconnoiter conditions in Montreal and St. John's. Brown reported back that St. John's was being fortified but had a small garrison, that the French in Quebec would not fight against the Americans, and that the Indians would remain neutral. Brown advocated an invasion. At the end of August, Schuyler's second in command, Gen. Richard Montgomery, reacting to the urgency of another scouting report from Brown, decided without orders from Schuyler to begin the march north. Montgomery sent Schuyler word that he had embarked on Lake Champlain with 1,200 men headed for St. John's. Schuyler received Montgomery's note, approved his decision, and set out from Ticonderoga with about 500 men to join him.[13]

Schuyler caught up with Montgomery at Île aux Noix, Quebec, and took charge of the attack on St. John's. Twice unsuccessful in dislodging the St. John's

Montgomery's troops embark at Crown Point. *(Library of Congress)*

garrison, he twice fell back to his encampment at Île aux Noix. While Schuyler struggled, Washington, without authorization from the Continental Congress, sent Benedict Arnold with a 1,050-man expedition to traverse Maine, cross the St. Lawrence River, and attack Quebec City. Too ill to carry on, Schuyler returned to Ticonderoga, leaving Montgomery in charge. His force augmented to 2,000 by the arrival of Seth Warner and 170 Green Mountain Boys, Montgomery posted 350 men in boats to prevent the British from moving south into Lake Champlain and, with his remaining troops, began laying siege to St. John's. In an action that would damage Montgomery's strategy, Ethan Allen, sent by Montgomery to Chambly to organize Canadian volunteers, precipitously launched a march on Montreal, became surrounded by a force sent out by Governor Sir Guy Carleton, and ended a prisoner of war transported to England for incarceration.

In late October, some 335 Connecticut and 225 New York troops arrived to reinforce Montgomery, and Warner's Green Mountain Boys prevented a relief expedition led by Carleton from crossing the St. Lawrence, so that the steadfast commander at St. John's, Maj. Charles Preston, had no choice but to surrender the garrison as November began. Montgomery could now march on toward Montreal, but Preston's defiance had cost him 55 days and delayed his thrust across the St. Lawrence into the winter months. As he marched northward, Arnold's expedition finally arrived at the St. Lawrence River, exhausted, half-starved, clothes tattered, bodies battered and torn. When he had sailed from Newburyport, Massachusetts, on September 19 for the mouth of the Kennebec River in Maine, Arnold anticipated a journey of 20 days, but traversing the 350 miles to Quebec—nearly twice the distance he had estimated—required 45 days. During this epic ordeal, his men transported thousands of pounds of food and ammunition, as well as boats, and other necessities, slept in rain-drenched and frozen clothing, survived violent storms, forged wild waters, slogged through menacing bogs, suffered dysentery and other ailments, and endured near-starvation. Not surprisingly, only 675 of his original force of 1,000 reached the St. Lawrence—the rest had succumbed to illness or death.

Accepting that he could not defend Montreal with his small force of 150 regulars and militia, Governor Carleton abandoned the city and sailed upriver under American fire. Montgomery then sent a deputation to confer with Montreal's residents, who surrendered; he occupied the city and awaited news from Arnold. At Sorel, the Americans attacked Carleton's flotilla, capturing the Gaspee, two armed vessels, and the troops that had garrisoned Montreal, but Carleton escaped by rowboat and continued on to Quebec. Concurrently, loading his men aboard canoes and dugouts, Arnold crossed the St. Lawrence, landed near Quebec, and occupied the Plains of Abraham. But the city's garrison of 1,200 British regulars and French-Canadian militia rejected Arnold's call for surrender with jeers. When British reinforcements arrived at Quebec, Arnold withdrew 20 miles to the west to encamp at Point aux Trembles. Carleton safely reached the city and took command of its defense.[14]

THE BATTLE OF QUEBEC

As December began, Montgomery learned of Arnold's arrival at Quebec and moved upriver to join him, bringing fresh clothes, artillery, ammunition, provi-

Troops withstand the attack of Arnold's men. *(Library of Congress)*

sions, and 300 troops for an assault on the city. Arnold posted his men to the north of Quebec, and Montgomery, now in command, occupied the Plains of Abraham. Faced with bitter winter weather, the expiration of their men's enlistments at year's end, and the prospect that the spring thaw would free the river for British ships to bring reinforcements, the two commanders confronted a dilemma: Should they attack or lay siege to the city? Initially, they began a siege. But as the end of December approached, the commanders decided on attack. After a false start on December 29, Montgomery launched the attack on the final day of the month.

In the early morning of that day, Montgomery assailed the Lower Town through a blinding blizzard as Arnold attacked from the north. Rockets signaled the advance at 4:00 A.M. but also alerted Carleton. Montgomery's troops floundered through snowdrifts and ice mounds tossed ashore by the river. Arnold's men, blinded by the driving snow, entered the city by the Palace Gate, but they had lost one cannon, and their second proved unusable. A ricocheting bullet wounded Arnold in the leg, and two men carried him to the rear for care. Daniel Morgan assumed command. Morgan's first assault failed, as bullets pierced his hat and beard. His second assault forced a breach into the Lower Town, where his men reassembled and failed in attempting to overcome another barricade. They paused to await Montgomery. But Montgomery had fallen dead with a bullet to the brain, and Carleton's counterattack forced his men to retreat across the frozen St. Lawrence or to surrender as British sorties captured 426 of the invaders. The defenders suffered only five dead and 13 wounded. Severely reduced by his losses in prisoners plus 60 casualties, the incapacitated Arnold withdrew his 600-man remnant army to concede victory to Carleton in the Battle of Quebec.[15]

POLITICAL IMPASSE

In early July, the Continental Congress made an effort at conciliation with the British government in approving the so-called Olive Branch Petition, which

General Montgomery dies in battle in Quebec. *(Courtesy of the National Archives and Records Administration)*

John Dickinson strongly advocated but John Adams, who circumspectly favored independence, disapproved. Addressed to George III, the petition reiterated the colonists' grievances while pursuing reconciliation and negotiation and requesting that the king forestall hostilities to allow negotiations to proceed. Congress dispatched Loyalist Richard Penn, a descendant of William Penn, to London to deliver the petition. Penn arrived in England in mid-August.

In the meantime, the Continental Congress received Lord North's proposals for reconciliation, grudgingly supported by George III and approved by Parliament at the end of February. North proposed that the royal government would cease taxing any colony that approved legislation to levy internal taxes that would adequately support British military personnel and civil and judicial officials operating within the colony. The proposal clearly suggested that the North ministry intended to deal individually with each of the colonies and thereby sidestep even tacit recognition of the authority of the Continental Congress. In addition, Parliament in early February had already approved a statement addressed to the king that declared the colonies in rebellion and mandated the use of force to ensure that the colonists obeyed Great Britain's laws and conceded its sovereignty. Consequently, at the end of July the Continental Congress rejected the North proposal, citing the "cruelty" of the North ministry's prosecution of hostilities while asserting the colonies' right to raise appropriations and to be involved in determining how they were expended. And in early November, the delegates to Congress learned that George III had not only rejected the Olive Branch Petition but also had declared the colonies in a state of rebellion. In December, the Continental Congress adopted an official reply, denying that the colonies were in rebellion and asserting that their actions had evidenced loyalty to the Crown, but also most notably opposing Parliament's "exercise of unconstitutional powers." There would be no conciliation.

Great Britain and her American colonies thus reached political impasse. But the Continental Congress's policies of establishing an army and a navy, recruiting troops, and raising funds, as well as its approval of ongoing hostilities, especially the invasion of Canada, had clearly foretold this outcome, whether individual delegates were prepared to admit as much or not. The next move also now seemed clear: to begin soliciting the aid of foreign nations in supporting the War of the Revolution. To this end, as November concluded, the Continental Congress appointed a committee of five members—John Dickinson, Benjamin Franklin, Benjamin Harrison, John Jay, and Thomas Johnson—to correspond with potential supporters overseas. Congress awarded the committee power to proceed on its own initiative, revealing its correspondence only when so directed by the Continental Congress, and voted to pay for any agents the committee might find it necessary to hire. Dubbing themselves the Committee of Secret Correspondence, the committee began to function as a rudimentary foreign service—a likely first step toward claiming nationhood.[16]

WAR EXPEDIENTS AND STRATAGEMS

A potentially momentous event—with significant political, military, and social implications—occurred in Virginia in November, when the die seemed already cast. Royal Governor Lord Dunmore, following an earlier meeting with a group of blacks who proposed fighting for the British, declared martial law and offered freedom to all slaves and indentured servants with the ability and the will to bear arms in His Majesty's military service. Many slaves flocked into the British army headquarters in Norfolk to accept the offer. Patriot forces thwarted Dunmore's tactics, however, when in December they routed a troop of Loyalists that included blacks wearing sashes bearing the motto "Liberty to Slaves"—Dunmore referred to these black men as "Loyal Ethiopians." Thereafter, Dunmore retreated into Norfolk, where he and many Loyalists and blacks boarded British ships anchored in the city's harbor—some of the blacks died of diseases that swept through the ships, notably smallpox, while others enlisted in the Royal Navy. Dunmore's subsequent military ventures would be confined to periodic coastal raids. But wherever Dunmore's flotilla appeared in the Chesapeake area, many slaves fled their masters in hopes of joining him; perhaps as many as 800 succeeded. In addition, other royal governors in the South considered adopting the tactic of promising freedom to slaves who would bear arms—a prospect that, of course, outraged and terrified white slaveholders. Consequently, some southern Patriot legislative bodies—the Virginia Convention, for example—instituted policies designed to intimidate or oppress slaves attempting to defect to the British.[17]

As Washington prepared for winter in the Boston area in late November, he observed that some of his wounded soldiers succumbed extraordinarily quickly to death. In truth, his troops faced an adversary potentially more deadly than their British opponents: smallpox. Once the disease surfaced, rumors that Howe pursued a devious scheme gained credibility. He reputedly had suggested but abandoned the tactic of launching arrows tainted with smallpox toxin into the rebel encampments. What Howe did do was send about 300 sickly Bostonian men, women, and children—supposedly among them prostitutes and slaves infected with smallpox—by boat across the Back Bay to Cambridge and into the rebel camps. Whether these hapless expellees spread smallpox or other virulent diseases, their presence in the Cambridge camp certainly represented for Washington and his men a heightened threat of ravaging illnesses. Throughout the war, unsanitary conditions in the American camps, especially exposed feces and rotting animal carcasses, and in their hospitals—so bad in the latter that the wounded preferred taking their chances by avoiding them—generated hundreds of fatal cases of smallpox, "putrid fever," dysentery, and other infectious maladies. By contrast, the better disciplined and sanitation-savvy British troops suffered minimally from such health menaces. Responding to the threat before the summer campaigns of 1777 could begin, Washington had all of his soldiers who had never had smallpox inoculated, a new medical technique strongly advocated by John Adams; the commander also mandated cleaning up camp sites, with some success. Nevertheless, smallpox would strike again during the encampment at Morristown in the winter of 1777. Still later, as Clinton prepared to attack Charleston in February 1779, the city experienced a smallpox epidemic; Patriot militiamen refused to enter the city, declaring that they feared the disease more than they feared the British.[18]

CHRONICLE OF EVENTS

1775

January 18: Georgia's First Provincial Congress convenes in Savannah, ostensibly to establish an independent government as a show of support for opponents of Britain in Massachusetts and other colonies. But revolutionary sentiments are largely localized in St. John's Parish, settled by New Englanders, and Loyalists prevail in most of the other parishes, so that only five of the 12 parishes have sent delegates.

January 27: Gen. Thomas Gage receives orders to maintain the Crown's authority in Massachusetts. He has assembled in Boston a force estimated at 4,000 men, comprising nine infantry regiments and segments of two others. The former include the 4th (King's Own), 5th, 10th, 23rd (Royal Welch Fusiliers), 38th, 43rd, 47th, 52nd, and 59th. There are three companies from the 18th Regiment (Royal Irish) and six from the 65th as well as five companies of Royal Artillery. The 14th and 29th regiments continue their garrison at Castle William. Four British ships—the *Scarborough,* the *Boyne,* the *Somerset,* and the *Asia*—each bearing at least 60 guns, and sundry frigates and other vessels lie at anchor in Boston Harbor. From these vessels, Gage has secured 460 marines. His combined force lacks only cavalry.

February 1: In London, William Pitt (now first earl of Chatham), joined by Edmund Burke, makes a final effort to persuade Parliament to conciliate the Americans by repealing the Intolerable Acts, withdrawing British troops from Boston, and approving legislation that stipulates the colonies will not be taxed without their consent. Pitt praises the correspondence received from the Continental Congress for "decency, firmness, and wisdom" and depicts the colonists' cause as based on "eternal" principles leading them to "die in defence of their rights as men, as freemen." But Parliament rejects the appeals and continues on course.

The illegal Second Massachusetts Provincial Congress convenes in Cambridge, across the Charles River from Boston, in defiance of Gage, who designated Salem as the capital in 1774. The congress hopes to formulate a policy response to the augmentation of the British garrison in Boston and to the Fisheries Act.

February 20: The Massachusetts Provincial Congress temporarily adjourns to reconvene in Concord. Delegates appoint William Heath and John Thomas to serve as officers with Hancock. In open rebellion, the congress also approves setting up a commissary for storing ordnance, arms, and other materials; sends an invitation to the Stockbridge Indians to enlist in serving Massachusetts; drafts rules of governance for an army; chooses delegates who will visit other colonies in New England to request that they provide militia to bolster the Massachusetts militia; and adopts other measures that anticipate armed conflict with British forces.

February 22: The American Manufactory of Woolens, Linens, and Cottons, the first joint stock manufacturing firm in the colonies, is founded. Shares are offered by subscription at 10 pounds each.

February 27: Parliament approves Lord North's proposal, which the king has reluctantly supported, to discontinue taxing any colony that passes legislation to levy internal taxes that will raise adequate funds to support British civil and judicial officials and military personnel within the colony. Intended as conciliatory, the proposal's stipulations clearly indicate that the ministry intends to deal with each colony individually and thereby obviate any tacit recognition of the Continental Congress's legitimacy. Furthermore, Parliament, during the first week of February, has already approved a statement addressed to the king that declares the American colonies in a state of rebellion and that mandates acts to enforce colonists' obedience of British laws and acceptance of British sovereignty.

March 10: Daniel Boone begins to blaze the Wilderness Road that will extend from Fort Chiswell in Virginia's Shenandoah Valley westward through the Cumberland Gap into Kentucky.

March 22: Edmund Burke addresses the House of Commons, pointing out that the colonies have no representation in Parliament but have nevertheless been obligated to pay taxes and other subsidies to the royal government. He recommends that, each colony has a legislature that has freely voted large subsidies for the royal government in past years, Parliament should leave the issue of subsidies to these separate legislatures. "Magnanimity in politics is not seldom the truest wisdom; and a great empire and little minds go ill together," he says. His words go unheeded.

March 23: At the convention meeting in Richmond following Lord Dunmore's suspension of the Virginia assembly, Patrick Henry passionately denounces Britain's military might in America as presaging, not reconciliation, but "war and subjugation." Noting that the Americans' many petitions have been for nought, he declares, "There is no longer any room for hope. If we

Patrick Henry was an eloquent orator. *(From* The Pictorial Field Book of the Revolution, *2 vols., by B. J. Lossing. New York: Harper Brothers, 1851 and 1852.)*

wish to be free . . . we must fight!" Arguing that no other choice remains, Henry declaims, "It is vain, sir, to extenuate the matter. Gentlemen may cry peace, peace, but there is no peace. The war is actually begun! The next gale that sweeps from the north will bring to our ears the clash of resounding arms! Our brethren are already in the field! Why stand we here idle? What is it that gentlemen wish? What would they have? Is life so dear or peace so sweet as to be purchased at the price of chains and slavery? Forbid it, Almighty God—I know not what course others may take; but as for me—give me liberty, or give me death!"

March 30: George III assents to the Fisheries Act, approved by Parliament, that strictly limits New England's commerce to trading only with Great Britain, Ireland, and the West Indies, an act certain to further exacerbate tensions with the colonists.

In Boston, Gen. Thomas Gage moves into action by sending a brigade of British troops on a practice march through Cambridge and Watertown. Col. Hugh Percy, who disagrees with government policies toward America but has nevertheless accepted duty with the royal forces here, leads the troops. The Massachusetts Provincial Congress, meeting in Concord, considers the march a hostile act and forewarns the local militia.

Members of the militia site a cannon at the Watertown bridge and remove the planks from the bridge at Cambridge. The royal troops return to Boston as concern grows among the Massachusetts Patriots.

April 5: The Massachusetts Provincial Congress adopts 53 articles of war, the preamble of which outlines colonial grievances and protests the colonists' innocence of the infractions imputed to them by the British government. The preamble states, ". . . our progenitors . . . fled from oppression for the sake of civil and religious liberty for themselves and their offspring, and . . . having seriously considered the duty we owe to God, to the memory of such invincible worthies, to the King, to Great Britain, our country, ourselves, our posterity, do think it our indispensable duty . . . to recover, maintain, defend, and preserve the free exercise of all those civil and religious rights and liberties for which many of our worthy forefathers fought, bled, and died."

April 8: At Newbern, North Carolina, Royal Governor Josiah Martin, having failed in his struggle to reconcile taxation and other issues, dissolves the provincial assembly. Despite the growing organization of the Patriots, Martin holds out hope that the Loyalists will prevail in North Carolina and royal governance will be restored. Even so, he sends his family to New York for safety.

April 14: Benjamin Franklin, Benjamin Rush, and others organize the Society for the Relief of Free Negroes Unlawfully Held in Bondage, the first antislavery society in the colonies, in Philadelphia.

At Boston, General Gage receives a letter from Lord Dartmouth, secretary of state for the American colonies, reproving him for inaction. Dartmouth instructs Gage to move circumspectly but to arrest the leaders of the Massachusetts Provincial Congress—an act likely to incite war.

April 15: General Gage issues orders creating a separate force of about 700 men derived from the elite units of his light infantry and grenadier companies to carry out extra assignments. Rather than having leaders of the Provincial Congress arrested, Gage determines to send troops to seize the Massachusetts militia's stores of powder, arms, or ammunition at Concord and Worcester. At Concord, the Provincial Congress adjourns, and the delegates leave town.

April 16: Dr. Joseph Warren sends Paul Revere, riding from Boston to Lexington, to warn John Hancock and Samuel Adams that General Gage may be planning to send troops to arrest them. They send warnings on to Concord, where the aroused Patriots load the militia's cache of arms and ammunition and send it to Worcester. Returning to Boston, Revere arranges with his cohorts in Charlestown for a system of signals from the steeple of Old North Church to warn them of the British troops' movements.

April 18: Despite his best efforts at secrecy, Patriots learn of General Gage's planned march on Concord. Before the British troops have even left their barracks, Dr. Warren receives news of the march and summons Revere and William Dawes. The two couriers race to bring their warning to Lexington. Skirting the enemy, Revere arrives in Lexington in time to warn Hancock and Adams. They prepare to flee while Revere awaits Dawes. Together, the two couriers start for Concord; Dr. Samuel Prescott joins them en route. Halted by British officers, Dawes and Prescott escape, but Revere is captured. Revere tells the officers that 500 militiamen are mustering at Lexington, and, gravely concerned, they leave him in Lexington without a horse and ride off. Revere returns to Parson Clark's house, finds Hancock and Adams ready for flight, and escapes with them to Burlington in a chaise.

April 19: General Gage's special force, commanded by Lt. Col. Francis Smith and Maj. John Pitcairn, marches toward Lexington in the early morning. At Lexington, 130 minutemen assemble on the village green under command of Capt. John Parker, but only 70 of them bear arms. Although outnumbered 10 to 1, Parker orders them to stand their ground, declaring he will shoot anyone who runs. Pitcairn orders the minutemen to disperse. The Patriots begin to move off but refuse to surrender their arms. Someone fires a shot, and the British send a volley over the minutemen's heads. Pitcairn shouts an order to cease firing, but the British troops fire another volley and charge the fleeing Patriots. Ten wounded minutemen escape with their cohorts, but eight lie dead on Lexington Green.

Smith's troops now join Pitcairn's advance force, and they move toward Concord as news of their march circulates through eastern Massachusetts, spread by a prearranged system of couriers, drums, and church bells. Minutemen summoned by the alarm bell muster in Concord. Some remove the armaments cache from Col. James Barrett's house, the objective of the British force. The Concord minutemen, numbering about 150, march forth to meet the British, but after sighting them, they wheel and return to Concord. The Brit-

ish enter the town, where their officers refresh themselves in the local taverns. Some of the troops fruitlessly search Barrett's and others' houses, while others under Capt. Walter Laurie stand guard at North Bridge. Barrett orders an advance, with his men instructed to hold their fire until fired upon. At North Bridge, Captain Laurie's men begin the shooting, wounding one Patriot. Then Laurie's men fire a volley, killing two Patriots and wounding two more. The minutemen open fire; their shots kill two British soldiers and wound several others, including officers. Laurie's men fall back in disarray but reform as reinforcements sent by Smith arrive. The minutemen press after them but founder for want of discipline. The Battle of Concord peters out.

At noon, the British troops begin their return trek to Boston. The first hour on the road proves uneventful, but during the next 16 miles of the march, minutemen run ahead of the British column and hide behind rocks, barns, houses, and trees. From these hidden posts, their sniping fire strafes the British ranks. Some Patriots lose their lives to the flanking troops; others leave as new arrivals take their places. Panicked by the sniping, the British retreat rapidly toward Lexington. Fortunately for them, Lord Percy arrives with reinforcements from Boston that nearly triple their force's strength. Struggling through Cambridge, the fatigued British find refuge on the hills known as Bunker and Breed's outside Charlestown. The day's toll of casualties seems modest—95 for the Patriots, including 49 dead; 273 for the British, including only 72 dead, out of a force of 2,000. American militiamen encircle Boston and lay siege to its garrison.

April 25: The Massachusetts Provincial Congress reconvenes in Concord and approves raising a militia force of 30,000, with an immediate recruitment of 13,600 in Massachusetts to be commanded by Artemas Ward. The Congress also votes to send delegates to the other New England colonies to ask their help in raising the full quota of 30,000 men. Militia from Rhode Island commanded by Nathanael Greene, from New Hampshire commanded by Nathaniel Folsom and led by Col. John Stark, and from Connecticut commanded by David Wooster join the Massachusetts militiamen encircling Boston—all under the command of Artemas Ward.

May 3: During a meeting of the Committee of Safety at Cambridge, Connecticut militia officer and merchant Benedict Arnold persuades the members of the importance of capturing Fort Ticonderoga. He contends that the fort is dilapidated and inadequately defended by only 50 soldiers and holds a prize of 50 cannon, 20 brass pieces, and a cache of small arms. The committee commissions Arnold as a colonel in the Massachusetts militia and authorizes him to raise 400 men for the expedition.

Benjamin Franklin, who is now almost 70 years old and has served in London since 1757 as an agent for Pennsylvania, Georgia, and Massachusetts, returns home to Philadelphia. Formerly an advocate of reconciliation, he has abandoned that policy since his scouring by the Privy Council in 1774 and is now in league with Samuel Adams and John Adams.

May 6: Franklin becomes a delegate to the Second Continental Congress. New England delegates, including John Hancock and Samuel Adams, arrive in New York en route to Philadelphia.

May 8: When the brigantine *Industry* arrives in Charleston with news of the battles at Lexington and Concord, the South Carolina assembly approves raising two infantry regiments of 750 men each and a squadron of 450 rangers and appropriating £1 million to support them.

At Bennington, Vermont, a small militia commanded by Col. Samuel H. Parsons of Connecticut joins with Ethan Allen and about 100 of his Green Mountain Boys. Arnold has convinced Parsons that if Fort Ticonderoga is taken, its cannon can be used by Artemas Ward's force at Boston. Parsons and Allen send men to Skenesboro and Panton to commandeer boats for crossing Lake Champlain. Apprised of this rival expedition, Arnold arrives to claim command, to which the Green Mountain Boys object. Arnold then travels to Shoreham (Hand's Cove), where Allen has already gone. The two men begrudgingly agree to cooperate.

May 10: With only two barges, Arnold and Allen decide to maintain the element of surprise by attacking Fort Ticonderoga immediately. Roused from sleep, Lt. Jocelyn Feltham awakens the commander, Capt. William De la Place. Arriving at the doorway of his room, Allen and Arnold confront Feltham, still holding his breeches. Feltham demands to know by what authority they have entered the fort, and Allen reputedly responds, "Come out of there, you sons of British whores, or I'll smoke you out." Allen demands surrender of the fort, threatening to kill every inhabitant otherwise. De la Place, entering from another room, agrees to surrender. With this easy victory, the Americans cap-

ture 50 prisoners, about 100 cannons, and other stores. Among the prisoners, however, are many invalids, and the fort's inhabitants include 24 women and children. Joined by their comrades arriving from Hand's Cove, the victorious Green Mountain Boys pillage and lay waste the fort—to Arnold's disgust.

The Second Continental Congress convenes in Philadelphia. The delegates include many members of the First Continental Congress but also some new faces: John Hancock representing Massachusetts; Benjamin Franklin and James Wilson, Pennsylvania; George Clinton, Francis Lewis, Robert R. Livingston, Lewis Morris, and Philip Schuyler, New York. Georgia, which had no representation in the previous congress, has sent Lyman Hall.

May 12: Without a shot fired, a company of Green Mountain Boys led by Lt. Col. Seth Warner captures Crown Point on Lake Champlain, taking nine prisoners.

May 17: Aboard a schooner captured at Skeneboro on May 14, Arnold and about 50 men set off for St. John's, Quebec, with Allen and 60 more men following later. Taking the fort on the Richelieu River and its garrison of 15 completely by surprise, Arnold destroys five boats and seizes stores, other boats, and the sloop *George III.* Heading back to Fort Ticonderoga, Arnold meets Allen, who is intent on occupying the fort at St. John's, although Arnold advises against doing so. A British relief force that arrived from Chambly repulses Allen's attack at St. John's, driving him and his force off while capturing three of his men.

May 18: Delegates to the Continental Congress elect Peyton Randolph of Virginia as president and Charles Thomson of Philadelphia as secretary, returning them to the posts they held in the First Continental Congress. Randolph reports the news of Fort Ticonderoga's capture, which the delegates welcome, because controlling Lake Champlain may enhance the opportunity to join forces with Canada, whose citizens are widely believed to sympathize with the American cause.

May 24: As Speaker of the Virginia House of Burgesses, Randolph must leave the Continental Congress to attend a session of the burgesses. The delegates first choice to succeed Randolph, Henry Middleton of South Carolina, declines to serve because of his health, so they elect John Hancock as president.

May 25: Generals William Howe, John Burgoyne, and Henry Clinton arrive at Boston aboard the *Cere-*

bus, bringing orders from the British Cabinet for General Gage to capture the Massachusetts militia's military stores at Concord and to pardon any rebel leaders who might be captured during the raid—orders clearly obviated by the battles at Lexington and Concord more than a month earlier.

May 27: Artemas Ward sends troops to Hog and Noodle Islands in Boston Harbor to disperse the livestock. They succeed on Hog Island, but Adm. Samuel Graves sends the *Diana* and some marines to thwart the effort on Noodle Island, where he has sizable stores. Before the British can attack, the Americans take away hundreds of animals, destroy others, and burn the hay stores. Then, as the opponents skirmish, dusk descends, and the *Diana,* beset by unfavorable winds, runs aground; the *Britannia* rescues the crew. Gen. Israel Putnam's soldiers board the *Diana,* loot the stores on board, and then torch the ship.

May 29: The Continental Congress issues a public appeal for Canada's support, drafted by John Jay, that states that taking the forts and stores at Ticonderoga and Crown Point "... was dictated by the great law of self-preservation ... you may rely on our assurances that these colonies will pursue no measures whatsoever but such as friendship and a regard for our mutual safety may suggest." The appeal concludes with a declaration of "hopes of your uniting with us in the defense of our common liberty...." Delegates to the Continental Congress hope that Canada will join their cause as the "fourteenth colony."

May 31: Meeting at Charlotte in Mecklenburg County, North Carolina, a committee drafts a statement of 20 resolutions for the colony's delegates to the Continental Congress to present in Philadelphia. The resolutions suspend all royal or Parliamentary laws and commissions and contend that executive and legislative authority in the future must rest with the colonies' individual assemblies under the Continental Congress. Known as the Mecklenburg Declaration of Independence, the statement of resolutions is never presented to the Continental Congress.

June 2: The Continental Congress begins to address two issues presented by the Massachusetts Provincial Congress: Should Massachusetts assume control of the colony's civil government, and should the Continental Congress assume control of the militia forces surrounding Boston? Although the second question remains unanswered, the Continental Congress creates an Army Pay Department.

June 6: Members of the local Sons of Liberty, led by Lt. Col. Marinus Willett, who has participated in an April attack on the city arsenal, seize five wagonloads of arms when British soldiers attempt to sneak them out of New York City.

June 8: At Yorktown, Virginia, Lord Dunmore finds refuge aboard the HMS *Fowey*—a signal that open conflict between Patriots and Tories in the colony has begun.

June 11: John Hancock sends a letter to the Massachusetts Provincial Congress informing its members that the Continental Congress has begun deliberations on the two issues they have presented. The Continental Congress sets up committees for soliciting loans and deciding how much money must be raised, while also urging each of the colonies to store powder for anticipated conflicts to come.

June 11–12: Boston Loyalist Ichabod Jones arrives at Machias, Maine, aboard the armed schooner *Margaretta,* accompanied by two transport sloops. Jones intends to negotiate a supply of lumber, but his demeanor offends the townspeople, who take him prisoner. Jones's midshipman escapes to the *Margaretta* and threatens to cannonade the town unless the residents free Jones. The townspeople demand the schooner's surrender. Sons of Liberty members capture the two sloops and fire on the *Margaretta* after it runs aground, but the midshipman manages to free the ship and anchor it. On the morning of the 12th, the midshipman attempts an escape, but Patriots follow the schooner in one of the seized sloops. They fire on and board the *Margaretta* after fatally wounding the midshipman, the sole casualty in the war's first naval engagement. Loss of the *Margaretta* enrages British commanders.

June 12: Fulfilling orders from the British Cabinet, General Gage declares martial law in Massachusetts. Because the declaration offers amnesty to all rebels who abandon their arms and switch allegiances back to the Crown, Gage hopes this move will prevent further conflicts. The amnesty offer, however, excludes Samuel Adams and John Hancock, who must stand trial and endure punishment because of the egregiousness of their offenses. And the pompous wording General Burgoyne uses in drafting the declaration evokes patriots' contempt and ridicule.

June 14: The Continental Congress approves a resolution to raise two companies of backcountry riflemen famed for marksmanship in each of three colonies—Pennsylvania, Maryland, and Virginia. The Continental

Congress also selects a committee to prepare rules for governing the Continental army, now comprised of militia forces in Massachusetts and New York, thereby answering the second question the Massachusetts Provincial Congress presented on June 2. Pennsylvania's quota subsequently will rise to six companies.

June 15: The Continental Congress approves a resolution to appoint a general "to command all the continental forces, raised or to be raised, for the defense of American liberty." Nominated by Thomas Johnson of Maryland with John Adams's telling support, George Washington of Virginia becomes the Continental Congress's unanimous choice to be commander in chief of the American forces.

The Committee of Safety in Cambridge, learning from intelligence reports that General Gage plans to occupy Dorchester Heights, orders Gen. Artemas Ward immediately to occupy Bunker Hill on the Charlestown peninsula and thereafter to occupy Dorchester Heights. (Curiously, although its strategic value as an overlook of Boston Harbor appears obvious, Dorchester Heights has been ignored by both the British and the American forces.)

George Washington became commander in chief of the American forces. *(From* The Pictorial Field Book of the Revolution, *2 vols., by B. J. Lossing. New York: Harper Brothers, 1851 and 1852.)*

June 16: Reluctant but honorably dutiful, Washington accepts command of the Continental army. The Continental Congress drafts a broad plan for organizing the army that entails appointing two major generals, five brigadier generals, one adjutant general, one commissary general, one quartermaster general, one paymaster general, and diverse engineers, aides, assistants, and other staff. Conscious of political needs—especially the necessity to solidify support of the southern colonies and to foster the sense of unity between the southern and New England colonies—the Continental Congress considers geographic distribution vital in choosing men to fill these army posts. Thus, the delegates select Artemas Ward of Massachusetts and Charles Lee of Virginia as the two major generals. But in trying to select brigadier generals, the delegates concern for geography falters, and they elect to increase the numbers as a remedy—there will be four major generals and eight brigadiers. Philip Schuyler of New York and Israel Putnam of Connecticut win the two added major generalships.

Advancing from Cambridge, Col. William Prescott just after 9:00 P.M. leads a force of 1,000 men, mostly Massachusetts militia plus men from a Connecticut regiment, under orders of Gen. Artemas Ward, to Bunker Hill just to fortify the hill. General Putnam meets them at the neck of the Charlestown peninsula with wagonloads of dirt and brushwood for this purpose. When they arrive on Bunker Hill, Prescott, Putnam, and chief engineer Col. Richard Gridley, disregarding Ward's orders, decide to leave a detachment there and move on to fortify Breed's Hill, closer to Boston Harbor. From midnight until dawn, the troops hastily dig trenches and build six-foot-high perimeter walls.

June 17: Once the Sun has risen, observers on British ships anchored in Boston Harbor quickly detect that the Americans are building fortifications on Breed's Hill. The *Lively*'s guns open fire, followed by those on other ships along with the battery emplaced on Copp's Hill. The bombardment has minimal effect, and the fortification work continues. Regiments from New Hampshire, led by John Stark and James Reed, arrive to reinforce the troops on Breed's Hill, but Prescott's force is actually weakened when, responding to Putnam's urging, he sends men with tools to fortify Bunker Hill.

At midday, a British assault force comprised of several regiments of regulars crosses the Charles River aboard barges as the British warships and batteries pro-

Soldiers clash in the Battle of Bunker Hill. *(Courtesy of Anne S. K. Brown Military Collection, Brown University Library)*

vide a protective cover of fire on the American positions. The regulars land unopposed, to be joined by another regiment as well as several light infantry and grenadier companies and a battalion of Royal Marines. Gen. William Howe's attack plan is simple: His well-trained soldiers will charge head-on into the rebel lines, and the untrained rebel militiamen, dismayed by a European-style bayonet charge, will break and scatter. Howe's ranks form and march toward the American fortifications, but the Americans hold and fire withering volleys.

Despite heavy losses, Howe and his officers rally their troops and attempt a second and then a third frontal assault. When their third assault reaches the Americans' position, Prescott's men have no ammunition left, and the British freely vault the fortifications and attack with bayonets. The Americans must abandon the fight, with many run through or shot at close range as they retreat. Dr. Joseph Warren, president of the Massachusetts Provincial Congress, falls among the dead. The Americans fall back to Bunker Hill under covering fire from Stark's men. At Bunker Hill, they join Putnam's troops in an orderly retreat, leaving the peninsula in British control. Having arrived in time for the final British assault, Gen. Sir Henry Clinton cannot regroup his troops in time to pursue the rebels, and the battle ends. The Americans, though defeated, learn a vital lesson—that the vaunted British regulars are vulnerable, even in the type of battle at which they are supposed to excel.

June 20: Washington receives his orders from the Continental Congress and adjudges them to require that he must not only solicit the counsel of his generals, but also secure their approval before pursuing any course of action. Unfortunately, his interpretation will hinder making incisive decisions. Washington reviews the Philadelphia militia, his first military ceremony as commander. Thomas Jefferson arrives in Philadelphia as Peyton Randolph's replacement in the Virginia delegation to the Continental Congress.

June 22: Georgia citizens meeting in Savannah form Committees of Safety, finally identifying the colony more firmly with the rebel cause.

The Continental Congress commits itself to funding the war with paper money by approving a sum not to exceed "two million of Spanish milled dollars" for defense of the colonies and pledging to the 12 currently confederated colonies—Georgia is still a holdout—that all present and future bills of credit will be redeemed.

June 23: In a ceremonial departure escorted by congressional delegates and accompanied by Philip Schuyler, Charles Lee, and aide-de-camp Thomas Mifflin, General Washington sets out from Philadelphia to New York. From there he will travel to Boston to take command of the army.

June 25: The Continental Congress appoints General Schuyler commander of the Northern Department, the Army of New York. Washington arrives in New York and sends Schuyler to assume command of the army in the colony and to occupy posts on Lake Champlain and Lake George. Concurrently with Washington's arrival, Royal Governor William Tryon returns to New York after a visit in England.

June 26: A committee comprised of John Rutledge, William Livingston, Benjamin Franklin, John Jay, and Thomas Johnson, appointed by the Continental Congress on June 23 to prepare a Declaration on Taking up Arms for Washington to publish at Boston, reports to the Continental Congress. Dissatisfied with the draft of the declaration, Congress adds Thomas Jefferson and John Dickinson to the committee. The enlarged committee assigns Jefferson to write a new declaration. When it is judged too harsh, he will ask Dickinson to assume the task.

June 27: The Continental Congress reverses its policy against invading Canada, reaffirmed as recently as June 1, and authorizes Schuyler to invade and to hold any captured areas whenever an invasion proves practicable.

June 30: The Continental Congress approves a statement of 69 articles of war, ironically based on the British Articles of War, to regulate actions of the Continental army. In an effort to enforce civil behavior among members of the army, the regulations affirm moral strictures and encourage church attendance. They impose death as the punishment for some major crimes, restrict courts-martial to ordering of no more than 39 lashes, fines not to exceed two-months' pay, or prison terms no longer than a month.

July 2: Washington arrives in Cambridge and assumes command of the Continental army. The army is supposed to total 16,000 men, but only 14,000 have reported for duty. Washington believes he cannot attack the British with fewer than 20,000 men. He decides to extend the arc of fortifications between the Mystic River and Dorchester, erected by Ward's troops as a means of containing the British in Boston, while the American army undergoes training and stockpiles supplies.

July 3: Aware of the enormous problems he confronts, Washington begins to issue general orders that will address every aspect of army life. An unruly lot of independent-minded volunteers, his troops abandon their posts and casually desert, disregard orders, chat with British sentries, or otherwise show disorderliness. To impose discipline, Washington's orders forbid drunkenness and profanity, establish food inspections, require replacing latrines every week, mandate attendance at worship services, and impose punishments for offenses. Exacerbating his task, the men's enlistments expire at year-end, and he must find means of persuading them to reenlist.

July 5: The Continental Congress approves the so-called Olive Branch Petition, addressed to George III, which reiterates the colonists' grievances while also pursuing reconciliation and negotiation and asking the king to prevent hostilities as negotiations proceed. John Dickinson strongly supports the petition, which John Adams views with contempt. Congress appoints Richard Penn, William Penn's descendant and a Loyalist, to sail for London and deliver the petition.

July 6: The Continental Congress adopts the much-revised Declaration of Causes of Taking up Arms, which explains the colonies' resort to arms, denies they intend to pursue independence, and advocates reconciliation. Its language, however, hardly sounds conciliatory, for the declaration impugns the British as ". . . unprovoked enemies, without any imputation or suspicion of offence. They boast of their privileges and civilization, and yet proffer no milder conditions than servitude or death." The declaration also asserts the justness of the colonies' cause and touts their union, while threatening that they may well receive "foreign assistance."

July 8: Maj. Benjamin Tupper and Capt. John Crane lead a group of American troops in attacking a British post on Boston Neck, routing the guard, and burning the guardhouse—the first of a series of probes that will continue throughout July.

July 10: Appointed by the Congress on June 17 as adjutant general with the rank of brigadier general, Horatio Gates issues instructions at Cambridge to guide recruiters seeking enlistees for the Continental army. No blacks, vagabonds, British deserters, or youths under 18 are acceptable. All must be either American-born or, if foreign-born, married and with children. Gates, formerly an officer in the British army, was born in England.

July 13: The Continental Congress begins to appoint commissioners assigned to negotiate with the Indians and, if possible, to obtain treaties that ensure their continuing peaceableness as a means of precluding the Indians from joining in hostilities on the British side.

July 18: General Schuyler and his entourage arrive at Fort Ticonderoga to find the garrison defenseless, the stores of food, ammunition, and other supplies inadequate; the available lumber insufficient for building boats; and the men a questionable lot from New York, Connecticut, and Massachusetts, along with a few Green Mountain Boys.

Josiah Martin, the royal governor of North Carolina, evacuates to Cape Fear and takes refuge aboard HMS *Cruzier.*

July 20: At New York, a party of Patriots raids a British storehouse and seizes the stores to send them to Boston and Lake Champlain.

July 21: American soldiers led by Maj. Joseph Vose row whaleboats to Boston's Nantasket Point. They drive off the British guard there and then destroy the lighthouse on Great Brewster Island.

At Philadelphia, Benjamin Franklin presents to the Continental Congress a draft of Articles of Confederation and Perpetual Union, written by himself and approved by Jefferson. With many members still unwilling to confront the issue of permanent union, the draft receives no entry in the official journal, in effect shelving the issue. The members also postpone discussion of a committee report and recommendations on the issue of opening American ports to trade in violation of the Continental Association's nonexportation agreement.

July 24: At Ticonderoga, General Schuyler sends Maj. John Brown with three soldiers to the north to gather information about St. John's, Montreal, and the views of Indians and Canadians.

July 25: At Cambridge, Dr. Benjamin Church, although suspected by Paul Revere of being a British informer, becomes the first surgeon general of the Continental army.

The Continental Congress, finally responding to the Massachusetts Provincial Congress's query of May 16, officially "adopts" the Continental army, thus assuming authority to regulate and direct its actions.

July 26: Responding to the report of a committee chaired by Franklin, and mandated to find a means of expediting distribution of information among the colonies, the Continental Congress establishes a post office department and appoints Franklin as postmaster general, a position he filled for many years under the royal government.

July 27: Meeting at Cephas Kent's tavern in Dorset, New Hampshire, the Green Mountain Boys, displeased with Ethan Allen, select Seth Warner as their lieutenant colonel, with Allen's former position as colonel remaining unfilled. General Schuyler, who hoped to see 500 Green Mountain Boys augment his force at Ticonderoga, will have to settle for Ethan Allen alone.

July 29: Having recently authorized 1 million Spanish dollars in addition to the 2 million earlier authorized and now being printed, the Continental Congress adopts a redemption plan for the currency that requires each colony, on the basis of population, to assume responsibility for its share and to create a means for redemption. The plan also provides for redemption in four installments, payable on the last day of November in 1779, 1780, 1781, and 1782.

July 31: The Continental Congress rejects Lord North's proposal, approved by Parliament on February 27, offering an end to taxes in any colony that provides internal taxes to support British officials and military personnel. The Continental Congress's statement of rejection asserts the colonies' right to raise appropriations and to determine their use.

August 2: A contingent of Virginia riflemen, led by Daniel Morgan, arrives at Cambridge for duty with the Continental army, joining Michael Cresap and his 1st Maryland Rifles, already in camp. These are the first two units of the 12 Congress authorized to be raised in Virginia, Maryland, and Pennsylvania. Although expert marksmen, the riflemen are also unruly and prone to refusing to obey regulations and work duties. Their presence exacerbates Washington's problems with discipline among the troops.

August 9–10: Off the coast near Gloucester, Massachusetts, HMS *Falcon,* commanded by Capt. John Linzee, pursues two American schooners on their return voyage to Salem from the West Indies. The *Falcon* captures one schooner and chases the other into Gloucester Harbor, coming under fire from American troops on shore. The *Falcon* returns fire but loses two barges and 35 men. It withdraws, leaving behind both schooners.

August 14: Returned from his mission, Major Brown reports to General Schuyler at Ticonderoga that the French residents of Quebec will not fight the Americans, that the Indians there will maintain neutrality, and that only 300 men garrison St. John's, which is being fortified (only 50 troops are stationed at Quebec). Brown urges Schuyler to invade Canada.

Richard Penn arrives in London.

August 23: George III proclaims the American colonies in a state of "open and avowed rebellion."

August 24: Under orders from the New York Provincial Congress, Capt. John Lamb leads about 60 men to New York City's Battery at about midnight to dismantle cannons and haul them to a safe site. Aboard HMS *Asia,* Capt. George Vandeput sends a bargeload of men to investigate—they fire a signal shot to warn the ship. Lamb's men fire on the barge and kill one man. The *Asia* fires on the Battery. As alarms sound in the city, many residents, fearful of attack, flee their homes in the first of a series of exoduses to New Jersey and Long Island.

August 26–28: Washington sends Gen. John Sullivan in command of a fatigue unit of 1,200 men accompanied by a guard detail of 2,400 (among them 400 of the Pennsylvania backwoods riflemen) to Ploughed Hill to erect fortifications for a commanding position on the Mystic River, from which the Continentals will have a clear shot at the British force on Bunker Hill. As day breaks on the 27th, two British floating batteries and another battery on Bunker Hill begin a daylong shelling of Sullivan's force. Sullivan makes effective use of his single cannon, which sinks one of the floating batteries and incapacitates the other. The Americans suffer four losses.

August 28: Reacting to the urgency of a second scouting report from Maj. John Brown received at Ticonderoga, General Schuyler's second in command, Gen. Richard Montgomery, without Schuyler's authorization, decides to begin the advance into Canada. Montgomery dispatches a notification of his decision to Schuyler and then, with a force of about 1,200 men, embarks on Lake Champlain for Île aux Noix on the Richelieu River to the south of Fort St. John.

August 30: General Schuyler, who has received Montgomery's notification in Albany, where he is participating in a council fire with Indians of the Six Nations, returns to Fort Ticonderoga. Schuyler approves of Montgomery's decision to invade Canada.

August 31: Although ill, Schuyler sets out with about 500 men to join Montgomery's expedition.

September 1: Washington has eight coastal vessels armed and manned by New England seamen, including some from Capt. John Glover's regiment from Essex County, Massachusetts. He assigns them the mission of interdicting British merchant ships that are bringing supplies to Boston for the occupying troops. Through the fall months, these privateers will seize 23 ships and, ignoring whether they carry military supplies, confiscate their cargoes, providing the Americans with large quantities of muskets and ammunition.

September 5: Schuyler joins Montgomery at Île aux Noix, Quebec, and orders the combined force to continue the advance. Leaving behind supplies that might slow their progress, the troops embark on the Richelieu River and make shore a mile and a half from the fort at St. John's. While attempting a flanking movement, they are ambushed by about 100 Indians led by Captain Tice, a New York Tory. The Indians kill eight Americans before being driven off. Warned during the night by an informant that the fort is impregnable, Schuyler leads his men back to Île aux Noix.

September 10: After fortifying the camp at Île aux Noix and welcoming 700 reinforcements that augment his force to 1,700, Schuyler begins a second advance with about 800 men. But his effort fails again as his men, fearful of being ambushed, flee when threatened. He retreats once more to Île aux Noix.

September 12: Without the authorization of the Continental Congress, Washington sends Benedict Arnold in command of a force of 1,050, including Capt. Daniel Morgan's riflemen, on a separate expedition to Canada. Ill prepared, inadequately provisioned, and lacking knowledge of any apt route to follow through the rugged wilderness that they must traverse by river and portage through Maine to the St. Lawrence River, Arnold's expedition begins its northward trek.

September 13: At Philadelphia, the Continental Congress convenes again with some members absent but a quorum that now includes a full delegation from Georgia.

September 16: Now too ill to continue, Schuyler sets out for Ticonderoga, leaving Montgomery in command at Île aux Noix. With reinforcements arriving, including 170 Green Mountain Boys led by Seth Warner, Montgomery's force swells to about 2,000.

September 18: After positioning 350 men in boats on the Richelieu River to prevent HMS *Royal Savage* from entering Lake Champlain, Montgomery embarks with the remainder of his force at St. John's and begins laying siege to the fort.

The Continental Congress establishes the Secret Committee, empowered to seek out sources of ammunition and powder and to negotiate contracts for their delivery to the army.

September 25: Sent by Montgomery to Chambly to organize a group of English Canadian volunteers, Ethan Allen overzealously anticipates capturing Montreal. When he meets Maj. John Brown returning with a force of Canadians he has organized at La Prairie, they agree to launch an attack on Montreal from two directions, with Brown sending a signal to Allen when his force is ready to move. Sir Guy Carleton, royal governor of Quebec province, learns that Allen's force is nearby and sends an attacking force of soldiers, volunteers, and Indians out of Montreal. Abandoned by many of his English Canadian volunteers and surrounded by the attack force, Allen surrenders. Although Allen narrowly escapes execution as a traitor and will be shipped to England for imprisonment, his impetuosity seriously imperils the Americans' strategy in Canada.

September 30: The Continental Congress appoints Benjamin Franklin, Thomas Lynch of South Carolina, and Benjamin Harrison of Virginia as a committee to visit General Washington in Cambridge and inquire into the status of the Continental army and its operations.

October 4: Charged with "criminal correspondence with the enemy," Dr. Church is court-martialed, with Washington presiding, and found guilty. His treachery was exposed when General Greene intercepted an encoded letter he had sent (he contended it was meant for his brother in Boston). When deciphered by two cryptologists, the letter proved to be an intelligence report. But the new Articles of War prescribe a punishment of cashiering, forfeiture of pay, and whipping only; in addition, treason has traditionally been defined as betrayal of the king—something all the rebels now stood guilty of—so Washington refers the issue of appropriate punishment to the Continental Congress.

The three-man committee appointed by the Continental Congress to visit the army leaves Philadelphia for Cambridge. With them Congress sends the judgment that, if it seems possible the British can be routed from Boston by the end of December, then Washington should attack them.

October 7: Annoyed by Burgoyne's and others' complaints that he fails to support the Boston garrison and by his incapacity to stop American privateering, Vice Adm. Samuel Graves responds with a series of punitive raids on eastern seaboard coastal towns—Bristol, Rhode Island, being the first target. Arriving at Bristol with a small British fleet from Newport Harbor, Capt. James Wallace sends an officer ashore with orders that the residents send a delegation to his ship to hear his demands or he will cannonade the town. William Bradford, as spokesman for the residents, responds that Wallace should come ashore. Wallace orders a bombardment that lasts an hour and a half, and the town capitulates, offering 40 sheep as a tribute.

October 10: Gen. William Howe replaces Gen. Thomas Gage as commander of the British forces in Boston. Ostensibly ordered to return to London for consultation but actually sacked from his post, Gage must remain in Boston for want of transport, adding to his humiliation.

October 12: The Continental Congress authorizes the outfitting of two swift ships—in effect, the beginning of an American navy.

October 18: Continuing the raids ordered by Vice Admiral Graves, Capt. Henry Mowat unsuccessfully tries to intimidate the residents of Falmouth (now Portland), Maine, and then orders his warships *Canceau* and *Halifax* to shell the town for nine hours. But no lives are lost because most of the residents have taken Mowat's warnings seriously and fled. After the bombardment, Mowat sends landing parties ashore. They torch the town, destroying 139 houses and 278 other structures, including the church, the courthouse, the town meetinghouse, the library, the wharves, and the warehouses. Outrage over the destruction spreads through the colonies. Washington sends a detachment of riflemen to help defend Portsmouth, New Hampshire, thought to be the next target. But a satisfied Graves terminates the raids.

Now equipped with cannons that have arrived during the night, Maj. John Brown, commanding 50 Americans, and Col. James Livingston, commanding 300 Canadians, attack the fort at Chambly. Their cannon fire suffices to convince Major Stopford, commander of the fort, to surrender the garrison of 10 officers and 78 privates of the Royal Fusiliers. Also residing in the fort are 81 women and children. Brown's and Livingston's men confiscate large stores of arms, powder, and ammunition and 138 barrels of foods.

October 19: Upon learning that the Continental Congress recommends that the colonial legislatures arrest "all persons who might endanger the liberties of Americans" and that plans for his own arrest are proceeding, Governor William Tryon chooses refuge aboard the warship HMS *Duchess of Gordon* in New York Harbor, where he will remain for nearly a year.

October 24–25: Royal Governor Lord Dunmore inflames his conflict with the Virginia rebels, sending six tenders under command of Captain Squire to destroy Norfolk. On the 24th, Squire's flotilla sails into Hampton Creek, bombards Hampton, and lands men to torch the town, but riflemen drive them off. At dawn on the 25th, Col. William Woodford leads 100 rebel militia into the town to defend it against a second attack. Marksmen among the militia pick off sailors on the decks and in the riggings of Squire's tenders, forcing their disorderly withdrawal. The rebels capture two sloops that run aground. The British suffer several deaths; the Americans, not a single casualty.

October 26: At St. John's, 335 Connecticut troops from the command of Gen. David Wooster and 225 4th New York troops commanded by Maj. Barnabas Tuthill reinforce the American siege.

October 27: Dr. Church is expelled from Massachusetts and imprisoned in Connecticut.

October 30: The Continental Congress appoints a seven-member "committee for fitting out armed vessels"—soon known as the Naval Committee—authorized to procure and outfit two more ships for the American navy.

Hoping to lift the American siege of St. John's, General Carleton leads a force of about 800 men—some from Lt. Col. Allan McLean's Royal Highland Emigrants, others from the Royal Fusiliers, and some Mohawk from Caughnawaga—in an effort to cross the St. Lawrence River to Longeuil. But Green Mountain Boys, joined by troops from the 2nd New York led by Seth Warner, frustrate his effort. Their musket firing

from the river's opposite bank forces Carleton's boats to turn back.

November 2: The British commander at St. John's, Maj. Charles Preston, faces reality—no help can be expected from Carleton; Montgomery's troops have destroyed the *Royal Savage,* ending his protection from the water; and Montgomery has a battery positioned overlooking the fort whose repeated shellings wreak devastation upon the fort. Preston surrenders, but his steadfast resistance has thwarted the Americans for 55 days, thereby forestalling their thrust toward Montreal into the winter months, while also buying valuable time to improve Canada's defenses. Among those taken prisoner by the Americans is a young officer of the 7th Royal Fusiliers, Maj. John André. Montgomery magnanimously permits the Canadian prisoners to return to their homes and allows the British regulars to depart for ports of embarkation.

Commodore Esek Hopkins poses on a ship. *(Courtesy of the National Archives and Records Administration)*

November 5: Montgomery's force begins its march to Montreal through cold rain and mud.

The Continental Congress appoints Rhode Islander Esek Hopkins commander in chief of the American navy, which is comprised of four ships assembling at Philadelphia. Brother of Stephen Hopkins, chairman of the original Naval Committee, Hopkins has been both a merchant captain and a privateer. His son John receives command of the brig *Cabot;* Dudley Saltonstall, of the *Alfred.* The *Columbus* and the *Andrew Doria* round out the fleet. John Paul Jones serves as one of Hopkins's lieutenants.

November 7: Proclaiming martial law in Virginia, Lord Dunmore appeals to all of the colony's loyal subjects to support the royal government or be considered traitors. He also offers freedom to indentured servants and to slaves residing on plantations owned by rebels if they will join British forces and fight against their masters. Many slaves will accept Dunmore's offer, but the threat of freed and armed slaves terrifies whites, solidifying their opposition to the governor.

Meeting at Providence, the Rhode Island General Assembly deposes Governor Joseph Wanton.

November 9: Benedict Arnold and a remnant of his original force finally reach the St. Lawrence River after traversing 350 miles, nearly twice the distance Arnold anticipated. Emerging from the Maine wilderness onto the river's shore, the men are exhausted and emaciated, their clothes in tatters and some shoeless. Of Arnold's original force of 1,000, only 675 have endured the journey—the others have turned back or succumbed to illness.

At Boston, about 500 British regulars cross from Charlestown Point to Lechmere's Point to confiscate sheep and cattle from the Phipps farm. They seize a drunken sentry, while other sentries fire on them and spread the alarm. Washington sends Col. William Thompson with a party of Pennsylvania riflemen to the attack, and the regulars withdraw with 10 captured cows. Two Americans receive wounds.

The Continental Congress receives news in Philadelphia that George III has not only rejected the Olive Branch Petition but also declared the American colonies in a state of rebellion. Congress authorizes creating two battalions of marines.

November 11–12: While attempting to blockade Hog Island Creek in Charleston Harbor, Capt. Simon Tuft's ship, *Defence,* encounters two British ships, HMS *Tamer* and HMS *Cherokee,* but nevertheless manages to

sink four hulks towed to the site to create the blockade and to avoid casualties.

November 13: Carleton, considering his position in Montreal untenable with only 150 regulars and some militia for defense, has sailed off with his troops and supplies two days earlier under American fire. Now Montgomery sends a deputation to the city, and the residents surrender. Montgomery's force occupies Montreal, and the American general promises respect for the residents' religion and fair prices for whatever supplies the Americans need, while he awaits word from Arnold. As Carleton's flotilla reaches Sorel, it falls under American attack. Two armed vessels, the *Gaspee,* and the troops with Carleton surrender; but Carleton manages to escape by rowboat and continue his flight to Quebec. At Quebec, after procuring more than 20 birch-bark canoes and a dozen dugouts, Arnold's force crosses the mile-wide river in darkness and embarks near the city, unthreatened by the British patrol boats or armed vessels in the harbor.

November 14: Having learned that Col. William Woodford is leading a march of 150 militiamen to join with another group of militia, Lord Dunmore hastens from Norfolk with a party of 350 regulars, Loyalists, sailors, and runaway slaves to prevent their meeting and accosts Woodford and his men at Kemp's Landing. Dunmore's superior force disperses the rebels, who suffer a few dead and wounded in the encounter.

November 15: Arnold's expeditionary force occupies the Plains of Abraham outside Quebec, where Arnold parades his troops in an effort to bluff the garrison of about 1,200 British and French-Canadian militia, along with a few sailors and marines from the ships in harbor, into surrendering. The defenders, unimpressed by exhibition, shout jeers from the city's walls. Arnold concludes that he will need cannons—he has none—and about 2,000 men to conquer the city.

November 16: On behalf of the Whig Party, Edmund Burke introduces a bill in the House of Commons stipulating that, because the American colonists have no representation in Parliament, no tax, levy, or other monetary burden should be imposed on the colonies by act of Parliament but only through voluntary authorization of the individual colonial legislatures. The bill, if enacted, would also repeal duties imposed on a variety of goods imported into the colonies and the punitive restrictions imposed on Boston and Massachusetts Bay Colony "for the suppression of riots and tumults." It would also confer pardons on all colonists accused of or imprisoned for treason, murders, felonies, or other crimes resulting from the recent hostilities. Burke delivers a speech advocating passage of the bill and conciliation with the Americans.

November 17: The bill introduced by Burke in the Commons the previous day is defeated by a vote of 210 to 105, indicating that at least a third of the House supports conciliation with the Americans.

November 19: Learning that Lt. Col. Allan McLean, who arrived in Quebec on the 13th with 80 of his Royal Highland Emigrants, plans to attack with a force of 800, Arnold orders his force on a quick march during the night to Point aux Trembles, 20 miles west of Quebec. For the next two weeks, he will wait here, allowing his men to recuperate but also giving McLean time to prepare a defense of the city. Meanwhile, Carleton arrives to assume command of the garrison.

About 1,800 Loyalists attack the fort at Ninety-Six, South Carolina, garrisoned by about 600 Patriots commanded by Maj. Andrew Williamson. A truce ensues after two days of gunfire and moderate casualties.

November 25: The Continental Congress declares British ships subject to seizure and creates admiralty courts to award prizes and prize money to those who succeed in capturing a ship.

November 28: The Continental Congress adopts Rules for the Regulation of the Navy of the United Colonies, drafted by the Naval Committee and primarily the work of John Adams.

November 29: The Continental Congress establishes a five-man committee—Benjamin Harrison, Benjamin Franklin, John Jay, Thomas Johnson, and John Dickinson—"for the sole purpose of corresponding with our friends in Great Britain, Ireland, and other parts of the world." The members may operate on their own initiative but must reveal their correspondence to Congress whenever directed to do so. Congress also approves paying for agents the committee decides to hire. Dubbing themselves the Committee of Secret Correspondence, the members will function as an elementary foreign service.

The American schooner *Lee,* commanded by Capt. John Manley, pursues and captures the *Nancy.* Much to Washington's pleasure, the 250-ton British ordnance brig provides a booty of 2,000 muskets with bayonets, scabbards, ramrods, 31 tons of musket balls, a 2,700-pound mortar, and other valuable military supplies.

December 2: Apprised two weeks earlier of Arnold's arrival at Quebec, Montgomery has floated down the St. Lawrence to join Arnold at Pointe aux Trembles. Montgomery arrives with fresh clothes confiscated at Montreal, artillery, ammunition, provisions, and 300 troops to augment the attack force, which he will now command. Montgomery and Arnold face a difficult decision because of severe winter weather, the expiration of their troops' enlistment period at year-end, and the prospect that the warm weather of spring will thaw the St. Lawrence, allowing British ships to bring reinforcements: can they afford to lay siege to Quebec or must they attack now?

December 6: The Continental Congress adopts an official reply to George III's rejection of the Olive Branch Petition—news of which the members received on November 9. Their reply denies that the colonies are in a state of rebellion and asserts that the colonies' actions demonstrate allegiance to the Crown, while also declaring opposition to the king's or Parliament's "exercise of unconstitutional powers." It makes no threat concerning independence.

At New York, Governor Tryon has public records confiscated and brought aboard HMS *Duchess of Gordon* for safekeeping.

December 8: Montgomery and Arnold begin to lay siege to Quebec, even though Montgomery realizes the tactic cannot succeed. Carleton summarily rejects Montgomery's calls for surrender.

December 9: Hoping to end Lord Dunmore's coastal raids and drive him out of Norfolk, the Virginia Council of Safety orders Col. William Woodford to station 1,000 militiamen at the southern end of the Great Bridge causeway spanning a swampy section of the Elizabeth River about 10 miles from Norfolk. At the opposite end of the causeway stands Dunmore and his force of about 200 regulars, some Loyalists and marines, and the "Loyal Ethiopians," as Dunmore calls the runaway slaves he recruited. Dunmore sends the regulars to the attack, but they afford an easy target when bottlenecked on the causeway. The Patriots' fire inflicts 60 casualties in a half hour, in effect neutralizing Dunmore's army, while suffering only a single minor wound among their own ranks. Pursued by the Patriots, Dunmore retreats to Norfolk, evacuates as many Loyalists as possible to British ships in the harbor, and then abandons the town to the rebels.

December 14: The Continental Congress establishes the Marine Committee, comprised of one member from each colony, to replace the Naval Committee and fulfill its responsibilities—organizing, outfitting, and directing the American navy.

December 22: Parliament approves the American Prohibitory Act, which terminates all trade with the colonies and subjects any ship involved in such trade to impoundment.

The Naval Committee submits to the Continental Congress the names of officers of the navy's four ships and Esek Hopkins as commander in chief.

At Cane Break, on the Reedy River in South Carolina, about 4,000 rebel militiamen and army troops commanded by Cols. Richard Richardson, William Thompson, Thomas Polk, and Alex Martin skirmish with and rout Loyalists led by William Cunningham—finishing the task of dispersing all the Loyalists since the victory at Ninety-Six.

December 28: A French agent named Archard de Bonvouloir arrives as a traveler in Philadelphia. Although disclaiming any official capacity, he advises the Committee of Secret Correspondence that the French government sympathizes with the Americans and will discreetly overlook their efforts to obtain supplies in France.

December 31: Following a false start on December 29, Montgomery now launches a genuine attack on Quebec as a blizzard rages. Montgomery approaches the city from the south along the St. Lawrence. Rocket launches signal the advance but also alert Carleton, who rouses his garrison to prepare for battle. Arnold's men attack from the north and enter the city by the Palace Gate. Arnold orders his men to storm the British barricades, but a ricocheting bullet breaks Arnold's leg, and two men carry him to the rear for care. Daniel Morgan assumes command and succeeds in entering the Lower Town. Driven back, Morgan's men hesitate, hoping Montgomery's force will join them, but Montgomery has been killed. Using the rebels' own Bunker Hill tactic of delayed fire, Carleton has thwarted Montgomery's advance, and the dead commander's surviving troops fall back in retreat. Some reach safety fleeing across the frozen St. Lawrence, but many are forced to surrender. Carleton sends a sortie party to capture Arnold's redoubt at St. Roche, but the hospitalized commander's artillery drives them off. Nevertheless, Carleton's successful defense of Quebec has netted 426 American prisoners, reducing Arnold's surviving command to only 600 men. The British defenders suffer only five dead and 15 wounded; the Americans, 60 dead and wounded.

EYEWITNESS TESTIMONY

1775

Sir, certain persons styling themselves delegates of several of His Majesty's colonies in America having presumed without His Majesty's authority or consent to assemble together at Philadelphia in the months of September and October last, and having thought fit amongst other unwarrantable proceedings to resolve that it will be necessary that another congress should be held at the same place on the 10th of May next unless redress for certain pretended grievances be obtained before that time and to recommend that all the colonies in North America should choose deputies to attend such congress, I am commanded by the King to signify to you His Majesty's pleasure that you do use your utmost endeavours to prevent any such appointment of deputies within the province under your government and that you do exhort all persons to desist from such an unjustifiable proceeding which cannot but be highly displeasing to the King.

The earl of Dartmouth, secretary of state for the American colonies, from a letter written at Whitehall, London, to the governors of each of the American colonies, January 4, 1775, in K. G. Davies, ed., Documents of the American Revolution, *vol. 9, p. 24.*

My Lord, it was thought impossible that the frenzy which had seized the people could be of very long duration unless constantly supported by new events and there was hopes, if tranquility could be for a time preserved, that people would have leisure for reflection and think seriously of their danger. . . . I find by accounts from several parts of the country that those hopes were not without foundation, that the people's minds are greatly cooled. . . .

. . . . .

The eyes of all are turned upon Great Britain waiting for her determination and it's the opinion of most people, if a respectable force is seen in the field, the most obnoxious of the leaders seized and a pardon proclaimed for all others, that government will come off victorious and with less opposition than was expected a few months ago.

Lt. Gen. Thomas Gage, from a letter written at Boston to the earl of Dartmouth, January 18, 1775, in K. G. Davies, ed., Documents of the American Revolution, *vol. 9, pp. 29–30.*

You will observe from what has already passed in Parliament on the subject of America how little ground there was for those assurances which had been artfully held out to the Americans of support here in the dangerous measures they have adopted, and the great majority which has appeared in both Houses upon every question that has been proposed for maintaining the supremacy of Parliament is such an evidence of the general sense of the nation as will I hope have the effect to prevent His Majesty's subjects in the colonies from committing themselves in any further acts of treason and rebellion; and I have the greater confidence in that hope as it appears by your dispatch of the 18th of last month which is just now received that the friends of government in the Massachusetts Bay are disposed to show themselves more openly and that the ill effects of an obstruction to the course of public justice begin to be felt.

The earl of Dartmouth, from a letter written at Whitehall, London, to Lt. Gen. Thomas Gage, February 22, 1775, in K. G. Davies, ed., Documents of the American Revolution, *vol. 9, p. 54.*

A few days ago a riot occurred at Elizabethtown in Jersey. The scene opened between twelve and one o'clock, with seizing a poor Staten Islander, for no other crime than because some people of that ever loyal island were supposed to have been ready to assist in landing some goods from Captain Watson's Scotch ship . . . having arrived at New York after the first of February, the day limited by the Congress for the importation of goods. The man's boat was dragged ashore, and his oysters distributed to the hungry vagabonds, who were visibly headed in the centre of the town, by Jonathan Hampton, a Justice of the Peace, a Judge of the county court, and chairman of the committee. . . . About four o'clock . . . the mob . . . proceeded to abuse all the people in the town who were known to be well affected to the constitution; they erected a gallows. . . . And fixed up a liberty pole in the middle of the town. It must be observed, that the worshipful Judge, Jonathan Hampton, was, as usual, completely drunk when the riot commenced. . . .

This was a glorious day to the sons of licentiousness; and it was also a glorious day to the sons of loyalty; for it has made in Elizabethtown more proselytes to the side of order and government, than all the other endeavors that have been exerted to abate the fever of the times.

From Rivington's New-York Gazetteer, *March 2, 1775, quoted in Frank Moore, compiler,* The Diary of the American Revolution, *pp. 4–5.*

Committee of Safety appointed by the Congress consisting of Handcock, Warren, Church, Heath and Gearey. These are to observe the motions of the army, and if they attempt to penetrate into the country immediately to communicate the intelligence to Colonel Ward, Colonel Bigelow and Colonel Henshaw who live in or near the towns of Worcester and Leicester, Colonel Warren of Plymouth and Colonel Lee of Marblehead. They are to send expresses round the country to collect the minute men who are to oppose the troops. The minute men amount to about 5000 and are the picked men of the whole body of militia and all properly armed. There are in the country thirty-eight field-pieces and nineteen companies of artillery, most of which are at Worcester, a few at Concord and a few at Watertown. Their whole magazine of powder, consisting of between ninety and a hundred barrels, is at Concord.

From a British intelligence report enclosed with a letter of March 4, 1775, sent by Lt. Gen. Thomas Gage to the earl of Dartmouth, in K. G. Davies, ed., Documents of the American Revolution, *vol. 9, pp. 63–64.*

The trade with America alone is now within less than £500,000 of being equal to what this great commercial nation, England, carried on at the beginning of this century with the whole world! If I had taken the largest year of those on your [inspector general's] table, it would rather have exceeded. But, it will be said, is not this American trade an unnatural protuberance that has drawn the juices from the rest of the body? The reverse. It is the very food that has nourished every other part into its present magnitude. Our general trade has been greatly augmented, and augmented more or less in almost every part to which it ever extended, but with this material difference, that of the six millions which in the beginning of the century constituted the whole mass of our export commerce the colony trade was but one twelfth part; it is now (as a part of sixteen millions) considerably more than a third of the whole. This is the relative proportion of the importance of the colonies at these two periods, and all reasoning concerning our mode of treating them must have this proportion as its basis, or it is a reasoning weak, rotten, and sophistical.

. . . . .

. . . But I confess . . . my opinion is much more in favor of prudent management than of force—consider-ing force not as an odious but a feeble instrument for preserving a people so numerous, so active, so growing, so spirited as this [Americans], in a profitable and subordinate connection with us.

First, sir, permit me to observe that the use of force alone is but *temporary.* It may subdue for a moment, but it does not remove the necessity of subduing again, and a nation is not governed which is perpetually to be conquered.

My next objection is its *uncertainty.* Terror is not always the effect of force, and an armament is not a victory. If you do not succeed, you are without resource, for, conciliation failing, force remains; but force failing, no further hope of reconciliation is left. Power and authority are sometimes bought by kindness, but they can never be begged as alms by an impoverished and defeated violence.

. . . . .

Sir, I shall open the whole plan to you together, with such observations on the motions as may tend to illustrate them where they may want explanation.

The first is a resolution: "That the colonies and plantations of Great Britain in North America, consisting of fourteen separate governments [including Province of Quebec] and containing two millions and upward of free inhabitants, have not had the liberty and privilege of electing and sending any knights and burgesses, or others, to represent them in the high court of Parliament."

This is a plain matter of fact, necessary to be laid down, and (excepting the description) it is laid down in the language of the constitution; it is taken nearly verbatim from acts of Parliament.

Edmund Burke, from a "Speech on Moving Resolutions for Conciliation with the Colonies," in Parliament, March 22, 1775, in Burke, Selected Writings and Speeches on America, *pp. 126, 130–131, 161–162.*

As the populace of Boston have thought fit to repeal the tarring and feathering act, the King's troops have thought fit to revive the said statute. . . . Yesterday [March 8], an honest countryman was inquiring for a forelock, when a soldier hearing him, said he had one he would sell. Away goes the ignoramus, and after paying the soldier very honestly for the gun . . . a dozen seized him and hurried the poor fellow away under guard, for a breach of the act against trading with the soldiers. After keeping him in duress all night . . . the officers condemned him without a hearing to be tarred and feathered, which sentence has been executed.

After stripping him naked and covering him with tar and feathers, they mounted him on a one-horse truck, and . . . exhibited him as a spectacle through the principal streets of the town. They fixed a label on the man's back, on which was written AMERICAN LIBERTY or A SPECIMEN DEMOCRACY; and to add to the insult they played Yankee Doodle:—Oh Britain, how art thou fallen! . . . What a wretched figure will the Boston expedition hereafter make in the historic page!

From the New-York Journal, *March 30, 1775, quoted in Frank Moore, compiler,* The Diary of the American Revolution, *pp. 11–12.*

It has come. The long expected blow has been struck, and by the British arm. How can I nerve myself to write of the horrors of yesterday; but I will do it.

At midnight of Tuesday we were awakened by the ringing of bells and beating of drums and the hurried tread of men arming for battle. The air was filled with cries of frightened women and children. "The regulars are out. To arms!" was the shout which, with lightning speed, went from mouth to mouth. Then we knew that the purposes of General Gage had ripened into deeds, and war was fairly upon us. Our minutemen were ready for action, and as the sun arose set off in the direction of Lexington, where the British troops had gone. For us at home there was the most terrible suspense to be endured. . . . Dr. Warren himself, they say, had a very narrow escape in the affray. He ran recklessly into it when the British were retreating, and a bullet whizzed past his head, taking off one of the side curls.

Dorothy Dudley, resident of Cambridge, Massachusetts, from diary entry of April 20, 1775, in Arthur Gilman, ed., Theatrum Majorum, *pp. 18–20.*

. . . On these companies' arrival at Lexington I understand from the report of Major Pitcairn who was with them and from many officers that they found on a green close to the road a body of country people drawn up in military order with arms and accouterments and, as appeared after, loaded; and that they had posted some men in a dwelling and meeting-house. As our troops advanced towards them without any intention of injuring them further than to inquire the reason of their being thus assembled, and if not satisfactory to

have secured their arms, but they in confusion went off principally to the left. Only one of them fired before he went off and three or four more jumped over a wall and fired from behind it among the soldiers, on which the troops returned it and killed several of them. They likewise fired on the soldiers from the meeting and dwelling-house: we had one man wounded and Major Pitcairn's horse shot in two places. . . . While at Concord we saw vast numbers assembling in many parts at one of the bridges. They marched down with a very considerable body on the light infantry posted there. On their coming pretty near, one of our men fired on them which they returned, on which an action ensued and some few were killed and wounded. In this affair it appears that after the bridge was quitted they scalped and otherwise ill treated one or two of the men who were either killed or severely wounded, being seen by party that marched by soon after. . . . On our leaving Concord to return to Boston they began to fire on us from behind the walls, ditches, trees etc., which as we marched increased to a very great degree and continued without the intermission of five minutes altogether for I believe upwards of eighteen miles, so that I can't think but that it must have been a preconcerted scheme. . . . Notwithstanding the enemy's numbers they did not make one gallant attempt during so long [an] action, though our men were so very much fatigued, but kept under cover on all occasions where much danger.

Lt. Col. Francis Smith, from his report written at Boston and submitted to Lt. Gen. Thomas Gage on the battles of Lexington and Concord, April 22, 1775, in K. G. Davies, ed., Documents of the American Revolution, *vol. 9, pp. 103–104.*

Accounts of the battle you may imagine instantly flew to all parts of the country and great numbers of their militia and minutemen are assembled at Cambridge and Roxborough and in its neighbourhood. They are at this time entrenching themselves at Roxborough and have absolutely prohibited every kind of provision being brought to Boston. They are so elated with having destroyed a few of the King's troops that they talk of erecting batteries at different places to destroy the men-of-war, of bombarding the town and taking Castle William. I have sent to acquaint the inhabitants of Charlestown with my determination to destroy it whenever I perceive them making any preparations for erecting batteries to annoy the King's ships, which

I shall most certainly do the moment I perceive them fairly at work....

Vice Adm. Samuel Graves, from a letter written aboard the Preston *in Boston Harbor to Philip Stephens, secretary of the Admiralty, April 22, 1775, in K. G. Davies, ed.,* Documents of the American Revolution, *vol. 9, p. 105.*

... For I am convinced that matters are now carried so far that the Americans in general are disposed to run the risk of a total ruin rather than suffer a taxation by any but their own representatives and that there is not the least reason to expect they will ever in this instance consent to acknowledge the right, even if they should be obliged to submit to the power, of Parliament. The plan now offered to them is happily a waiving of the exercise of that right on conditions corresponding with their own former declarations and which I cannot therefore but hope the reasonable part of them will think it the duty of this country to adopt.

Governor William Franklin, from a letter written at Perth Amboy, New Jersey, to the earl of Dartmouth, May 6, 1775, in K. G. Davies, ed., Documents of the American Revolution, *vol. 9, pp. 127–128.*

It's admirable to see alteration of the Tory class in this place [Philadelphia], since the accounts of the engagement in New England. Their language is quite softened, and many of them have so far renounced their former sentiments as that they have taken up arms, and are joined in the association; nay, even many of the stiff Quakers, and some of those who drew up the Testimony, are ashamed of their proceedings....

Christopher Marshall, Philadelphia merchant, official, and Quaker, from diary entry of May 7, 1775, in Marshall, Extracts from the Diary of Christopher Marshall, *p. 23.*

Within this week we have received the unhappy news of an action of considerable magnitude the king's troops and our brethren of Boston.... This accident has cut off our last hopes of reconciliation, and phrenzy of revenge seems to have seized all ranks of people. It is a lamentable circumstance that the only mediatory power acknowledged by both parties ... should pursue the incendiary purpose of still blowing up the flames as we find him constantly doing in every speech and public declaration. This may perhaps be intended to intimidate into acquiescence, but the effect has been most unfortu-

nately other wise. A little knolege [*sic*] of human nature and attention to it's [*sic*] ordinary workings might have foreseen that the spirits of the people here were in a state in which they were more likely to be provoked than frightened by haughty deportment.... When I saw Lord Chatham's bill I entertained high hope that a reconciliation could have been brought about. The difference between his terms and those offered by our congress might have been accomodated if entered on by both parties with a disposition to accomodate. But the dignity of parliament it seems can brook no opposition to it's power. Strange that a set of men who have made a sale of their virtue to the minister should yet talk of retaining dignity! ...

Thomas Jefferson, from a letter written to William Small, May 7, 1775, in Julian P. Boyd, ed., The Papers of Thomas Jefferson, *vol. 1, pp. 165–166.*

You will have heard before this reaches you of the Commencement of a Civil War; the End of it perhaps neither myself, nor you, who are much younger, may live to see. I find here all Ranks of People in Arms, disciplining themselves Morning and Evening, and am informed that the firmest Union prevails throughout North America; New York as hearty as any of the rest....

Benjamin Franklin, from a letter written in Philadelphia, May 8, 1775, to David Hartley, in William B. Willcox, ed., The Papers of Benjamin Franklin, *vol. 22, p. 34.*

A party headed by a certain Patrick Henry, one of the delegates of this colony, a man of desperate circumstances and one who has been very active in encouraging disobedience and exciting a spirit of revolt among the people for many years past, advanced to within a few miles of this place and there encamped with all the appearances of actual war ...; Henry, their leader, dispatching letters all over the country to excite the people to join him; and he sent one particularly to direct that the people of the County of York should prevent at all events any succour being sent to me from the man-of-war lying at York or my retreat to the man-of-war.

The earl of Dunmore, governor of Virginia, from a letter written at Williamsburg to the earl of Dartmouth, May 15, 1775, in K. G. Davies, ed., Documents of the American Revolution, *vol. 9, p. 133.*

All People here feel themselves much oblig'd by your Endeavours to serve them. I hear your propos'd

Resolves were negativ'd by a great Majority; which was denying the most notorious Truths; and a kind of national Lying, of which they may be convicted by their own Records.

The Congress is met here, pretty full. I had not been here a Day before I was return'd a Member. We din'd together on Saturday, when your Health was among the foremost. With the sincerest Esteem. . . .

Benjamin Franklin, from a letter written in Philadelphia, May 15, 1775, to Edmund Burke, in William B. Willcox, ed., The Papers of Benjamin Franklin, *vol. 22, p. 41.*

. . . The state of the inhabitants of . . . Boston and their distresses no language can paint—imprisoned with their Enemies, suffering hunger and famine, obliged to endure insults and abuses from breach of faith plited to them in the most solemn manner by the General [Gage], that if they would deliver up their arms, both they and their effects should be sufferd to depart, and then treachously deceived. . . .

We have lamented the infatuation of Britain and have wished an honourable reconsilation with her till she has plunged her Sword into our Bosoms and laid 40 of our Brethren in the Dust. Tyranny, oppression and Murder have been the reward of all the affection, the veneration and the loyalty which has heretofore distinguished Americans. . . . We have received in the course of the last three Months every indignity that it was possible for humane nature to endure. The Troops of Brittain, once the pride and Glory of Europe, have descended to become a Mob. . . .

The Spirit that prevails among Men of all degrees, all ages and sex'es is the Spirit of Liberty. For this they are determined to risk all their property and their lives. . . . Tis Thought we must now bid a final adieu to Britain, nothing will now appease the Exasperated Americans but the heads of those trators who have subverted the constitution, for the blood of our Breathren crys to us from the Ground. . . .

Abigail Adams, from a letter written to Edward Dilly, May 22, 1775, in L. H. Butterfield, ed., Adams Family Correspondence, *vol. 1, pp. 200–202.*

The body of the troops, in the mean time, under the command of Lieutenant-Colonel Smith, had crossed the river an landed at Phipps' farm. They proceeded with great silence to Lexington, six miles below Concord. A company of militia, numbering about eighty men, had mustered near the meeting house. Just before sunrise the King's troops came in sight, when the militia began to disperse. The troops then set out upon the road, hallooing and huzzaing, and coming within a few rods of them, the commanding officer cried out in words to this effect, "Disperse, you damned rebels! Damn you, disperse!" upon which the troops again huzzaed, and at the same time one or two officers discharged their pistols, which were instantaneously followed by the firing of four or five of the soldiers, and then there seemed to be a general discharge from the whole. It is to be noticed, they fired upon the militia as they were dispersing agreeably to their command, and that they did not even return the fire. Eight of our men were killed, and nine wounded. The troops then laughed, and damned the Yankees, and said they could not bear the smell of gunpowder.

From the Pennsylvania Journal, *Philadelphia, May 24, 1775, reporting on the battles of Lexington and Concord, quoted in Frank Moore, compiler,* The Diary of the American Revolution, *pp. 24–25.*

Oh that I was a Soldier—I will be.—I am reading military Books.—Every Body must and will, and shall be a soldier.

John Adams, from a letter written in Philadelphia to Abigail Adams, May 29, 1775, in L. H. Butterfield, ed., Adams Family Correspondence, *vol. 1, p. 207.*

Before this Letter can reach you, you must, undoubtedly, have received an Account of the engagement in the Massachusetts Bay between the Ministerial Troops (for we do not, nor cannot yet prevail upon ourselves to call them the King's Troops) and the Provincials of that Government; But as you may not have heard how that affair began, I inclose you the several Affidavits that were taken after the Action.

. . . . .

From the best Accounts I have been able to collect of that affair; indeed from every one, I believe the fact, stripped of all colouring, to be plainly this, that if the retreat had not been as precipitate as it was (and God knows it could not well have been more so) the Ministerial Troops must have surrendered, or been totally cut off: For they had not arrived in Charlestown (under cover of their Ships) half an hour, before a powerful body of Men from Marblehead and Salem were at their heels, and must, if they had happened to have been up one hour sooner, inevitably intercepted their retreat to Charlestown. Unhappy it is though to reflect, that a Brother's Sword has been sheathed in a Brother's breast, and that, the once happy and peaceful plains of America are either drenched with Blood, or Inhabited by Slaves. Sad alternative! But can a virtuous Man hesitate in his choice?

George Washington, from a letter written at Philadelphia to George William Fairfax, May 31, 1775, in John C. Fitzpatrick, ed., The Writings of George Washington, *vol. 3, pp. 291–292.*

There are still many friends to government here but they begin to think they are left to fall a sacrifice to the resentment of the people for want of proper support and protection, and for their own safety and other prudential reasons are falling off and lessening every day. Pardon me, my lord, but a few troops 12 months ago would have kept all the southern provinces *out of rebellion,* and I much fear many will now be necessary. My lord, the King has not a servant better disposed to support his honour and just rights than I am and I can lay my hand on my heart and say with an honest and good conscience that I have done everything in my power to support the just sovereignty of Great Britain, law, government and good order. But I cannot continue in this very uncomfortable situation without the means of protection and support, and therefore must humbly request that His Majesty will be graciously pleased to give me leave to return home, which I would propose to do next spring or sooner as things may be circumstanced, and would therefore hope to have it as soon as may be.

Governor Sir James Wright, from a letter written at Savannah, Georgia, to the earl of Dartmouth, June 9, 1775, in K. G. Davies, ed., Documents of the American Revolution, *vol. 9, pp. 167–168.*

Mr. President: Tho' I am truly sensible of the high Honour done me in this Appointment, yet I feel great distress from a consciousness that my abilities and Military experience may not be equal to the extensive and important Trust: However, as the Congress desires I will enter upon the momentous duty, and exert every power I Possess In their Service for the Support of the glorious Cause: I beg they will accept my most cordial thanks for this distinguished testimony of their Approbation.

But lest some unlucky event should happen unfavorable to my reputation, I beg it may be remembered by every Gentn. in the room, that I this day declare with the utmost sincerity, I do not think my self equal to the Command I am honoured with.

As to pay, Sir, I beg leave to Assure the Congress that as no pecuniary consideration could have tempted me to have accepted this Arduous employment [at the expence of my domesstt. Ease and happiness] I do not wish to make any proffit from it: I will keep an exact Account of my expences; those I doubt not they will discharge and that is all I desire.

George Washington, acceptance of appointment as general and commander in chief, June 16, 1775, in John C. Fitzpatrick, ed., The Writings of George Washington, *vol. 3, pp. 292–293.*

As the enemy approached, our men was not only exposed to the attack of a very numerous musketry, but to the heavy fire of the battery on Corps-Hill, 4 or 5 men of war, several armed boats or floating batteries in Mistick-River, and a number of field pieces. Notwithstanding we . . . sustained the enemy's attacks with great bravery and resolution . . . and after bearing, for about 2 hours, as sever and heavy a fire as perhaps ever was known . . . we ware over-powered by numbers and obliged to leave the intrenchment, retreating about sunset to a small distance over Charlestown Neck.

. . . I received a wound in my rite arm, the bawl gowing through a little below my elbow breaking the little shel bone. Another bawl struck my back, taking a piece of skin about as big as a penny. But I got to Cambridge that night. . . .

Amos Farnsworth, corporal in the Massachusetts militia, from a diary entry on the Battle of Bunker Hill, June 17, 1775, in Henry Steele Commager, ed., The Spirit of 'Seventy Six, *vol. 1, pp. 122–123.*

I can now inform you that the Congress have made Choice of the modest and virtuous, the amiable, generous and brave George Washington, Esqr., to be General of the American Army, and that he is to repair as soon as possible to the Camp before Boston. This Appointment will have a great Effect, in cementing and securing the Union of these Colonies. . . .

John Adams, from a letter written in Philadelphia to Abigail Adams, June 17, 1775, in L. H. Butterfield, ed., Adams Family Correspondence, *vol. 1, p. 215.*

My Dearest: I am now set down to write to you on a subject, which fills me with inexpressible concern, and this concern is greatly aggravated and increased, when I reflect upon the uneasiness I know it will give you. It has been determined in Congress, that the whole army raised for the defence of the American cause shall be put under my care, and that it is necessary for me to proceed immediately to Boston to take upon me the command of it.

You may believe me, my dear Patsy, when I assure you, in the most solemn manner that, so far from seeking this appointment, I have used every endeavor in my power to avoid it. . . . But as it has been a kind of destiny, that has thrown me upon this service, I shall hope that my undertaking it is designed to answer some good purpose. . . . I shall feel no pain from the toil or the danger of the campaign; my unhappiness will flow from the uneasiness I know you will feel from being left alone. I therefore beg, that you will summon your whole fortitude, and pass your time as agreeably as possible. . . . My earnest and ardent desire is, that you would pursue any plan that is most likely to produce content, and a tolerable degree of tranquillity. . . .

As life is always uncertain, and common prudence dictates to every man the necessity of settling his temporal concerns, while it is in his power, and while the mind is calm and undisturbed, I have . . . got Colonel [Edmond] Pendleton to draft a will for me . . . which will I now enclose. The provision made for you in case of my death will, I hope, be agreeable.

George Washington, from a letter written in Philadelphia to his wife, Martha, June 18, 1775, in John C. Fitzpatrick, ed., The Writings of George Washington, *vol. 3, pp. 293–295.*

How can I write of the great and terrible loss which has come to us in the death of our beloved Dr. Warren. Yes, he is killed, pierced through the brain by a British bullet, and left dead on the field. When he was hurrying to the battle, and someone warned him to spare himself, he replied: "Dulce et decorum est pro patria mori." [It is sweet and glorious to die for one's country.] At Bunker Hill, though tendered the command by both Putnam and Prescott, he declined, and took his place with the common soldiers, musket in hand, to do his part in defending the hill. When they were driven to surrender, he was the last to leave the ramparts, and fell bravely fighting. Many others of our brave men are gone, but none so valuable to the country as General

Warren. He was appointed major-general only three days ago.

Dorothy Dudley, resident of Cambridge, Massachusetts, from diary entry of June 18, 1775, in Arthur Gilman, ed., Theatrum Majorum, *p. 24.*

Early in the morning of the 17th the *Lively* discovered several thousand rebels on the hills near Charlestown who had thrown up an entrenchment the preceding night. Capt. Bishop instantly fired among them, and upon his alarm they were attacked from Copse Hill battery on Boston side. Preparations were also immediately made to dislodge them; the troops accordingly landed in the afternoon under the cover of His Majesty's ships *Lively, Glasgow* and *Falcon,* and a transport, a sloop and some scows fitted by the General but manned and supplied with ammunition from the squadron. They attacked the rebels and after a very obstinate defence carried their entrenchments and drove them with great slaughter. The King's troops are now encamped on the heights of Charlestown and the rebels are digging entrenchments and erecting other works at some distance apparently with a view to dispute every foot of ground. Their lordships may be assured that every possible assistance has and shall be given to the army by His Majesty's ships under my command.

Vice Adm. Samuel Graves, from a letter written aboard the Preston *in Boston Harbor to Philip Stephens, secretary of the Admiralty, June 22, 1775, K. G. Davies, ed.,* Documents of the American Revolution, *vol. 9, pp. 192–193.*

. . . Washington set out from here on Friday last as Generalissimo of all Provincial troops in North-America. Ward and Lee are appointed major Generals, and Gates Adjutant. We are exceedingly anxious till we hear of their arrival at Boston, as it is evident to every one that the provincial encampment is the most injudicious that can possibly be conceived. For the sole purpose of covering two small towns near Boston they have encamped so near the line of the ministerial army that the centries may converse. Gage too being well fortified is in little danger of an attack from them, while their situation is such that he may attack them when he pleases, and if he is unsuccessful they cannot pursue him a foot scarcely, on account of the ships and floating batteries bearing on the neck of Boston. . . .

Thomas Jefferson, from a letter written at Philadelphia to Francis Eppes, June 26, 1775, in Julian P. Boyd, ed., The Papers of Thomas Jefferson, *vol. 1, p. 175.*

The name of Howe the Yankees dread,
We see it very plainly.
And now my song is at an end,
And to conclude my ditty,
It is the poor and ignorant
And only them I pity:
As for their king John Hancock,
And Adams if they're taken,
There heads for signs shall hang up high,
Upon that hill call'd Beacon.

From the Battle of Bunker Hill, *a broadside published
at Providence, R.I., June 1775, quoted in Frank Moore,
complier,* The Diary of the American Revolution,
pp. 50–51.

Happy some land, which all for freedom gave,
Happier the men whom their own virtues save;
Thrice happy we who long attacks have stood,
And swam to Liberty thro' seas of blood;
The time shall come when strangers rule no more,
Nor cruel mandates vex from Britain's shore;
When Commerce shall extend her short'ned wing,
And her free freights from every climate bring;
When mighty towns shall flourish free and great,
Vast their dominion, opulent their state;
When one vast cultivated region teems,
From ocean's edge to Mississippi's streams;
While each enjoys his vineyard's peaceful shade,
And even the meanest has no cause to dread;
Such is the life our foes with envy see,
Such is the godlike glory to be free.

*Philip Freneau, from "American Liberty, A Poem,"
July 1775, in Fred Lewis Pattee, ed.,*
The Poems of Philip Freneau, *vol. 1,
pp. 151–152.*

From the moment this blow was struck and the town of Boston invested by the rebels there was no longer any room to doubt of the intention of the people of Massachusetts Bay to commit themselves in open rebellion. The other three New England governments have taken the same part and in fact all North America (Quebec, Nova Scotia and the Floridas excepted) is in arms against the King in every sense of that expression.

In this situation every effort must be made both by sea and land to subdue rebellion should the people persist in the rash measures they have adopted. But I still entertain a hope from some favourable circumstances that may be collected from the last advices that, when the middle colonies have recovered from the prejudices and consternation which were created by the artful misrepresentations of the affair of the 19th of April, they will be induced to take up the consideration of the resolution of the House of Commons of the 20th [27th] of February . . . upon some ground that may lead to reconciliation.

*The earl of Dartmouth, from a letter written at
Whitehall, London, to Lt. Gen. Thomas Gage,
July 1, 1775, in K. G. Davies, ed.,*
Documents of the American Revolution,
vol. 11, p. 25.

Parole Abington. Countersign Bedford.

Exact returns to be made by the proper Officers of all the Provisions Ordnance, Ordnance Stores, Powder, Lead working Tools of all kinds, Tents, Camp Kettles, and all other Stores under their respective care, belonging to the Armies at Roxbury and Cambridge. The commanding Officer of each Regiment to make a return of the number of blankets wanted to compleat every Man with one at least.

The Hon: Artemus Ward, Charles Lee, Philip Schuyler, and Israel Putnam Esquires are appointed Major Generals of the American Army, and due obedience is to be paid them as such. . . .

The Continental Congress having now taken all the Troops of the several Colonies . . . into their Pay and Service. They are now the Troops of the UNITED PROVINCES of North America; and it is hoped that all Distinctions of Colonies will be laid aside; so that one and the same Spirit may animate the whole, and the only Contest be, who shall render, on this great and trying occasion, the most essential service to the Great and common cause in which we are all engaged.

It is required and expected that exact discipline be observed, and due Subordination prevail thro' the whole Army, as Failure in these most essential points must necessarily produce extreme Hazard, Disorder and Confusion; and end in shameful disappointment and disgrace.

The General most earnestly requires, and expects, a due observance of those articles of war, established for the Government of the army, which forbid profane cursing, swearing and drunkeness; And in like manner requires and expects, of all Officers, and Soldiers, not engaged on actual duty, a punctual attendance on divine Service, to implore the blessings of heaven upon the means used for our safety and defence.

George Washington, from his first General Orders, issued at his Cambridge, Massachusetts, headquarters, July 4, 1775, in John C. Fitzpatrick, ed., The Writings of George Washington, vol. 3, pp. 308–309.

The battle of Charlestown I expect you have heard, but perhaps not so as you may depend on. The provincials sustained two attacks in their trenches, and twice repulsed the ministerial forces, with immense slaughter. The third attack, however, being made with fixed bayonets, the provincials gave around, retires a little way, and rallied ready for their enemy; but they, having been pretty roughly handled, did not choose to pursue. We lost between 60 and 70 killed, and about 150 wounded. The enemy had 1400 killed and wounded, of whom were about 500 killed. Major Pitcairn was among the slain; an event at which every one rejoices, as he was the commanding-officer at Lexington, first fired his own piece, and gave command to fire. On our side doctor Warren fell, a man immensely valued to the north. The New Englanders are fitting out privateers, with which they expect to be able to scour the seas and bays of every thing below ships of war; and may probably go to the European coasts, to distress British trade there. The enterprising genius and intrepidity of these people are amazing. They are now intent on burning Boston, in order to oust the regulars; and none are more eager for it than those who have escaped out, and who have left their whole property in it: So that, their rage has got the better of every interested principle.

Thomas Jefferson, from a letter written at Philadelphia to George Gilmer, July 5, 1775, in Julian P. Boyd, ed., The Papers of Thomas Jefferson, vol. 1, pp. 185–186.

The two defeats near Boston seem to have made little impression on the Ministry. They still talk of great things to be expected from their Generals and Troops when united. One of your judgment will draw more information from the single word *Rebels* usd in the [London] Gazette, than from any thing I can say. Far from retracting they mean to exasperate, in perfect confidense of being successful. It is the curse of fools to be secure; and I trust their fate will prove, that the end of the wicked is punishment.

Arthur Lee, from a letter written in London, July 6, 1775, to Benjamin Franklin, in William B. Willcox, ed., The Papers of Benjamin Franklin, vol. 22, p. 89.

Your Description of the Distresses of the worthy Inhabitants of Boston, and the other Sea Port Towns, is enough to melt an Heart of stone. Our Consolation must be this, my dear, that Cities may be rebuilt, and a People reduced to Poverty, may acquire fresh Property: But a Constitution of Government once changed from Freedom, can never be restored. Liberty once lost is lost forever. When the People once surrender their share in the Legislature, and their Right of defending the Limitations upon the Government, and of resisting every Encroachment upon them, they can never regain it.

John Adams, from a letter written in Philadelphia to Abigail Adams, July 7, 1775, in L. H. Butterfield, ed., Adams Family Correspondence, vol. 1, p. 241.

I had the pleasure of seeing both the Generals and their Aid de camps soon after their arrival and of being personally made known to them. They very politely express their regard for you....

I was struck with General Washington. You had prepaired me to entertain a favorable opinion of him, but I thought the one half was not told me. Dignity with ease, and complacency, the Gentleman and Soldier look agreeably blended in him. Modesty marks every line and feture of his face.... General Lee looks like a careless hardy Veteran and from his appearance brought to my mind his namesake Charls the 12, king of Sweeden. The Elegance of his pen far exceeds that of his person....

Abigail Adams, from a letter written in Braintree, Massachusetts, to John Adams, July 16, 1775, in L. H. Butterfield, ed., Adams Family Correspondence, vol. 1, pp. 246–247.

...They [rebels in the Assembly] are ripe for any violence and I am determined whatever is done shall be acted before them; in fact it will be their own deed, as the Assembly almost to a man are members of the Congress and Committee. No subterfuge should be left them; things are come to such a pass, my lord, that the whole world ought to know that the present measures proceed not from a mob fired by oppression, but that they are the result of a concerted plan and firm determination of a powerful party to establish an independency by acts as unprovoked as they are unjustifiable. It is with real sorrow I write this of a people with whom I am so connected but my duty, my honour, and the trust reposed in me by my Sovereign obliges me to be explicit. I did hope the madness had not gone so far, but I meet with nothing but violence and frenzy where I flattered myself I should have found temper and moderation.

Governor Lord William Campbell, from a letter written at Charleston, North Carolina, to the earl of Dartmouth, July 19 and 20, in K. G. Davies, ed., Documents of the American Revolution, *vol. 11, p. 50.*

Dr. Franklin has been very constant in his Attendance on Congress from the Beginning. His conduct has been composed and grave. . . . He has not assumed any Thing, nor affected to take the lead; but has seemed to choose that the Congress should pursue their own Principles and sentiments and adopt their own Plans: yet he has not been backward. . . . He does not hesitate at our boldest Measures, but rather seems to think us, too irresolute, and backward. . . . But he thinks that We shall soon assume a Character more decisive.

He thinks, that We have the Power of preserving ourselves, and that even if We should be driven to the disagreeable Necessity of assuming a total Independency, and set up a separate state, We could maintain it. The People of England, have thought that the Opposition in America, was wholly owing to Dr. Franklin . . . but there cannot be a greater Mistake. He has had but little share farther than to co operate and assist. He is however a great and good Man. I wish his Colleagues from this City were All like him, particularly one [John Dickinson], whose Abilities and Virtues, formerly trumpeted so much in America, have been found wanting.

John Adams, from a letter written in Philadelphia to Abigail Adams, July 23, 1775, in L. H. Butterfield, ed., Adams Family Correspondence, *vol. 1, p. 253.*

My Lord, though your lordship must from all quarters be informed of the revolted and hostile state of America you may not possibly be acquainted how far some of those who now exercise the usurped powers of government evidently mean to pursue their dangerous designs. Independency is shooting from the root of the present contest: it is confidently said if Great Britain does not within six months adopt some new plan of accommodation the colonies will be severed from her, . . . that the standard of freedom and independency may be erected on this continent when all those who have not taken an active part in the commotions (though inimitable to the principle

of Parliamentary taxation) will far a sacrifice to the resentment of their rulers and their estates confiscated to defray in part the expense of the civil war. At the same period it is believed the ports of America will be declared free and the powers of Europe invited to guarantee the independency of the colonies. It is also whispered propositions have been made for that purpose and that a French officer of distinction was at Philadelphia a few weeks ago on some important embassy. Large supplies of ordnance, arms and ammunition have been procured from Hispaniola and Martinico. Calamitous as this conduct must prove to the confederate colonies, the chief rulers seem determined to drive on their measures.

Governor William Tryon, from a letter written in New York to the earl of Dartmouth, August 7, 1775, in K. G. Davies, ed., Documents of the American Revolution, *vol. 11, p. 69.*

It is a matter of exceeding great Concern to the General, to find, that at a time when the united efforts of America are exerting in defence of the common Rights and Liberties of mankind, that there should be in an Army constituted for so noble a purpose, such repeated Instances of Officer's, who lost to every sense of honour and virtue, are seeking by dirty and base means, the promotion of their own dishonest Gain, to the eternal Disgrace of themselves, and Dishonour of their country—practices of this sort will never be overlooked, whenever an Accusation is lodged, but the Authors brought to most exemplary punishment. . . .

George Washington, from a general order issued at his Cambridge, Massachusetts, headquarters, August 10, 1775, in John C. Fitzpatrick, ed., The Writings of George Washington, *vol. 3, p. 412.*

I cannot but observe to your lordship the great importance I conceive the preserving this province will be to His Majesty's interests in America, the only port where ships can be cleaned and have a supply of masts and other timber, all other resources in America being entirely at an end, and where the troops can retreat should than happen to be the case, but is at present the only place from whence they can be supplied with any kind of refreshments. . . .

Upon all these considerations, my lord, I think it absolutely necessary that fortifications for the security of the naval yard, the protection of the magazines in the town, cannon and other military stores, should be erected, for I conceive that the magazines when thus protected will be the only safe place in America for their deposit.

Governor Francis Legge, from a letter written in Halifax, Nova Scotia, to the earl of Dartmouth, August 19, 1775, in K. G. Davies, ed., Documents of the American Revolution, *vol. 11, p. 79.*

The People of this government have obtained a Character which they by no means deserved; their officers generally speaking are the most indifferent kind of People I ever saw. I have already broke one Colo. and five Captains for Cowardice and for drawing more Pay and Provisions than they had Men in their Companies; there is two more Colos. now under arrest, and to be tried for the same offences.... I dare say the Men would fight very well (if properly Officered) although they are an exceeding dirty and nasty people; had they been properly conducted at Bunkers Hill (on the 17th of June) or those that were there properly supported, the Regulars would have met with a shameful defeat ...; it was for their behaviour on that occasion that the above Officers were broke, for I never spared one that was accused of Cowardice bot brot 'em to immediate Tryal.

George Washington, from a letter written at his Cambridge, Massachusetts, headquarters to Lund Washington, August 20, 1775, in John C. Fitzpatrick, ed., The Writings of George Washington, *vol. 3, p. 433.*

I am sorry the situation of our country should render it not eligible to you to remain longer in it. I hope the returning wisdom of Great Britain will e'er long put an end to this unnatural contest. There may be people to whose tempers and dispositions Contention may be pleasing.... But to me it is of all states, but one, the most horrid. My first wish is a restoration of our just rights; my second a return of the happy period when, consistently with duty, I may withdraw myself totally from the public stage and pass the rest of my days in domestic ease and tranquility, banishing every desire of afterwards ever hearing what passes in the world.... Looking with fondness towards a reconciliation with Great Britain, I cannot help hoping you may be able to contribute towards expediting this good work. I think it must be evident to yourself that the ministry have been deceived by their officers on this side the water, who (for what purposes I cannot tell) have constantly represented the American opposition as that of a small faction, in which the body of the people took little part. This you can inform them of your own knolege to be untrue. They have taken it into their heads too that we are cowards and shall surrender at discretion to an armed force. The past and future operations of the war must confirm or undeceive them on that head.... Even those in parliament who are called friends to America seem to know nothing of our real determinations.... If indeed Great Britain, disjoined from her colonies, be a match for the most potent nations of Europe with the colonies thrown into their scale, they may go on securely. But if they are not assured of this, it would be certainly unwise ... to risque our accepting a foreign aid which perhaps may not be obtainable but on a condition of everlasting avulsion from Great Britain. This would be thought a hard condition to those who still wish for reunion with their parent country. I am sincerely one of those, and would rather be in dependance on Great Britain, properly limited, than on any nation upon earth, or than on no nation. But I am one of those too who rather than submit to the right of legislating for us assumed by the British parliament ... would lend my hand to sink the whole island in the ocean.

Thomas Jefferson, from a letter written at Monticello to John Randolph, August 25, 1775, in Julian P. Boyd, ed., The Papers of Thomas Jefferson, *vol. 1, p. 241.*

Sir: You are intrusted with a Command of the utmost Consequence to the Interest and Liberties of America. Upon your Conduct and Courage and that of the Officers and Soldiers detached on this Expedition, not only the Success of the present Enterprize, and your own Honour, but the Safety and Welfare of the Whole Continent may depend. I charge you, therefore, and the Officers and Soldiers under your Command, as you value your own Safety and Honour and the Favour and Esteem of your Country, that you consider yourselves, as marching, not through an Enemy's Country; but that of our Friends and Brethren, for such the Inabitants of Canada, and the Indian Nations have approved themselves in this unhappy Contest between Great Britain and America.... Should any American Soldier be so base and infamous as to injure any Canadian or Indian, in his Person or Property, I do most earnestly enjoin you to bring him to such severe and exemplary Punishment as the Enormity of the Crime may require.... But I hope and trust, that the brave Men who have voluntarily engaged in this Expedition, will be governed by far different Views. that Order, Discipline and Regularity of Behaviour will be as conspicuous, as their Courage and Valour. . . .

George Washington, from a letter and orders written at Cambridge, Massachusetts, to Benedict Arnold concerning his expedition into Canada, September 14, 1775, in John C. Fitzpatrick, ed., The Writings of George Washington, *vol. 3, pp. 491–492.*

However, as he [John Joachim Zubly] is the first Gentleman of the Cloth who has appeared in Congress, I can not but wish he may be the last. Mixing the sacred Character, with that of the Statesman, as it is quite unnecessary at this Time of day, in these Colonies, is not attended with any good Effects. The Clergy are universally too little acquainted with the World, and the Modes of Business, to engage in civil affairs with any Advantage. Besides those of them, who are really Men of Learning, have conversed with Books so much more than Men, as to be too much loaded with Vanity, to be good Politicians.

John Adams, from a letter written in Philadelphia to Abigail Adams, September 17, 1775, in L. H. Butterfield, ed., Adams Family Correspondence, *vol. 1, p. 281.*

Dr. Rush came in. He is an elegant, ingenious Body. Sprightly, pretty fellow. He is a Republican. He has been much in London. Acquainted with Sawbridge, McCaulay, Burgh, and others of that Stamp. . . . He complains of D[ickinson]. Says the Committee of Safety are not the Representatives of the People, and therefore not their Legislators; yet they have been making Laws, a whole Code for a Navy. This Committee was chosen by the House, but half of them are not Members and therefore not the Choice of the People. All this is just. He mentions many Particular Instances, in which Dickenson has blundered. He thinks him warped by the Quaker Interest and the Church Interest too. Thinks his Reputation past the Meridian, and that Avarice is growing upon him. Says that Henry and Mifflin both complained to him very much about him. But Rush, I think, is too much of a Talker to be a deep Thinker. Elegant not great.

John Adams, from diary entry of September 24, 1775, in L. H. Butterfield, ed., Diary and Autobiography of John Adams, *p. 182.*

. . . before we left our last encampment, it became a resolution of the whole party that the pork in the possession of each one should be eaten raw, and to eat but in the morning and evening. As we could not obtain food in this miserable portion of the globe, even for money, if we had it, and having nothing else than our arms and our courage to depend on; unacquainted with the true distance of our expedition, for we had neither map nor chart, yet resolved to accomplish our orders at the hazard of our lives—we prudently began to hoard our provision; half a biscuit and half an inch square of raw pork, became this evening's meal. . . .

John Joseph Henry, a rifleman from Lancaster, Pennsylvania, with the Arnold expedition along the Dead River in Maine, from diary entry of September 30, 1775, in Henry, Account of Arnold's Campaign against Quebec, *p. 29.*

1st. Whether we should push the war with our whole force in the next campaign on the side of New England?

I am of opinion that no offensive operations can be carried on to advantage from Boston: on the supposition of a certainty of driving the rebels from their entrenchments, no advantage would be gained but reputation; victory could not be improved through the want of every necessary to march into the country. The loss of men would probably be great and the rebels be as numerous in a few days as before their defeat. Besides the country is remarkably strong and adapted to their way of fighting.

2nd. Whether viewing the whole state of America it would not be more advisable to make Hudson's River the seat of the war and for that purpose immediately take possession of the city of New York. . . .?

It has always appeared to me most advisable to make Hudson's River the seat of the war. Its situation between the eastern and western colonies is advantageous, besides being commodious in transporting the necessaries of an army. . . . I am, however, of opinion that the force now in Boston cannot be divided and is too weak to hold Boston and New York at the same time.

Lt. Gen. Thomas Gage, from a letter written in Boston to the earl of Dartmouth, October 1, 1775, in K. G. Davies, ed., Documents of the American Revolution, *vol. 11, p. 135.*

Lord Dunmore is exceedingly offended with the Virginia printers, for presuming to furnish the public with a faithful relation of occurrences, and now and then, making a few strictures upon his lordship's own conduct, as well as that of some of his delightful associates. . . . Some of their actions have certainly deserved the severest reprehension, . . . for which the printers appeal to the whole world, even Freddy North himself, and the immaculate Johnny Bute. It seems his lordship has it much at heart to destroy every channel of public intelligence that is inimical to his designs upon the liberties of this country, alleging that they poison the minds of the people; or, in other words, lay open to them the tyrannical designs of a wicked ministry, which hath been supported in character by most of their slavish dependents. . . .

From the Virginia Gazette, *Williamsburg, October 7, 1775, quoted in Frank Moore, compiler,* The Diary of the American Revolution, *p. 69.*

. . . By an unlucky stroke of some of our paddles . . . the canoe was thrown a little out of its true course, just as it was entering the prongs of the fork. . . . to us it was the signal of death. One of the prongs took the right hand side of the canoe, within six inches of the bow, immediately below the gunwale. Quick as lightning that side of the canoe was laid open from stem to stern, and water was gushing in upon us, which would inevitably have sunk us in a second of time, but for that interference of Providence, which is atheistically called presence of mind. . . . Instinctively leaning to the left, we sunk the gunwale of that side down to the water's edge, by which we raised the broken side an inch and more out of it. . . . Carefully and steadily sitting, and gently paddling, many hundreds yards, we landed safely. . . .

John Joseph Henry, with the Arnold expedition on the Chaudière River, from diary entry of October 11, 1775, in Henry, Account of Arnold's Campaign against Quebec, *p. 39.*

We now found it necessary to erect a building for the reception of our sick, who had now increased to a very formidable number. A block house was erected and christened by the name of Arnold's Hospital, and no sooner finished than filled. Not far from this was a small bush hut provisionally constructed by Morgan's division of riflemen, who were gone forward. In this they left a young gentleman by name Irvin, a native of Pennsylvania. . . . The case of this young gentleman was truly deplorable. In the first of our march from

Cambridge, he was tormented with a dysentery, for which he never paid any medical attention. When he came to wading in the water every day, then lodging on the ground at night, it kept him in a most violent rheumatism I ever saw, . . . every joint in his extremities inflexible and swelled to an enormous size. . . .

Isaac Senter, physician from Londonderry, New Hampshire, who had been studying medicine in Newport, Rhode Island, when the war began, now on the Kennebec River with the Arnold expedition to Quebec, from diary entry of October 16, 1775, in Senter, The Journal of Isaac Senter, *pp. 11–12.*

Several of the men towards evening were ready to give up any thoughts of ever arriving at the desired haven. Hunger and fatigue had so much the ascendancy over many of the poor fellows, added to their despair of arrival, that some of them were left in the river, nor were heard of afterwards. In turn with Col. Greene, I carried the compass the greater part of this day. In this condition we proceeded with as little knowledge of where we were or where we should get to, as if we had been in the unknown interior of Africa, or the deserts of Arabia.

Dr. Isaac Senter, from diary entry written during the Quebec expedition, October 30, 1775, in Henry Steele Commager, ed., The Spirit of 'Seventy Six, *vol. 1, p. 199.*

. . . In a very misrabel Sittuation / nothing to eat but dogs / hear we killed a nother and cooked / I got sum of that by good [luck] with the head of a Squirll with a parsol of Candill wicks boyled up to gether wich made very fine Supe without Salt / hear on this we made a nobel feast without bread or Salt thinking it was the best that ever I eat & so went to Sleep contented. . . .

Volunteer soldier Jeremiah Greenman from Newport, Rhode Island, then on the Chaudière River with the Arnold expedition, from diary entry of November 1, 1775, in Greenman, Diary of a Common Soldier in the American Revolution, 1775–1783, *p. 18.*

We live my Friend in a most important Age, wch demands that every Moment should be improvd to some serious Purpose. It is the Age of George the Third, and to do Justice to our *most gracious King,* I will affirm it as my opinion, that his Councils and Administration will necessarily produce the grandest Revolutions the

World has ever seen.... Events succeed each other so rapidly, that the most industrious and able politicians can scarcely improve them to the full Purposes for which they seem to be designd. You must send your best Men here [Congress]; therefore recall me from this Service. Men of moderate abilities, especially when weakened with Age are not fit to be employd in *founding Empires.*

Samuel Adams, from a letter written in Philadelphia, November 4, 1775, to James Warren, in Harry Alonzo Cushing, ed., The Writings of Samuel Adams, *vol. 3, pp. 234–235.*

Sir: At a time when some of our Seaport Towns are cruelly and Wantonly laid in Ashes; and ruin and Devastation denounced against others.... When General Howe by Proclamation, under the threat of Military Execution, has forbid the Inhabitants of Boston to leave the Town without his permission.... When by another proclamation he strictly forbids any person's bringing out of that place more than Five pounds Sterlg. of their property in Specie ... and when by a third Proclamation, (after the inhabitants no alternative) he calls upon them to take Arms, under Officers of his appointing; 'tis evident, that the most Tyrannical, and cruel system is adopted for the destruction of the rights, and liberties of this Continent, that ever disgraced the most despotick Ministry, and ought to be opposed by every Means in our Power.

George Washington, from a letter written at Cambridge, Massachusetts, to Brig. Gen. John Sullivan, November 5, 1775, in John C. Fitzpatrick, ed., The Writings of George Washington, *vol. 4, p. 67.*

... things were now hurried with all possible speed. The enemy had advantageously posted two vessels of war in the river, in order to obstruct our passing the river to the Plains of Abraham. The mechanicks had now finished their works. Ladders, lannuts, &c., were in readiness for crossing.... 2 o'clock at night assembled at a certain place ... when the boats were to be drawn from the cave of the Chandiere [sic] to receive us.... The canoes were but few in number; therefore were obliged to cross and return three times ere the army got over. The night being exceeding dark, every thing was conducted with the utmost secrecy, no lights, no noise.... I went in the first division, and in the Pilot boat, in which was General Arnold, Captain Morgan with some riflemen, and one boat

load of savages, with others to the amount of six boats. Crossed between the two vessels, notwithstanding the armed barges were plying every hour from ship to ship....

Isaac Senter, physician with the Arnold expedition to Quebec, describing crossing the St. Lawrence River to Wolfe's Cove, from diary entry of November 13, 1775, in Senter, The Journal of Isaac Senter, *pp. 26–27.*

He [Burke] next considered the proposition for repealing all the acts since 1763. This he showed to be impossible without ruining the whole system of the trade laws, and some of those laws also, which are extremely beneficial to America. That all the laws which leaned upon the colonies, and were the cause or consequence of the quarrel, were to be repealed in this bill, which made provision likewise for authorizing such a negotiation as might tend to the settlement of all those lesser matters to the mutual advantage of the parties. That the congress did not require this sweeping repeal as a preliminary to peace; but that even if it had, he was for treating of peace with and making concessions to the colonies, and not receiving laws from them. That he did not conceive that when the men come to treat of peace they must of course persevere in demanding everything which they claimed in the height of the quarrel. That the cause of the quarrel was taxation; that being removed, the rest would not be difficult. For he denied that the desire of absolute dependency was or could be general in the colonies. It was so contrary to their clearest interests, provided their liberties were preserved, that so far from disbelieving them when they denied such a design, he could scarcely credit them if they should assert it. He then stated five or six capital facts to prove that independency neither was or could be their objective.

Edmund Burke, from a "Second Speech on Conciliation," in Parliament, November 16, 1775, as summarized in the Parliamentary History *(vol. 18, pp. 963–982), from Burke,* Selected Writings and Speeches on America, *pp. 199–200.*

My Lord, after the taking of St. John's I waited but for a fair wind to bring the few troops that were at Montreal to this town in the *Gaspe* and two armed vessels detained there for that purpose. All communication but by water was rendered impracticable by the rebels who had crossed over the Berthier where they were joined by many Canadians. They also crossed over in large bodies with cannon above the town. . . .

Governor Guy Carleton, from a letter written in Quebec to the earl of Dartmouth, November 20, 1775, in K. G. Davies, ed., Documents of the American Revolution, *vol. 11, p. 185.*

The second class of people, for whose sake a few remarks upon this proclamation [of Lord Dunmore] seem necessary, is the Negroes. They have been flattered with their freedom, if they be able to bear arms, and will speedily join Lord Dunmore's troops. To none, then, is freedom promised, but to such as are able to do Lord Dunmore service. The aged, the infirm, the women and children, are still to remain the property of their masters; masters who will be provoked to severity, should part of their slaves desert them. . . . But should there be any among the Negroes weak enough to believe that Dunmore intends to do them a kindness, and wicked enough to provoke the fury of the Americans against their defenceless fathers and mothers, their wives, their women and children, let them consider the difficulties of effecting their escape. . . . Long have the Americans, moved by compassion, and actuated by sound policy, endeavored to stop the progress of slavery. Our assemblies have repeatedly passed acts laying heavy duties upon imported Negroes, by which they meant altogether to prevent the horrid traffic; but their humane intentions have been as often frustrated by the cruelty and covetousness of a set of English merchants, who prevailed upon the King to repeal our kind and merciful acts. . . . Can it then be supposed that the Negroes will be better used by the English, who have always encouraged and upheld this slavery, than by their present masters, who pity their condition, who wish, in general, to make it as easy and comfortable as possible, and who would willingly, were it in their power, or were they permitted, not only prevent any more Negroes from losing their freedom, but restore it to such as have already unhappily lost it?

From the Virginia Gazette, *Williamsburg, November 25, 1775, quoted in Frank Moore, compiler,* The Diary of the American Revolution, *pp. 81–82.*

I am more and more convinced that Man is a dangerous creature, and that power whether vested in many or a few is ever grasping, and like the grave cries give, give. The great fish swallow up the small, and he who is most strenuous for the Rights of the people, when vested with power, is as eager after the perogatives of Government. You tell me of degrees of perfection to which Humane Nature is capable of arriving, and I believe it, but at the same time lament that our admiration should arise from the scarcity of the instances.

Abigail Adams, from a letter written to John Adams, November 27, 1775, in L. H. Butterfield, ed., Adams Family Correspondence, *vol. 1, p. 329.*

. . . We have been till this time enlisting about three thousand five hundred men. To engage these I have been obliged to allow furloughs as far as fifty men a regiment, and the Officers I am persuaded indulge as many more. The Connecticut troops will not be prevailed upon to stay longer than their term (saving those who have enlisted for the next campaign, and mostly on furlough), and such a dirty, mercenary spirit pervades the whole, that I should not be surprised at any disaster that may happen. In short, after the last of this month our lines will be so weakened, that the minute-men and militia must be called in for their defence; these, being under no kind of government themselves, will destroy the little subordination I have been laboring to establish, and run me into one evil whilst I am endeavoring to avoid another; but the lesser must be chosen. Could I have foreseen what I have, and am likely to experience, no consideration upon earth should have induced me to accept this command. . . .

George Washington, from a letter written at Cambridge, Massachusetts, to Joseph Reed, November 28, 1775, in John C. Fitzpatrick, ed., The Writings of George Washington, *vol. 4, pp. 124–125.*

It is an immense misfortune to the whole empire to have a king of such a disposition at such a time. . . . To undo his empire he has but one truth more to learn, that after colonies have drawn the sword there is but one step more they can take. That step is now pressed upon us by the measures adopted as if they were afraid we would not take it. Believe me Dear Sir there is not in the British empire a man who more cordially loves a Union with Gr. Britain than I do. But by the god that made me I will cease to exist before I yield to a connection on such terms as the British parliament propose and in this I think I speak the sentiments of America. We want neither inducement nor power to declare and assert a separation. It is will alone which is wanting and that is growing apace under the fostering hand of our king. One bloody campaign will probably decide everlastingly our future course; I am sorry to find a bloody campaign is decided on. . . .

Thomas Jefferson, from a letter written in Philadelphia to John Randolph, November 29, 1775, in Julian P. Boyd, ed., The Papers of Thomas Jefferson, *vol. 1, p. 269.*

Dear Sir: Your much esteemed Favour of the 22nd Ulto., covering Colonel Arnolds Letter, with a Copy of one to General Montgomery and his to you, I received yesterday Morning. It gave me the highest Satisfaction to hear of Colonel Arnold's being at Point Levi, with his Men in great Spirits, after their long and fatiguing March, attended with almost insuperable Difficulties, and the discouraging Circumstances of being left by near one Third of the Troops that went on the Expedition. The Merit of this Gentleman is certainly great, and I heartily wish that Fortune may distinguish him as one of her Favourites. I am convinced that he will do every Thing that Prudence and Valour shall suggest, to add to the Success of our Arms, and for reducing Quebec to our Possession. . . .

George Washington, from a letter written at Cambridge, Massachusetts, to Gen. Philip Schuyler, December 5, 1775, in John C. Fitzpatrick, ed., The Writings of George Washington, *vol. 4, p. 147.*

My Lord, since my last letter . . . we have advice by the way of Boston that Montreal is in the hands of the rebels, that they were assisted by the Canadians in this attempt and supplied by them with provisions. I have only to add that Canada being in the hands of the rebels will deprive this province of every resource for supplying the army, navy, and the inhabitants of this colony with bread; and the only supplies of provisions are to be had from Great Britain and Ireland. And your lordship will be convinced of the rectitude of the measure of sending the quantity of provision to arrive here early in the spring. . . .

My reason for urging this measure is that the Americans have fitted out vessels of war and have lately been cruising in these seas and intercepted several vessels bound from Europe to Boston. . . .

Governor Francis Legge, from a letter written in Halifax, Nova Scotia, to the earl of Dartmouth, December 5, 1775, in K. G. Davies, ed., Documents of the American Revolution, *vol. 11, p. 202.*

By order of his Excellency General Washington, a Board of General Officers sat yesterday in Cambridge, and unanimously recommended the following Rations to be delivered in the manner hereby directed—Viz: Corn'd Beef and Pork, four days in a week. Salt Fish one day, and fresh Beef two days. As Milk cannot be procured during the Winter Season, the Men are to have one pound and a half of Beef, or eighteen Ounces of Pork pr. day. Half pint of Rice, or a pint of Indian Meal pr Week—One Quart of Spruce Beer pr day, or nine Gallons of Molasses to one hundred Men pr week. Six pounds of Candles to one hundred Men pr week, for guards. Six Ounces of Butter, or nine Ounces of Hogs-Lard pr week. Three pints of Pease, or Beans pr man pr week, or Vegetables equivalent, allowing Six Shillings pr Bushel for Beans, or Pease—two and eight pence pr Bushel for Onions—One and four pence pr Bushel for Potatoes and Turnips—One pound of Flour pr man each day—Hard Bread to be dealt out one day in a week, in lieu of Flour.

George Washington, from general orders issued at Cambridge, Massachusetts, December 24, 1775, in John C. Fitzpatrick, ed., The Writings of George Washington, *vol. 4, p. 180.*

At Quibbletown, New Jersey, Thomas Randolph, cooper, who had publicly proved himself an enemy to his country, by reviling and using his utmost endeavors to oppose the proceedings of the continental and provincial conventions, in defence of their rights and liberties; and being judged a person not of consequence enough for a severer punishment, was ordered to be stripped naked, well coated with tar and feathers, and carried in a wagon publicly around the town—which punishment was accordingly inflicted. As soon as he became duly sensible of his offence, for which he earnestly begged pardon, and promised to atone, as far as he was able, by a contrary behavior for the future, he was released and suffered to return to his house, in less than half an hour. The whole was conducted with that regularity and decorum that ought to be observed in all public punishments.

From the New-York Journal, *December 28, 1775, quoted in Frank Moore, compiler,* The Diary of the American Revolution, *pp. 85–86.*

. . . Not more than an hour had the action continued before the wounded came tumbling in, that the grand ward was directly filled. They continued coming until the enemy rushed out at St. John's Gate and St. Roque's suburbs and captured the horses and carriages, which were employed in the service. . . . Daylight had scarce made its appearance ere Colonel Arnold was brought in, supported by two soldiers, wounded in the leg, with a piece of musket ball. The ball had probable come in contact with a cannon, rock, stone or the like. Ere it entered the leg which had cleft off nigh a third. The other two-thirds entered the outer side of the leg, about midway, and in an oblique course passed between the tibia and fibula, lodged in the gastroennmea muscle at the rise of the tendon achilles, where upon examination I easily discovered and extracted it. . . .

Isaac Senter, physician with the Arnold expedition to Quebec, describing Arnold's wound incurred during the attack on Quebec City, from diary entry of December 31, 1775, in Senter, The Journal of Isaac Senter, *pp. 33–34.*

3 Declaring Independence
1776

A SOUTHERN STRATEGY

As 1776 opened, the British focus for hostilities shifted abruptly to the South. On the very first day of the year, the despised Lord Dunmore, the former royal governor of Virginia who had fled Williamsburg to safety aboard a British ship the previous June, anchored with his small fleet off Norfolk and demanded that the town supply him with provisions. The resident Patriots refused. Dunmore ordered a cannonade of the town that continued into the night, and then he disembarked some of his troops to set afire houses and warehouses lining the shore. The Patriots retaliated by torching the homes of prominent local Loyalists. The conflagration swept through the town, killing three civilians, injuring several, and destroying so many buildings that the local Council of Safety ordered all of Norfolk razed to prevent its use by either Dunmore or the patriots. By early February, the once-thriving commercial center of 6,000 inhabitants stood empty and desolate.[1]

Also in early January, Gen. William Howe, who had succeeded Sir Henry Clinton as British commander in chief and had strained relations with his predecessor, ordered Clinton to take two companies of light infantry and sail from Boston to Cape Fear, North Carolina. At Cape Fear, Clinton was to rendezvous with a fleet arriving from Cork, Ireland, under command of Com. Sir Peter Parker and transporting an army under Charles, earl of Cornwallis. Howe's orders were for Clinton to assume command of this combined military and naval force and use it to secure British authority in Virginia, Georgia, and the Carolinas. He was then to place Loyalists in control of these colonies and to return to Boston.

Clinton arrived at Cape Fear in mid-March to discover that some 1,500 Loyalists had been overwhelmed by Patriot troops at Moore's Creek Bridge, shattering Tory strength in North Carolina and that in South Carolina the Loyalist movement had dissipated, its leaders held prisoner by the Patriots. Parker's fleet in its entirety did not reach Cape Fear until the end of May, and the Clinton-Parker force immediately set sail for Charleston. In late June, Parker's fleet sailed up the channel of Charleston Harbor to bombard the fort on Sullivan's Island in preparation for a British conquest. But some of Parker's frigates ran aground, Col. William Moultrie's fortifications held firm against Parker's cannons, and Moultrie's own cannons, though outnumbered by more than four to one, shelled the fleet with such effectiveness as to render it unfit for further combat. Howe's southern strategy came undone—for now at least. Cornwallis and Parker lingered until late July and then sailed for New York.[2]

THE EVACUATION OF BOSTON

Gen. George Washington, in command of the Continental army from his headquarters at Cambridge, issued general orders on January 1 noting that the day marked the beginning of "the new army." He had hoisted for the first time a "union flag" of 13 alternating red and white stripes. In a little more than three weeks the commander's artillery expert, Col. Henry Knox, arrived with the cannons captured at Fort Ticonderoga. And by mid-February, the restive commander felt ready to take the offensive, convinced that his combined force of 16,000 militiamen and Continentals held a great chance of success in ending the war before General Howe's force of an estimated 5,000 received reinforcements. But Washington's proposal of attack evoked solid opposition at a council of war, and the commander bowed to his officers' arguments that he had underestimated Howe's strength, overestimated his own troops' capabilities, and lacked sufficient powder for Knox's artillery.[3]

Disappointed, Washington agreed to wait. He ordered Knox to emplace the artillery on Dorchester Heights, which for some unaccountable reason Howe had left unoccupied, to erect defenses there, and to prepare for bombarding both Boston and the harbor. At the beginning of March, as the American artillery fired cannonades for three nights to create a distraction, Gen. John Thomas, with 2,000 men, secretly occupied Dorchester Heights and hurriedly constructed fortifications. Anticipating an attack on Dorchester Heights since March 5 marked the anniversary of the Boston Massacre, Washington prepared for a counterattack on Howe's Boston garrison. At the urging of Rear Adm. Molyneux Shuldham, who

Colonel Henry Knox advances with artillery from Fort Ticonderoga. *(Courtesy of Anne S. K. Brown Military Collection, Brown University Library)*

General William Howe and the British forces evacuate Boston. *(Courtesy of Anne S. K. Brown Military Collection, Brown University Library)*

perceived an extreme peril to both his ships in Boston Harbor and the troops in Boston from the cannons emplaced on Dorchester Heights, Howe prepared to attack immediately. But after a violent storm prevented launching the attack, Howe changed his mind, deciding instead to evacuate Boston.

While Howe's troops prepared to leave Boston, both Loyalists and Patriots pleaded with him not to burn the city when departing; consequently, Howe entered into a tacit agreement with Washington to leave the city intact if Washington's forces left the British unmolested. By March 17, the British commander had completed preparations, with 9,000 troops and officers, 1,000 women and children associated with the troops, 1,100 Loyalists, and tons of arms and supplies loaded aboard 125 vessels in Boston Harbor. On March 20, Washington's army occupied Boston to discover the city intact but many homes plundered by the departed British troops. Howe's fleet paused temporarily at Nantasket Roads, only five miles below Boston, as Washington pondered Howe's final destination but assumed it to be New York. Near the end of March, the British fleet set sail for Halifax, Nova Scotia, where the Loyalists would disembark and the ships would be refitted and resupplied.[4]

FAILURE IN CANADA

At the request of General Schuyler, the Continental Congress voted in January to reinforce the Canada expeditions and requested New Hampshire, New York, Connecticut, Pennsylvania, and New Jersey to send troops for this purpose. Congress also authorized Washington to send a battalion from Cambridge and Moses Hazen to raise a regiment within Canada. In addition, in March the Congress appointed Benjamin Franklin, Samuel Chase, Charles Carroll, and the Rev. John Carroll as commissioners to carry word to the Canadians that the American invasion's only intent was to frustrate British plans, that the Americans would provide all possible aid to Canada in achieving independence, that Canadian and American interests were "inseparably united," and that the Continental Congress desired to adopt Canada into the American union. The commissioners began their journey north on March 25.[5]

As April opened, Maj. Gen. David Wooster, who had assumed command of the Continental army in Canada following General Montgomery's death, arrived at Quebec City with reinforcements from Montreal to continue the American siege of the city. He assumed command from Benedict Arnold—promoted to brigadier general by Congress for his services in Canada—who left for Montreal. During April, Wooster positioned batteries on the Heights of Abraham and bombarded Quebec but to no avail, as Carleton returned still heavier fire against the Americans. Wooster's plan to burn British vessels in the city's harbor also failed. In consequence, Gen. John Thomas replaced Wooster on May 1. Thomas discovered, however, that the American force had been reduced to 1,900, with only 1,000 fit for duty, and of these, only 500 were considered reliable. Thomas was besieging a city whose inhabitants outnumbered his troops by 10 to 1. Thomas also discovered that 15 British ships had arrived in the St. Lawrence River bearing Gen. John Burgoyne's army of seven Irish regiments, one English regiment, and 4,300 German mercenaries to reinforce Carleton's garrison. Thomas began preparations to leave. On May 6, with Burgoyne's fleet in harbor, Carleton sallied forth with 900 troops to the Plains of Abraham, and Thomas's troops fled in panic, abandoning 200 ill comrades. Thus, the American siege of Quebec was suddenly aborted.[6]

In mid-May, the American garrison of 400 stationed at The Cedars, about 30 miles west of Montreal, surrendered to a force of 150 British and Canadian troops and 500 Indians commanded by Captain Forster without firing a shot. At the same time, near the mouth of the Richelieu River at Sorel, Thomas's men gathered with other Americans retreating in disarray, and in a council of war, the smallpox-ravaged Thomas and other officers concluded they had no choice but to continue retreating toward Chambly. A few days later, about 100 men led by Maj. Henry Sherburne arrived from Montreal to relieve The Cedars, which was already lost. They fell into an ambush by Forster and surrendered. Forster learned that Arnold was approaching with a relief force and sent Sherburne to tell Arnold that Forster would turn his prisoners over to the Indians if Arnold attacked. In negotiations Arnold agreed to accept the prisoners and return to Montreal.[7]

In early June, Gen. John Sullivan sent 2,000 troops under command of Gen. William Thompson to cross the St. Lawrence River and attack the British stronghold at Trois-Rivières, halfway between Montreal and Quebec. Thompson crossed at night, left 250 men to guard his boats, and set out at 3:00 A.M. on June 8 intending a surprise attack; but, misled by their guide, his men became mired in a swamp, emerging to reach the shore at daybreak only to be fired on by British vessels. They sought safety in a woods but mired again in a swamp and became separated. Thompson and his main force finally reached Trois-Rivières but confronted solid entrenchments. Unbeknownst to them, many of Burgoyne's troops had already arrived, so heavy fire met their attack and sent them scurrying for safety into a woods and then into flight toward Sorel, pursued by Indians and Canadian irregulars. Not wanting the Americans as prisoners, Carleton allowed them to cross the bridge at Rivière du Loup and reach Sorel; 236 of the Americans nevertheless surrendered, and another 400 died, strayed, or fell into enemy hands in their effort to escape.

In mid-June, General Sullivan ordered a retreat from Sorel to Lake Champlain, transporting 2,500 men by bateaux—the British arrived in Sorel an hour after the withdrawal. Arnold joined Sullivan in retreat at Île aux Nois. Many of their 8,000 men suffered from smallpox, dysentery, or malaria, and all succumbed to exhaustion, hunger, and demoralization. After rowing the length of Lake Champlain, they reached safety on July 7 at Crown Point—3,000 needed hospitalization. Some 5,000 of their fellows remained behind in Canada as casualties. Disaster thus terminated the American invasion of Canada. Its final chapter played out in October, when Carleton's fleet of five ships and 20 gunboats pounded Arnold's so badly in battle on Lake Champlain that Arnold had to withdraw his surviving ships all the way back to Ticonderoga, losing 11 of his 16 vessels.[8]

THE DECLARATION OF INDEPENDENCE

As the war proceeded in the South, in Boston, and in Canada, the Continental Congress convened at the State House (now called Independence Hall) in Philadelphia, where delegates began to consider the issue of American independence from Great Britain. Already in early January, New Hampshire became

This shows an exterior view of Independence Hall. *(Courtesy of the National Archives and Records Administration)*

the first of the colonies to establish an independent government, whereas the Maryland Convention had joined the assemblies of Pennsylvania, New Jersey, and Delaware in continuing advocacy of an ameliorative stance that avoided any support of independence for the colonies. At the same time, however, the impetus toward independence received a huge boost with the publication in Philadelphia of Thomas Paine's *Common Sense,* which argued the futility of efforts at reconciliation and strongly urged creation of an independent, continental republic with a constitution that provided governance by a president and a congress. Widely distributed and read, *Common Sense* favorably impressed and persuaded not only such leaders as Adams and Washington, but also tens of thousands of their fellow Americans.[9]

Nearing the end of January, the Continental Congress responded to accusations from George III and the royal governor of New Jersey, William Franklin, that the colonies were pursuing independence by appointing a committee, headed by James Wilson of Pennsylvania, assigned to draft a statement that would prepare the American public for independence. In mid-February, Wilson showed the drafted statement—a labored, 6,000-word address—to congressional colleagues not belonging to his committee. But Congress as a whole tabled the statement, and it was never published, the judgment being that public response to *Common Sense* had obviated the need for such a publication. As February concluded, the Continental Congress for the third time during the month debated, without resolution, the feasibility, or even propriety, of entering into trade agreements with other nations. The question of independence loomed behind their discussions.[10]

That question finally came into focus for the Continental Congress in May. On May 10, Congress adopted a resolution recommending that each of the individual colonies establish an independent government and appointed John Adams, Edward Rutledge, and Richard Henry Lee as a committee to draft a preamble for the resolution's public release. On May 15, following heated debate, Congress adopted the preamble, whose wording, prepared by John Adams, clearly implied that the Continental Congress favored independence. Notably, on the preceding day, Thomas Jefferson, after an absence of four and a half months, returned to serve in Congress as a delegate from Virginia. Thus, May proved pivotal to the Continental Congress's open shift toward declaring independence.

With a mandate from the Virginia Convention, and spurred by his own outrage over British treaties with the German states to provide mercenaries to fight the Americans, Richard Henry Lee on June 7 introduced a resolution in Congress that called for American independence. The resolution contained three proposals, the first beginning with the words "That these United Colonies are, and of right ought to be free and independent states," and concluding that all political connection between the colonies and Great Britain be "totally dissolved." The second proposal favored pursuing alliances with other nations; the third, preparing a plan for confederation to submit to the 13 colonies. The Continental Congress voted to postpone considering the resolution for a day, debated as a committee of the whole on that day, and decided to continue the debate on June 10, when conservatives maneuvered to postpone further consideration until July. But preliminary preparations continued.

On June 11, the Continental Congress appointed a committee—John Adams, Benjamin Franklin, Thomas Jefferson, Robert R. Livingston, and Roger Sherman—to prepare a draft of a declaration of independence. Congress also resolved to appoint another committee to draft a proposal for confederation of the colonies and a third committee to prepare "a plan of treaties" to propose to other nations. Congress made these committee appointments the following day, with the committee on confederation to be chaired by John Dickinson, who would also serve on the foreign treaties committee along with Adams, Franklin, and others. On June 28, the committee assigned to draft a declaration of independence presented for the Continental Congress's consideration a proposed statement written by Jefferson and revised by him in response to recommendations by Adams and Franklin. Debate ensued.[11]

After John Dickinson had spoken in opposition to independence and John Adams in favor, the new delegation from New Jersey arrived on July 1. The New Jersey Provincial Congress had deposed and arrested William Franklin and dispatched delegates to the Continental Congress with instructions to support the three proposals earlier presented by Richard Henry Lee. These new delegates now requested that the arguments in favor of independence be summarized, and Adams complied. The canvass that followed showed only nine colonies firmly in favor of independence. Throughout the afternoon and night, the delegates negotiated, bargained, remonstrated, and maneuvered with one another in anticipation of the crucial vote scheduled for the next day. Richard Henry Lee persuaded Rutledge that he and the other South Carolina delegates should vote in favor if Delaware and Pennsylvania did so.

On the rainy morning of July 2, the Continental Congress assembled and pursued routine business to await the arrival of Caesar Rodney, a delegate from Delaware known to be returning to Philadelphia after a visit home to tend his ill wife. A supporter of independence, Rodney arrived spattered with mud following a furious ride, and the voting proceeded. Delaware supported independence, as did Pennsylvania, South Carolina, and every other delegation except New York, which abstained. Richard Henry Lee's resolution carried by a vote

Delegates to the Continental Congress approve the Declaration of Independence, held by Thomas Jefferson. *(Declaration of Independence, courtesy of the National Archives and Records Administration)*

of 12-0. Congress formed into a committee of the whole to resume discussion of Jefferson's declaration.

Following two days of debate, deletion of one passage that denounced the people of Great Britain instead of its government and another that condemned the slave trade, and modest revisions of wording, the Continental Congress on July 4 approved the Declaration of Independence, with Thomas Jefferson's original wording largely intact. On the following day, in compliance with Congress's directive, President John Hancock began to disseminate copies of the declaration, authenticated by his and Secretary of Congress Charles Thomson's signatures, to the colonies to be publicly proclaimed. On July 8, in Philadelphia, the Declaration of Independence was read for the first time to a large public gathering. Its public proclamation in other cities and towns occurred on following days and to the Continental army in New York on July 9, by order of General Washington. As the Revolutionary War raged on, its most vital and glorious cause seemed now clearly defined.[12]

LIBERTY V. SLAVERY

As noted, however, the original proposal had contained a statement condemning the slave trade, thereby defining a crucial future issue for the American states. With the concurrence of Franklin and Adams and of legislators from Virginia and the upper South, Jefferson, himself a slaveowner and a believer in the inferiority of blacks, had among his many articles indicting King George a lengthy one that excoriated the king for pursuing the African slave trade, outlining the horrors it entailed, and for preventing the colonies from outlawing that trade. But then Jefferson had agreed to the article's deletion at the behest of South Carolina and Georgia. The justly famous words of the Declaration's preamble—"We hold these truths to be self-evident, that all men are created equal"—thus evidenced an apparent hypocrisy and an inherent paradox or dilemma that would plague the future of the new nation.[13]

In at least one recorded instance, the paradox generated a quick resolution. In summer 1777, a Continental soldier from Portsmouth, New Hampshire, Captain William Whipple, wrote that his slave Prince had dejectedly declared, "Master, *you* are going to fight for your *liberty,* but I have none to fight for." Thunderstruck by the validity of Prince's statement, Whipple quickly granted his freedom. (Prince had been one of the oarsmen who rowed Washington across the Delaware River on Christmas night, 1776.) The paradox of liberty v. slavery, and the grim irony inherent in that paradox, profoundly evidenced itself in the Patriots' frequent public declarations equating denial of their own liberty with slavery and invoking Patrick Henry's famous evocation of liberty or death as the only viable choices. As more Patriots perceived the paradox their own rhetoric evoked, growing numbers of slaves might expect to receive freedom in return for joining the struggle for independence.

While the Revolutionary War proceeded, and especially in its aftermath, thousands of slaves received their freedom largely for such reasons as Prince's protest evinced; but the paradox of liberty v. slavery was simply displaced by the contradictory and insidious ideology of racial inferiority inherent in Jefferson's view. Although Jefferson rejected the idea that blacks and whites were equivalently capable and endowed and never freed any of his own slaves, he did nevertheless believe in the basic philosophic truth given voice in that famous line of the Declaration. And his effort, supported by a majority of his contemporaries, to condemn the slave trade in the Declaration had at least introduced the promise of an eventual end of the slave trade and the abolition of slavery.[14]

THE BATTLE OF LONG ISLAND

Convinced that Howe's fleet would head for New York and aware that reinforcements were en route from England, General Washington hastened south in mid-April, ahead of his army, to begin planning resistance to a British attack on the city. The commander in chief feared that if the British gained control of New York, they could totally disrupt commerce and communications between the northern and southern colonies. His surmise of Howe's destination and purpose proved accurate. At the end of June, Howe's fleet of 127 ships, bearing 10,000

Spirit of '76 was painted by A. M. Willard in 1876. *(Courtesy of the National Archives and Records Administration)*

troops, appeared off Sandy Hook. On July 3, the British commander landed 9,300 troops on Staten Island. Howe waited for the arrival of his brother Adm. Richard Howe, commanding a fleet of 150 ships carrying 11,000 fresh troops. The admiral arrived on July 12 and immediately sent five frigates sailing up the Hudson River to Tappan Zee in defiance of American artillery. And on the first day of August, Com. Peter Parker's fleet arrived from Charleston with the 2,500 troops commanded by Clinton and Lord Cornwallis. General Howe now had amassed nearly 32,000 troops (including 8,000 German mercenaries), the largest expeditionary force Great Britain had ever shipped out. Believing that Brooklyn Heights provided the key to the American defense of New York City, General Howe landed a total of 15,000 troops with arms and supplies at Gravesend Bay in preparation for an attack. Against Howe's professional, well-trained, well-disciplined, and well-equipped army, Washington could field only 19,000 largely untrained, undisciplined, and poorly equipped amateurs.[15]

Washington at first had placed Maj. Gen. Nathanael Greene in charge of troops on Long Island, but Greene fell ill, Sullivan took his place, and then in late August, Maj. Gen. Israel Putnam, who knew nothing of the area's topography, received the command. When Washington arrived on the island, he quickly realized that he had underestimated the size of Howe's force and augmented his garrison of Brooklyn Heights to 9,000 men from 5,800. Washington had fortifications extending from Brooklyn to Gowanus Creek and from there to Wallabout Bay, both of the latter sites protected by salt marshes, with a defense line a mile forward of these fortifications that stretched across the wooded Heights of Guan. But there were gaps in this line, and the one at Jamaica Pass, giving access to the Americans' left flank, was guarded by only five men. In the darkness of night on August 26, under orders from General Howe, a force led by General Clinton and Sir Hugh, Lord Percy, marched directly toward Jamaica Pass.

In silence, Clinton's troops, followed by the main army and artillery under Lord Percy, crossed a causeway and Shoemaker's Bridge, encountered no American defense, and before daybreak on August 27 secured control of Jamaica Pass by occupying the heights at the intersection of the Jamaica and Flushing Roads. General Sullivan led 400 men to check the security of Bedford Road, walked straight into Clinton's force, and surrendered. William Alexander, Lord Stirling, moved forward reinforcements to protect the American right as British troops led by Gen. James Grant attacked, but Clinton's men suddenly attacked from the American rear as Hessian troops commanded by Gen. Philip von Heister launched a frontal assault. Totally surprised and greatly outnumbered, the majority of the Americans broke and fled toward Brooklyn Heights, leaving Lord Stirling with about 950 men to hold fast. His retreat closed off, Lord Stirling surrendered to von Heister. The Americans suffered 970 casualties and 1,079 lost to capture, while the British numbered only 400 casualties. Although the Battle of Long Island ended by noon, leaving many daylight hours for pursuit, General Howe halted his troops' advance.[16]

THE BATTLE OF NEW YORK

The day after the battle, Washington ferried across the East River with reinforcements from Manhattan. Prevented from attacking by a fierce storm, the British dug in and prepared for an artillery barrage of Brooklyn Heights. Although at first determined to hold fast, Washington accepted his officers' judgment that the American position on Brooklyn Heights was untenable and ordered his troops to begin evacuating during the night of August 29. By dawn the next day, the evacuation was completed, with 9,500 men and their equipment, horses, and artillery successfully transported to Manhattan. But Washington sent word to the Continental Congress that many of his militiamen had deserted, and he feared that their behavior would spread insubordination among the remainder. The Continental Congress responded with instructions that Washington alone could decide whether to evacuate New York but that, if he chose to evacuate, the city must not be burned.[17]

At the beginning of September, while the pause in battle continued, General Howe sent the captive General Sullivan as an emissary to the Continental Congress to request a meeting with some of the members as private citizens—Howe could not recognize the entire Continental Congress as an official entity. After debate, Congress concluded that it would be improper for any members to meet with Howe as private citizens but authorized a committee to confer with the general and appointed Benjamin Franklin, John Adams, and Edward Rutledge as its members. The committee left Philadelphia on September 9, the very day that the Continental Congress adopted the name *United States of America* for the united colonies. The committee returned from New York on September 13 to report that the colonies must restore their allegiance to the Crown before Howe could consult with them and that their response had been that the Congress could not rescind the Declaration of Independence because it had been approved in fulfillment of their constituents' wishes. The die was now irrevocably cast.

On September 7, Washington called a council of war to discuss evacuating New York, and the council decided on compromise: Israel Putnam's division of 5,000 men would remain in the city, while five brigades under Nathanael Greene would be posted at Turtle Bay and Kip's Bay and 9,000 troops commanded by

The British engage American troops in the Battle of Harlem Heights. *(Courtesy of Anne S. K. Brown Military Collection, Brown University Library)*

William Heath would garrison Harlem. Howe finally renewed the offensive on September 15. Early in the morning, five British warships moved into position broadside to the shore at Kip's Bay; at 11:00 A.M., their cannons began to fire on the American militia entrenchments commanded by Capt. William Douglas. The militia fled in disarray. Then 4,000 British troops sent from Long Island disembarked without resistance and moved inland. Alarmed by the sounds of the ships' cannons, Washington rode south out of Harlem to reconnoiter and encountered Douglas's men in flight. Unable to rally them, the enraged commander flogged officers and privates with his riding crop—to no avail; the troops fled on. Left behind as Hessian troops approached, Washington narrowly escaped death or capture when an aide grabbed his horse's bridle and hastened him away. General Putnam rode into the melee, organized the fleeing troops, and led them in orderly retreat to the west side of Manhattan, guided by his aide-de-camp Aaron Burr. Simultaneously, British troops hastened up the east side of Manhattan, unaware that their enemy's flight paralleled their own movement. The Americans escaped 12 miles northward to Heath's encampment at Harlem Heights, and once again, General Howe halted his troops' pursuit. The routed Americans left behind supplies, artillery, and 367 lost men, nearly all captives.[18]

WITHDRAWAL TO WHITE PLAINS

The Americans now had about 10,000 troops on the plateau of Harlem Heights on a neck of land between the Hudson and Harlem Rivers and about 18,000 further north at Kingsbridge, but of the total only about 16,000 were fit for duty. The British encamped two miles to the south with control of McGowan's Pass, portal to the only road connecting Harlem and lower Manhattan. British troops forced into retreat a reconnaissance of 120 Rangers sent out under Capt. Thomas Knowlton and then paused at the base of the Harlem Heights plateau and taunted the Americans with bugle blasts signaling the end of a fox hunt. Washington sent out both frontal and flanking sorties that drove back the British—a minor vic-

British troops occupy New York City. *(Courtesy of Anne S. K. Brown Military Collection, Brown University Library)*

tory that briefly lifted the Americans' spirits. A fire in Whitehall, a section at the southern tip of Manhattan, apparently set by incendiaries, distracted the British soldiers and sailors, who were ordered by Howe to help stanch the flames, which caused widespread destruction. The British troops were further distracted by the execution of Nathan Hale for espionage on September 22.[19]

They soon returned to action, however. On October 12, General Howe embarked with the bulk of his army aboard 80 vessels to cross the treacherous Hell Gate and disembark 4,000 troops on Throg's Neck with the intention of outflanking the American position on Harlem Heights. As these troops attempted to cross a causeway to Manhattan, musket fire from a small band of Rangers commanded by Col. Edward Hand drove them back. American reinforcements arrived, and both sides began to dig in as Howe disembarked the remainder of his army.

Washington called a council of war to consider how best to respond to Howe's actions. Gen. Charles Lee advised withdrawing the troops to safer positions—counsel Washington heeded. On October 18, the commander began to evacuate his 13,000 troops, with all artillery, baggage, and supplies, northward, many of them destined for White Plains. Washington left 2,000 troops posted at Fort Washington to interdict British navigation on the Hudson River for as long as possible. Howe pursued the offensive, landing troops headed for Pell's Point, a peninsula on Pelham Bay that offered advantages for attacking the Americans. Col. John Glover hastened forward with 750 men to confront the British advance and to protect the Continental army's withdrawal. They repeatedly fired and withdrew, frequently pushing back the British troops until nightfall and then withdrew to Dobbs Ferry. The action cost 21 casualties but afforded Washington time to reach White Plains.[20]

THE CAPTURE OF FORT WASHINGTON

In pursuit of Washington, Howe encamped first at New Rochelle and then at Mamaroneck. Advancing to assault White Plains, his troops encountered Brig. Gen. Joseph Spencer, commanding about 1,500 American troops. Spencer's men fired from behind stone walls to slow the British march. Forced back across the Bronx River, Spencer's men positioned themselves on Chatterton's Hill, where a brigade under Gen. Alexander McDougall reinforced their line; but a British artillery cannonade, followed by a bayonet charge, sent the militia units into panicked retreat, and the remainder of the American force staged an orderly withdrawal to White Plains. On the last day of October, Washington pulled his army back to North Castle Heights and built new entrenchments. On November 5, General Howe concluded that Washington's position was impregnable and withdrew his army to encamp at Dobbs Ferry on the east bank of the Hudson River.[21]

In mid-November, after British ships had handily passed around the sunken hulks and chevaux-de-frise meant to obstruct navigation on the Hudson at Fort Washington, Howe's troops overwhelmed the fort's 3,000-man garrison. The assault cost Howe 450 casualties but gained him 2,858 American prisoners and the fort's artillery, ammunition, and supplies. The American defenders suffered 150 casualties in succumbing to total defeat. A few days later Lord Cornwallis led an attack on Fort Lee. Forewarned by an officer on patrol, General Greene managed to evacuate most of his men safely. Cornwallis pursued Washington—who was retreating with a small force through New Jersey—until Howe ordered him to halt on December 1 at New Brunswick, where Howe would join forces a few days later. Of great concern to Washington, the enlistments of some 2,000 Maryland and New Jersey militiamen expired at the end of November, and they left for home; others from Pennsylvania simply deserted. Now in total control of New York City, most of the Hudson River, and a major part of New Jersey, General Howe and his brother issued a proclamation offering pardons to all Americans who declared allegiance to the Crown within 60 days. Prospects for the Continental army and the American cause appeared alarmingly imperiled.[22]

WASHINGTON CROSSES THE DELAWARE

The sense of peril increased. Washington retreated to Trenton and ordered that all boats along the Delaware River be assembled to ferry his troops across to the west bank. On December 7, Washington led 1,200 troops back toward Princeton and encountered Lord Stirling in retreat before the oncoming Cornwallis. Hastening to Trenton, the Americans crossed the Delaware to safety in Pennsylvania. Unable to follow—the Americans had confiscated all boats within 75 miles up and down the river and destroyed those not needed—Cornwallis received Howe's

Washington prepares to cross the Delaware. *(Courtesy of Anne S. K. Brown Military Collection, Brown University Library)*

permission to halt at the river. Nevertheless, panic swept Philadelphia; many residents packed belongings and fled into the countryside. Washington dispatched Gen. Israel Putnam to impose martial law and to fortify the city. The anxious Continental Congress approved a resolution granting Washington near dictatorial power to prosecute the war and then on December 12 adjourned to depart for Baltimore. The next day, British troops killed or captured all of Gen. Charles Lee's staff officers and took the general prisoner. (Ignoring Washington's wishes, Lee had lingered in northern New Jersey with 5,500 troops.) Both defeat and desperation now menaced the Continental army.[23]

Reprieve blessed Washington in mid-December, as Howe terminated the pursuit, ordered his troops into winter quarters, and granted Cornwallis permission to return to England. Leaving Hessian troops under command of Col. Carl von Donop posted at Amboy, New Brunswick, Princeton, and Trenton and the 42nd Black Watch at Bordentown, Howe returned to New York City with the bulk of his army. Washington encamped at Newtown, Pennsylvania, where reinforcements joined him. The commander in chief called Generals Greene, Sullivan, Mercer, Lord Stirling, Roche de Fermoy, and St. Clair and several colonels into a council of war and proposed a surprise attack, with Trenton as the principal objective. His officers concurred with the plan.[24]

On Christmas Day, three American divisions set forth to cross the Delaware River for the attack on Trenton. Severe weather and ice floes clogging the river caused the division commanded by Gen. James Ewing, embarking at Trenton Ferry, to abandon the effort. Col. John Cadwalader, believing the river impassable at Bristol, marched his division to Dunk's Ferry and managed to cross, but, after failing to get his artillery across, he returned to the Pennsylvania side. The third division, 2,400 men commanded by General Washington and divided into two corps under Greene and Sullivan, assembled at McKonkey's Ferry after dark. Among the troops were seasoned veterans John Stark and Aaron Burr and new recruits John Marshall and James Monroe. Knox brought 18 artillery pieces; Alexander Hamilton commanded one of the batteries. The men clambered into flat-bottomed boats to be rowed across the Delaware River by Col. John Glover's oarsmen from Marblehead. Defying the weather and the ice floes, all, including Knox's artillery, reached the New Jersey bank by 3:00 A.M. and formed for the 19-mile march to Trenton. Sullivan's corps approached the town along the river from the south; Greene's, from the north, was accompanied by Washington. Four cannons preceded each column, with the others accompanying the reserve troops. As day broke the Continentals entered Trenton. Knox placed his artillery at the junction of Trenton's main thoroughfares, King and Queen Streets, as Sullivan's and Greene's troops sealed off other streets and moved to the attack.[25]

The 1,500 Hessians and their commander, Col. Johann Rall, garrisoning the town awakened, many of them stupefied from their Christmas celebration. Unable to organize a defense, they retreated before the American troops. Knox's artillery fire rained death on the Hessians as they raced through the streets, but Rall reformed some of them on the edge of town in an orchard and tried to organize a counterattack. Knox's artillery found them again, mortally wounded Rall, and sent his men into flight. In a fight lasting an hour and a half, the Americans captured Trenton and 900 prisoners; 22 Hessians lay dead, 93 suffered wounds, and about 400 escaped to Bordentown. The Americans counted no dead and only a few wounded, among them James Monroe and Washington's

Hessian troops surrender to General Washington following the Battle of Trenton. *(Courtesy of the National Archives and Records Administration)*

nephew William Washington, both struck by musket balls when they charged and captured a Hessian cannon emplacement. Concerned that his exhausted troops could not withstand an advance on Princeton or a counter-attack without the support of his other two divisions, Washington ordered their withdrawal to the river; they recrossed to Pennsylvania with their prisoners and confiscated supplies. Victory in the Battle of Trenton revived the Continental army's morale and led the Continental Congress to rejoice.[26]

FOREIGN AFFAIRS

Although the Continental Congress had addressed the issue of independence tentatively, it approached the solicitation of foreign support forthrightly, as if the nation and its government were already securely autonomous. The Committee of Secret Correspondence, appointed at the end of November 1775, decided at the beginning of March 1776 to send an agent to France with the mandate to try to obtain supplies for the war effort and also to ascertain how the French foreign minister, Charles Gravier, count de Vergennes, felt about the American cause. They chose Silas Deane as the agent. Deane arrived in Paris on July 7. His dual task may have been eased by the fact that at the beginning of May the count de Vergennes, who had already obtained the Spanish government's support for clandestine French aid to the Americans, secured a provision of funds from Louis XVI for Pierre-Augustin Caron de Beaumarchais to create Roderigue Hortalez et Cie, a dummy company allowing Beaumarchais to pose as a merchant and buy arms and ammunition to ship to America. But Deane's final success would depend on the Continental army's viability, proven by victory in battle.[27]

In June, following consideration of Richard Henry Lee's resolution, the Continental Congress appointed a committee to plan foreign treaties—John Adams, John Dickinson, Benjamin Franklin, Benjamin Harrison, and Robert Morris. It could hardly have been coincidental that Dickinson, Franklin, and Harrison also served on the Committee of Secret Correspondence. With these two

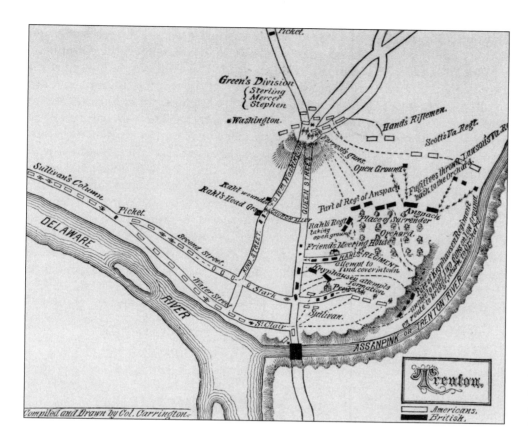

The Battle of Trenton began on
Christmas Day, 1776. *(Courtesy of
Anne S. K. Brown Military Collection,
Brown University Library)*

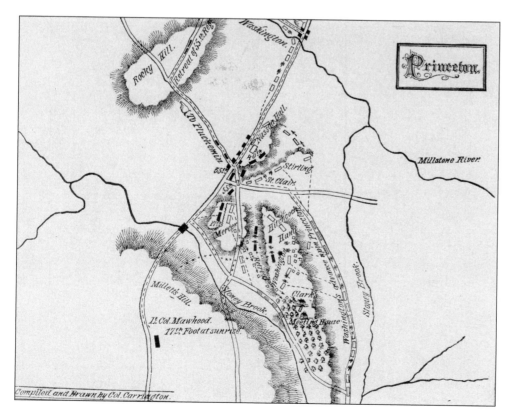

This map details the Battle of
Princeton. *(Courtesy of Anne S. K.
Brown Military Collection, Brown
University Library)*

committees in place, a full-fledged pursuit of supportive relations with foreign nations could proceed more aggressively. In mid-September, the Continental Congress adopted a Plan of Treaties intended to enhance the potential for negotiating a treaty of alliance with France. And in its most important move of all, on September 26 Congress appointed two additional commissioners to send to France with a mandate to negotiate a treaty. The new commissioners were Benjamin Franklin and Thomas Jefferson. The Continental Congress instructed the new commissioners to vigorously pursue a treaty in accord with the Plan of Treaties; to assure the French that the United States would never restore its allegiance to the British Crown; to agree that, if France supported the United States in the war, neither ally would make peace with Great Britain for six months after notifying the other that negotiations were under way; and to request that France immediately supply arms, ammunition, and engineers. Later this mandate expanded to include a request for eight line-of-battle ships and to try persuading other European nations to recognize American independence. Franklin left for Paris on October 26 and arrived in France on December 4, to be joined by Arthur Lee, who replaced Jefferson as commissioner.[28]

CHRONICLE OF EVENTS

1776

January 1: At Cambridge, Massachusetts, General Washington issues general orders for the Continental army; and a new flag for the American colonies, with a field bearing 13 alternating red-and-white stripes, is raised for the first time.

At Norfolk, Virginia, Lord Dunmore, with his fleet anchored offshore, demands provisions from the town. After the Norfolk rebels refuse, Dunmore orders a cannonade launched on the town that continues into the night. Dunmore lands men to set fire to the houses and warehouses lining the Norfolk shoreline; the rebels retaliate by torching the homes of prominent local Loyalists.

At Montreal, Maj. Gen. David Wooster assumes command of the Continental army in Canada, succeeding Montgomery.

January 2: The conflagration begun the previous day at Norfolk continues for 54 hours, sweeping through the city and leaving three noncombatants dead and seven wounded. The rebels' Council of Safety orders razing of what remains of the town to leave Norfolk useless to Dunmore and the Loyalists.

January 5: Delegates meeting in Portsmouth, New Hampshire, decide on independence—the first colony to do so—adopting a constitution that provides for a government with a president and a general court composed of a house of representatives and a senate.

January 6: In Philadelphia, where he had arrived in late 1774 with letters of introduction from Benjamin Franklin, Thomas Paine publishes his rousing pamphlet *Common Sense.*

Alexander Hamilton, native of St. Croix who became a student at King's College in 1773, founds the Provincial Company of Artillery of the Colony of New York in New York City.

In Boston, Gen. William Howe orders Lt. Gen. Sir Henry Clinton to set sail for Cape Fear, North Carolina, directing him to prepare a military and naval attack on Charleston. Clinton is to rendezvous at Cape Fear with Com. Peter Parker, who is commanding a fleet that will arrive from Cork, Ireland, with troops commanded by Gen. Charles, Lord Cornwallis. Howe has ordered this combined force to secure Virginia, Georgia, and the Carolinas and then return to Boston, leaving Loyalists in charge of the subdued colonies.

January 8: During a performance of Gen. John Burgoyne's play *The Blockade of Boston* in Charlestown, Massachusetts, an actor, ironically costumed as a rebel sergeant, announces that rebel troops are raiding the town. The audience assumes he's simply opening the performance. In fact, rebel raiders, led by Col. Thomas Knowlton, take five prisoners, torch eight houses, and return unscathed to camp.

January 10: Still confident of wide support in North Carolina yet judiciously refuged aboard HMS *Scorpion,* Royal Governor Josiah Martin promulgates an appeal to all Loyalists to help him put down the rebellion in the colony perpetrated by "certain traitorous, wicked and designing men," whose property he promises to have confiscated. As he had earlier informed General Gage and the government in London, Martin fully expects that 20,000 Loyalists will come forward, with especially strong support from Scottish Highlanders. He urges these potential supporters to gather near Brunswick by February 15 to join in a British offensive in the South.

January 11: Meeting at Annapolis, the Maryland Convention joins with the assemblies of Delaware, New Jersey, and Pennsylvania to advocate moderation and reject independence. The convention instructs the colony's delegates to the Continental Congress to favor efforts to reconcile with Great Britain and to support any conciliatory proposals from the king or Parliament, while "taking care to secure the Colonies against the exercise of the right assumed by Parliament to tax them, and to alter and change their Charters, Constitutions, and internal polity, without their consent."

January 12: Having taken possession of Rhode Island in December without opposition, British forces now raid Prudence Island.

January 17: A force of 3,000 militia dispatched by Gen. Philip Schuyler arrives at Johnson Hall, the home of Sir John Johnson, a renowned Loyalist and son of the deceased former superintendent of Indian affairs Sir William Johnson. Sir John has assembled at Johnson Hall about 200 Loyalist Highlanders and some Mohawk, along with an armaments supply, and is assumed to endanger Patriots in the area. The militia compels Johnson to disarm his followers, surrender his armaments supply, and accept imprisonment leading to parole under orders of the Congress—in effect, eliminating Loyalist resistance in the Albany area.

January 19: The Delaware Continentals is organized by native Irishman Col. John Haslet as Delaware's only regiment supporting the revolution. Equipped with imported English muskets, the regiments are among the very few American troops with bayonets.

Responding to a letter from General Schuyler brought to Philadelphia by Edward Antil, the Continental Congress approves sending reinforcements to the army in Canada. Antil has been sent from Quebec by Benedict Arnold, who hopes to resume the siege of the city. Antil has already failed to win reinforcements from General Wooster in Montreal, from Chambly or St. John's, and from General Schuyler in Albany. Congress now requests that New Hampshire, Connecticut, New York, Pennsylvania, and New Jersey send reinforcements to Arnold as soon as possible and authorizes Washington to send a battalion from Cambridge and Moses Hazen to raise a regiment in Canada, with Antil serving as lieutenant colonel.

January 20: General Clinton sails from Boston with two companies of light infantry to rendezvous at Cape Fear, North Carolina, with the Loyalists assembled by Governor Martin and a naval squadron, commanded by Commodore Parker, that is bringing troops under Lord Cornwallis. They plan to make a swift incursion into the Carolinas, which they assume will solidify presumed Loyalist support, strengthen the British position,

Henry Knox was Washington's artillery expert. *(From* The Pictorial Field Book of the Revolution, *2 vols., by B. J. Lossing. New York: Harper Brothers, 1851 and 1852.)*

and secure a base for operations in the South—all at minimal output of effort.

January 22–23: Receiving word that a British supply ship, HMS *Blue Mountain Valley,* lies off the coast, the Committee of Safety of Elizabethtown, New Jersey, authorizes its capture. Volunteers manning four small craft sight the ship about 40 miles out from Sandy Hook, New York. The British assume that the Americans are fishermen and allow them alongside. The rebels seize the ship in a surprise attack.

January 24: Col. Henry Knox, Washington's artillery expert, arrives at Cambridge with the guns captured at Fort Ticonderoga. (Washington sent him to retrieve the guns in November to support the siege of Boston.) Without benefit of wagons or roads, Knox's men have transported 44 cannons, 14 mortars, and one howitzer across nearly 300 miles. They used flat-bottom scows to convey the guns across Lake George; specially built sleds to cross snow, ice, hills, and frozen lakes; and finally trains pulled by horses and oxen.

The Continental Congress, responding to charges by the king and by Gov. William Franklin of New Jersey that the colonies seek independence, appoints a committee to draft a statement to prepare the American public for the prospect of independence from Great Britain. Chaired by James Wilson of Pennsylvania, the committee's other members are Robert Alexander of Maryland, James Duane of New York, William Hooper of North Carolina, and John Dickinson of Pennsylvania. Having received news the previous week of the Canadian expedition's failure, the Congress also begins serious consideration of creating a war office.

February 4: Withdrawn from the siege of Boston to recruit volunteers in Connecticut for the defense of New York City, Maj. Gen. Charles Lee arrives in the city after a period of recuperation from a gout attack.

Under General Howe's orders to command the Charleston expedition, Lt. Gen. Sir Henry Clinton arrives off Sandy Hook while sailing from Boston to Cape Fear, North Carolina. New Yorkers, uncertain of Clinton's purposes, react anxiously.

February 6: The militia troops commanded by Col. Robert Howe that forced Lord Dunmore from Norfolk abandon the town after evacuating all the inhabitants to safety, destroying the entrenchments Dunmore's force has built, and burning all the houses and other buildings that remain. Once a thriving commercial center with a population of 6,000, Norfolk now lies totally desolate.

February 7: Col. William Alexander, an American officer who prefers to be known as Lord Stirling, arrives in New York with 1,000 New Jersey troops.

February 13: James Wilson has drafted the 6,000-word address intended to prepare the American public for the prospect of independence. He shows it to other delegates to the Continental Congress besides his fellow committee members. Although straddling the issue of independence, the address concludes strongly, "That the colonies may continue connected, as they have been, with Britain is our second wish. Our first is—*That America may be free.*" Because the reception of Thomas Paine's *Common Sense* has obviated the need for the address, however, Congress tables it without publication.

February 16: Frustrated by weeks of inactivity, Washington holds a war council and proposes taking advantage of the extremely cold temperatures that have frozen over the Back Bay in Boston by sending a force across the bay in a surprise attack on the British. Attacking now, he argues, "might put a final end to the war." But his officers oppose the idea on the grounds that Washington underestimates the British strength, overestimates his own troops' capabilities, and lacks adequate powder for an artillery barrage. They present a counterproposal to seize and fortify a site that will draw the British out of the city for an attack. In the meantime, more powder for the artillery can be acquired. Although disappointed, Washington pursues this proposal and decides to have Knox's artillery from Fort Ticonderoga emplaced on Dorchester Heights, from which the cannons can bombard Boston and its harbor.

February 17: Esek Hopkins, commander of the Continental navy, embarks the small American fleet from Philadelphia and heads for open water through the Delaware Bay. His squadron includes the *Cabot,* the *Alfred,* the *Columbus,* the *Andrew Doria,* the *Providence,* the *Hornet,* and the *Wasp.* Under orders from the Continental Congress to drive Dunmore's fleet out of the Chesapeake Bay, to disperse British ships off the coast of the Carolinas, and to chase the Royal Navy from Rhode Island's waters, Hopkins faces a formidable task—his eight ships mount a total of only 110 guns, while the 78 British ships he must oppose mount 2,000 guns. Hopkins takes advantage of a clause in his orders allowing him discretion to use his own judgment about the best course of action: He sets sail for Nassau, the Bahamas.

The Continental Congress orders Maj. Gen. Charles Lee, currently preparing the defense of New York City, to succeed General Schuyler as commander of the Northern Department.

February 27: Responding to Governor Martin's call, some 1,500 Highlanders and other Loyalists, led by Col. Donald McLeod, approach the coast of North Carolina for the designated rendezvous at Brunswick with Clinton and Parker. Patriot North Carolina militia led by Col. James Moore, with the assistance of Colonels Alexander Lillington, John Ashe, and Richard Caswell, have entrenched at Moore's Creek Bridge, which the Loyalists must cross to reach the coast. After removing planks from the bridge floor, they wait massed 1,000 strong on the east bank of the creek. With bagpipes and drums playing and 80 Scots armed with muskets, broadswords, and dirks in the vanguard, McLeod leads the Loyalists onto the bridge. The Patriots unleash a fusillade, and 50 of the Loyalists, McLeod reportedly among them, fall dead or wounded. The remainder flee, but the Patriots take nearly half of them prisoner. The Patriots' victory, at a cost of only one man dead and another wounded, shatters Loyalist strength in North Carolina.

February 29: During a discussion of commercial trading, members of the Continental Congress, for the third time during February, debate the feasibility and propriety of entering into trade alliances with other nations, principally France and Spain. The debate once again raises the question of independence. The issues remain unresolved.

March 1: Acceding to pressures from New York delegates who support Gen. Philip Schuyler, the Continental Congress reverses its orders of February 17 and restores Schuyler to command of the Northern Department while awarding command of the Southern Department to Maj. Gen. Charles Lee.

March 2: During the night, American artillery bombard Boston from positions at Lechmere Point, Cobble Hill, and Roxbury—a stratagem to distract British forces from anticipating the American occupation of Dorchester Heights.

March 3: The Continental Congress's Committee of Secret Correspondence decides to send an agent to France who will try to achieve two purposes: procuring supplies for the war effort and discerning the attitude of the French foreign minister, Charles Gravier, count de Vergennes, toward the American cause. They select Silas Deane, a former congressional delegate from Connecticut, for the task.

March 3–4: For the American navy's first planned operation, Esek Hopkins sails his fleet into New Providence, the port town of Nassau, the Bahamas, and sends a landing party of 200 marines under Samuel Nicholas to occupy the town; its principal stronghold, Fort Nassau; and another fort. The raid is the marines' first experience of "combat," although they actually encounter no resistance. The Americans seize 71 cannons and 24 casks of powder.

March 4: Under cover of a third night of artillery fire and the concealment of fog and hay bales spread along Dorchester Neck, a force of 2,000 men led by Gen. John Thomas secretly occupies Dorchester Heights and begins to build entrenchments with materials hauled to the site by 360 oxcarts. The men work through the moonlit night—supplanted by a relief party at 3:00 A.M.—digging trenches, erecting barricades, and strengthening breastworks at Nook's Hill and Castle William that surmount the heights. By daybreak, the fortifications stand complete and occupied by five companies of riflemen and companies of other troops who marched over from Cambridge during the night.

Washington expects an immediate British attack on Dorchester Heights and plans a counterattack in Boston. In the view of Rear Adm. Molyneux Shuldham, now commanding the British fleet in Boston Harbor, the artillery on Dorchester Heights so greatly imperils both his ships and the troops in Boston that Howe must order either an immediate attack or a rapid evacuation of the city and harbor. Responding to the admiral's sense of urgency, Howe orders 2,200 men to disembark from the Long Wharf for a night attack on Castle William, begun from the extremity of Dorchester peninsula. Two other regiments—grenadiers and light infantry to be ferried across on flatboats—are to attack simultaneously from the north. Howe's orders specify using bayonets only. But before the troops set out, a violent storm of high winds and heavy squalls sweeps in, preventing the launching of the boats. Meanwhile, at the recommendation of a council of war but unbeknownst to his troops, Howe reverses himself and opts for evacuating Boston. The preparations will begin immediately.

March 7: Georgia Patriots seize Hutchinson's Island across the Savannah River from Savannah and threaten the jurisdiction of Gov. Sir James Wright.

March 9: As the British prepare to leave Boston, the Americans bolster their fortification of Dorchester Heights and station troops on Nook's Hill, which British artillery then bombards. The American artillery responds, but the Continentals withdraw from the hill after suffering five deaths.

Near Chariton Creek, Virginia, in the Chesapeake Bay, militiamen from Maryland and the Maryland ship *Defence* attack and drive off HMS *Otter,* a ship belonging to Dunmore's "navy."

March 12: Gen. Sir Henry Clinton's small fleet arrives off the coast at Cape Fear, North Carolina, where he learns the discouraging news of the Loyalists' defeat at Moore's Creek Bridge and their captivity or dispersal by the rebels. He leads two companies of foot soldiers ashore, sightsees along the coast, replenishes his supplies, and waits for Admiral Parker and General Cornwallis to arrive.

March 17: In response to the pleas of both Tories and Patriots not to burn Boston as the British force evacuates, Howe has arranged a tacit agreement with Washington that the British will leave the city intact if Washington's forces leave the British unmolested, and the last of his supplies and troops come aboard ship this day. A fleet of 125 ships in Boston Harbor awaits the order to set sail. The ships hold 9,000 troops and officers, more than 1,100 Loyalists, 1,000 women and children connected with the soldiers, and tons of arms and supplies. The departing soldiers have fulfilled Howe's orders to seize all supplies in the city that might be useful to Washington and to destroy whatever of these supplies cannot be accommodated by the ships. Violating Howe's orders, the soldiers have also plundered many homes, exacerbating the animosity of Boston's residents. Anticipating that Howe will sail for New York, Washington has been sending Continental army units to the environs of New York to prepare for battle.

March 19: The Continental Congress, which tabled a motion submitted on February 13 by Samuel Chase that would have authorized Admiral Hopkins to seize British merchant ships and encouraged the colonies to outfit privateers—a response to the American Prohibitory Act—responds to public petitions by resolving "That the inhabitants of these colonies be permitted to fit out armed vessels to cruize on the enemies of these United Colonies."

March 20: American troops occupy Boston. The British fleet, however, has anchored at Nantasket Roads, only five miles below Boston, causing Washington and his officers concern over their intentions. But the fleet has paused simply to shift cargoes and to take on fresh water.

The Continental Congress adopts instructions for its commission to Canada—Benjamin Franklin, Samuel Chase, Charles Carroll, and the Rev. John Carroll—to advise the Canadians that the American invasion was intended only to frustrate British plans, that the Americans will assist Canada toward independence in any way possible, that Canadian and American interests "are inseparably united," that Congress wishes to adopt the Canadian provinces into the union of the colonies, and that the Americans "hold sacred the rights of conscience, and . . . the free and undisturbed exercise of their [Canadians'] religion."

March 25: Receiving word from General Washington that the British have left Boston, the Continental Congress directs that, as a token of its thanks, a gold medal be struck commemorating Washington's achievement. Members of the commission to Canada depart from Philadelphia.

March 26: At Charleston, the South Carolina assembly declares a temporary constitution, effectively establishing the colony's independence.

March 27: The British fleet finally sets sail from Nantasket Roads, bound not for New York but for Halifax, Nova Scotia—there to deposit the Loyalists, refit the ships, and take on fresh supplies.

April 2: Maj. Gen. David Wooster arrives at Quebec with reinforcements from Montreal to continue the siege of the city and to assume command from Benedict Arnold. Promoted by Congress to the rank of brigadier general as a reward for his Canada expedition, Arnold, still recovering from his wound and a fall from his horse, departs for Montreal.

April 4: Off the coast of New York, Hopkins's American fleet, having returned from Nassau and with the capture of a half-dozen British ships to its credit, now seizes the small British schooner HMS *Hawk.*

April 5: Hopkins's command ship *Alfred* captures the British brigantine HMS *Bolton.*

April 6: Off the coast near Block Island, Rhode Island, HMS *Glasgow* sails into the midst of Hopkins's fleet after midnight. Throughout the ensuing, fierce three-hour battle, Capt. Tryingham Howe of the *Glasgow* moves boldly with superior seamanship, inflicting 24 casualties while experiencing only four, as its guns also destroy the *Alfred's* wheelblock and rake its deck with shot. As the battle rages, Captain Howe throws overboard dispatches he carries from Gen. Wil-

liam Howe in Halifax that are addressed to General Clinton. Greatly outnumbered and badly damaged, the *Glasgow* manages to escape. Hopkins lamely explains that some 30 of his best seamen were "on board the Prizes, and some that were on board had got too much Liquor out of the Prizes to be fit for Duty."

The Continental Congress finally makes a decision in response to the American Prohibitory Act, which has technically ended foreign commerce with the colonies while also creating a naval blockade of commercial shipping. Congress decides that American ports will be open to trade from all nations except Great Britain and her dominions. Some cautious members continue to voice concern that this decision may propel the colonies toward independence—the very outcome that others, John Adams notably among them, hope for.

April 12: Meeting in Halifax following the rebels' victory at Moore's Creek Bridge, the Fourth Provincial Congress of North Carolina becomes the first among the colonies to officially endorse independence from Great Britain by adopting the so-called Halifax Resolves, which authorize the colony's delegates to the Continental Congress to concur with delegates from the other colonies "in declaring independency" and entering into foreign alliances, while reserving to North Carolina the right to formulate its own constitution and laws.

April 13: After more than a year of immobility at Boston, the main army under General Washington's command marches for New York. Washington oversees the march's start and then hastens ahead, convinced that defending the city against an anticipated attack by General Howe is crucial to the American cause. He fears that if the British secure control of New York and the North River, then they can disrupt vital commerce and communication between the northern and southern colonies. He also knows that Howe's forces in Halifax will be reinforced and that another expedition is en route to America from Great Britain.

April 15: At Providence, Rhode Island, two new American warships, the *Warren* and the *Providence,* are launched.

April 17: The *Lexington,* commanded by Capt. John Barry, engages the British sloop HMS *Edward* in battle off the Virginia coast. British naval experience tells once more, despite the *Edward's* being outgunned by the *Lexington,* which endures a heavy battering and four casualties while severely damaging the British ship's sails and rigging. But the *Edward* finally strikes its colors in surrender, making Barry the first American naval captain to capture a British ship in actual battle.

April 18: Although Com. Sir Peter Parker still remains many days out to sea, the first ship of his long-awaited fleet arrives at Cape Fear, North Carolina.

May 1: The inept Gen. David Wooster's siege of Quebec ends in failure. Gen. John Thomas now relieves Wooster of command. Thomas quickly learns that his new command has been reduced to 1,900 men—only 1,000 of them fit for duty, and a mere half of these being reliable. This small force has laid siege to a city whose residents outnumber them by 10 to 1, but for some reason Carleton's force has remained within the city's walls and never attempted an attack.

May 2: Count de Vergennes has secured assurances of support from the Spanish government for clandestine French aid of both arms and money to the Americans and also approval of his efforts on the Americans' behalf from a reluctant King Louis XVI of France and the comptroller general Baron Turgot, who has been vehemently opposed but finds himself outvoted by the king's other ministers. On May 2, the king directs that Pierre-Augustin Caron de Beaumarchais be provided with 1 million livres to create a dummy company, Roderigue Hortalez et Cie. Beaumarchais will pose as a merchant for the purpose of buying arms and munitions to send to the Americans.

General Thomas learns that a fleet of 15 British ships has arrived in the St. Lawrence River carrying Gen. John Burgoyne, seven Irish regiments, one English regiment, and 4,300 German mercenaries commanded by Gen. Baron Friedrich von Riedesel to reinforce the garrison in Quebec. The American siege of Quebec collapses.

May 3: At the urging of Lord North, George III appoints a peace commission of two members, Gen. Sir William Howe and his brother Adm. Lord Richard Howe, to negotiate separately with each of the colonies. Lord Howe will also assume command of British naval forces in America, and, by the king's directive, the military operations must proceed. Although his dual roles apparently conflict, Lord Howe has credibility for having offered himself as peacemaker in 1774 and for his affectionate regard for the colonies, especially New England. But, by Lord George Germain's devising, the commissioners must invoke one nonnegotiable stipulation: "that no colony should be restored to the

King's peace till it had acknowledged the supremacy of Parliament."

Commodore Parker and Lord Cornwallis arrive off the coast at Cape Fear, North Carolina, although many ships in their convoy still remain well out to sea.

The Rhode Island General Assembly, meeting in Providence, approves an act declaring the colony independent, with designation as the State of Rhode Island and Providence Plantations.

May 6: The British fleet arrives at Quebec. General Carleton, learning that the Americans plan to withdraw from the Plains of Abraham, forms a reconnaissance mission of 900 men, including the first 200 to disembark from the ships, and four cannons. As his mission approaches the American encampment, General Thomas can muster only 250 troops to oppose them. In a panic, the American troops abandon 200 ill comrades and their muskets and artillery and flee to the west. Carleton decides against pursuit and waits for the full complement of reinforcements, led by Burgoyne, that swells the Quebec garrison to 13,000.

The Continental Congress finally responds to Washington's inquiry of March 24 about the course he should follow if a British peace commission arrives in Boston. Congress directs that, in effect, Washington should await events. If a commission is to be sent, the instructions read, then Great Britain will apply for passports of safe conduct for the commissioners, and at that time Congress will decide the appropriate course of action.

May 8–9: Near the mouth of Christiana Creek in the vicinity of Wilmington, Delaware, 13 Pennsylvania galleys attack two British ships, forcing their withdrawal downriver.

May 10: John Paul Jones receives command of the recently launched sloop *Providence*.

The Continental Congress adopts the following resolution, encouraging each of the colonies to establish independent governments: "That it be recommended to the respective assemblies and conventions of the United Colonies, where no government sufficient to the exigencies of their affairs have been hitherto established, to adopt such government as shall, in the opinion of the representatives of the people, best conduce to the happiness and safety of their constituents in particular, and America in general." In addition, Congress appoints John Adams, Edward Rutledge, and Richard Henry Lee as a committee to prepare a preamble for the resolution before it is made public.

May 14: Following an absence of four-and-a-half months, Thomas Jefferson returns to the Continental Congress as a delegate from Virginia.

May 15: The Continental Congress adopts the preamble to its resolution encouraging independent governments for the individual colonies, but only after heated debate because the preamble more pointedly calls for independence than the resolution itself does and sparks greater opposition. Composed by John Adams—according to his own assertion—the preamble reflects his bias for immediate independence for the united colonies. The preamble recounts the king's and Parliament's transgression against the colonies and then asserts that "it appears absolutely irreconcilable to reason and good conscience" for the colonists to take oaths supporting the British government and that it is "necessary" that all authority of the Crown "should be totally suppressed. . . ." It concludes by asserting the necessity that all governmental powers should be "exerted, under the authority of the people of the colonies, for the preservation of internal peace, virtue, and good order, as well as for the defence of their lives, liberties, and properties, against the hostile invasions and cruel depredations of their enemies; therefore, resolved, etc."

The Virginia Convention responds to a deluge of petitions (some angrily denouncing Great Britain) from many of the colony's counties requesting that the colony's delegates to the Continental Congress be instructed to support independence. The convention adopts a resolution that instructs the Virginia delegates to propose that the Continental Congress "declare the United Colonies free and independent States, absolved from all allegiance to, or dependence upon, the Crown or Parliament of Great Britain; and that they give the assent of this Colony to such declaration, and to whatever measures may be thought necessary by the Congress for forming foreign alliances, and a Confederation of the Colonies . . . ," reserving to each colony the power to form its government and regulate its internal affairs.

May 16: Having earlier requested that local families turn in objects made of lead "to be employed in the defence of this country," the Philadelphia Committee of Safety announces that, to expedite procurement of lead objects, a team of four men will go from house to house and pay six pence per pound for objects they receive.

The Continental Congress, apparently convinced that the American Revolution must proceed, sends a request to General Washington to come to Philadelphia "in order to consult with Congress upon such measures as may be necessary for the carrying on the ensuing campaign."

Col. Moses Hazen, left temporarily in command at Montreal while Arnold is away with Gen. Thomas's force, has ordered Col. Timothy Bedel, with 400 men, to defend The Cedars, a small post about 40 miles west of Montreal. Discovering the previous day that a company of 650 British troops led by Capt. Forster approaches, Hazen has left Maj. Isaac Butterfield in command and hastened to Montreal for reinforcements. As the reinforcements, commanded by Maj. Henry Sherburne, are en route, Butterfield surrenders The Cedars without offering resistance after Forster provides assurances that the Americans will be protected from the Indians accompanying the British troops.

May 17: General Thomas and his troops, having encountered other Americans including a regiment from Pointe Levis and a party from Trois-Rivières, assemble as a disorganized mob at the mouth of the Richelieu River near Sorel. Thomas, ravaged by smallpox, and his council of war accept that continuing the retreat is their only recourse. They begin a march toward Chambly along the Richelieu.

Off the coast at Nantasket Roads the *Franklin,* commanded by Capt. James Mugford, seizes HMS *Hope,* a British supply ship carrying entrenching tools and 1,500 barrels of powder to Boston. Enraged by the seizure, the British command in Boston Harbor sends 13 boats bearing more than 200 men to board the *Franklin* during the night. Mugford's sailors, armed with muskets and spears, drive them off, but Mugford is killed during the clash.

May 20: As they approach within four miles of The Cedars, the American relief column of 100 men from Montreal commanded by Major Sherburne falls prey to ambush, forcing their surrender. Their captors execute two of the prisoners.

May 24–25: General Washington confers with members of the Continental Congress on the conduct of the war. Congress appoints a committee of 14—two from Virginia and one each from the other colonies—to devise a plan for carrying on the campaign, and it also approves a resolution supporting recruitment of Indians for service in the Continental army.

May 26: As the British force of 150 English and Canadian troops and 500 Indians that captured The Cedars and Sherburne's troops pauses near Quinze

Chiens, word arrives of Arnold's approach with a relief force. Captain Forster sends Major Sherburne to inform Arnold that, if Arnold attacks, Forster will turn his American prisoners over to the Indians. During the ensuing negotiations, Arnold and Forster agree that Arnold will accept the American prisoners, who can be exchanged later, and return to Montreal.

May 31: The last ships of Commodore Parker's fleet arrive at Cape Fear, North Carolina, and the fleet immediately sets sail for Charleston.

June 1: Maj. Gen. Charles Lee, commander of the Southern Department, sends word to the Continental Congress from Wilmington, North Carolina, that Parker's fleet has sailed, presumably for Charleston, and that he himself plans to leave the next day for Charleston.

With orders to assume command from Maj. Gen. John Thomas, Gen. John Sullivan arrives at St. John's with 3,300 men from New York and there joins forces with Brig. Gen. William Thompson's brigade of four regiments sent by Washington. Supplied with food, ammunition, and arms, Sullivan and his troops expect to launch a second attack against Quebec.

June 2: During the Americans' retreat march up the Richelieu River, General Thomas dies of smallpox near Chambly.

June 4: Gen. Charles Lee arrives at Charleston to an enthusiastic welcome by Col. William Moultrie of the Second South Carolina Colonial Regiment. Moultrie has been overseeing construction of a fort on Sullivan's Island at the entrance to the city's harbor.

June 6: Under Sullivan's orders, Thompson leaves St. John's with 2,000 troops aboard bateaux to attack the fortress at Trois-Rivières, strategically sited about halfway between Montreal and Quebec. Anthony Wayne, William Irvine, Arthur St. Clair, and William Maxwell serve as Thompson's regimental commanders.

June 7: After a delay caused by inclement weather, Parker's fleet enters Charleston's outer harbor and drops anchor. General Clinton begins reconnaissance of the waterways surrounding the city as the American troops hasten to carry out Lee's many directives for accelerating the defense preparations.

Off the coast at Newburyport, Massachusetts, the British frigate *Melford,* commanded by Capt. John Burr, attacks the American privateer *Yankee Hero,* bound for Boston. Although outnumbered four to one, the *Yankee Hero*'s crew gallantly resists the attack for two hours before surrendering.

Richard Henry Lee, with a mandate from the Virginia Convention and spurred by his and other delegates' outrage over British treaties with German states to provide mercenaries, introduces a resolution to the Continental Congress calling for independence. The resolution has three propositions:

> That these United Colonies are, and of right ought to be free and independent States, that they are absolved from all allegiance to the British Crown, and that all political connection Between them and the State of Great Britain is, and ought to be, totally dissolved.

> That it is expedient forthwith to take the most effectual measures for forming foreign Alliances.

> That a plan of confederation be prepared and transmitted to the respective Colonies for their Consideration and approbation.

Congress postpones considering Lee's resolution for a day.

June 8: The Continental Congress meets as a committee of the whole to discuss Lee's resolution but concludes by deciding to resume consideration of the resolution on the following Monday, June 10.

June 8–10: Having arrived at Trois-Rivières, Thompson leaves 250 men to guard the bateaux and sets out at 3:00 A.M. with the remainder of his force, intent on a surprise attack; but, misled by their local guide, the Americans wander into a swamp and become mired down. They finally reach shore near daybreak, endure a shelling from enemy vessels, and seek safety in the woods—only to become separated and mired down in another swamp. Wayne leads 200 men who reach firm ground after 8:00 A.M. and drive off a party of British regulars. Leading the main force, Thompson finally finds solid ground in sight of Trois-Rivières but confronts a line of intervening entrenchments, and many of Burgoyne's 8,000 troops have already arrived on their march up the St. Lawrence. Thompson's force attacks but falls back under heavy fire; their retreat cut off, they scatter into the woods hoping to flee to Sorel; they flounder northward for two days. American hopes of annexing Canada evaporate.

June 9: Recognizing the hopelessness of their position, Arnold and his 300 men holding Montreal hastily abandon the city, cross the St. Lawrence to Longueil, and head for St. John's with the British hard on their heels.

June 10: Under an order Vergennes issued on June 5, Roderigue Hortalez et Cie, Beaumarchais's dummy company, receives 1 million livres in gold coins from the French treasury. The Spanish government, with King Charles III's consent and to fulfill a prior agreement made with the French government, approves another 1 million livres for Beaumarchais.

Conservative members of the Continental Congress succeed in having consideration of independence postponed until July, as the necessary preliminary preparations continue.

June 11: The Continental Congress appoints Thomas Jefferson, John Adams, Benjamin Franklin, Roger Sherman, and Robert R. Livingston as a committee to prepare a draft proposal of a declaration of independence. Congress also approves a resolution to appoint a committee to draft a proposal on confederation and another "to prepare a plan of treaties to be proposed to foreign powers."

June 12: The Continental Congress appoints the committee for drafting a confederation proposal composed of one delegate from each colony, with John Dickinson as chairman, and the committee to plan for treaties with foreign powers, which includes John Dickinson, John Adams, Benjamin Franklin, Benjamin Harrison, and Robert Morris. Congress also resolves to establish a war office, under supervision of a five-man congressional committee, calling it the Board of War and Ordnance.

Meeting at Williamsburg, the Virginia Convention adopts a Declaration of Rights, largely George Mason's work, the first article of which states, "That all men are by nature equally free and independent, and have certain inherent rights, of which, when they enter into a state of society, they cannot by any compact deprive or divest their posterity; namely, the enjoyment of life and liberty, with the means of acquiring and possessing property, and pursuing and obtaining happiness and safety." The other 15 articles affirm the sovereignty of the people, the right of the people to alter or to abolish any government that does not serve them, the need for periodic elections, the principle of due process, trial by jury, a free press, and "the free exercise of religion."

June 14: Ordering a retreat to Lake Champlain, General Sullivan evacuates Sorel and embarks with his 2,500 men aboard bateaux. Within an hour of the Americans' departure, the British fleet arrives at Sorel.

June 15: Thomas Hickey, a member of Washington's Life Guard, and Michael Lynch, a Continental soldier, appear before the provincial assembly in New York City, charged with having passed counterfeit bills.

June 16: Fighting a rearguard action against the British near Chambly, Arnold's force continues retreating.

Having finished his reconnaissance at Charleston, General Clinton dispatches 2,000 regulars and 500 seamen to Long Island in the city's harbor, confident they can wade across from there to attack Sullivan's Island under cover of a bombardment from Parker's ships. But much to Clinton's dismay, the troops discover in the breach between the two islands deep potholes that prevent their passage across.

June 17: The Continental Congress receives the news in Philadelphia of the disastrous defeat at Trois-Rivières and instructs Washington to place Gen. Horatio Gates in command of American troops in Canada—those troops, of course, being in rapid retreat homeward.

June 21: The bragging of defendants Thomas Hickey and Michael Lynch about their involvement reveals an ostensible plot to abduct or assassinate Washington, apparently masterminded by Governor Tryon, acting through paid agents in New York from aboard his warship-refuge in the city's harbor.

After deposing and arresting royal governor William Franklin, the New Jersey Provincial Congress sends a new delegation to the Continental Congress—Richard Stockton, Abraham Clark, John Hart, Francis Hopkins, and Dr. John Witherspoon—instructed to support, at their own discretion, the resolutions for declaring independence, creating a confederation, and forming treaties with foreign nations.

June 24: Arnold's and Sullivan's forces, now combined in retreat, pause at Île aux Noix. Although numbering 8,000, the majority of the troops suffer from smallpox, dysentery, or malaria, and all experience such extreme exhaustion, hunger, and demoralization after their defeat and flight that they barely manage to repulse even a modest probe by a British advance guard. Accepting the Canada expedition's final failure, Sullivan orders that the retreat continue.

June 26: The court-martial of Thomas Hickey in New York judges him guilty of mutiny and sedition and sentences him to be hanged.

June 28: In a public execution witnessed by 20,000 spectators, including, by Washington's orders, all the Continentals in New York not on duty, Thomas Hickey is hanged in a field near Bowery Lane just before noon.

Commodore Parker's fleet of nine ships, including two mounting 50 guns each, sails up the channel of Charleston Harbor with orders for three of the frigates to pass by Sullivan's Island and bombard the island's fort from the southwest, the fort's incomplete side, while the remaining ships attack from the southeast. But the frigates run aground, dooming the attack by forcing Parker to launch only a frontal bombardment of the fort. One hundred guns rain shells upon the fort, which has only 21 guns to return fire. Col. William Moultrie's fortifications endure, as their composition of spongy palmetto logs and sand absorbs the British cannonballs; Moultrie's cannons inflict heavy damage on the British ships. Low on powder by early afternoon, Moultrie receives new supplies from General Lee and continues the shelling. After nightfall, Parker abandons one of his frigates and withdraws the remainder of his fleet, now unfit for further combat. Parker reportedly has 64 dead and 131 wounded, while Moultrie's force has 17 dead and 20 wounded. Fort Sullivan's improvised flag, with a blue field bearing a white crescent and the word *Liberty,* still flies.

Meeting in Annapolis, the Maryland Convention votes unanimously to instruct the colony's delegation to the Continental Congress to support a resolution for independence.

The committee assigned to draft a declaration of independence presents its proposed declaration to the Continental Congress. Jefferson, who drafted the original statement, has amended it modestly, following recommendations from Adams and Franklin.

June 29: American sentinels sight a British fleet off Sandy Hook at New York. The mass of ships carrying Gen. William Howe and 10,000 troops from Halifax, Nova Scotia, says one sentinel, resembles "a fleet of pine trees trimmed. . . . I could not believe my eyes." By afternoon, nearly 100 ships anchor in the Hook, where Howe will await the arrival of the rest of his fleet and another fleet sailing from England that his brother Richard commands.

At Williamsburg, the Virginia House of Burgesses adopts a constitution transforming the colony into an independent state. The constitution delineates grievances against George III and then defines a government of three departments: executive, legislative, and judicial. The legislature will be bicameral—a House of Delegates and a Senate—with two members elected by freeholders representing each county in the House and 24 members indirectly elected by the county delegates serving in the Senate. The governor, elected by the legislature, will serve a maximum of three one-year terms. The document also specifies diverse other offices, including delegates to the Continental Congress, their methods of selection, and their duties.

June 30: The remainder of Howe's fleet from Halifax arrives at Sandy Hook, swelling the assemblage to 127 ships.

July 1: Following a debate in the Continental Congress on the issue of independence, the new delegation from New Jersey arrives at Independence Hall and requests a summation of the arguments favoring independence. Prodded by South Carolina's Edward Rutledge, who opposes independence, and New Jersey's John Witherspoon, John Adams provides a summary. A subsequent canvass of the delegates indicates that only nine colonies firmly support independence. An afternoon and night of bargaining, maneuvering, and cajoling follows.

July 2: As a heavy rain falls, the delegates to the Continental Congress assemble in Independence Hall and devote the morning hours to routine business while awaiting the arrival of Caesar Rodney, a delegate from Delaware who has been at home ministering to his ill wife but is known to be en route back to Philadelphia. After a furious ride and splattered with mud, Rodney, who favors independence, arrives at the hall. Delaware votes for independence, followed by South Carolina and Pennsylvania. New York abstains. Richard Henry Lee's resolution carries by a vote of 12 in favor and none opposed. The Congress forms itself into a committee of the whole to resume discussion of the proposed Declaration of Independence.

July 3: General Howe lands 9,300 British troops on Staten island.

July 4: After nearly two days of debate and discussion, the Continental Congress approves a final draft of the Declaration of Independence. The final version of the declaration preserves most of Thomas Jefferson's eloquent original wording. The vote for approval is 12 to none, with New York abstaining. John Hancock signs the declaration as president of the Continental Congress. Congress directs that the declaration be authenticated and printed, with copies to "be sent to the several assemblies, conventions and committees, or councils of safety, and to the several commanding officers of the continental troops; that it be proclaimed in each of the United States, and at the head of the army."

July 5: In compliance with the Continental Congress's directive, Hancock begins to send out copies of the Declaration of Independence, authenticated by his signature and the signature of the secretary of the Continental Congress, Charles Thomas. With each copy, Hancock includes the request that the declaration be proclaimed universally.

Patrick Henry is sworn in as governor of Virginia, following his election to the post on June 29.

Generals Gates and Schuyler arrive at Crown Point, New York.

July 7: After rowing the length of Lake Champlain, the last remnants of Arnold's and Sullivan's force reach refuge at the fort at Crown Point, from which 10 months earlier Gen. Richard Montgomery had set out to conquer Canada. Of the 8,000 survivors of Montgomery's expedition now arrived at Crown Point, 3,000 require hospitalization; they have left behind in Canada 5,000 casualties. General Schuyler orders the entire northern army to withdraw to Fort Ticonderoga, 10 miles farther south.

Silas Deane arrives in Paris, France, on his diplomatic mission representing the Continental Congress's Committee of Secret Correspondence.

July 8: In Philadelphia, the Declaration of Independence is proclaimed in public for the first time.

July 9: At New York, the Declaration of Independence is read to the assembled army by Washington's orders, which state that he "hopes this important Event will serve as a fresh incentive to every officer and soldier . . . knowing that now the peace and safety of his Country depends (under God) solely on the success of our arms."

July 9–10: A brigade of Virginia troops commanded by Gen. Andrew Lewis attacks Lord Dunmore's base on Gwynn Island, Virginia, which the former royal governor has set up with his small fleet and about 500 Tory troops and runaway slaves as a means of keeping a foothold in Virginia. Lewis's cannons bombard the fleet, wounding Dunmore. While some of Dunmore's ships run aground trying to flee, Dunmore and the remainder of his fleet escape. When they cross to the island, the Patriots find many graves and dead or dying victims of smallpox.

July 10: The Declaration of Independence is publicly proclaimed in New York City.

July 12: Adm. Richard Howe arrives at New York with a fleet of 150 ships carrying 11,000 troops to join his brother Gen. William Howe. Two British frigates, the *Phoenix* and the *Rose,* sail up the Hudson River to Tappan Zee, unharmed by the American artillery along the river that is supposed to prevent such an outflanking movement.

The committee charged with preparing a proposal on confederation submits to the Continental Congress the Articles of Confederation and Perpetual Union, drafted largely by John Dickinson. The draft contains 13 articles.

July 15: Because the New York Convention on July 9 adopted a resolution approving the Declaration of Independence, the New York delegates to the Continental Congress now present the resolution to this Congress, making support of the declaration unanimous.

July 16: Lord Dunmore and the remnant of his force begin a raid up the Potomac River, with the apparent intention of reaching Mount Vernon and attempting to capture Martha Washington.

July 21: Parker and Clinton abandon hope of taking Charleston and set sail for New York.

July 29: Commanding a force of 2,400 men, Gen. Griffith Rutherford begins an invasion of the Cherokee Nation's territory in North Carolina in an effort to end both Cherokee attacks on American frontier settlements and their alliance with the British. Rutherford's effort is complemented by South Carolina troops commanded by Maj. Andrew Williamson and Virginia troops led by Col. William Christian.

August 1: Commodore Parker's fleet of nine warships and 30 transports carrying General Clinton, General Cornwallis, and 2,500 troops arrives at New York.

August 2: Until now, copies of the Declaration of Independence signed only by Hancock and Thomson have been sent out for the public proclamations. The other members of the Continental Congress now join them in signing a copy of the declaration engrossed on parchment.

August 3: Lt. Col. Benjamin Tupper commands five small boats in an abortive attack on the British ships at Tappan Zee, now numbering five, that three weeks earlier sailed up the Hudson unscathed.

August 7: Off the coast at Portsmouth, New Hampshire, the American privateer *Hancock* captures the British ship *Reward* and brings it into port to unload the cargo, which includes turtles that were to be delivered to Lord North.

August 16: The Americans again attack the British ships at Tappan Zee, sending fire rafts against them, but failing once again. Alarmed by the assault, the commander of HMS *Phoenix* orders the ships to return down the Hudson to rejoin the British fleet at New York.

August 22: With the Howe brothers' efforts to negotiate a peaceful resolution heading nowhere, General Howe decides to attack in New York. Howe's army of 32,000 men includes 8,000 mercenaries from the German principalities of Hesse, Brunswick, Ansbach, Waldeck, and Anhalt-Zerbst, but the Americans refer to all of them as Hessians. Among the most professional soldiers in the world, these troops have the additional advantage of being under the command of the highly experienced Generals Howe, Clinton, Percy, Cornwallis, and Philip von Heister. Mustered against this imposing array of force stands Washington's ragtag army of 19,000. Howe lands 15,000 troops with arms and suppliers at Gravesend Bay on Long Island. In response, Washington sends six regiments to reinforce the garrison on Brooklyn Heights and orders Gen. William Heath, stationed at the north end of Manhattan Island, to be ready to send several regiments under his command there, if necessary.

August 23: Near Bedford Pass on Long Island, American troops commanded by Col. Edward Hand attack a Hessian outpost commanded by Col. Carl von Donop. The Hessians withdraw but counterattack, forcing the Americans to retreat.

August 24: Washington has replaced the ill Maj. Gen. Nathanael Greene with Maj. Gen. John Sullivan in command of troops on Long Island, and now he replaces Sullivan with Maj. Gen. Israel Putnam. Underestimating the size of the British force there, Washington has only about 5,800 troops on Long Island for the defense of Brooklyn Heights, and two-thirds of these men are militia. Expecting a simultaneous attack on Brooklyn Heights and Manhattan, Washington keeps the bulk of his force on Manhattan.

In command of a fleet of schooners, sloops, and gondolas, Gen. Benedict Arnold sets sail from Crown Point ready to do battle on Lake Champlain.

August 25: General Howe augments his force on Long Island with two brigades of Hessians commanded by General von Heister.

August 26: Washington arrives on Long Island and orders reinforcements sent to Brooklyn Heights, increasing the American force there to 9,000. The for-

tifications at Brooklyn Heights extend around Brooklyn from Gowanus Creek and its salt marshes north to Wallabout Bay, also protected by salt marshes. About one mile in front of this line, a forward defense position stretches along the wooded hills of the Heights of Guan, although gaps exist at Gowanus, Flatbush, Bedford, and Jamaica Passes. Only five men stand guard at Jamaica Pass, the access point of the American left flank. General Howe orders General Clinton and Lord Percy to lead a force to Jamaica Pass, and they begin their march after nightfall.

August 27: Moving in silence, Clinton's troops, followed by Percy's main army and artillery, traverse a causeway and Shoemaker's Bridge, so narrow they must proceed in single file. They remain undetected and, before daybreak, occupy the heights at the intersection of the Jamaica and Flushing Roads. Meanwhile, von Heister's Hessians have created a distraction with a diversionary maneuver at Flatbush Pass. Concerned about the security of the Bedford Road, General Sullivan leads 400 men to reconnoiter the site and marches straight into Clinton's army. Sullivan quickly surrenders. Lord Stirling moves up reinforcements and succeeds in defending the American right against an assault led by Gen. James Grant, but Clinton's unopposed troops suddenly swarm over his men from the rear while von Heister's Hessians storm their front. Surprised and outnumbered, most of the Americans flee toward Brooklyn Heights. Lord Stirling holds fast, but the vastly superior British force overwhelms his men and prevents retreat, and Lord Stirling surrenders to von Heister. The Battle of Long Island ends abruptly before noon. American losses include 970 casualties and 1,079 taken prisoner; British casualties number 400.

August 28: Determined to hold Brooklyn Heights, Washington ferries across the East River with reinforcements from Manhattan and assumes command of the effort to strengthen the American defenses. The British, prevented from attacking by a raging northeaster storm, dig in and plan to pummel the Americans on Brooklyn Heights with an artillery bombardment.

August 29: A council of war the previous night has concluded that the Brooklyn Heights position is untenable, so Washington orders his troops to begin evacuating during the dark of night.

August 30: The Americans successfully evacuate Brooklyn Heights before dawn, transporting, without British awareness, equipment, horses, cannons, and 9,500 men to Manhattan. But Washington fears, that

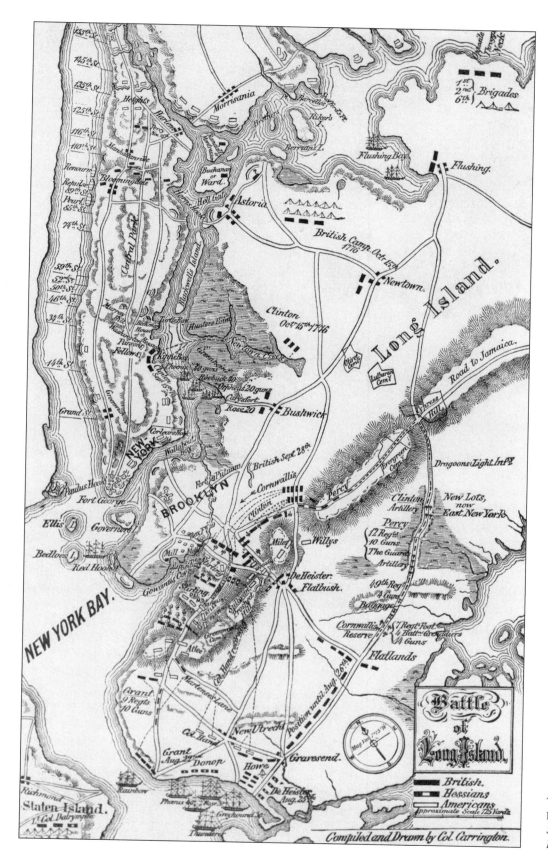

This map depicts the Battle of Long Island. *(Courtesy of Anne S. K. Brown Military Collection, Brown University Library)*

Henry Lee led his own legion in battle. *(From* The Pictorial Field Book of the Revolution, *2 vols., by B. J. Lossing. New York: Harper Brothers, 1851 and 1852.)*

his troops sink with dismay, fear, and demoralization and that the many desertions will infect the remaining soldiers with the desire to sneak away.

September 2: General Sullivan arrives in Philadelphia as an emissary from General Howe to the Continental Congress, bringing a message from his captor that requests a meeting with some of the congress's members as private citizens—Howe cannot recognize the Continental Congress itself as an official body. Congress debates a response to the request.

September 3: Washington receives an answer to his query sent to the Continental Congress: He is instructed not to burn New York if he evacuates the city; whether to evacuate is his decision.

September 5: Following four days of debate, the Continental Congress decides that as "representatives of the free and independent states of America" it would be improper for any of its members to meet with General Howe as private citizens; Congress will, however, send an authorized committee to meet with him.

September 6: The Continental Congress appoints Benjamin Franklin, John Adams, and Edward Rutledge as a committee to confer with General Howe.

At New York, David Bushnell of Connecticut has an opportunity to demonstrate his invention, a "water machine" christened the *Turtle* because of its shape. The craft—constructed of oak timbers that are caulked, bound with iron bands, and coated with tar to prevent leaks—is operated by one man, who submerges it by pulling a hand spring that flushes water into a compartment in the hull and raises it with a foot pump whose action expels the water from the compartment. Hand devices allow the operator to propel the craft in four directions. The *Turtle*'s purpose is to maneuver beneath an enemy ship and attach a bomb (timed to explode after the *Turtle* has moved off) to the ship's hull by using a large screw. Sergeant Ezra Lee, trained by Bushnell, dives under a British ship off Staten Island to screw a bomb to its hull. Failing, Lee withdraws and sets the bomb loose. It floats into the East River and explodes harmlessly.

September 7: Washington calls a council of war to decide whether New York should be evacuated. The council reaches a compromise: Israel Putnam's 5,000-man division will remain in the city; five brigades under Nathanael Greene will be posted at Turtle Bay and Kip's Bay; and 9,000 troops under William Heath will hold Harlem.

September 9: Franklin, Adams, and Rutledge leave Philadelphia to confer with General Howe at New York. The Continental Congress approves a resolution adopting the name *United States of America* for the united colonies.

September 13: Franklin, Adams, and Rutledge return to Philadelphia after a three-hour conference with General Howe and report to the Continental Congress that Howe has stipulated that the colonies must restore their allegiance to the Crown before he can consult with them, but that at present he can only assure the colonies of the British government's good will toward them. The three-man committee has informed Howe that the Continental Congress cannot rescind the Declaration of Independence because it was approved in fulfillment of instructions from the delegates' constituents. Neither side will reverse course.

September 15: During the early morning, five British warships move into position broadside to the shore at Kip's Bay. At 10:00 A.M., 85 flatboats carrying about 4,000 British troops set out from Long Island. At 11:00 A.M., the ships at Kip's Bay begin to cannonade American entrenchments manned by militia under the command of Capt. William Douglas. The militiamen flee. The British troops from Long Island disembark and meet no resistance. Alarmed by sounds of the bombardment, General Washington rides south from Harlem and encounters Douglas's men in confused flight. Washington fails to rally them. General Putnam rides into the melee, reforms the fleeing militiamen, and leads them in an orderly retreat up the west side of Manhattan. They successfully escape 12 miles northward to an encampment at Harlem Heights. The rout costs the Americans 367 men lost, nearly all of them prisoners of the British, as well as hastily abandoned supplies and artillery.

September 16: An American force of about 10,000 men occupies the plateau of Harlem Heights on a neck of land stretching between the Harlem and Hudson Rivers; the remainder of the army's troops are farther north at Kingsbridge. (The entire army now numbers about 28,000, but only 16,124 are considered "fit for duty.") The British control McGowan's Pass, through which runs the only road connecting Harlem and lower Manhattan. Capt. Thomas Knowlton leads 120 volunteer Rangers on a reconnaissance of the British. To their surprise, they encounter light infantry at an advance post and exchange fire with them. A Black Watch troop advances against the Americans' left flank, and Knowlton orders a retreat. The British halt at the base of the Harlem Heights plateau and taunt the Americans. Washington sends forward one force to make a frontal assault and another to outflank the British. Aware of the flanking movement, the British repeatedly fall back as more American troops rush into the fray. The small American victory partially redeems the Kip's Bay fiasco, but the American casualties include two valued officers, Captain Knowlton and Maj. Andrew Leitch.

September 17: The Continental Congress adopts a Plan of Treaties designed primarily to enhance the prospects of negotiating a treaty with France.

September 21: Fire is discovered in Whitehall at the southern tip of Manhattan before 1:00 A.M., but no alarm can be sounded because Washington's army has carried off the city's bells. Other fires break out, apparently set by incendiaries, some of whom the British claim to have captured. Although Lord Howe orders British soldiers and sailors to help fight the fires, extensive destruction occurs. Whoever started the fires, their destructiveness serves the American cause, as some of General Howe's supplies go up in flames and the general is temporarily distracted.

British authorities arrest Nathan Hale for spying. After the Battle of Long Island, Washington called for paid volunteers to spy on the British and try to ascertain their plans and tactics. Hale volunteered out of a sense of patriotism. Dressed as a Dutch schoolmaster, he has slipped behind the British lines on Long Island. But a New Hampshire relative, the Tory Samuel Hale, recognizes him at a tavern and reveals his identity. Documents he carries clearly expose Hale as a spy.

September 22: In the early morning, Nathan Hale confesses and is sentenced to be executed without trial. He writes letters to his brother and to a fellow officer, but the British deny him the visit of a clergyman. At 11:00 A.M., Hale walks to the gallows. With the noose around his neck, Hale calmly tells the spectators that it is a good soldier's duty to obey any order of his commanding officer. A British officer praises Hale's dignity in facing death and reports that his final words were, "I only regret that I have but one life to lose for my country."

September 23: On September 10, the British captured Montresor's Island, a vantage point from which they can land troops above Harlem or flank the Americans at Kingsbridge. Brig. Gen. William Heath later secured Washington's permission to dispatch 240 men under Lt. Col. Michael Jackson to attempt retaking the island. They set out in three boats, with Jackson and the soldiers in the first boat landing near dawn. The British attack immediately, but instead of coming to their cohort's aid, the other two boats withdraw. The Americans suffer 14 losses. When the two boatloads of "delinquents" return, they are arrested and held for court-martial.

General Arnold anchors his fleet in the harbor at Bay St. Amand, about 10 miles south of Valcour Island, in Lake Champlain.

September 26: The Continental Congress appoints Benjamin Franklin, Thomas Jefferson, and Silas Deane (already in France) as commissioners to France, with instructions to make every possible effort to attain a treaty compliant with the Plan of Treaties but also with limited discretion to make concessions. Congress directs them to request France to supply arms, ammunition, and some engineers immediately and to promise the French that the United States will never endorse an allegiance to the British Crown and that, if France joins the war effort, neither nation shall make peace with Great Britain until six months after notifying the other that negotiations are under way.

October 4: Gen. Sir Guy Carleton, now having a total force of 13,000 with the addition of 5,000

German mercenaries, sets sail from St. John's with a fleet of five ships, 20 gunboats, and 28 longboats carrying field pieces and supplies. He has 42 guns to Arnold's 32 and can deliver nearly twice the poundage of Arnold's firepower.

October 11: Carleton's fleet encounters Arnold's near Valcour Island. They exchange a furious cannonade lasting several hours. Carleton lands detachments of Canadian troops and Indians on both the mainland and the island to fire upon the Americans from the shore. At dusk, the shellings end. Arnold's ships have sustained severe damage, his ammunition is three-fourths used up, and he has 60 casualties. Recognizing that resuming the battle is impossible, Arnold chooses to escape during the night. His fleet quietly sails off unseen by the British.

October 12: At dawn, five of Arnold's ships anchor at Schuyler's Island, as the others sailed on ahead. Arnold discovers two of the anchored ships so badly damaged from yesterday's battle that they must be scuttled, and a third ship runs aground. He sets sail with the two remaining ships and rejoins his fleet. Carleton hastens after and finds Arnold at Split Rock. The British capture two ships and another runs aground, but Arnold's ship *Congress* escapes to Crown Point, where the remainder of his fleet has already arrived.

General Howe embarks with most of his army aboard 80 vessels. They pass the treacherous Hell Gate and reach Throg's Neck, where Howe lands 4,000 troops in an effort to outflank the American position on Harlem Heights. As the regulars attempt to cross a causeway and a ford to reach Manhattan, 25 Rangers led by Col. Edward Hand rake them with musket fire and drive them back. American reinforcements arrive, and both sides dig in. Howe lands the remainder of his force.

October 14: Aware that they cannot defend Crown Point, Arnold and Col. Thomas Hartley, commander of the fort's garrison, have the buildings torched and retreat to Ticonderoga. As they are arriving at Ticonderoga, British rowboats under a flag of truce deliver 110 captured American sailors whom Carleton magnanimously paroled. Arnold has lost 80 of his men and 11 of his 16 vessels, but to some positive effect, as Carleton decides Ticonderoga cannot be conquered. He will return to St. John's.

October 16: Washington calls a council of war to decide a response to Howe's flanking movement. Gen. Charles Lee, who recently returned from Charleston, urges withdrawing the army to safer positions.

October 18: Washington begins to evacuate Harlem Heights, moving his army to White Plains. Because Congress wants navigation on the Hudson River interdicted for as long as possible, 2,000 men remain at Fort Washington. As the Americans evacuate, Howe loads his men on transports and heads for Pell's Point, a peninsula on Pelham Bay that affords an advantageous site from which to attack the Americans. Col. John Glover commands 750 American troops, who race into position behind a stone wall in advance of the British march. They repeatedly fire and fall back as the British charge until night falls, when Glover leads his men to Dobbs Ferry to make camp. Glover has 21 casualties.

The Continental Congress grants to Tadeusz Kościuszko a commission as a colonel of engineers. Kościuszko graduated from the Royal School in Warsaw, Poland, and studied at the school of artillery and military engineering at Mezières, France. He arrived in Philadelphia in August and was hired to help plan the construction of forts along the Delaware River.

October 22: Washington's army completes the withdrawal to White Plains.

Col. John Haslet leads about 750 men in attacking the Queen's American Rangers, Maj. Robert Rogers's 500-man corps of Tories. Haslet's men capture 36 of the Tories and some muskets to bring to White Plains.

Tadeusz Kościuszko was trained in engineering in Poland. *(From* The Pictorial Field Book of the Revolution, *2 vols., by B. J. Lossing. New York: Harper Brothers, 1851 and 1852.)*

October 26: Benjamin Franklin embarks from Philadelphia for France. Arthur Lee now serves in Jefferson's place, and the commission has additional instructions from the Continental Congress to procure eight line-of-battle ships from the French court by either purchase or loan and to try to obtain recognition from other European nations for the United States's independence.

October 28: While Washington bolsters his defenses at White Plains, Howe encamps first at New Rochelle and then at Mamaroneck. Howe now launches an attack, but a 1,500-man advance guard led by Brig. Gen. Joseph Spencer, firing from behind stone walls, slows his troops' advance. Spencer's men fall back to avoid being outflanked, cross the Bronx River, and take posts on Chatterton's Hill, where a regiment commanded by Colonel Haslet and a brigade under Gen. Alexander McDougall reinforce them. British artillery bombards the American position, and British troops attack with bayonets. A light dragoons cavalry charge panics some of the American militiamen, who flee, many into death or capture. Haslet holds fast as McDougall begins an orderly retreat. Haslet then joins the retreat to White Plains. The British advance stalls temporarily.

October 31: Washington withdraws his army to North Castle Heights, and the troops begin constructing a new line of entrenchments.

November 4: Carleton's fleet leaves Crown Point to return to St. John's.

November 5: After deciding that Washington's position on North Castle Heights is impregnable, Howe moves his army to the east bank of the Hudson River and encamps at Dobbs Ferry, where reinforcements brought from Manhattan by Lord Percy swell his total ranks to 20,000.

November 7: On the Hudson near Fort Washington, three British ships skirt the sunken hulks and chevaux-de-frise the Americans have stretched across the river to impede navigation—proving the obstruction's ineffectualness. The ships' easy passage seems to obviate the purpose served by Fort Washington and Fort Lee across the river in New Jersey, but the garrisons remain. General Putnam staunchly believes that Fort Washington is impregnable, even though it has only open earthworks and lacks an internal water source, outworks, and barracks.

About 180 rebels, mostly New Englanders, begin to lay siege to Fort Cumberland, Nova Scotia.

November 8: Washington sends a letter from North Castle Heights to Gen. Nathanael Greene, who is in charge of Forts Washington and Lee, advising him that the British ships' passage upriver proves the forts' inefficacy, but he gives Greene discretion to decide whether to abandon them.

November 10: At Fort Cumberland, the rebel leader Jonathan Eddy sends the fort's commander, Col. Joseph Goreham, a summons to surrender.

John Paul Jones, promoted to captain on October 10, sails his ship *Providence* out of Philadelphia. He will ply the sea-lanes from Nova Scotia to Bermuda, intending to capture British ships as prizes.

November 12: Washington visits Greene at Fort Lee to discuss the forts; they make no decision.

November 13: Eddy begins an attack on Fort Cumberland after Goreham rejects his surrender demand.

November 16: Fort Orange, the Dutch outpost on St. Eustatius, fires an 11-gun salute in response to a salute from the USS *Andrew Doria,* flying the red-and-white striped flag of the Continental Congress. It is the first official salute of the American flag by a foreign nation.

In the early morning, Washington, Greene, Putnam, and Mercer row from Fort Lee across to Fort Washington to make a final decision about evacuating the fort. They arrive just as a British cannonade begins, signaling an attack by Howe's army. They turn about and row back to Fort Lee. With his 3,000-man garrison at Fort Washington outnumbered at least three to one, Col. Robert Magaw posts three detachments commanded by Lt. Col. Lambert Cadwalader, Colonel Baxter, and Lt. Col. Moses Rawlings in a ring before the fort. British troops led by Lord Percy and Gen. Edward Matthews and Hessians led by Gen. Wilhelm Knyphausen attack simultaneously. The American line holds for nearly three hours before collapsing. His position hopeless, Magaw surrenders the fort. Although British casualties number 450, they capture 2,858 prisoners and all the artillery, ammunition, and supplies, including hundreds of entrenching tools, at the fort. The Americans suffer more than 150 casualties and a total defeat, brightening British prospects.

November 20: Crossing the Hudson during the night, General Cornwallis, with a force of 4,000 British and Hessian soldiers, arrives at Closter, New Jersey, at daylight and begins an immediate march south toward Fort Lee. Cornwallis intends to block any American attempt to escape toward Hackensack, but a Continental officer on patrol spots the British advance and rides in haste to warn General Greene. Greene sends word to Washington and orders the immediate evacuation of Fort Lee. During their withdrawal, the Americans lose more than 100 men to death or capture, but most make their way to safety. Cornwallis takes possession of the fort.

November 21: Washington leads his small force from Hackensack to Newark. Despite Washington's recommendation to move his men to the New Jersey side of the Hudson, General Lee remains at the North Castle Heights with 5,000 troops. General Heath commands about 3,200 duty-fit troops at Peekskill.

November 28: After five days of rest at Newark, Washington's force breaks camp and marches toward New Brunswick. Cornwallis occupies Newark.

November 29: Washington and his weary, demoralized men arrive at New Brunswick, where they find Lord Stirling with about 1,200 equally wretched troops—some even shoeless and shirtless.

British reinforcements arrive at Fort Cumberland, Nova Scotia, and end the rebel siege. More than 100 rebels surrender and express regret for the siege; Goreham pardons them.

November 30: The enlistment period for about 2,000 militiamen from Maryland and New Jersey expires, and they leave New Brunswick for home; other militiamen from Pennsylvania desert. Believing the American cause now gravely endangered, Washington has no choice but continued flight before Cornwallis's oncoming army.

Seeing an opportunity emerging from recent British victories, William and Richard Howe issue a proclamation at New York that promises pardons to all Americans who declare allegiance to the Crown within 60 days.

December 1: Cornwallis very nearly catches the beleaguered Washington, who spirits his men across the Raritan River and has the timbers supporting the bridge they have crossed destroyed. General Howe orders Cornwallis to halt his advance at New Brunswick.

December 2: General Lee and his troops abandon North Castle Heights and cross the Hudson River to New Jersey.

December 3: Washington's troops reach the Delaware River, whose west bank affords hope for safety. The commander orders that all the boats along the river be assembled to ferry his men across the river.

The first official American flag, known as Congress Colors, is raised on the *Alfred,* Esek Hopkins's flagship, on the Delaware River.

December 4: Carried safely across the Atlantic aboard Capt. Lambert Wickes's *Reprisal,* Benjamin Franklin disembarks at St. Nazaire on his mission to France and other European nations. Accompanying him are his grandsons William Temple Franklin (age 16) and Benjamin Franklin Bache (age seven). William, whose father, William Franklin, is under house arrest after being deposed as royal governor of New Jersey, will serve as his grandfather's clerk.

December 5: The Pennsylvania Associators, a Patriot military organization formed before the war, together with part of Col. Nicholas Haussegger's regiment of Germans from Pennsylvania and Maryland, arrive at Washington's encampment near Trenton, adding some strength to the commander's depleted army.

At the College of William and Mary, the first social fraternity at an American college, Phi Beta Kappa, is founded, with five students as members.

December 6: General Howe joins Cornwallis at New Brunswick and orders him to resume the pursuit of Washington.

The Virginia state legislature, meeting at Williamsburg, incorporates the County of Kentucky.

December 7: With about 1,200 troops, Washington marches toward Princeton, but on the way, he encounters Lord Stirling in retreat before Cornwallis's advance approaches. They return to Trenton.

A combined force of Loyalists and British marauders, called cowboys, pillages Tappan, New York, harassing local Patriots and cutting down their liberty pole.

December 8: Cornwallis's army enters Trenton, but Washington's force has already crossed the Delaware. The Americans have commandeered every boat within 75 miles up and down the river and destroyed those not needed for their escape, so that to pursue Washington further, Cornwallis must first have boats made to carry his men across the river. Washington deploys his troops in a thin line along a 25-mile front on the Pennsylvania side of the river. Cornwallis receives Howe's permission to halt at the Delaware; even so, panic strikes in Philadelphia—where residents pack their belongings and flee into the countryside. Washington sends Gen. Israel Putnam to impose martial law in Philadelphia.

Under orders of General Howe, who finds his insistent advice annoying, Gen. Sir Henry Clinton sails into Newport, Rhode Island, with 6,000 troops and occupies the town.

December 12: Concerned over the British troops' proximity to Philadelphia, the Continental Congress votes to adjourn and reassemble in Baltimore. The delegates approve a resolution awarding Washington virtually dictatorial powers: "... that until Congress shall otherwise order, General Washington be possessed of full power to order and direct all things relative to the department, and the operations of war." In response to Washington's recommendation, they also authorize creation of a regiment of light dragoons, the 2nd Dragoons, composed of a Connecticut light horse battalion that Washington has already recruited, and commission Elisha Sheldon of Connecticut as a colonel in command of the dragoons—the first cavalry unit in the American army.

December 13: Gen. Charles Lee, who despite Washington's counsel has held his 5,500 men in northern New Jersey awaiting an opportunity to attack Howe's army from the rear, falls prey to the British. A British reconnaissance patrol of the Queen's Light Dragoons surprises Lee at White's Tavern in Basking Ridge, and subaltern Banastre Tarleton orders him to surrender or

Charles Lee was a general in the Continental army. *(From* The Pictorial Field Book of the Revolution, *2 vols., by B. J. Lossing. New York: Harper Brothers, 1851 and 1852.)*

they will torch the tavern and put everyone inside to the sword. Lee attempts to escape, but the dragoons kill or wound all of his staff officers and take him prisoner.

December 14: General Howe ceases his advance and orders his troops into winter quarters. Howe returns to New York City with the largest contingent of his army, leaving the Hessian troops commanded by Carl von Donop encamped at Amboy, New Brunswick, Princeton, and Trenton and the 42nd Black Watch at Bordentown. Howe grants Lord Cornwallis permission to return to England.

December 19: Now serving as a volunteer assistant aide-de-camp to Gen. Nathanael Greene, Thomas Paine publishes the first of his American Crisis series in the *Pennsylvania Journal.* Its opening lines declare, "These are the times that try men's souls. The summer soldier and the sunshine patriot will, in this crisis, shrink from the service of his country; but he that stands it *now* deserves the love and thanks of man and woman." Paine recounts the retreat through New Jersey, reports on the status of the army, and praises Washington's steadfastness. Paine wrote his piece on a drumhead by a campfire during the retreat. Washington orders that it be read at the head of every regiment in the army.

December 20: The Continental Congress reconvenes at Baltimore, with fewer than half the members present. Washington writes to the Congress his assurance that he has "no lust after power" and will use the powers granted him only to prosecute the war; he also orders up recruits and militiamen and requests money from the state legislatures.

Maj. Gen. John Sullivan, who has assumed Lee's command, arrives at Washington's encampment at Newtown, Pennsylvania, with 2,000 troops. General Gates also arrives with 500 men from Schuyler's command; Col. John Cadwalader, with 1,000 Philadelphia Associators; and Col. Nicholas Haussegger, with the Maryland and Pennsylvania Germans he commands. But most of these new arrivals are ill, poorly clothed, or otherwise unfit.

Pleased that his offer of a pardon had drawn hundreds of Pennsylvania and New Jersey residents into allegiance to the Crown and consequently convinced that capturing Philadelphia will end the rebellion in the Middle Colonies, General Howe writes to Germain and proposes sending 10,000 men to invade the city. This proposal would change the British strategy, followed since Bunker Hill, of attacking from both Canada and the Atlantic to suppress the rebellion in New England; would force postponement of the planned offensive against Boston from Rhode Island; and would divert troops from the campaign against Albany, New York.

December 21: Benjamin Franklin arrives in Paris, France, joining Silas Deane and Arthur Lee in pursuit of negotiating treaties with European nations and securing loans from France.

December 23: Paine's *The American Crisis I* is issued as a pamphlet.

December 24: Washington calls a council of war at Newtown to discuss his plan for a surprise attack, with the Hessians at Trenton as the primary target. The council of Generals Greene, Sullivan, Mercer, Lord Stirling, Roche de Fermoy, and St. Clair, with several colonels, approves the plan. Washington issues the operation's password: "Victory or Death."

December 25: Three divisions set forth from Newtown to cross the Delaware River. One division, discouraged by severe weather and ice floes in the river, abandons the effort. Another manages to cross at Dunk's Ferry but then, failing to get supporting artillery across, returns to the Pennsylvania side. Only Washington's division—2,400 men in two corps commanded by Greene and Sullivan—succeeds in crossing the Delaware as planned. Col. Henry Knox's artillery brings 18 field pieces. Col. John Glover's Marblehead oarsmen transport them in flat-bottomed Durham boats designed to haul grain and iron ore. Washington crosses in the advance party.

December 26: At about 3:00 A.M., Washington's assembled force begins the nine-mile march to Trenton in a driving sleet storm. About 1,500 Hessians under Col. Johann Rall and six cannons compose the Trenton garrison, but they have no fortifications. The Americans enter Trenton by daybreak. The Hessians awake to total surprise. They retreat before the advancing Americans, using bayonets or muskets as clubs—some have wet firing pans and cannot shoot their muskets. The Americans possess Trenton as Colonel Rall and some of his men reform in an orchard on the town's outskirts to prepare a counterattack, but Knox trains his cannons on the orchard and unleashes a barrage of grape and canister. Rall collapses with a mortal wound, and his men flee. The Americans round up their prisoners, 900 in all, with 22 Hessians killed and 92 wounded. About 400

Washington's artillery and troops rout the Hessian garrison during the Battle of Trenton. *(The Battle of Trenton, courtesy of Anne S. K. Brown Military Collection, Brown University Library)*

Hessians escape to Bordentown. American casualties include no dead and only a few wounded. Washington decides that trying to attack Princeton and New Brunswick without support from Ewing's and Cadwalader's divisions is too risky. The Americans return to their boats and cross the river to McKonkey's Ferry. Washington's stunning victory rattles the other Hessian and British outposts in New Jersey. Von Donop withdraws his troops from Mount Holly to Allentown and orders the Hessians at Bordentown to join him. The troops stationed at Burlington evacuate the town—some moving to Princeton, others to New Brunswick.

December 27: At Baltimore, the Continental Congress rejoices over the victory at Trenton and adopts a resolution extending Washington's "dictatorial powers" and defining them in more detail. Washington has full power to raise more battalions, infantry, artillery, dragoons, and engineers and to appoint all officers below the rank of brigadier general. In addition, the Congress resolves to raise 16 new at-large regiments.

Learning of the Americans' success at Trenton, Cadwalader leaves Bristol, Pennsylvania, and recrosses the Delaware with his 1,800 men. In New Jersey, he receives a letter from Washington expressing regret for Cadwalader's and Ewing's failure to cross the river the previous day and apprising him that the army has returned to Pennsylvania. Col. Joseph Reed persuades Cadwalader that his men want action, and despite the presumed danger, he pushes forward to discover that the Hessians have evacuated Burlington and Bordentown.

December 30: Washington, who embarked the previous day to recross the Delaware, arrives in Trenton. He discovers that Cornwallis and Gen. James Grant have gathered artillery and a force of 8,000 men at Princeton and have sent advance troops now en route to Trenton. Washington sends for General Mifflin's 1,600 Philadelphia militia posted at Bordentown and Cadwalader's troops (now 2,100) at Crosswicks. They bring his force to 5,000 men and 40 cannons. Many of these men, however, lack training and are poorly clothed, hungry, and exhausted; also for nearly half of them, enlistments expire today. Washington addresses those whose enlistments expire and persuades most to remain for another six weeks, offering a $10 bounty as a reward.

The Continental Congress reacts to the report of a committee appointed on December 24 to study means of obtaining assistance from foreign nations by resolving to send commissioners "to the courts of Vienna, Spain, Prussia, and the Grand Duke of Tuscany." Congress's instructions for these new commissioners and those already in Europe are to pursue the help of other European nations in preventing Great Britain from sending more troops to America and to offer in return to France the sharing of the Newfoundland fisheries and any territorial conquests and to Spain the harbor and town of Pensacola.

EYEWITNESS TESTIMONY

1776

This day giving commencement to the new army, which, in every point of View is entirely Continental, The General flatters himself, that a laudable Spirit of emulation, will now take place, and pervade the whole of it. . . . His Excellency hopes that the Importance of the great Cause we are engaged in, will be deeply impressed upon every Man's mind, and wishes it to be considered, that an Army without Order, Regularity and Discipline, is no better than a Commission'd Mob; Let us therefore, when every thing dear and valuable to Freemen is at stake; when our unnatural Parent is threat'ning of us with destruction from every quarter, endeavour by all the Skill and Discipline in our power, to acquire the knowledge, and conduct, which is necessary in War—Our Men are brave and good; Men who with pleasure it is observed, are addicted to fewer Vices than are commonly found in Armies; but it is Subordination and Discipline (the Life and Soul of an Army) which next under providence, is to make us formidable to our enemies, honorable in ourselves, and respected in the world; and herein is to shewn the Goodness of the Officer—

> *George Washington, from his general orders issued at Cambridge, Massachusetts, January 1, 1776, in John C. Fitzpatrick, ed.,* The Writings of George Washington, *vol. 4, p. 202–203.*

. . . It was on this day that my heart was ready to burst with grief, at viewing the funeral of our beloved general [Richard Montgomery]. [General Guy] Carleton had, in our former wars with the French, been the friend and fellow-soldier of Montgomery. Though political opinion, perhaps ambition or interest, had thrown these worthies on different sides of the great question, yet the former could not but honor the remains of his quondam friend. About noon the procession passed our quarters. It was most solemn. The coffin covered with a pall, surmounted by transverse swords—was borne by men. . . . For many of us it drew tears of affection for the defunct, and speaking for myself, tears of greeting and thankfulness, towards General Carleton. . . .

> *John Joseph Henry, then a prisoner of the British in Quebec City (in fall 1776, Henry was repatriated to New York) commenting on the funeral of General Montgomery, from diary entry of January 3, 1776, in Henry,* Account of Arnold's Campaign against Quebec, *pp. 134–135.*

We hope our countrymen will not be at all dispirited at the destruction of Norfolk, but rather rejoice that half the mischief our enemies can do us is done already. They have destroyed one of the first towns in America, and the only one (except two or three) in Virginia, which carried on any thing like a trade. We are only sharing part of the sufferings of our American brethren, and can now glory in having received one of the keenest strokes of the enemy, without flinching. They have done their worst, and to no other purpose than to harden our soldiers, and teach them to bear without dismay, all the most formidable operations of a war carried on by a powerful and cruel enemy. . . .

> *"An American," from the* Virginia Gazette, *Williamsburg, January 5, 1776, in Frank Moore, compiler,* The Diary of the American Revolution, *pp. 94–95.*

Having undoubted Intelligence of the fitting out of a Fleet at Boston, and of the Imbarkation of Troops from thence, which from the Season of the year and other Circumstances, must be destined for a Southern Expedition. And having such Information as I can rely on, that the Inhabitants, (or great part of them) on Long Island in the Colony of New York, are not only Inemical to the Rights and Liberties of America; but by their Conduct and Publick professions, have discoverd a disposition to aid and assist in the reduction of that Colony to Ministerial Tyranny: And as it is a matter of the utmost Importance to prevent the Enemy from taking Possession of the City of New York and the North River, as they will thereby Command the Country, and the communication with Canada; it is of too much consequence . . . to hazard such a Post at so alarming a crisis.

You will, therefore, with such Volunteers as are willing to join you, and can be expeditiously raised, repair to the City of New York . . . to put that City into the best Posture of Defence which the Season and Circumstances will admit of. Disarming all such persons upon Long Island and elsewhere (and if necessary otherwise securing them), whose conduct, and declarations have renderd them justly suspected of Designs unfriendly to the Views of Congress.

> *George Washington, from his instructions to Gen. Charles Lee, January 8, 1776, in John C. Fitzpatrick, ed.,* The Writings of George Washington, *vol. 4, pp. 221–222.*

The object contended for, ought always to bear some just proportion to the expense. The removal of North, or the whole detestable junto, is a matter unworthy the millions we have expended … but if the whole continent must take up arms, if every man must be a soldier, 'tis scarcely worth our while to fight against a contemptible ministry only. Dearly, dearly do we pay for the repeal of the acts, if that is all we fight for; for, in a just estimation 'tis as great a folly to pay a Bunker Hill price for law as for land. As I have always considered the independency of this continent, as an event which sooner or later must arrive, so from the later rapid progress of the continent to maturity, the event cannot be far off. Wherefore, on the breaking out of hostilities, it was not worth the while to have disputed a matter which time would have finally redressed, unless we meant to be in earnest. … No man was a warmer wisher for a reconciliation than myself, before the fatal nineteenth of April, 1775, but the moment the event of this day was made known, I rejected the hardened, sullen-tempered Pharaoh of England for ever; and disdain the wretch, that with the pretended title of FATHER OF HIS PEOPLE can unfeelingly hear of their slaughter, and composedly sleep with their blood upon his soul.

Thomas Paine, from Common Sense, *January 9, 1776, in Van der Weyde,* The Life and Works of Thomas Paine, *vol. 2, pp. 137–138.*

… the Officers who are out inlisting, having reported, that few men who have Arms will engage in the Service, and that they are under the disagreable alternative of taking men without Arms, or of getting none. Unhappy situation Indeed and much to be deplored! Especially when we know, that we have to contend with a formidable Army, well provided of every necessary, and that there will be a most vigorous exertion of Ministerial vengence against us, as soon as they think themselves in a condition for it. I hope it is in the power of Congress to afford us relief; If it is not, what must, what can be done?

Our Treasury is almost exhausted … a constant supply of money to answer every claim and exigency, would much promote the good of the Service; in the common affairs of Life, it is useful: In War, it is absolutely necessary and essential. I would beg leave too, to remind you of Tents and of their importance; hoping if an opportunity has offered, you have procured them.

George Washington, from a letter written at Cambridge, Massachusetts, to the president of the Congress, John Hancock, January 14, 1776, in John C. Fitzpatrick, ed., The Writings of George Washington, *vol. 4, pp. 238–239.*

Thomas Paine was the author of *Common Sense. (From* The Pictorial Field Book of the Revolution, *2 vols., by B. J. Lossing. New York: Harper Brothers 1851 and 1852.)*

Dear Sir: On the 17th. Inst. I received the melancholy Account of the unfortunate Attack on the City of Quebec, attended with the Fall of General Montgomery and other brave officers and Men, and of your being wounded. This unhappy Affair affects me in a very sensible Manner and I sincerely condole with you upon the Occasion. … I am happy to find, that suitable Honors were paid to the Remains of Mr. Montgomery; and our Officers and Soldiers, who have fallen into their Hands, treated with Kindness and Humanity.

… I need not mention to you the great Importance of this Place, and the consequent Possession of all Canada, in the scale of American Affairs. You are well apprized of it. To whomsoever it belongs, in their Favour probably, will the Ballance turn. If it is in ours, Success, I think will most certainly crown our virtuous Struggles. if it is in theirs, the Contest at best, will be doubtful, hazardous and bloody. The glorious Work must be accomplished in the Course of this Winter, otherwise it will become difficult; most probably, impracticable. . . . I am fully convinced that your Exertions will be invariably directed to this grand Object, and I already view the approaching Day, when you and your brave Followers will enter this important Fortress with every Honor and Triumph, attendant on Victory, and Conquest. . . .

> *George Washington, from a letter written at Cambridge, Massachusetts, to Col. Benedict Arnold, January 27, 1776, in John C. Fitzpatrick, ed.,* The Writings of George Washington, *vol. 4, pp. 281–282.*

Some people among us seem alarmed at the *name of Independence,* while they support measures and propose plans that comprehend all the *spirit* of it. Have we not made laws, created courts of judicature, established magistrates, made money, levied war, and regulated commerce, not only without his Majesty's intervention, but absolutely against his will? Are we not as criminal in the eye of Britain for what we have done as for what we can yet do? If we institute any government at all, for heaven's sake let it be the best we can. We shall be as certainly hanged for a bad as a good one. . . . If, therefore, we incur the danger, let us not decline the reward. . . .

> *Letter from a member of the Virginia Convention written February 10, from the* New York Packet, *April 3, 1776, in Frank Moore, compiler,* The Diary of the American Revolution, *p. 99.*

I am now in a very promising course of experiments on *metals,* from all of which dissolved in spirit of nitre, I get first nitrous air as before, and then distilling to dryness from the same materials *fixed air,* and dephlogisticated air. This proves that fixed air is certainly a modification of the nitrous acid. I have, however, got no fixed air from gold or silver. You will smile when I tell you I do not absolutely despair of the transmutation of metals.

> *Joseph Priestley, from a letter written in London, February 13, 1776, to Benjamin Franklin, in William B. Willcox, ed.,* The Papers of Benjamin Franklin, *vol. 22, p. 349.*

The preparations increase and something great is daily expected, something terrible it will be. I impatiently wait for, yet dread the day.—I received a Letter from you wrote at Watertown, and a Book [*Common Sense*] Last week; for which I am much obliged, tis highly prized here and carries conviction wherever it is read. I have spread it as much as it lay in my power, every one assents to the weighty truths it contains. I wish it could gain Credit enough in your assembly to be carried speadily into Execution.

> *Abigail Adams, from a letter written to John Adams, February 21, 1776, in L. H. Butterfield, ed.,* Adams Family Correspondence, *vol. 1, p. 350.*

As the Season is now fast approaching, when every man must expect to be drawn into the Field of action, it is highly necessary that he should prepare his mind, as well as every thing necessary for it. It is a noble Cause we are engaged in, it is the Cause of virtue, and mankind, every temporal advantage and comfort to us, and our posterity, depends upon the Vigour of our exertions; in short, Freedom, or Slavery must be the result of our conduct, there can therefore be no greater Inducement to men to behave well:—But it may not be amiss for the Troops to know, that if any Man in action shall presume to skulk, hide himself, or retreat from the enemy, without the orders of his commanding Officer; he will be *instantly shot down,* as an example of cowardice;—Cowards having too frequently disconcerted the best form'd Troops, by their dastardly behaviour.

> *George Washington, from his general orders issued at Cambridge, Massachusetts, February 27, 1776, in John C. Fitzpatrick, ed.,* The Writings of George Washington, *vol. 4, p. 355.*

You will only preserve the peace you desire, Sire, by preventing it at all price from being made between England and America, and in preventing one from completely triumphing over the other; and the only means of attaining this end is by giving assistance to the Americans which will put their forces on an equality with those of England, but nothing beyond. And believe me, Sire, that the economy of a few millions at present may, before long, cost a great deal of blood and money to France.

> *Pierre-Augustin Caron de Beaumarchais, from a letter written to Louis XVI, February 29, 1776, to be delivered by Foreign Minister Count de Vergennes, in Henry Steele Commager, ed.,* The Spirit of 'Seventy Six, *vol. 2, p. 669.*

. . . Our People I hear will have Liberty to enter Boston, those who have had the small pox. The Enemy have not yet come under sail. I cannot help suspecting some design which we do not comprehend; to what quarter of the World they are bound is wholy unknown, but tis generally Thought to New York. Many people are elated with their quitting Boston. I confess I do not feel so, tis only lifting the burden from one shoulder to the other which perhaps is less able or less willing to support it. . . . I feel glad however that Boston is not distroyed. I hope it will be so secured and guarded as to baffel all future attempts against it. . . .

From Pens Hill we have a view of the largest Fleet ever seen in America. You may count upwards of 100 & 70 Sail. They look like a Forrest. . . .

Abigail Adams, from a letter written in Braintree, Massachusetts, to John Adams, March 17, 1776, in L. H. Butterfield, ed., Adams Family Correspondence, *vol. 1, p. 358.*

Sir: It is with the greatest pleasure I inform you that on Sunday last the 17th. Instant, about 9th O'Clock in the forenoon the Ministerial Army evacuated the Town of Boston, and that the Forces of the United Colonies are now in actual Possession thereof. I beg leave to congratulate you Sir, and the Honorable Congress on this happy event, and particularly as it was effected without endangering the Lives and property of the remaining unhappy Inhabitants.

George Washington, from a letter written at Cambridge, Massachusetts, to the president of the Continental Congress, John Hancock, March 19, 1776, in John C. Fitzpatrick, ed., The Writings of George Washington, *vol. 4, p. 403.*

You ask, what is thought of Common sense. Sensible Men think there are some Whims, some Sophisms, some artfull Addresses to superstitious Notions, some keen attempts upon the Passions, in this Pamphlet. But all agree there is a great deal of good sense, delivered in a clear, simple, concise and nervous Style.

His Sentiments of the Abilities of America, and of the Difficulty of a Reconciliation with G.B. are generally approved. But his Notions, and Plans of Continental Government are not much applauded. Indeed this Writer has a better Hand at pulling down than building.

John Adams, from a letter written to Abigail Adams, March 19, 1776, in L. H. Butterfield, ed., Adams Family Correspondence, *vol. 1, p. 363.*

Proceed, great chief, with virtue on thy side,
Thy every action let the goddess guide.
A crown, a mansion, and a throne that shine,
With gold unfading, WASHINGTON! be thine.

Phillis Wheatley, freed slave and poet, the concluding lines of her poem "To His Excellency General Washington," first published in the Virginia Gazette, *March 20, 1776, at the request of Washington's adjutant Joseph Reed—the manuscript of the poem had greatly pleased the general and elicited a gracious letter of thanks and praise from him to Wheatley, in William H. Robinson,* Phillis Wheatley and Her Writings, *p. 289.*

This morning, about two o'clock, departed my honored and worthy friend, Governor Ward, by the small pox, which he bore with manly and great patience. His loss will be deplored by all true friends of liberty in these colonies, who knew his merits. . . . Dined at home with Thomas Paine. . . . We hear, that on the seventeenth instant, about nine in the forenoon, the Ministerial army evacuated Boston . . . and that they [the British] have left effects by their sudden departure to between Thirty and Forty Thousands Pounds.

Christopher Marshall, Philadelphia merchant, official, and Quaker, from diary entry of March 26, 1776, in Marshall, Extracts from the Diary of Christopher Marshall, *p. 64.*

This morning [March 17] the British army in Boston, under General Howe, . . . after suffering an ignominious blockade for many months past, disgracefully quitted all their strongholds in Boston and Charlestown, fled from before the army of the United Colonies, and took refuge on board their ships. . . .

. . . . .

We are told that the Tories were thunder-struck when orders were issued for evacuating the town, after being many times assured, that such reinforcements would be sent, as to enable the King's troops to ravage the country at pleasure. Thus are many of those deluded creatures, those vile traitors to their country, obliged at last, in their turn, to abandon their once delightful habitations, and go they know not where. Many of them, it is said, considered themselves as undone, and seemed, at times, inclined to throw themselves on the mercy of their offended country, rather than leave it. One or more of them, it is reported, have been left to end their lives by the unnatural act of suicide.

From the Pennsylvania Evening Post, *Philadelphia, March 30, 1776, in Frank Moore, compiler,* The Diary of the American Revolution, *pp. 107 and 109.*

. . . I long to hear that you have declared an independancy—and by the way in the new Code of Laws which I suppose it will be necessary for you to make I desire you would Remember the Ladies, and be more generous and favourable to them than your ancestors. Do not put such unlimited power into the hands of the Husbands. Remember all Men would be tyrants if they could. If perticuliar care and attention is not paid to the Laidies we are determined to foment a Rebelion, and will not hold ourselves by any Laws in which we have no voice, or Representation.

That your Sex are Naturally Tyrannical is a Truth so thoroughly established as to admit of no dispute, but such of you as wish to be happy willingly give up the harsh title of Master for the more tender and endearing one of Friend. Why then, not put it out of the power of the vicious and the Lawless to use us with cruelty and indignity with impunity. . . .

Abigail Adams, from a letter written at Braintree, Massachusetts, to John Adams, March 31, 1776, in L. H. Butterfield, ed., Adams Family Correspondence, *vol. 1, p. 370.*

. . . If the [British peace] commissioners do not come over with full and ample powers to treat with Congress, I sincerely wish they may never put their feet on American ground, as it must be self-evident, (in the other case,) that they come over with insidious intentions; to distract, divide, and create as much confusion as possible; how then can any man, let his passion for reconciliation be never so strong, be so blinded and misled, as to embrace a measure evidently designed for his destruction? No man does, no man can, wish the restoration of peace more fervently than I do, but I hope, whenever made, it will be upon such terms, as will reflect honor upon the councils and wisdom of America. . . . My countrymen I know . . . will come reluctantly into the idea of independence, but time and persecution bring many wonderful things to pass; and by private letters, which I have lately received from Virginia, I find "Common Sense"

is working a powerful change there in the minds of many men.

George Washington, from a letter written at Cambridge, Massachusetts, to Joseph Reed, April 1, 1776, in John C. Fitzpatrick, ed., The Writings of George Washington, *vol. 4, pp. 454–455.*

As to your extraordinary Code of Laws, I cannot but laugh. We have been told that our Struggle has loosened the bands of Government every where. That Children and Apprentices were disobedient—that schools and Colledges were grown turbulent—that Indians slighted their Guardians and Negroes grew insolent to their Masters. But your Letter was the first Intimation that another Tribe more numerous and powerfull than all the rest were grown discontented.—This is rather too coarse a Compliment but you are so saucy, I wont blot it out.

Depend upon it, We know better than to repeal our Masculine systems. Altho they are in full Force, you know they are little more than Theory. We dare not exert our Power in its full Latitude. We are obliged to go fair, and softly, and in Practice you know We are the subjects. We have only the Name of Masters, and rather than give up this, which would compleatly subject Us to the Despotism of the Peticoat, I hope General Washington, and all our brave Heroes would fight. . . .

John Adams, from a letter written to Abigail Adams, April 14, 1776, in L. H. Butterfield, ed., Adams Family Correspondence, *vol. 1, p. 382.*

The designs of the Enemy are too much behind the Curtain, for me to form any accurate opinion of their Plan of Operations for the Summers Campaign; we are left to wander in the field of conjecture, and as no place, all its consequences considered, seemed of more Importance in the execution of their grand Plan, than possessing themselves of Hudsons River; I thought it advisable to remove, with the Continental Army to this City, as soon as the Kings Troops evacuated Boston, but if the Congress from their knowledge, information, or believe, think it best for the general good of the Service, that I should go to the Northward, or elsewhere, they are convinced I hope, that they have nothing more to do, than signify their Commands. . . .

George Washington, from a letter written at New York to the president of the Continental Congress, John Hancock, May 5, 1776, in John C. Fitzpatrick, ed., The Writings of George Washington, *vol. 5, pp. 19–20.*

G[reat] B[ritain] has at last driven America, to the last Step, a compleat Seperation from her, a total absolute Independence, not only of her Parliament bout of her Crown, for such is the Amount of the Resolve of the 15th.

Confederation among ourselves, or Alliances with foreign Nations are not necessary, to perfect Seperation from Britain. That is effected by extinguishing all Authority, under the Crown, Parliament and Nation as the Resolution for instituting Governments, has done, to all Intents and Purposes. Confederation will be necessary for our internal Concord, and Alliances may be so for our external Defence.

John Adams, from a letter to Abigail Adams, May 17, 1776, in L. H. Butterfield, ed., Adams Family Correspondence, *vol. 1, p. 410.*

No Person whatever, belonging to the Army, is to be innoculated for the Small-Pox—those who have already undergone that operation, or who may be seized with Symptoms of that disorder, are immediately to be removed to the Hospital provided for that purpose on Montresor Island. Any disobedience to this order, will be most severely punished—As it is at present of the utmost importance, that the spreading of that distemper, in the Army and City, should be prevented.

George Washington, from general orders issued at his New York headquarters, May 20, 1776, in John C. Fitzpatrick, ed., The Writings of George Washington, *vol. 5, p. 63.*

This morning the Indian Treaty was again Opened. Our great Warrior (Col. [Elias] Dayton) told the Mohawks by the Interpretor that if they offered to take up the Hatchet or oppose his Warriors in their present Expedition He would break the Covenant Chain, He would burn their upper & lower Castles on the Mohawk River, would burn all their houses, destroy their Towns & Cast the Mohawks with their Wifes & Children off of the face of the Earth; on the contrary if they would be still and let us alone in a Family Quarrel [the war with Britain], his Young Men (meaning the Soldiery) Should not come near nor molest their Castles &c.... I believe this had a good effect, these savages cant bear to be supplicated, it makes them think they are of great consequence. The only way is to strike terror into them. This is the way the brave & politic good old Sr. Wm. Johnson used to treat them. Upon this the Indian Chiefs & Warriors withdrew for

one hour, then returned appeared more mild, submissive & peaceable. Said they were determined not to meddle with our Family Quarrell; all they wanted was to be assured Sr. John [Sir William's son and a Loyalist] should not be killed. We might do as we pleased with the Highlanders, upon which our Chief (Col. Dayton) told them not a hair of Sr. John's head should fall to the ground. We loved him also for his Father's sake, what we was a going to do would be for Sr. John's benefit. We should destroy ... Those Indians who opposed us only, after which some friendly speeches past. The Covenant Chain was promised by both to be brightened and the Hatchet buried....

Captain Joseph Bloomfield of the Continental army's 3rd New Jersey Regiment, on an expedition near Johnstown, New York, from journal entry of May 21, 1776, in Mark E. Lender and James Kirby Martin, eds., Citizen Soldier, *pp. 50–51.*

By the present demand for Flints, by some of the Troops, the General has reason to apprehend, that due care has not been taken of those lately deliver'd to the Soldiers, who have had no occasion to make an extraordinary use of them—and it is well known, that a good flint, well screw'd in, will stand the firing of sixty rounds (after which it may still be repaired) 'tis therefore presumed, that the men have either lost their Flints through negligence, or abused them by that worst of practices, *Snapping their pieces continually,* which not only spoils their Lock, softens the Hammer, and destroys the Flint, but frequently causes the death of many a man, by the Gun being unknowingly loaded—The Officers are therefore required, to pay strict attention to this particular, and have their men's Flints examined when they review their Ammunition; for Men being surprized with bad flints in their Guns, mat be attended with fatal consequences....

George Washington, from general orders issued at his New York headquarters, May 21, 1776, in John C. Fitzpatrick, ed., The Writings of George Washington, *vol. 5, pp. 72–73.*

Your Sentiments of the Duties We owe to our Country, are such as become the best of Women, and the best of Men. Among all the Disappointments, and Perplexities, which have fallen to my share in Life, nothing has contributed so much support to my Mind, as the choice Blessing of a Wife, whose Capacity enabled her to comprehend, and whose pure Virtue obliged her to approve the Views of her Husband. This has been the cheering Consolation of my Heart, in my most solitary, gloomy and disconsolate Hours. In this remote Situation, I am deprived in a great Measure of this Comfort. Yet I read, and read again your charming Letters, and they serve me, in some faint degree for the Company and Conversation of the Writer.

John Adams, from a letter written to Abigail Adams, May 22, 1776, in L. H. Butterfield, ed., Adams Family Correspondence, *vol. 1, pp. 412–413.*

The dignity and stability of government in all its branches, the morals of the people, and every blessing of society, depend so much upon an upright and skilful administration of justice, that the judicial power ought to be distinct from both the legislative and executive, and *independent* upon both, that so it may be a *check* upon both, as both should be checks upon that. The judges, therefore, should always be men of learning and experience in the laws, of exemplary morals, great patience, calmness, coolness and attention; their minds should not be *distracted with jarring interests; they should not be* dependent upon any man, or body of men. To these ends they should hold *estates for life* in their offices, or, in other words, their commissions should be *during good behaviour,* and their salaries ascertained and established by law.

For *misbehaviour . . .* the house of representatives, should impeach them before the governor and council, when they should have time and opportunity to make their defence; but *if convicted,* should be *removed* from their offices, and subjected to such other punishment as shall be thought proper.

Thomas Jefferson, from a letter to George Wythe, June 1776, in Julian P. Boyd, ed., The Papers of Thomas Jefferson, *vol. 1, p. 410.*

. . . Arrived at 5 in John's Town. Was informed by the Colonel [Elias Dayton] that in consequence of his Proclamation for the Torys & others disaffected to the cause to come in & deliver themselves up on Monday last, 195 came in accordingly, of whom the following is an Acct: English 11, Scots 32, Irish 6, Germans 74, Poles 1, Swiss 3, Prussians 1, Americans 67. . . .

Captain Joseph Bloomfield of the Continental army's 3rd New Jersey Regiment, from journal entry of June 5, 1776, when he returned to camp near Johnstown, New York, in Mark E. Lender and James Kirby Martin, eds., Citizen Soldier, *p. 59.*

. . . New York still acts in Character, like a People without Courage or sense, or Spirit, or in short any one Virtue or Ability. There is neither Spunk nor Gumption, in that Province as a Body. Individuals are very clever. But it is the weakest Province in point of Intellect, Valour, public Spirit, or any thing else that is great and good upon the Continent. It is incapable of doing Us much good, or much Hurt, but from its local situation. The low Cunning of Individuals, and their Prostitution plagues Us, the Virtues of a few Individuals is of some Service to Us. But as a Province it will be a dead Weight upon any side, ours or that of our Enemies.

John Adams, from a letter written in Philadelphia to Cotton Tufts, physician and uncle of Abigail Adams, June 23, 1776, in L. H. Butterfield, ed., Adams Family Correspondence, *vol. 2, p. 22.*

Our Misfortunes in Canada, are enough to melt an Heart of Stone. The Small Pox is ten times more terrible than Britons, Canadians and Indians together. This was the Cause of our precipitate Retreat from Quebec, this the Cause of our Disgraces at the Cedars—I don't mean that this was all. There has been Want, approaching to Famine, as well as Pestilence. And these Discouragements seem to have so disheartened our Officers, that none of them seem to Act with prudence and Firmness.

. . . . .

The small Pox! The small Pox! What shall We do with it? I could almost wish that an inoculating Hospital was opened, in every Town in New England. It is some small Consolation, that the Scoundrell Savages have taken a large Dose of it. They plundered the Baggage, and stripped off the Cloaths of our Men, who had the Small Pox, out full upon them at the Cedars.

John Adams, from a letter written in Philadelphia to Abigail Adams, June 26, 1776, in L. H. Butterfield, ed., Adams Family Correspondence, *vol. 2, pp. 23–24.*

Congress, I doubt not, will have heard of the Plot that was forming among many disaffected persons in this City and Government for aiding the Kings Troops on their arrival. The matter I am in hopes, by a timely discovery, will be suppressed, and put a stop to, many Citizens and others, among whom is the May or, are now in confinement. It has been traced up to Governor Tryon, and the Mayor appears to have been a principal Agent, or go between him and the persons concerned in it. The plot had been communicated to some of the Army and part of my Guard engaged in it. Thomas Hicky, one of them, has been tried and by the unanimous opinion of a Court Martial, is sentenced to die having inlisted himself and engaged others. . . .

George Washington, from a letter written at New York to the president of the Continental Congress, John Hancock, June 28, 1776, in John C. Fitzpatrick, ed., The Writings of George Washington, *vol. 5, p. 193.*

Yesterday the greatest Question was decided, which ever was debated in America, and a greater perhaps, never was or will be decided among Men. A Resolution was passed without one dissent Colony "that these united Colonies, are, and of right ought to be free and independent States, and as such, they have, and of Right ought to have full Power to make War, conclude Peace, establish Commerce, and do all the other Acts and Things, which other States may rightfully do." You will see in a few days a Declaration setting forth the Causes, which have impell'd Us to this mighty Revolution, and the Reasons which will justify it, in the sight of God and Man. A Plan of Confederation will be taken up in a few days.

John Adams, from a letter written in Philadelphia to Abigail Adams, July 3, 1776, in L. H. Butterfield, ed., Adams Family Correspondence, *vol. 2, pp. 27–28.*

But the Day is past. The Second Day of July 1776, will be the most memorable Epocha, in the History of America.—I am apt to believe that it will be celebrated, by succeeding Generations, as the great anniversary Festival. It ought to be commemorated, as the Day of Deliverance by solemn Acts of Devotion to God Almighty. It ought to be solemnized with Pomp and Parade, with Shews, Games, Sports, Guns, Bells, Bonfires and Illuminations from one End of this Continent to the other from this Time forward forever more.

You will think me transported with Enthusiasm but I am not.—I am well aware of the Toil and Blood and Treasure, that it will cost Us to maintain this Declaration, and support and defend these States.—Yet through all the Gloom I can see Rays of ravishing Light and Glory. I can see that the End is more than worth all the Means. And that Posterity will tryumph in that

Days Transaction, even alto We should rue it, which I trust in God We shall not.

John Adams, from a second letter written in Philadelphia to Abigail Adams, July 3, 1776, in L. H. Butterfield, ed., Adams Family Correspondence, *vol. 2, pp. 30–31.*

Another anniversary, not of a contest of arms, but of an occasion of very great importance to the country. Just one year to-day since General Washington, under the superb elm which we love to call by his name, formally assumed the command of our immense body of armed men. An army it could scarcely be called, it was so sadly in need of all the requisite implements of war, and the discipline which his firm hand and wise head brought to the disorderly mass. At this distance of time we can more easily understand the dreadful difficulties he had to surmount to preserve the appearance of a well-equipped army in the eyes of the Redcoats under Sir William Howe. . . .

Dorothy Dudley, resident of Cambridge, Massachusetts, from diary entry of July 3, 1776, in Arthur Gilman, ed., Theatrum Majorum, *p. 83.*

. . . We have a government, you know, to form; and God only knows what it will resemble. Our politicians, like some guests at a feast, are perplexed and undetermined which dish to prefer. Our affairs in Canada have lately become much the subject of animadversion; and the miscarriages in that country are, with little reserve, imputed to the inattention of the Congress. Indeed, there is reason to believe that certain military gentlemen who reaped no laurels there are among the patrons of that doctrine. It is to me amazing that a strict inquiry has not been made into the behaviour of those under whose direction we have met with nothing but repeated losses in that country. . . .

John Jay, from a letter written in Philadelphia, July 6, 1776, to Edward Rutledge, in William Jay, The Life of John Jay, *vol. 1, pp. 62–63.*

Our Army at Crown Point is an Object of Wretchedness, enough to fill a humane Mind, with Horror. Disgraced, defeated, discontented, dispirited, diseased, naked, undisciplined, eaten up with Vermin—no Cloaths, Beds, Blanketts, no Medicines, no Victuals, but Salt Pork and flour. . . .

John Adams, from a letter written in Philadelphia to Abigail Adams, July 7, 1776, in L. H. Butterfield, ed., Adams Family Correspondence, *vol. 2, p. 38.*

John Jay represented New York at the First Continental Congress. *(From* The Pictorial Field Book of the Revolution, *2 vols., by B. J. Lossing. New York: Harper Brothers 1851 and 1852.)*

Since my last, General Howe's Fleet from Halifax has arrived; in Number about 130 Sail. His Army is between nine and ten Thousand, being joined by some of the Regiments from the West Indies, and having fallen in with Part of the Highland Troops, in his Passage. He has landed his Men on Staten Island, which they mean to secure, and is in daily Expectation of the Arrival of Lord Howe, with one Hundred and fifty Ships, with a large and powerful Reinforcement. This we have from four Prisoners which fell into our Hands and some Deserters. . . . From every Appearance, they mean to make a most vigorous Push, to subdue us this Campaign. . . . Our utmost Exertions must be used, and I trust, thro' the Favour of divine Providence, they will be disappointed in their Views.

George Washington, from a letter at his New York headquarters to Gen. Philip Schuyler, July 11, 1776, in John C. Fitzpatrick, ed., The Writings of George Washington, *vol. 5, p. 258.*

Our Declaration of Independency has given Vigor to the Spirits of the People. Had this decisive Measure been taken Nine Months ago, it is my opinion that Canada would at this time have been in our hands. But what does it avail to find fault with what is past. Let us do

better for the future. We were more fortunate than expected in having 12 of the 13 Colonies in favor of the all important Question. The delegates of N York were not empowered to give their Voice on either Side. Their Convention has since acceded to the Declaration. . . . So mighty a Change in so short a Time! . . .

Samuel Adams, from a letter written in Philadelphia, July 15, 1776, to Richard Henry Lee, in Harry Alonzo Cushing, ed., The Writings of Samuel Adams, *vol. 3, pp. 297–298.*

At twelve o'clock to-day [July 8], the Committees of Safety and Inspection of Philadelphia, went in procession to the State House, where the Declaration of the Independency of the United States of America was read to a very large number of the inhabitants of the city and county, and was received with general applause and heartfelt satisfaction. And, in the evening, our late King's coat-of-arms was brought from the hall in the State House, where the said King's courts were formerly held, and burned amidst the acclamations of a crowd of spectators.

From the Constitutional Gazette, *New York, July 17, 1776, in Frank Moore, compiler,* The Diary of the American Revolution, *p. 130.*

Last Thursday [July 18] after hearing a very Good Sermon I went with the Multitude into Kings Street to hear the proclamation for independence read and proclamed. Some Field pieces with the Train were brought there, the troops appeard under Arms and all the inhabitants assembled there (the small pox prevented many thousand from the Country). When Col. Crafts read from the Belcona [balcony] of the State House the Proclamation, great attention was given every word. As soon as he ended, the cry from the Belcona, was God Save our American States and then 3 cheers which rended the air, the Bells rang, the privateers fired, the forts and Batteries, the cannon were discharged, the platoons followed and every face appeard joyfull. Mr. Bowdoin then gave a Sentiment, Stability and perpetuity to American independance. After dinner the kings arms were taken down from the State House and every vestage of him from every place in which it appeared and burnt in King Street. Thus ends royall Authority in this State, and all the people shall say Amen.

Abigail Adams, from a letter written in Boston to John Adams, July 21, 1776, in L. H. Butterfield, ed., Adams Family Correspondence, *vol. 2, p. 56.*

Lord Dunmore, driven from Gwins, retreated to St. George's island in Potowmack, a station we hear he found no less unquiet than what he left, so that he hath gone up that river, distressed, it is imagined for want of water. Ought the precept, 'if thine enemy thirst give him drink,' to be observed towards such a fiend, and in such a war? Our countrymen will probably decide in the negative; and perhaps such casuists as you and I shall not blame them. . . .

George Wythe, from a letter written at Williamsburg to Thomas Jefferson, July 27, 1776, in Julian P. Boyd, ed., The Papers of Thomas Jefferson, *vol. 1, p. 476.*

The great attention serious, solemn & devout Behaviour of those poor Savages, with the sweetest, best & most harmonious singing I ever heard, excited the attention & admiration of all present, & was an Example to the whites & at the same time a Reproof to the Chistians, who . . . frequently behave with the greatest Rudeness during Divine service. . . .

When I observed & Reflected with what reverence & solemnity the almost naked Savages, (the Men haveing a Clout only round them & the Women a skirt & Blanket wh. they covered themselves except their faces entirely) . . . I say, their devout Behaviour struck me with Astonishment & made me blush with shame for myself and my own People. . . .

It is worth remarking that Very early in the Morning I heard the Dutch Domine preach in the High-German-Language, so that I heard Divine-Worship Delivered in three Tongues today [German, English, and Oneida]. Besides I heard in the different Companies I was in, the following Languages spoke—1st. English, 2d. High-Dutch, 3d. Low-Dutch, 4th. French, 5th. the Mohawk, 6th. Oneydoes, 7th. Senekas, 8th. Caygas, 9th. Tuscaroras & 10th. The Onandagoe-Languages. . . .

Captain Joseph Bloomfield of the Continental army's 3rd New Jersey Regiment, then at the so-called German Flats on the Mohawk River, from journal entry of Sunday, July 28, 1776, in Mark E. Lender and James Kirby Martin, eds., Citizen Soldier, *pp. 90–91.*

Wilson. If the War continues 2 Years, each Soul will have 40 dollars to pay of the public debt. It will be the greatest Encouragement to continue Slave keeping, and to increase them, that can be to exempt them from the Numbers which are to vote and pay. . . . Slaves are Taxables in the Southern Colonies. It will be partial

and unequal. Some Colonies have as many black as white. . . . These will not pay more than half what they ought. Slaves prevent freemen cultivating a Country. It is attended with many Inconveniences.

Lynch. If it is debated, whether their Slaves are their Property, there is an End of the Confederation. Our Slaves being our Property, why should they be taxed more than the Land, Sheep, Cattle, Horses, &c. Freemen cannot be got, to work in our Colonies. It is not in the Ability, or Inclination of freemen to do the Work that the Negroes do. Carolina has taxed their Negroes. So have other Colonies, their Lands.

Dr. Franklin. Slaves rather weaken than strengthen the State, and there is therefore some difference between them and Sheep. Sheep will never make any Insurrections.

Rutledge. . . . I shall be happy to get rid of the idea of Slavery. The Slaves do not signify Property. The old and the young cannot work. The Property of some Colonies are to be taxed, in others not. The Eastern

Thomas Jefferson was the primary author of the Declaration of Independence. *(Courtesy of the National Archive and Records Administration)*

Colonies will become the Carriers for the Southern. They will obtain wealth for which they will not be taxed.

John Adams, from a diary entry, notes on the Continental Congress's debates on the Articles of Confederation, July 30, 1776, in L. H. Butterfield, ed., Diary and Autobiography of John Adams, *pp. 245–246.*

. . . The Shawanese and Delawares are disposed to peace. I believe it, for this reason. We [Congress] had by different advices information from the Shawanese that they should strike us, that this was against their will, but that they must do what the Senecas bid them. At that time we knew the Senecas meditated war. We directed a declaration to be made to the six nations in general that if they did not take the most decisive measures for the preservation of neutrality we would never cease waging war with them while one was to be found on the face of the earth. They immediately changed their conduct and I doubt not have given corresponding information to the Shawanese and Delawares. I hope the Cherokees will now be driven beyond the Missisipi and that this in future will be declared to the Indians the invariable consequence of their beginning a war. Our contest with Britain is too serious and too great to permit any possibility of avocation from the Indians. This then is the season for driving them off. . . .

Thomas Jefferson, from a letter written in Philadelphia to Edmund Pendleton, August 13, 1776, in Julian P. Boyd, ed., The Papers of Thomas Jefferson, *vol. 1, pp. 493–494.*

If you complain of neglect of Education in sons, What shall I say with regard to daughters, who every day experience the want of it. With regard to the Education of my own children, I find myself soon out of my debth, and destitute and deficient in every part of Education.

I most sincerely wish that some more liberal plan might be laid and executed for the Benefit of the rising Generation, and that our new constitution may be distinguished for Learning and Virtue. If we mean to have Heroes, Statesmen and Philosophers, we should have learned women. The world perhaps would laugh at me, and accuse me of vanity. But you I know have a mind too enlarged and liberal to disregard the Sentiment. If much depends as is allowed upon the early Education of youth and the first principals which are instilld take

the deepest root, great benefit must arise from literary accomplishments in women.

Abigail Adams, from a letter written in Boston to John Adams, August 14, 1776, in L. H. Butterfield, ed., Adams Family Correspondence, *vol. 2, p. 94.*

. . . As Lord Dunmore and his Squadron have join'd the Fleet at Staten Island, you will, I should think, have a favourable oppertunity of sending of your Flour, Midlings, Ship stuff &ca. Corn will, more than probably, sell well sometime hence; especially if your Crops should be as short as you apprehend. If your Ship stuff and Middlings should have turnd Sower it will make exceeding good Bisquet notwithstanding. Your Works abt. the Home House will go on Slowly I fear as your hands are reduced. . . . [R]emember that the New Chimneys are not to smoke. Plant Trees in the room of all dead ones in proper time this Fall. and as I mean to have groves of Trees at each end of the dwelling House . . . these Trees to be Planted without any order or regularity (but pretty thick, as they can at any time be thin'd) and to consist that at the North end, of locusts altogether. and that at the South, of all the clever kind of Trees (especially flowering ones) that can be got, such as Crab apple, Poplar, Dogwood, Sasafras, Laurel, Willow. . . .

George Washington, from a letter written at New York to Lund Washington, August 19, 1776, in John C. Fitzpatrick, ed., The Writings of George Washington, *vol. 5, pp. 460–461.*

The Temper of the Colonies as professed in their several Petitions to the Crown was sincere. The Terms they proposed should then have been closed with, and all might have been Peace. I dare say your Lordship as well as my self, laments they were not accepted. I remember I told you that better would never be offered. . . . But the Contempt with which those Petitions were treated, none of them being vouchsaf'd an Answer; and the cruel Measures since taken, have chang'd that Temper. It could not be otherwise. To propose now to the Colonies a Submission to the Crown of Great Britain, would be fruitless. The Time is past. One might as well propose it to France, on the Footing of a former title.

Benjamin Franklin, from a letter written in Philadelphia, August 20, 1776, to Lord Richard Howe, in William B. Willcox, ed., The Papers of Benjamin Franklin, *vol. 22, p. 575.*

Yesterday Morning I took a Walk, into Arch Street, to see Mr. Peele's [Charles Willson Peale] Painters Room. Peele is from Maryland, a tender, soft, affectionate Creature. . . .

He shewed me one moving Picture. His Wife, all bathed in Tears, with a Child about six months old, laid out, upon her Lap. This Picture struck me prodigiously.

He has a Variety of Portraits—very well done. But not so well as Copeleys [John Singleton Copley] Portraits. Copeley is the greatest Master, that ever was in America. His Portraits far exceed [Benjamin] Wests.

Peele has taken General Washington, Dr. Franklin, Mrs. Washington, Mrs. Rush, Mrs. Hopkinson. Mr. Blair McClenachan and his little Daughter in one Picture. His Lady and her little son, in another.

. . . . .

He is ingenious. He has Vanity—loves Finery—Wears a sword—gold Lace—speaks French—is capable of Friendship, and strong Family Attachments and natural Affections.

John Adams, from a letter written in Philadelphia to Abigail Adams, August 21, 1776, in L. H. Butterfield, ed., Adams Family Correspondence, *vol. 2, pp. 103–104.*

The Enemy have now landed on Long Island, and the hour is fast approaching, on which the Honor and Success of this army, and the safety of our bleeding Country depend. Remember officers and Soldiers, that you are Freemen, fighting for the blessings of Liberty. . . . Remember how your Courage and Spirit have been dispised, and traduced by your cruel invaders; though they have found by dear experience at Boston, Charlestown and other places, what a few brave men contending in their own land, and in the best of causes can do, against base hirelings and mercenaries—Be cool, but determined; do not fire at a distance, but wait for orders from your officers—It is the General's express orders that if any man attempt to skulk, lay down, or retreat without Orders he be instantly shot down as an example, he hopes no such Scoundrel will be found in this army; but on the contrary, every one for himself resolving to conquer, or die, and trusting to the smiles of heaven upon so just a cause, will behave with Bravery and Resolution. . . . And if this Army will but emulate, and imitate their brave Countrymen, in

other parts of America, he has no doubt they will, by a glorious Victory, save their Country, and acquire to themselves immortal Honor.

George Washington, from general orders issued at his New York headquarters, August 23, 1776, in John C. Fitzpatrick, ed., The Writings of George Washington, *vol. 5, pp. 479–480.*

. . . The fantastical idea of virtue and the public good being a sufficient security to the state against the commission of crimes, which you say you have heard insisted on by some, I assure you was never mine. It is only the sanguinary hue of our penal laws which I meant to object to. Punishments I know are necessary, and I would provide them, strict and inflexible, but proportioned to the crime. Death might be inflicted for murther and perhaps for treason if you would take out of the description of treason all crimes which are not such in their nature. Rape, buggery &c. punish by castration. All other crimes by working on high roads, rivers, gallies &c. a certain time proportioned to the offence. But as this would be no punishment or change of condition to slaves (me miserum!) let them be sent to other countries. By these means we should be freed from the wickedness of the latter, and the former would be living monuments of public vengeance. Laws thus proportionate and mild should never be dispensed with. . . .

Thomas Jefferson, from a letter written in Philadelphia to Edmund Pendleton, August 26, 1776, in Julian P. Boyd, ed., The Papers of Thomas Jefferson, *vol. 1, p. 505.*

A general Action is every day expected at New York. If the Enemy is beaten, it will probably be decisive as to them; for they can hardly produce such another Armament for another Campaign: But our growing Country can bear considerable Losses, and recover them, so that a Defeat on our part will not by any means occasion our giving up the Cause. Much depends upon the Bravery of you who are posted at Ticonderoga. If you prevent the Junction of the two Armies, their Project for this Year will be broken, and the Credit of the British Arms thro'out Europe and of the Ministry in England will be demolish'd, and the Nation grow sick of the Contest.

Benjamin Franklin, from a letter written in Philadelphia, August 28, 1776, to Gen. Anthony Wayne, in William B. Willcox, ed., The Papers of Benjamin Franklin, *vol. 22, p. 584.*

Sir: Inclination as well as duty, would have induced me to give Congress, the earliest information of my removal of the Troops from Long Island and its dependencies to this City, the night before last; but the extreme fatigue . . . since the incampment of the 27th rendered me entirely unfit to take pen in hand. Since Monday, we have scarce any of us been out of the Lines, till our passage across the East River was effected yesterday Morning, and for the 48 hours preceeding that; I had hardly been off my horse and had never closed my Eyes, so that I was quite unfit to write or dictate till this Morning.

Our Retreat was made without any loss of Men or Ammunition and in better order than I expected, from Troops in the Situation ours were. . . .

In the Engagement of the 27th Generals Sullivan and Stirling were made prisoners; The former has been permitted on his parole to return for a little time. From Lord Stirling I had a Letter by General Sullivan. . . . General Sullivan says Lord Howe is extremely desirous of seeing some of the Members of Congress, for which purpose he was allowed to come out and to communicate to them what has passed between him and his Lordship. . . .

George Washington, from a letter written at his New York headquarters to the president of the Continental Congress, John Hancock, August 31, 1776, in John C. Fitzpatrick, ed., The Writings of George Washington, *vol. 5, pp. 506–507.*

Our situation is truly distressing. The Check our Detachment sustained on the 27th Ulto. has dispirited too great a proportion of our Troops and filled their minds with apprehension and dispair. The Militia, instead of calling forth their utmost efforts to a brave and manly opposition, in order to repair our Losses, are dismayed, Intractable and Impatient to return. Great numbers of them have gone off, in some instances almost by whole Regiments, by half ones and by Companies at a Time. This circumstance of itself . . . would be sufficiently disagreeable, but when their example has Infected another part of the Army . . . [and] produced a like conduct but too common to the whole, and an entire disregard of that order and Subordination necessary to the well doing of an Army . . . our Condition is still more Alarming, and with the deepest concern I am obliged to con-

fess my want of confidence, in the generality of the Troops. . . .

George Washington, from a letter written at New York to the president of the Continental Congress, John Hancock, September 2, 1776, in John C. Fitzpatrick, ed., The Writings of George Washington, *vol. 6, pp. 4–5.*

. . . I have felt uneasy to Hear from you. The Report of your being dead, has no doubt reach'd you by Bass who heard enough of it before he came away. It took its rise among the Tories who as Swift said of himself "By their fears betray their Hopes." . . . I am sometimes ready to suspect that there is a communication between the Tories of every State, for they seem to know all news that is passing before tis known by the Whigs.

Abigail Adams, from a letter written in Braintree, Massachusetts, to John Adams, September 7, 1776, in L. H. Butterfield, ed., Adams Family Correspondence, *vol. 2, p. 122.*

The loss of the Enemy yesterday, would undoubtedly have been much greater, if the Orders of the Commander in Chief had not in some instances been contradicted by inferior officers, who, however well they may mean, ought not to presume to direct—It is therefore ordered, that no officer, commanding a party, and having received Orders from the Commander in Chief, depart from them without Counter Orders from the same Authority. . . .

George Washington, from his general orders issued at his Harlem Heights headquarters, September 17, 1776, in John C. Fitzpatrick, ed., The Writings of George Washington, *vol. 6, p. 65.*

thare came on board an officer told us we should all be landed a munday at Night / a very great fire broke out in the town and by looks of it burnt the biger part of the town / the river & harbor full of Shiping going up to the town / we hear that the 200 housand burnt down in ye City / we hear that ye man was cetched that set the housend on fire by the Sentry and run throu by a bayinet & then the next day he was hung.

Volunteer soldier Jeremiah Greenman of Newport, Rhode Island, who had been a prisoner in Quebec City and was now being repatriated to New York City, describing the fire in that city that consumed 493 houses, diary entry of September 21–22, 1776, in Greenman, Diary of a Common Soldier in the American Revolution, 1775–1783, *p. 32.*

A Soldier reasoned with upon the goodness of the cause he is engaged in, and the inestimable rights he is contending for, hears you with patience, and acknowledges the truth of your observations, but adds, that it is of no more Importance to him than others. The Officer makes the same reply, with this further remark, that his pay will not support him, and he cannot ruin himself and Family to serve his Country, when every Member of the community is equally Interested and benefitted by his Labours. The few therefore, who act upon Principles of disinterestedness, are, comparatively speaking, no more than a drop in the Ocean. It becomes evidently clear then, that as this Contest is not likely to be the Work of a day; as the War must be carried on systematically, and to do it, you must have good Officers, there are, in my Judgment, no other possible means to obtain them but by establishing your Army upon a permanent footing; and giving your Officers good pay. . . .

George Washington, from a letter written at Harlem Heights to the president of the Continental Congress, John Hancock, on the difficulties of recruiting troops and officers, September 24, 1776, in John C. Fitzpatrick, ed., The Writings of George Washington, *vol. 6, pp. 107–108.*

The plan of foreign treaty is just finished, and yourself, with Doctor Franklin, and Mr. Deane now in France, are the Trustees to execute this all important business. The great abilities and unshaken virtue, necessary for the execution of what the safety of America does so capitally rest upon, has directed the Congress in their choice; and tho ambition may have no influence in this case, yet that distinguished love for your country that has marked your life, will determine you here. In my judgement, the most eminent services that the greatest of her sons can do America will not more essentially serve her and honor themselves, than a successful negotiation with France. With this country, every thing depends upon it, and if we may form a judgement of what is at a distance, the dispositions of that Court are friendly in a high degree, and want only to be properly acted upon, to be wrought into fix attachment and essential good. . . .

Richard Henry Lee, from a letter written in Philadelphia to Thomas Jefferson, September 27, 1776, in Julian P. Boyd, ed., The Papers of Thomas Jefferson, *vol. 1, p. 522.*

The Only Sourse of uneasiness amongst us arises from the Number of Tories we find in every State. They are More Numerous than formerly and Speak more openly but Tories are now of various kinds and various principles, some are so from real attachment to Britain, some from interested views, many very many from fear of the British Force, some because they are dissatisfied with the General Measures of Congress, more because they disapprove of the Men in power and the measures of their respective States . . . and if America falls it will be oweing to such divisions more than the force of our Enemies. . . .

Benjamin Franklin and Robert Morris, from a letter of the Committee of Secret Correspondence written in Philadelphia, October 1, 1776, to Silas Deane, in William B. Willcox, ed., The Papers of Benjamin Franklin, *vol. 22, p. 643.*

The Spirit of Venality, you mention, is the most dreadfull and alarming Enemy, that America has to oppose. It is as rapacious and insatiable as the Grave. We are in the Faece Romuli, non Republica Platonis. This predominant Avarice will ruin America, if she is ever ruined. If God almighty does not interpose by his Grace to controul this universal Idolatry to the Mammon of Unrighteousness, We shall be given up to the Chastisements of his Judgments. I am ashamed of the Age I live in.

John Adams, from a letter written in Philadelphia to Abigail Adams, October 8, 1776, in L. H. Butterfield, ed., Adams Family Correspondence, *vol. 2, p. 140.*

So vast a fleet was never before seen together in the port of New York, or perhaps in all America. The ships are stationed up the East River or Sound, as far as Turtle Bay, and near the town. The multitude of masts carries the appearance of a wood. Some are moored up the North River, others in the bay between Red and Yellow Hook; others, again, off Staten Island, and several off Powle's Hook, and towards the kills. The men-of-war are moored chiefly up New York Sound, and make, with the other ships, a very magnificent and formidable appearance. . . .

From an article in the Freeman's Journal, *Portsmouth, N.H., October 29, 1776, in Frank Moore, compiler,* The Diary of the American Revolution, *p. 169.*

It is with astonishment the General hears, that some officers have taken Horses, between the Enemy's

Camp and ours, and sent them into the Country for their private use: Can it be possible, that persons bearing Commissions, and fighting in such a Cause, can degrade themselves into Plunderers of horses?—He hopes every officer will set his face against it, in future; and does insist that the Colonels, and commanding Officers of the Regiments, immediately enquire into the matter, and report to him, who have been guilty of these practices....

George Washington, from his general orders issued at his White Plains, New York, headquarters, October 31, 1776, in John C. Fitzpatrick, ed., The Writings of George Washington, *vol. 6, pp. 234–235.*

...I heared with much regret that you had declined both the voyage [to France], and your seat in Congress. No Man feels more deeply that I do, the love of, and the loss of, private enjoyments; but let attention to these be universal, and we are gone, beyond redemption lost in the deep perdition of slavery. By every account from lake Champlain we had reason to think ourselves in no danger on that water for this Campaign. Nor did Gen. Arnold seem to apprehend any until he was defeated by an enemy four times as strong as himself. This Officer, fiery, hot and impetuous, but without discretion, never thought of informing himself how the enemy went on, and he had no idea of retiring when he saw them coming, tho so much superior to his force! Since his defeat, our people evacuated Crown point, and joined their whole strength at Ticonderoga. We do not hear the enemy have thought proper to visit them there, and the Season must now stop operations on the Lake....

Richard Henry Lee, from a letter written in Philadelphia to Thomas Jefferson, November 3, 1776, in Julian P. Boyd, ed., The Papers of Thomas Jefferson, *vol. 1, p. 589.*

I was last week [October 1] on board the American privateer called the *Yankee* ... and, as an Englishman, I earnestly wish your lordship [Lord Mayor of London] ... would be pleased to go likewise ... to see the truly shocking, and I may say, barbarous and miserable condition of the unfortunate American prisoners, who, however criminal they may be thought to have been, are deserving of pity, and entitled to common humanity.

They are twenty-five in number, and all inhumanly shut close down, like wild beasts, in a small, stinking apartment, in the hold of a sloop ... without a breath of air....

I do not exaggerate, my lord; I speak the truth; and the resemblance that this barbarity bears to the memorable black hole at Calcutta ... strikes everyone at the sight. All England ought to know that the same game is now acting out upon the Thames on board this privateer, that all the world cried out against, and shuddered at the mention of in India, some years ago....

From an article published in the London Gazette, *October 1, and reprinted in the* Pennsylvania Journal, *Philadelphia, November 6, 1776, in Frank Moore, compiler,* The Diary of the American Revolution, *pp. 166–167.*

By every information I can obtain, and the accounts I had last night, by two deserters who were very intelligent and particular, Genl. Howe still has in view an expedition to the Jersey's and in preparing for it with great industry. I have detached the first division of our Troops, which was thought necessary to be sent, and which I hope will cross the River at Peekskill to day. The Second I expect will march this Evening, and tomorrow Morning I propose to follow myself, in order to put things in the best train I can and to give him every possible opposition. I hope ... to check his progress and prevent him from penetrating any distance from the River if not to oblige him to return immediately with some loss. Whatever is in my power to effect, shall be done....

George Washington, from a letter written at White Plains, New York, to the president of the Continental Congress, John Hancock, November 9, 1776, in John C. Fitzpatrick, ed., The Writings of George Washington, *vol. 6, pp. 261–262.*

There is very good intelligence that the British intend to make a push for Philadelphia. We hear part of their force is embarked, either to go up the Delaware, and make their attacks on both sides at once, or else to amuse the Southern States, and prevent their sending any assistance to Philadelphia. We have not force enough to oppose their march by land. We look to New Jersey and Pennsylvania for their militia, and on their spirit depends the preservation of America. If in this hour of adversity they shrink from danger, they deserve to be slaves indeed! If the freedom that success will insure us, if the misery that awaits our subjection, will not rouse them, why let them sleep till they awake in bondage.

From the Pennsylvania Journal, *Philadelphia, November 27, 1776, in Frank Moore, compiler,* The Diary of the American Revolution, *p. 183.*

... were it not for the weak and feeble state of the force I have, I should highly approve of your hanging on the Rear of the Enemy. . . . But when my situation is directly opposite to what you suppose it to be, and when Genl. Howe is pressing forward with the whole of his Army, except the Troops that were lately embarked and a few besides, left at New York, to possess himself of Philadelphia; I cannot but request and entreat you and this too, by the advice of all the Genl. Officers with me, to march and join me with all your whole force, with all possible expedition. The utmost exertions that can be made, will not be more than sufficient to save Philadelphia. Without the aid of your force, I think there is but little, if any, prospect of doing it. . . .

George Washington, from a letter written at the Falls of Trenton to Maj. Gen. Charles Lee, December 10, 1776, in John C. Fitzpatrick, ed., The Writings of George Washington, *vol. 6, pp. 340–341.*

10. Our people in confusion, of all ranks, sending all their goods out of town into the country. News brought that our army had sent their heavy baggage from Trenton [to] this side of the river; the enemy advancing in great order, and was at Brunswick. This day, attended forenoon and afternoon [at] the aforesaid office. Great numbers of sick soldiers arriving into the town.

11. Further accounts of the rapid progress of Gen. Howe. Our Congress leaves this City for Baltimore. The militia going out fast for Trenton: streets full of wagons, going out with goods.

Christopher Marshall, Philadelphia merchant, official, and Quaker, who would leave Philadelphia with his wife for Lancaster, where they had a home, as the British approached—his children, however, remained in the city, diary entries of December 10 and 11, 1776, in Marshall, Extracts from the Diary of Christopher Marshall, *p. 107.*

The General, to his great astonishment, has been informed that several of the inhabitants of this city [Philadelphia] have refused to take the Continental

Currency in payment for goods. In future, should any of the inhabitants be so lost to public virtue and the welfare of their country as to presume to refuse the currency of the American States in payment for any commodities they may have for sale, the goods shall be forfeited, and the person or persons so refusing committed to close confinement.

Major General Israel Putnam, from his General Orders issued on December 14, 1776, recorded in Christopher Marshall, Extracts from the Diary of Christopher Marshall, *p. 297.*

Since I came on this side, I have been join'd by about 2000 of the City Militia, and understand that some of the Country Militia (from the back Counties) are on their way; *but we are in a very disaffected part of the Provence, and between you and me, I think our Affairs are in a very bad situation; not so much from the apprehension of Genl. Howe's Army, as from the defection of New York, Jerseys, and Pennsylvania. In short, the Conduct of the Jerseys has been most Infamous. Instead of turning out to defend their Country and affording aid to our Army, they are making their submissions as fast as they can. . . .*

. . . . .

Before this reaches you, you will no doubt have heard of the Captivity of Genl. Lee; this is an additional misfortune, and the more vexatious, as it was by his own folly and Imprudence (and without a view to answer any good) he was taken. . . .

George Washington, from a letter written at camp near the Falls of Trenton to John Augustine Washington, December 18, 1776, in John C. Fitzpatrick, ed., The Writings of George Washington, *vol. 6, pp. 397–398.*

These are the times that try men's souls. The summer soldier and the sunshine patriot will, in this crisis, shrink from the service of their country; but he that stands it *now*, deserves the love and thanks of man and woman. Tyranny, like hell, is not easily conquered; yet we have this consolation with us, that the harder the conflict, the more glorious the triumph. What we obtain too cheap, we esteem too lightly: it is dearness only that gives every thing its value. Heaven knows how to put a proper price upon its goods; and it would be strange indeed if so celestial an article as FREEDOM should not be highly rated. . . .

... By perseverance and fortitude we have the prospect of a glorious issue; by cowardice and submission, the sad choice of a variety of evils—a ravaged county—a depopulated city—habitations without safety, and slavery without hope—our homes turned into barracks and bawdy-houses for Hessians, and a future race to provide for, whose fathers we shall doubt of. Look on this picture and weep over it! And if there yet remain one thoughtless wretch who believes it not, let him suffer it unlamented.

COMMON SENSE

Thomas Paine, from The American Crisis I, *December 19, 1776, from Van der Weyde,* The Life and Works of Thomas Paine, *vol. 2, pp. 263–264 and 277–278.*

The Enemy like locusts Sweep the Jerseys with the Besom of destruction. They to the disgrace of a Civilisd Nation Ravish the fair Sex, from the Age of Ten to Seventy. The Tories are Baneful in pointing out the friends to the American Cause, and giving Notice of every Motion we make.

· · · · ·

Genl. [Charles] Lee had the misfortune to be taken prisoner to the 13th Inst. He had Saunterd about three miles and a half from his Army—lodged the night before at a house recommended to him by a Colo. Vanhorn, a person in the Enemys Service . . . and Stayd at the place until ten O'Clock on the 13th when 50 light horsemen Supposed to be detachd by Advice of Vanhorn, came to the house and carry him off. He had thirteen men of a Guard but they were Stragling and Absent except three.

By accounts from Old France of Octob 1st. That Nation is on the Eve of a War with England.

I expect that we shall have hot Work as soon as the Delawar is frozen over.

If we lose Philadelphia and let it Stand, it will go near to Ruin us. They will open the port, give great prices for Wheat and flour and Seduce the Body of the People.

Brig. Gen. Adam Stephen, from a letter written at an encampment on the Delaware River, 30 miles from Philadelphia, to Thomas Jefferson, December [20 ?], 1776, in Julian P. Boyd, ed., The Papers of Thomas Jefferson, *vol. 1, p. 659.*

Dear Sir: Notwithstanding the discouraging Accounts I have received from Col. Reed of what might be expected from the Operations below, I am determined, as the Night is favourable, to cross the River and make the attack upon Trenton in the Morning. If you can do nothing real, at least create as great a diversion as possible. I am, etc.

George Washington, a letter written at McKonkey's Ferry to Col. John Cadwalader, 6:00 P.M., December 25, 1776, in John C. Fitzpatrick, ed., The Writings of George Washington, *vol. 6, pp. 440–441.*

... In justice to the Officers and Men, I must add, that their Behaviour upon this Occasion [attack on Trenton], reflects the highest honor upon them. The difficulty of passing the River in a very severe Night, and their march thro' a violent Storm of Snow and Hail, did not in the least abate their Ardour. But when they came to the Charge, each seemed to vie with the other in pressing forward, and were I to give a preference to any particular Corps, I should do great injustice to the others. . . .

George Washington, from a letter written at Newton, Pennsylvania, to the president of the Continental Congress, John Hancock, December 27, 1776, in John C. Fitzpatrick, ed., The Writings of George Washington, *vol. 6, p. 444.*

4 Victories and Losses
1777

THE BATTLE OF PRINCETON

As General Washington sought to preserve some advantage from the American victory at Trenton, so General Howe attempted to remedy the British defeat. With his return to England canceled by Trenton, Lord Cornwallis rode the 50 miles from Manhattan to arrive at Princeton with 6,000 troops on the first day of the year. On the same day, Gen. James Grant brought 1,000 troops from New Brunswick, leaving behind only 600 men to guard the town. These reinforcements swelled to 8,000 the force Cornwallis assumed command of, while Washington had only about 5,100 troops. On January 1, Washington dispatched the French volunteer Brig. Gen. Alexis Roche de Fermoy in command of a brigade assigned to slow Cornwallis's anticipated march toward Trenton. De Fermoy positioned his men to the south of Maidenhead.[1]

Washington leads the Continental troops at Princeton, January 3, 1777. *(Courtesy of the National Archives and Records Administration)*

On January 2, Cornwallis posted 1,200 men under Lt. Col. Charles Mawhood to protect Princeton and, with 5,500 men and 28 artillery pieces, marched toward Trenton, impeded by deep mud created by the previous night's heavy rainfall. At about 10:00 A.M. the British encountered the American advance guard, now commanded by Col. Edward Hand since de Fermoy had returned to Trenton. The Americans fulfilled their mission, firing and falling back to hamper Cornwallis's progress. They held the British for three hours at Shabbakonk Creek and for another hour at the north of Trenton, finally withdrawing to join Washington's force positioned behind earthworks at Assunpink Creek. Cornwallis's advance guard of 1,500 men reached the creek at about 5:00 P.M., but American fire prevented their three attempts at crossing a bridge. Having arrived on the scene with his main force, Cornwallis decided that he had Washington entrapped, with his back to the Delaware River, and encamped to prepare for attack the following day. In a council of war during the night Washington and his officers decided on boldness. Leaving 400 men to stoke the campfires and to erect entrenchments noisily, the main American force quietly withdrew from Trenton at 1:00 A.M. on January 3 and moved through the early morning darkness around Cornwallis's left flank and on toward Princeton, to be stealthily followed after daybreak by the 400 decoys. A fortunate drop in temperature had

Continental army troops advance against British forces at the Battle of Princeton. *(The Battle of Princeton, courtesy of Anne S. K. Brown Military Collection, Brown University Library)*

frozen the roads, easing the passage of both men and cannons; with their wheels wrapped in rags, the gun carriages rolled along quietly.

The element of surprise failed, however, because Mawhood, ordered to march most of his men to join General Leslie at Maidenhead, had already mounted his horse and had begun his march. About 350 American troops under Gen. Hugh Mercer—sent to guard Stony Brook bridge—approached the bridge just as Mawhood's British troops had crossed over. The Americans succeeded in the race to occupy a nearby orchard, crouched behind trees and hedges, and fired on Mawhood's troops. Mawhood responded with a bayonet charge that scattered the rebels into flight. Lambert Cadwalader's men appeared and joined Mercer's retreat before Mawhood. Hearing the shots, Washington and his staff broke off from the main force of Sullivan's division that was advancing toward Princeton and galloped into the fray to rally the Americans. Washington, waving his hat, raced toward the British troops, who fired on him at a range of 30 yards. An aide to Washington covered his eyes. The musket smoke cleared. The American commander, unscathed astride his white horse, urged his troops into an attack that forced Mawhood and many of his men into retreat toward Trenton and finally into a scattering rout, while their 194 cohorts left behind surrendered. The British who had remained in Princeton fled to New Brunswick. The Americans counted 100 wounded and 40 dead, including Mercer, but their stunning victory in the Battle of Princeton cost the British 250 casualties.

With his troops weary, and with Cornwallis likely fast marching to Princeton, Washington decided against attacking New Brunswick and withdrew toward Morristown. Cornwallis's men, forced to wade Stony Brook's breast-deep waters because Washington's men had destroyed the bridge, reached Princeton only to see Washington's force withdrawing in the distance. Assuming Washington's objective to be New Brunswick, Cornwallis marched all night to arrive at the town on January 4. Washington sent word to Gen. William Heath in the Hudson Highlands to move down closer to New York to threaten the British garrisoned there and then settled into winter quarters at Morristown. His successes at Trenton and Princeton and the subsequent capture of Hackensack and Elizabethtown left the British in control only of Amboy and New Brunswick, with 5,000 troops in each town, rather than the entire state, as before. And so 1777 began promisingly for the Americans.[2]

SOME REVERSALS OF FORTUNE

Washington's hope that General Heath could menace the British in New York was unrealized. After gathering a total force of about 6,000 men at Spuyten Duyvil, Heath attempted to capture Fort Independence on the approach to Manhattan. But the fort's garrison of 2,000 Hessians held off the Americans for more than a week and then sallied forth in an assault that forced them into flight. His efforts frustrated, Heath decided at the end of January to withdraw to Spuyten Duyvil.[3]

By mid-March, Washington's force at Morristown diminished to fewer than 3,000 men, two-thirds of them militia whose enlistments ended on the last day of March, reducing his efforts to harassing attacks on British foraging parties and sentinels. In mid-April, Lord Cornwallis attacked the American outpost at Bound Brook, New Jersey, garrisoned by 500 troops under Maj. Gen. Benjamin Lincoln.

Taken by surprise, Lincoln withdrew, ceding some prisoners and all his artillery to be taken by the British to New York. In the meantime, General Howe sent Gen. William Tryon with about 2,000 British and Tory troops to raid Danbury, Ridgefield, and Norwalk, Connecticut; they destroyed caches of supplies, houses, storehouses, and barns before reboarding their ships to sail back to New York. In early May, Gen. John Burgoyne arrived at Quebec to assume command of British forces in Canada and to pursue his orders to launch an invasion of New York, secure control of the entire Hudson River, and sever the New England states from the rest of the union.[4]

Despite the victories at Trenton and Princeton, Washington's army remained severely distressed; the commander and other leaders consequently solicited help from all sources, including women. During the years leading to war, many American women had become politicized through involvement in boycotting tea and other British imports. For example, 51 North Carolina women organized in October 1774 the Edenton Ladies' Tea and Party agreed to adhere to the tenets of the nonimportation resolutions as a means of supporting the "publick good." Such patriotic women adopted substitutes for tea by brewing the leaves of the loosestrife plant, a drink that came to be known as "liberty tea."[5]

Even though men continued to view their wives, mothers, and sisters as unsuited to actual revolution, warfare, or politics, with the Continental army struggling to overcome the deprivations of the previous winter, women increasingly came to play a more active role—not as combatants, but as providers of some basic necessities. Women responded en masse to requests to become spinners, turning out clothing and blankets for the troops individually or as groups in spinning bees, thus earning the sobriquet "Daughters of Liberty." They also saved rags for making bandages and paper. They removed lead weights from window sashes to be melted for bullets, and they saved their families' urine for making saltpeter. In some cities, women assumed the task of policing local merchants to ensure that they were not hoarding needed commodities, in a few cases even breaking into homes and warehouses owned by Loyalists to confiscate goods for the Continental army. (Patriots of course also considered Loyalists' wives as suspect, since it was presumed, often falsely, that they agreed with their husbands' politics.)[6]

Many women had, in effect, joined the army, especially wives with children who had no other means of support when their husbands became soldiers. They migrated with the troops, caring for their men and earning their upkeep by serving as cooks and clothes washers, often with children in tow. Officers often regarded these women as a nuisance, since they had to be transported by wagons needed for other purposes and they had to be fed; unmarried women camp followers often represented a yet more serious problem. The only officially employed women were those who served as nurses, freeing men to fight; but their duties were largely confined to those of contemporary orderlies—only men, unless none were present, could administer medicines. The vast majority of women remained at home and found diverse ways to support themselves. Some transformed their homes into boardinghouses—an especially viable option in Philadelphia as delegates to the Continental Congress arrived and needed places to live. During occupations, however, this option soured, as military officers simply commandeered homes without providing compensation.[7]

BURGOYNE'S INVASION

By mid-June, Burgoyne had assembled a force of more than 7,200 men, mostly British and German regulars but including small units of Indians, French Quebecois, and Loyalists, augmented by 138 artillery. In addition, he had nine ships, 28 gunboats, and many bateaux to carry this formidable force down Lake Champlain. His advance guard under command of Brig. Gen. Simon Fraser reached Crown Point on June 16. A week later, Lt. Col. Barry St. Leger departed from Montreal with 2,000 men, about 340 of them British and Hessian regulars and the remainder Indians and Tories, on his march south to juncture with Burgoyne at Albany.[8]

On the first day of July, Burgoyne positioned his British troops on the west bank of Lake Champlain and his Hessian troops on the east bank only three miles above Fort Ticonderoga and began preparations to attack the fort. The following day, he sent British troops against Mount Hope; the American defenders torched the post and fled. Meanwhile Hessians under Baron von Riedesel moved to the rear of Mount Independence. Then Burgoyne had artillery hauled up Sugar Loaf Hill and emplaced overlooking both Ticonderoga and Independence. Gen. Arthur St. Clair, commander of the American garrison of about 2,500 men, and his officers concurred that the artillery would overwhelm their defenses and decided to abandon the fort. In the early morning darkness of July 6, the

General John Burgoyne addresses Indians at their war feast in Canada. *(Courtesy of Anne S. K. Brown Military Collection, Brown University Library)*

garrison crossed the bridge to Mount Independence, placed ill soldiers in bateaux for transport to Skenesboro under the leadership of Col. Pierce Long, and pushed southeast to Hubbardton. Leaving a small force under Col. Seth Warner to await the arrival of his rear guard and then to follow after him, St. Clair marched his main force to Castleton.

His force augmented to 1,000 by the rear guard's arrival, Warner ignored St. Clair's orders and remained overnight at Hubbardton. A British advance party under Fraser discovered Warner's encampment and launched a surprise attack at dawn on the morning of July 7. A ferocious battle raged for two hours, with the Americans gaining the upper hand, until von Riedesel suddenly arrived with a detachment of Hessians. The Hessians assaulted the Americans' flanks, collapsing their defense, and Warner ordered his men to disperse. The Continentals fled, leaving more than 40 dead and 300 captured; Fraser suffered 183 casualties, among them 35 dead. Learning of Warner's loss, St. Clair set out for Fort Edward intent on saving the remainder of his force.

Burgoyne arrived at Skenesboro, which Long had realized to be indefensible and ordered burned before hastening toward Fort Anne. The British commander had sent his gunboats, artillery, and burdensome supplies on to the head of Lake George and stationed von Riedesel and his Germans at Castleton. After pausing at Skenesboro, Burgoyne pushed on to Fort Anne, but through the three weeks leading to July's end, his advance slowed greatly to about one mile per day because General Schuyler's men had compounded the natural hazards of the terrain by felling trees, dislodging boulders and rolling them down hills to block passages, and digging ditches to create swamps. As the month ended, Burgoyne arrived at Fort Edward to find that Schuyler had abandoned it as untenable. A few days later, St. Leger arrived at Fort Stanwix, New York, and, failing to win surrender from the fort's commander, Col. Peter Gansevoort, began to lay siege to the garrison. But the siege cost precious time, halting his advance toward Albany to join Burgoyne.[9]

THE BATTLE OF BENNINGTON

Having encountered little opposition but experiencing supply shortages because of his delayed march, Burgoyne made a fateful choice. At the urging of General von Riedesel, he decided to send out a foraging party into the Connecticut River valley to acquire horses and meat, but, against von Riedesel's counsel, he ordered that the party push farther out toward Manchester in search of Seth Warner. With about 800 men—mostly Germans but including 300 Tories, Canadians, and Indians—Lt. Col. Friedrich Baum set out on the foraging expedition, with the American military supply depot at Bennington as his initial objective. As Baum marched toward Bennington, Burgoyne crossed the Hudson River with his main force and headed for Saratoga.

At the same time, Brig. Gen. John Stark, having returned to service with the understanding that his command was exempt from the Continental Congress's orders, had recruited 1,500 militiamen equipped with their own clothes and guns and had begun to march them from Portsmouth, New Hampshire. They reached Bennington ahead of Baum. Reinforced by the arrival of Seth Warner and his 400 militiamen, Stark devised with Warner a plan to encircle Baum and attack his front, rear, and flanks simultaneously. The attack commenced at noon on August

Continental troops march toward the Battle of Bennington. *(Courtesy of Anne S. K. Brown Military Collection, Brown University Library)*

16, following a rainstorm. When the two detachments sent to outflank Baum to the right and left approached, Baum observed that they wore civilian clothes, assumed they were Loyalists come to his aid because he had been assured that local sympathies were pro-British, and withdrew his guards. Stark led the frontal attack, sending Baum's Canadians, Indians, and Tories into flight, some to join Baum's regulars dug in on a hilltop. After a two-hour battle, Baum's ammunition ran low, and he led his dragoons with drawn sabers charging into the Americans' midst. Baum received a fatal wound; his men surrendered. German reinforcements under command of Lt. Col. Heinrich von Breyman, sent by Burgoyne in response to Baum's request, arrived on the outskirts of the battlefield, but Stark's men and a contingent of Warner's men that arrived from Manchester forced them to retreat. The Battle of Bennington ended with the Americans enduring fewer than 70 casualties while killing 200 of their enemy and capturing 700 more—an initial disaster for Burgoyne.[10]

THE BATTLE OF BRANDYWINE

As Burgoyne pursued his invasion and experienced his first setback at Bennington, General William Howe launched his own expedition to capture Philadelphia. Howe had withdrawn all of his troops from New Jersey and reassembled them in New York and on Staten Island as June ended. In the third week of July, with 18,000 troops and horses, artillery, and supplies loaded aboard 260 ships, Howe set sail, passed beyond Sandy Hook, and disappeared into the Atlantic, his destination unknown to the Americans. General Washington's officers, however, surmised that Howe's destination was Philadelphia, and, although doubtful, the commander ordered four of his divisions, commanded by Generals Sullivan, Lord Stirling, Stephen, and Lincoln, along with Daniel Morgan's riflemen and three dragoon squadrons, to march immediately for Philadelphia. But Washington quickly changed his mind and halted Sullivan at Hanover, New Jersey, and his own main army, now restored in strength and well supplied, at the falls of the Schuylkill River near Germantown.[11]

During the third week of August, Washington learned that Howe's armada had entered the Chesapeake Bay; he ordered General Sullivan to rejoin the main army as quickly as possible and Gen. Francis Nash to hasten to Chester. On August 24, in a show of force meant to intimidate Loyalists and uplift patriots, Washington marched his 16,000-man army in a single column through the streets of Philadelphia, led by the commander, with the marquis de Lafayette, who had arrived from France a month earlier, riding beside him. The next day, the vanguard of Howe's fleet anchored at the head of the Elk River in Maryland and began to disembark troops. By the end of the month, Howe's entire force was on the march: One division, under Lord Cornwallis and accompanied by Howe, moved toward Philadelphia via Elkton, and a second division, under Wilhelm von Knyphausen, traveled via Cecil Courthouse on the east side of the Elk River.

Initially, Washington pursued a tactic of harassment. The Continentals' first encounter with Howe's advancing regulars occurred on September 3 at Iron Hill, Delaware, where about 100 rebels commanded by Brig. Gen. William Maxwell skirmished with Cornwallis's vanguard before withdrawing to the main American encampment. Both sides suffered about 30 casualties. Howe marched on. Believing Howe intended to outflank him, Washington moved his army to Chadd's Ford on Brandywine Creek. As Howe approached on the road from Kennett Square, Washington deployed his troops along Brandywine Creek, a natural barrier, with Generals Wayne and Greene in command at the center of the line, Armstrong at the left, and Lord Stirling, Stephen, and Sullivan at the right, but this deployment left Trimble's Ford on the creek's west branch and Jeffrie's Ford on the east branch unprotected.

While von Knyphausen engaged the American center in an artillery duel at Chadd's Ford, Howe and Cornwallis crossed the creek at the unprotected fords and positioned their troops at Osborne's Hill, outflanking Washington, who had been misled by conflicting reports on their movements. Lord Stirling and Stephen moved to confront the British but unintentionally created a gap between their lines that the British surged through in a bayonet attack. Greene's brigade raced forward to stem the breach but were forced back in furious fighting. At the same time, von Knyphausen sallied across the Brandywine, withstood the Continentals' stubborn defense and deadly fire, captured the American artillery, and turned the cannons on the retreating Continentals. As darkness fell, the battle terminated. Washington withdrew to Chester. The victorious Howe encamped on the battlefield. By General Greene's estimate, the American losses numbered 1,200, including 400 prisoners; the British losses, under 600. Apprised by a dispatch from Washington of the American defeat at the Battle of Brandywine, the Continental Congress immediately requested reinforcements for the army from New York, New Jersey, Maryland, and Pennsylvania, but anxiety over Howe's approach also prodded the delegates to begin leaving Philadelphia on September 18 to reconvene in Lancaster.[12]

PHILADELPHIA AND GERMANTOWN

Concerned again that he might be outflanked, Washington moved his army to the White Horse Tavern near Malvern. Howe followed. The enemies positioned themselves for battle, but a fierce downpour precluded fighting and ruined the Americans' ammunition. Washington marched in the rain toward Reading Furnace to acquire fresh ammunition. That achieved, he marched back to the east side of the Schuylkill River to encamp by Perkiomen Creek. Von Knyphausen and Cornwallis marched to Valley Forge and discovered an American cache of flour, soap, and other supplies. Howe set up a post at Valley Forge. Forewarned by local Tories, Howe dispatched troops in a surprise attack against about 1,500 men under Gen. Anthony Wayne sent to harass the British. Put to flight, Wayne's force suffered 150 dead and more than 70 captured.

Washington moved once again to avoid being outflanked and encamped near Pott's Grove (now Pottstown). In response, Howe shifted directions, crossed the Schuylkill River, and marched to Norristown, arriving on September 23—the same day that Lord Cornwallis took possession of Philadelphia, encamping near Howe's main force at Germantown. Washington marched to encamp at Pennypacker's Mill (now Schwenksville). At dawn on October 4, Washington's army attacked Howe's main force at Germantown and drove back the British advance units. One of the retreating units holed up in Benjamin Chew's stone house and fired on the Continentals, halting their advance. Knox persuaded Washington not to continue the attack until the house was captured, causing an hour's delay. Knox's artillery barrage of Chew's house attracted General Stephen's attention; confused by a heavy fog, he shifted directions, approached the rear of General Wayne's force, and opened fire, bringing both forces to a standstill. With General Greene's progress also delayed, Washington's plan for a coordinated attack came totally undone, and the commander ordered a general withdrawal after losing 673 men plus 400 taken prisoner. Howe's casualties numbered 535. Although a disappointment for Washington, the Battle of Germantown was his first attack on the major force of the British army and that army's first retreat before the Americans in open battle.[13]

This portrait of Henry Knox was painted by Charles Wilson Peale. *(Courtesy Anne S. K. Brown Military Collection, Brown University Library)*

THE BATTLE OF SARATOGA

At Fort Stanwix, Col. Peter Gansevoort received word on August 6 that Gen. Nicholas Herkimer would soon arrive from Oriskany with 800 militiamen. The colonel sent out 200 men to distract St. Leger's troops and to meet Herkimer. They chanced upon one of St. Leger's camps, killed 15 soldiers, and drove off the remainder, but the skirmish exposed their movements and prevented their rendezvousing with Herkimer. St. Leger sent Joseph Brant and 400 of his Mohawk along with two Tory units to ambush Herkimer's force. The ambuscade decimated the surprised Americans, who fought back ferociously in hand-to-hand combat, inflicting serious casualties but losing perhaps 200 men.

The next day, St. Leger, conferring under a flag of truce, offered Gansevoort and his garrison safe conduct following a surrender but threatened a massacre by the Indians otherwise. Offended by the threat, Gansevoort rejected surrender but accepted the offer of a three-day truce. During the truce, he sent a courier secretly through the British lines to Fort Dayton to request reinforcements. Meanwhile at Stillwater, General Schuyler learned of the siege of Fort Stanwix and decided to send reinforcements, an expedition Benedict Arnold quickly volunteered to command. At Fort Dayton, Arnold's brigade was joined by 100 militiamen but still lacked adequate numbers to challenge St. Leger. As a ruse, Arnold sent Hon Yost Schuyler to spread the rumor among St. Leger's men that Arnold was approaching Fort Stanwix with a superior force. Arnold promised Schuyler pardon of a death sentence for trying to recruit troops for the British; Schuyler had bullet holes shot through his coat, and he convinced St. Leger that he had escaped from Arnold's troops and come to warn him. The ruse succeeded. St. Leger abandoned the siege and, on August 22, began marching back to Montreal.[14]

In the meantime, Gen. Horatio Gates arrived at Stillwater to assume command of the Northern Department from General Schuyler. Gates ordered the fortification of Bemis Heights, a bluff above the Hudson River protected by ravines and forests. Arnold and Col. Tadeusz Kościuszko devised the fortifications to be built. On September 13, General Burgoyne abandoned his plan to cross the Hudson at Albany as presenting too many difficulties and began to cross over a bridge made of bateaux near Fort Miller—his destination, Saratoga. At 10:00 A.M. on September 19, a cannon shot signaled the beginning of Burgoyne's advance, launched in three columns under Hamilton, Fraser, and von Riedesel. As Hamilton's column moved toward Bemis Heights, Arnold urged Gates to send a foray into the British center line in the woody terrain to prevent Burgoyne from using his artillery to entrap and bombard the American lines on the heights. Gates pondered this counsel for two hours before acceding. First, he sent Morgan's men forth and then most of Arnold's force to assault Burgoyne's center. The opponents battled throughout the afternoon, each side repeatedly charging and withdrawing across the 350-yard clearing that separated them. General Fraser's column, sent to the north to search for high ground, remained too distant to join the battle, but part of von Riedesel's column struggled up the bluffs from the river in time to prevent the collapse of Hamilton's force. When darkness arrived, Arnold withdrew, leaving the battlefield in possession of Burgoyne but at a serious cost to the British of 556 casualties, while Arnold had 287.[15]

As October began, Gen. Sir Henry Clinton, left by Howe in command of the New York garrison, which had been reinforced to 7,000 British and German regulars in addition to 3,000 Loyalists, led a force of 4,000 toward Tarrytown to create a diversion in support of Burgoyne. He handily seized the American post at Verplanck's Point, whose defenders withdrew without offering opposition. Leaving 1,000 men to guard the post, Clinton crossed the Hudson River, marched

Col. Benedict Arnold was leader of the Continental army forces on the Canada expedition. *(Colonel Arnold, courtesy of Anne S. K. Brown Military Collection, Brown University Library)*

up the east bank, divided his force into two divisions, sent one division to attack Fort Campbell, and led the second division in attacking Fort Clinton. Successful in both attacks, the British inflicted severe casualties on the American defenders, who escaped after dark; the British also burned the Americans' vessels in the river.[16]

After a two-week pause at Bemis Heights, during which Gates received reinforcements that augmented his total force to 11,000 while Burgoyne received none and consumed needed supplies, the British commander rejected Fraser's and von Riedesel's counsel to retreat and instead, on October 7, organized and led a reconnaissance detachment of 1,500 men to probe Gates's left flank. They failed to find the Americans and formed in a wheatfield to wait. Continentals led by Daniel Morgan and Enoch Poor launched a surprise attack and outflanked the waiting troops. Arnold, although earlier relieved of duty by Gates, spurred his horse into the ensuing battle, inspiring the Americans to charge wildly and repeatedly. The British defense crumbled. As the British retreated, Fraser took a mortal wound. Arnold rashly swept on in pursuit, until, his horse shot from under him and his leg badly wounded, he had to be carried to the rear, depriving the Americans of a brash leader and ending the attack. With 600 casualties against fewer than 150 for the Americans, Burgoyne had no choice but retreat. During the night, he withdrew his force toward Saratoga, abandoning tents, wagons, baggage, and even bodies of his dead en route.

On October 9, Burgoyne's army, constantly harassed by Gates's advance troops in hot pursuit, reached the heights at Saratoga. His force of 13,000 greatly outnumbering Burgoyne's 5,800 troops, Gates positioned his men to cut off any possibility of retreat for Burgoyne, blocking his access to the Hudson River. On October 13, Burgoyne conceded the hopelessness of his situation and requested a halt to hostilities. Negotiations for a surrender began. On October 16, Gates and Burgoyne reached final agreement on the terms of their "Convention" for the British surrender: All troops in Burgoyne's force would be considered British, regardless of nationality; they would be returned to England by way of Boston; and they must never again participate in the American war. On the same day, Gen. Sir Henry Clinton dispatched 1,700 troops under Gen. John Vaughan to move upriver from Kingston in search of Burgoyne's army. On the following day at 2:00 P.M., Burgoyne surrendered his army, and he and Gates lunched together, with Burgoyne offering a toast to Washington and Gates a toast to George III. A few days later, Clinton received orders from Howe to abandon his quest for Burgoyne and to send reinforcements to Pennsylvania.[17]

This portrait of General Horatio Gates was painted by John Morris. *(Courtesy of National Archives and Records Administration)*

THE DELAWARE RIVER OFFENSIVE

On October 19, General Howe withdrew his troops from Germantown to concentrate his entire army in Philadelphia. Determined to gain control of the

General Burgoyne surrenders at Saratoga. *(Courtesy of the National Archives and Records Administration)*

Delaware River as the best supply route for his army, he sent detachments to clear the river of chevaux-de-frise the Americans had created across the river that could rip open the hulls of ships passing over. Throughout October and November, he dispatched troops to conquer American posts along the river. His troops quickly routed the American garrison at Billingsport, New Jersey. At Fort Mercer, however, the 2,000 Hessian troops commanded by Col. Carl von Donop sent to the attack fared less well. Approaching the fort by land, they traversed its outer defenses without a shot being fired but suddenly experienced a shattering hail of bullets and subsequent firing from galleys in the river that forced their withdrawal, with the mortally wounded von Donop left on the field.[18]

Fort Mifflin, Pennsylvania, also presented a formidable resistance. On October 23 the fort's artillery shelled six British ships sent to clear the chevaux-de-frise from the Delaware; two of the ships ran aground and were destroyed. But the river's current created a new channel that allowed the British to move a floating battery of 22 24-pound cannons within 40 yards of the fort, and on November 10, the battery began a five-day continuous cannonading of the fort's defenses. This horrendous pounding knocked out all but two of the fort's cannons, inflicted high casualties, and laid waste major parts of the fort. To finish the job, the British moved six ships into range that fired hundreds of cannonballs every 20 minutes and reduced the fort to rubble. During the night of November 15, the American commander had the fort's ruins torched and withdrew his men across the river to Red Bank. Only 150 of the fort's original 450 defenders escaped death or wounding. The British endured 12 casualties. The fort's demolition allowed Howe to send Cornwallis with 2,000 troops to attack Fort Mercer again. This time the British succeeded, as the Americans accepted their incapacity to protect the fort and evacuated, burning the fort's buildings and supplies. Howe gained control of the Delaware River.[19]

In early December, General Howe led most of his army from Philadelphia for a surprise attack on Washington at Whitemarsh. But a scout observing Howe's movements forewarned the American commander, who prepared a defense. Howe first encamped at Chestnut Hill and then at Edge Hill. On December 8, his troops pushed back Washington's right and left wings until repulsed by American cavalry. Deciding that Washington held an impregnable position, Howe marched his army back to Philadelphia. During the third week of December, Washington moved his army to Valley Forge and began building winter quarters. Hostilities had ended for 1777.[20]

THE ARTICLES OF CONFEDERATION

The Continental Congress divided the majority of its attentions among financial, military, and foreign relations issues, but as the year progressed, the latter became of increasing importance and influenced the delegates' determinations of vital policies, including the question of forming a new national government. The growing significance of foreign relations evidenced itself on the very first day of 1777, when Congress appointed Benjamin Franklin commissioner to the court of Spain—a clear indication of the importance that Congress placed on negotiations with that nation. In April, the delegates confirmed the importance of cultivating relations with other nations by renaming the Committee of Secret Correspondence as the Committee for Foreign Affairs. And in May, the Continental Congress appointed Arthur Lee to replace Franklin as commissioner to Spain, while also appointing Ralph Izard to replace Franklin as commissioner to the court of the grand duke of Tuscany and William Lee as commissioner to the courts of Berlin and Vienna. This emphasis on foreign relations complemented the pursuit of a plan of confederation.[21]

As early as 1775, Benjamin Franklin had introduced a plan entitled Articles of Confederation and Perpetual Union. In January 1776, the Continental Congress had debated whether to consider the plan but had shelved it because the issue of separation from Great Britain remained unresolved. But interest in such a plan endured. For example, in May 1776, while Congress was considering independence, the Virginia Convention had instructed its delegates to support not only independence but also the securing of foreign alliances along with the forming of a confederation. In mid-June, the Continental Congress had appointed a committee to draft a constitution. And when Richard Henry Lee submitted the resolution to draft a declaration of independence, he included advocating creation of a confederation and establishing of foreign alliances. Soon after Congress had approved and announced independence, the delegates began to debate provisions for a confederation based on a draft plan generated by the Constitution Committee and largely the work of committee member John Dickinson. The debates stretched over many months, and Congress frequently put aside the issue to address more pressing concerns.

In April 1777, the Continental Congress returned to the issue with vigor. As September began, following innumerable debates on the provisions of a confederation plan, the members disapproved a motion to consider the issue on a daily basis. Preoccupation with military operations and the delegates' September evacuation of Philadelphia intermittently sidetracked their deliberations. The debates resumed in October while Congress met in York. The delegates settled the question of how the new Congress would vote by awarding a single vote to each state. They next turned their focus on taxation.

In mid-October, following nearly a week of debate on whether taxes should be proportioned on the basis of population, land values, or general property values, they chose the basis of land values and their improvements. They also decided that each state should have at least two delegates and no more than seven, with three-year terms of office. By mid-November, although many of the delegates had already returned home, those remaining in York approved and had recorded in the journals of the Continental Congress 13 Articles of Confederation. On November 17, the Congress sent out copies of the Articles of Confederation to the various states with the hope that their legislatures would quickly and unanimously ratify them. The delegates believed confederation, as a consummation of the union, vital to successful prosecution of the war.[22]

THE ALLIANCE WITH FRANCE

As matters unfolded, military victory proved more crucial than confederation to the success of the American effort to secure overt and official foreign support. In the context of that effort at least, the pivotal Battle of Saratoga decided the ultimate course of the Revolutionary War. Tentative American negotiations with the court of France had been ongoing since the summer of 1776 and had intensified with Benjamin Franklin's arrival in Paris in December of that year. But their

Benjamin Franklin visits the Court of France. *(Courtesy of the National Archives and Records Administration)*

final success depended on some positive catalytic event. News of General Howe's occupation of Philadelphia reached France in November 1777 and effectively derailed the American commissioners' pursuit of an alliance, but on December 4, an envoy from the Continental Congress arrived at the Versailles court with news of the American victory and capture of Gen. John Burgoyne and his army at Saratoga. The American commissioners had their positive catalytic event.

On December 6, Charles Gravier, count de Vergennes, the French foreign minister, sent his congratulations on the Saratoga victory to Silas Deane, Benjamin Franklin, and Arthur Lee; of greater import, he invited them to reinstate their request for establishing a formal alliance between the United States and France. The following day, Franklin sent his grandson William Temple Franklin, who served as Franklin's clerk, to deliver to Vergennes a proposal for an alliance that he had drafted. On December 12, the three American commissioners met secretly with Vergennes, who informed them that France's overt participation in the war depended on Spain's concurrence, yet to be received. But on December 17, an official from the foreign office brought word to Franklin that Louis XVI's ministers had approved a formal alliance with the United States that would remain secret until receipt of Spain's presumptive assent. Although news of these developments could not reach the United States for several weeks, Franklin and his fellow commissioners now had assurances that France would join the American side in fighting the Revolutionary War. These three Americans, at least, knew that as the year ended, prospects for the war's outcome looked much brighter.[23]

CHRONICLE OF EVENTS

1777

January 1: His trip to England canceled by the Trenton debacle, Charles, Lord Cornwallis, completes the 50-mile ride from New York City, arriving at Princeton with 6,000 soldiers as Gen. James Grant also arrives with 1,000 troops. (Grant has left a guard of only 600 at New Brunswick.) Cornwallis's command at Princeton totals 8,000 men.

With a force of about 5,100 men gathered at Trenton, Washington sends a brigade commanded by the French volunteer Brig. Gen. Roche de Fermoy toward Princeton in the hope of forestalling Cornwallis's anticipated march on Trenton. De Fermoy stations his men south of Maidenhead.

The Continental Congress appoints Benjamin Franklin commissioner to the court of Spain, emphasizing the importance placed on negotiating with the Spaniards.

January 2: Leaving behind 1,200 men under Lt. Col. Charles Mawhood to guard Princeton, Cornwallis begins a march to Trenton in the early morning with 5,500 soldiers and 28 artillery pieces. At about 10:00 A.M., the British encounter the American advance guard, now commanded by Col. Edward Hand. Retreating slowly, the Americans pause at advantageous sites to skirmish with the British and delay their progress. Hand's men fall back to a ridge along the south bank of Assunpink Creek, where Washington's force waits behind earthworks. The 1,500-man British advance guard reaches the creek at about 5:00 P.M. Cornwallis's main force arrives; deciding that he has Washington entrapped, the British general withdraws his troops to encamp and to prepare an attack for the next day. Washington calls a council of war that decides on an audacious plan to withdraw under cover of darkness, march around Cornwallis's left flank, and move on to attack the British forces remaining at Princeton and New Brunswick. Washington leaves 400 men assigned to deceive Cornwallis by stoking the campfires and noisily building entrenchments.

January 3: At 1:00 A.M., Washington begins the march to Princeton. At Stony Brook, Washington leaves 350 men commanded by Gen. Hugh Mercer to hold a stone bridge in case Cornwallis comes in pursuit. Meanwhile, the main army pushes on to Princeton. But the element of surprise is lost, as Mawhood,

under orders to march with most of his men to join General Leslie at Maidenhead, has already begun to move out. Mawhood's men cross Stony Brook bridge and spot Mercer's troops approaching. They race to a nearby orchard. Mawhood orders a bayonet attack. Unnerved, the American troops flee. Mercer tries to rally them but falls mortally wounded by seven bayonet thrusts. Cadwalader's men arrive on the scene and enter the skirmish. Hearing the musket shots, Washington and his staff leave Sullivan's division behind to gallop into the fray. Many of Mercer's and Cadwalader's retreating men rally and, joined by men from Sullivan's division, charge into the midst of the British, firing at point-blank range. Mawhood and many of his men manage to break free and retreat toward Trenton, as Washington leads a party of Philadelphia dragoons hard after them. The retreating British troops finally scatter and run, throwing away muskets and equipment to unburden themselves as they flee. The Americans drive back to Princeton the 194 men Mawhood has left behind and force their surrender. The British lose more than 250 men in the battle. American casualties are 100 wounded and 40 dead, including Mercer and Col. John Haslet. Washington decides to withdraw to Morristown. Cornwallis's troops enter Princeton in time to see the rear guard of Washington's army withdrawing in the distance. Cornwallis assumes that Washington is marching to New Brunswick and hastens there.

January 4: Cornwallis's army enters New Brunswick after marching all night, while Washington's army pauses to rest in Pluckemin.

January 5: In the hope of maximizing whatever advantage accrues from his victories at Trenton and Princeton, Washington writes a letter at Pluckemin to send to Gen. William Heath in the Hudson Highlands, instructing Heath to move his troops toward New York and feign an attack on the city.

January 6: Washington settles his army into winter quarters in the Watchung Mountains near Morristown. From here, the Americans can observe New York and the roads leading to New England and Philadelphia. Contingents of American troops capture Hackensack and Elizabethtown, reducing former British control of New Jersey to their garrisons of 5,000 men each in New Brunswick and Amboy.

January 9: Without explanation, the Continental Congress dismisses Dr. John Morgan as director-general of the army's hospitals. He has made enemies through his strenuous efforts to organize an effective medical service.

January 13: Thomas Paine publishes *The American Crisis II,* addressed to Lord Howe.

January 16: Because New Hampshire has granted Vermont a declaration of independence, a convention meeting at Westminster, New Hampshire, votes in favor of requesting recognition from the Continental Congress as an independent state.

January 18: Because three divisions commanded by Generals Benjamin Lincoln, Charles Scott, and David Wooster and Samuel Parsons have joined with his own force at Spuyten Duyvil, General Heath now has nearly 6,000 troops. He launches an attack (by Washington's orders) against Fort Independence north of Kingsbridge as he marches toward New York. About 2,000 Hessians defend the fort, and their commander refuses Heath's demand to surrender within 20 minutes, ordering a cannonade of the Americans instead. The cautious and sluggish Heath pauses to consider his options.

January 20–22: British troops, headed for Somerset Courthouse, New Jersey, in search of provisions, skirmish with Americans encamped at nearby Morristown. About 400 Continentals led by Brig. Gen. Philemon Dickinson drive off the British foragers, seizing some prisoners, wagons, and horses.

January 29: At Fort Independence, after 10 days of sporadic artillery shots and feints and a sally by the Hessians that sent his men into flight, Heath decides to withdraw and encamp north of Spuyten Duyvil Creek.

February 2: Troy militiamen stationed near the Florida-Georgia border attack Fort McIntosh, Georgia, a small stockade on the bank of the Satilla River, commanded by Continental Capt. Richard Winn.

February 4: A two-day siege of Fort McIntosh forces Captain Winn's surrender. The victorious Tories parole all their captives except two officers whom they take to St. Augustine as hostages.

February 15: After lengthy intermittent discussions generated by concerns over the inflationary prices that have resulted from their excessive but necessary issuance of paper money, the members of the Continental Congress condone a New England convention's response that recommends imposing rigid regulations on pricing. Congress encourages other states to meet in convention and follow the New England example.

February 19: The Continental Congress promotes Lord Stirling, Thomas Mifflin, Adam Stephen, Arthur St. Clair, and Benjamin Lincoln to the rank of major general. Enraged over being omitted from the promotions, Benedict Arnold submits his resignation, but Washington persuades him to withdraw it.

February 25: Disregarding King George III's message to Lord North that George, Viscount Germain, will propose placing General Clinton in charge of the forces in Canada and General Burgoyne will be sent to join General Howe, the North cabinet approves sending Burgoyne to Canada to serve in a dual command with General Carleton.

February 27: The Continental Congress adjourns in Baltimore to reconvene in Philadelphia on March 4.

February 28: General Burgoyne presents his plan for the 1777 campaign in America to Germain in London. Burgoyne proposes to send a force of 8,000 men from Canada across Lake Champlain and a smaller force through Oswego and down the Mohawk River, with the two uniting on the Hudson River above Albany for an attack on that city. His proposal rejects the option of employing a strike force from the sea. Burgoyne states, "I do not conceive any expedition from the sea can be so formidable to the enemy, or so effectual to close the war, as an invasion from Canada by Ticonderoga." The campaign's goal is to gain control of the Hudson and to seal off New England from the other states in order to free General Howe for attacks on Philadelphia and other objectives farther south or for pursuit of some alternative plan.

March 3: Lord Germain writes to General Howe approving his plan to attack Philadelphia and continue moving southward, but Germain makes no promises concerning the additional 20,000 troops Howe has requested, telling him that reinforcements may be limited to 5,500.

March 12: Lacking a quorum on March 4, the Continental Congress now reconvenes in Philadelphia, but some states remain unrepresented.

March 13: Distracted and annoyed by problems arising from the large numbers of foreign officers (many of them assumed to be mercenaries with suspect motives) who seek commissions to serve in the Continental army, the Continental Congress orders the Committee of Secret Correspondence to write immediately to instruct "all their ministers and agents abroad, to discourage all gentlemen from coming to America with expectation of employment in the service, unless they are masters of our language, and have the best of recommendations."

March 14: Washington's army at Morristown has dwindled to 3,000 men through desertions and the end of the six-week reenlistment period that he persuaded many to accept. Many of those remaining are militiamen whose enlistments expire at the end of March. Although the Continental Congress has authorized raising an army of 75,000 and offering bounties of $20 plus 100 acres at the end of each enlistee's period of service, recruitment efforts fall well below needs. Washington keeps his few troops occupied in harassing the enemy with raids on their foraging parties and sentinels as a means of convincing General Howe that the American army is larger than it really is. Exacerbating his recruitment worries, Washington must commandeer supplies from civilians.

March 23: During the past November, Washington left 3,300 troops at Peekskill, New York, to keep watch on the Hudson Highlands. Now, the great majority of these troops have dissipated, even as large quantities of military supplies have been brought to the post for storage. Massachusetts has ignored Washington's request for eight regiments to defend the post; only 250 men commanded by Gen. Alexander McDougall remain for that task. About 500 British soldiers disembark to launch an attack on the post, and McDougall withdraws from the town, dispatching a request to Col. Marinus Willett to send troops from Fort Montgomery on the opposite side of the river. The British advance guard burns the American barracks and some of the military supplies. Arriving with 80 men, Willett fails to persuade McDougall to attack but gains his permission to lead an assault of his own. When Willett's men open fire and begin a bayonet charge, the British fall back to their boats and escape.

March 26: Lord Germain signs orders for General Carleton that incorporate General Burgoyne's plan; Burgoyne will carry them to Quebec, and a copy will go to General Howe. Germain also orders Carleton, after evicting the Americans from Canada, to keep enough troops in Quebec to defend the province and to send the remainder south to aid Burgoyne's army in the invasion of the colonies. Lt. Barry St. Leger will lead this force on a diversionary march through the Mohawk Valley as Burgoyne marches to Albany.

April 12: General Howe writes to Lord Germain to advise him that, lacking the reinforcements he has requested, Howe cannot move overland to attack Philadelphia. Instead, Howe plans to load his troops aboard ships in New York Harbor to transport them to Phila-

delphia for an assault from the water. If fulfilled, this plan would mean that Howe's army will not be available to support Burgoyne's invasion from Canada, but Germain has not yet made the nature of this invasion clear to Howe.

April 11: The Continental Congress names Philadelphia physician William Shippen to succeed Dr. John Morgan as director-general of the Continental army's hospitals. Shippen has served as director-general of the army's hospital in New Jersey, and in March, he submitted a plan for reorganizing the medical service that Congress accepted.

April 13: British troops commanded by Lord Cornwallis stage a surprise attack on the American outpost at Bound Brook, New Jersey, that Maj. Gen. Benjamin Lincoln commands. Lincoln succeeds in withdrawing most of his 500 men, but the British capture some prisoners along with the post's artillery to transport back to New York.

April 17: The Continental Congress resolves to rename the Committee of Secret Correspondence as the Committee for Foreign Affairs and appoints Thomas Paine to serve as the committee's secretary.

April 19: On this first anniversary of the Battle of Lexington, Thomas Paine publishes *The American Crisis III.*

April 20: With the official blessing of Silas Deane, Marie-Joseph du Motier (the marquis de Lafayette) and Johann Kalb ("baron de Kalb") set sail from France to offer their services to the American Revolution.

April 25: William Tryon, now a major general under orders from Howe to destroy an American supply at Danbury, Connecticut, lands at the mouth of the Saugatuck River with a force of about 2,000, including about 300 Loyalists, to carry out his mission.

April 26: Tryon encounters no opposition and arrives at Danbury to discover that the small detachment of Continentals assigned to guard the post there has already withdrawn and taken some of the supplies along. His men begin to destroy those supplies left behind.

April 27: Tryon's men continue their work of destruction, in the end burning 19 houses, 22 storehouses and barns, and quantities of meats, flour, clothing, and tents. Their work completed, Tryon begins a return march to Norwalk, Connecticut.

Benedict Arnold, sulking at his sister's home in New Haven, Connecticut, over not being promoted to major general, learns of Tryon's raid on Danbury and rides to Redding, where General Wooster and Connecticut militia Gen. Gold Silliman camp with 600 troops. They march to Bethel, Connecticut. Learning that Tryon's force is returning to Norwalk, they divide into two units—Arnold and Silliman leading 400 men to Ridgefield, Connecticut, and Wooster taking 200 men to harass Tryon's rear guard.

Wooster's men skirmish repeatedly with Tryon's until Wooster falls mortally wounded and the Americans retreat. About 100 militiamen join Arnold's and Silliman's force at Ridgefield. They barricade the road leading into the north side of the town and fire on the approaching British troops, who move to outflank them, sending the Americans into retreat. Arnold's horse is shot from under him, and he becomes entangled in his stirrups. Arnold shoots an attacking Tory who demands his surrender, untangles himself, and narrowly escapes.

April 28: Tryon's men arrive at Compo Hill, near to the site where they will board their ships. Arnold forms his men to prepare an attack, but General Erskine leads 400 British troops in a bayonet attack against them, and the Americans scatter. Tryon's men go aboard ship and sail off. The two-day encounter leaves the Americans with about 60 casualties, including 20 dead; the British suffer at least 60 dead, although their exact losses remain unclear.

May 1: The Continental Congress appoints Arthur Lee to replace Benjamin Franklin as commissioner to Spain.

May 2: With praise for Benedict Arnold for his "gallant conduct" at Danbury, the Congress promotes him to the rank of major general, but he remains junior to the five men promoted in February.

Lt. William Linn arrives at Fort Henry, Virginia, bringing 98 barrels of powder for the fight against Indians and Tories on the frontier.

May 3: The *Surprise,* commanded by Gustavus Conyngham, "the Dunkirk pirate," attacks and captures the British packet *Prince of Orange* off the French coast at Dunkirk and brings her into port. The American commissioners in Paris appointed Conygham as ship commander in early March.

May 6: Welcomed by Sir Guy Carleton, Gen. John Burgoyne arrives at Quebec aboard HMS *Apollo* to assume command of British forces in Canada.

May 7: The Continental Congress appoints Ralph Izard to replace Benjamin Franklin as commissioner to the court of the Grand Duke of Tuscany.

May 8: Washington issues a general order forbidding gambling of any kind by his officers and soldiers.

May 9: The Continental Congress appoints William Lee commissioner to the courts of Berlin and Vienna.

May 10: Maj. Gen. Adam Stephen attempts a surprise attack on the 42nd Highlanders (the Black Watch) at Piscataway, New Jersey, and suffers a rout, inflicting fewer than 30 casualties while suffering 27 dead and twice as many taken prisoner—much to Washington's displeasure.

May 15: With an increased recruitment effort, Washington's army at Morristown now numbers 9,000 men, and he is able to outfit them properly because in March he received 12,000 muskets, 1,000 barrels of powder, and clothing surreptitiously sent from France. Washington organizes his army into five divisions commanded by Major Generals Greene, Stephen, Sullivan, Lincoln, and Lord Stirling.

May 17: Col. Augustine Prevost leads a combined force of British regulars, Rangers, and Indians in an attack on Col. John Baker's small force of 109 Americans near Thomas's Swamp, Florida, routing the rebels, killing eight, and taking 31 prisoners. But the Indians begin to massacre the American prisoners, killing more than half of them before Prevost's struggling regulars manage to regain control.

May 29: Concerned over what moves General Howe might make, Washington moves his army southward to the Middlebrook Valley in the Watchung Mountain range and stations a force at Princeton under Sullivan's command. From his new encampment Washington can watch the roads leading to New Brunswick and Philadelphia.

June 12: General Howe assembles an 18,000-man army at Amboy with orders to march to New Brunswick. There the army separates; Lord Cornwallis leads one column to Somerset, and Gen. Philip von Heister leads a second column to Middlebrook. Howe's purpose is to separate Sullivan from Washington's main army and to egg Washington into battle, but his strategy fails.

By orders of General Gates, Maj. Gen. Arthur St. Clair arrives at Fort Ticonderoga to assume command of the garrison of perhaps 2,500 men. Three brigadier generals—Alexis Roche de Fermoy, John Paterson, and Enoch Poor—serve under St. Clair.

June 13: General Burgoyne has assembled an army of 7,200 men at St. John's, Quebec. The main force is

3,724 British and 3,016 German regulars; about 150 French Quebecois, 100 Loyalists, and 400 Indians fill out the ranks. His artillery numbers 139 cannons. He has also assembled nine ships (including three captured from Arnold), 28 gunboats, and a sizable number of bateaux to carry his army across Lake Champlain for the invasion of the United States. All the guns in the fort and the fleet present a massive salute to the Union flag.

The marquis de Lafayette and Johann de Kalb arrive at Georgetown, South Carolina. They carry written agreements from Silas Deane to the effect that the Continental Congress will commission them as major generals in the Continental army.

June 14: The Continental Congress authorizes creation of an official flag of the United States. The resolution specifies that the flag "be thirteen stripes alternative red and white; that the Union be thirteen stars, white in a blue field, representing a new constellation." Congress also appoints John Paul Jones as commander of the sloop *Ranger*.

June 16: Burgoyne's advance guard, under the command of Brig. Gen. Simon Fraser, reaches Crown Point.

June 17: The American regiment commanded by Col. Daniel Morgan, recently released by the British and awarded the command by Washington, harasses British troops trying to build entrenchments at a redoubt near Somerset Courthouse, New Jersey.

June 18: Burgoyne's main army assembles at Cumberland Head at Lake Champlain to prepare for crossing the lake.

June 19: Conceding that his strategy to lure Washington into battle has failed, General Howe withdraws von Heister's troops from Middlebrook to New Brunswick. Washington sends a detachment commanded by Gen. William Maxwell to establish a position between New Brunswick and Amboy as a means of forestalling any effort by Howe's army to attack the Americans' exposed left flank.

June 20: At Cumberland Head, General Burgoyne issues a pompous proclamation accusing the American rebels of inflicting upon "suffering" Loyalists "the completest system of Tyranny that God ever in his displeasure suffer'd for a time to be exercised over a froward and stubborn Generation." He threatens to unleash on the rebels the vengeance of the Indians and the "devastation, famine and every concomitant horror that a reluctant but indispensable prosecution of military duty must occasion." The proclamation's hyperbole invites

ridicule of Burgoyne, even by Britons. Burgoyne and his army set off for Crown Point.

Maj. Gen. Philip Schuyler, still in command of the Northern Department despite being unpopular, arrives at Fort Ticonderoga for a council of war. The officers all agree the fort should be held as long as possible but then must be abandoned—the garrison will escape by boat to Mount Independence across the lake.

June 22: General Howe leaves New Brunswick for Amboy, and American troops commanded by Daniel Morgan and Anthony Wayne attack his rear guard of Hessians. Although Washington's generals argue that Howe is staging a genuine withdrawal, the commander moves his main army to Quibbletown along the left flank of Howe's army. Howe shifts directions and heads for Scotch Plains in the hope of outflanking Washington; his army occupies the ridges above Middlebrook.

June 23: Lt. Col. Barry St. Leger leads his force of about 2,000 men and a dozen cannons out of Montreal on a march to conjoin with Burgoyne at Albany. Indians make up half of St. Leger's force, along with about 340 British and Hessian regulars and at least an equal number of Tories.

June 26: Sending Cornwallis's detachment through Woodbridge in an outflanking effort and another detachment to Bonham Town to confront Greene and Wayne, Howe moves the remainder of his army to Metuchen Meeting House. Cornwallis encounters a division led by Lord Stirling on the outskirts of Woodbridge. Although outnumbered two to one, Stirling's men fight tenaciously and suffer perhaps 100 dead. Washington uses Stirling's delaying of Cornwallis to withdraw his main army to protected positions at Middlebrook. Conceding that his tactics have failed, Howe begins the withdrawal of all his troops to Staten Island.

General Burgoyne has established a magazine and a hospital at Crown Point and has issued supplies to his men. General Fraser's advance guard of Indians, Loyalists, and Canadians sets out from Crown Point for Ticonderoga.

June 27: While returning to France after a successful foray against British merchantmen in the Irish Channel—they seized 18 ships, destroyed 10, and kept eight as prizes—Capt. Lambert Wickes and his two accompanying raiders run upon the British warship *Burford* off the French coast. Ordering his two companions to scatter, Wickes attempts to effect the *Reprisal's* escape, initially keeping the ship out of range. The *Bur-*

ford closes and turns to fire a broadside. Wickes turns the *Reprisal* to prevent exposing its sides, has some beams sawed off to enhance the ship's buoyancy, and speeds away to safety.

June 30: Howe's entire army completes reassembling in New York and on Staten Island, leaving the Continental army in control of all of New Jersey.

Burgoyne's army disembarks at a landing site on Lake Champlain secured by Fraser's advance guard.

July 1: Burgoyne divides his force, placing his British troops on the west side of Lake Champlain and his Hessians on the east side—a flotilla that nearly covers this mile-wide stretch of the lake. The two divisions disembark and encamp on opposite shores of the lake about three miles above Fort Ticonderoga. Although the fort is actually sited on both sides of the lake, its entrenchments on the west bank are in disrepair.

July 2: Burgoyne begins his assault on Fort Ticonderoga, with Gen. William Phillips leading a force that includes Fraser's advance guard against Mount Hope. The American defenders torch the post and flee. Simultaneously, Baron von Riedesel leads his division to the rear of Mount Independence, where the Americans fire on them.

July 3: General Phillips's force occupies Mount Hope. Burgoyne sends his chief engineer, Lieutenant Twiss, to reconnoiter Sugar Loaf Hill (Mount Defiance), and Twiss reports back that the hill overlooks and is within artillery range of both Ticonderoga and Independence. Burgoyne orders the building of a road up Sugar Loaf Hill and begins to move his artillery into position.

July 4: At Philadelphia and throughout the states, Americans celebrate the first anniversary of their independence with bell ringing, fireworks, and toasts.

July 5: From Fort Ticonderoga, General St. Clair observes the British emplacing cannons on Sugar Loaf Hill. He calls a council of war that quickly and unanimously decides to abandon the fort.

July 6: Having loaded supplies and ill soldiers under command of Col. Pierce Long aboard bateaux for transport to Skenesboro, St. Clair marches his men out of Fort Ticonderoga under cover of morning darkness across the bridge to Mount Independence and on to Hubbardton. There he orders Lt. Col. Seth Warner to wait with 150 men until the rear guard appears and then to follow after the main body of the troops to Castleton, six miles distant. The rear guard's arrival swells Warner's force to 1,000. He

disregards St. Clair's orders, remaining for the night in Hubbardton. Quickly apprised of the Americans' evacuation of Fort Ticonderoga, the British send out an advance party of about 850 men, commanded by Gen. Simon Fraser, that encamps for the night only three miles from Warner. Fraser's Indian scouts discover Warner's encampment (Warner has posted no pickets). Fraser plans a surprise attack for the next morning.

Long arrives at Skenesboro and quickly realizes that the weak stockade is untenable. He torches the buildings and three of his transports and hastens toward Fort Anne. Burgoyne arrives and sends men in pursuit of the fleeing Long.

July 7: At dawn, Fraser's force surprises Warner's at Hubbardton. The unprepared Americans respond ferociously, inflicting heavy losses during a two-hour battle. But a detachment of Hessians commanded by Riedesel has heard the sounds of battle and hastens to outflank the Americans, and Warner orders them to scatter. (St. Clair has also heard the sounds, but his militia refuse to obey the order to march to the fray.) The Continentals suffer 40 dead and 300 captured; the British, 183 casualties, with 35 dead. Informed of the outcomes at Skenesboro and Hubbardton, St. Clair heads for Fort Edward in hopes of saving his troops.

July 8: At Fort Anne, the British overtake Long, whose 150 men have been reinforced by 400 militia under Col. Henry van Rensselaer dispatched by Schuyler. A two-hour skirmish ensues, until Long hears a single war whoop and, fearing Indian warriors are reinforcing the British, withdraws his troops after setting fire to the fort. They march to Fort Edward.

Meeting at Windsor, the Vermont Convention adopts a constitution as an independent state. The document mandates manhood suffrage and abolition of slavery.

General Howe begins to load his troops aboard ships in New York Harbor.

July 9: During the night, with 40 volunteers, militia Lt. Col. William Barton enters the Newport headquarters of Gen. Richard Prescott, commander of British forces in Rhode Island, and fulfills his plan to capture the general, along with his aide, to exchange him for Gen. Charles Lee.

After sending his gunboats, artillery, and heavy supplies toward the head of Lake George, Burgoyne arrives at Skenesboro. He stations Riedesel and his German troops at Castleton to obscure his plan of advance.

July 16: Now a captain in the Continental navy and in command of the *Revenge,* Gustavus Conyngham sets sail from Dunkirk, France, to prey on British ships.

July 17: The New Hampshire General Court, convened at Portsmouth, accepts John Langdon's proposal to fund a militia commanded by John Stark, who resigned from the Continental army in April, disgruntled over not being promoted to brigadier general. Stark stipulates that he will accept no orders from either Congress or Continental officers.

July 23: Howe sets sail from New York with 18,000 troops, artillery, horses, and supplies aboard 260 warships and transports, destination unknown, although most of Washington's staff believe it to be Philadelphia. Although doubtful, Washington orders four divisions under Generals Sullivan, Lord Stirling, Stephen, and Lincoln, plus Morgan's riflemen and three squadrons of dragoons to Philadelphia immediately.

July 24: At Portsmouth, New Hampshire, Stark has already recruited nearly 1,500 men.

July 25: Congress commends Lt. Col. William Barton for his capture of Prescott and approves awarding him "an elegant sword."

Burgoyne's men have cleared a passageway to allow an advance to Fort Anne. Reinforced by St. Clair's and Long's detachments and about 600 Continentals commanded by Brig. Gen. John Nixon, Schuyler now has a force of about 2,600 regulars and 1,600 militia. Washington has also sent him Generals Benedict Arnold and Benjamin Lincoln, but the officers agree that their force is insufficient to hold Fort Edward.

July 26: Lt. Col. Barry St. Leger leads his force from Oswego to begin his southern offensive.

July 27: Indians from Burgoyne's force capture Jane McCrea, whose Loyalist fiancée serves with Burgoyne, and a Mrs. McNeil, cousin of Gen. Simon Fraser, at Fort Edward. They return to Burgoyne's headquarters at Fort Anne with McNeil and McCrea's scalp. Although the evidence implicates a Wyandot (Huron) man in McCrea's death, Burgoyne can impose no penalty for fear of losing the Indians' allegiance. He thus provides outraged Americans a propaganda issue.

The marquis de Lafayette and Johann de Kalb arrive in Philadelphia with Silas Deane's promise of commissions as major generals. Beleaguered by foreigners seeking commissions in the Continental army, the Continental Congress stalls on honoring Deane's promise.

July 29: Schuyler abandons Fort Edward and moves down the Hudson River to Saratoga. To delay the enemy, marching through a naturally rugged terrain of ravines and swamps, he has his men fell numerous trees, dig ditches to extend swamps, and roll boulders down hills to block passages, so that Burgoyne's army consumes 24 days in traversing only 23 miles. The retreating Americans also burn crops and pastures and incorporate settlers and their cattle into the withdrawal to deny the British forage, horses, and meat.

July 30: Burgoyne's army occupies Fort Edward.

Stark and his militiamen, bearing their own weapons and wearing their own clothes, leave Portsmouth headed for Manchester.

July 31: Congress commissions the marquis de Lafayette a major general but with no command.

At Corryell's Ferry, New Jersey, Washington receives word, first dispatched to Congress by Henry Fisher, a pilot from Lewes, that Howe's fleet has been sighted off the Delaware capes. He orders his army to cross the Delaware River and march to Philadelphia.

August 1: Temporarily headquartered at Chester, Pennsylvania, Washington welcomes Lafayette and, greatly taken with him, invites the young Frenchman to join his staff.

August 2: Now at Germantown, Washington receives word from Henry Fisher that Howe's fleet has sailed away, apparently without a destination. Washington surmises that Howe is sailing for the North River to join forces with Burgoyne and orders his generals to reassemble their troops at Peekskill.

St. Leger arrives at Fort Stanwix, New York, and begins to lay siege to the fort, garrisoned by about 750 men under Col. Peter Gansevoort.

August 3: Deciding to await certain word of Howe's destination, Washington changes his orders to have Sullivan halt at Hanover, New Jersey, while holding his main army at the falls of the Schuylkill near Germantown.

Schuyler arrives with his army of 4,500 intact at Stillwater, New York, about 12 miles below Saratoga on the Hudson.

August 4: Indians with St. Leger encircle Fort Stanwix, yelling to frighten the occupants.

Congress issues orders replacing Schuyler with Gen. Horatio Gates as commander of the Northern Department.

August 6: Three militiamen sent by Gen. Nicholas Herkimer from Oriskany sneak past the Indians and enter Fort Stanwix to inform Gansevoort that Herkimer is en route with 800 militiamen. Gansevoort fires three cannons, as instructed, to apprise Herkimer the message is received and sends out 200 men under Lt. Col. Marinus Willett to distract the British and meet Herkimer. Willett's men chance upon one of St. Leger's camps and kill more than 15; in so doing, they expose their own presence. St. Leger sends 400 Mohawk led by Joseph Brant, John Butler's Tory Rangers, and John Johnson's Royal Greens to prepare an ambush, which Herkimer's own Oneida allies fail to detect. Entrapped at a causeway and raked by deadly fire, the Americans fight ferociously, with Herkimer suffering a shattered leg. A thunderstorm ends the hand-to-hand combat after nearly an hour. Both sides count severe losses, especially among the Indians; American casualties may total over 200.

August 7: St. Leger sends a delegation with a truce flag to urge Gansevoort to surrender Fort Stanwix and offer safe conduct, while threatening an Indian massacre if the fort does not surrender. Offended by the threat, Gansevoort refuses to surrender but accepts a preferred three-day truce. At night, he sends Willett and Major Stockwell through the enemy lines to seek reinforcements from Fort Dayton.

August 8: Ending a pause at Manchester, the post of Seth Warner and Benjamin Lincoln, Stark marches to Bennington, a vital depot for American military supplies.

August 10: At Stillwater, New York, Schuyler learns of the siege at Fort Stanwix, decides to send a relief detachment of about 900 men, and asks for a brigadier general to lead the detachment. Benedict Arnold quickly volunteers, with Brig. Gen. Ebenezer Learned as second in command.

Although returned by uncertainty to Corryell's Ferry, Washington has learned that Howe's fleet was sighted off the Maryland coast sailing southward and is heading for Philadelphia; Howe halts 30 miles north of the city on Neshaminy Creek.

August 11: Short of supplies, Burgoyne accepts Riedesel's suggestion to send out a foraging party as far as the Connecticut River. But he overrides Riedesel's protests and decides on the more ambitious move of sending the expedition to Manchester enlisting Tories en route, and then changes the objective to Bennington. Lt. Col. Friedrich Baum sets out with about 800 men, nearly half of them Germans, but including about 300 Tories, Canadians, and Indians. The Germans' cumbersome uniforms and equipment impede movement through the rugged terrain and complicate fighting,

John Stark played a key part in the Battle of Bennington. *(From* The Pictorial Field Book of the Revolution, *2 vols., B. J. Lossing. New York: Harper Brothers, 1851 and 1852.)*

but Burgoyne believes that the Americans will not fight and that many Loyalists or sympathizers will come to Baum's assistance.

August 13: Burgoyne leaves Fort Edward to cross the Hudson and march on Saratoga.

August 14: Learning that Baum's Indians are looting, killing cows, and pillaging as they advance before the main column, Stark sends 200 men to a mill on Owl Creek to oppose the Indians, but Baum's column arrives and drives them away. Baum now suspects there are more militiamen at Bennington than Burgoyne has surmised; he sends Burgoyne a letter informing him of the capture of supplies at the mill and assuring him of an attack on the militiamen the next day.

August 15: About 400 Vermont militia led by Seth Warner reinforce Stark at Bennington, increasing his force to about 2,000. Rain prevents an engagement, but Baum positions his men and erects breastworks.

August 16: Stark and Warner plan to encircle Baum and attack his front, rear, and flanks. The Americans' opening volley sends most of Baum's Tories, Indians, and Canadians into flight. Two hours of fierce fighting nearly exhaust Baum's ammunition, and all but his dragoons flee. Ordering them to draw sabers, he leads a charge into the Americans' midst and falls fatally wounded. Baum's men surrender. Stark's men scatter to chase the fleeing troops and to plunder their encampment, but German reinforcements under Lt. Col. Heinrich von Breymann, who were sent by Burgoyne at Baum's request, arrive, and skirmishes ensue as Stark desperately tries to regroup his men. A contingent of Warner's men arrives from Manchester to join Stark and force von Breymann into retreat. The Americans have fewer than 70 casualties, while 200 of Baum's and von Breymann's troops lie dead and 700 are prisoners.

August 17: Apprised of the disaster at Bennington, Burgoyne orders his troops into readiness at Fort Miller.

August 19: Gates arrives at Stillwater to assume command of the Northern Department and finds about 4,500 encamped there near the mouth of the Mohawk River.

August 21: About 100 militiamen arrive at Fort Dayton to reinforce Arnold's brigade, but he learns that St. Leger has 1,700 men and concludes that he needs still more troops.

Still bewildered over Howe's movements, Washington calls a council of war at his encampment on Neshaminy Creek that concludes that Charleston must be Howe's destination.

August 22: With news that Howe's armada is in the Chesapeake Bay, Washington cancels orders to move the main army toward the Hudson River and instead orders Sullivan to hastily join him and Gen. Francis Nash to hurry to Chester. He also announces news of the victory at Bennington, bolstering his troops' morale.

August 23: Apprised of Fort Stanwix's peril, Arnold leads part of his force up the Mohawk River to relieve the fort. To his delight, Arnold soon learns that a ruse he concocted with a local German, Hon Yost Schuyler, has succeeded. Arnold promised Schuyler a pardon of his death sentence for trying to recruit troops for the British. In return, Arnold expected Schuyler to travel to St. Leger's camp to tell the British commander that a huge American relief force was approaching Fort Stanwix. Schuyler convinced St. Leger, who lifted the siege on August 22 and began marching back to Montreal.

Marching toward Philadelphia, Washington's army encamps at Germantown for the night.

August 24: Astride his white horse, with Lafayette beside him and his mounted staff immediately following, Washington marches his 16,000-man army single file through Philadelphia, down Front Street and up Chestnut Street, intimidating the local Tories and lifting the spirits of the Patriots.

August 25: The vanguard of Howe's fleet drops anchor in the Elk River; troops begin to disembark.

August 28: After a rest and a pause to await the end of rainy weather, Cornwallis, accompanied by Howe, leads a division of British troops to Elkton, while Wilhelm von Knyphausen leads a second division across the Elk River to encamp at Cecil Courthouse.

September 1: Four hundred Indians lay siege to Fort Henry (now Wheeling, West Virginia), Virginia, named for Patrick Henry, killing a few soldiers in skirmishes. As American reinforcements arrive, the Indians kill livestock, burn the settlement, and withdraw, leaving the settlers unharmed within the fort.

September 2: The Continental Congress defeats a motion to make the issue of confederation part of each day's business.

September 3: Under Washington's orders to harass the advancing British army, Brig. Gen. William Maxwell leads about 100 Continentals in a surprise attack on Cornwallis's division, firing from behind trees at the Hessian and Anspach troops in the forefront. As Lt. Col. Ludwig von Crumb leads his men in a bayonet charge, the Americans fall back, repeatedly pause to fire, and flee back to Green's and Stephen's encampment on White Clay Creek. Each side has about 30 casualties.

September 6: Greene's and Stephen's divisions move to encamp at Newport, Pennsylvania, while Maxwell's corps remains on guard at White Clay Creek.

September 9: Believing Howe intends to move around his right flank and on to Philadelphia, Washington moves his army to Chadd's Ford on Brandywine Creek.

September 10: Howe assembles his entire army at Kennett Square on the road to Philadelphia passing through Chadd's Ford.

September 11: Washington's deployment of his troops in a line at Chadd's Ford on Brandywine Creek leaves Trimble's Ford and Jeffrie's Ford unguarded. Von Knyphausen's Germans open an artillery duel with the American center, while Howe and Cornwallis lead their troops across the unguarded fords and into position on Osborne's Hill, outflanking Washington. Sullivan sends Stephen's and Lord Stirling's troops against the British, but they unknowingly leave a wide gap between their forces, and Howe launches a bayonet attack through this gap. Greene's brigade rushes into the breach but must fall back. Von Knyphausen charges across the Brandywine to capture the Americans' artillery and train it on them as they fall back. Darkness ends the battle, and Washington withdraws to Chester. Howe encamps on the battlefield. British casualties are fewer than 600; Greene estimates the American casualties at 1,200.

September 12: With a force of 6,000 men, General Gates fortifies Bemis Heights, a strategic bluff above the Hudson River.

Washington sends news to the Congress in Philadelphia about the Battle of Brandywine, describing his troops as "in good spirits," and moves his army to the falls of the Schuylkill near Germantown. Congress sends orders to New York, New Jersey, and Pennsylvania requesting reinforcements for Washington.

September 13: Recognizing the difficulty of crossing the Hudson at Albany, Burgoyne creates a bridge of bateaux at Fort Miller and begins to move his troops across to Saratoga.

September 14: Capt. Lambert Wickes, detained by the French in response to British ambassador Lord Stormont's vehement protests over American privateers' use of French ports, is allowed to embark from St.-Malo to sail the *Reprisal* to America.

Hoping to avoid being outflanked again, Washington moves his army to White Horse Tavern near Malvern.

September 15: Congress commissions Baron de Kalb a major general and Kazimierz Pulaski, who had been a volunteer aide with Washington at Brandywine, a brigadier general. Following Washington's recommendation, Congress also creates the position of Commander of the Horse, to be filled by Pulaski, who served in the Polish cavalry. While crossing the Schuylkill River by ferry, but astride his horse, another European claimant to a commission—the troublesome and arrogant Phillipe Tronson du Coudray—drowns when his nervous horse leaps into the river.

September 16: As Howe marches toward White Horse Tavern, von Knyphausen's column encounters Wayne and Maxwell, who withdraw. The two armies position themselves for battle, but a huge cloudburst precludes any encounter. Because the deluge ruins hundreds of thousands of the Americans' cartridges, Washington marches his troops toward Reading Furnace to acquire replacement ammunition, pausing for the night at Yellow Springs.

September 17: Washington encamps at Reading Furnace.

September 18: Anxious over Howe's approach, members of the Continental Congress begin to leave Philadelphia to reconvene in Lancaster. The Liberty Bell that rang out American independence on July 8, 1776, is shipped by army baggage train to Allentown to be hidden in Zion Reformed Church.

Von Knyphausen joins Cornwallis to march to Valley Forge, where they find a rebel cache of flour, soap, horseshoes, entrenching tolls, and other supplies.

An American patrol attacks one of Burgoyne's foraging parties near Bemis Heights, so the British commander has a clearer idea of the American army's location. Arnold, with the help of Col. Tadeusz Kościuszko, has completed the Americans' fortifications, extending from Bemis's Tavern to the three-sided breastworks on the heights of the bluff above the river.

September 19: With his ammunition restored, Washington marches his army 29 miles to encamp beside Perkiomen Creek on the east side of the Schuylkill River, placing his force once more between Philadelphia and Howe's army.

At 10:00 A.M., Burgoyne sends his men in three separate columns to advance on the Americans' breastworks at Bemis Heights. Arnold urges General Gates to send troops out to encounter the British and prevent Burgoyne from using his artillery to entrap Gates's army on the heights. Gates finally sends out Morgan's men and then Arnold's own force to confront Burgoyne's center column under Brig. Gen. Henry Hamilton at Freeman's Farm, a mile north of the heights. The battle rages through the afternoon. General Fraser's column is too far off to aid Hamilton, but part of the third column, under von Riedesel, struggles up the bluffs from the river to shore up his force. With the coming of darkness, Arnold withdraws, leaving the battlefield to the British, who have suffered 556 casualties to the Americans' 287.

September 20–21: Howe establishes a post at Valley Forge.

Washington has sent four cannons and 1,500 men, commanded by Anthony Wayne, to Warren's Tavern near Paoli to harass the British rear guard and baggage train, but Loyalists warn the British. Howe sends troops commanded by Maj. Gen. Charles Grey in a surprise nighttime attack that kills about 150 of Wayne's men and sends the rest into flight. Local residents, who find mangled bodies at the site, immediately term the fray the Paoli Massacre.

September 22: Still concerned about being out-flanked, Washington moves his army to Pott's Grove (now Pottstown), Pennsylvania, causing Howe to march to Fatland Ford and begin to cross the Schuylkill.

September 23: Howe marches to Norristown, Pennsylvania. Unable to follow, Washington sends Alexander Hamilton to Philadelphia and Clement Biddle through the countryside to obtain blankets and clothing for his troops.

To the cheers of Loyalists, Lord Cornwallis leads four British and two Hessian units into Philadelphia to take possession of the city. The main body of Cornwallis's army encamps at Germantown. Washington moves to encamp at Pennypacker's Mill (Schwenksville) on the Perkiomen River.

September 24: After capturing 300 British troops on Lake George's west shore, Col. John Brown's Continentals successfully attack Diamond Island but fail to take Fort Ticonderoga.

September 27: Still fearful of Howe's movements, the Continental Congress convenes once in Lancaster and adjourns to cross the Susquehanna River and reconvene in York, Pennsylvania.

September 30: The Continental Congress convenes at York.

October 1: Captain Wickes and all the crew of the *Reprisal* but the cook are lost when the ship founders off the Newfoundland Banks.

October 2: Aware of the Delaware River's value as a supply route, General Howe decides to have it cleared of obstacles, including a double line of chevaux-de-frise stretched by the Americans across the river at Billingsport, New Jersey, that can rip open a ship's hull; so he sends troops to attack the Billingsport garrison and remove the obstacle. The American defenders torch the barracks, spike the guns, and flee.

October 3: Having received reinforcements of German and British regulars that increase his force to 7,000 (plus 3,000 Tories), Gen. Sir Henry Clinton, left in command at New York, sends 4,000 men toward Tarrytown to attack Forts Clinton and Montgomery and create a diversion for Burgoyne.

October 4: After a 16-mile night march from Skippack Creek, Washington attacks the British at Germantown, Pennsylvania, at dawn, driving back the advance units of Howe's 9,000-man force—the American commander's first advance to attack the major force of

the British army and the first retreat by British troops in open battle with the Americans. Attracted by the sounds of battle but confused by fog, General Stephen approaches the rear of General Wayne's force and opens fire, immobilizing both his and Wayne's units. With General Greene's advance delayed, no hope exists of a coordinated attack, and Washington orders a general withdrawal after suffering 673 casualties and 400 taken prisoner of his 7,000 troops. Howe's army has only 535 casualties but finds the battle demoralizing.

October 5: Launching his attack force aboard flatboats, galleys, and bateaux, Clinton captures Verplanck's Point near Tarrytown as the American defenders flee without offering resistance.

Admiral Lord Howe's fleet begins to arrive in Delaware Bay a month after leaving Head of Elk.

October 6: Leaving a guard of 1,000, mostly Loyalists, at Verplanck's Point, Sir Henry Clinton crosses the Hudson River, marches up the east bank, sends a division under Lt. Col. Archibald Campbell to attack Fort Montgomery, and leads a second division to Fort Clinton. When Gen. George Clinton refuses to surrender, the British attack both forts. As night falls, the defeated Americans escape, after suffering 250 casualties out of a force of 600 and leaving vessels in the river that the victors burn. The British have 200 casualties.

October 7: Burgoyne refuses to retreat and instead leads a reconnaissance of 1,500 men to test the strength of Gates's left at Bemis Heights. The British form in a wheatfield and are unexpectedly attacked by American troops led by Enoch Poor and Daniel Morgan, who outflank and nearly surround Burgoyne's force. Arnold rides recklessly into the battle, inspiring the Continentals to attack wildly. British resistance crumbles; as Fraser tries to cover their retreat, he falls mortally wounded. Arnold and his men relentlessly sweep ahead to Freeman's Farm and seize the redoubt on Burgoyne's right flank. But Arnold, his horse shot from under him, suffers a leg wound and must be carried from the field. Burgoyne's casualties number 600; the Americans, only 150. His position now untenable, Burgoyne begins to withdraw toward Saratoga during the night.

At York, the Continental Congress resumes the debate on confederation, with the focus on voting in Congress. The members resolve the issue by deciding that each state will have one vote. Although some delegations vote in favor in order to move the debates ahead to other difficult issues, such as taxation, only the Virginia delegation votes no.

October 8: American troops commanded by Generals George Clinton and James Clinton join Putnam's force at New Windsor, New York.

Responding to a September 28 letter from Burgoyne concerning orders, Sir Henry Clinton at Fort Montgomery writes that only General Howe can send Burgoyne orders and expresses hope that his own success will bolster Burgoyne's effort, which Clinton cannot know is already doomed. Clinton puts his message in a hollow silver bullet to be delivered by Daniel Taylor.

October 9: Harassed by the advance troops of Gates's pursuing army, Burgoyne's retreating force reaches the heights of Saratoga, but by now Burgoyne's force, with fewer than 5,800 men, is greatly outnumbered by Gates's 13,000 men.

October 10: British artillery opens a bombardment of the land side of Fort Mifflin on Mud Island in the Delaware River.

October 12: Gates blocks Burgoyne's access to the Hudson River, denying him any hope of further retreat and forcing him to consider beginning discussions of surrender terms.

October 13: Burgoyne requests a cessation of hostilities; Gates agrees, and surrender negotiations begin.

October 14: At Saratoga, Americans troops capture Daniel Taylor, who swallows the silver bullet containing Sir Henry Clinton's message. Gen. George Clinton orders an emetic for Taylor. With the bullet recovered, Taylor is executed as a spy.

After nearly a week of debate at York on whether taxes under the confederation will be proportional to population or based on land values or general property values, the Continental Congress, in a narrowly divided vote, selects a basis of land values and their improvements. The members also decide that each state shall have at least two but no more than seven congressional delegates, whose terms will be limited to three years.

October 16: Gates and Burgoyne meet to determine the final details of the surrender. Their agreement stipulates that Burgoyne's army will return to England via Boston, that all persons with the army will be considered British citizens regardless of their nationality, and that all must pledge never again to be involved in the American war.

Sir Henry Clinton has sent 1,700 troops under Gen. John Vaughan and a flotilla under Sir James Wallace up the Hudson to find and support Burgoyne.

They burn Kingston, where they anchored the previous day, and head for Livingston's Manor.

October 17: Accompanied by the beat of drums, the British march out of their fortifications at Saratoga at 2:00 P.M., and Burgoyne surrenders his army to Gates. Then the two commanders and their staffs eat a simple lunch together. Surprising everyone, Burgoyne proposes a toast to Washington, and Gates responds with a toast to George III.

Congress adopts a resolution to create a Board of War comprised of noncongressional members with certain supervisory powers over army operations. Washington's critics see the board as a possible means of undermining his authority.

October 19: General Howe withdraws his troops from Germantown to concentrate his entire force in Philadelphia.

October 22: With news from Vaughan that he cannot make contact with Burgoyne and with orders from Howe to abandon the expedition and send reinforcements to Philadelphia, Clinton sends orders to Vaughan to withdraw.

Pursuing his plan to free the Delaware River for navigation, Howe sends Col. Carl von Donop with 2,000 Hessians to attack Fort Mercer at Red Bank and dislodge its American garrison. Under command of Col. Christopher Greene, the fort is among those whose fortifications have been strengthened under supervision of Chevalier de Mauduit de Plessis. Crossing the river at Philadelphia, the Hessians attack by land. Refusing to surrender, Greene orders his men to hold fire as the Hessians advance across an abatis of felled trees, cross a ditch, and ascend to the fort's parapets; then they shatter the Hessians with a murderous musket volley. Trying to launch a second attack from the south, the Hessians take fire from galleys in the river, forcing their withdrawal. They leave behind the mortally wounded von Donop.

October 23: At Fort Mifflin, Pennsylvania, American artillery opens fire on six British ships that had broken through the chevaux-de-frise in the Delaware; the *Augusta* and the *Merlin* run aground and are destroyed.

October 28: James Wilkinson, an aide to General Gates, stops in Reading on his way to York to inform the Continental Congress of Burgoyne's surrender. Gates disdains to follow proper procedure and channel his report through Washington to the Congress. Wilkinson compounds this affront to the commander in chief by telling Lord Stirling's aide, Maj. William

McWilliam, about a letter Thomas Conway, a brigadier general from Ireland, has sent Gates, praising Gates while derogating Washington.

October 31: Wilkinson arrives in York and confirms rumors circulating among members of the Continental Congress that Burgoyne has surrendered, but he offers only a verbal report, asking for more time to "digest and arrange" the written dispatches Gates has sent with him.

John Hancock resigns as president of the Continental Congress.

November 1: The Continental Congress elects Henry Laurens of South Carolina as president. Most of the members have departed for home; the remainder continue discussing confederation.

November 2: Capt. John Paul Jones sails his sloop *Ranger* out of Portsmouth, New Hampshire, bound for France.

At Whippany Township, Pennsylvania, Washington orders a court-martial of Gen. Adam Stephen on charges that he lied about a skirmish at Piscataway and was drunk during the battles at Brandywine and Germantown, conduct "unlike an officer." Then Washington breaks camp and marches his troops to encamp at Whitemarsh, 12 miles from Philadelphia.

November 3: Outraged by what his aide McWilliams has told him, Lord Stirling writes to Washington recounting the story and denouncing Conway's "duplicity." News that two of his subordinates are attempting to discredit him shocks Washington. This is his first knowledge of the so-called Conway Cabal, whose reputed intent is to replace Washington with Gates as commander in chief.

At York, Wilkinson presents to the Continental Congress Gates's dispatches about Saratoga and Burgoyne's surrender.

November 6: To the newly created Board of War, the Continental Congress appoints Gen. Thomas Mifflin, who has recently resigned as quartermaster general, Col. Thomas Pickering, and Col. Robert H. Harrison.

November 7: Assured that the final form of the Articles of Confederation has been approved, except for word revisions, Samuel Adams and John Adams receive requested leaves of absence to return home.

Washington writes a two-sentence letter at Whitemarsh informing Conway that he has received a letter stating that Conway wrote of Gates, "Heaven has been determined to save your Country; or a weak General and bad Counsellors would have ruined it." Washington's intent is clear.

November 10: Since the Delaware's current opened a new channel between Mud Island and the Pennsylvania shore, the British are able to move a floating battery of 22 24-pound cannon within 40 yards of Fort Mifflin, and they begin a daylong shelling of the fort.

November 11: The congressional committee to which proposed additions to the Articles of Confederation are referred reports that seven additions have been approved, meaning that the document's provisions are not yet final.

November 14: Thomas Conway submits his resignation to the Continental Congress, citing as his reasons criticism of his request for promotion, denial of promotion, Baron de Kalb's promotion ahead of him (de Kalb had been his junior in the French army, so Conway's reputation in France will be demeaned), and the unfortunate letter to Gates to which Washington referred. Congress sends his letter to the Board of War.

November 15: After five days of shelling, Fort Mifflin's defenders have suffered many casualties and major destruction of the fort, and they have only two cannons in service. Moving six ships into firing range to complement the shore artillery and the floating battery, the British begin a horrendous bombardment, with perhaps 1,000 balls fired every 20 minutes, that levels the fort. During the night Maj. Simeon Thayer, Col. Samuel Smith's replacement as commander, torches the ruins and escapes across the river to Red Bank with the remnants of his garrison—only 150 out of 450 remain alive and unwounded. The British have only 12 casualties.

At York, the 13 Articles of Confederation are recorded in the journals of the Continental Congress as finally adopted.

November 17: The Continental Congress sends copies of the Articles of Confederation to the states to consider for ratification, along with a circular letter from Richard Henry Lee depicting the articles as best "adapted to the circumstances of all" and urging the state legislators to study their provisions with liberality, wisdom, and magnanimity and to prove "capable of rising superior to local attachments, when they may be incompatible with the safety, happiness, and glory of the general Confederacy." Considering the confederation vital to successful prosecution of the war, Congress hopes for a quick and unanimous outcome.

November 18: With the site of Fort Mifflin captured, Howe sends Cornwallis with 2,000 men to New Jersey to again attack Fort Mercer. Washington places Nathanael Greene in charge of the Continentals in New Jersey with orders to prevent the fort's loss, if possible. Cornwallis crosses the Delaware and lands at Billingsport.

November 20: With Howe in effective control of the Delaware River as far as Red Bank, Greene believes that holding Fort Mercer will prove impossible. With Greene's approval, Col. Christopher Greene, who also believes his fort is untenable, orders an evacuation along with burning the fort's buildings and supplies. Cornwallis takes Fort Mercer without a shot being fired, giving Howe control of the Delaware to Philadelphia. The Americans burn their ships positioned upriver to prevent their capture by the British.

Accepting the court-martial's judgment that Gen. Adam Stephen is guilty of misconduct, Washington dismisses Stephen from his command.

November 21: Reacting to charges of embezzlement brought against Silas Deane by Arthur Lee, the Continental Congress recalls Deane to America to make a response.

November 25: Lafayette leads a 300-man reconnaissance force in a successful skirmish with a troop of Hessians, to harass Cornwallis's position at Gloucester, New Jersey.

November 27: The Continental Congress issues a recommendation that the states confiscate the property of Loyalists. Colonel Harrison has declined to serve on the Board of War, so Congress appoints three new members, Gen. Horatio Gates, Joseph Trumbull, and Richard Peters, with Gates to serve as president. As Gates and Mifflin are hostile and Pickering is lukewarm toward Washington, the board appears to threaten the commander in chief.

November 28: The Continental Congress appoints John Adams to succeed Silas Deane as commissioner to France.

December 1: With the blessing of Benjamin Franklin and an introductory letter from him to Washington, Baron Friedrich Wilhelm von Steuben arrives at Portsmouth, New Hampshire, from France to volunteer his services with the Continental army. Formerly on Frederick the Great's general staff, von Steuben also has the blessing of the French minister of war, the comte de St. Germain, and Beaumarchais's Roderigue Hortalez et Cie is paying his travel expenses.

December 2: John Paul Jones and his USS *Ranger* arrive at Nantes, France.

December 4: Sent by the Continental Congress, Jonathan Austin arrives at Versailles with news of Burgoyne's surrender and capture at Saratoga. The news revives French interest in pursuing an alliance with the United States, which seriously flagged after news arrived in November that Howe had captured Philadelphia.

Hoping to surprise Washington at Whitemarsh, Howe marches his entire army from Philadelphia, but Capt. Allen Marsh has been continuously scouting British movements and reports Howe's march to Washington, giving him time to mount a defense and to send McLane's cavalry to harass the British front and flank.

December 6: Vergennes sends a message from Versailles to congratulate Franklin, Deane, and Lee on the American victory at Saratoga and, more important, to invite them to revive their request for creating a formal alliance between France and the United States.

December 7: Howe marches to Edge Hill, placing him within a mile of Washington's left flank, but then during the night pushes on to Jenkintown.

December 8: As Howe advances Washington's right and left lines fall back, the left in disarray; but Captain McLane's cavalry repulses a British bayonet attack. The skirmishing ends, but Howe decides that Washington's position is too strong and returns to Philadelphia.

Franklin sends his grandson Temple to Vergennes with a draft proposal for an alliance.

December 11: Washington's army leaves Whitemarsh to cross the Schuylkill River by bridge at Matson's Ford and proceed to Valley Forge. General Sullivan's division and half of another division have already crossed the river when 3,500 British regulars in an advance unit led by Cornwallis appear. Washington orders his men to return across the bridge and then burn it. The enemy forces briefly face each other in battle formations on opposite sides of the river, until Cornwallis withdraws to forage for supplies and Washington to return to Whitemarsh.

December 12: The American commissioners meet secretly with Vergennes at Versailles. He tells them that France can openly enter the war only with Spain's agreement and that the courier he has sent to Madrid will need three weeks to return with Spain's decision.

December 13: The Continental Congress appoints Thomas Conway to major general, passing over 23 other brigadier generals senior to him, and approves creating the post of inspector general for the Continental army, which will be independent of the commander in chief and report directly to the Board of War.

December 14: The Board of War has taken no action on Thomas Conway's letter of resignation, and the Continental Congress appoints him inspector general of the army in an apparent triumph for the Conway Cabal partisans.

December 17: A French foreign office official brings word to Franklin at Passy that Louis XVI's ministers have agreed to a formal alliance, but it must remain secret until Spain makes a decision. With this knowledge of France's recognition of the United States's independence, Franklin can reject British agent Paul Wentworth's appeal to visit London with his fellow commissioners to negotiate a cease-fire based on British-American relations prior to 1763.

December 19: Washington's army arrives at Valley Forge to establish winter quarters.

December 23: Washington writes a letter suggesting that the Continental Congress send a few members of the Board of War or a congressional committee to Valley Forge to discuss and resolve the issues of leadership and organization of the Continental army raised by his detractors.

December 27: Acting as a committee of the whole, the Continental Congress resolves that Burgoyne and his army, now awaiting embarkation at Boston, be detained until the Crown ratifies the convention agreed to at Saratoga and sends instructions to General Heath in Boston to make certain that transport ships are adequately provisioned and all outstanding accounts are liquidated—another delaying tactic.

EYEWITNESS TESTIMONY

1777

The future and proper disposition of the Hessian Prisoners, struck me in the same light in which you view it, for which Reason I advised the Council of Safety to seperate them from their Officers, and canton them in the German Counties. If proper pains are taken to convince them, how preferable the Situation of their Countrymen, the Inhabitants of those Counties is to theirs, I think they may be sent back in the Spring, so fraught with a love of Liberty and property too, that they may create a disgust to the Service among the remainder of the foreign Troops and widen that Breach which is already opened between them and the British.

George Washington, from a letter written at his Trenton headquarters to Robert Morris, George Clymer, and George Walton, delegates to the Continental Congress, January 1, 1777, in John C. Fitzpatrick, ed., The Writings of George Washington, *vol. 6, p. 464.*

We have made a successful attack upon Princeton. Genl. Howe advanced upon Trenton, we evacuated the Town, and lay on the otherside of the Mill Creek, until dark, then Stole a march and attacked Princeton about nine O'Clock in the Morning. There was three Regiments Quartered there, the killed, wounded, and taken prisoners amounts to about 500. The Enemy are in great consternation, and as the Panick affords us a favourable Opportunity to drive them out of the Jerseys, It has been determined in Council, that you should move down towards New York with a considerable force, as if you had a design upon the city. That being an Object of great importance, the Enemy will be reduced to the Necessity of withdrawing a considerable part of their force from the Jerseys, if not the whole, to secure the City. I shall draw the force on this side the North River together at Morristown, where I shall watch the motions of the Enemy and avail Myself of every favourable Circumstance.

George Washington, from a letter written at Pluckemin, New Jersey, to Maj. Gen. William Heath, January 5, 1777, in John C. Fitzpatrick, ed., The Writings of George Washington, *vol. 6, p. 472.*

The affairs of America seem to be drawing toward a crisis. The Howes are at this time in possession of or are able to awe the whole middle coast of America, from Delaware to the western boundary of Massachusetts Bay; the naval barrier on the side of Canada is broken; a great tract of country is open for the supply of troops; the river Hudson opens a way into the heart of the provinces; and nothing can, in all probability, prevent an early and offensive campaign. What the Americans *have* done is, in their circumstances, truly astonishing; it is, indeed, infinitely more than I expected from them. . . . It is now, however, evident that they cannot look standing armies in the face. They are inferior in everything, even in numbers—I mean, in the numbers of those whom they keep in constant duty and in regular pay. . . . An army that is obliged at all times and in all situations to decline engagement may delay their ruin but can never defend their country. Foreign assistance they have little or none, nor are likely soon to have more. France, in effect, has no king, nor any minister accredited enough either with the court or the nation to undertake a design of great magnitude.

In this state of things, I persuade myself Franklin is come to Paris to draw from that court a definitive and satisfactory answer concerning the support of the colonies. If he cannot get an answer (and I am of opinion that at present he cannot), then it is to be presumed he is authorized to negotiate with Lord Stormont on the basis of dependence on the Crown. This I take to be his errand. . . . On this supposition, I thought it not wholly impossible that the Whig party might be made a sort of mediators of the peace. . . . If the congress could be brought to declare in favor of those terms for which one hundred members of the House of Commons voted last year, with some civility to the party which held out those terms, it would undoubtedly have an effect to revive the cause of our liberties in England and to give the colonies some sort of mooring and anchorage in this country. It seemed to me that Franklin might be made to feel the propriety of such a step, and as I have an acquaintance with him, I had a strong desire of taking a turn to Paris. . . . But when I had conversed with the very few of your Lordship's friends who were in town. . . . I laid aside the design, not being desirous of risking the displeasure of those for whose sake alone I wished to take that fatiguing journey at this severe season of the year.

Edmund Burke, from a "Letter to the Marquess of Rockingham," January 6, 1777, from Burke, Selected Writings and Speeches on America, *pp. 207–209.*

... Do not think that the whole or even the uninfluenced majority of Englishmen in this island are enemies to their own blood on the American continent. Much delusion has been practiced, much corrupt influence treacherously employed. But still a large, and we trust the largest and soundest, part of this kingdom perseveres in the most perfect unity of sentiments, principles, and affections with you....

. . . . .

We disclaim also any sort of share in that other measure which has been used to alienate your affections from this country, namely, the introduction of foreign mercenaries. We saw their employment with shame and regret....

We likewise saw with shame the African slaves, who had been sold to you on public faith and under sanction of acts of Parliament, to be your servants and your guards, employed to cut the throats of their masters.

You will not, we trust, believe ... we could have thought of letting loose upon you, our late beloved brethren, these fierce tribes of savages and cannibals, in whom the traces of human nature are effaced by ignorance and barbarity. We rather wished to have joined with you in bringing gradually that unhappy part of mankind into civility, order, piety, and virtuous discipline, than to have confirmed their evil habits and increased their natural ferocity by fleshing them in the slaughter of you, whom our wiser and better ancestors had sent into the wilderness with the express view of introducing, along with our holy religion, its humane and charitable manners....

We do not call you rebels or traitors. We do not call for the vengeance of the Crown against you....

Edmund Burke, from an "Address to the British Colonists in North America," January 6, 1777, from Burke, Selected Writings and Speeches on America, pp. 234 and 237–239.

Finding the small pox to be spreading much and fearing that no precaution can prevent it from running thro' the whole of our Army, I have determined that the Troops shall be inoculated. This Expedient may be attended with some inconveniences and some disadvantages, but yet I trust, in its consequences will have the most happy effects. Necessity not only authorizes but seems to require the measure, for should the disorder infect the Army, in the natural way, and rage with its usual Virulence, we should have more to dread from it, than from the Sword of the Enemy....

George Washington, from a letter written at Morristown, New Jersey, to Dr. William Shippen, Jr., January 6, 1777, in John C. Fitzpatrick, ed., The Writings of George Washington, vol. 6, p. 473.

You have heard of the captivity of General Lee. Congress have directed General Washington to offer six Hessian field-officers in exchange for him. It is suspected that the enemy choose to consider him as a deserter, bring him to trial in a court-martial, and take his life. Assurances are ordered to be given to General Howe, that five of those officers, together with Lieutenant-Colonel [Archibald] Campbell, will be detained, and all of them receive the same measure that shall be meted to him. This resolution will most certainly be executed.

Samuel Adams, from a letter written in Baltimore, January 9, 1777, to John Adams, in Harry Alonzo Cushing, ed., The Writings of Samuel Adams, vol. 3, p. 343.

... We crossed the Delaware on the 25 of December at night 8 miles above the town [Trenton] in one of the severest Hails and rain storms I ever saw. We reached the town the next morning about 8 oclock and surprized it. We attacked it by storm and soon carried the garrison. The number of the killed and wounded and prisoners amounts to upwards of 1200. We crossed the Delaware again that night. I was out 30 hours in all the storm without the least refreshment. Our loss was inconsiderable in carrying the place. The troops behaved incomparably well. We took 6 field pieces and a large number of small arms and a considerable quantity of stores.

Nathanael Greene, from a letter written at Morristown, New Jersey, January 10, 1777, to Nicholas Cooke, governor of Rhode Island, in Richard K. Showman, ed., The Papers of General Nathanael Greene, vol. 2, p. 4.

By what means, may I ask, do you expect to conquer America? If you could not effect it in the summer, when our army was less than yours, nor in the winter, when we had none, how are you to do it? In point of generalship you have been outwitted, and in point of fortitude outdone; your advantages turn out to your loss, and show us that it is in our power to ruin you by gifts: like a game of drafts, we can move out of *one* square to let you come in, in order that we may after-wards take two or three for one; and as we can always keep a double corner for ourselves, we can always pre-vent a total defeat. You cannot be so insensible as not to see that we have two to one the advantage of you, because we conquer by a drawn game, and you lose by it. Burgoyne might have taught your lordship this knowledge; he has been long a student in the doctrine of chances.

Thomas Paine, from The American Crisis II, *addressed to Lord Howe, January 13, 1777, from Van der Weyde,* The Life and Works of Thomas Paine, *vol. 2, pp. 295–296.*

It is now generally believed here that G. Washington has killed and taken at least two Thousands of Mr. Howes Army since Christmas. Indeed the Evidence of it is from the Generals own Letters. You know I ever thought Mr. Hows [sic] march through the Jerseys a rash Step. It has proved so—but how much more so would it have been thought if the Americans could all have viewed it in that light and exerted themselves as they might and ought. The whole Flock would infal-libly have been taken in the Net.

John Adams, from a letter written at Hartford, Connecticut, to Abigail Adams, January 14, 1777, in L. H. Butterfield, ed., Adams Family Correspondence, *vol. 2, pp. 145–146.*

My Lord, it is with much concern that I am to inform your lordship the unfortunate and untimely defeat at Trentown has thrown us farther back than was at first apprehended, from the great encouragement it has given to the rebels.

I do not now see a prospect of terminating the war but by a general action, and I am aware of the difficul-ties in our ways to obtain it as the enemy moves with so much more celerity than we possibly can with our for-eign troops, who are too much attached to their baggage which they have in amazing quantities in the field.

Gen. Sir William Howe, from a private letter written at New York to Lord George Germain, January 20, 1777, in K. G. Davies, ed., Documents of the American Revolution, *vol. 14, p. 33.*

This retreat was censured by some as pusillanimous and disgraceful; but, did they know that our army was at that time less than a thousand effective men, and never more than 4000,—that the number of the enemy was at least 8000, exclusive of their artillery and light horse,—that this handful of Americans retreated *slowly* above 80 miles without losing a dozen men—and that suffering themselves to be forced to an action, would have been their entire destruction—did they know this, they would never have censured it at all—they would have called it prudent—posterity will call it glorious—and the names of Washington and Fabius will run par-allel to eternity.

Thomas Paine, from "Retreat across the Delaware," January 29, 1777, in Van der Weyde, The Life and Works of Thomas Paine, *vol. 3, pp. 259–260.*

The extent of country from Ticonderoga to the inhab-ited country upon that river opposite to Charles Town is about sixty miles and, . . . should the object appear worthy it is to be hoped resources might be found. In that case it would be advisable to fortify with one or two strong redoubts the heights opposite to Charles Town and establish posts of savages upon the passage from Ticonderoga to those heights to preserve the com-munication, and at the same time prevent any attempt from the country above Charles Town . . . from molest-ing the rear or interrupting the convoys of supply while the army proceeded down the Connecticut. Should the junction between the Canada and Rhode Island armies be effected upon the Connecticut, it is not too sanguine an expectation that all the New England provinces will be reduced by their operations.

Lt. Gen. John Burgoyne, from thoughts for conducting the war from the side of Canada, written in London, February 28, 1777, in K. G. Davies, ed., Documents of the American Revolution, *vol. 14, pp. 44–45.*

The disagreeable occurrence at Trenton is I must own extremely mortifying, and it gives me real concern that your successes should suffer an interruption or have their brilliancy in the least tarnished at the close of your campaign, especially as I fear with you that even this affair may elate the enemy and encourage them, notwithstanding the pardon held out to them, to per-severe in their rebellion.

Lord George Germain, from a letter written at Whitehall, London, to Gen. Sir William Howe, March 3, 1777, in K. G. Davies, ed., Documents of the American Revolution, *vol. 14, pp. 46–47.*

. . .The mild and gentle treatment the Hessian Prisoners have receivd since they have been in our possession

John Burgoyne served as a general in the British army. *(From* The Pictorial Field Book of the Revolution, *2 vols., by B. J. Lossing. New York: Harper Brothers, 1851 and 1852.)*

has produced a great alteration in their disposition. Desertion prevails among them. One whole Brigade refusd to fight or do duty and were sent Prisoners to New York. Rancour and hatred prevails between them and the British Soldiery. It should be our policy to increase this hatred, not take a measure that may heal the difference. General How has been spreading papers among the Hessians with accounts of our haveing sold the Hessians Prisoners for slaves. This [proposed policy of] severity to their Officers will but too strongly confirm them in the account. . . .

Nathanael Greene, from a letter written at Baskenridge, New Jersey, March 3, 1777, to John Adams, in Richard K. Showman, ed., The Papers of General Nathanael Greene, *vol. 2, p. 31.*

This City is a dull Place, in Comparison of what it was. More than one half the Inhabitants have removed into the Country, as it was their Wisdom to do—the Remainder are chiefly Quakers as dull as Beetles. From these neither good is to be expected nor Evil to be apprehended. They are a kind of neutral Tribe, or the Race of the insipids.

How [General Howe] may possibly attempt this Town, and a Pack of sordid Scoundrels male and female, seem to have prepared their Minds and Bodies, Houses and Cellars for his Reception: but these are few, and more despicable in Character than in Number. America will loose nothing, by Hows gaining this Town. No such Panick will be spread by it, now as was spread by the Expectation of it in December.

John Adams, from a letter written in Philadelphia to Abigail Adams, March 7, 1777, in L. H. Butterfield, ed., Adams Family Correspondence, *vol. 2, pp. 169– 170.*

His Majesty intends to open this year's campaign with ninety thousand Hessians, Tories, Negroes, Japanese, Moors, Exquimaux, Persian archers, Laplanders, Feejee Islanders, and light horse. With this terrific and horrendous armament, in conjunction with a most tremendous and irresistible fleet, he is resolved to terminate this unnatural war the next summer. . . . His Majesty has also the strongest assurances that France will cooperate with him in humbling his seditious subjects. . . . For Heaven's sake, ye poor, deluded, misguided, bewildered, cajoled, and bamboozled Whigs! ye dumfounded, infatuated, back-bestridden, nose-led-about, priest-ridden, demagogue-beshackled, and Congress-becrafted independents, fly, fly, oh fly, for protection to the royal standard. . . .

From a letter sent from London in January, published in Freeman's Journal, *March 22, 1777, in Frank Moore, compiler,* The Diary of the American Revolution, *p. 190.*

I was in an Engagement this day on Strawberry Hill in Woodbridge. Fired Eight rounds myself being the first time I ever was in action or saw the Enemy in the field, notwithstanding I have been in the Continental service near fifteen Months. After the Battle which was very inconsiderable more than skirmishing, I went over the Creek. Dined with Mrs. & Miss Abbe Smith, Mr. [William] Smith being gone to the Enemy. Engaged in the Evenning in moving the Goods of Justice [Ellis] Barron also gone to the Enemy or at least as the Enemy were oblidged to leave this day on our approach.

Major Joseph Bloomfield (he was promoted in November 1776), now encamped at Morristown, New Jersey, journal entry of March 30, 1777, in Mark E. Lender and James Kirby Martin, eds., Citizen Soldier, *p. 124.*

Great Efforts are now making by the British Ministry, to procure more Troops from Germany. The Princes in Alliance with France, have refused to lend any, or to enter into any Guarrantee of Hanover, which England has been mean enough to ask, being apprehensive for that Electorate if she should draw from it, any more of its Troops.

Four more Regiments (two of them to be light Horse) are raising in Hesse, where there has been an Insurrection, on Account of drafting the People: and now great sums of Money, are distributed for procuring Men. They talk of Ten thousand Men in all to be sent over this Spring.

The Hearts of the French are universally for Us, and the Cry is strong for immediate War with Britain. Indeed every Thing tends that Way, but the Court has Reasons for postponing it, a little longer. In the mean Time, Preparations are making. . . .

John Adams, from a letter written in Philadelphia to Abigail Adams, April 2, 1777, in L. H. Butterfield, ed., Adams Family Correspondence, vol. 2, pp. 195– 196.

Restricted as I am from entering upon more extensive operations by the want of force, my hopes of terminating the war this year are vanished. Still, I think it probable that by the latter end of the campaign we shall be in possession of the provinces of New York, the Jerseys and Pennsylvania, though this in some measure must depend upon the successes of the northern army. For, notwithstanding it is my opinion the rebels will not be able to raise their army voted last autumn, yet they will have a numerous militia in the field, in addition to their standing force, with a tolerable train of artillery.

Gen. Sir William Howe, from a letter written in New York to Lord George Germain, April 2, 1777, in K. G. Davies, ed., Documents of the American Revolution, vol. 14, p. 65.

There is one Subject, which I would wish you to turn your Thoughts to, for your Amusement, as soon as possible. It is likely to be the most momentous political Subject of any. It is the Subject of Money. You will find in Mr. Locks Works a Treatise concerning Coins, and in Postlethwait, another of Sir Isaac Newton under the Terms, Coin, Money, &c.

It is a Subject of very curious and ingenious Speculation, and of the last Importance at all Times to Society, but especially at this Time, when a Quantity of Paper more than is necessary for a Medium of Trade, introduces so many Distresses into the Community, and so much Embarrasses our public Councils and Arms.

John Adams, from a letter written in Philadelphia to John Thaxter, April 8, 1777, in L. H. Butterfield, ed., Adams Family Correspondence, vol. 2, p. 205.

Should anyone among you require the force of example to animate you on this glorious occasion, let him turn his eyes to that bright luminary of war, in whose character the conduct of Emillus, the coolness of a Fabius, the intrepidity of a Hannibal, and the indefatigable ardor and military skill of a Caesar, are united. Let not the name of Brutus or Camillus be remembered whilst that of Washington is to be found in the annals of America. Great in the cabinet as in war, he shines with unrivaled splendor in every department of life; and whilst his abilities as a statesman and a general excite our wonder, his disinterested patriotism and domestic virtues command universal veneration. . . .

From commentary written in January, published in Freeman's Journal, April 12, 1777, in Frank Moore, compiler, The Diary of the American Revolution, pp. 198–199.

Some days ago, the daughter of Mr. Jonathan Kniffen, of Rye, in Connecticut, was murdered by a party of rebels. . . . She was carrying some clothes to her father in company of two men who had the charge of a herd of cattle. They were fired upon by the rebels from behind a stone wall. The poor young woman received a ball in her head, of which she instantly died. The men escaped unhurt. They plundered her dead body of its clothes, cut one of her fingers almost off in order to take a ring, and left the corpse indecently exposed in the highway. Such are the advocates of this cursed rebellion! Yet the officer (so called) who commanded the party . . . gloried in the exploit, and swore it was better to kill one woman than two men. . . .

From the New York Gazette and Weekly Mercury, April 14, 1777, in Frank Moore, compiler, The Diary of the American Revolution, p. 214.

Britain, like a gamester nearly ruined, has now put all her losses into one bet, and is playing a desperate game for the total. If she wins it, she wins from me my life; she wins the continent as the forfeited property of rebels; the right of taxing those that are left as reduced subjects; and the power of binding them slaves: and the single die which determines this unparalleled event is, whether we support our independence or she overturn it. Here is the touchstone to try men by. *He that is not a supporter of the independent States of America in the same degree that his religious and political principles would suffer him to support the government of any other country, of which he called himself a subject, is, in the American sense of the word,* A TORY; *and the instant that he endeavors to bring his toryism into practice, he becomes* A TRAITOR. The first can only be detected by a general test, and the law hath already provided for the latter.

> *Thomas Paine, from* The American Crisis III, *April 19, 1777, from Van der Weyde,* The Life and Works of Thomas Paine, *vol. 2, pp. 315–316.*

The committee appointed by Congress some time ago to inquire into the conduct of the British troops in their different marches through New York and New Jersey, have to-day [April18] reported:—

. . . . .

The whole track of the British army is marked with desolation, and a wanton destruction of property, particularly through Westchester County, in the State of New York, the towns of Newark, Elizabethtown, Woodbridge, Brunswick, Kingston, Princeton, and Trenton, in New Jersey. . . .

. . . . .

The prisoners, instead of that humane treatment which those taken by the United States experienced, were in general treated with the greatest barbarity. . . .

. . . . .

The committee had authentic information of many instances of the most indecent treatment and actual ravishment of married and single women. . . .

> *From the* Pennsylvania Evening Post, *April 24, 1777, in Frank Moore, compiler,* The Diary of the American Revolution, *pp. 215–217.*

My friends, I hope . . . that you are convinced that it is your interest and duty to yourselves to oppose any invasion of this province or of the neighbouring nations by the rebels. I was frequently applied to by your nation and also by the Creeks to mediate between you and put an end to the bloodshed caused by your quarrel. This I did twice but your own people and the Creeks spoiled the path again; but upon the breaking out of the present rebellion and seeing my children in so much danger, I again endeavoured to compose your differences and make peace between you. . . . It is the interest and duty of all nations to join like one people to support themselves and oppose the enemies of the Great King, to whose protection they are indebted for their trade and every other advantage they enjoy.

> *John Stuart, British superintendent for Indian affairs in the southern district, conclusion of a speech to the Chickasaw and Choctaw at Mobile, May 14, 1777, in K. G. Davies, ed.,* Documents of the American Revolution, *vol. 14, p. 82.*

. . . That the office of first magistrate [governor] of this State [New York] will be more respectable as well as more lucrative, and consequently more desirable, than that place I now fill [delegate to Congress], is very apparent. But, sir, my object in the course of the present great contest neither has been, nor will be, either rank or money. I am persuaded that I can be more useful to the State in the office I now hold than in the one alluded to, and therefore think it my duty to continue in it. . . .

> *John Jay, from a letter written in New York State, May 16, 1777, to Abraham Yates, Jr., delegate to the New York provincial congress, in William Jay,* The Life of John Jay, *vol. 1, p. 73.*

Continuing in morristown till the 25 of may 3 milds from head Quarters / our men all most ye biger part of them old Country men wich are very bad / we are [forced?] to flog them night & morning a hunder[d] lashes a piece / Sum will git drunk stab the genl horses wen [when] on Sentry at the door / others wen on Sentry at the Comesary will leave the[i]r post and git drunk. . . .

> *Jeremiah Greenman, recently reenlisted in the Continental army and now a sergeant with Col. Israel Angell's 2nd Rhode Island Regiment, encamped at Morristown, New Jersey, from diary entry of April 25–May 25, 1777, in Greenman,* Diary of a Common Soldier in the American Revolution, 1775–1783, *pp. 72–73.*

There is a very evil spirit opperating and an encreasing Bitterness between the Town and Country. The Town of Boston has lost its leaders, and the respectable figure it once made is exchanged for party squables, for Avarice, venality, Animosity, contention, pride, weakness and dissapation. I wish I could say this spirit was confined to the Capital, but indeed too much of it prevails in the cottage.

Really we are a most ungratefull people, favour'd as we have been with peculiar Blessings and favours to make so poor returns. With the best opportunities for becomeing a happy people, and all the materials in our power, yet we have neither skill nor wisdom to put them together.

Abigail Adams, from a letter written in Braintree, Massachusetts, to John Adams, June 15, 1777, in L. H. Butterfield, ed., Adams Family Correspondence, *vol. 2, p. 265.*

The army is in the fullest powers of health and spirit. I have a large body of savages and shall be joined by a larger in a few days. Ticonderoga reduced, I shall leave behind me proper engineers to put it in an impregnable state and it will be garrisoned from Canada where all the destined supplies are safely arrived. My force therefore will be left complete for future operations.

Lt. Gen. John Burgoyne, from a letter written at a camp near Ticonderoga, New York, to Gen. Sir William Howe, July 2, 1777, in K. G. Davies, ed., Documents of the American Revolution, *vol. 14, p. 125.*

Yesterday [July 4], being the first anniversary of the Independence of the United States of America, was celebrated in Philadelphia with demonstrations of joy and festivity. About noon all the armed ships and galleys in the river were drawn up before the city, dressed in the gayest manner. . . . At one o'clock . . . they began the celebration of the day by a discharge of thirteen cannon from each of the ships, and one from each of the thirteen galleys, in honor of the thirteen United States.

In the afternoon an elegant dinner was provided for Congress, to which were invited the President and the supreme executive council . . . the general officers and colonels of the army, and strangers of eminence. . . . The Hessian band of music, taken in Trenton the twenty-sixth of December last, attended and heightened the festivity with some fine performances . . . while a corps of British deserters, taken into the service of the conti-

nent by the State of Georgia, . . . filled up the intervals with *feu de joie.* . . .

From the Pennsylvania Journal, *July 9, 1777, in Frank Moore, compiler,* The Diary of the American Revolution, *p. 229.*

As the War in which your Country is engaged will probably hereafter attract your Attention, more than it does at this Time, and as the future Circumstances of your Country, may require other Wars, as well as Councils and Negotiations, similar to those which are now in Agitation, I wish to turn your Thoughts early to such Studies, as will afford you the most solid Instruction and Improvement for the Part which may be allotted you to act on the Stage of Life.

Ther is no History, perhaps, better adapted to this usefull Purpose than that of Thucidides, an Author, of whom I hope you will make yourself perfect Master, in original Language, which is Greek, the most perfect of all human Languages. In order to understand him fully in his own Tongue, you must however take Advantage, of every Help you can procure and particularly of Translations of him into your own Mother Tongue.

You will find in your Fathers Library, the Works of Mr. Hobbes, in which among a great deal of mischievous Philosophy, you will find a learned and exact Translation of Thucidides, which will be usefull to you.

John Adams, from a letter written in Philadelphia to his son John Quincy Adams, August 11, 1777, in L. H. Butterfield, ed., Adams Family Correspondence, *vol. 2, p. 307.*

The Surrender of Tyconderoga has deeply wounded our Cause. The Grounds of it must be thoroughly inquired into. The People at large have a Right to demand it. They do demand it and Congress have orderd an Inquiry to be made. This Matter must be conducted with Impartiality. The Troops orderd for the Defence of that Post were chiefly from New England. It is said there was a great Deficiency in Numbers—and General Schuyler tells us that a third Part of the Army there were Boys Negroes and aged Men not fit for the Field or indeed any other Service, that a great Part of them were naked, without Blanketts, ill armed & very deficient in Accoutrements. . . .

Samuel Adams, from a letter written in Philadelphia, August 12, 1777, to Maj. Gen. William Heath, in Harry Alonzo Cushing, ed., The Writings of Samuel Adams, *vol. 3, p. 407.*

No one half of them can not be termed fit for duty on any immergency; Of those, who of them went with me on a late expedition near to Kings bridge many were bare foot, in consequence of which its probable they won't be fir for duty again for many week 5 of them there deserted to ye enemy. . . . In fine ye Regiment is scandalous in its appearance in ye view of every one—and has because of this incurred from surrounding regiments from ye inhabitants of Towns thro which they have lately passed, ye disagreeable and provoking Epithets of the Ragged Lousey Naked Regiment. . . .

Col. Israel Angell, commenting on the quality and appearance of the men under his command in the 2nd Rhode Island Regiment, in a letter of August 22, 1777, to the governor of Rhode Island, from Angell, Diary of Colonel Israel Angell, *p. xii.*

I like this Movement of the General [Washington], through the City, because, such a show of Artillery, Waggons, Light Horse and Infantry, which takes up a Line of 9 or 10 Miles upon their March and will not be less than 5 or 6 Hours passing through the Town, will make a good Impression upon the Minds of the timorous Whiggs for their Confirmation, upon the cunning Quakers for their Restraint and upon the rascally Tories for the Confusion.

John Adams, from a letter written in Philadelphia to Abigail Adams, August 23, 1777, in L. H. Butterfield, ed., Adams Family Correspondence, *vol. 2, p. 326.*

This morning the Light Troops, British and Hessian Grenadiers, 1st, 2d and 5th Brigades marched to the head of Elk. The remainder of the Army under Lieutenant General Knyphausen changed the disposition of their Encampment. The advanced part of the Army took a considerable quantity of tobacco, Indian corn, oats and other articles. It seems the Rebels had a very large store there, and had been employed since the landing of the Troops in carrying them away. Washington had been there on the 27th and dined at the house now General Howe's Quarters. . . .

Major John André, from diary entry of August 28, 1777, in André, Major André's Journal, *p. 38.*

This afternoon, the two thieves, who stole Col. White's cash and trunk, were marched about a mile and a half out of town, in order, it's said, to be hanged, but upon the Colonel's lady's intercession, it's said, they were pardoned from death, but received two or three hundred

lashes each, well laid on their backs and buttocks. A great number of spectators, it's said, were assembled.

Christopher Marshall, merchant and Quaker then in Lancaster, Pennsylvania, diary entry of September 6, 1777, in Marshall, Extracts from the Diary of Christopher Marshall, *p. 125.*

One of the Field-Officers of the day. At 7 A.M., a true alarm. At Eight the Enemy appeared, fought & drove in our advanced parties from the heighths on the south side of Chad's Ford. Immediately a severe cannonade of Shells, Bombs &c. &c. &c. opened from each side, which exhibited the grandest scene I ever Saw, a sight beyond description grand.

At 2 P.M. Our division marched towards Jones' Ford. At 3. Lord Stirling and Genl. Sullivan's divisions engaged Lord Cornwallis's light corps & the British Main Army. We broke and Rallied and Rallied & broke from heighth to heighth till we fell on our main Army, who reinforced us & about sunset we made a stand, when I was wounded, having a Ball with the Wad shot through my left forearm & the fuse set my coat and shirt on fire. Soon after this I left the field and road about two Miles. By the assistance of a stranger dressed my Wound with some tow . . . and wrapped my Arm in my handerkerchief. . . .

It is well known that after we rallied the first time & broke . . . Capt. Bellard of our Regt. who was wounded in the leg & would have fallen into the hands of the Enemy had I not (though I have the Modesty to say it myself) went back upon his crying for assistance, taken him behind me & brought him from the Field of Battle: & must undoubtedly have been killed had not the Enemys fire been expended & they relyed on their Bayonetts in their pursuit as their front was within a few Yards of us when I rode off with Capt. Bellard.

Major Joseph Bloomfield of the 3rd New Jersey Regiment describing the Battle of Brandywine, from journal entry of September 11, 1777, in Mark E. Lender and James Kirby Martin, eds., Citizen Soldier, *pp. 127–128.*

We live in critical Moments! Mr. Howes Army is at Middleton and Concord. Mr. Washington, upon the Western Banks of Schuylkill, a few Miles from him. I saw this Morning an excellent Chart of the Schuylkill, Chester River, the Brandywine, and this whole Country, among the Pensilvania Files. This City [Philadelphia] is the Stake, for which the Game is playd. I think, there is a Chance for saving it, although the Probability is against Us. Mr. Howe I conjecture is waiting for his Ships to come into the Delaware. Will W. attack him? I hope so—and God grant him Success.

John Adams, from diary entry of September 15, 1777, in L. H. Butterfield, ed., Diary and Autobiography of John Adams, *p. 262.*

. . . What you now enjoy is only a respite from ruin; an invitation to destruction; something that will lead on to our deliverance at your expense. We know the cause which we are engaged in, and though a passionate fondness for it may make us grieve at every injury which threatens it, yet, when the moment of concern is over, the determination to duty returns. We are not moved by the gloomy smile of a worthless king, but by the ardent glow of generous patriotism. We fight not to enslave, but to set a country free, and to make room upon the earth for honest men to live in. In such a case we are sure that we are right; and we leave to you the despairing reflection of being the tool of a miserable tyrant.

Thomas Paine, a comment addressed to Lord Howe, from The American Crisis IV, *September 12, 1777, from Van der Weyde,* The Life and Works of Thomas Paine, *vol. 2, p. 368.*

It was a false alarm which occasioned our Flight from Philadelphia. Not a Soldier of Howes has crossed the Schuylkill. Washington has again crossed it, which I think is a very injudicious Maneuvre. I think, his Army would have been best disposed on the West Side of the Schuylkill. If he had sent one Brigade of his regular Troops to have heald the Militia it would have been enough. With such a Disposition, he might have cutt to Pieces, Hows Army, in attempting to cross any of the Fords. How will not attempt it. He will wait for his Fleet in Delaware River. He will keep open his Line of Communication with Brunswick, and at last, by some Deception or other will slip unhurt into the City.

Burgoine has crossed Hudsons River, by which Gen. Gates thinks, he is determined at all Hazards to push for Albany, which G. Gates says he will do all in his Power to prevent him from reaching. But I confess I am anxious for the Event, for I fear he will deceive Gates, who seems to be acting the same timorous, defensive Part, which has involved us in so many Disasters.—Oh, Heaven! grant Us one great Soul! One leading Mind

would extricate the best Cause, from that Ruin which seems to await it, for the Want of it.

John Adams, diary entry of September 21, 1777, in L. H. Butterfield, ed., Diary and Autobiography of John Adams, *vol. 2, p. 265.*

I am much distressed at Gen. Arnold's determination to retire from the army at this important crisis. His presence was never more necessary. He is the life and soul of the troops. Believe me, Sir, to him and to him alone is due the honor of our late victory. Whatever share his superiours may claim they are entitled to none. He enjoys the confidence and affection of officers and soldiers. They would, to a man, follow him to conquest or death. His absence will dishearten them to such a degree as to render them of but little service.

Col. Henry Brockholst Livingston of the Continental army, from a letter written at Bemis Heights, New York, September 23, 1777, to Gen. Philip Schuyler, in Henry Steele Commager, ed., The Spirit of 'Seventy Six, *vol. 1, p. 583.*

. . . The Rebels were each equipped with a piece of white paper in his hat, which made us imagine they meant a surprise by night. Their disposition for the attack is not easily traced; it seems to have been too complicated; nor do their Troops appear to have been sufficiently animated for the execution of it in every part, altho' the power of strong liquor had been employed. Several, not only of their Soldiers but Officers, were intoxicated when they fell into our hands. . . . We supposed the Rebels to have lost between 200 and 300 killed, with the proportion of wounded. On our side about 300 were killed or wounded. . . . We took 380 prisoners, whereof fifty were Officers. . . .

Major John André, from diary entry of October 4, 1777, describing the Battle of Germantown, in John André, Major André's Journal, *p. 57.*

In my son's letter are many instances of the wanton cruelty they [British] exercised in his [Philadelphia] neighborhood, amongst which is the burning of the house where Col. [Joseph] Reed did live, the house where Thompson kept tavern, with every thing in it, all the hay at Col. Bull's, fifteen hundred bushels of wheat, with other grain, his powder mill and iron works; destroyed all the fences for some miles, with the Indian corn and buckwheat, emptied feather beds, destroyed furniture, cut books to pieces. . . .

Christopher Marshall, from a diary entry written in Lancaster, Pennsylvania, October 8, 1777, in Marshall, Extracts from the Diary of Christopher Marshall, *pp. 133–134.*

Toward evening, we at last came to Saratoga. . . . I was wet through and through by the frequent rains, and was obliged to remain in this condition the entire night, as I had no place whatever where I could change my linen. I, therefore, seated myself before a good fire, and undressed my children; after which, we laid ourselves down together upon some straw. I asked General [William] Phillips, who came up to where we were, why we did not continue our retreat. . . . "Poor woman," answered he . . . "Would that you were only our commanding general! He halts because he is tired, and intends to spend the night here and give us a supper." In this latter achievement, especially, General Burgoyne was very fond of indulging. He spent half the nights in singing and drinking, and amusing himself with the wife of the commissary, who was his mistress. . . .

Baroness Frederika Charlotte von Riedesel, wife of Baron Friedrich von Riedesel, from journal entry about October 9, 1777, in Hugh F. Rankin, ed., Narratives of the American Revolution, *pp. 330–331.*

At last, my husband sent to me a groom with a message that I should come to him with our children. . . . [I]n the passage through the American camp, I observed, with great satisfaction, that no one cast at us scornful glances. On the contrary, they all greeted me, even showing compassion. . . . I confess that I feared to come into the enemy's camp. . . . When I approached the tents, a noble looking man [Gen. Philip Schuyler] came toward me, took the children out of the wagon, embraced and kissed them, and then with tears in his eyes helped me also to alight. "You tremble," said he to me, "fear nothing." "No," replied I, "for you are so kind . . . that it has inspired me with courage." He then led me to the tent of General Gates, with whom I found Generals Burgoyne and Phillips. . . .

Baroness von Riedesel, from journal entry about October 17, 1777, in Hugh F. Rankin, ed., Narratives of the American Revolution, *pp. 343–344.*

. . . I have to report to your lordship the proceedings of the army under my command . . . a series of hard

toil, incessant effort, stubborn action, till disabled in the collateral branches of the army by the total defection of the Indians, the desertion or the timidity of the Canadians and provincials, some individuals excepted, disappointed in the last hope of any timely cooperation from other armies, the regular troops reduced by losses . . . to three thousand five hundred fighting men, not two thousand of which were British, only three days provisions, . . . invested by an army of sixteen thousand men, and no apparent means of retreat remaining, I called into council all the generals, field officers, and captains commanding corps, and by their unanimous concurrence and advice I was induced to open a treaty with Major-General Gates.

Lt. Gen. John Burgoyne, from a letter written at Albany, New York, to Lord George Germain, October 20, 1777, in K. G. Davies, ed., Documents of the American Revolution, *vol. 14, pp. 228–229.*

. . . they attacked on the North & South Sides, the North Side was a brea[st] work within a nother which we cut off and made the Fort small as we had but few men to man it . . . a row of strong pallesaids sallied out from the parapet on the gate on the South Side / we had a small place big enough for eight men to fight in which overlooked all the ground round the Fort which was surrounded with double abattis / both of the attacks where such as was expected / . . . they advanced as far as the abbatis, but they could not remove it (tho sum got over) being repulsed with great loss / they left their Command'g officer [Col. Carl von Donop] dying on the Ground in his glacis, and retreated with hurry & Confusion . . . we feched in to the fort all the Wounded & dressed them shewing as [much] humanity as posable. Colo. Donop was attended with care

Continental army sergeant Jeremiah Greenman, describing the October 22 Hessian attack on Fort Mercer, from diary entry of October 22, 1777, in Greenman, Diary of a Common Soldier in the American Revolution, 1775–1783, *p. 82.*

I wrote you about ten days ago that General Gates had obtain'd a Signal Victory over General Burgoyne on the 7th. Inst. and now have the pleasure of informing you that a few days after this defeat Burgoyne with his whole Army Surrend'd themselves prisoners of War to the American General. It is said the prisoners Stores &c. taken are as followeth Viz. 1 Lt.

General, 2 Major Generals, 7 Brigadier Do. 5000 privates, 2 English noblemen, 1 Irish Do. 15000 Stand of Arms 40 Brass Cannon and a Considerable Quantity of Cloathing. This great and Important News I transmit to you on the Authority of the Committee of Albany, Governor Clinton and General Washington's Letters to Congress (except the Enumeration of Officers &c. which we have from another Quarter). No one doubts the truth of this happy Event Yet many feel the greatest Anxiety for a Confirmation of it under General Gates's own hand. Almost every day brings us News of some advantage or other over the Enemy. . . .

John Harvie, from a letter written in York, Pennsylvania,
where the Continental Congress convened, to Thomas
Jefferson, October 25, 1777, in Julian P. Boyd, ed.,
The Papers of Thomas Jefferson,
vol. 2, pp. 37–38.

Burgoine is expected in by the middle of the week. I have read many Articles of Capitulation, but none which ever contain so generous Terms before. Many people find fault with them but perhaps do not consider sufficently the circumstances of General Gates, who (*perhaps*) by delaying and exacting more might have lost all. This must be said of him that he has followed the golden rule and done as he would wish himself in like circumstances to be dealt with.—Must not the vapouring Burgoine who tis said possesses great Sensibility, be humbled to the dust. He may now write the Blocade of Saratoga. I have heard it proposed that he should take up his quarters in the old South [Meeting House], but believe he will not be permitted to come to this Town. . . .

Abigail Adams, from a letter written in Boston to John
Adams, October 25, 1777, in L. H. Butterfield, ed.,
Adams Family Correspondence, *vol. 2, p. 358.*

I feel my self particularly happy in the honor of transmitting the inclosed Vote of Thanks by Congress in their own Name & and on behalf of their Constituents to Your-Self, to Major General Lincoln, Major General Arnold & the rest of the rest of the Officers & Troops under your Command, with an additional Vote for perpetuating the remembrance of this great event [Saratoga] by a Medal.

Your Name Sir will be written in the breasts of the grateful Americans of the present Age & sent down to Posterity in Characters which will remain

Horatio Gates was appointed president of the Board of War in 1777. *(From* The Pictorial Field Book of the Revolution, *2 vols., by B. J. Lossing. New York: Harper Brothers, 1851 and 1852.)*

indelible when the Gold shall have changed its appearance. . . .

Henry Laurens, president of Congress, from a letter
written in York, Pennsylvania, November 5, 1777, to
Horatio Gates, in David R. Chesnutt and C. James
Taylor, eds., The Papers of Henry Laurens, *vol. 12,*
pp. 21–22.

Last night [September 25], the royal army, under the command of his Excellency Sir William Howe, Knight of the Bath . . . entered Philadelphia, marched through Second street, and . . . encamped to the southward of the town.

The fine appearance of the soldiery, the strictness of their discipline, the politeness of the officers, and the orderly behavior of the whole body, immediately dispelled every apprehension of the inhabitants . . . and has given the most convincing refutation of the scandalous falsehoods which evil and designing men have been long spreading to terrify the peaceable and innocent. A perfect tranquility now prevails in the city. . . .

From Rivington's Gazette, *November 8, 1777, in*
Frank Moore, compiler, The Diary of the American
Revolution, *pp. 252–253.*

Sir: A Letter which I received last Night, contained the following paragraph.

In a Letter from Genl. Conway to Genl. Gates he says: "Heaven has been determined to save our Country; or a weak General and bad Councellors would have ruind it."

I am Sir Yr. Hble Servt.

George Washington, from a letter written at White Marsh, New Jersey, November 9, 1777, to Brig. Gen. Thomas Conway, in John C. Fitzpatrick, ed., The Writings of George Washington, *vol. 10, p. 29.*

My Lord, by the death of Major Barret, late of the artillery, the command of the troops in this island has devolved upon me, which makes it my duty to represent to your lordship the situation of affairs in this country, as the absence of the *Active* frigate which was to have wintered in this harbour, and the unfortunate event that has happened to General Burgoyne's army, has rendered an attack on this island early in the spring more probable and has greatly weakened the resources for our defence.

Capt. Robert Pringle, from a letter written in St. John's, Newfoundland, to Lord George Germain, November 22, 1777, in K. G. Davies, ed., Documents of the American Revolution, *vol. 14, p. 256.*

. . . Our Situation, as you justly observe is distressing . . . more especially from the impracticability of answering the expectations of the world without running hazards which no military principles can justify, and which, in case of failure, might prove the ruin of our cause; patience, and a steady perseverance in such measures as appear warranted by sound reason and policy, must support us under the censure of the one, and dictate a proper line of conduct for the attainment of the other; that is the great object in view. This, as it ever has, will I think, ever remain the first wish of my heart, however I may mistake the means of accomplishment; that your views are the same, and that your endeavours have pointed to the same end, I am perfectly satisfied of. . . .

George Washington, from a letter written at White Marsh, New Jersey, November 26, 1777, to Maj. Gen. Nathanael Greene, in John C. Fitzpatrick, ed., The Writings of George Washington, *vol. 10, pp. 106–107.*

My Lord, in consequence of the misfortune that has fallen upon the troops under Lieutenant-General Burgoyne's command, a considerable reinforcement from General Gates's corps has joined General Washington. The hopes of the people at large as well as of the rebel army are greatly raised from this event, and I am free to own I do not apprehend a successful termination to the war from any advantages His Majesty's troops can gain, while the enemy is able to avoid or unwilling to hazard a decisive action, which might reduce the leaders in rebellion to make an overture for peace; or that this is to be expected unless a respectable addition to the army is sent from Europe to act early in the ensuing year. . . .

Gen. Sir William Howe, from a letter written in Philadelphia to Lord George Germain, November 30, 1777, in K. G. Davies, ed., Documents of the American Revolution, *vol. 14, p. 264.*

We have the Honour to acquaint your Excellency that we have just receiv'd an Express from Boston, in 30 Days, with Advice of the total Reduction of the Force under General Burgoyne, himself and his whole Army having surrendered themselves Prisoners. General Gates was about to send Reinforcements to Gen. Washington, who was near Philadelphia with his Army. Gen. Howe was in Possession of that City, but having no Communication with his Fleet, it was hoped he would soon be reduced to submit to the same Terms with Burgoyne, whose Capitulation we enclose. . . .

The American Commissioners Benjamin Franklin, Silas Deane, and Arthur Lee, from a letter to Count de Vergennes, December 4, 1777, in William B. Willcox, ed., The Papers of Benjamin Franklin, *vol. 25, p. 236.*

I have heard with great pleaure that you are about to new-model the army. For God's sake, do not forget to take the medical system under your consideration. It is a mass of corruption and tyranny and has wholly disappointed the benevolence and munificence of the Congress. It would take up a volume to unfold all the disorders and miseries of the hospitals. What do you think of 5000 being supported with stores, hospital furniture, etc., sufficient for only 1500 men? What do you think of 600 men in a village without a single officer to mount a guard over them or punish irregularities. This is the case at this time in Princetown, and the consequences are: Old disorders are prolonged, new ones are contracted, the discipline of the soldiers

...is destroyed, the inhabitants are plundered, and the blankets, clothes, shoes, etc., of the soldiers are stolen or exchanged in every tavern and hut for spiritous liquors.

Dr. Benjamin Rush, from a letter written at Princeton, New Jersey, December 13, 1777, to William Duer, New York delegate to the Continental Congress, in Henry Steele Commager, ed., The Spirit of 'Seventy Six, *vol. 2, p. 834.*

Prisoners & Deserters are continually coming in. The Army which has been surprisingly healthy hitherto, now begins to grow sickly from the continued fatigues they have suffered this Campaign. Yet they still show a spirit of Alacrity & Contentment not to be expected from so young Troops. I am Sick—discontented—and out of humour. Poor food—hard lodging—Cold Weather—fatigue—Nasty Cloaths—nasty Cookery—Vomit half my time—smoak'd out of my senses—the Devil's in't—I can't Endure it—Why are we sent here to starve and Freeze. . . .

Albigence Waldo, Continental surgeon with 1st Connecticut Infantry Regiment, from diary entry written at Valley Forge, December 14, 1777, in Hugh F. Rankin, ed., Narratives of the American Revolution, *p. 181.*

. . . We are now five of us in this City [three commissioners, Ralph Izard, and William Lee], all honest and capable Men (if I may include myself in that Description) and all meaning well for the Public, but our Tempers do not suit, and we are got into Disputes and Contentions that are not to our Credit, and which I have sometimes feared would go to Extremes. You know the natural Disposition of some of us, how jealous, how captious, how suspicious even of real Friends, and how positive, after suspecting a while, that the Suspicions are certain Truths. . . . You will therefore, I am persuaded, if Complaints of one another should come to your hands, make due Allowance for such Tempers, and suffer no Man to be comdemn'd unheard. I do not write thus on my own Account, as I am not apprehensive of your receiving any Complaints of me. . . .

Benjamin Franklin, from a letter written in Paris, December 21, 1777, to Robert Morris, in William B. Willcox, ed., The Papers of Benjamin Franklin, *vol. 25, pp. 330–331.*

Our affairs wear a very gloomy aspect. Great part of our army gone into winter quarters; those in camp wanting breeches, shoes, stockings, [and] blankets, . . . in want of flour, yet being in the land of plenty; our farmers having their barns and barracks full of grain; hundreds of barrels of flour lying on the banks of the Susquehanna perishing for want of care in securing it from the weather . . . ; our enemies revelling in balls, attended with every degree of luxury and excess in the City; rioting and wantonly using our houses, utensils and furniture. . . . Add to this their frequent excursions round about for twenty miles together, destroying and burning what they please, pillaging, plundering men and women, stealing boys above ten years old, deflowering virgins, driving into the City for their use, droves of cattle, sheep [and] hogs; poultry, butter, meal, meat, cider, furniture and clothing of all kinds, loaded upon our own horses. All this done in the view of our Generals and our army, who are careless of us, but carefully consulting where they shall go to spend the winter in jollity, gaming, and carousing. O tell this not in France or Spain! Publish it not in the streets of London, Liverpool or Bristol, lest the uncircumcised there should rejoice, and shouting for joy, say "America is ours, for the rebels are dismayed and afraid to fight for us any longer! O Americans, where is now your virtue? O Washington, where is your courage?" . . .

Christopher Marshall, merchant and Quaker then in Lancaster, Pennsylvania, from diary entry of December 28, 1777, in Marshall, Extracts from the Diary of Christopher Marshall, *pp. 152–153.*

Your Supply of Cloathing came very Opportunely to Cover the Shivering Limbs of our poor Naked Soldiers. Thousands of them are now in the Hospitals for the want of even Wrags to keep them from the Cold. We hear Two Hundred thousand pounds worth of Goods (at Exorbitant prices) has been purchased in the Massachusetts. We hope they will be soon forwarded to the Army.

There is no late Interesting Intelligence from either of our Army's. General Washingtons is now in Forge Valley about twenty three Miles from Philadelphia where they will probably remain Inactive the greatest part of the Winter. The Waste of the Enemy wherever they move is a Scene of Cruelty and distress. This dreadful Calamity is only Alleviated to the Whig by seeing the Torys property made one Common Ruin with his own, for all their late Ravages is Indiscriminate.

John Harvie, from a letter written in York, Pennsylvania, to Thomas Jefferson, December 29, 1777, in Julian P. Boyd, ed., The Papers of Thomas Jefferson, *vol. 2, p. 126.*

Your favour of Yesterday conveyed to me fresh proof of that friendship and attachment which I have happily experienced since the first of our acquaintance, and for which I entertain sentiments of the purest affection. It will ever constitute part of my happiness to know that I stand well in your opinion, because I am satisfied that you can have no views to answer by throwing out false colours, and that you possess a Mind too exalted to condescend to dirty Arts and low intrigues to acquire a reputation. Happy, thrice happy, would it have been for this Army and the cause we are embarked in, if the same generous spirit had pervaded all the Actors in it. But one Gentleman [Maj. Gen. Horatio Gates] . . . had, I am confident, far different views. His ambition and great desire of being puffed off as one of the first Officers of the Age, could only be equalled by the means which he used to obtain them; but finding that I was determined not to go beyond the line of my duty to indulge him in the first, nor, to exceed the strictest rules of propriety, to gratify him in the second, he became my inveterate Enemy. . . .

George Washington, from a letter written at Valley Forge, December 31, 1777, to the marquis de Lafayette, in John C. Fitzpatrick, ed., The Writings of George Washington, *vol. 10, pp. 236–237.*

5
From Valley Forge to Vincennes
1778

WINTER AT VALLEY FORGE

As Commander in Chief George Washington and his army had begun to settle in at Valley Forge in December 1777, the so-called Conway Cabal overtook the commander. This ostensible plot to undermine his authority and perhaps replace him can be traced to the Continental Congress's appointment of Col. Timothy Pickering, Gen. Thomas Mifflin, and Gen. Horatio Gates as members of the newly created Board of War and designation of Gates as the board's president in November 1777. The appointments appeared to threaten Washington, as both Gates and Mifflin had evidenced hostility toward him, and Pickering indifferent support. Then, in mid-December, the Continental Congress had overlooked 23 other brigadier generals who were Thomas Conway's seniors to promote him to

George and Martha Washington visit the troops at Valley Forge on Christmas Day, 1777. *(Courtesy of Anne S. K. Brown Military Collection, Brown University Library)*

major general. He was also appointed to the newly created position of inspector general of the army, an agency independent of the commander in chief that reported directly to the Board of War—an apparent victory for Washington's detractors.

In response, Washington wrote to the Continental Congress and suggested that a few members of the Board of War or a committee of congressmen visit the Valley Forge encampment to resolve concerns about his leadership and the organization of the Continental army that his detractors had raised. Conway visited the camp in December; and in January, Washington sent his and Conway's correspondence to Congress with a letter that made clear his displeasure with Conway. Congress then resolved to send a committee of its own members along with Gates, Mifflin, and Pickering to Valley Forge; but the three members of the Board of War, after reviewing the correspondence Washington had sent to the Continental Congress, asked to be excused from visiting the camp.

Congress complicated this stew by envisioning a bizarre "irruption" (a euphemism for invasion) into Canada and placing Lafayette in command of the expedition, with Conway as his second in command. Lafayette wrote to the Board of War and to President Henry Laurens expressing his abhorrence of and contempt toward Conway; as a result, Laurens, a strong supporter of Washington, began to suspect the Conway Cabal partisans of treachery. Finally, in February, the exasperated and angry commander in chief wrote a series of letters to Gates chastising him for ambiguous statements on the matter and denouncing Conway's malignity. These letters had the desired effect of ending the presumed Conway Cabal.[1]

During this sideshow, the congressional committee arrived at Valley Forge for a two-month review. Only 8,200 of the 11,000 soldiers in winter quarters there were fit for duty, and all lacked adequate provisions. Many needed hats, shoes, and coats. Their rations frequently consisted only of a mixture of bread flour and water baked over a campfire. Fearful that their deprivations would generate a mutiny, Washington had sent pleading letters to Congress and to Gov. George Clinton of New York requesting provisions. In early March, the visiting committee presented recommendations for reform of the army and the Quartermaster General's Department, and the Continental Congress appointed Nathanael Greene as quartermaster general to effect the recommendations. In April, pursuing the effort at reform, Congress appointed Jeremiah Wadsworth as commissary general of purchases to reorganize the Commissary Department. These changes would prove of some value in bringing order and consistency to the army's transportation and supply systems, but unfortunately the visiting committee also interfered with Washington's plan for an exchange of prisoners with General Howe that eventuated in the plan's failure and a congressional rebuke of Washington that the commander chose to ignore.[2]

Greene undertook several initiatives to improve supply systems, including ordering that stores of hay and grain be set up at intermediate sites along the Continental lines for feeding horses and other livestock. Thus sizable stocks of hay and grains were stored at Trenton, New Jersey; Reading, Allentown, and Lancaster, Pennsylvania; Head of Elk, Maryland; and at posts along the Delaware and Hudson Rivers. These stocks would facilitate movement of artillery and wagons drawn by draft horses and also troops of cavalry. Greene also drew up careful estimates of the numbers of wagons and teams needed to move a single brigade of troops. Estimates in 1778 placed the number of horses serving as wagon teams and as cavalry or officer mounts for the main army at 10,000.[3]

BOOSTING MORALE

Unfortunately for the troops at Valley Forge, Congress's efforts begun in 1777 to improve the commissary system had not reached fruition by the time the Continental army encamped for the winter. Consequently, supplies of flour and salted meats and fish that had been stored at Lebanon and Carlisle in Pennsylvania proved insufficient. Difficulties in transporting supplies occurred because wagons, boats, and horses had been moved south to prevent their falling into British hands, thus forcing extended journeys in sometimes perilous winter weather. Furthermore, the British army occupying Philadelphia competed for supplies of grains and beef in the same region where Washington's army attempted to purchase such supplies. Local farmers who had grains refused to sell to Washington, fearing that they would not be paid because of the devalued Continental currency. And the British, whose currency largely retained its value, could make purchases of beef cattle from unscrupulous agents who had previously sold to the Patriots. These and other circumstances deprived Washington's men at Valley Forge of proper nutrition—from December 1777 to June 1778 nearly one-fourth of them died.[4]

Curiously, one means that Washington chose for distracting his men's attention from their sufferings and demoralization was a production of Joseph Addison's play *Tragedy of Cato.* The play depicts the doomed senator and general Cato on the frontier of the Roman Republic awaiting with his army and African allies the onslaught of Julius Caesar's legionnaires. Although Cato serves the cause of liberty and endures hardships in that service, he faces annihilation and the defection of some of his commanders. Furthermore, Cato commits suicide after securing clemency for his troops who wish to join Caesar and sending the rest to an uncertain destiny aboard ships heading into the open seas. How Washington's troops responded to such a drama may only be guessed. Perhaps the commander in chief at least gained some succor from performances of his favorite play during this bleak winter.[5]

Baron von Steuben visits Valley Forge, 1777. *(Courtesy of the National Archives and Records Administration)*

Perhaps the most propitious occurrence for both Washington and the Continental army during this bleak winter was Baron Friedrich Wilhelm von Steuben's arrival at Valley Forge in late February. Well trained in the military arts—he had been instructed by Frederick the Great—von Steuben quickly won the trust and admiration of Washington, who assigned Alexander Hamilton and John Laurens, son of the president of the Continental Congress, as his aides. Von Steuben set about organizing and training a drill company of 100 men. Once these men attained proficiency, they trained other men, so by the time spring arrived, the entire army had mastered improved military methods and discipline. In addition, during the winter von Steuben wrote the army's first manual of regulations and drills. His colorful appearance and behavior also helped boost the morale of the ill-fed and ill-clothed troops. The Battle of Monmouth Courthouse would reveal their new firmness.[6]

A FINAL PEACE INITIATIVE

The American victory at the Battle of Saratoga resounded not only at Versailles and Paris but also in London. Dismayed by the British loss and concerned by rumors of an American alliance with France, Lord North launched a final effort at reconciliation. On February 16 he submitted a plan for Parliament's consideration that included repeal of the Tea Act and the Coercive Acts, a promise that no revenue taxes would be imposed on the American colonies, appointment of a commission to negotiate a peaceful settlement with the Continental Congress, and, if necessary, suspension of all relevant legal acts approved by Parliament since 1763. Charles James Fox responded by asking North whether France and the United States had concluded a treaty of commerce, which in fact they had on February 6, along with a treaty of alliance. Edmund Burke rose to repeat Fox's question and to point out that North's plan was virtually identical to one that Burke had proposed two years previously. The shaken North answered equivocally. But North would pursue his peace plan while also ordering a new military strategy.[7]

Parliament approved the reconciliation plan—Royal Instructions to the Peace Commission of 1778—in mid-March. The North ministry entrusted the plan's fulfillment to a commission composed of Frederick Howard, earl of Carlisle, a friend of Fox; Richard and William Howe; William Eden, commissioner for trade and plantations; and George Johnstone, former governor of West Florida. The members, it was thought, would appeal to the Americans, but Carlisle himself lacked ability, and his colleagues appeared as secret intelligence agents. The Carlisle Commission, as it was known, received the ministry's mandate to negotiate every issue extant between the two belligerents and to offer numerous concessions, including removal of standing armies from the colonies during peacetime, acceptance of the Continental Congress, and a guarantee of American charters. But what could not be conceded foredoomed the Carlisle Commission: American independence and Parliament's sovereignty.

The Carlisle Commission embarked for America in mid-April aboard the same ship on which Lord Cornwallis sailed to assume his duties as second in command to Gen. Sir Henry Clinton, appointed in early March to succeed General Howe as commander in chief in America. They were less than a week out of port when the Continental Congress, with many members having seen a

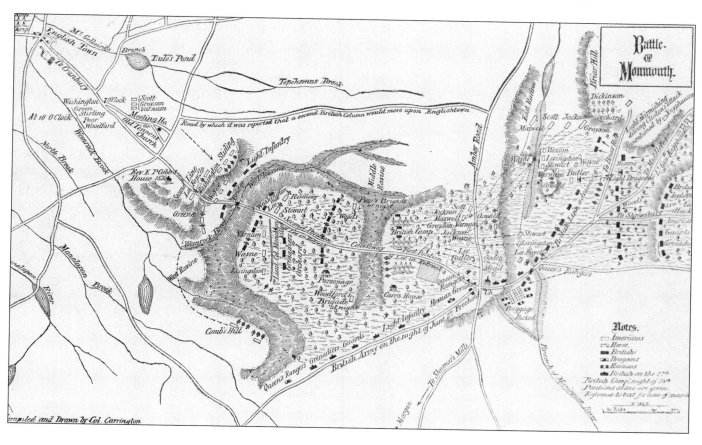

The Battle of Monmouth did not have a clear victor. (*Courtesy of Anne S. K. Brown Military Collection, Brown University Library*)

draft of North's speech introducing his plan in Parliament, approved a resolution declaring any group or individual who negotiated terms with the commission to be an enemy of the United States. Congress continued to insist that no negotiations could proceed until Great Britain withdrew its armed forces or unequivocally recognized American independence. The Carlisle Commission arrived in Philadelphia on June 6 to certain failure.[8]

Responding to letters outlining terms received from the commission in mid-June and discussed by the delegates for three days, the Continental Congress evoked its longstanding terms: Withdraw military forces or recognize American independence. No movement occurred for two months. Perhaps desperate to overcome Congress's intransigence, George Johnstone offered bribes to three congressmen that, when publicly revealed, forced his removal from the commission and spread suspicion of its purposes. Finally, in early October, the Carlisle Commission tried to sidestep the Continental Congress by publishing a proclamation offering pardons to both civilians and military personnel who replied favorably within 40 days. Near the end of November, their efforts proven totally fruitless, the members of the Carlisle Commission set sail for Great Britain. The war raged on before, during, and after their mission.[9]

THE BATTLE OF MONMOUTH COURTHOUSE

The return to combat in 1778 emerged slowly. The initial American offensive occurred outside the United States' borders when, near the end of January, Capt.

John Peck Rathbun's USS *Providence* captured the two British forts at Nassau and, for the first time, flew the American flag over a conquered foreign post. This easy victory, however, paled in early March when the USS *Randolph* exploded during battle off the West Indies, killing Capt. Nicholas Biddle and all but four of his 315 officers and crewmen—a significant loss for the American navy. Then, during the second week of April, across the Atlantic, John Paul Jones set sail from Brest for a series of moderately successful raids along the Scottish coast.[10]

The war on land, however, appeared reluctant to resume. Except for a small skirmish in New Jersey in mid-March and another in Pennsylvania at the beginning of May, the British army remained sequestered in Philadelphia and the Continental army at Valley Forge well into June, without confrontation. But then, on June 16, Gen. Sir Henry Clinton, now commander in chief, began the evacuation of the British army from Philadelphia. While crossing the Delaware River, the 10,000 soldiers plus 3,000 Loyalists, with wagons, horses, supplies, and artillery, would have been a vulnerable prey to the Continental army. But the Americans remained at Valley Forge. Clinton's force crossed to Gloucester, and his ships sailed down the river unmolested on June 18, restoring Philadelphia to the rebels. When a courier brought the news to Washington that day, he immediately began to move his army—now increased to 13,500 men, better clothed and better equipped, and well disciplined—toward Coryell's Ferry to cross the Delaware and pursue Clinton.[11]

On June 24, with the Continental army encamped within 15 miles of Clinton's camp at Allentown, Pennsylvania, Washington called a council of war. Gen. Charles Lee, supported by the majority of the officers, opposed attack; instead, Brig. Gen. William Maxwell would lead 1,300 Continentals and Gen. Philemon Dickinson 800 New Jersey militiamen in harassing Clinton's flanks. Concerned that Washington might attack while his troops crossed the Raritan River at New Brunswick, Clinton sent half his army and his baggage train commanded by General von Knyphausen in advance and accompanied a second division commanded by Lord Cornwallis to follow after. Both divisions headed toward Monmouth Courthouse. Washington, displeased over the decision not to attack, sent an advance guard of 4,000 troops, including both Maxwell's and Dickinson's men, under Lafayette to strike at Clinton's rear. Then Lee, as second in command, insisted on assuming command of this strike force, and with Washington's assent, marched off with another 1,000 men to join Lafayette at Englishtown. On June 27, now encamped near Englishtown, Washington ordered an attack on Clinton's rear to be led by Lee and also ordered Lee to send troops during the night to observe Clinton's movements, but the impulsive Lee delayed carrying out the latter order for hours.[12]

In the early morning of the following day, Clinton sent von Knyphausen's division toward Middletown, a movement Dickinson observed and reported to both Lee and Washington. Some hours later, Lee began a halting advance, impeded by skirmishes with Cornwallis's rear guard. Near Monmouth Courthouse after 11:00 A.M., Lee's 5,000-man force engaged the 2,000-man rear guard, but confusion prevailed, as Lee lacked an attack plan and had no orders for his generals—Maxwell, Anthony Wayne, Charles Scott, and William Woodford. Sensing a greater menace than the Americans' earlier harassment tactics, Clinton wheeled his army about and marched to attack, sending Lee's force into retreat toward Englishtown. Advancing with his main army from Englishtown, Wash-

Molly Pitcher cleans a cannon at the Battle of Monmouth. *(Courtesy of the National Archives and Records Administration)*

ington encountered Lee's force in retreat and, outraged, accosted and denounced Lee for failing to attack Clinton's rear. Washington swore, Gen. Charles Scott declared, "till the leaves shook on the trees. . . . [H]e swore like an angel from heaven."

Washington assumed command. Riding up and down the lines, he inspired and rallied the troops to return to battle. General Greene and Lord Stirling created a defensive position along a ridge above West Ravine, separated from Clinton's force by a morass, and Knox sited his artillery on the American right on Comb's Hill. The enemy forces battled throughout the afternoon, their struggle punctuated by an artillery duel. (Heroine Molly Pitcher reputedly loaded and fired her fallen husband's cannon.) Clinton's troops attacked repeatedly, but the Americans held fast and forced the British back. At about six o'clock, Clinton withdrew his troops, and the American soldiers slept on their arms. Washington slept wrapped in his cloak, with Lafayette beside him. The American commander planned to attack in the morning, but during the night, Clinton's army quietly moved off to Middletown en route to Sandy Hook and finally New York City. Clinton had 358 casualties, including 217 dead; Washington lost 356 men, including 72 dead and 132 missing. Although neither side could claim a clear victory, the Battle of Monmouth Courthouse evidenced Washington's and the Continental army's resolve.[13]

THE CLARK EXPEDITION

As the year began, George Rogers Clark visited Williamsburg, Virginia, to press his case with Governor Patrick Henry and other officials for an expedition to drive the British out of the northwestern territory of the Ohio-Mississippi River valley. With support from Thomas Jefferson, George Mason, and Richard Henry Lee, Clark won Henry's approval. The Virginia governor appointed Clark as a colonel in the militia and commander of the proposed expedition, with authority to raise seven companies. Henry also provided some funding and authorized Clark to acquire supplies at Fort Pitt. Publicly, the governor announced that Clark's orders were to defend Virginia's Kentucky Territory, threatened by marauding Shawnee and Cherokee, but Clark's secret orders were to attack Kaskaskia and, if possible, the British army post at Detroit.

In mid-May, Clark traveled down the Monongahela River headed for a rendezvous at the falls of the Ohio (at present-day Louisville) with the frontiersmen that Maj. W. P. Smith had recruited for the expedition. Clark arrived in late May to discover that Smith had failed to raise the four expected companies and that only part of one company from the Holston settlement had appeared. With four captains in his service, Clark began to train the men recruited from western Pennsylvania, Kentucky, and Tennessee without revealing the true nature of their mission. When he did reveal the mission, many of the men tried to desert, but Clark's forcefulness earned the loyalty of the majority. In late June, Clark left about 20 men to guard the supplies and the blockhouse on the island they occupied at the falls of the Ohio and set out in flatboats with 175 men bound for Kaskaskia.[14]

The expedition left the river at Fort Massaic and proceeded overland for 120 miles to preserve the advantage of surprise in their approach. On July 4, Clark procured boats, crossed the Kaskaskia River, positioned half his troops surrounding the village of Kaskaskia, and marched with the other half straight through an open gate of the fort and to the house of the commandant Chevalier de Rocheblave, a French officer in service with the British, who immediately surrendered. Clark then sent Capt. Joseph Bowman with 30 men to obtain the surrender of Prairie du Rocher and Cahokia. By the end of the day, Clark held control of all three posts without a shot having been fired. He gained the support of Kaskaskia's French residents, and Father Pierre Gibault with a group of Frenchmen visited Vincennes on Clark's behalf to persuade the French residents there to surrender—the British regulars had departed. On July 20, the residents of Vincennes granted their support to Clark without resistance.

Hopeful of attacking Detroit if he could win the Indians' neutrality, Clark negotiated with Ottawa, Chippewa, Miami, and Fox warriors during the remainder of the summer. But in early October, Governor Henry Hamilton of Detroit set out from that British post with 175 troops, mostly French, and 60 Indians to recapture Vincennes. Hamilton approached Vincennes in mid-December, having been joined en route by more than 400 Indian warriors. Capt. Leonard Helm, left in charge of the fort at Vincennes, had sent out scouting parties that Hamilton captured, so Helm had only one soldier as his garrison. Lacking support of the local French residents, Helm surrendered to Hamilton without offering resistance. The final fate of the Clark expedition remained unresolved as 1778 ended.[15]

INDIAN AND TORY RAIDERS

Although not determinative of the war's ultimate course, raids conducted by Tory militiamen and Indian warriors, frequently in combined forces, intensified in 1778. These raids were encouraged by British commanders in the aftermath of Saratoga and made a galling and fretful problem for Americans living on the frontier. For example, in March, Lt. Col. Charles Mawhood and his Tory troops, who had seen action at the Battle of Princeton, maneuvered about 300 militia-men into a trap at Quinton's Bridge in New Jersey, killing about 40 and routing the remainder; they also brutally killed militia sentries, a patrol, and the Han-cocks, known to be Loyalists, at Hancock's Bridge. Both of these attacks outraged residents of the state.[16]

From the beginning of June and throughout the rest of the year, the Mohawk chief Joseph Brant led his Tory and Mohawk raiders in a series of attacks on settlements in New York. As June began, they routed Continental troops, killed their commander, and then massacred residents of and burned Cobbleskill on the Susquehanna River about 20 miles west of Albany. In July, Brant's Mohawk burned and looted Andrustown, killing many members of the seven families who lived there. In September, Brant and 150 Mohawk, joined by 300 Tories under Capt. William Caldwell, raided German Flats (Herkimer); they killed only three men but burned 100 houses, barns, and mills and departed with hundreds of horses, sheep, and cows. This raid engendered a reprisal, when Lt. Col. William Butler led his Pennsylvania Continentals in attacking Unadilla, Brant's base of operations abandoned by the Mohawk before the attack, and burning all but one of its buildings. But in November, Brant led Seneca and Mohawk warriors, along with Tories commanded by Capt. Walter Butler, in raiding Cherry Valley, mas-sacring more than 30 settlers, mostly women and children; they failed to capture the fort, however, even after killing its commander.[17]

Probably the most vicious of such raids occurred in the Wyoming Valley of Pennsylvania. Maj. Sir John Butler commanded a force of 1,200 Tory rangers and Indians that came down from Fort Niagara in the summer of 1778 to loot and burn their way through western Pennsylvania. During the first week of July, they attacked Forty Fort. When the defenders, led by Zeb Butler, refused to surrender, Sir John used a ruse to entice them out of the fort by setting fire to Fort Winter-mot, which had surrendered earlier, to convince Zeb Butler and his cohorts that Sir John's force was departing. Fooled by the ruse, Zeb Butler and his men raced out of Forty Fort to pursue Sir John's raiders, and the Indians ambushed them in the woods. Using spears and tomahawks, the Indians induced panic among Zeb Butler's men, some of whom in fleeing dove into the Susquehanna River; the Indians killed them in the water. The Indians also chased down and killed other men trying to reach the safety of their forts; they took some captive, tied them to trees, and burned them alive. The Wyoming Valley Massacre, as it became known, generated widespread outrage among the American frontier settlements.[18]

FRANCE'S NAVAL ROLE

On March 13, in London, the French ambassador informed Great Britain's sec-retary of state, Thomas, Viscount Weymouth, of the treaty of commerce, although not the treaty of alliance, between the United States and France. The North ministry recalled from France Britain's ambassador, Lord Stormont, and canceled orders issued to General Clinton. The British saw France, not the rebellious Americans, as the greater enemy. Consequently, new orders to Clinton reflected the North ministry's view that the West Indies constituted a more important commercial prize than the American colonies did: Clinton was to send an expe-dition of 5,000 troops against St. Lucia; reinforce the garrisons at St. Augustine and Pensacola to secure Florida and to provide a base for defending Jamaica or attacking New Orleans; withdraw totally from Philadelphia to concentrate his army in New York City; and, if New York proved untenable, send that garrison to Halifax, while holding Newport.[19]

The French government also saw the West Indies as the great prize. France's initial participation in the Revolutionary War involved its navy, but Washington and other American commanders may well have doubted the efficacy of the French naval role. The French fleet based at Toulon—11 ships of the line, one 50-gun ship, and several frigates—set sail in the second week of April under command of Count d'Estaing. The North ministry remained in a quandary about its destination, and d'Estaing's fleet did not pass through the Straits of Gibraltar and head into the open sea until more than a month later. D'Estaing finally arrived at Sandy Hook, New Jersey, in July, three months after leaving Toulon Harbor. Fearful of attack in both the English Channel and North America, the North ministry in June dispatched Adm. John Byron to take command of the American fleet and Adm. Augustus Keppel commanding the channel fleet to protect British ships sailing from Gibraltar. Near the end of July, Keppel's fleet of 30 ships with 2,280 guns engaged the French fleet of 27 ships bearing 1,950 guns out of Brest, commanded by Admiral D'Orvilliers. The French effectively disabled the British ships but suffered 736 casualties to Keppel's 408 and withdrew to leave the British in control of the English Channel. Attention then shifted to American waters.[20]

At the end of July, d'Estaing's fleet arrived at Newport, which had been held by the British since December 1776. The ships began to enter Narragansett Bay, while Gen. John Sullivan assembled a force of 10,000 troops and militia to attack the British garrison from land. Although somewhat antagonistic toward each other, the general and the admiral agreed on their strategy for conquest through a coordinated attack. D'Estaing initially sent two frigates up the Providence River that panicked the British into running four of their own ships aground, destroying them, and scuttling several other vessels in a futile hope of preventing the French fleet from entering Newport Harbor.

As the second week of August began, Sullivan learned that the British had abandoned their defenses on the north end of Newport's island. He crossed the river to occupy the site before the time appointed for the coordinated attack, angering d'Estaing. Then Admiral Lord Howe's fleet appeared off the coast, and d'Estaing sailed out of Newport Harbor into the open sea to do battle. The two fleets maneuvered for two days before being widely dispersed by ferocious winds. As the third week of August ended, d'Estaing, ignoring the appeals of Lafayette, set sail with his 4,000 troops, abandoning the effort to recapture Newport. Sullivan, who had been inching closer to the British lines and entrenching, had no choice but to withdraw, especially after his militia units, dismayed by d'Estaing's departure, deserted and thereby reduced his force by half. Attacked by the British as he retreated, Sullivan managed to escape disaster as a second British fleet arrived with 5,000 troops to reinforce the 6,000-man Newport garrison.[21]

In November, abandoning a proposed though poorly conceived plan for a joint American-French naval attack on Halifax and Newfoundland, d'Estaing set sail from Boston for the West Indies. The admiral chose not to inform Washington of his destination. D'Estaing's fleet arrived at Martinique the second week of December, while Com. William Hotham's fleet from New York arrived at

Barbados with 5,800 troops to reinforce Adm. Samuel Barrington's fleet for an attack against the French island of St. Lucia. On December 13, Adm. John Byron, greatly delayed by foul weather but finally arrived to replace Admiral Howe, also sailed from Newport to join this British effort to capture the Lesser Antilles. That same day, Barrington's and Hotham's combined fleets captured St. Lucia only an hour before d'Estaing arrived from Martinique with 9,000 troops; his fleet outnumbered the British fleet by three ships to one. The British force of 5,800 divided into three units, dug in to the north of the harbor at Cul-de-Sac and on the Morne Fortune mountain and successfully defended their new conquest against d'Estaing's assaults, inflicting 1,200 wounded and 400 dead on the admiral. D'Estaing lingered for 10 days and then sailed back to Martinique. To this point, French naval action in the Americas afforded scant hope of tipping the war's balance in favor of the United States.[22]

MISSTEPS AND MISTAKES

Other events of 1778 also appeared to menace the American cause. The farcical Canada "irruption" suggested that the Continental Congress might not be facing up to reality. Congress further clouded the outlook by reneging on the Saratoga Convention, finally allowing General Burgoyne and two members of his staff to return to England but detaining his entire army (known as the Convention Army) as prisoners in Boston—on the grounds that Burgoyne intended to abrogate the convention but clearly to prevent the British from sending replacements once the repatriated troops reached England. Then the delegates embroiled themselves in partisan bickering over Silas Deane's role while in France: Had he or had he not been involved in suspect dealings?

In addition, Congress interfered in Washington's conduct of the war, not only with the Conway Cabal episode, but also in such actions as appointing Gen. Benjamin Lincoln as commander of the Continental army in the South without even consulting the commander in chief. And Congress waffled for nearly four months before carrying out the decision reached by the court-martial of Gen. Charles Lee that he be suspended for a year for disobeying orders, misconduct, and disrespect for Washington. Unsuccessful in persuading the states to adopt the Articles of Confederation, the Continental Congress also returned in disappointment to considering the stipulations in the articles. Most states came belatedly to adoption, but at the end of the year Maryland still held out, leaving this desired means of legitimizing the union and Congress in limbo.[23]

While the Continental Congress dithered or meddled, the Continental army registered signs of strain. One of the strains derived from Congress's indecisiveness over the issue of officers' compensation. The committee that Congress had sent to Valley Forge to investigate army conditions and recommend reforms had worked out a proposal with Washington that provided officers with half-pay for life and their widows with pensions. Although a slight majority of congressmen favored the proposal, others expressed concern about the officers' motives (patriotism or greed?) and anxieties about the threat of a standing army. Washington wrote to President Henry Laurens in support of the proposal, arguing that the quality and morale of the officer corps—and therefore the fate of the war—depended on its approval. After nearly two months of debate, the Continental Congress finally approved the compensation proposal with the compromise that officers would receive half-pay for seven years following the war if they served for the war's duration.[24]

In other ways the army also evidenced confusion or at least uncertainty. Apparently reacting with sympathy but poor judgment to Lafayette's dismay over the Canada "irruption," Washington gave the marquis command of 2,200 troops (one-third of the army) in May with orders to interdict British foraging parties, gather intelligence, and patrol the area between the Delaware and Schuylkill Rivers. Pursuing this dangerous and probably pointless assignment, Lafayette moved his division across the Schuylkill to Barren Hill, only two miles from British outposts at Chestnut Hill. Apprised of this move almost immediately, General Clinton dispatched a force of 5,000 that encircled and trapped Lafayette's force, which managed a miraculous escape via a perilously steep slope to the river and back across to the west bank. At the same time, in Georgia, a planned attack by Maj. Gen. Robert Howe, commanding 550 Continentals plus Georgia militia, on Gen. Augustine Prevost's army in East Florida abruptly foundered when the Georgia militia officers refused to accept orders. And in late December, the hapless Howe tried to defend Savannah against British assault only to experience a crushing defeat. As the year 1778 ended, the euphoric optimism with which the Continental Congress and the Continental army had greeted news of the alliance with France in early May and the presumed boost it would afford the American cause appeared groundless.[25]

CHRONICLE OF EVENTS

1778

January 2: George Rogers Clark, a frontier fighter against the Indians and thereafter the British in the Kentucky Territory, visits Williamsburg, Virginia, to advocate support for his plan, first proposed in 1775, to seize control of the northwestern territory of the Mississippi-Ohio River valley, with Detroit as the final objective. Several factors now serve Clark: the withdrawal of British troops from Kaskaskia in summer 1777; Virginians' keen interest in land speculation; concern over Shawnee and Cherokee attacks, and the support of Thomas Jefferson, George Mason, and Richard Henry Lee. Consequently, Governor Patrick Henry now acquiesces. Not wanting to divulge the true nature of Clark's expedition, Henry publicly announces that its goal is to defend the Kentucky Territory.

Following two visits to Valley Forge by Inspector General Conway and an exchange of letters, an exasperated and angry Washington writes to the Continental Congress, enclosing Conway's captious letters and his own cool responses, to make clear his views of Conway in hopes of resolving the "cabal."

January 5: David Bushnell, inventor of the so-called American Turtle, launches his torpedoes (powder-filled kegs with fuses meant to generate explosions when they contact ships) into the Delaware River to drift toward the British fleet. But icy water impedes their progress, and at daylight, the British spot them and blow them up.

January 8: In a meeting at Versailles, Charles Gravier, count de Vergennes, informs Franklin, Deane, and Lee that the French government is prepared to form an alliance with the United States.

The Continental Congress completes the resolution delaying Burgoyne's departure from Boston until the British government has ratified the Saratoga Convention. Accompanying resolutions accuse Burgoyne of not fulfilling some terms of the convention and object to his contention that the Americans are guilty of breach of faith, which, the resolutions state, reveal Burgoyne's intent to abrogate the convention.

January 10: The Continental Congress responds to Washington by resolving to send a committee composed of congressional members, along with Gates, Mifflin, and Pickering from the Board of War, to Valley Forge.

January 13: Washington's men complete the last of the log huts to house themselves at Valley Forge. The encamped army numbers 11,000, although only 8,200 are fit for duty; many lack hats, shoes, and coats and frequently have only firecake (a thin bread of flour and water baked over a campfire) for food. Washington, who promised to share their hardships, quartered in a tent until completion of the huts and now moves into the Isaac Potts house. He writes letters to Congress pleading for food and clothing for his men.

January 14: The Continental Congress sends its resolutions on the Saratoga Convention to General Heath in Boston.

January 19: General Gates arrives to a warm welcome in York to assume his duties as president of the Board of War.

January 20: Granting his request, the Continental Congress excuses Gates—and Mifflin and Pickering as well—from serving on the committee to visit Valley Forge.

January 21: Poet, congressman, and now commissioner on the Continental Navy Board, Francis Hopkinson, inspired by Bushnell's failed torpedoes, publishes the "Battle of the Kegs" in the *New Jersey Gazette* of Bordentown.

January 22: As the army suffers deprivations at Valley Forge, the Continental Congress resolves to support an apparently madcap "irruption" in Canada and to provide the requisite funding.

January 23: The Board of War chooses Lafayette to head the Canada "irruption," with Thomas Conway as second in command and John Stark serving with them.

January 27: The 50-man crew of the USS *Providence,* commanded by Capt. John Peck Rathbun, seizes control of the two British forts at Nassau and raise the Stars and Stripes in place of the Union flag—the first flying of the American flag over a conquered foreign post.

January 28: After receiving letters from Lafayette expressing his abhorrence of Conway and refusal to serve with him, President Henry Laurens write apologetically to the marquis. A strong supporter of Washington, Laurens begins to suspect the Conway Cabal of foul play, especially because Conway has already left for Albany, with the Board of War's approval, to begin to prepare for the Canada expedition.

January 31: Lafayette voices his objections to serving with Conway to the Board of War and gives it an ultimatum: He threatens to return to France, taking most of the other French officers with him, thereby presumably ending the Canada expedition.

February 4: At Boston, General Heath delivers the Continental Congress's resolutions on the Saratoga Convention to Burgoyne, preventing the British army's departure and the possibility that, on their arrival in Britain, other troops will be substituted for them in America.

February 5: Baron Friedrich von Steuben arrives in New York, and Congress temporarily accepts his offer to serve the Continental army as an unpaid volunteer.

February 6: Meeting in Paris, the American commissioners and French officials approve two treaties. With the Treaty of Amity and Commerce, the French officials make war with Britain inevitable by recognizing the United States's independence and publicly sanctioning the heretofore clandestine French trade with the states; the Treaty of Alliance will become effective whenever that war breaks out. The second treaty stipulates mutual guarantees that the United States will recognize French claims in the West Indies and that each nation will recognize the other's territorial gains resulting from the war, excepting that Louis XVI renounces forever any claims to Bermuda, Canada, and any areas of North America east of the Mississippi River. In addition, neither nation may make a separate peace with Great Britain or cease fighting until American independence has been secured.

February 9: Angry and determined to end the Conway Cabal plot to replace him, Washington writes to Gates, rebuking him for issuing ambiguous statements and for not making public Conway's original letter as a means of clearing the air. Washington denounces Conway for his "malignity," "disappointed vanity," and "personal aggrandizement." This and other scathing letters from Washington terminate the presumed plot against him.

February 14: John Adams, accompanied by his son John Quincy, sets sail aboard the *Boston* out of Hough's Neck, Massachusetts, bound for Bordeaux, France. Adams is destined for Paris to assume his duties as commissioner from the United States.

February 16: Lord George Germain responds to a letter he received in London the previous December from General Howe in which Howe asked to be relieved of his duties. Germain accepts Howe's resignation but requires him to remain in America until his successor arrives.

February 17: Concerned by the stunning defeat at Saratoga and rumors of a French-American alliance, Lord North presents to Parliament a plan for reconciliation that offers to repeal the Tea Act and the Coercive Acts, promises no revenue taxes will be imposed on the colonies, stipulates appointing a commission to negotiate a peace settlement with the Continental Congress, and provides for suspending all acts passed since 1763, if necessary.

February 19: Sent by Washington to direct the Canada "irruption," Lafayette, who arrived in Albany two days earlier, writes to tell Washington that the expedition is hopeless. Conway has already reached this conclusion after receiving letters from Schuyler, Lincoln, and Arnold declaring such an expedition impossible (no soldiers are available). Lafayette expresses his disgust over being sent on a hopeless mission in the winter and his resentment against the Board of War for conceiving a farcical undertaking that has humiliated him. He informs Washington that he has sent a full account of the matter to the Continental Congress.

February 23: Invited by Washington, Baron von Steuben arrives at Valley Forge with a secretary-translator

Friedrich Wilhelm von Steuben volunteered in the Continental army. *(From* The Pictorial Field Book of the Revolution, *2 vols, by B. J. Lossing. New York: Harper Brothers, 1851 and 1852.)*

(the baron does not speak English), two aides, and a German servant. The baron has claimed to have been a lieutenant general when his real rank in Prussia was captain and he was discharged from the Prussian army 14 years ealier. However, he was instructed by Frederick the Great himself and is well trained and knowledgeable. Washington assigns Alexander Hamilton and John Laurens, the Continental Congress president's son, as von Steuben's aides.

February 24: Believing that the presumed plot against him has been precluded, Washington writes a conciliatory letter to Gates, who has backed away from any hint of involvement in a plot and blamed his aide, Col. James Wilkinson, for creating the misunderstanding. Washington expresses the desire to consign the matter to oblivion, thus ending the Conway Cabal affair.

March 2: The committee visiting Valley Forge submits recommendations to the Continental Congress for reforming the army, including a major reorganization of the department of quartermaster general. To implement this reorganization, Congress appoints as quartermaster general the capable Nathanael Greene, who reluctantly accepts.

March 7: Germain signs orders in London appointing Gen. Sir Henry Clinton as General Howe's replacement.

In the West Indies, HMS *Yarmouth* and USS *Randolph* battle fiercely for 20 minutes. Although outgunned by more than two to one, the *Randolph* appears headed for victory when it suddenly explodes, killing the already-wounded Capt. Nicholas Biddle and all but four of his 315 officers and crewmen.

March 8: Pressured by George III to review its American strategy thoroughly, the North ministry has concluded that a land war is unlikely to succeed, making a different strategy necessary. Consequently, Germain sends Clinton new orders to cooperate with Adm. Lord Richard Howe in disengaging the fleet from supporting military operations and instead enforcing a blockade enhanced by military raids on coastal locations from Nova Scotia to New York. Clinton is to prepare an invasion of the Carolinas and Georgia in an effort to separate the southern and northern states. This new plan obviates Philadelphia's strategic value, so Clinton is to withdraw the army to New York.

March 12: A new government elected on March 3 takes office in Montpelier in the now independent state—in fact, free republic—of Vermont.

Sir Henry Clinton replaced General Howe. (*From* The Pictorial Field Book of the Revolution, *2 vols., by B. J. Lossing. New York: Harper Brothers, 1851 and 1852.*)

March 13: Reacting to reports from Lafayette, Congress suspends the Canada "irruption" and authorizes Washington to order Lafayette and de Kalb to rejoin the main army immediately.

In London, the French ambassador informs Secretary of State Thomas Thynne, Lord Weymouth, of the Treaty of Commerce between France and the United States but not the Treaty of Alliance. The North ministry recalls Lord Stormont from Paris and cancels the orders Germain had signed for Clinton on March 8.

March 16: Lord North's conciliation plan is adopted under the title Royal Instructions to the Peace Commission of 1778. Frederick Howard, earl of Carlisle, and the Howe brothers make up the commission, known as the Carlisle Commission. They will have broad authority to negotiate.

March 18: Col. Charles Mawhood has led a small British force into New Jersey to counter Gen. Anthony Wayne's foraging excursions, and at Quinton's Bridge, they manipulate about 300 militia into a trap. Believing the British are retreating, the Americans restore planks in the bridge and leave 100 men to guard it while 200 men under Captain Smith pursue the British. Suddenly cut off when rangers stationed in a brick house emerge to fire on their rear, Smith's men flee in disarray, leaving perhaps 40 dead behind. The British lose one man.

March 20: As a formal act of recognition, French king Louis XVI receives Franklin, Deane, and Lee, along with William Lee and Ralph Izard, all wearing formal court clothes, at Versailles. In a private audience, the king asks Franklin to assure the Continental Congress of his friendship for the Americans. Franklin tells the king he can be assured of Congress's gratitude and determination to fulfill its treaty agreements. Vergennes treats the Americans to a sumptuous dinner and introduces them to the royal family. Franklin charms Queen Marie Antoinette.

March 21: Mawhood stages an attack at Hancock's Bridge, from which all but 20 of 200 militia have been withdrawn. Mawhood's Tories kill the sentries, a patrol, and inhabitants of the Hancock house. The ruthlessness of this and Mawhood's earlier assault at Quinton's Bridge, which local residents term *massacres,* incite outrage in New Jersey.

Germain issues new orders to Clinton, who now is to send 5,000 troops to attack St. Lucia, a French island in the West Indies, and another 3,000 to reinforce St. Augustine and Pensacola to secure Florida and provide a base for a possible attack on New Orleans. He is to withdraw any remaining forces from Philadelphia to New York City because holding New York should enhance the Carlisle Commission's negotiations; if it cannot be held, then Clinton is ordered to maintain the garrison at Newport and withdraw the New York garrison to Halifax, Nova Scotia. Germain's new orders clearly indicate that the government sees the West Indies as more important commercially than the American colonies; in fact, the West Indies trade is more lucrative, and merchants involved in it have pressured the North ministry for protection. Capturing St. Lucia and its excellent harbor would give the British a solid base from which to attack the French islands in the Lesser Antilles.

Thomas Paine publishes *The American Crisis V, To General Sir William Howe,* over the signature Common Sense, in Lancaster, Pennsylvania.

March 26: Francis Dana and Nathaniel Folsom, members of the committee sent to Valley Forge, introduce in the Continental Congress a proposal devised by the committee and Washington to provide Continental army officers with half-pay for life and their widows with pensions. The proposal generates furious debate.

March 30: The committee sent to Valley Forge completes its work, which interfered with a plan for a general exchange of prisoners that Washington's agents had been negotiating with Howe, causing consternation and debate in Congress. The delegates create a committee that devises instructions for Washington to complete an agreement with Howe, entailing that Gen. Charles Lee must be exchanged for Maj. Gen. Richard Prescott or no exchange may occur without further orders from Congress and also requiring that Ethan Allen be exchanged. Furthermore, all congressional resolutions concerning Tories who have served with the British must be respected (for example, such Tories would be handed over to states for trial as traitors); all exchanges will have no relation to rank; and Washington must approve the terms of the exchange agreement.

March 31: John Adams and his 10-year-old son, John Quincy Adams, arrive at Bordeaux, France.

April 4: Washington writes from Valley Forge to inform President Laurens that he judges that Howe can never accept some of the requirements the congressional committee has mandated for a prisoner exchange, including vindictive treatment of Tories.

April 5: Congress permits Burgoyne and two of his staff to sail from Boston for England but requires that his troops (known as the Convention Army) must remain behind as prisoners.

April 8: Adams arrives in Paris to assume his commissioner duties as Deane's replacement.

April 9: Pursuing its efforts to reform the army, the Continental Congress appoints Jeremiah Wadsworth as commissary general of purchases to head and reorganize the trouble-plagued Commissary Department.

April 10: John Paul Jones and his crew of about 140 men set sail from Brest in the *Ranger,* equipped with 18 six-pounder cannons, to make raids in British waters.

Washington writes to President Laurens supporting the Dana-Folsom proposal on officers' compensation and asserting that he has no personal interest in the proposal, which will not benefit him but will, he believes, increase the honorableness of army commissions and the order and regularity among officers.

April 11: The French fleet at Toulon, including 11 ships of the line, one 50-gun ship, and several frigates, sets sail under command of Charles-Hector Théodat, count d'Estaing. British officials discuss its destination. If d'Estaing joins the fleet at Brest, the French navy could threaten the British Isles, so commander of the home fleet Adm. Augustus Keppel strenuously opposes dividing the British fleet to send ships to America or to counter the French at the Straits of Gibraltar. John Montagu, fourth earl of Sandwich and first lord of the Admiralty, supports Keppel's view. Germain strongly favors halting the French at the Straits to prevent their sailing for America. Thus the North ministry faces a dilemma.

April 12: The North ministry appoints two other members to the Carlisle Commission: William Eden, a friend of Carlisle and member of the Board of Trade; and George Johnstone, former governor of West Florida and an American supporter in Parliament. Because Carlisle is a close friend of opposition leader Charles Fox, North expects the commission's composition to please the Americans, but he is not optimistic about their success.

April 14: President Laurens sends Washington a letter drafted by the Continental Congress following acrimonious debate that rebukes the commander for objecting to congressional resolutions on exchanging prisoners and again insists on the Lee-for-Prescott exchange as a prerequisite. But negotiations with Howe collapse, rendering the issue moot, and Washington chooses to ignore the rebuke, thanking Congress for "their confidence."

April 16: The Carlisle Commission embarks from Portsmouth, England, aboard the man-of-war *Trident.* Accompanying them are the pregnant Mrs. Eden and Lord Cornwallis, who will be Clinton's second in command in America.

April 21: At Washington's request, Elias Boudinot, commissary of prisons, has secured the exchange of Gen. Richard Prescott for Gen. Charles Lee. Actually released on parole on April 5, Lee stayed briefly at Valley Forge, where Washington greeted him warmly and Martha Washington provided him an elegant dinner and a room. Lee now visits the Congress in York to complain that other officers have been promoted during his absence. His exchange now official, Lee departs for Virginia after telling Boudinot that Washington is "not fit to command a sergeant's guard."

April 22: Members of the Continental Congress have seen a draft of North's speech introducing his conciliatory measures in Parliament and a draft of the bill but remain unimpressed by the ministry's change of heart. They approve a resolution branding anyone who comes to terms with the Carlisle Commission an enemy of the United States, precluding negotiations.

The *Ranger* enters the harbor at Whitehaven, Scotland, at night, and Captain Jones rows ashore with a raiding party. They spike the cannon at the entrance to the port, set fire to vessels in the harbor, and then return to the *Ranger* as local residents quell the fires. Little harm occurs beyond British consternation over this first "assault" on a British port since 1667.

April 23: Jones lands on St. Mary's Isle planning to kidnap the earl of Selkirk, owner of the island, and take him to France as a hostage to exchange for American prisoners in England; but the earl is not home. Jones seizes Lady Selkirk's family silver.

April 24: The *Ranger* sails into Carrickfergus, Ireland. The captain of HMS *Drake,* a 21-gun warship at anchor in the harbor, assumes it to be a British privateer, and sends an officer by longboat to visit while he prepares to leave harbor. Jones takes the officer prisoner. As the *Drake* leaves harbor and hails the *Ranger,* Jones identifies himself and fires a broadside. Badly shot up in a battle of more than an hour and diminished by 30 casualties, including the captain, the *Drake* surrenders. The *Ranger* has eight casualties.

April 27: Intelligence reports from Paris, confirmed by bankers in Amsterdam, convince the king, North, and most of the cabinet that d'Estaing is sailing to America, headed for either Boston or the Delaware. Germain foresees his efforts in ruins, with the enemy in control of Philadelphia, Halifax, and even Quebec; he urges North to dispatch part of the home fleet to America at once.

April 29: After the earl of Sandwich proves hesitant, a desperate Germain writes protests to the king and the cabinet. The cabinet immediately decides to send 13 ships of the line to America under command of Adm. John Byron to reinforce Adm. Lord Richard Howe's fleet, and Germain relays the orders to the Admiralty. The question remains how to warn Howe that d'Estaing is en route because no notice was sent during debate over the French fleet's destination.

May 1: At Crooked Billet, Pennsylvania, a force of 450 militia under Brig. Gen. John Lacey, posted here to harass British foraging parties, has been reduced by expired enlistments to under 60 men, now nearly surrounded by 400 light infantry under Lt. Col. Robert Abercrombie at their front and 300 rangers under Maj. John Graves Simcoe at their rear. Withdrawing into a woods, the militiamen hold their ground briefly and then retreat, abandoning their baggage, after suffering

36 casualties, including 26 dead. The British suffer nine casualties.

May 2: After adjourning for the sabbath, the Continental Congress is recalled on this Saturday evening because Simeon Deane, brother of Silas, has received copies of the treaties of commerce and alliance from a messenger sent by the American commissioners in France. The congress members hear the treaties read and again adjourn.

May 4: The Continental Congress reconvenes and unanimously ratifies the treaties with France but also decides to request that France rescind two treaty articles.

May 5: Acting on Washington's recommendation, the Continental Congress confirms appointment of Baron von Steuben as major general and inspector general of the army. The baron has been instructing the Continental army at Valley Forge in military drill and training, including use of the bayonet, with marked success. He has also imposed hygiene standards and has written the army's first military manual, translated into English by an aide and then revised by Alexander Hamilton for clarity.

May 6: Troops of the Continental army joyfully celebrate news of the treaties with France, loudly, as Lafayette has advocated. They march in review, demonstrating for the commander in chief the new order and precision taught by von Steuben.

May 8: The *Ranger* returns to Brest with the captured *Drake* and about 200 British prisoners.

The Continental Congress publishes the "necessary" parts of the treaties with France for public dissemination and includes an address to the American people by Gouverneur Morris that warns of losing independence through acceptance of peace with the enemy and also depicts and reviles the enemy's evil ways.

Gen. Sir Henry Clinton arrives at Philadelphia from New York to succeed General Howe as commander in chief.

More than 600 British troops from Philadelphia enter Bordentown, New Jersey, to destroy American military stores. They burn Joseph Borden's estate, plunder some properties, destroy the stores, and then some small vessels at White Hills.

May 11: The earl of Chatham, William Pitt, a long-time supporter of American interests in Parliament, dies in London.

May 12: George Rogers Clark sets out from the Redstone Settlement to travel down the Monongahela River for a rendezvous at the falls of the Ohio with men recruited by Maj. W. P. Smith for his northwestern expedition.

May 14: Still dubious, as Keppel is also, about d'Estaing's destination, especially because his fleet was spotted in the Mediterranean Sea off Algiers on April 28, two weeks after setting sail, the earl of Sandwich hastily orders Admiral Byron not to embark.

May 15: After strenuous debate, the Continental Congress adopts the officers' compensation proposal, with an approved compromise specifying that officers will receive half-pay for seven years following the war's conclusion, if they serve for the war's duration.

May 16: Sighted by HMS *Proserpine* and HMS *Enterprise,* d'Estaing's fleet passes the Straits of Gibraltar and heads for the open sea.

May 18: An extravagant party and mock tournament, known as a Meschianza and organized by Capt. John André, honors Gen. William Howe, soon to depart Philadelphia. The party's lavishness, occurring in an occupied city with the half-starved American army encamped nearby, seems in such bad taste that even some Loyalists object, among them Thomas Jones, who declares that, had Howe's conduct been properly rewarded, "an execution, and not a Meschianza, would have been the consequence."

Apparently to placate Lafayette, Washington gives him command of a 2,200-man division with orders to approach British lines, gather intelligence, and protect the area between the Delaware and Schuylkill Rivers. The assignment is dangerous and may be pointless because the force is too large for intelligence gathering and too small to protect a large area. Lafayette crosses the Schuylkill and positions his men at Barren Hill, two miles from British outposts at Chestnut Hill.

May 19: Apprised almost immediately of Lafayette's deployment, Clinton plans a surprise attack to capture the marquis, humiliating him and France. At 10:30 P.M., Maj. Gen. James Grant leads a force of 5,000 British troops out of Philadelphia toward the intersection of Whitemarsh and Ridge Roads to cut off Lafayette's retreat to fords across the Schuylkill. Maj. Gen. Charles Grey simultaneously leads 2,000 troops straight down the road to Barren Hill to assault Lafayette's left flank. Clinton, accompanied by Howe, marches up the Ridge Road from the south. Learning of Clinton's approach, the resourceful raider Capt. Allen McLane dispatches a company of riflemen to harass and delay Clinton while he hastens to warn Lafayette.

May 20: Lafayette prepares a defense and sends scouts in all directions. One scout reports that a second road to Matson's Ford descends the steep slope from Barren Hill so abruptly that Lafayette's troops could be quickly hidden from Grant's view on the heights above. Lafayette feigns an attack on Grant as his troops slip away, followed by the marquis and a rear guard. Clinton arrives to find Lafayette and his men on a height on the west bank of the Schuylkill. In disgust, Clinton orders his troops to return to Philadelphia.

Maj. Gen. Robert Howe, leading about 550 Continentals plus Georgia militia under Governor William Houston and Colonels Pinkney, Bull, and Williamson, arrives at the Altahama River. He plans to invade East Florida and attack a British force under Gen. Augustine Prevost, with St. Augustine as the first objective, but the Georgia militia officers refuse to take orders.

May 25: Gen. William Howe sails out of Philadelphia bound for England.

British marauders in Rhode Island commanded by Maj. Gen. Richard Prescott, recently exchanged for Gen. Charles Lee, raid Bristol and Warren, torching buildings, harassing residents, plundering, and seizing livestock.

May 27: The Continental Congress adopts proposals for reorganizing and regulating the army prepared by the committee that visited Valley Forge to review army operations with General Washington.

George Rogers Clark arrives at the falls of the Ohio and learns that Major Smith has failed to raise four companies of recruits from the Holston settlements—only part of one company will join him. Clark encamps on an island in the Ohio River and begins to train his men before revealing the true nature of their expedition. Four captains, Joseph Bowman, Leonard Helm, William Harrod, and John Montgomery, are in his service.

May 28: Washington appoints Benedict Arnold, who arrived at Valley Forge weeks earlier to a warm welcome, as governor and commander of troops in Philadelphia—when the British evacuate. Partly mollified by the Continental Congress's restoration of his rank and seniority, Arnold suffers from the Saratoga leg wound, which shortened his leg by two inches and prevents his assuming a field command.

May 31: After Prescott and his 150 raiders torch several mills at Tiverton, Rhode Island, about two dozen defenders prevent their doing further damage.

June 1: After driving off Continental troops, Tories and Indian warriors led by Mohawk chief Joseph Brant burn Cobbleskill, New York, a settlement of about 20 families on the Susquehanna River west of Albany, and massacre many of the settlers. The only military recourse for the British after Saratoga, such raids are launched mostly from Detroit, Niagara, and Oswego.

June 2: HMS *Proserpine* sails into Falmouth, England, bringing the news that d'Estaing's fleet has cleared the Straits of Gibraltar and is headed for America.

June 6: The members of the Carlisle Commission arrive in Philadelphia.

June 9: In response to the cabinet's hasty decision and new orders of June 7, Admiral Byron sets sail from Plymouth, England, for New York.

June 13: The channel fleet under command of Adm. Augustus Keppel sails out of Plymouth with orders to protect British ships sailing homeward from Gibraltar—forced to pass by Brest, where part of the French fleet remains in harbor—to reinforce the home fleet.

June 16: The British remove the artillery from all their redoubts around Philadelphia, and several regiments begin the evacuation, crossing the Delaware River at Cooper's Point. Clinton must evacuate 10,000 troops and all the army's wagons, horses, artillery, provisions, and supplies, which are vulnerable to American

George Rogers Clark led troops at the Kaskaskia River. *(From* The Pictorial Field Book of the Revolution, *2 vols., by B. J. Lossing. New York: Harper Brothers, 1851 and 1852.)*

attack while on the river. He also has to evacuate 3,000 Loyalists and their possessions.

June 17: Off the English coast at the Lizard, Keppel sights two French frigates, which by custom may proceed safely if they respond peaceably to his hailing. But one of the frigates fires a broadside, the opening salvo in a new Franco-British war. The French ship surrenders, and the British find aboard a list of the fleet at Brest that indicates 27 ships are ready to sail and five others are making preparations. Keppel returns to harbor to obtain reinforcements.

After three days discussing letters from the Carlisle Commission, outlining terms for reconciliation, but deploring the American alliance with France, the Continental Congress unanimously approves a response of readiness to consider a peace treaty whenever George III shows his sincere intention to acknowledge American independence or withdraws his fleets and armies.

June 18: The last of Clinton's troops leave Philadelphia, marching to Gloucester Point to cross the Delaware to Gloucester, as the British fleet hoists anchor and sails downriver. A courier brings the news to Washington at Valley Forge. He immediately begins to move his army to Coryell's Ferry.

June 19: General Arnold enters Philadelphia accompanied by a regiment of light horse to begin a military occupation.

June 20: The Continental Congress resumes consideration of the Articles of Confederation, chagrined that the states have not adopted the articles to legitimize the union and Congress's authority before a minister arrives from France. Only Virginia, New York, and New Hampshire have ratified.

June 24: Pursuing Clinton, Washington's entire army has crossed the Delaware at Coryell's Ferry and encamps for the night near Hopewell, New Jersey, about 15 miles northeast of the British encampment at Allentown. During a council of war, Gen. Charles Lee and a majority again oppose attacking. Continentals commanded by Brig. Gen. William Maxwell and Jersey militiamen under Gen. Philemon Dickinson will continue harassing Clinton's flanks.

June 25: Concerned that Washington will intercept him at New Brunswick, Clinton divides his force, with half of the army under Lieutenant General von Knyphausen marching in advance followed by the baggage train and the other half under Lord Cornwallis, accompanied by Clinton. Both halves head for Monmouth Courthouse and then Sandy Hook. Washington

places Lafayette in command of an advance guard of 4,000 to assault Clinton's flank. Lee claims the command, and Washington acquiesces. Lee takes an additional 1,000 men and marches to join Lafayette at Englishtown. Washington moves his remaining force from Kingston to Cranbury during the night.

June 26: Clark leaves about 20 men to guard the supplies and blockhouse on the island at the falls of the Ohio and sets out with 175 men in flatboats to shoot the rapids at the falls during an eclipse of the sun, which he sees as an omen of good luck. Because some of his men have tried to desert on learning of the expedition's objectives, Clark has had to force them to serve; but the majority, swayed by Clark's forceful personality, have pledged their loyalty to him.

June 27: Congress adjourns at York, complying with a June 24 resolution to reconvene in Philadelphia on July 2, hold a public celebration of independence there on July 4, and attend church en masse on July 5 to give thanks for independence.

Keppel anchors at the Isle of Wight to seek reinforcements, but the king and the cabinet express dismay over his return, believing it leaves the Gibraltar fleet and merchant ships from India and the West Indies easy prey for French raiders from Brest. The Admiralty orders him to return to sea off Brest once he has added four ships, increasing his fleet to 26.

Encamped about five miles from Englishtown, Washington calls a council to order an attack on Clinton's rear. He places Lee in command and sends him orders to dispatch a unit to observe Clinton's army for any signs of movement, but Lee delays fulfilling the order for two hours.

June 28: Near 4:00 A.M., Clinton orders von Knyphausen to begin the march to Middletown. Dickinson reports their movement to Lee and Washington. After 11:00 A.M., Lee's force of 5,000 confronts 2,000 troops of Cornwallis's rear guard, but Lee has no plan of attack. Clinton turns back to do battle. Misconstruing Lafayette's movements, Maxwell and Scott retreat to prevent dangerous exposure, joined by Lee and his entire force. Washington arrives leading the main army, expresses his outrage to Lee, assumes command, and rallies the troops. The two armies clash all afternoon. The weary British army withdraws around 6:00 P.M. The exhausted Americans sleep on their arms. During the night, Clinton slips away to Middletown. The inconclusive battle leaves 356 American casualties, including 72 dead and 132 missing, many disabled by heat exhaustion or sunstroke. The British suffer 358 casualties, including 217 dead, perhaps 50 of them felled by sunstroke.

June 30: Clinton's army arrives at Sandy Hook to await transport to New York City, but 600 men (440 of them Hessians) have deserted during their march.

July 1: Washington begins a series of short daily marches toward White Plains, halting for the night in New Brunswick.

July 2: The Continental Congress reconvenes in Philadelphia, lacking a quorum.

July 3–4: Maj. Sir John Butler's 1,200-man force of Tory Rangers and Indians has been pillaging western Pennsylvania and attacks Forty Fort in the Wyoming Valley. The fort's defenders, led by Zeb Butler, refuse to surrender, so Sir John sets fire to Fort Wintermont to trick the defenders into thinking his raiders are leaving. Zeb Butler's men race from the fort to pursue the raiders and are surprised and killed by Indians. News of this "Wyoming Valley Massacre" generates outrage among frontier settlers.

July 4: George Rogers Clark and his Tennessee, Kentucky, and western Pennsylvania recruits have hidden their boats beside the river at Fort Massaic and trekked 120 miles overland to maintain the advantage of surprise. Clark procures boats, crosses the Kaskaskia River, has half of his men surround the fort at Kaskaskia, and leads the rest through an open gate and to the house of the commandant, who surrenders immediately. Clark sends Captain Bowman with 30 men to Prairie du Rocher and Cahokia, which surrender. Not a single shot has been fired.

Responding to Charles Lee's letters complaining of Washington's treatment of him, demanding reparations, and requesting a court-martial, Washington agrees to a court-martial. With Lord Stirling presiding, the court-martial opens at New Brunswick. Lee is charged with disobeying orders by not attacking at Monmouth Courthouse, misbehavior in the battle by a disorderly and shameful retreat, and disrespect for the commander in chief, revealed in his letters.

July 6: British navy ships transport Clinton's army and its supplies, horses, wagons, and baggage from Sandy Hook to New York.

July 7: The Continental Congress finally musters a quorum at Philadelphia.

July 8: Delayed by unfavorable winds while crossing the Atlantic, d'Estaing's fleet finally arrives off the coast at the Capes of Delaware—days too late to pre-

vent Admiral Howe's fleet from sailing to New York. D'Estaing has 12 ships with 834 guns; Howe, nine ships with 534 guns.

July 9: The Continental Congress receives the newly engrossed Articles of Confederation, and members from eight states that have ratified sign their names. North Carolina and Georgia have ratified but have no delegates at Congress now; and delegates from New Jersey, Maryland, and Delaware have yet to receive authority to sign. Adoption of the articles must wait.

July 10: Admiral d'Orvilliers sets sail from Brest commanding a fleet of 32 ships, although three are unfit for combat. His orders are to cruise for a month but not to search for or attack the British fleet.

July 11: D'Estaing's fleet arrives at Sandy Hook.

July 14: French settlers at Kaskaskia promise Clark their support. Father Pierre Gibault has agreed to seek the surrender of Vincennes and its Fort Sackville on Clark's behalf. He leaves for Vincennes with other Frenchmen with letters from Clark addressed to the French settlers there. (All the British regulars have been withdrawn from Vincennes.)

July 15: Washington's army arrives at Haverstaw, New York, to prepare for crossing the Hudson River.

July 18: Mohawk led by Joseph Brant burn and plunder Andrustown, New York, a settlement of seven families, massacring many of the residents.

July 20: Persuaded by Father Gibault and Clark's letters, Vincennes residents agree to shift their allegiance to Virginia and to support Clark—another surrender without a single shot being fired.

July 21: North Carolina delegates to the Continental Congress sign the Articles of Confederation.

July 22: Prevented from attacking Howe's fleet by a sandbar that extends from Staten Island to Sandy Hook that renders the water too shallow for his ships, d'Estaing agrees with Washington on a strategy and sets sail for Newport, Rhode Island. Washington directs Gen. John Sullivan, commanding 1,000 troops at Providence, to request that Rhode Island, Massachusetts, and Connecticut raise 5,000 men to join him and to obtain boats and pilots for an attack on Newport coordinated with d'Estaing. Washington sends Lafayette to Providence with two brigades, while Maj. Gen. John Hancock leads 6,000 New England militia to Providence.

July 23: Admiral d'Orvilliers sights Admiral Keppel's fleet about 66 miles off the coast of Ushant Island, the outermost French island in the English Channel, and maneuvers to avoid an encounter.

July 24: Georgia's delegates to the Continental Congress sign the Articles of Confederation. Delaware, New Jersey, and Maryland hold back, with Maryland demanding that all states with western land claims cede them to the United States before ratification can occur.

July 27: D'Orvilliers has avoided Keppel for three days, but the wind shifts to his disadvantage, allowing Keppel to close on his rear. Two of d'Orvilliers's ships have sailed off the previous night, leaving him with 27 ships with 1,950 guns against Keppel's 30 ships with 2,280 guns. D'Orvilliers turns about to face Keppel but wishes to avoid close action, and the fleets pass each other in opposed directions. Langrage fired from the French ships shatters the masts of the British ships, immobilizing them, but Keppel cannot give chase when d'Orvilliers withdraws in the night. Both sides claim victory, but the French suffer 736 casualties to the British 408. Keppel's fleet occupies the battle scene, suggesting that the British will maintain control of the channel.

July 28: Silas Deane, recently returned from France, requests an audience with the Continental Congress to report on the commissioners' activities in Paris and Versailles and to justify his own conduct. Arthur Lee has accused Deane of pursuing excessive commercial ventures for his own profit, misusing public funds, and advocating payment for the supplies Beaumarchais has provided instead of accepting them as gifts; Lee has pressed Congress to investigate Deane.

July 29: D'Estaing's fleet arrives off Newport, Rhode Island, but Sullivan's force is not yet assembled. Sir Robert Pigot commands 3,000 British troops in control of the large island site of Newport between the Sakonnet and Middle passages of the Providence River.

July 30: Washington's army arrives and encamps at White Plains, New York, beginning a land blockade of the British army in New York City.

D'Estaing's fleet begins to enter the Narragansett Bay.

August 1: D'Estaing lands a small number of troops on Conanicut Island west of Newport.

August 5: Sullivan has assembled at Tiverton, Rhode Island, a force of 10,000, with Gen. James Varnum's Rhode Island troops and Gen. John Glover's Marblehead troops as the core. Initiating the strategy that he and Sullivan have adopted, d'Estaing sends Adm. Pierre-André de Suffren with two frigates sailing up the Sakonnet Passage of the Providence River. The British panic, run four of their ships aground, and then destroy them. They scuttle several vessels to block the French fleet's entry into Newport Harbor.

August 6: Receiving word in New York that Newport is under siege, Clinton orders Lord Howe's fleet to Newport. With the recent arrival of four ships from Adm. John Byron's fleet, Howe now has 20 ships with 914 guns to confront d'Estaing's 16 ships and 834 guns.

August 8: Sullivan awaits the arrival of more militia before beginning an attack on Newport planned for August 9 in coordination with d'Estaing, but he learns that the British have abandoned defenses on the north end of Newport's island and, fearing they may return, crosses the river immediately without first consulting d'Estaing. His precipitate move angers d'Estaing, exacerbating their already strained relations and endangering their cooperation.

August 9: Howe's fleet arrives off the coast at Newport, and d'Estaing orders his men posted on land to reboard their ships and prepare for battle.

August 10: With the wind in his favor but under fire from the shore batteries, d'Estaing sails out of Newport Harbor for open sea to engage Howe, who avoids contact in hopes that the wind will shift.

Responding to Georgia's foundering from lack of an effective government, members of the state assembly meet in Augusta and elect an executive council of nine men headed by John Wereat, who immediately appeals to Gen. Benjamin Lincoln for money, supplies, and soldiers before British troops join the Indians to overrun the state.

August 12: Following two days of maneuvers that forestall a battle, a sudden, furious wind disperses both Howe's and d'Estaing's fleets from their formations.

At Paramus, New Jersey, the court-martial of Gen. Charles Lee concludes, finding him guilty on all charges and suspending him from command for a year.

August 15: Sullivan moves his troops forward at Newport, builds entrenchments, and positions two batteries of artillery, forcing Pigot to withdraw his outposts back to his main lines. Both sides exchange ineffectual cannonades.

Silas Deane has his first hearing before the Continental Congress; subsequent discussions will reveal two strong factions favoring either Deane or Arthur Lee.

August 16: Washington forwards results of Lee's court-martial to the Continental Congress for review.

August 20: Following several days of sporadic fighting between individual ships, Howe has reassembled his fleet to return to New York for refitting, and d'Estaing reassembles his fleet off Newport. Sullivan requests that d'Estaing join him in fulfilling their original plan of attack, but the disgruntled admiral rejects the request, contending that his orders and his staff's counsel oblige him to sail for Boston to have his ships refitted before the severe hurricane season begins.

August 21: Rejecting an appeal from Lafayette, who believes Newport can be taken in two days with d'Estaing's support, d'Estaing sets sail at midnight, taking 4,000 French troops with him.

August 23: Keppel's fleet sails out of Portsmouth, England, to search for d'Orvilliers's fleet at the entrance to the English Channel, but the French fleet is in the Bay of Biscay and eludes detection.

August 26: Carlisle Commission member George Johnstone's attempt to bribe Congressmen Joseph Reed, Robert Morris, and Francis Dana to break the logjam in peace negotiations is exposed, forcing his resignation from the commission.

August 27: British agent John Berkenhout arrives in Philadelphia to pursue George Johnstone's underhanded tactics. He introduces himself to Richard Henry Lee as a friend of Arthur Lee, but Richard Henry Lee has been forewarned by Gen. William Maxwell, whose suspicions were aroused when Berkenhout passed through Elizabethtown en route from New York.

August 28: Discouraged by d'Estaing's departure, the militia serving with Sullivan have deserted, reducing his force's strength by half and precluding an attack on Pigot's well-entrenched garrison of 6,000. Sullivan begins to withdraw. Pigot sends troops in pursuit.

August 29: Sullivan's force is in full retreat, with his main line spread across the north end of Newport's island and a strong position at Butt's Hill, when Pigot's troops attack. Although outflanked at Quaker Hill and fired on from British frigates that have moved upriver, the Americans persistently repulse British advances. At about 4:00 P.M., the British begin to withdraw. Nathanael Greene, whose men have protected Sullivan's right flank, sallies forth to counterattack and rout the retreating British and Hessian troops.

August 30: Receiving word that Clinton is sending 5,000 troops to relieve the Newport garrison, Sullivan realizes his peril, and during the night he begins to ferry his men across the river to Bristol and Howland.

August 31: A fleet of 100 British ships carrying 5,000 troops commanded by Clinton and Maj. Gen. Charles Grey appears off the coast at Newport, but by early morning Sullivan has his entire force safely across the river.

September 3: Congress has learned from a London newspaper that Berkenhout and Sir John Temple, his colleague in New York, are British agents; the Council of Pennsylvania questions Berkenhout and has him jailed.

September 5: Returned to New York after deciding that d'Estaing cannot be successfully attacked at Boston, Clinton sends Gen. Charles Grey with a force to make raids on the coast of Massachusetts. Grey lands at Clark's Neck, Massachusetts, and raids New Bedford and Fair Haven, burning many buildings in both towns and 70 vessels in the Acushnet River. Then he sails for Martha's Vineyard.

September 7: Indian and Tory raiders attack Fort Boonesborough, Kentucky. Daniel Boone, who recently escaped from Shawnee taking him to Detroit, returns in time to warn of the attack and help prepare the fort's defense.

As Adm. Samuel Barrington's fleet, sent from England in May to protect Great Britain's Leeward Islands, waits at Barbados for an expedition supposedly being sent by Admiral Howe, the governor of the French island of Martinique takes advantage of Barrington's absence. He lands a force of 2,000 men on British Dominica, garrisoned by only 60 men. Possession of Dominica augments France's network of islands, providing a wedge between British-controlled islands to the north and south.

September 8: General Grey's raiders invade Martha's Vineyard, seizing thousands of sheep and cattle, public funds, and militia weapons, and destroying vessels and equipment to cripple the local whaling industry.

September 13: Joseph Brant leads 150 Indians and Capt. William Caldwell, 300 Tories, in a raid on German Flats (now Herkimer), New York. They kill three men; burn more than 100 houses, barns, and mills; and make off with hundreds of horses, cattle, and sheep. But they apparently commit no such atrocities against women and children as occurred at the Wyoming Valley Massacre.

September 14: Fulfilling a unanimous decision of September 11 that the United States needs a minister plenipotentiary at the French court, the Continental

Congress appoints Benjamin Franklin to the post, replacing the previous three-man commission.

The Council of Pennsylvania paroles John Berkenhout.

September 19: Berkenhout returns to New York. The Continental Congress is now convinced not to negotiate with the Carlisle Commission.

September 22: After weeks of testimony from Deane and others, the Continental Congress decides to investigate the dealings of the mission to France.

September 26: Without consulting Washington, the Continental Congress appoints Gen. Benjamin Lincoln as commander of the Continental army in the South, replacing Gen. Robert Howe, who remains as commander of the Savannah garrison.

September 28: Pursuing Washington's plan to harass British foraging parties, Gen. Anthony Wayne has stationed New Jersey militia at Old Tappan, New Jersey. During the night, British troops sent by Cornwallis under Gen. Charles Grey surround three barns where 100 of the militia lie sleeping, charge in with bayonets, kill 30, and capture 50, including their commander Lt. Col. George Baylor and nine other officers.

October 3: The Carlisle Commission attempts to bypass the Continental Congress, publishing a proclamation that offers a general pardon of disloyalty to all Americans and a full pardon to all military and civil officeholders who accept the pardon within 40 days.

October 7: Because George Rogers Clark's small force is vulnerable to attack by Indian or British forces, he has been negotiating with Ottawa, Chippewa, Miami, and Fox warriors hoping to gain their neutrality. Now Lt. Gen. Henry Hamilton sets out from Detroit with 175 troops, mostly French, and 60 Indians to attack Vincennes.

October 6–8: The 4th Pennsylvania Continentals, a group of Daniel Morgan's sharpshooters, and some rangers led by Lt. Col. William Butler raid Joseph Brant's base at Unadilla, New York, but find that the Mohawk have fled. Butler's men burn all but one of the stone and frame houses, a sawmill, and a grist mill in this formerly white settlement that was abandoned after Brant seized the settlers' crops and cattle. The destruction of Unadilla culminates more than two weeks of reprisal attacks, and the soldiers return to their base at Schoharie, New York.

October 14: Three British sloops and six smaller vessels attack Little Egg Harbor, New Jersey, a favorite port of American privateers, while 300 regulars and Tories led by Capt. Patrick Ferguson assist on land. They burn 10 privateering ships and several houses and storehouses. Informed by a French deserter that Pulaski's Legion is encamped on nearby Mincock Island, Ferguson sets out in rowboats with 250 of his men during the night to land on the island and prepare an attack.

October 15: Before daylight, Ferguson's men enter three houses on Mincock Island, where Pulaski's legionnaires lie asleep, and with bayonets kill 50 of them, including two French officers. Apprised of the raid, Pulaski attacks with his dragoons. The British escape under fire in their boats.

October 23: The Continental Congress finally begins to discuss the findings of Gen. Charles Lee's court-martial.

October 26: Completing the letter of credence and instructions to Benjamin Franklin as minister plenipotentiary to the French court, the Continental Congress authorizes Franklin to assure the court that the United States values French aid and is committed to fulfilling terms of the two nations' alliance, to solicit French financial aid, and to advocate French attacks on Halifax and Quebec to cripple British fisheries off the Newfoundland banks, but Franklin must not commit the United States to any stipulations without Congress's consent.

October 28: The Committee for Foreign Affairs dispatches the Continental Congress's instructions to Franklin and a letter to John Adams, whose role as commissioner now ends, encouraging him to turn his efforts to improving American finances.

October 31: Plagued by ill health and the illness of 1,000 of his seamen, Adm. Augustus Lord Keppel returns to Spithead at Portsmouth, England, to harbor his fleet for refitting over the winter.

November 4: With the plan to mount a French-American naval attack on Halifax and Newfoundland abandoned, d'Estaing sets sail from the West Indies, without informing Washington of his destination.

November 6: Col. Ichabod Alden, the commander of 250 troops of the 7th Massachusetts Regiment at Cherry Valley, New York, receives a warning from Fort Stanwix that a force of Tories and Indians plans an attack on the settlement and its fort, built by Alden's men to protect the settlers.

November 10: Refusing to prepare a defense or to allow settlers inside the fort at Cherry Valley, Col. Alden does send out reconnaissance teams. Seneca and Mohawk warriors led by Joseph Brant and Tories led by Capt. Walter Butler capture one of the teams and acquire information about disposition of the troops and houses at Cherry Valley.

November 11: Brant's warriors attack houses in Cherry Valley, where Alden and his officers are billeted, and kill Alden. Failing to take the fort after several hours of skirmishing, the warriors withdraw to attack settlers in their houses and massacre more than 30, mostly women and children. Captain McDonnell leads a sortie from the fort to rescue settlers hiding in a nearby woods, while Brant and Butler withdraw with 71 prisoners.

November 12: Walter Butler releases most of his prisoners and heads for Niagara with two women and their seven children as hostages, possibly to make an exchange for his mother and aunt and the wives of Tory officers being held prisoner in Albany.

November 19: Near Spencer's Hill, Georgia, British troops led by Colonel M'Girth, Lt. Col. James Mark Prevost's subordinate, ambush American troops led by Col. John Baker, attempting to harass Prevost's plundering expedition. Baker receives a wound, and the Americans retreat.

November 21: Thomas Paine publishes *The American Crisis VII, To the People of England* in Philadelphia.

November 24: Prevost's troops skirmish with American troops led by Col. John White at Medway Church, Georgia, and burn the church and other buildings.

November 26: New Jersey delegates to the Continental Congress ratify the Articles of Confederation, but Maryland holds out.

November 27: With Admiral Howe returned to England and Adm. John Byron having succeeded him in command of the British fleet at New York, General Clinton orders Col. Archibald Campbell to set sail from Sandy Hook with 3,500 regular, Hessian, and Loyalist troops in a squadron of ships commanded by Com. Hyde Parker, to join Gen. Augustine Prevost to attack Savannah.

Admitting failure, the members of the Carlisle Commission board the *Roebuck* at Philadelphia and set sail for England.

November 30: Washington has now deployed his army in a semicircle around New York City within a radius of about 40 miles to observe British troop movements. Headquartered himself at Middlebrook, he has units posted in winter quarters at West Point and Fishkill, New York; Danbury, Connecticut; and Middlebrook, Elizabeth, and Ramapo, New Jersey.

December 4: Gen. Benjamin Lincoln arrives in Charleston, South Carolina, to assume command of Continental army forces in the South.

December 5: The Continental Congress finally orders fulfillment of the recommended sentence by the court-martial of Gen. Charles Lee, relieving him of duty for a year.

Frustrated by his inability to secure an audience to defend himself before the Continental Congress, Silas Deane publishes in the *Pennsylvania Packet* an address "To the Free and Virtuous Citizens of America," which contains vituperative charges against Arthur Lee, William Lee, and some members of Congress, setting off a raging controversy.

December 10: Com. William Hotham's ships arrive at Bridgetown, Barbados, with a force of 5,800 troops commanded by Gen. James Grant and dispatched from New York by Clinton to reinforce Adm. Samuel Barrington, who has been resupplying his ships here. The British can now begin their offensive against St. Lucia.

Recently reelected as a delegate from New York, John Jay becomes president of the Continental Congress.

December 11: Admiral d'Estaing's fleet arrives at Martinique, Lesser Antilles.

December 12: The expedition commanded by Admirals Barrington and Hotham and General Grant anchors off St. Lucia. Hotham lands Grant's troops to begin a sweep of the island.

December 13: Admiral Byron's fleet, which had been scattered or forced to turn back twice by storms, sails from Newport, Rhode Island, to search for d'Estaing's fleet in the West Indies.

Grant's troops secure control of St. Lucia by capturing the French naval base only an hour before d'Estaing's fleet, outnumbering the British by three ships to one, arrives from Martinique carrying 9,000 troops. Divided into three units, Grant's force digs in at Vigie Point on the harbor's north side, Morne Fortune mountain, and Cul-de-Sac Bay.

December 17: While marching toward Vincennes, Henry Hamilton has been joined by more Indians, now numbering 500, and he has captured small scouting parties sent out by Capt. Leonard Helm, whom Clark left in command of the fort at Vincennes and whose garrison is reduced to one soldier. Offered no support by the local French, Helm surrenders Vincennes to Hamilton.

December 18: Despite his superior force, d'Estaing has failed to dislodge the British from Cul-de-Sac Bay, so he lands his troops at Anse de Choc to try to overpower British defenses at Vigie Point and open the bay to his ships. During a three-hour encounter, the British repulse two French attacks, wounding 1,200 and killing 400 of d'Estaing's force; among their own 1,300 defenders at the point, only 13 are killed and 158 wounded.

December 21: General Washington leaves Middlebrook to confer with the Continental Congress in Philadelphia.

December 23: Com. Hyde Parker's squadron, which is transporting soldiers commanded by Lt. Col. Archibald Campbell, arrives at Tybee Island at the mouth of the Savannah River just 15 miles below Savannah to await Gen. Agustine Prevost's arrival. Gen. Robert Howe marches from Sunbury to Savannah with 700 Continentals and 150 militia to defend the city, whose 20-year-old fortifications lie in ruins.

December 25: Lt. Col. Archibald Campbell sends ashore Capt. Sir James Baird with a company of light infantry. Baird discovers that Howe has only a small force but expects Gen. Benjamin Lincoln to join him once Lincoln learns that the British have arrived and that Howe has stationed his men on the road to Giradeau, with both their flanks protected by swamp. Campbell decides to attack instead of waiting for Prevost, who will assume command when he arrives.

December 28: After a 10-day pause, St. Lucia falls to British control when the French garrison surrenders following d'Estaing's withdrawal to sail to Martinique.

At Savannah, Georgia, Campbell orders Parker to move downriver to Girardeau's plantation, but a shifting tide prevents disembarking his troops.

December 29: Gen. Robert Howe assumes that the swamp will protect his flank and force Campbell's troops to attack him head-on, but Campbell has learned from a slave named Quamino Dolly about a secret trail through the swamp. Campbell sends men under Baird up the trail to attack Howe's flank while he leads a frontal assault. Howe's men are forced to retreat across a causeway in Musgrove Swamp and to swim Musgrove Creek, where many drown or are taken prisoner. The British chase the remainder through Savannah's streets, bayoneting many. The British suffer only 26 casualties but kill 83, wound 11, and capture 453 along with 48 cannons, 23 mortars, ammunition supplies, and the ships in the harbor.

EYEWITNESS TESTIMONY

1778

Great Advantages are often Attended with Great Incoveniences, And Great Minds Called to severe trials. If your Dearest Friend [John Adams] had not Abilities to Render such important services to his Country, he would not be Called to the self Denying task of leaving for a time His Beloved Wife and Little pratling Brood. Therefore while I Weep with my Friend the painful abscence, I Congratulate her that she is so Nearly Connected with a Gentleman Whose Learning, patriotism And prudence qualify Him to Negotiate at Foreign Courts the affairs of America at this Very Critical period.

Mercy Otis Warren, from a letter written in Plymouth, Massachusetts, to Abigail Adams, January 2, 1778, in L. H. Butterfield, ed., Adams Family Correspondence, *vol. 2, p. 376.*

As some Indian Tribes, to the westward of the Mississippi have lately, without any provocation, massacred many of the Inhabitants upon the Frontiers of this Commonwealth, in the most cruel and barbarous Manner, and it is intended to revenge the Injury and punish the Aggressors by carrying the War into their own Country.

We congratulate You upon your Appointment to conduct so important an Enterprize in which We most heartily wish You Success; and we have no Doubt but some further Reward in Lands, in that Country, will be given to the Volunteers who shall engage in this Service, in addition to the usual Pay: if they are so fortunate to succeed, We think it just and reasonable that each Volunteer entering as a common [soldier] in this Expedition, shou'd be allowed three hundred Acres of Land, and the Officers in the usual Proportion, out of the Lands which may be conquered in the Country now in the Possession of the said Indians; so as not to interfere with the Claims of any friendly Indians, or of any People willing to become Subjects of this Commonwealth; and for this we think You may safely confide in the Justice and Generosity of the Virginia Assembly.

George Wythe, George Mason, and Thomas Jefferson, a letter written at Williamsburg to George Rogers Clark, January 3, 1778, in Julian P. Boyd, ed., The Papers of Thomas Jefferson, *vol. 2, pp. 132–133.*

I was call'd to relieve a Soldier tho't to be dying—he expir'd before I reach'd the Hutt. He was an Indian—an excellent Soldier—and an obedient good natur'd fellow. He engaged for money doubtless as others do;—but he has serv'd his country faithfully—he has fought for those very people who disinherited his forefathers—having finished his pilgrimage, he was discharged from the War of Life & Death. His memory ought to be respected, more than those rich ones who supply the world with nothing better than Money and Vice. There the poor fellow lies not Superior to a clod of earth—his Mouth wide open—his Eyes staring. . . .

Albigence Waldo, Continental surgeon with 1st Connecticut Infantry Regiment, from a diary entry written at Valley Forge, January 4, 1778, in Hugh F. Rankin, ed., Narratives of the American Revolution, *p. 201.*

By the conversation with those gentlemen [George Bryan and Dr. Benjamin Rush] to night [sic], there appears to be a general murmur in the people . . . against the weak conduct of Gen. Washington. His slackness and remissness in the army are so conspicuous that a general langor must ensue, except that some heroic action takes place speedily, but it's thought by me that G. W. must be the man to put such a scheme into practice. Notwithstanding, a cry begins to be raised for a Gates, a Conway, a DeKalb, a Lee, but those men can't attain it. Such is the present concern of fluctuating minds.

Christopher Marshall, merchant and Quaker then in Lancaster, Pennsylvania, from diary entry of January 7, 1778, in Marshall, Extracts from the Diary of Christopher Marshall, *p. 159.*

The Commander in Chief is informed that gaming is again creeping into the army; in a more especial manner among the lower staff in the environs of the camp. He therefore in the most solemn terms declares, that this Vice in either Officer or soldier, shall not when detected, escape exemplary punishment; and to avoid discrimination between play and gaming forbids Cards and Dice under any pretence whatsoever. Being also informed that many men are render'd unfit for duty by the Itch, He orders and directs the Regimental Surgeons to look attentively into this matter. . . .

George Washington, from General Orders issued at Valley Forge, January 8, 1778, in John C. Fitzpatrick, ed., The Writings of George Washington, *vol. 10, p. 276.*

My mind seems anxiously concerned on account of our distressed friends and acquaintance, with our brave Gen. Washington, as he and his army are now obliged to encounter all the inclemency of this cold weather, as they with him are living out in the woods with slender covering; our poor friends in town, many of them in want of fuel and other necessaries, while our internal enemies, under the protection of that savage monster Howe, are revelling in luxury, dissipation and drunkenness, without any feelings for the distress of their (once happy) bleeding country. . . .

Christopher Marshall, from a diary entry written in Lancaster, Pennsylvania, January 17, 1778, in Marshall, Extracts from the Diary of Christopher Marshall, *pp. 161–162.*

I suppose you have heard of the appointments of Colonel [James] Wilkinson to a Brigadier and General [Thomas] Conway to a Major General. Is it possible to conceive the policy or justice of these appointments? The Army has been greatly convulsed—the Colonels and Brigadiers have sent in a memorial to Congress representing their grievances. If these appointments are not recinded, there will be a general resignation of two capital lines of the Army; but it is said Wilkinson is appointed Secretary to the board of war; what will be done with Conway I don't know. I think him a very dangerous man in this Army; he has but small talents, great ambition, and without any uncommon spirit of enterprize, naturally of a factious make and of an intrigueing temper. . . .

Nathanael Greene, from a letter written at Valley Forge, January 25, 1778, to Gen. Alexander McDougall, in Richard K. Showman, ed., The Papers of General Nathanael Greene, *vol. 2, p. 260.*

It is not indeed consistent with reason or justice, to expect that one set of Men should make a sacrifice of property, domestic ease and happiness, encounter the rigors of the field, the perils and vicissitudes of war to obtain those blessings which every Citizen will enjoy, in common with them, without some adequate compensation. It must also be a comfortless reflection to any Man, that after he may have contributed to securing the rights of his country at the risk of his life and the ruin of his fortune, there will be no provision made to prevent himself and family from sinking into indigence and wretchedness. Besides adopting some methods to make provision for officers equal to their pres-

Nathanael Greene became a major general in the Continental army. *(From* The Pictorial Field Book of the Revolution, *2 vols., by B. J. Lossing. New York: Harper Brothers, 1851 and 1852.)*

ent exigencies, a due regard should be paid to futurity. Nothing, in my opinion, would serve more powerfully to reanimate their languishing zeal, and interest them thoroughly in the service, than a half pay and pensionary establishment. . . .

George Washington, from a letter written at Valley Forge, January 29, 1778, to the Committee of Congress with the Army, in John C. Fitzpatrick, ed., The Writings of George Washington, *vol. 10, pp. 364–365.*

. . . But when your Nation is hiring all the Cut Throats it can collect of all Countries and Colours to destroy us, it is hard to persuade us not to ask and accept of Aid, from any Power that may be prevail'd with to grant it; and this only from the hope that tho' you now thirst for our Blood and pursue us with Fire and Sword, you may in some future time treat us kindly. This is too much Patience to be expected of us; indeed I think it is not in Human Nature. The Americans are received and treated here in France with a Cordiality, a Respect and Affection, they never experienced in England when they most deserved it, and which is now . . . less to be expected there than ever. And I cannot see why we may not upon an Alliance hope for a continuance of it.... America has been *forc'd* and *driven* into the Arms of France. She was a dutiful and virtuous Daughter. A cruel Mother-in-Law turn'd her out of Doors, defamed her, and sought her life. All the world knows her Innocence and takes her part....

Benjamin Franklin, from a letter written at Passy, France, February 12, 1778, to David Hartley, opposition member of Parliament, in William B. Willcox, ed., The Papers of Benjamin Franklin, *vol. 25, p. 651.*

My desire was you know to have run all hazards and accompanied him [John Adams], but I could not prevail upon him to consent. The Dangers from Enemies was so great, and their treatment to prisoners so inhumane and Brutal, that in case of a Capture my sufferings would enhance his misiry, and perhaps I might be subjected to worse treatment on account of my connection with him. These arguments prevaild upon me to give up the favorite wish of my Heart. Master John was very happy in his pappa's consent to accompany him, But young as he is a Mothers Heart will feel a thousand Fears and anxieties upon the occasion. There are many snares and temptations.... But to exclude him from temptation would be to exclude him from the World in which he is to live, and the only method which can be pursued with advantage is to fix the padlock upon the mind.

Abigail Adams, from a letter written in Braintree, Massachusetts, to John Thaxter, February 15, 1778, in L. H. Butterfield, ed., Adams Family Correspondence, *vol. 2, pp. 390–391.*

The public may be assured it is an undoubted fact that the court of France is positively, and has in earnest determined, that they will show no countenance whatever to the rebellion in America—have given the most satisfactory assurances that they will not assist the Americans in any manner, or suffer their vessels to trade at their ports.

From the New York Gazette and Weekly Mercury, *February 23, 1778, in Frank Moore, compiler,* The Diary of the American Revolution, *pp. 288–289.*

Exhibited such Scenes as were new to me. We lost Sight of our Enemy it is true but We found our selves in the Gulph Stream, in the Midst of an epouvantable Orage [*sic*], the Wind N.E. then N., and then North West.

It would be fruitless to attempt a Description of what I saw, heard and felt, during these 3 days and nights. To describe the Ocean, the Waves, the Winds, the Ship, her Motions, Rollings, Wringings and Agonies—the Sailors, their Countenances, Language and Behaviour, is impossible. No Man could keep upon his Legs, and nothing could be kept in its Place—an universal Wreck of every Thing in all parts of the Ship, Chests, Casks, Bottles &c. No Place or Person was dry.

On one of these Nights, a Thunder bolt struck 3 Men upon deck and wounded one of them a little, by a Scorch upon his Shoulder. It also struck our Main Topmast.

John Adams, diary entry describing a storm at sea while voyaging to France to serve as a commissioner with Benjamin Franklin and Arthur Lee representing the United States, February 23, 1778, in L. H. Butterfield, ed., Diary and Autobiography of John Adams, *pp. 275–276.*

... I am as averse to controversy, as any Man, and had I not been forced into it, you never would have had occasion to impute to me, even the shadow of a disposition towards it. Your repeatedly and Solemnly disclaiming any offensive views, in those matters, which have been the subject of our past correspondence, makes me willing to close with the desire, you express, of burying them hereafter in silence, and as far as future events will permit, oblivion. My temper leads me to peace and harmony with all Men; and it is particularly my wish, to avoid any personal feuds or dissension with those, who are embarked in the same great National interest with myself, as every difference of this kind must in its consequences be very injurious.

George Washington, from a letter written at Valley Forge, February 24, 1778, to Maj. Gen. Horatio Gates, in John C. Fitzpatrick, ed., The Writings of George Washington, *vol. 10, pp. 508–509.*

The rebel army continues in the same situation as when I had last the honour of writing to your lordship, hutted at Valley Forge, where their men suffer exceedingly from the very inclement weather that has prevailed this winter which has induced numbers to desert. Great struggles are making throughout the provinces to assemble a numerous army in the spring and the most oppressive and arbitrary means exercised to draw the people to the field, who almost generally show extreme backwardness to their service and in some instances have forcibly resisted the tyranny of their rulers.

Gen. Sir William Howe, from a letter written in Philadelphia, March 5, 1778, to Lord George Germain, in K. G. Davies, ed., Documents of the American Revolution, *vol. 15, p. 53.*

That a man whose soul is absorbed in the low traffic of vulgar vice, is incapable of moving in any superior region, is clearly shown in you by the event of every campaign. Your military exploits have been without plan, object or decision. Can it be possible that you or your employers suppose that the possession of Philadelphia will be any ways equal to the expense or expectation of the nation which supports you? What advantages does England derive from any achievements of yours? To *her* it is perfectly indifferent what place you are in, so long as the business of conquest is unperformed and the charge of maintaining you remains the same.

. . . At the close of the campaign, in 1775, you were obliged to retreat from Boston. In the summer of 1776, you appeared with a numerous fleet and army in the harbor of New York. By what miracle the continent was preserved in that season of danger is a subject of admiration! If instead of wasting your time against Long Island you had run up the North River, and landed any where above New York, the consequence must have been, that either you would have compelled General Washington to fight you with unequal numbers, or he must have suddenly evacuated the city with the loss of nearly all the stores of his army, or surrendered for want of provisions; the situation of the place naturally producing one or the other of these events.

Thomas Paine, from "The American Crisis V., To General Sir William Howe," March 21, 1778, in Van der Weyde, The Life and Works of Thomas Paine, *vol. 3, pp. 9–11.*

My Colleague, Mr. Deane, being recall'd by Congress, and no Reasons given that have yet appear'd here, it is apprehended to be the Effect of some Misrepresentations from an Enemy or two at Paris and at Nantes. I have no doubt that he will be able clearly to justify himself; but having lived intimately with him now fifteen Months . . . and been a constant Witness of his Public Conduct, I cannot omit giving this Testimony, tho' unask'd, in his Behalf, that I esteem him a faithful, active and able Minister, who to my Knowledge has

done in various ways great and important Services to his Country. . . .

Benjamin Franklin, from a letter written at Passy, France, March 31, 1778, to president of the Continental Congress Henry Laurens, in William B. Willcox, ed., The Papers of Benjamin Franklin, *vol. 26, pp. 203–204.*

. . . If I have receiv'd and borne your Magisterial Snubbings and Rebukes without Reply, ascribe it to the right Causes, my Concern for the Honour and Success of our Mission, which would be hurt by our Quarrelling, my Love of Peace, my Respect for your good Qualities, and my Pity of your Sick Mind, which is forever Tormenting itself, with its Jealousies, Suspicions and Fancies that others mean you ill, wrong you, or fail in Respect for you. If you do not cure your self of this Temper it will end in Insanity. . . .

Benjamin Franklin, from a letter written at Passy, France, April 3, 1778, to Arthur Lee, although probably not sent, in William B. Willcox, ed., The Papers of Benjamin Franklin, *vol. 26, p. 223.*

Rode through Orleans, &c. and arrived at Paris, about 9 O Clock. For 30 Miles from Paris or more the Road is paved, and the Scaenes extreamly beautifull.

At Paris We went to several Hotels which were full. . . . Then We were advised to the Hotell de Valois, where We found entertainment. But we could not have it without taking all the Chambers upon the floor which were four in Number, very elegant and richly furnished, at the small Price of two Crowns and a Half a Day, without any Things to eat or drink. We send for Victuals to the Cooks. I took the Apartments only for two or three days.

John Adams, from diary entry of April 8, 1778, in L. H. Butterfield, ed., Diary and Autobiography of John Adams, *p. 296.*

Dr. Franklin presented to me the Compliments of Mr. Turgot, lately Comptroller of the Finances, and his Invitation to dine with him. Went with Dr. Franklin and Mr. Lee and dined in Company with the Duchess D'Anville, the Mother of the Duke De Rochefoucault, and twenty of the great People of France.—It is in vain to Attempt a Description of the Magnificence of the House, Gardens, Library, Furniture, or the Entertainment of the Table. Mr. Turgot has the Appearance of a grave, sensible and amiable

Man. Came home and supped with Dr. Franklin on Cheese and Beer.

John Adams, from diary entry of April 9, 1778, in L. H. Butterfield, ed., Diary and Autobiography of John Adams, *p. 297.*

The increasing warmth of the Season requires that the greatest Care should be taken to keep the Hutts of the men clean, their beding air'd every day and the Streets and Alleys of the Camp free from all kind of Filth; The Commander in Chief therefore earnestly requests both the Brigade and Regimental officers of the day to see these duties regularly and punctually performed; All bones, putrid meat, dirty straw and any other kind of filth to be every day collected and burnt.

George Washington, from General Orders issued at Valley Forge, April 10, 1778, in John C. Fitzpatrick, ed., The Writings of George Washington, *vol. 11, p. 232.*

Continuing in Grinage [East Greenwich, Rhode Island] exersis[ing] our Recrutes / thick Clowdy Wether/ in ye after part of the day turn'd out our black [troops] rec'd sum orders picked out a guard of 20 men & a sub. then marcht down to Quidneset ware we made a guard house [out] of a dwelling house half a mild from ye Shore ware we set 5 Sentinels. . . .

Sergeant Jeremiah Greenman, commenting on the training of black troops whom he had been sent to Rhode Island to recruit, since the Rhode Island assembly had authorized enlistment of Indian and black slaves, to be compensated as other troops and to also receive their freedom, with their owners being indemnified by the state, from diary entry of April 14, 1778, in Greenman, Diary of a Common Soldier in the American Revolution, 1775–1783, *p. 114.*

Sir, We [Congress] have within a Month past—improved many whole days & some tedious Nights by hammering upon a plan for half pay establishment for Officers who shall continue in the Army to the end of the present War—a most momentous engagement—in which all our labour has not yet matured one single Clause nor even determined the great leading questions to be, or not to be. [T]he Combatants have agreed to meet to morrow vis a vis & by the point of Reason & by somethings proxies for Reason put an end to the Contest.—I'll be hanged they do—

Henry Laurens, from a letter written in York, Pennsylvania, April 19, 1778, to William Livingston, governor of New Jersey, in David R. Chesnutt and C. James Taylor, eds., The Papers of Henry Laurens, *vol. 13, p. 148.*

It is with much Grief and Concern that I have learned from my first landing in France, the Disputes between the Americans, in this Kingdom. The Animosities between Mr. D[eane] and Mr. L[ee]—between Dr. F[ranklin] and Mr. L.—between Mr. Iz[ard] and Dr. F.—between Dr. B[ancroft] and Mr. L.—between Mr. C[armichael] and all. It is a Rope of Sand. . . .

I am at present wholly untainted with these Prejudices, and will endeavor to keep myself so. Parties and Divisions among the Americans here, must have disagreeable if not pernicious Effects.

Mr. D. seems to have made himself agreable here to Persons of Importance and Influence, and is gone home in such Splendor, that I fear, there will be Altercations,

Henry Laurens was a member of Congress. *(From* The Pictorial Field Book of the Revolution, *2 vols., by B. J. Lossing. New York: Harper Brothers, 1851 and 1852.)*

in America about him. . . . Sir J[ames] J[ay] insinuated that Mr. D. had been at least as attentive to his own Interest, in dabbling in the English Funds, and in Trade, and fitting out Privateers, as to the Public . . . and said that Dr. B. too had made a Fortune. . . . What shall I say? What shall I think?

John Adams, from diary entry of April 21, 1778, in L. H. Butterfield, ed., Diary and Autobiography of John Adams, *p. 304.*

I thank you for your kind caution, but having nearly finished a long life, I set but little value on what remains of it. Like a draper, when one chaffers with him for a remnant, I am ready to say, "As it is only the fag-end, I will not differ with you about it, take it for what you please." Perhaps the best use such an old fellow can be put to, is to make a martyr of him.

Benjamin Franklin, a letter written at Passy, France, April 29, 1778, to David Hartley, in William B. Willcox, ed., The Papers of Benjamin Franklin, *vol. 26, p. 374.*

From the Situation in which I found the Quarter Master General's Department on my entering upon the Office, which is not unknown to your Excellency, It appeared to be absolutely necessary to make very extensive and speedy Preparations for the ensuing Campaign, especially in Horses, Teams, Tents, and other Articles of high Price. In Consequence of this apparent Necessity, I have given extensive Orders, almost without Limitation, for the Purchase of these Articles; apprehending, from the Prospects at that Time, the utmost Exertions we could make would not procure more than a Sufficiency for the necessary Accomodation of the Army.

Nathanael Greene, from a letter written at Valley Forge, May 3, 1778, to George Washington, in Richard K. Showman, ed., The Papers of General Nathanael Greene, *vol. 2, p. 372.*

Having detained the Express that he might carry you the news that we heard was on its way from France, I am furnished with an opportunity of congratulating you on the important event of a Treaty of Commerce, and one of Alliance and Amity, having been signed at Paris on the 6th of February last, between France and the United States. . . . Great Britain has now two Cards to play but which she will choose we cannot tell, altho we certainly ought in wisdom to be prepared for the

worst. She may either acknowledge the Independency of America and make a Treaty of Commerce with her and thus be at peace with us and with all the World; or she may submit to the uninterrupted progress of French commerce to avoid a war with that Power and yet push her whole force against us this Campaign and thereby injure us extremely if we are not prepared with a strong force to prevent it. . . .

Richard Henry Lee, from a letter written at York, Pennsylvania, to Thomas Jefferson, May 3, 1778, in Julian P. Boyd, ed., The Papers of Thomas Jefferson, *vol. 2, p. 176.*

I very much fear that we, taking it for granted that we have nothing more to do, because France has acknowledged our Independency and formed an alliance with us, shall relapse into a state of supineness and perfect security. I think it more than probable, from the situation of affairs in Europe, that the Enemy will receive no considerable, if any, reinforcements. But suppose they should not, their remaining force, if well directed, is far from being contemptible. In the desperate state of British Affairs, it is worth a desperate attempt to extricate themselves, and a blow at our main Army, if successful, would have a wonderful effect upon the minds of a number of people still wishing to embrace the present terms or indeed any terms offered by Great Britain. It behoves us therefore to make ourselves as respectable as possible, that if the Enemy continue in their detached State, we endeavour to destroy them by piecemeal, and if, on the contrary, they collect, they may not fall heavily upon us in some quarter. . . .

George Washington, from a letter written at Valley Forge, May 5, 1778, to Maj. Gen. Alexander McDougall, in John C. Fitzpatrick, ed., The Writings of George Washington, *vol. 11, p. 352.*

Agreably to the above Orders [to assemble for review and thanksgiving], his Excellency Genl. Washington, his amiable lady & suite, Lord Stirling, the Countess of Stirling, with other general officers & ladys, attended at Nine O'Clock at the Jersey Brigade. . . .

Upon the signal at half past eleven the whole army repaired to their Alarm posts; upon which Genl. Washington & the Genl. Officers reviewed the whole Army at their respective posts; & after the firing of the Cannon & Musketry & huzza's were given agreably to the orders, the Army returned to their respective brigade-parades, & were dismissed.

All the officers of the Army assembled, & partook of a collation provided by the Genl., at which several patriotic toasts were given, accompanied by three cheers. His Excellency took leave of the officers at five O'Clock, upon which there was a universal huzzaing, *Long live Genl. Washington!* & clapping of hands until the Genl. rode some distance.

Major Joseph Bloomfield of the 3rd New Jersey Regiment, then encamped at Valley Forge, from his journal entry of May 6, 1778, in Mark E. Lender and James Kirby Martin, eds., Citizen Soldier, *p. 134.*

This Morning Dr. Franklin, Mr. Lee, and Mr. Adams, went to Versailles, in Order that Mr. Adams might be presented to the King.—Waited on the Count De Vergennes, at his office, and at the Hour of Eleven the Count conducted Us, into the Kings Bed Chamber where he was dressing—one officer putting on his Sword, another his Coat &c.

The Count went up to the King, and his Majesty turned about, towards me, and smiled. Ce est il Monsieur Adams, said the King and then asked a Question, very quick, or rather made an Observation to me which I did not fully understand. The Purport of it was that I had not been long arrived. . . . The Count told the King, that I did not yet take upon me to speak French. The King asked, whether I did not speak *at all* as yet—and passed by me, into the other Room.

John Adams, from diary entry of May 8, 1778, in L. H. Butterfield, ed., Diary and Autobiography of John Adams, *pp. 309–310.*

General Washington keeps his station at the Valley Forge. I was there when the army first began to build huts; they appeared to me like a family of beavers: every one busy; some carrying logs, others mud, and the rest fastening them together. The whole was raised in a few days, and is a curious collection of buildings in the true rustic order.

Thomas Paine, from "Letter to Franklin, in Paris," May 16, 1778, in Van der Wayde, The Life and Works of Thomas Paine, *vol. 3, p. 277.*

. . . I am glad of the alliance of France but it behoves us to look about us with Wisdom & firmness—we ought now to prepare for more serious contest than we have experienced—If Great Britain has declared War against France the whole Nation will be engaged & the whole Nation is Mighty, their full power when exerted, & well directed, is almost Almighty—I am however more afraid of ourselves than I am of their allmightiness—afraid we shall lull ourselves into a fatal security in the mistaken weakness of Britain & Strength of our Ally. . . .

Henry Laurens, from a letter written in York, Pennsylvania, May 16, 1778, to his son John Laurens, in David R. Chesnutt and C. James Taylor, eds., The Papers of Henry Laurens, *vol. 13, p. 309.*

Every piece of intelligence from Philadelphia makes me think it more and more probable, that the Enemy are preparing to evacuate it. Whether they intend to leave the Continent, or only go to some other part of it must be uncertain. There are some reasons that induce a suspicion they may intend for New York. In any case it is absolutely necessary, we should be ready for an instant movement of the army. . . .

George Washington, from a letter written at Valley Forge, May 17, 1778, to Maj. Gen. Nathanael Greene, in John C. Fitzpatrick, ed., The Writings of George Washington, *vol. 11, p. 403.*

At length we have intelligence from France that the Congress have concluded a treaty of alliance with the King of the French:—His Most Christian Majesty guarantees the independence, sovereignty, liberties, and all the possessions of the United States of America; and they, on their part, guarantee all the dominions of that prince in the West Indies. The part he has acted upon this occasion is truly noble and magnanimous. No monopoly of our trade is desired; it is left open to all we choose to trade with. This is wise as it is generous, it being undoubtedly the interest of France that this treaty should be durable, which would not have been so likely had hard terms been exacted of us. We are, moreover, liberally assisted there with all kinds of supplies. The treaties were signed on the sixth of February, but were not publicly known when the frigate which brought them to Congress, sailed. . . .

From the New-York Journal, *May 18, 1778, in Frank Moore, compiler,* The Diary of the American Revolution, *p. 291.*

Yesterday [May 18] the British army, anxious to give Sir William Howe the most public and splendid testimony of the high esteem they entertain of him as a general, and of the affection and attachment which his popular conduct has secured to him from all ranks . . . prepared a magnificent entertainment to grace his departure from Philadelphia. It consisted of a variety of parts, and was therefore called the MISCHIANZA. . . . The fete began at four o'clock in the afternoon, by a grand procession on the Delaware. . . . Three flatboats, with bands of music in each, led the procession.

. . . . .

After the fireworks the company sat down to a supper consisting of a thousand and twenty-four dishes, in a magnificent apartment built for the occasion. . . .

From the Pennsylvania Ledger, *May 23, 1778, in Frank Moore, compiler,* The Diary of the American Revolution, *pp. 305–307.*

The reasons which you assign for selling your Lotts in Williamsburg and James City . . . may be good, if you can get an adequate price for them and the Money is immediately vested in the funds, or laid out in other lands; but, if this is not done be assured, it will melt like Snow before a hot Sun, and you will be able to give as little acct. of the going of it; to which I may add . . . that Lands are permanent, rising fast in value, and will be very dear when our Independency is established, and the Importance of America better known. . . .

George Washington, from a letter written at Valley Forge, May 26, 1778, to John Parke Custis, in John C. Fitzpatrick, ed., The Writings of George Washington, *vol. 11, p. 457.*

Tho' much of my time is employed in the councils of America I have yet a little leisure to indulge my fondness for philosophical studies. I could wish to correspond with you on subjects of that kind. It might not be unacceptable to you to be informed for instance of the true power of our climate as discoverable from the Thermometer, from the force and direction of the winds, the quantity of rain, the plants which grow without shelter in the winter &c. On the other hand we should be much pleased with contemporary observations on the same particulars in your country, which will give us a comparative view of the two climates. Farenheit's thermometer is the only one in use with us. I make my daily observations as early as possible in the morning and again about 4. o'clock in the afternoon, these generally showing the maxima of cold and heat in the course of 24 hours. I wish I could gratify your Botanical taste; but I am acquainted with nothing more than the first principles of that science, yet myself and

my friends may furnish you with any Botanical subjects which this country affords. . . . The greatest difficulty will be the means of conveyance during the continuance of the war.

Thomas Jefferson, from a letter written at Williamsburg to Italian scientist Giovanni Fabbroni, June 8, 1778, in Julian P. Boyd, ed., The Papers of Thomas Jefferson, *vol. 2, pp. 195–196.*

I am further directed to inform Your Excellencies that Congress are inclined to Peace notwithstanding the unjust Claims from wh. this War originated and the Savage manner in wh. it hath been conducted; they will therefore be ready to enter upon the consideration of a Treaty of Peace and Commerce . . . when the King of Great Britain shall demonstrate a sincere disposition for that purpose. The only solid proof of this disposition will be an explicit acknowledgment of the Independence of these States or the withdrawing his Fleets and Armies. . . .

Henry Laurens, from a letter written in York, Pennsylvania, June 17, 1778, to the Carlisle Commission, in David R. Chesnutt and C. James Taylor, eds., The Papers of Henry Laurens, *vol. 13, p. 471.*

Sir: You are immediately to proceed to Philadelphia and take the command of the troops there. The principal objects of your command you will find specified in the inclosed resolve of Congress of the 4th. instant; which you will carefully execute. You will take every prudent step in your power, to preserve tranquillity and order in the city, and give security to individuals of every class and description; restraining, as far as possible, 'till the restoration of civil government, every species of persecution, insult, or abuse, either from the soldiery to the inhabitants, or among each other. . . .

George Washington, from orders written at Valley Forge, June 19, 1778, to Maj. Gen. Benedict Arnold, in John C. Fitzpatrick, ed., The Writings of George Washington, *vol. 12, pp. 94–95.*

But . . . if the power of the Crown within the province must be trampled down to exalt the sway of inferior servants and scribblers . . . unconcerned for the interests of the King our master, his authority must be here destroyed, . . . I will venture to prognosticate that instead of subordination, tranquility and obedience, your lordship will soon perceive faction and sedition among both troops and people and this great province run headlong into the same disorders our neighbours have experienced, with no less detriment to the interests of Great Britain.

Governor Sir Guy Carleton, from a letter written in Quebec, June 25, 1778, to Lord George Germain, in K. G. Davies, ed., Documents of the American Revolution, *vol. 15, p. 148.*

This night I lay with Capt. Voorhees Lieuts. Wm. Pyatt & Bloomfield with 50 Contl. Soldiers & 40 Militia on Taylor's heights within a quarter of a Mile of [Gen. Henry] Clinton's Main-Army. Fired upon & alarmed them several times in the night, and in the morning followed their rear. Capt. Voorhees party took 15 Prisoners & had several skirmishes with the Jagars [Jaegers, German troops]. Took three Jagars myself Prisoners when we was reconnitreing within sight of the Enemys Rear. The Jersey Brigade with the Marquis D. la Feayette, Genl. Wayne & [Charles] Scott's chosen corps lay together this Night in Upper-Freehold.

Major Joseph Bloomfield of the 3rd New Jersey Regiment, reconnoitering near Maidenhead, New Jersey, journal entry of June 25, 1778, in Mark E. Lender and James Kirby Martin, eds., Citizen Soldier, *p. 136.*

Breakfasted and dined at Stephen Collin's with my children. In the interval, engaged in viewing some of our and others' houses with wonder and amazement on the scenes of malice and wanton cruelty, yet my late dwelling house was not so bad as many others, yet grief seized me in beholding the ruins, viz., houses quite demolished, of which ours near [the Bettering House was] quite gone with the brick-walls, chimneys, &c., the doors, cases, windows and cases, etc., either destroyed or carried away entirely.

Christopher Marshall, merchant and Quaker, diary entry of June 26, 1778, describing homes in Philadelphia following the British departure from the city and his own temporary return, in Marshall, Extracts from the Diary of Christopher Marshall, *p. 190.*

...The Guards first fell into action by receiving a very heavy fire from a wood on their right. They soon dislodged the Enemy from it, and drove them as far as they had strength to pursue. The Enemy had yet cannon and Troops on an advantageous height in front, from which it was necessary to force them. The Grenadiers were therefore led on, and the Reb-

els were driven back across a deep morass, upon their main Army. This was not effected without loss, but more from heat and fatigue under which many died, than from the Enemy's shot. To this height our cannon. Consisting of twelve 6-pounders, two medium 12-pounders, and two howitzers, were brought and opposed to that of the Enemy, whose whole force occupied the opposite hills. . . .

Major John André, from his diary entry of June 28, 1778, describing the Battle of Monmouth (Freehold), in André, Major André's Journal, *pp. 79–80.*

Englishtown / this morn att two oClock we slung our packs / advanc'd towards the enemy about 3 milds from ware we lay / part of the militia & light hores that was on the wright engag'd the enemy / then our Division under the Command of Genl Lee advanced towards the enemy / thay form'd in a Sollid Collom then fir'd a voley att us / thay being so much Superier to our Number we retreated / . . . then we form'd again under a fence ware the light horse advanced on us / we began a fire on them very heavy / then the foot-men rushed on us / after firing a Number of rounds we was obliged to retreat. a Number of our men died with heat a retreating. a Number of troops form'd in the rear of us and sum artilira wich cover'd our retreat. thay began a fire on the enemy, than thay [the British] retreat'd / Left the Ground with about a thousand kil'd & wounded. on our Side about two hundred kil'd & wounded & died with heat. . . .

Sergeant Jeremiah Greenman describing the Battle of Monmouth, diary entry of June 28, 1778, in Greenman, Diary of a Common Soldier in the American Revolution, 1775–1783, *pp. 121–122.*

The Enemies Loss upon their March through the Jerseys by Desertion, in Skirmishing, by Sickness and Heat, and in the last Action [Monmouth Courthouse] is estimated at upwards of 3000 Men. We have suffered considerably by the Heat. We marched through a Country from Monmouth to Brunswick not unlike the Deserts of Arabia for Soil and Climate. The Enemy embarked their Troops at Hows Harbor [at Sandy Hook] opposite Staten Island. It is the opinion of Many that the Enemy will give us but Little more Trouble this Summer.

Nathanael Greene, from a letter written at Brunswick, New Jersey, July 2, 1778, to his brother Jacob Greene, in Richard K. Showman, ed., The Papers of General Nathanael Greene, *vol. 2, p. 451.*

The arrival of a Fleet, belonging to his most Christian majesty on our coast, is an event that makes me truly happy; and permit me to observe, that the pleasure I feel on the occasion, is greatly increased by the command being placed in a Gentleman of such distinguished talents, experience and reputation as the Count D'Estaing. I am fully persuaded that every possible exertion will be made by you to accomplish the important purposes of your destination, and you may have the firmest reliance, that my most strenuous efforts shall accompany you in any measure which may be found eligible.

George Washington, from a letter written at his camp at Haverstraw Bay, New York, July 17, 1778, to Charles, count d'Estaing, in John C. Fitzpatrick, ed., The Writings of George Washington, *vol. 12, pp. 185–186.*

Writing to a philosopher, I may hope to be pardoned for intruding some thoughts of my own, tho' they relate to him personally. Your time for two years past has, I believe, been principally employed in the civil government of your country. Tho' I have been aware of the authority our cause would acquire with the world from it's being known that yourself and Doctr. Franklin were zealous friends to it, and am myself duly impressed with a sense of the arduousness of government,... yet I am also satisfied there is an order of geniusses above that obligation, and therefore exempted from it. No body can conceive that nature ever intended to throw away a Newton upon the occupations of a crown. It would have been a prodigality for which even the conduct of providence might have been arraigned, had he been by birth annexed to what was so far below him. Cooperating with nature in her ordinary economy, we should dispose of and employ the geniusses of men according to their several orders and degrees. I doubt not there are in your country many persons equal to the task of conducting government: but you should consider that the world has but one Ryttenhouse, and that it never had one before....

Thomas Jefferson, from a letter written at Monticello to astronomer and treasurer of Pennsylvania David Rittenhouse, July 19, 1778, in Julian P. Boyd, ed., The Papers of Thomas Jefferson, *vol. 2, pp. 202–203.*

The lavish manner, in which rank has hitherto been bestowed on these gentlemen [foreign volunteers], will certainly be productive of one or the other of these evils, either to make it despicable in the eyes of Europe, or become a means of pouring them in upon us like a torrent, and adding to our present burden. But it is neither the expense nor the trouble of them that I most dread. There is an evil more extensive in its nature, and fatal in its consequences, to be apprehended, and that is, the driving of all our own officers out of the service, and throwing not only our army, but our military councils, entirely into the hands of foreigners.

George Washington, from a letter written at White Plains, New York, July 24, 1778, to Gouverneur Morris, in John C. Fitzpatrick, ed., The Writings of George Washington, *vol. 12, p. 226.*

Britain, at last to arrest your lawless hand,
Rises the genius of a generous land,
Our injured rights bright Gallia's prince defends,
And from this hour that prince and we are friends;
Feuds, long upheld, are vanished from our view.
Once we were foes—but for the sake of you—
Britain, aspiring Briton, now must bend—
Can she at once with France and us contend,
When we alone, remote from foreign aid,
Her armies captured, and distressed her trade?
Britain and we no more in combat join,
No more, as once, in every sea combine;
Dead is that friendship which did mutual burn,
Fled is the scepter, never to return;
By sea and land perpetual foes we meet,
Our cause more honest, and our hearts as great;
Lost are these regions to Britannia's reign,
Nor need these strangers of their loss complain,
Since all, that here with greedy eyes they view,
From our own toil to wealth and empire grew.

Philip Freneau, from "America Independent," August 1778, in Fred Lewis Pattee, The Poems of Philip Freneau, *vol. 1, pp. 277–278.*

Arose early, eat breakfast; then went in our chair to Dr. Kennedy's. Sent Charles back with [the] chair; stayed till the Dr.'s carriage was ready, in which with his negro man (past nine) we set out for Philada. Stopped at the sign of the Hart; served horses; then proceeded; stopped on [the] road; eat some gammon, drank some toddy; so went forward through a heavy rain to the sign of [the] Wagon, not much wet, as the carriage had a very good covering. I slept here, or, I would say, lodged.

Christopher Marshall, diary entry of August 16, in Marshall, Extracts from the Diary of Christopher Marshall, *p. 196.*

I dind with Gen [Nathanael] Greene to day, the french fleet Left us to day bound to Boston and I think left us in a most Rascally manner and what will be the Event God only knows we had one man kill'd and one or two wounded, one Eighteen pounder and one Brass ten inch morter was split to day but kild no man.

Col. Israel Angell, from his diary entry of August 23, 1778, recorded at Newport, Rhode Island, in Angell, The Diary of Colonel Israel Angell, *p. 4.*

This [August 6] being the day appointed by Congress for the reception of Sieur Gerard, Minister Plenipotentiary from his Most Christian Majesty, that Minister received audience accordingly. In pursuance of the ceremonial established by Congress, the Honorable Richard Henry Lee, Esquire, one of the Delegates from Virginia, and the Honorable Samuel Adams, Esquire, one of the Delegates from Massachusetts Bay, in a coach and six provided by Congress, waited upon the Minister at his house. . . . The carriages being arrived at the state house, Philadelphia, the two members of Congress, placing themselves at the Minister's left hand, a little before one o'clock, introduced him to his chair in the Congress chamber, the President and Congress sitting; the chair was placed fronting the President. The Minister being seated, he gave his credentials into the hand of his Secretary, who advanced and delivered them to the President. The Secretary of Congress then read and translated them, which being done, Mr. Lee announced the Minister to the President and Congress; at this time, the president, the Congress, and the Minister rose together: he bowed to the President and Congress, they bowed to him. . . . In a moment the Minister arose and made a speech to the Congress, they sitting. . . .

From the New-York Journal, *August 24, 1778, in Frank Moore, compiler,* The Diary of the American Revolution, *p. 319.*

The unfortunate circumstance of the French Fleet having left Rhode Island at so critical a moment, I am apprehensive, if not very prudently managed, will have many injurious consequences, besides merely the loss of the advantages we should have reaped from succeeding in the Expedition. It will not only tend to discourage the people, and weaken their confidence in our new alliance, but may possibly produce prejudices and resentments, which may operate against giving the

Fleet such Zealous and effectual assistance in its present distress, as the exigence of affairs and our true interest demand. . . .

George Washington, from a letter written at White Plains, New York, August 28, 1778, to Maj. Gen. William Heath, in John C. Fitzpatrick, ed., The Writings of George Washington, *vol. 12, p. 364.*

. . . If they [Great Britain] really are coming to their senses at last, and it should be proposed to treat of peace, will not the Newfoundland fisheries be worthy particular attention, to exclude them and all others from them except our tres grands et chers amies et alliées. Their great value to whatever nation possesses them is as a nursery for seamen. In the present very prosperous situation of our affairs I have thought it would be wise to endeavor to gain regular and acknoleged access in every court in Europe, but most the Southern. The countries bordering on the Mediterranean I think will merit our earliest attention. They will be the important markets for our great commodities of fish (as Roman catholics) wheat, tobacco and rice. The two last commodities particularly may be vended in any quantities in turkey. This power is moreover likely to be in our scale in the event of a general war. Emigrants too from the Mediterranean would be of much more value to our country in particular than from the more Northern countries. They bring with them a skill in agriculture and other arts better adapted to our climate. . . .

Thomas Jefferson, from a letter written at Monticello to Richard Henry Lee, August 30, 1778, in Julian P. Boyd, ed., The Papers of Thomas Jefferson, *vol. 2, p. 210.*

. . . Let me entreat you therefore my dear Marquis to take no exception at unmeaning expressions, uttered perhaps . . . in the first transport of disappointed hope. Every body, Sir, who reasons, will acknowledge the advantages which we have derived from the French Fleet, and the Zeal of the Commander of it, but in a free, and republican Government, you cannot restrain the voice of the multitude; every Man will speak as he thinks, or more properly without thinking, consequently will judge of Effects without attending to the Causes. The censures which have been leveled at the Officers of the French Fleet, would more than probable, have fallen in a much higher degree upon a Fleet of our own (if we had one) in the same situation. . . .

> *George Washington, from a letter written at White Plains, New York, September 1, 1778, to marquis de Lafayette, in John C. Fitzpatrick, ed.,* The Writings of George Washington, *vol. 12, p. 383.*

. . . this morning there Came an Express from beadford [New Bedford] informing us that the british troops had landed and burnt beadford I dind with the Marquis de La ffiat and while we was at the table there Came another Express with four Deserters from beadford informing us that all the houses and Stores and Shipping were Destroyed at Beadford and that the troops were all Embarked on board of their Ships while I was at the Marquises my brother Jason Came to me and brought the agreeable news that my family and friends were all well. . . .

> *Col. Israel Angell, from his diary entry of September 6, 1778 while encamped at Bristol, Rhode Island, in Angell,* The Diary of Colonel Israel Angell, *pp. 13–14.*

Yesterday [August 28], the fleet of his Most Christian Majesty, commanded by Admiral Count D'Estaing, arrived safe in Nantasket Road, and this morning three of his frigates anchored off Boston. The fleet has received considerable damage in the late storm; the count's ship (the *Languedoc,* of ninety guns) is particularly damaged, her masts and bowsprits being carried away, and her rudder injured. . . . The damaged ships are repairing with the utmost expedition, and in all probability will soon be in a condition to give the dastardly Britons a drubbing, should they have the effrontery to attempt to stand before them.

This afternoon the Count D'Estaing, with his suite, came up to Boston in his barge. He was saluted on his landing by the cannon of the American fortresses and ships in the harbor, and all respects were paid him that time and circumstances would allow. The count and his officers, General Heath, the Marquis de Lafayette, the principal officers of the American marine, and other gentlemen, dined with General Hancock.

> *From the* New Hampshire Gazette, *September 8, 1778, in Frank Moore, compiler,* The Diary of the American Revolution, *pp. 325–326.*

The 17th, 37th and 40th Regiments embarked. More arms, sheep and oxen were brought in. Two men having deserted, the inhabitants were required to restore them, on pain of having a double number of their friends seized. A Tender arrived from Lord Howe with Orders to the Fleet to return to New York. The Nantucket Expedition was of course set aside.

> *Major John André, diary entry of September 13, 1778, while with the fleet commanded by Gen. Charles Grey that General Clinton sent to make raids on the Massachusetts coast, in André,* Major André's Journal, *p. 93.*

In no light, therefore, that I view your situation do I see anything but good to the King's affairs in prospect, for the high opinion I have of Lord Howe's conduct, the intrepidity of the British seamen, and other circumstances, banishes every apprehension of failure; and therefore I am persuaded you will very soon after the date of your last dispatch have seen abundant cause for relinquishing all ideas of evacuating New York, and His Majesty and all his confidential servants concur so entirely in this opinion that the destination of all supplies for the fleet and army will continue to be New York until General [James] Robertson arrives, by whom I am to expect your determination.

> *Lord George Germain, from a letter written at Whitehall, London, September 25, 1778, to Gen. Sir Henry Clinton, in K. G. Davies,* Documents of the American Revolution, *vol. 15, p. 208.*

The question of the Canadian expedition in the form it now stands appears to me one of the most interesting that has hitherto agitated our National deliberations. I have one objection to it, untouched in my public letter [to Congress], which is in my estimation, insurmountable, and alarms all my feelings for the true and permanent interests of my country. This is the introduction of a large body of French troops into Canada, and putting them in possession of the capital of that Province [Quebec], attached to them by all the ties of blood, habits, manners, religion and former connexion of government. I fear this would be too great a temptation, to be resisted by any power actuated by the common maxims of national policy. Let us realize for a moment the striking advantages France would derive from the possession of Canada. . . .

> *George Washington, from a private letter written at Fredericksburg, Virginia, November 14, 1778, to the president of the Continental Congress Henry Laurens, in John C. Fitzpatrick, ed.,* The Writings of George Washington, *vol. 13, p. 254.*

. . . It has been the crime and folly of England to suppose herself invincible. . . . The arm of Britain has been spoken of as the arm of the Almighty, and she has lived of late as if she thought the whole world created for her diversion. Her politics, instead of civilizing, has tended to brutalize mankind, and under the vain, unmeaning title of "Defender of the Faith," she has made war like an Indian against the religion of humanity. Her cruelties in the East Indies will *never* be forgotten, and it is somewhat remarkable that the produce of that ruined country, transported to America, should there kindle up a war to punish the destroyer. . . .

When information is withheld, ignorance becomes a reasonable excuse; and one would charitably hope that the people of England do not encourage cruelty from choice but from mistake. Their recluse situation, surrounded by the sea, preserves them from the calamities of war, and keeps them in the dark as to the conduct of their armies. They see not, therefore they feel not. . . . They are made to believe that their generals and armies differ from those of other nations, and have nothing of rudeness or barbarity in them. They suppose them what they wish them to be. . . . There was a time when I felt the same prejudices; . . . but experience . . . has taught me better. What the conduct of former armies was, I know not, but what the conduct of the present is, I well know. It is low, cruel, indolent and profligate; and had the people of America no other cause for separation than what the army has occasioned, that alone is cause sufficient.

Thomas Paine, from "The American Crisis VII, To the People of England," November 21, 1778, in Van der Weyde, The Life and Works of Thomas Paine, *vol. 3, pp. 68–70.*

. . . By a faithful labourer then in the cause. By a Man who is daily injuring his private Estate without even the smallest earthly advantage not common to all in case of a favourable Issue to the dispute. By one who wishes the prosperity of America most devoutly and sees or thinks he sees it, on the brink of ruin, you are beseeched most earnestly my dear Colo. Harrison, to exert yourself in endeavouring to rescue your Country, by, (let me add) sending your ablest and best Men to

Congress. . . . If I was to be called upon to draw A picture of the times, and of Men . . . I should in one word say that idleness, dissipation and extravagance seem to have laid fast hold of most of them. That Sepculation, peculation, and an insatiable thirst for riches seems to have got the better of every other consideration and almost of every order of Men. That party disputes and personal quarrels are the great business of the day whilst the momentous concerns of an empire . . . are but secondary considerations and postponed from day to day . . . I am alarmed and wish to see my Countrymen roused. . . .

George Washington, from a postscript to a letter written at Middle Brook, New Jersey, December 30, 1778, to Benjamin Harrison, former Virginia delegate to the Continental Congress, in John C. Fitzpatrick, ed., The Writings of George Washington, *vol. 13, pp. 466–467.*

. . . The enemy, eight hundred in number, consisting of five hundred Indians, commanded by Brant, fifty Regulars under Captain Colvill, and another captain with some of Johnson's Rangers, and above two hundred Tories, the whole under Colonel Butler's command immediately surrounded the fort; . . . they commenced a very heavy fire upon the fort, which held three and a half hours, and was as briskly returned. . . .

The next day [November 12] they made it their whole business to collect horses, cattle, and sheep, which they effected, and at sunset left the place. The enemy killed, scalped, and most barbarously murdered, thirty-two inhabitants, chiefly women and children, also Colonel Alden. . . . They committed the most inhuman barbarities on most of the dead. Robert Henderson's head was cut off, his skull bone was cut out with the scalp. Mr. Willis' sister was ripped up, a child of Mr. Willis', two months old, scalped, and arm cut off; the clergyman's wife's leg and arm cut off, and many others as cruelly treated. . . .

From an account of the attack on Cherry Valley, New-Jersey Gazette, *December 31, 1778, in Frank Moore, compiler,* The Diary of the American Revolution, *pp. 331–332.*

6

A Great Sea Battle
1779

The Battle of Stony Point

The apparent malaise that settled upon American arms in the second half of 1778 prevailed through the first half of 1779, until Washington decided on a response to Clinton. Persuaded by the exiled renegade congressman Joseph Galloway and Gen. James Robertson that Loyalists actually composed the majorities in New York, New Jersey, and Pennsylvania, the North ministry decided on a new strategy. Gen. Sir Henry Clinton received orders from Lord George Germain to push Washington into the upper Hudson Highlands and to isolate New York from the other colonies as a bastion of Loyalist power and royal governance and a base for extending similar campaigns into the Middle Colonies. Germain believed the task would require 29,000 troops; as Clinton had only 22,000, he would be sent 1,000 from Halifax and the remainder from England.

At the end of May, Clinton assembled 6,000 crack British and Hessian troops at Spuyten Duyvil; they embarked aboard 70 sailing vessels and 150 flat-bottomed boats to move up the Hudson River and attack Washington's army headquartered at West Point. The British quickly captured the American posts at Stony Point and Fort Lafayette on both sides of the river 12 miles below West Point. In July, Clinton sent a force of 2,600 troops out of Whitestone, New York, to raid Connecticut in order to shut off supplies to the Continental army from that source and to end harassment of British shipping. This force successfully raided New Haven, Fairfield, and Norwalk.[1]

As the Connecticut raids proceeded, General Washington and Gen. Anthony Wayne personally reconnoitered Stony Point and planned an assault on the fort. They received detailed observations on the status of the fortifications from Capt. Allen McLane, Maj. Henry Lee's scout, who obtained entry to the fort through a ruse. And they sent McLane with a few other soldiers to monitor from hiding the daily routine at the fort. Wayne also had the assistance of a slave, Pompey Lamb, a Patriot spy who delivered fruits and vegetables to the fort and arranged for a nighttime delivery—the password given to him by the British would facilitate access by Wayne's men after the British guards opened the gate for Lamb's entry. (His effort earned Lamb freedom and a horse in payment.) During the night of July 15, General Wayne assembled 1,350 Continentals at Donderberg. He revealed to his colonels the true purpose of their mission. He ordered his troops to place white slips of paper in their hats for identification in the dark, explained their duties in detail, stressed that none might carry a loaded weapon except the men he designated, insisted on absolute obedience, and specified that no one remove his musket from his shoulder under threat of death—anyone who retreated or hesitated would be shot by the nearest officer. As a positive incentive, Wayne offered cash prizes beginning at $500 to the first five men to enter the fort at Stony Point.[2]

Wayne divided his men into two main columns to attack from the right and the left, with a third unit to assault the center. He chose 150 men to lead the right column and wield axes against the two lines of British abatis, freeing the way for the right column, accompanied by Wayne, to rush into the fort. In the early hours of July 16, the Continentals crossed a marsh and a sandbar leading to the fort and, in a perilous and courageous charge, surged into the fort under protective fire from their left—only Maj. Hardy Murfree's men in this column had loaded weapons. The fort's commandant, Col. Henry Johnson, led some of the 625 defenders to confront Murfree; the Americans' right column, led by Wayne and Lt. Col. Christian Febiger, stormed across the outer abatis before Johnson realized what was occurring and his men went out of control. Wayne, his head grazed by a bullet, fell at the second abatis but had two officers hoist and carry him up the hill. A bullet tore through Febiger's nose and cheek, but with blood spurting into his mouth he persisted. Francis McDonald, with the American left column, climbed on a comrade's shoulders, hoisted himself over a parapet, and dropped into the midst of the British. He unbolted the heavy gate, and the Continentals swarmed inside. They captured the summit and raised the flag with triumphant shouts. Realizing his defenses had failed, Johnson surrendered. The overwhelmed British garrison numbered 63 dead and 70 wounded and 543 taken prisoner, while Wayne's force suffered 15 dead and 80 wounded. Wayne's totally unexpected and stunning victory forced Clinton to cancel the Connecticut raids and assemble all available men-of-war to sail upriver and recapture the fort. Wayne destroyed and abandoned the fort, leaving it for Clinton to reoccupy and rebuild. The two winners of the prize money as first inside the fort donated the money to the enlisted men. Wayne's triumph at Stony Point demoralized Clinton but propelled a leap in morale among the Continentals.[3]

Stony Point proved the highwater mark of the year for the war in the North, which settled into near stasis, except for Maj. Henry (Light Horse Harry) Lee's surprising but temporary triumph at Paulus Hook in August. Inspired by Wayne's triumph at Stony Point, Lee persuaded Washington to let him attack the garrison of 200 British troops and 40 Hessians on this peninsula in the Hudson across from New York City. Capt. Allen McLane's talents were again used to scout the redoubt. In the early morning of August 19, Lee's men waded across the marshes, their splashes alerting the defenders; but Lee's "suicide squad" of axmen succeeded in destroying the British abatis nevertheless. The Americans raced ahead to capture a blockhouse in a quick triumph effected without firing a single shot, while bayoneting 50 of the garrison and taking 158 prisoners. But commander Maj. William Sutherland and some 40 Hessians barricaded themselves in another blockhouse and refused to surrender. Since the huge British garrison in New York had already received an alarm, Lee had no choice but withdrawal—leaving the barracks and cannons intact and taking no booty. He headed for Douwe's Ferry with his men and prisoners. The triumphant Americans had only two dead and three wounded, and Lee's lightning victory gave another boost to the Continentals' morale.[4]

FOCUS ON THE SOUTH

In the South, however, events proved far from uplifting, as continual encounters awarded the advantage to the British. During January, Gen. Augustine Prevost moved from triumph to triumph in Georgia, beginning with the capture of Fort Morris on January 9 that, with the earlier occupation of Savannah, gave the British effective control of eastern Georgia. By the end of January, having joined forces with Col. Archibald Campbell, Prevost attained control of Augusta, the capital since 1776. Sent by Prevost and joined by Loyalist troops from South Carolina en route, Campbell captured the town without opposition. Many patriots fled to South Carolina. Those who remained in Georgia either acquiesced to signing an oath of allegiance to the king or witnessed their property seized or burned. And so the British began 1779 in control of Georgia.

The British hold on Georgia appeared to weaken when Col. Andrew Pickens, with a combined force of about 350 of his own South Carolina militia and Capt. John Dooley's Georgia militia, won a victory over 700 Tories at Kettle Creek in mid-February. This victory, along with Gen. William Moultrie's successful defense in early February of Port Royal Island, South Carolina, against an attack force of British troops sent by General Prevost, energized Maj. Gen. Benjamin Lincoln to mount an effort to recapture Augusta. Lincoln posted troops across the Savannah River from Augusta, at Black Swamp, and at Briar Creek—the latter force composed of 1,400 North Carolina militia, 100 Georgia Continentals, and 200 light-horse militia commanded by Gen. John Ashe.[5]

This threat to Augusta induced Campbell to withdraw from the town and to burn the bridge across Briar Creek to impede Ashe from following. On March 3, as Ashe's troops rebuilt the bridge, a force of 900 grenadiers, dragoons, and militia sent by Prevost attacked their rear. When Ashe's Continentals began firing, his militia panicked and fled; the deserted Continentals then retreated in disarray. Most of the fleeing Americans cast away their weapons; some tried to escape in the river and drowned—altogether, 150 died in the encounter. The British, while enduring only 16 casualties, captured 11 officers and 162 soldiers, seven cannons, other weapons, and ammunition—a disaster for the Americans that crushed any hope of regaining control of Georgia.[6]

The action shifted to South Carolina and Virginia. At the end of April, Prevost crossed the Savannah River with 2,500 troops apparently intending to attack Charleston. His advance forced Col. Alexander McIntosh and his small force of 220 to withdraw from Purysburg and join Moultrie, who commanded 1,000 troops at Black Swamp. Regarding Black Swamp as untenable, the Americans retreated to Coosahatchie Bridge. Prevost followed hard after. Moultrie's force, now reduced to 600 men, reached Charleston in the second week of May. Although his original purpose had been simply to distract Lincoln, Prevost decided that his unopposed advance recommended the seizure of Charleston; he bottled up the town and demanded its surrender. While negotiating, Gov. John Rutledge sent out troops to reinforce the outer abatis without informing Moultrie, whose men fired on them, killing 13. The enraged Moultrie received full command of Charleston's defense from the governor's council and vowed never to surrender.

Learning that Lincoln's army had left Georgia and reentered South Carolina, Prevost withdrew to Johns Island to avoid being trapped between Lincoln and Moultrie and began to construct fortifications on the mainland at Stono Ferry. In mid-June, however, he evacuated most of his force to Savannah, leaving 900 troops under command of Col. John Maitland at the island. A few days later, General Lincoln led 1,200 of his 6,500 man Charleston garrison in a poorly executed attack on Maitland, whose force held fast until Prevost arrived with reinforcements; Lincoln ordered a retreat. Maitland had 129 casualties, while Lincoln suffered 146 casualties and 155 missing men, most of them deserters. In the aftermath of this battle, Maitland withdrew his force to Beaufort on Port Royal Island.[7]

In Virginia, the British achieved easy success. An expedition commanded by Adm. John Collier and Gen. Edward Matthews arrived at Hampton Roads during the second week of May. The British force conquered Fort Nelson, meant to protect Portsmouth, Norfolk, and the naval yard at Gosport, when the American garrison evacuated and withdrew toward the Dismal Swamp. The capture of Portsmouth, Norfolk, Gosport, and Suffolk quickly followed. At these towns, the British confiscated huge quantities of naval supplies, ordnance, and tobacco; they also seized or destroyed 137 vessels as well as many privateers; total losses to the Americans were estimated at £2 million. Their venture accomplished without the loss of a single life, Collier and Matthews set sail for New York.[8]

RECRUITING BLACKS

Since the British army now felt increasing strains from a growing manpower shortage, Gen. Sir Henry Clinton in June 1779 adopted Lord Dunmore's earlier tactic for recruitment of blacks. He promised freedom to all slaves (excluding those belonging to Loyalists who would leave their masters and bolster the British forces. As the British effort in the South expanded into 1779, many more slaves would take advantage of the promise. Lord Dunmore in fact even advocated formation of a black army of 10,000 men to help bring the rebels to heel, but his proposal failed of implementation.[9]

Northern states, especially in New England, had been pursuing the same tactic for the Patriot cause from the beginning of the war; and Rhode Island had organized the first all-black regiment, the 132-man 1st Rhode Island in 1778 under the command of Colonel Christopher Greene. Hundreds of blacks did in fact join the Patriot cause, serving in both the army and the navy alongside their white compatriots. Although initially, at the urging of South Carolina, the Continental Congress had barred blacks from service in the Continental army, with Washington's total concurrence, the delegates—and the commander in chief—had quickly rescinded that directive when, in December 1776, disaster had portended and the advantages of black support became clear. Washington himself had strongly urged the about-face. The shift resulted largely from the advocacy of two prominent South Carolinians, Henry Laurens and his son John, both opponents of slavery, which they viewed as not only morally abhorrent but also in violation of the liberty, equality, and freedom for which the Patriots fought—ironic since Henry owned slaves. Only South Carolina and Georgia continued to bar blacks from military service.[10]

THE SIEGE OF SAVANNAH

In September, at the urging at Moultrie and others, Adm. Charles-Hector-Théo-dat, Count d'Estaing reappeared to rescue American hopes. Despite Washington's appeal for his help in attacking Newport or New York, the French admiral chose to intervene at Savannah, sailing into Savannah River on September 8 with 22 warships, 10 frigates, and other vessels carrying 4,000 troops. He landed 3,000 troops at Beaulieu in preparation for laying siege to Savannah. Lincoln and Gen. Kazimierz Pulaski soon arrived with 1,350 men to support d'Estaing. The admiral requested Prevost's surrender, and the British general asked for a 24-hour truce to prepare terms of capitulation. D'Estaing granted the request, and Prevost used the time to significantly buttress his defenses and to welcome Maitland with reinforcements from Port Royal Island.

The siege began during the third week of September. For nearly two weeks, the Americans dug trenches, pushed slowly forward, emplaced cannons and mortars, and began to shell the British garrison but to little effect except to destroy the city itself. With d'Estaing grown impatient and demanding an immediate attack, contrary to Lincoln's counsel, the allied force of 3,500 French soldiers, 600 Continentals, and 350 militia launched a predawn assault on October 9. Leading the Continentals, Count Pulaski's cavalry reached the

The attack on Savannah occurred on October 8, 1779. *(Courtesy of the National Archives and Records Administration)*

British abatis, when a canister shot mortally wounded the count. Continentals led by Lt. Col. John Laurens foundered in a ditch too steep to scale, and grenadiers drove them off. D'Estaing suffered an arm wound. Gen. Lachlan McIntosh's Continentals floundered in a swamp while advancing—blasted by British artillery fire, they could only withdraw. A general retreat ensued. The allies suffered grievous losses—700 French and 450 American dead and wounded. Prevost's force of 3,200 had only 150 casualties. On October 20, d'Estaing loaded the remnant of his army aboard his ships and embarked, leaving Lincoln with no recourse but retreat to Charleston. Calamity stalked the Continental army and the American cause in the South.[11]

GEORGE ROGERS CLARK'S TRIUMPH

For unknown reasons, after recapturing Vincennes in December of 1778, Lt. Col. Henry Hamilton made no effort to attack George Rogers Clark at Kaskaskia. By early February, having regained the support of the French residents, Clark decided to move against Hamilton. Because of expired enlistments, Clark's force had declined to about 100 men. He dispatched 40 of them under Lt. Col. John Rogers aboard a row-galley bearing two four-pounder cannons and four swivel guns up the Ohio and Wabash rivers with orders to prevent the British from retreating down the Mississippi River. Then, with 127 men, about half of them French, he began a 180-mile overland trek to Vincennes. Impeded by heavy rains, floods, and hunger, Clark's force needed two days just to ferry across the Little Wabash River and reach the Wabash.[12]

On February 23, 17 days after leaving Kaskaskia, the weary and famished band arrived at the lake at Horseshoe Plain on the approach to Vincennes. Assigning Capt. James Bowman and 25 trusted men to bring up the rear with orders to shoot any man who refused to continue, Clark plunged into the lake's shoulder-deep waters and urged his men onward. They traversed the lake and came to a rest two miles from Vincennes, where they built fires and dried their clothes. From a French prisoner, Clark learned that although Hamilton remained ignorant of the Americans' approach, his troops had been reinforced by 200 Indians. Clark sent the Frenchman to Vincennes with the message that townspeople favoring the United States should remain in their homes and those on Great Britain's side should join Hamilton in Fort Sackville because Clark intended to conquer the fort during the night. Then he divided his force into two units to march separately on the town to create an impression of superior strength. Both subterfuges succeeded. The townspeople remained indoors or brought Clark ammunition, and many of the Indians

George Rogers Clark rallies his men for the attack on Vincennes. *(Courtesy of the National Archives and Records Administration)*

either fled or joined Clark. His men marched unopposed through the town and besieged Fort Sackville, maintaining their fire throughout the night.

The following morning, the fort's cannons stood silent as the exceptional accuracy of Clark's Long Rifles had inflicted such heavy casualties on the defenders. Clark had only one wounded man. At about 9:00 A.M., Clark demanded Hamilton's surrender, but the well-supplied British commander refused. Clark's men resumed firing, and two hours later Hamilton agreed to surrender if given suitable terms. Clark rejected the offer but agreed to negotiate. An Indian raiding party allied with Hamilton returned to the town with two American captives and some scalps, and Clark's men killed or seized the raiders, including the son of Pontiac. Clark had the prisoners taken to a site clearly visible from the fort and had them executed with tomahawks to perturb the Indians in the fort. Now, doubtful of his Indians' resolve and certain that he would receive no support from the town's French residents, Hamilton first tried to negotiate and finally capitulated. The next day, he surrendered Fort Sackville, his troops, and himself to Clark's custody. Clark's astonishing victory won him effective control of the Illinois territory.[13]

THE SULLIVAN EXPEDITION

Dismayed and angered by Indian raids on the frontier, Commander in Chief Washington in June ordered Maj. Gen. John Sullivan to rendezvous with Brig. Gen. James Clinton at Tioga, Pennsylvania, and, with their combined force of 3,700 men, to invade the territory of the Six Nations of the Iroquois Confederation. Sullivan lingered in Wyoming Valley, Pennsylvania, for more than a month, ostensibly acquiring supplies for his men. Meanwhile, Clinton assembled his men, boats, and supplies at Otsego Lake, New York and by the end of June was awaiting Sullivan's orders. At the end of July, Sullivan began the march to Tioga with 2,300 men. Under his orders from Washington, Sullivan held a mandate to effect the "total destruction and devastation" of the Iroquois settlements and to capture as many prisoners as possible. Sullivan arrived at Tioga on August 11 as Col. Daniel Brodhead marched out of Pittsburgh with 600 men to lay waste Indian settlements on the Pennsylvania frontier in the Allegheny River valley in support of his mission. During the following month Brodhead covered 400 miles and destroyed 10 villages and their croplands.[14]

In the final week of August, Sullivan and Clinton left 250 men at Tioga to defend their base and heavy baggage and began to march up the Chemung River. Initially, they discovered villages abandoned by the Iroquois, but on August 29, they thwarted an attempted ambush on the river by a sizable force of British and Tory troops under Capt. Walter Butler and 500 Iroquois led by Joseph Brant. Learning of the ambush in advance of their arrival, Sullivan encircled the ambuscade and unleashed his artillery. The British and Iroquois forces fled into the woods, abandoning 12 dead and two prisoners. The skirmish cost Sullivan three dead and 39 wounded. His men scalped their dead enemies and skinned the legs of two Iroquois to make boot legs for Lt. William Barton and his commanding major. Then they moved on to destroy the Iroquois settlement of Newtown, its orchards, and its field crops.[15]

Sullivan's expedition pursued its course of devastation through September. Along the Chemung River in New York, they laid waste Catherine's Town, two

This painting depicts the surrender
of Fort Sackville. *(Courtesy of
the National Archives and Records
Administration)*

Iroquois villages with their croplands, and Appletown. During the second week of September, Sullivan reached and destroyed the major Iroquois settlement of Canandaigua, noted for its 23 frame houses. Here Sullivan's men needed two days to ruin the vast orchards and croplands totally. Then they headed for Genesee, the grand capital of the Six Nations. Approaching Genesee, Sullivan's advance guard of 26 men under Lt. Thomas Boyd fell into an ambush by Maj. John Butler's troops, who killed 22 of Boyd's men. Taken prisoner, Boyd suffered death from torture, and the Iroquois with Butler hacked to death Boyd's Oneida guide.

On September 14, Sullivan's expedition entered Genesee, abandoned by the Iroquois. The Americans burned the entire old town of 128 houses that Sullivan described as "most very large and elegant." They also destroyed all the crops. Aware that Brodhead would not rendezvous with him, Sullivan decided against a planned march to Niagara and instead began a return to Wyoming Valley, Pennsylvania, via the southern shore of Lake Ontario, Cayuga territory. On the final day of September, having destroyed Iroquois towns around Cayuga Lake en route, Sullivan's expedition arrived back in Wyoming Valley. The general reported that, although his expedition brought back no prisoners, it had succeeded in devastating 40 Iroquois villages, an estimated 160,000 bushels of corn, extensive orchards, and large quantities of other crops. This wholesale ruination doomed the Iroquois to a winter of severe deprivation. Worse still for them, it left their entire community in that area effectively destroyed.[16]

THE INDIANS AT WAR

The Sullivan expedition may have been the single greatest catastrophe to befall any Indian tribe during the Revolutionary War, but the war itself wrought major changes for all the eastern and southern tribes that predicated the eventual demise of Indian control in any areas of the former colonies and eventually in the transmountain frontier extending to the Mississippi River. Indians largely perceived the struggle between British and American armies as a civil war. As such, it compelled most tribes to choose sides, leading almost inevitably to disastrous consequences. In colonial America during the 17th and early 18th centuries, Indians and white settlers had mingled in cities and towns, conducted commerce with each other, and joined in planting, hunting, and other endeavors. Intermarriages often resulted from such communion, as did much strife, resulting most especially from white settlers' growing acquisition of Indian lands, frequently through fraud. Finally, in the years leading to the outbreak of revolution, violence (rather than accommodation) came largely to typify white-Indian relations.[17]

The war itself exacerbated all the elements of strife and accelerated whites' encroachments on Indian territory. Demographic, economic, religious, and tribal intergenerational conflicts ripped the fabric of Indian culture and tradition and eroded the authority of tribal chieftains, generating confusion and influencing decisions on which side to choose in the war. Some tribes allied themselves with the British in hopes that the king's colonial governors would enforce bans on whites' land encroachments, especially on the western frontier, and also in an effort to preserve what remained of their cultures. The Stockbridge and Mohegan Indians became staunch allies of the Patriots. The Mohawk and the Seneca, the latter under their great war leader Cornplanter, supported the British, as did the Shawnee after a group of Patriots foolishly murdered their leader Cornstalk. Many individual Indians, for diverse reasons, joined the rebel forces.[18]

Both American and British governments supposedly chose to enlist Indian support only when necessary, but they also deliberately encouraged friction among tribes that joined their opponents, thereby encouraging both internecine violence and cultural disintegration. The Iroquois League of the Six Nations (Mohawk, Oneida, Tuscarora, Onondaga, Cayuga, and Seneca) perhaps typified the results of such developments. After attempting to remain neutral in 1775, the league discovered that tactic lacked viability; the Oneida and Tuscarora sided with the Patriots, destroying the league's unity—a boon for the Patriots as that unity would have served the British well; and by 1777, the six tribes were at war among themselves. The Sullivan Expedition sealed their fate. The Revolutionary War, in short, proved catastrophic for the majority of Indians.[19]

SUCCESS AT SEA

In early February, after nearly a year of sumptuous living in Paris while lobbying the minister of marine, John Paul Jones received the award of a ship. The ministry had purchased for his use an East Indiaman named *Duc de Duras.* Jones renamed the ship the *Bonhomme Richard* in honor of his benefactor, Benjamin Franklin, whose *Poor Richard's Almanac* enjoyed wide popularity in France. Jones sailed out of L'Orient in mid-August with a fleet of ships financed by the French government and mostly commanded by French officers who resented being subordinate to him as their commander. Pierre Landais commanded the American frigate *Alliance;* three French ships—the frigate *Pallas,* the brig *Vengeance,* and the cutter *Le Cerf*—rounded out the small fleet. Jones initially headed for the west coast of Great Britain.[20]

As September began, Jones planned to attack Leith, the port serving Edinburgh, and Newcastle-on-Tyne, England's major coal-shipping port. In mid-September, Jones's fleet stood off Flamborough Head, England. After capturing two brigs, Jones learned of a large fleet of British merchantmen accompanied by a frigate sailing up from the mouth of the Humber River. On September 23, still off Flamborough Head and accompanied by the *Pallas* and the *Alliance,* Jones sighted 41 merchant ships headed north. He gave chase. Perceiving Jones's approach, the merchantmen hastened for shore, while HMS *Serapis* and HMS *Countess of Scarborough* left the convoy to do battle with Jones's three ships.

The *Pallas* and the *Alliance* engaged the *Countess of Scarborough.* The *Bonhomme Richard* and the *Serapis* fought one on one. Commanded by Capt. Richard Pearson, the *Serapis* presented Jones a formidable opponent—a new frigate with double decks, a copper

John Paul Jones captures the *Serapis. (Courtesy of the National Archives and Records Administration)*

bottom, and 54 cannons, including 20 18-pounders that favored the *Sera-pis* by almost a three-to-two ratio in firepower over the *Bonhomme Richard*. The *Serapis*'s cannon fire tore at the *Bonhomme Richard*'s rigging and hull and silenced its battery of 12-pounders; two of Jones's nine-pounders exploded on firing and killed most of their crewmen. As the ships maneuvered, a miscalculation by Pearson allowed the *Bonhomme Richard* to ram the *Serapis*'s stern. The *Serapis* wheeled about. Hit by a sudden wind, both ships ended together, bow to stern and stern to bow. The *Serapis*'s jibstay shattered and plummeted to the *Bonhomme Richard*'s deck, where Jones and his helmsman lashed it to their mizzenmast as Jones's crew strained to bind the two ships together with grappling hooks.

The enemy crews battled ferociously, breaking apart occasionally to douse fires in their ships' riggings. The ships' closeness prevented use of their main batteries, but the *Serapis*'s bow guns fired point-blank. Blood and bits of flesh splattered the *Bonhomme Richard*'s bulkheads below decks, where the wounded and dying writhed in agonizing pain and fear of death from sudden bursts of flame or cascades of water rushing through gaps in the hull. As night fell under a full moon the battle raged on. The *Alliance* suddenly appeared off the *Serapis*'s bow. But instead of aiding Jones, the errant Landais ignored his ally's frantic signals and, apparently quite purposefully, fired repeated broadsides into the *Bonhomme Richard*'s stern, killing nearly 20 crewmen. Confronting their now hopeless state, Jones's officers urged him to surrender. In this crucial instant, one of Jones's sail-

The *Bon Homme Richard* and the *Serapis* lock in deadly combat. *(Courtesy of the National Archives and Records Administration)*

ors lobbed a grenade that fell into a hatchway on the *Serapis* and ignited powder on the gundeck. The resulting monstrous explosion killed 20 men and shivered the *Serapis*'s mainmast. Assuming certain defeat, Pearson struck his colors and conceded victory to Jones. Moments later the *Countess of Scarborough* surrendered to the *Pallas*.

The brutal four-hour battle exacted a horrendous human toll. Of the *Bonhomme Richard*'s crew of more than 300, one-half lay dead; the *Serapis*, with an equivalent crew, suffered 49 dead and 68 wounded. No commander in previous naval history had endured such heavy losses in battle as Jones took and still achieved victory. During the two days following the battle, Jones's carpenters repaired the *Serapis*. But, finding the *Bonhomme Richard* beyond salvaging, Jones transferred his crew to the *Serapis*, abandoned his flagship, and sunk its ravaged hulk in the waters off Flamborough Head. Accompanied by the *Pallas* and the *Countess of Scarborough*, Jones sailed for Holland. Hounded by eight British warships and impeded by rough weather, Jones's tiny fleet reached the safety of Texel's harbor on October 3.[21]

THE PHILADELPHIA STORY

Although obliged to abandon the expedition to Canada—the "irruption" that Lafayette and Conway were to have led the year before—delegates to the Continental Congress continued to harbor a desire to "emancipate" Canada and to bring it into the nation. The idea had revived when William Lee of the Committee for Foreign Affairs learned that Nova Scotia wished to be "adopted." The new alliance with France appeared to make an expedition to Nova Scotia possible. But General Washington and President Laurens opposed any such expedition involving France out of concern that, when the war terminated, the French would retain control of Canada—an undesirable outcome for the United States. The commander and the president prevailed, and as 1779 began Congress reluctantly relinquished hope of bringing Canada into the union.[22]

Concerned that some opposition to the alliance with France existed among the congressmen, the French minister to the United States, Rayvenal de Gérard, pressured the Continental Congress to issue a declaration of commitment. In mid-January, Congress finally complied by unanimously approving a resolution committing the United States to conclude no truce or peace with Great Britain without France's prior approval. Questions remained, however. Gérard wanted Congress to decide on specific peace terms, especially relating to navigation on the Mississippi River and the postwar status of the Floridas, as these were major concerns of the Spanish. During the second half of February, the Continental Congress appointed a committee to draft peace terms and report

This portrait of John Paul Jones was painted by Charles Wilson Peale. *(Courtesy of Anne S. K. Brown Military Collection)*

their conclusions, which the delegates discussed and debated for months, with the critical point of disagreement involving fishing rights off the Newfoundland banks, a major issue for the New England states. Finally, in mid-August, Congress issued instructions for the as yet unappointed official who would negotiate a peace settlement. The main nonnegotiable issues were recognition of American independence and, with French approval, the immediate withdrawal of British troops. The instructions also recommended the official's abiding by "the advice of our allies."[23]

The most difficult and crucial issue that the Continental Congress struggled with throughout 1779 was the ongoing problem of financing the war. As the year began, Congress approved an issue of $50 million in bills of credit, and within about six weeks, the members approved issuance of another $10 million, followed by approval of yet another issue of $5 million on April 1. Clearly, a financial crisis impended. By May, the crisis required Congress's attention for three days of each week. The Continental Congress issued a request to the states to fulfill their quotas of $45 million and appointed a committee to devise the best means of procuring a foreign loan. War profiteers and speculators compounded the crisis; consequently, Congress made a modest effort to reform procurement processes and to prosecute those suspected of malfeasance.

Finally, on September 1, the Continental Congress moved toward fiscal responsibility by resolving not to issue bills of credit exceeding a total of $200 million; two days later, the delegates voted not to approve even the $40 million this first resolution allowed beyond the $160 million already issued. In mid-September, the new congressional president, John Jay, issued a letter to accompany copies of these resolutions to be sent to the states in which he forcefully contended that the Continental Congress would never renege on paying its debts. Such resolutions and letters, however, did not establish fiscal soundness—that required revenues. And so, in October Congress decided to levy a $15 million assessment on the states between February 1 and October 1, 1780, and to charge interest on inadequate payments. The delegates also chose Henry Laurens as their agent to negotiate a loan from Holland.[24]

The Patriot women of Philadelphia, determined to make a contribution to the Revolutionary effort, during the spring and summer of 1779 put together a campaign to collect funds for the Continental troops—the most widely known and ably organized political action by women during the entire war. Esther De Bert Reed, wife of the Pennsylvania Council's president, and Sarah Franklin Bache, daughter of Benjamin Franklin, established and led this campaign. They were joined by such other worthies as the wives of Robert Morris and Benjamin Rush. The women collected money by going door to door. In early July, Reed wrote to General Washington that they had collected a total of 300,000 paper dollars. Washington suggested the money be deposited with the Bank of the United States, but Reed politely demurred, responding that the women's intention had been to provide the troops with something special and they preferred exchanging the paper for hard specie in order to give each soldier $2 to use as he pleased. Washington rejected that idea on the grounds that his men had always received paper (and that of doubtful value) and might grow discontented if they now got some hard money; he also worried that his men might squander the hard specie on hard liquor. Finally, the women determined to use the money to buy linen cloth to be made into shirts for the soldiers. Following Reed's death in the fall of 1780, Bache assumed leadership of the Ladies' Association; she sent Washington 2,200 shirts in December of that year. Before her death, Reed had published a broadside, *The Sentiments of an American Woman,* which, through references to Old Testament women, female monarchs, and heroines like Joan of Arc and Boadicea, provided a philosophic platform for rousing patriotic women throughout the United States to mobilize in support of the Glorious Cause.[25]

THE TRIALS OF BENEDICT ARNOLD

In addition to the Continental Congress's deliberations, residents of Philadelphia found distraction in the fortunes of Benedict Arnold. In May 1778, General Washington had appointed Arnold, whose injuries prevented his further involvement in combat, as governor and military commandant in Philadelphia; Arnold had assumed his duties in late June after Gen. Sir Henry Clinton evacuated the city. In early February 1779, Joseph Reed, a former aide to Washington and member of Congress, brought charges against Arnold before the Continental Congress on behalf of the Pennsylvania Council and the state. Arnold evoked disfavor because of his arrogance and tactlessness and his social involvement with Loyalist sympathizers in Philadelphia, including Peggy Shippen, and he was suspected of and then charged with misuse of equipment, workmen, and facilities available to him as commandant and with financial speculation. The charges were vague, however, and Washington and others came to Arnold's defense. Delayed for months, the court-martial of Arnold finally convened in December, with the charges reduced to minor offenses because of lack of documentation. Arnold conducted his own defense. In January 1780, he was found guilty of two minor offenses, punishable by a reprimand from Washington, but Arnold was enraged at not receiving complete exoneration.[26]

In the meantime, Arnold's private life changed dramatically. He ardently courted Peggy Shippen, and the two were married in the Shippens' Philadelphia home on April 8. Within the first month of his marriage, Arnold began the secret contacts that would eventuate in his treason, sending Philadelphia Loyalist Joseph Stansbury as his representative to contact Maj. John André, General Clinton's aide, in New York City and to inform André that Arnold was prepared to offer his services to Clinton. In late May, Arnold provided Clinton with information on Washington's movements to prove his good faith and to aid Clinton's assessment of Washington's plans. Disgruntlement over the charges brought against him and the later court-martial solidified Arnold's intentions. The American hero, had determined to turn traitor long before 1779 ended with his commander-in-chief moving the Continental army into winter quarters at Morristown, New Jersey. The day following Christmas, however, General Clinton shifted his view southward, left 10,000 British troops to garrison New York under command of Lt. Gen. Wilhelm von Knyphausen, and set sail with 8,500 troops and a fleet of 14 ships commanded by Adm. Marriot Arbuthnot—their goal: conquest of the South.[27]

CHRONICLE OF EVENTS

1779

January 1: At George III's instructions, Gen. Sir Henry Clinton has assured the Continental Congress, which continues to accuse Gen. John Burgoyne of breach of faith, that the king has ratified the Saratoga Convention. But Congress disputes Clinton's assurances, contends that the king's signature may be forged, and reneges on fulfilling the convention's terms. Burgoyne's army is sent from Boston to Rutland, with Virginia their final destination.

Washington's conferences with the Continental Congress result in abandoning a plan to "emancipate Canada" that had been revived when William Lee of the Committee for Foreign Affairs received word that Nova Scotia wished to be "adopted" by the United States. Washington and Laurens oppose becoming involved in an invasion with the French (proposed by Lafayette) out of concern that the French will retain control of Canada after the war.

January 2: Congress decides to cancel some bills of credit previously issued and substitute a new issue of $50 million.

January 6: While marching to join Campbell at Savannah, General Prevost, with a force of about 2,000 that includes some Indians, attacks Fort Morris (now Sunbury), Georgia, where Maj. Joseph Lane, left in control when Howe left for Savannah, mounts a defense with only 200 men.

January 9: After Prevost moves his artillery into place to bombard Fort Morris, Lane surrenders—he has 11 casualties to Prevost's four. Their victory here and at Savannah gives the British effective control of eastern Georgia.

January 10: The French minister to the United States, Conrad Alexandre Rayvenal de Gérard, who has discovered some opposition to the alliance with France among members of the Continental Congress, again requests a declaration of positive commitment from Congress.

January 11: With congressional approval of his request to return to France to explore possibilities for service there or in Canada, the Marquis de Lafayette sales aboard the *Alliance,* the only Continental navy warship commanded by a Frenchman, Capt. Pierre Landais, who has orders to join John Paul Jones in France.

January 14: Responding to Gérard's request, the Continental Congress unanimously approves a resolution pledging that the United States will not conclude a truce or peace with Great Britain "without the formal consent of their ally first obtained."

January 23: The Continental Congress adopts a proposal made by Washington to generate enlistments in the Continental army, approving payment of a bounty not to exceed $200 to anyone who reenlists and bounties to all new recruits in amounts decided by Washington but not to exceed $200.

In London, Lord Germain writes orders to General Clinton detailing the 1779 campaign, whose initial strategy is restoring a government loyal to the king and Parliament in at least one of the former colonies. The campaign's military objective is to drive Washington's army into the upper Hudson Highlands, sever New York from the other colonies, reestablish a royal government there, and use it as a stepping stone toward doing the same in the Middle Colonies.

January 29: Joined with Col. Archibald Campbell at Ebenezer, Georgia, Gen. Augustine Prevost sends Campbell to capture Augusta. South Carolina Loyalists join Campbell's force en route, and they occupy the abandoned town without firing a shot, giving the British control of the state capital established in 1776 and of the entire state.

January 31: The conferences between Washington and the Continental Congress conclude.

February 2: Washington leaves Philadelphia for Middlebrook, while Martha Washington remains behind as a guest in Henry Laurens's home.

February 3: On behalf of the Pennsylvania Council, of which he is president, Joseph Reed, former aide to Washington and former member of the Continental Congress, brings charges against Gen. Benedict Arnold before Congress. But the eight charges Reed states against him are vague, and Washington and many members of Congress come to Arnold's defense.

Gen. William Moultrie has been sent by General Lincoln to prevent Port Royal Island, South Carolina, from being captured by two companies of British troops under Major Gardiner dispatched by General Prevost. Moultrie occupies Beaufort with 300 Charleston militia, only 10 Continentals, and three field pieces posted on both sides of the road that Gardiner must use for his approach. The British troops scurry for cover in a nearby woods following an American cannon blast, and an hour of fighting ensues. The Americans run out of ammunition as they realize the British are in retreat, and dragoons give chase, taking a few prisoners. Moultrie has 30 casualties.

The Continental Congress authorizes issuing another $5 million in bills of credit.

February 4: The Continental Congress authorizes General Washington to take whatever measures he deems expedient to reform and enhance the Continental army and to resolve all questions of officer rank below brigadier while adhering to the rules Congress established by an act of November 24, 1778.

Encouraged by Benjamin Franklin, John Paul Jones has been lobbying the French minister of marine Gabriel de Sartine, who informs Jones in Paris that an East Indiaman named the *Duc de Duras* has been purchased for his use.

February 5: George Rogers Clark has survived at Kaskaskia. Although he has only 100 men because of expired enlistments, Clark has regained support of the French locals with the aid of Father Gibault. Deciding to attack Vincennes, Clark sends Lt. Col. John Rogers with 40 men up the Ohio and Wabash Rivers in the *Willing,* a row-galley armed with two four-pounder cannons and four swivel guns, to prevent a British retreat down the Mississippi River.

February 6: Clark begins an overland march from Kaskaskia with 127 men, nearly half of them French, to attack the British at Vincennes, some 180 miles distant.

The Continental Congress fetes French Minister to the United States Gérard with a banquet and a public entertainment to celebrate the one-year anniversary of the two countries' alliance.

February 8: The Continental Congress resumes discussion of whether to seek d'Estaing's help in the defense of Georgia and South Carolina and to compensate France for such aid. Gerard brings President John Jay the secret news that Spain appears likely to join the Franco-American alliance.

February 10: At Carr's Fort, Georgia, Col. Andrew Pickens leads about 350 men from his South Carolina militia and Capt. John Dooley's Georgia militia in attacking 200 Loyalists commanded by Lt. Col. John Hamilton, Scottish patrician and veteran of the Battle of Culloden. Although victorious, Pickens learns that Loyalist Colonel Boyd approaches with 700 men marched from North Carolina to join Hamilton, and he breaks away to attack Boyd.

February 13: Colonel Boyd crosses the Savannah River near Kettle Creek and encamps, unaware that Pickens has made a full circle, crossed the river, and occupies his rear.

February 14: At Kettle Creek, the Patriots attack Boyd from three directions simultaneously, Pickens leading the center, Dooley the right, and Lt. Col. Thomas Clark the left. Though surprised, Boyd's Tories form and hold fast for nearly an hour, then falter and run when Boyd falls mortally wounded. The Tories suffer 40 dead and 75 captured; the Patriots, 32 casualties.

February 15: French minister Gérard urges the Continental Congress to decide on definitive peace terms and emphasizes the question of navigation rights on the Mississippi River and the future status of Florida—both major concerns of Spain as a potential ally.

February 18: Having slogged through swamps and muddy prairies, spending two days ferrying across the Little Wabash River, and then being impeded by heavy rains, floods, and hunger, George Rogers Clark's rugged band arrives at the Wabash River.

February 19: The Continental Congress again authorizes issuing $5 million in bills of credit.

February 23: Clark's exhausted and half-starved men reach the lake at Horseshoe Plain. A captured Frenchman informs Clark that Lt. Col. Henry Hamilton remains unaware of his approach but has been reinforced by 200 Indians. Hoping to frighten the British into surrender, Clark sends the Frenchman to Vincennes with the message that residents who favor the United States should remain in their homes and those who favor Great Britain should join Hamilton inside Fort Sackville because Clark's force will overwhelm the fort during the night. At sunset Clark deploys his men in two divisions to march toward Vincennes in such a way as to create the appearance of greater strength than he actually has. Clark marches his men straight through Vincennes and begins the assault on the fort.

The committee appointed to define final peace terms—Gouverneur Morris of New York, Thomas Burke of North Carolina, John Witherspoon of New Jersey, Samuel Adams of Massachusetts, and Meriwether Smith of Virginia—reports to the Continental Congress. They specify one absolute condition: Great Britain's recognition of American independence. They also propose six other terms as ultimatums: the establishment of minimum boundaries, the evacuation of British forces from the United States, a grant of fishing rights off Newfoundland, free navigation on the Mississippi to the United States' southern boundary, free commerce with one or more ports south of that boundary, and the ceding of Nova Scotia to the United States if the allies so request. In addition, the committee proposes six negotiable terms. Congress begins to discuss the report.

February 24: By dawn the accuracy of Clark's Long Rifles has exacted such a heavy toll in dead and wounded that Fort Sackville's cannons lie silent. At about 9:00 A.M., Clark demands Hamilton's surrender; Hamilton refuses. The firing resumes for two hours, and Hamilton offers to surrender if the terms are agreeable. Clark and Hamilton agree to confer at the French church. The conference recesses, and Hamilton returns to the fort to consult his officers. An Indian raiding party returns to Vincennes with two American captives and some scalps, and Clark's men kill or capture all of them. Clark has the prisoners brought to a site in clear view from the fort and executed with tomahawks to unnerve the Indians inside the fort. Hamilton returns to negotiations. Clark detests Hamilton as a reputed buyer of American scalps and insists on unconditional surrender or he will attack mercilessly. At day's end, Hamilton capitulates.

February 25: Hamilton surrenders himself, his troops, and Fort Sackville to Clark, presenting Clark with a stunning victory and virtual control of the entire Illinois territory.

February 26: Gov. William Tryon with 600 troops raids Horseneck Landing, Connecticut, defended by only two cannons and 150 militia commanded by Gen. Israel Putnam. The raiders destroy the local salt works, three vessels in the port, and a store and plunder the village, taking about 200 cows and horses. Putnam barely escapes capture by riding breakneck down a hill so steep that the British troops fear following him. Tryon has two dead and 20 captured.

March 3: Maj. Gen. Benjamin Lincoln has sent a unit of troops to the eastern bank of the Savannah River across from Augusta, another unit to the Black Swamp, and a third under Gen. John Ashe to Briar Creek. In response, Lt. Col. Archibald Campbell has withdrawn his troops from Augusta, crossed the Savannah River, and marched for Savannah after burning a bridge at Briar Creek to impede Ashe's pursuit. While Ashe's men rebuild the bridge 900 infantry, grenadiers, dragoons, and militia sent by Gen. Augustine Prevost cross the creek above Ashe's camp and attack the Americans' rear. Ashe's Continentals open fire, frightening his militiamen into flight; the deserted Continentals retreat in disorder. The combined American force suffers 150

dead and 11 officers and 162 soldiers captured. The British have only 16 casualties.

March 9: With state bounties limiting enlistments in the Continental army, the Continental Congress amends its January 23 resolution to repeal the sections on both new enlistments and reenlistments and to substitute a general $200 bounty for anyone enlisting for the duration of the war. States that award an equivalent or larger bounty will receive credit for Congress's bounty. Congress also calls on the states to raise 80 battalions for the infantry, with each state having a quota, and encourages the states to raise recruits through drafts.

March 12: President Jay sends copies of the March 9 resolutions to the states with a letter that expresses his view that the 1779 campaign, "if successful, will be the last," so that the states should be forthcoming in doing whatever they can to ensure its success.

March 23: The Continental Congress has mostly settled the issue of boundaries to be stipulated in any peace treaty but now bogs down in considering a resolution on fishing rights off Newfoundland, with delegates from the New England and southern states voicing conflicting views.

March 29: The Continental Congress unsuccessfully urges gravely imperiled South Carolina and Georgia to enlist 3,000 slaves, paying their owners $1,000 per slave, and granting those slaves who perform well their freedom and $50 at the war's end.

April 1: Yet again, the Continental Congress authorizes the issuance of $5 million in bills of credit.

Many Cherokee led by Chief Dragging Canoe and other chiefs who have rejected treaties, negotiated in 1777, that would have ceded their lands east of the Blue Ridge Mountains and north of the Nolichucky River, move to Chickamauga, Georgia, and continue waging war. Believing that the Cherokee resistance endangers the southern frontier, Virginia and South Carolina send out a force of 900 men under command of Col. Evan Shelby that begins a monthlong series of raids destroying Indian villages along the Clinch, Powell, and Tennessee Rivers.

April 3: At Madrid, the Spanish foreign minister Count Floridablanca offers Spain's services to Great Britain to mediate between Britain and France and remain neutral in exchange for Gibraltar, suggesting that Gibraltar is the price for Spain's not allying with France.

April 8: Benedict Arnold and Peggy Shippen are married at the Shippens' Philadelphia home.

April 12: Meeting in Aranjuez, Spain, ministers of France and Spain sign the Convention of Aranjuez, which commits both nations to pursue the war with Great Britain until the Britain cedes Gibraltar to Spain. The convention specifies that France recover Senegal and Dominica, be awarded Newfoundland, and be readmitted to India as war objectives, and it forbids either nation to make a separate peace with Great Britain. But the alliance does not obligate Spain to recognize American independence because Floridablanca sees an independent United States as a menace to Spain's possessions in Louisiana and Mexico and a bad example to Spain's colonies. Spain's slight financial aid to the United States reflects a desire for revenge and for possible recovery of Gibraltar, Florida, Jamaica, and other territories lost to Great Britain in previous wars.

April 21: With Washington's approval, 550 Continentals commanded by Col. Gose Van Schaik have marched 180 miles to attack the Onondaga Indian settlement as Onondaga Creek, New York. Although most of the Indians escape into the woods, Van Schaik's troops destroy the Onondaga Castle of 50 houses, kill more than 20 warriors, take 37 prisoners, among them a white man, seize 100 guns, and pillage the settlement, destroying whatever they cannot carry away. They then return to Fort Schuyler.

April 23: South Carolina governor John Rutledge, given nearly dictatorial powers to protect the state following the disastrous American defeats in Georgia, has bolstered the militia so that Gen. Benjamin Lincoln now has about 4,000 troops. He crosses the Savannah River to attack Augusta.

April 24: After numerous delays, a fleet commanded by Adm. Marriot Arbuthnot, assigned to replace Adm. John Byron as commander of the British navy in America, sails out of Torbay for New York with British and German soldiers to reinforce General Clinton's army. But the delayed sailing means that Arbuthnot will arrive too late to greatly aid the 1779 campaign.

April 29: Countering Lincoln's move, General Prevost crosses the Savannah River with 2,500 men, apparently to attack Charleston. Col. Alexander McIntosh, defending Purysburg with only 220 men, quickly withdraws to join Gen. William Moultrie's 1,000 troops at Black Swamp, with Prevost in pursuit. Thinking his post indefensible, Moultrie withdraws to Coosahatchie Bridge.

May 5: A British force commanded by Adm. Sir John Collier and Maj. Gen. Edward Matthews embarks

from New York to raid Virginia ports and hinder Virginia's supplying of commodities to the rebels and shipping of tobacco that supports foreign credit.

May 9: Collier's and Matthews's expedition reaches Hampton Roads and overwhelms Fort Nelson, constructed to protect Portsmouth, Norfolk, and the navy yard at Gosport. Fort Nelson's 100 soldiers commanded by Maj. Thomas Matthews hastily withdraw toward the Dismal Swamp.

May 10: Philadelphia Loyalist and shopowner Joseph Stansbury meets in New York with Maj. John André, aide to Gen. Henry Clinton, at the behest of Benedict Arnold, who has asked him in utmost secrecy to inform the British of Arnold's intention to offer his services to Clinton. Arnold requests and receives assurances that the British are committed to victory, and Clinton accepts his offer, indicating that Arnold can best serve in his Philadelphia post.

May 11: Without opposition, the Collier-Matthews expedition invades Portsmouth, Norfolk, Gosport, and Suffolk, capturing large quantities of naval supplies, ordnance, and tobacco, while also seizing or burning 137 vessels and many privateers—£2 million worth of damage altogether. Their mission completed with no loss of life, the British sail for New York.

To counter Lincoln's move against Augusta, Prevost crosses the Ashley River and pushes toward Charleston with 900 troops, following hard after Moultrie's retreat to the city. Moultrie has only about 600 men now, but Governor John Rutledge joins him with some militiamen. They find the Charlestonians terrorized by Prevost's approach. Prevost cuts the city off and demands its surrender. Moultrie receives full command from the governor's council and insists Charleston will not surrender.

May 12: In the early morning, Moultrie sends Prevost a message canceling surrender negotiations. It is undelivered because Prevost has learned from an intercepted letter that Lincoln is again in South Carolina and has withdrawn two miles south of Charleston to James Island to avoid being trapped between Moultrie's and Lincoln's forces.

May 13: Prevost moves his troops to Johns Island, adjoining James Island, and begins to build fortifications on the mainland at Stono Ferry.

May 21: The Continental Congress has devoted three days each week to discussing solutions to the financial crisis and now passes a resolution calling on the states to pay their $45 million in quotas by January 1, 1780.

May 23: To indicate the seriousness of his intentions, Benedict Arnold sends Clinton information on Washington's movements, aiding Clinton's attempts to evaluate Washington's plans.

May 26: Realizing that their resolution requesting the states pay their quotas will require the states to impose burdensome taxes (a major cause of the American Revolution), the Continental Congress adopts a persuasive address by John Dickinson to include with the copies of the resolution being sent out.

May 28: Uncertain about the states' response to the resolution about financial quotas, the Continental Congress appoints a committee to study and report on the best means of negotiating a foreign loan, the size of the loan, and the use of the loan money.

At Kingsbridge, where the Post Road crosses the Spuyten Duyvil Creek, Clinton assembles 6,000 British and Hessian grenadiers, light infantry, and dragoons plus units of Tory troops, including Simcoe's Queen's Rangers, in preparation for an attack on West Point.

May 30: Clinton's force at Kingsbridge embarks on the Hudson River aboard 70 sailing vessels and 150 flat-bottomed boats.

June 1: Clinton's expedition captures the unfinished fort at Stony Point on the Hudson's west bank after the mere 40 Americans posted there torch the blockhouse and flee. From this vantage point and their boats in the Hudson, the British cannonade Fort Lafayette at Verplanck's Point across the river. Although protected by palisades, abatis, and a double ditch, the fort's vastly outnumbered garrison of 70 North Carolina troops is forced to surrender. Clinton's men immediately begin work on completing the fort at Stony Point. Capture of these two forts gives the British control over Kings Ferry, a vital link in the Americans' communications system and gateway to the Hudson River Highlands, sited only 12 miles below West Point.

June 12: The Continental Congress receives a memorial from a group of officers strongly advocating Washington's original recommendation of lifetime compensation for officers and submits it to the Committee of Conference with instructions "to report speedily" on the compensation issue.

Headquartered at New Windsor, New York, Washington instructs Maj. Henry Lee to gather intelligence on the strength of British forces and fortifications at Stony Point.

June 16: Prevost begins evacuating his troops to Savannah, leaving behind a rear guard of 900 men on Johns Island under command of Lt. Col. John Maitland.

In London, the Spanish ambassador delivers a declaration to Lord Germain that lists numerous alleged grievances, deplores the "rejection" of Spain's offer to mediate the war, and concludes that Spain now must use any available means to procure "justice." On the basis of the Convention of Aranjuez, the North ministry accepts the statement as effectively a declaration of war.

June 17: In response to the Spanish declaration, Lord John Cavendish proposes in Parliament a resolution that all of Great Britain's forces be mobilized for war with Spain and France. Although the resolution fails by a two-to-one vote, other members of Parliament join with Cavendish to advocate abandoning the war in America to muster Britain's strength against the Bourbon allies.

June 18: Preparing to attack Barbados, Admiral d'Estaing captures St. Vincent.

June 20: Gen. Benjamin Lincoln leads a force from Charleston across the Ashley River to march 18 miles for a dawn attack on Maitland's garrison on James Island. Assuming a simultaneous attack by Moultrie on Johns Island to prevent Maitland from moving reinforcements across Stono Inlet, Lincoln divides his force into a right wing of Carolina militia under Brig. Gen. Jethro Sumner and a left wing of Continentals under Brig. Gen. Isaac Huger. Against fierce resistance they struggle to the abatis encircling Maitland's fortifications. Lincoln orders a bayonet attack, which founders as the British rally. Maitland brings reinforcements from Johns Island, and Prevost arrives with reinforcements. Lincoln orders a retreat. Maitland's troops move to assault the withdrawing Americans, but Colonel Mason leads a force of Virginians against them, and Lincoln's men escape to safety. Lincoln's inept attack leaves him with 146 casualties and 155 missing men, mostly deserters. Maitland suffers 129 casualties and one missing man.

June 23: Now having the needed ships for a planned withdrawal, Maitland begins a retreat to Beaufort (Port Royal Island).

Troops led by Maj. Gen. John Sullivan arrive at Wyoming Valley, Pennsylvania, en route to join with Brig. Gen. James Clinton's troops at Tioga. Their combined force of 3,700 will march north into the territory of the Six Nations of the Iroquois Confederation.

June 28: American troops led by Col. John Twiggs capture an entire unit of 40 British grenadiers under Captain Muller at Hickory Hill, Georgia.

June 30: Commodore la Motte-Picquet arrives at Martinique from Brest with five ships giving the French naval superiority in the Leeward Islands.

Gen. James Clinton sends word to General Sullivan that his entire force with all needed supplies and boats is assembled at Otsego Lake and awaits further orders from Sullivan about their rendezvous, but Sullivan lingers at Wyoming Valley, claiming he needs more provisions.

July 1: Virginia governor Thomas Jefferson issues a proclamation that states, in effect, that all residents still regarding themselves as subjects of the British Crown must appear before him at a meeting in council to be processed for deportation from the commonwealth.

July 2: Some 360 British and German troops commanded by Lt. Col. Banastre Tarleton raid Pound Ridge, 20 miles northeast of White Plains, intent on capturing patriot Maj. Ebenezer Lockwood and overwhelming Col. Elisha Sheldon's 90 soldiers of the 2nd Continental Dragoons encamped nearby. Apprised of their approach, Sheldon forms his men but must retreat before Tarleton's advance. Then local militiamen fire on Tarleton's men from behind fences and buildings, forcing their retreat, with Sheldon in pursuit. The retreating British torch the church and some houses in Pound Ridge; they have two casualties to Sheldon's 10.

July 3: With a fleet of transports and a convoy of four ships of war assembled at Whitestone, New York, Sir Henry Clinton embarks 2,600 troops (a division of guards and jaegers under Brig. Gen. Garth and a second division of Royal Welch Fusiliers, Hessians, and Tories under Gen. William Tryon) for raids on Connecticut to penalize its residents for supplying the Continentals and harassing British commerce.

July 4: While Admiral Byron is absent on convoy duty, Count d'Estaing captures the British island of Grenada in the West Indies.

July 5: Clinton's expedition anchors in the harbor at New Haven, Connecticut. Garth's division marches on the town with four cannons and meets modest opposition, while Tryon's division disembarks at East Haven and routs the opposition. The two divisions join together. Garth desires to burn New Haven but is content with plundering the town and taking about 40 prisoners before reboarding the ships to sail for Fairfield.

July 6: Reinforced by a squadron brought from France by Adm. Frangois-Joseph, count de Grasse, d'Estaing battles inclusively with the British but prevents their retaking Grenada.

July 8: Clinton's raiders occupy the abandoned village of Fairfield, plunder the houses, and burn two churches, 83 houses, more than 100 barns and storehouses, two schools, the jail, and the courthouse.

July 9: Modestly attacking procedural problems affecting procurement, the Continental Congress approves a resolution requesting state executives to examine the conduct of persons involved with the supply departments and to remove those suspected of misconduct or to have them prosecuted at the Continental government's expense.

July 10: Washington has given Brig. Gen. Anthony Wayne command of the Light Infantry, and both generals have personally reconnoitered British fortifications at Stony Point. General Lee's able scout Capt. Allen McLane has even gained entry to the fort and provides detailed descriptions of the fortifications. Wayne has also stationed soldiers in hiding to observe the garrison's daily routine for several days. Local residents reveal the existence of a sandbar that troops could use to cross the marsh separating Stony Point from the mainland. Convinced by all this intelligence that the Light Infantry can capture Stony Point in a night bayonet attack, Washington orders Wayne to make needed preparations.

The Spanish government authorizes Count Bernardo de Gálvez, the 23-year-old governor of Louisiana and Florida stationed at New Orleans, to make raids on British colonial towns along the Mississippi River to weaken the British presence in the West.

July 11: Clinton's raiders descend on Norwalk, which is unsuccessfully protected by only 50 militiamen. The raiders loot the town and torch 130 houses, more than 100 barns and storehouses, two churches, more than 20 shops and mills, and five vessels. With their mission completed, they return to New York.

July 15: With McLane's and other units secreted near Stony Point to intercept anyone approaching the fort, General Wayne has mustered his main force at Donderburg. He issues strict orders. His men must overrun two lines of abatis and several artillery batteries and then overwhelm the garrison of 625 commanded by Col. Henry Johnson. Wayne divides his troops into two main columns. The right column, accompanied by Wayne, will attack from the south; the left, from the north, with Maj. Hardy Murfree's men (alone having loaded muskets) to detach themselves and attack the center with sustained fire to create the impression the Americans are attacking straight-in en masse. Heading the right column will be 150 handpicked men under Lt. Col. François de Fleury; the left column, a similar group under Maj. John Stewart—both groups armed with axes to destroy the abatis in advance of the attacking columns. Accompanying each group of axeman are 20 fearless men commanded by Lt. George Knox on the right and Lt. James Gibbons on the left assigned to hurtle through the openings the axeman make and engage the British defenders in hand-to-hand combat. Wayne's advance begins at half past 11 and reaches the morass below Stony Point by midnight.

Off Newfoundland, the American frigates *Providence, Queen of France,* and *Ranger* become lost in dense fog and sail into the midst of a British squadron of 150 merchant ships convoyed by a single 74-gun ship of the line and several smaller vessels. Capt. John Rathburn successfully feigns that his *Queen of France* is a British man-of-war and captures several of the merchant ships. Commodore Abraham Whipple's *Providence* fires several broadsides at the escort ship *Holderness,* which surrenders with a large booty of allspice, coffee, sugar, and rum. The American frigates seize 11 ships with total cargoes worth $1 million to return with them to Boston.

July 16: Approaching the fort at Stony Point, General Wayne's right column traverses the muddy road crossing the marsh as the left column struggles across the sandbar. Although Murfree's men begin to fire before the columns are in position to attack, their ruse succeeds. Finding the gap in the British defenses described by McLane, they race through. The Continentals capture the summit, and Johnson surrenders. One British soldier escapes by diving into the Hudson and swimming to HMS *Vulture.* But the victorious Americans turn the fort's 15 cannons on the ship and Verplanck's Point, securing their win, which has cost 15 dead and 80 wounded against British losses of 63 dead, 70 wounded, and 543 captured along with 31 tents and copious supplies. Wayne sends word of the victory to Washington.

July 17: General Washington inspects the fort at Stony Point, concludes that its defense will require too many men, and consequently orders Wayne to remove all the guns and stores and then to destroy the fortifications. Alarmed at the loss, General Clinton ends the Connecticut raids, assembles all available men-of-war, and sails up the Hudson intent on retaking Stony Point.

July 18: With destruction of the fortifications at Stony Point completed, Wayne abandons the site, leaving Clinton free to effect its reoccupation and refortification.

July 19: Joseph Brant sets out from Oquaga, New York, with a band of Mohawk and Tories to travel down the Delaware River and raid villages on its banks. Brant posts most of his men at Grassy Brook and with 60 Indians and 27 Tories heads for Minisink.

July 20: During the early morning, Brant and his men enter Minisink and set fire to buildings. The village's residents awake and flee. Brant's men take several prisoners, plunder houses and barns, round up the cattle, and return to Grassy Point with their loot.

July 21: Without consulting the Continental Congress, Massachusetts sends 1,000 militia under Generals Solomon Lovell and Peleg Wadsworth toward Castine at Maine's Penobscot Bay, where Col. Francis MacLean commands about 800 British troops from Halifax in constructing a base from which to protect lumber shipments for the Halifax shipyards, interdict American military expeditions against Nova Scotia, and send raiding parties into the nearby countryside. At the same time, Capt. Dudley Saltonstall of the Continental navy also sets sail with 2,000 troops aboard a flotilla of three navy ships, three brigantines, 13 privateers, 20 Massachusetts transports, and a New Hampshire vessel to attack the British base from sea.

July 22: Lt. Col. Benjamin Tusten commands 149 militiamen, joined by Col. John Hathorn and a group of his men, in pursuing Brant. Coming upon a campsite that reveals that Brant's force is larger than expected, the men override Tusten's and Hathorn's objections and move ahead to discover Brant's men approaching a ford across the Delaware. Trying to intercept Brant's men, the militiamen become outmaneuvered and outflanked. The ensuing massacre leaves only 30 of their original force as survivors, including Hathorn.

July 25: The Lovell-Wadsworth-Saltonstall expedition reaches Castine, but MacLean's troops hold them off.

July 28: General Lovell's militiamen land on the southwest side of the peninsula in Penobscot Bay to prepare at attack on MacLean, but Saltonstall refuses them naval support until they take the fort, which is not possible.

July 31: Gen. John Sullivan finally leaves Wyoming Valley, Pennsylvania, with 2,300 men to join with

Gen. James Clinton at Tioga for a vindictive expedition against the Six Nations of the Iroquois Confederation.

August 3: The French minister to the United States, Chevalier Anne-César de la Luzerne, and his staff and John Adams, returning from his sojourn as commissioner to the French court, arrive in Boston aboard a French frigate. Luzerne and his staff lodge at John Hancock's home.

August 5: Brig. Gen. John Glover's cavalry and local militia skirmish with Oliver De Lancey's Loyalists, taking five prisoners, at Morrisania, the Morris family seat in the Bronx.

August 11: In conjunction with Sullivan's expedition, Col. Daniel Brodhead sets out from Pittsburgh with 600 men to march up the Allegheny River and destroy Indian villages on the Pennsylvania frontier. Sullivan's army arrives at Tioga.

August 13: Comdr. Sir George Collier arrives at Castine with ten vessels and 1,600 soldiers to reinforce MacLean. Their position now untenable, the American militiamen hold a council of war, reboard their ships to retreat up the Penobscot River, then abandon and burn the ships, and flee into the Maine woods. The Americans suffer a loss of 474 men, plus all their ships, against the British loss of only 13 men.

August 14: John Paul Jones sets sail from L'Orient, France, with his fleet flying American flags but funded by France and mostly commanded by French officers, who are resentful of serving under him. The name of Jones's command ship, *Bonhomme Richard,* honors his benefactor Benjamin Franklin, whose *Poor Richard's Almanac* is highly popular in France. Included in the fleet are the American frigate *Alliance* captained by Pierre Landais, the frigate *Pallas,* the brig *Vengeance,* and the cutter *Le Cerf.* Their destination is the west coast of Great Britain.

Following months of debate, the Continental Congress approves final instructions for the as yet unnamed minister who will negotiate a peace settlement. They insist on the immediate withdrawal of British forces and advise the minister to be guided by counsel of the allies, knowledge of American interests, and "your own discretion, in which we repose the fullest confidence."

August 18: Inspired by Wayne's victory at Stony Point, Maj. Henry (Light Horse Harry) Lee has persuaded Washington to let him attack Paulus Hook. Its central redoubt, 150 feet in diameter, is protected by a ditch, abatis, and six heavy cannons; there are four cannons and a blockhouse to the northeast and a block-

house to the southeast and at the drawbridge—all garrisoned by 200 British troops and 48 Hessians under command of Maj. William Sutherland. Lee assembles 100 men of Woodford's Virginia brigade under Maj. Jonathan Clark as his right wing; two Maryland companies under Capt. Levin Handy as his center; and 100 of Muhlenberg's Virginians and Capt. Allen McLane's dismounted dragoons commanded by himself as his left. Planning to attack shortly after midnight, Lee leaves Paramus, New Jersey, at 10:30 A.M. on a feigned foraging expedition but is misled by a guide and delayed for three hours; about half of the Virginians under Major Clark, disgruntled at being subordinate to Lee, abandon the march.

August 19: Lee finally arrives at Paulus Hook at 4:00 A.M. and orders a bayonet attack. Clark and the residue of his Virginians form the right; Capt. Robert Forsyth, McLane's men, and the other Virginians, the right; Handy's men form a reserve. Lt. Michael Rudolph and Lt. Archibald McAllister lead a "suicide" squad that succeeds in hacking a route through the abatis, allowing Clark's men to surge through into

John Sullivan was ordered by Washington to subdue the Iroquois. *(From* The Pictorial Field Book of the Revolution, *2 vols., by B. J. Lossing. New York: Harper Brothers, 1851 and 1852.)*

the circular redoubt, with Forsyth and McLane close after. They bayonet 50 of the defenders and take 158 prisoners, while enduring only two killed and three wounded. With the British garrison in New York alerted by the battle sounds, Lee is forced to withdraw to Douwe's Ferry, where boats were to await him but have left on the assumption the battle was called off because Lee is hours late. Lee orders his men on to New Bridge with Col. Abraham Van Buskirk's men in pursuit and dispatches a rider to request Lord Stirling, at New Bridge with 300 men, to send aid. Capt. Thomas Catlett arrives with the 50 Virginians who had abandoned the attack; a detachment sent by Lord Stirling also appears; they repulse an attack on Lee's left by Van Buskirk. Lee reaches safety in New Bridge with his prisoners by one o'clock.

August 22: Gen. James Clinton arrives at Tioga to join Sullivan for their expedition against the Indians. While awaiting him, Sullivan has raided and burned nearby Iroquois villages, some comprised of log houses with glass windows, whose inhabitants took flight.

August 25: Long delayed, the British fleet with 3,000 reinforcements for Clinton commanded by Adm. Marriot Arbuthnot, whose orders are to succeed Admiral Byron as naval commander in America, arrives in New York Harbor.

August 26: Sullivan and James Clinton leave most of their heavy baggage and 250 men to guard their base at Tioga, Pennsylvania, and begin to march up the Chemung River.

August 27: In a show of support for the Franco-American alliance, Spanish governor Count Bernardo de Gálvez sets out from New Orleans with a motley force of Spanish regulars, militia, Americans, and Indians to attack British outposts at Manchac Post, Baton Rouge, and Natchez.

August 29: The Iroquois and their British allies have built a hidden breastwork on a hilltop above the path Sullivan's and Clinton's troops follow along the bank of the Chemung River to ambush the advancing Americans. In wait are two battalions of rangers, a detachment of the 8th Regiment, and about 200 Tories commanded by Capt. Walter N. Butler, and about 500 Indians under Joseph Brant. But the American advance, led by Maj. James Parr and three companies of Morgan's riflemen, discovers the breastwork and returns to halt the main column. Troops under Brig. Gen. Enoch Poor circle behind the enemy to cut off their retreat, and American artillery bombards the breastworks. After

a brief skirmish the British and Indian forces flee into the woods.

September 1: Confronted with depreciating bills of credit, the Continental Congress adopts fiscal responsibility with a resolution to authorize issuing bills of credit not to exceed $200 million in total. Since to date issuances amount to $160 million, only $40 million more may be authorized.

September 3: The Continental Congress now resolves to authorize no further bills of credit at all unless absolutely necessary. Gérard sends Congress notice of his intention to step down as French minister, as his successor, Chevalier Anne-César de la Luzerne, arrived in Boston in August.

After sailing on their own, the *Alliance* and the *Pallas* rejoin Jones's fleet off the coast of Scotland, and the squadron turns south to attack Leith, the port of Edinburgh, and the major coal-shipping port at Newcastle-on-Tyne.

September 4: With the destruction completed of Catherine's Town, Pennsylvania, two Iroquois villages, and the surrounding croplands, Sullivan's troops burn Appletown and march toward Kindaia.

September 5: About 150 dismounted Continental dragoons in a surprise attack led by Maj. Benjamin Tallmadge against 500 Tories at Lloyd's Neck, Long Island, capture most of the garrison without loss of a single man and then return with their prisoners to their base at Shippan Point near Stamford, Connecticut.

September 7: Gálvez captures Manchac Post at the northern boundary of the Isle of Orleans, giving him control of a water route traversing the Amite River and Lakes Maurepas, Ponchartrain, and Borgne into the Gulf of Mexico.

September 8: Ignoring appeals from Washington for aid against Newport or New York, Admiral d'Estaing instead responds to requests to help Charleston by the marquis de Bretigny and southern Patriots such as John Rutledge and William Moultrie. He arrives at the mouth of the Savannah River with 22 warships, 10 frigates, and other vessels carrying 4,000 troops.

September 10: Sullivan's expedition destroys the major Iroquois settlement at Canandaigua, New York, notable for its 23 frame houses. Sullivan's men need two days to lay waste the extensive cornfields and orchards. With the task finished, they head for Genesee, the Six Nations' "grand capital."

September 13: Maj. John Butler and his troops ambush the 26 men led by Lt. Thomas Boyd in Sullivan's advance guard as they approach to reconnoiter Genesee, killing 22 while capturing Boyd and an Oneida guide named Hanyerry. The Iroquois with Butler hack Hanyerry to pieces and, after Boyd has been questioned, torture him until he dies.

D'Estaing lands 3,000 troops at Beaulieu, preparing to lay siege to Savannah.

The Continental Congress unanimously approves sending out with the resolution on bills of credit issuance copies of a letter by Pres. John Jay touting the confederacy's credibility and future capability of reimbursing purchasers of the bills and asserting the surety of the revolution's success and Congress's never reneging on its debts. Congress authorizes the printing of 200 copies of the letter in English and 200 in German.

September 14: Col. Daniel Brodhead and his men return to Pittsburgh from a month's raids on the Iroquois in conjunction with Sullivan's expedition. They have burned 10 villages and destroyed crops during their 400-mile march; their booty includes many furs.

Sullivan's expedition enters the abandoned Iroquois capital of Genesee. Sullivan's men burn the entire town and destroy all the crops, foreshadowing a bleak winter for the Iroquois, as Genesee is the Six Nations' granary. Sullivan begins the trek back to Wyoming Valley through the Cayuga Indian territory along Lake Ontario's southern shore.

September 16: Gen. Benjamin Lincoln's force joins d'Estaing and Pulaski's legion at Savannah, providing a total force of 1,350 American troops from Georgia, Virginia, and South Carolina. Certain of victory, d'Estaing requests Gen. Augustine Prevost's surrender. Prevost requests a 24-hour truce to prepare articles of capitulation, and d'Estaing agrees. During the truce, Prevost strengthens his fortifications, and Col. John Maitland brings reinforcements from Port Royal. Prevost informs d'Estaing that he intends to defend Savannah "to the last extremity."

September 21: Count Bernardo de Gálvez captures Baton Rouge, the former French outpost ceded to the British in 1763 as part of West Florida. In surrendering, the British also grant Gálvez control of Natchez and other outposts on the Mississippi River.

John Paul Jones captures two British brigs off the coast at Flamborough Head and discovers that a large fleet of merchant ships with a British frigate lies at the mouth of the Humber River.

The Chevalier de la Luzerne arrives in Philadelphia to succeed Gérard as French minister to the United States.

September 23: With heavy cannons brought ashore from his ships to bombard the British garrison, d'Estaing, along with Lincoln and Pulaski, begins the siege of Savannah. Quarrels between the French admiral and the American officers, as well as the approaching hurricane season, threaten their effort.

Off the English coast at Flamborough Head, John Paul Jones's *Bonhomme Richard* along with the French cruisers *Pallas* and *Alliance* sight 41 British merchant ships headed north and give chase. Seeing their approach, the merchantmen run toward shore, leaving their convoy ships HMS *Serapis* and HMS *Countess of Scarborough* to do battle. The *Pallas* and the *Alliance* engage the *Countess of Scarborough,* while the *Bonhomme Richard* closes with the *Serapis,* a new double-decked frigate under command of Capt. Richard Pearson. The ships maneuver, with each attempting to cross and fire into the other's bow; but Pearson miscalculates, allowing Jones's crippled ship to ram his stern. The *Serapis* wheels about; a sudden wind gust pivots both ships together, stern to bow and bow to stern. The battle continues into the night. With their situation hopeless, Jones's officers urge him to surrender. But at this crucial moment one of his sailors lobs a grenade into a hatchway on the *Serapis,* igniting powder on the gundeck that sets off a huge explosion. Captain Pearson, now convinced the battle is lost, strikes his colors. Half of the *Bonhomme Richard's* crew of more than 300 have perished in the four-hour battle, while the *Serapis* is left with 49 dead and 68 wounded. The *Countess of Scarborough* surrenders to the *Pallas.*

September 25: Jones's carpenters repair the *Serapis,* but the *Bonhomme Richard* proves beyond salvaging, so Jones abandons ship and scuttles the hulk.

September 27: The Continental Congress appoints John Jay minister to Spain, with a mandate to negotiate treaties of alliance and commerce—and hopes of securing a loan. Pursuing compromise between Jay's and John Adam's supporters, Congress also names Adams as chief negotiator of treaties of peace and commerce with Great Britain following the Revolution.

September 28: The Continental Congress elects Samuel Huntington of Connecticut to succeed Jay as president.

Jones sets sail for Holland in the *Serapis,* accompanied by the *Pallas* and the *Countess of Scarborough.*

September 30: Having devastated the Indian settlements bordering Cayuga Lake during his march homeward, Sullivan arrives in Wyoming Valley, Pennsylvania, without a single hostage. He reports that his expedition laid waste 40 Indian towns, an estimated 160,000 bushels of corn, vast orchards, and huge quantities of other vegetables and crops.

October 3: Although delayed by rough weather and pursued by eight British warships, John Paul Jones's small squadron arrives safely in harbor at Texel, Holland.

October 4: Simon Girty, former interpreter for the Continental army who defected to the British, and his Indian band ambush Col. David Rogers on the Ohio River, killing 57 of the 70 men with Rogers and capturing 600,000 Spanish dollars and various supplies Rogers was taking to Fort Pitt from New Orleans.

American sappers have dug trenches, inching closer to Savannah, and sited three battering cannons and 14 mortars that now begin to bombard the city. The bombardment's ferocity prompts Prevost to request a truce so that women, children, and the aged can be evacuated, but, disillusioned by Prevost's past actions, d'Estaing and Lincoln reject the request.

October 6: The Continental Congress decides to levy a monthly assessment of $15 million on the states between February 1 and October 1, 1780, and to charge interest for insufficient payments.

October 9: The American cannonade at Savannah has mostly sailed over the British lines to devastate the city, leaving Prevost confident of his defenses and hopeful. The impatient d'Estaing demands an immediate attack or he will depart. Before dawn an allied force of 3,500 French troops and 600 Continentals begins an attack across a swamp and into Prevost's right, with 350 Charlestown militia striking at his center. Under Maitland's command, the British right rakes the attackers with grapeshot and musket fire. Repulsed and shattered by the British defense, the allied force withdraws, having endured 700 French and 450 American casualties. British casualties number fewer than 150 out of a force of 3,200.

October 11: Concerned about d'Estaing's presence at Savannah, Georgia, Gen. Sir Henry Clinton orders withdrawal of the British garrison of 3,000 troops from Newport, Rhode Island, to New York.

After ineffective surgery to remove grapeshot from his groin during the attack on Savannah, Count Kazimierz Pulaski dies aboard the USS *Wasp*.

Count Kazimierz Pulaski led a cavalry charge in Savannah. *(From The Pictorial Field Book of the Revolution, 2 vols., by B. J. Lossing. New York: Harper Brothers, 1851 and 1852.)*

October 20: Admiral d'Estaing and his troops return to their ships and set sail from Savannah, forcing Lincoln to retreat to Charleston.

October 21: The Continental Congress chooses Henry Laurens to serve as its agent in negotiating a loan from Holland.

October 22: New York's Provincial Congress, convened in Kingston, approves a law mandating the forfeiture and sale of property belong to Loyalists and declares Governor Lord Dunmore, General Tryon, Oliver DeLancey, and 57 others to be public enemies. (Some 15,000 New Yorkers serve with the British army, and another 8,000 serve in Loyalist militias.)

November 1: The Continental Congress authorizes Henry Laurens to negotiate treaties of amity and commerce with Holland.

November 2: An Act of Emancipation authored by George Bryan, with a preamble ostensibly written by Thomas Paine, is introduced into the Pennsylvania Assembly, for which Paine becomes clerk on this day.

November 7: At Jeffer's Neck, New York, the marquis de la Rouerie Tuffin, a French aristocrat volunteer known to the Americans as Col. Charles Armand and now in command of Pulaski's Legion, surprises and captures Maj. Mansfield Bearmore and five other Tories.

November 25: Parliament convenes in London, with George III's opening speech appealing for unity, denouncing the Americans for an "unprovoked war," and urging support for his ministers and their prosecution of the war. Opposition in both the Commons and the Lords heaps criticism on the government's policies and failures in Ireland, the West Indies, the Mediterranean, and America, but the North ministry manages to survive no-confidence votes in both houses.

December 1: Washington arrives at Morristown, New Jersey, to set up his army's winter quarters, using the home of the widowed Mrs. Theodosia Ford as his headquarters.

December 5: Washington's guard arrives in Morristown, and his troops begin to arrive and to fell trees for building huts.

December 23: Following months of delay, the court-martial of Gen. Benedict Arnold reconvenes, with three of the original 14 jurors having been replaced, Col. John Laurence in charge of prosecution, and Arnold conducting his own defense. Since available documents do not support many of the original charges, the court can accuse Arnold of only minor offenses and three serious offenses for which proof is lacking.

December 26: Convinced by the British victory at Savannah that conquering the South is now opportune, General Clinton places Lt. Gen. Wilhelm von Knyphausen in charge of a garrison of 10,000 British troops in New York and, with the remainder of his army and Lord Charles Cornwallis as second in command, sets sail for Charleston, South Carolina. Ninety transports carry his 8,500 troops from eight British and five Hessian regiments and five Tory corps, along with artillery and cavalry. Adm. Marriot Arbuthnot commands the convoy of five ships of the line and nine frigates bearing 5,000 crewmen and 650 guns.

EYEWITNESS TESTIMONY

1779

'Tis an honour to serve the bravest of nations,
And be left to be hang'd in their capitulations—
Then scour up your mortars
And stand to your quarters,
'Tis nonsense for Tories in battle to run,
They never need fear sword, halberd, or gun;
Their hearts should not fail 'em,
No balls will assail 'em
Forget your disgraces
And shorten your faces,
For 'tis true as the gospel, believe it or not,
Who are born to be hang'd, will never be shot.

Philip Freneau, from "Sir Harry's [Clinton] Invitation,"
1779, in Fred Lewis Pattee, The Poems of Philip
Freneau, *vol. 2, p. 8.*

There is something in this concealment of papers that looks like an embezzlement. Mr. Deane came so privately from France, that he even concealed his departure from his colleague Arthur Lee, of which he complainers by a letter in my office, and consequently the papers are not in his hands; and had he left them with Dr. Franklin he would undoubtedly have taken the Doctor's receipt for them, and left nobody to *"guess,"* at what Mr. Deane meant by a *safe place:* A man may leave his own private affairs in the hands of a friend, but the papers of a nation are of another nature, and ought never to be trusted with any person whatever out of the direct line of business. This I conceive to be another reason which justifies Congress in not granting Mr. Deane an audience of leave and departure till they are assured where those papers are.... Many accidents might have happened by which those papers and accounts might have been totally lost, the secrets got into the hands of the enemy, and the possibility of settling the expenditure of public money forever prevented. No apology can be made for Mr. Deane, as to the danger of the seas, or their being taken by the enemy, in his attempt to bring them over himself, because it ought always to be remembered that he came in a fleet of twelve sail of the line.

Thomas Paine, from "To the Public on Mr. Deane's
Affair," January 8, 1779, in Van der Weyde,
The Life and Works of Thomas Paine,
vol. 3, pp. 315–316.

... I like all but your Reflections against the King of France for assisting us. In my Mind, the Coming to the Relief of an innocent People under the bloody Oppression your Ministers were exercising over them ... was not only what any Prince had a Right to do for the sake of common Humanity, but was a magnanimous & heroic Action, that is admired at present by the wise & good through all Europe, and will hand his Name down with Glory to Posterity! Our different ways of thinking in this particular will not however diminish our private Friendship. . . .

Benjamin Franklin, from a letter written at Passy, France,
January 25, 1779, to David Hartley, in Barbara B.
Oberg, ed., The Papers of Benjamin Franklin, *vol.*
28, p. 420.

You wish to know how I live. It is in a fine House, situated in a neat Village, on high Ground, half a Mile from Paris, with a large Garden to walk in. I have abundance of Acquaintance, dine abroad Six Days in seven. Sundays I reserve to dine at home, with such Americans as pass this Way; & I then have my Grandson Ben, with some other American Children from his School: If being treated with all the Politeness of France, & the apparent Respect & Esteem of all Ranks, from the highest to the lowest, can make a Man happy, I ought to be so. . . .

Benjamin Franklin, from a letter written at Passy, France,
January 25, 1779, to his former housekeeper Margaret
Stevenson, in Barbara B. Oberg, ed., The Papers of
Benjamin Franklin, *vol. 28, pp. 422–423.*

A fine Clear and Pleasant morning in the Afternoon Col. Webbs Regt. Mutined and turned out under Arms but was with Some Difficulty Desperst but at Night they all paraded and Marched to the Barracks where my men was and about forty of my Regt Joined them after talking some time with them they all Disperst and Remained in peace the night.

Col. Israel Angell, diary entry of January 28, 1779,
while encamped at Warren, Rhode Island, in Angell,
The Diary of Colonel Israel Angell,
pp. 47–48.

This morning [February 2], his Excellency General Washington set off from Philadelphia to join the army in New Jersey. During the course of his short stay, (the only relief he has enjoyed from service since he first entered into it,) he has been honored with every mark of esteem which his accomplished fortitude as a soldier, and his exalted qualities as a gentleman and a citizen, entitle him to. Among other instances, he was welcomed at his first coming by an address from the Supreme Executive Council and the magistrates of the city, and politely entertained by the President of Congress, the President of the State, his Excellency the Minister of France, Don Juan Marrailles, a Spanish gentleman of distinction and amiable character.... The council of this State being desirous of having his picture in full length, requested his sitting for that purpose, which he politely complied with, and a striking likeness was taken by Mr. Peale of Philadelphia. The portrait is to be placed in the Council Chamber. Don Juan Marrailles has ordered five copies, four of which, we hear, are to be sent abroad....

From the Pennsylvania Packet, *February 4, 1779, in Frank Moore, compiler,* The Diary of the American Revolution, *p. 342.*

In Conversation with Dr. Franklin, in the Morning I gave him my Opinion, of Mr. Deanes Address to the People of America, with great Freedom and perhaps with too much Warmth. I told him that it was one of the most wicked and abominable Productions that ever sprung from an human Heart. That there was no safety in Integrity against such a Man. That I should wait upon The Comte de Vergennes, and the other Ministers, and see in what light they considered this Conduct of Mr. Deane. That if they, and their Representatives in America, were determined to countenance and support by their Influence such Men and Measures in America, it was no matter how soon the Alliance was broke. That no Evil could be greater, nor any Government worse, than the Toleration of such Conduct. No one was present, but the Doctor and his Grandson.

John Adams, from diary entry of February 8, 1779, in L. H. Butterfield, ed., Diary and Autobiography of John Adams, *p. 345.*

The Wisdom of Solomon, the Meekness of Moses, and the Patience of Job, all united in one Character, would not be sufficient, to qualify a Man to act in the Situation in which I am at present—and I have scarcely a Spice of either of these Virtues.

On Dr. F. the Eyes of all Europe are fixed, as the most important Character, in American Affairs in Europe. Neither L. nor myself, are looked upon of much Con-

sequence. The Attention of the Court seems most to F. and no Wonder. His long and great Rep[utation] to which L's and mine are in their infancy, are enough to Account for this. His Age, and real Character render it impossible for him to search every Thing to the Bottom, and L. with his privy Council, are evermore, contriving. The Results of their Contrivances, render many Measures more difficult.

John Adams, from diary entry of February 9, 1779, in L. H. Butterfield, ed., Diary and Autobiography of John Adams, *p. 347.*

I have the pleasure of acquainting you, that the Congress have been pleased to honor me with a Sole Appointment to be their Minister Plenipotentiary at this Court, & I have just received my Credentials. This Mark of public Confidence, is the more agreable to me, as it was not obtained by any Solicitation or Intrigue on my Part, nor have I ever written a Syllable to any Person in or out of Congress, magnifying my own Services or diminishing those of others.

Benjamin Franklin, from a letter written at Passy, France, February 13, 1779, to his cousin Jonathan Williams, Jr., in Barbara B. Oberg, ed., The Papers of Benjamin Franklin, *vol. 28, p. 522.*

Be it remembered that my good wife constantly milks the cow night and morning, and, besides her daily house work, makes us cheeses, besides supplying our family with plenty of good cream and two poor families with milk. Here is prudence and industry.

Christopher Marshall, from a diary entry written in Lancaster, Pennsylvania, March 7, 1779, in Marshall, Extracts from the Diary of Christopher Marshall, *p. 213.*

Whereas it hath been represented, that many of those Soldiers, who have been induced, from divers Motives, to desert their Corps, and are now dispersed in different Parts of these States, having seen their Error, would be glad to return to their Duty, but are restrained by the Fear of Punishment: In order to quiet such Apprehensions, and give them an Opportunity to put in Practice these good Dispositions, I do hereby proclaim full PARDON to all who shall rejoin their respective Corps by the first of May next; at the same Time declaring to all such who ... shall persist in their Delinquency ... that the most effective Measures shall be pursued to detect them . . . and to bring them to the most rigorous and exemplary Punishment.

George Washington, from a proclamation issued at Middle Brook, New Jersey, March 10, 1779, in John C. Fitzpatrick, ed., The Writings of George Washington, *vol. 14, pp. 222–223.*

When I am on the subject of Southern affairs, you will excuse the liberty I take, in saying, that I do not think measures sufficiently vigorous are persuing for our defence in that quarter. Except the few regular troops of South Carolina, we seem to be relying wholly on the militia of that and the two neighbouring states. These will soon grow impatient of service and leave our affairs in a very miserable situation. No considerable force can be uniformly kept up by militia. . . .

Alexander Hamilton, from a letter written at Middlebrook, New Jersey, March 14, 1779, to John Jay, president of the Continental Congress, in Harold C. Syrett, ed., The Papers of Alexander Hamilton, *vol. 2, p. 18.*

The policy of our arming Slaves is, in my opinion, a moot point, unless the enemy set the example; for should we begin to form Battalions of them, I have not the smallest doubt . . . of their following us in it, and justifying the measure upon our own ground; the upshot then must be, who can arm fastest, and where are our Arms? besides, I am not clear that a discrimination will not render Slavery more irksome to those who remain in it; most of the good and evil things of this life are judged by comparison; and I fear a comparison in this case will be productive of much discontent in those who are held in servitude. . . .

George Washington, from a letter written at Middle Brook, New Jersey, March 20, 1779, to Henry Laurens, in John C. Fitzpatrick, ed., The Writings of George Washington, *vol. 14, p. 267.*

Yesterday [March17], the anniversary of Saint Patrick, the tutelar saint of Ireland, was celebrated in New York by the natives of that kingdom, with their accustomed hilarity. The volunteers of Ireland, preceded by their band of music, marched into the city, and formed before the house of their colonel, Lord Rawdon, who put himself at their head, and, after paying his compliments to his Excellency General Knyphausen, and to General Jones, accompanied them to the Bowery,

where dinner was provided, consisting of five hundred covers. . . . The soldierly appearance of the men, their order of march, hand in hand, being all natives of Ireland, had a striking effect.

From the New York Gazette and Weekly Mercury, *March 22, 1779, in Frank Moore, compiler,* The Diary of the American Revolution, *p. 353.*

The astonishing activity and success of Joseph Brant's enterprises and the important consequences with which they have been attended give him claim to every mark of our regard and which you think will be pleasing to him. What has occurred to me as most likely to gratify him has been done, and enclosed herewith you will receive a commission signed by His Majesty appointing him a colonel of Indians and on board of the *Three Brothers* storeship is a box with prints taken from Lord Warwick's picture of him which he was particularly pleased with, some of which you will send into his nation. . . .

Lord George Germain, from a letter written at Whitehall, London, April 16, 1779, to Gen. Frederick Haldimand, governor of Quebec, in K. G. Davies, ed., Documents of the American Revolution, *vol. 17, p. 105.*

Joseph Brant attempted to convince the Six Nations to support the British. *(From* The Pictorial Field Book of the Revolution, *2 vols., by B. J. Lossing. New York: Harper Brothers, 1851 and 1852.)*

The Zeal, The Ardor, the Enthusiasm, the Rage, for the new American Connection I find is much damped, among the Merchants since the loss of so many of their East and West India Ships. The Adventurers to America, have lost so many Ships, and have received so small Returns for those which went Safe, that they are discouraged, and I cannot learn that any Expeditions are formed or forming for our Country.—But all their Chagrine cannot prevent the Court from continuing the War. The Existence of french Commerce and Marine both, are at Stake, and are wholly undone without American Independance.

The Pleasure of returning home is very great, but I confess it is a Mortification to leave France. I have just acquired enough of the Language to understand a Conversation, as it runs at a Table at Dinner, or Supper, to conduct all my Affairs myself. . . .

John Adams, from diary entry of April 22, 1779, in L. H. Butterfield, ed., Diary and Autobiography of John Adams, *pp. 360–362.*

. . . I do not doubt but before the receipt of this you will he[ar] of my late success against Governor [Henry] Hamilton at post St. Vincenne. That gentleman with a body of men possessed himself of that post on the 15th of December last, . . . where he was to be joined by 200 Indians from Mechetemachinoi and 500 cherokees chiccasaws and other nations. With this body he was to penetrate the Ohio to Fort Pitt, sweeping Kentuckey on his way. . . . I made all the preparations I possibly could for the attack, . . . but in the height of the hurry a Spanish merchant who had been at St. Vincenne arrived and gave the following intelligence. That Mr. Hamilton had weakened himself by sending his Indians against the Frontiers and to block up the Ohio. . . . My situation and circumstances induced me to fall on the resolution of attacking him before he could collect his Indians again. I was sensible the resolution was as desperate as my situation but I saw no other probability of securing the country. . . . I marched across the country with 130 men being all I could raise after leaving this place garrisoned by the militia. . . . The inclemency of the season high waters &c. seemed to threaten the loss of the expedition. When within three leagues of the Enemy it took us five days to cross the drowned lands of the Wawbash river having to wade often upwards of two leagues to our breast in water. Had not the weather been warm we must have perished. But on the evening of the 23d we got on dry land in sight of the Enemy

and at seven Oclock made the attack before they knew any thing of us. The Town immediately surrendered with joy and assisted in the seige. . . .

George Rogers Clark, from a letter written at Kaskaskia, Illinois, to Patrick Henry, April 29, 1779, in Julian P. Boyd, ed., The Papers of Thomas Jefferson, *vol. 2, pp. 256–257.*

After Dinner walked out, with C[aptain John Paul] Jones and [Captain] Landais to see Jones's Marines—dressed in English Uniform, red and white. A Number of very active and clever Serjeants and Corporals are employed to teach them the Exercise, and Maneuvres and Marches &c.

After which Jones came on Board our ship.

This is the most ambitious and intriguing Officer in the American Navy. Jones has Art, and Secrecy, and aspires very high. You see the Character of the Man in his uniform, and that of his officers and Marines, variant from the Uniforms established by Congress. Golden Button holes, for himself—two Epauletts—Marines in red and white instead of Green.

Eccentricities, and Irregularities are to be expected from him—they are his Character, they are visible in his Eyes. His voice is soft and still and small, his Eye has keenness, and Wildness and Softness in it.

John Adams, from a diary entry written while in harbor at Lorient, France, May 13, 1779, in L. H. Butterfield, ed., Diary and Autobiography of John Adams, *pp. 370–371.*

15. Went and visited Wilson Peale's pictures, a curious collection.

17. Saw our Poll [runaway servant], but she flew away, so could not speak [to] her.

20. Col. Proctor's regiment marched out of [the] city for [the] back woods.

21. Signed [a] petition to Congress respecting our Continental money.

Christopher Marshall, Philadelphia merchant and Quaker, complete diary entries for May 15–21, 1779, in Marshall, Extracts from the Diary of Christopher Marshall, *p. 217.*

After you have very thoroughly completed the destruction of their settlements; if the Indians should shew a disposition for peace, I would have you to encourage it, on condition that they will give some decisive evidence of their sincerity by delivering up some of the principal instigators of their past hostility into our hands. Butler, Brandt, the most mischievous of the tories that have joined them. . . .

*George Washington, from his instructions for the
expedition against the Six Nations written at
Middle Brook, New Jersey, May 31, 1779, to Maj.
Gen. John Sullivan, in John C. Fitzpatrick, ed.,*
The Writings of George Washington,
vol. 15, p. 191.

The honor which the General Assembly have been pleased to confer on me, by calling me to the high office of Governour of this commonwealth, demands my most grateful acknowledgments. . . . In a virtuous and free state, no rewards can be so pleasing to sensible minds, as those which include the approbation of our fellow citizens. My great pain is, lest my poor endeavors should fall short of the kind expectations of my country; so far as impartiality, assiduous attention, and sincere affection to the great American cause, shall enable me to fulfil the duties of any appointment, so far I may, with confidence undertake; for all beyond, I must rely on the wise counsels of the General Assembly, and of those whom they have appointed for my aid in those duties. . . .

*Thomas Jefferson, from his message accepting election as
governor of Virginia, June 2, 1779, in Julian P. Boyd,
ed.,* The Papers of Thomas Jefferson, *vol. 2,
pp. 277–278.*

The Military character you mention [General Gates] is without principle honor or honesty. He is a child of vanity, and a dupe to his foolish ambition. So little does he know his own standing that he conceives himself in the high road to the cheif Command, while he is dispised by the great part of the continent. Had he been content with his good fortune he would have been respected, but aspiring to dignities for which he had no talents he has lost even the consequence that his good fortune gave him. I both pity and despise him, and shall give myself no further trouble about him; unless he throws out openly personal reflections; in that case I shall speak to him in language he is not fond of.

*Nathanael Greene, from a letter written at Camp Smiths
Clove, New York, June 21, 1779, to Col. Ephraim
Bowen, in Richard K. Showman, ed.,* The Papers
of General Nathanael Greene, *vol. 4,
pp. 173–174.*

Should America continue firmly to oppose the tyranny of Britain, says a correspondent, may not the promise of the present day sanctify a conjecture, that in a few years the rising grandeur of this new world will invite every man from Europe who is not attached to it by landed property or other similar cause. There is a field opening for every species of manufacture, art and science, trade and commerce. Finely situated for the encouragement and cultivation of business, every artificer will fly here and transplant with him the art he possesses. Secure from tyrannical burdens, he will apply himself assiduously in the prospect of reaping what he sowed, and will assist in rearing this new republic to a pitch of grandeur superior, perhaps, to any state now existing.

From the New Hampshire Gazette, *June 29, 1779,
in Frank Moore, compiler,* The Diary of the American
Revolution, *pp. 367–368.*

The measure you propose of putting deserters from our Army to immediate death would probably tend to discourage the practice. But it ought to be executed with caution and only when the fact is very clear and unequivocal. I think that that part of your proposal which respects cutting off their heads and sending them to the Light Troops had better be omitted. Examples however severe ought not to be attended with an appearance of inhumanity otherwise they give disgust, and may excite resentment rather than terror. . . .

*George Washington, from a letter written at New
Windsor, New York, July 9, 1779, to Maj. Henry Lee,
in John C. Fitzpatrick, ed.,* The Writings of
George Washington, *vol. 15, p. 388.*

. . . the Enemy went immediately to plundering, and at seven oClock set fire to the Town [Fairfield] which now remains a heap of rubbish—This Village was large & as beautiful as any in this State, the buildings large and elegant, to add to the misfortune, the Inhabitants had not time to remove any of their property, so that many reputable worthy familys are reduced from a State of affluence to Poverty. . . . [A] Child of three years old was taken from the Arms of its mother and thrown into the flames. . . . [A] Man who was taken prisoner being an old Countryman, was rolld in a sheet bound fast—the sheet wet with rum and set fire to . . . several negro servants who were left to take care of their Masters property were burnt alive for attempting to extinguish the fire. . . .

Samuel Blachley Webb, Continental regimental commander and former aide to General Washington, from a letter written at Wethersfield, Connecticut, July 11, 1779, to his half brother Joseph Barrell, in Worthington Chauncey Ford, ed., Correspondence and Journals of Samuel Blachley Webb, *vol. 2, p. 180.*

I regret the loss of the two places of public worship at Fairfield which took fire unintentionally by the flames from other buildings, and I gave strict orders and set guards for the preservation of that burnt at Norwalk; but it is very difficult where the houses are close and of very combustible materials, of boards and shingles, to prevent the spreading of the flames.

Maj. Gen. William Tryon, from a letter written in New York, July 20, 1779, to Gen. Sir Henry Clinton, in K. G. Davies, ed., Documents of the American Revolution, *vol. 17, pp. 164–165.*

Perhaps the fittest condition any countries can be in to make a peace, calculated for duration, is when neither is conquered, and both are tired. The first of these suits England and America. I put England first in this case, because she began the war. And as she must be and *is* convinced of the impossibility of conquering America, and as America has no romantic ideas of extending her conquests to England, the object on the part of England is lost, and on the part of America is so far secure, that, unless she unwisely conquers herself, she is certain of not being conquered; and this being the case, there is no visible object to prevent the opening a negotiation. But how far England is disposed thereto is a matter wholly unknown, and much to be doubted.

Thomas Paine, from "Peace, and the Newfoundland Fisheries," July 21, 1779, in Van der Weyde, The Life and Works of Thomas Paine, *vol. 4, pp. 35–36.*

. . . To the encomium he [Brig. Gen. Anthony Wayne] has deservedly bestowed on the officers and men under his command, it gives me pleasure to add that his own conduct, throughout the whole of this arduous enterprise, merits the warmest approbation of Congress. He improved upon the plan recommended by me and executed it in a manner that does signal honor to his judgment and to his bravery. In a critical moment of the assault he received a flesh wound in the head with a musket-ball; but continued leading on his men with unshaken firmness.

George Washington, from a letter about the Battle of Stony Point written at New Windsor, New York, July 21, 1779, to the president of the Continental Congress, in John C. Fitzpatrick, ed., The Writings of George Washington, *vol. 15, p. 447.*

We think ourselves justified in Governor [Henry] Hamilton's strict confinement, on the general principle of National retaliation. To state to you the particular facts of British Cruelty to American prisoners, would be to give a melancholy history from the capture of Colo. Ethan Allen, at the beginning of the war, to the present day. . . . I with pleasure do you the justice to say that I believe these facts to be very much unknown to you, as Canada has been the only Scene of your service, in America, and, in that quarter, we have reason to believe that Sr. Guy Carleton, and the other officers commanding there, have treated our prisoners (since the instance of Colo. Allen) with considerable lenity. . . . I would only observe to you, Sir, that the confinement, and treatment, of our officers, soldiers, and Seamen, have been so rigorous, and

Anthony Wayne was a general in the Continental army. *(From* The Pictorial Field Book of the Revolution, *2 vols., by B. J. Lossing. New York: Harper Brothers, 1851 and 1852.)*

cruel, as that a very great proportion of the whole of those captured in the course of this war, and carried to Philadelphia, while in possession of the British army, and to New York have perished miserably, from that cause only; and that this fact is as well established, with us, as any historical fact which has happened in the course of the War. . . .

Governor Thomas Jefferson, from a letter written in Williamsburg to William Phillips, July 22, 1779, in Julian P. Boyd, ed., The Papers of Thomas Jefferson, *vol. 3, pp. 44–45.*

Nothing can exceed the spirit and intrepidity of our brave countrymen in storming and carrying the British fortress at Stony Point. It demonstrates that the Americans have soldiers equal to any in the world; and that they can attack and vanquish the Britons in their strongest works. No action during the war, performed by the British military, has equalled this *coup de main.* The generosity shown by our men to the vanquished, when the parties of our enemy are repeating their savage barbarities . . . is unexampled. How much more honorable and manly is it to carry fortresses sword in hand, than to burn defenceless towns, and distress unarmed citizens, and even women and children? What action has Clinton to boast of, this campaign, that may be compared with this master-piece of soldiership by General Wayne? . . . .

From the New Hampshire Gazette, *July 27, 1779, in Frank Moore, compiler,* The Diary of the American Revolution, *pp. 384–385.*

Was our strength equal to the attempt, Offensive opperations would be by far the most eligible. This would give security to our Sea Coast and by finding the Enemy employ[ed] at Home, prevent their depradations abroad.

But it is a melancholy truth that we have neither force or ammunition to commence any serious opperations against New York or its dependencies except Ver Planks Point; and therefore we must accommodate our measures to our circumstances.

To attempt to insult the Enemy in New York, in such a secure position as they are, strongly fortified withal, and of superior strength, aided by a large Naval force, will be madness in the extreme.

Nathanael Greene, from a letter written at West Point, New York, July 27, 1779, to George Washington, in Richard K. Showman, ed., The Papers of General Nathanael Greene, *vol. 4, p. 269.*

Many and pointed orders have been issued against that unmeaning and abominable custom of *Swearing,* notwithstanding which, with much regret the General observes that it prevails, *if possible,* more than ever; His feelings are continually wounded by the Oaths and Imprecations of the soldiers whenever he is in hearing of them.

George Washington, from general orders issued at West Point, New York, July 29, 1779, in John C. Fitzpatrick, ed., The Writings of George Washington, *vol. 16, p. 13.*

. . . The General has the pleasure to inform the army that on the night of the 18th instant, Major Lee at the head of a party composed of his own Corps and detachments from the Virginia and Maryland lines, surprized the Garrison of Powles Hook and brought off a considerable number of Prisoners with very *little loss on our side.* The Enterprise was executed with a distinguished degree of Address, Activity and Bravery and does great honor to Major Lee and to all the officers and men under his command, who are requested to accept the General's warmest thanks.

George Washington, from General Orders issued at West Point, New York, August 22, 1779, in John C. Fitzpatrick, ed., The Writings of George Washington, *vol. 16, p. 149.*

. . . You will have heard of the declaration of Spain against our Enemy. The combined fleets of France and Spain, have been some time in the British Channel searching in vain for that of G. Britain, which has slipt out of the Channel and escaped. As it is not thought prudent to invade England till their fleet is beaten, the french troops which were ready for that enterprise are not embarked. Two french frigates have taken the Ardent of 64 Guns, off Plymouth, after a very feeble resistance.

Arthur Lee, from a letter written in Paris to Thomas Jefferson, September 4, 1779, in Julian P. Boyd, ed., The Papers of Thomas Jefferson, *vol. 3, p. 82.*

. . . But if any individuals have been imprudent, or unprincipled, let them answer for themselves. I am responsible, only for my own conduct. Your feasts for the injury, which the indiscretions of such persons might do to the General [Washington], were kind, but I hope unnecessary. The decided confidence of Congress & the hearts of the people of America are the witnesses to his integrity. The blame of the unmeaning petulance of a few impatient spirits will never rest upon him; for whoever knows his character will be satisfied, that an officer would be ashamed to utter in his hearing, any sentiments, that would disgrace a citizen.

Alexander Hamilton, from a letter written at West Point, New York, September 5, 1779, to Congregational clergyman Rev. William Gordon, in Harold C. Syrett, ed., The Papers of Alexander Hamilton, *vol. 2, p. 156.*

This morn cule / order'd to see our mens arms clean to march in the morn to be reviewed by Barron Stuban, a Major Genl. who hold the Rank of a inspector Genl. of the American army / he is a prusan / first brought the Prusan Excercise into our army.

Ensign Jeremiah Greenman, commenting on a drill for Baron von Steuben while encamped near North Kingston, Rhode Island, diary entry of September 5, 1779, in Greenman, Diary of a Common Soldier in the American Revolution, 1775–1783, *p. 139.*

. . . I received a letter from General Sullivan yesterday informing me of a victory over the Savages at a place called new town beyond Chemung. They had collected their whole force under the two Butlers Brandt and one McDonald. . . . The Genl. . . . put them to the route with every symptom of terror and precipitation. They left eleven warriors and one female dead; and it is reported by two prisoners taken, had sent off a number of wounded in Canoes and on horseback during the action. . . . The prisoners add that this was intended as their principal stand; and for this purpose they had waited eight days. The settlement of New Town is one of the most considerable in the Indian Country abounding in rich and extensive fields of every sort. This made the fourteenth which had been destroyed since commencement of the expedition. We had three men killed and thirty nine wounded. The intelligence is agreeable and important.

George Washington, from a letter written at West Point, New York, September 8, 1779, to Brig. Gen. Anthony Wayne, in John C. Fitzpatrick, ed., The Writings of George Washington, *vol. 16, pp. 252–253.*

I am certain no man set out with a warmer heart or a better disposition to render public service than myself, in everything which lay in my power. My first endeavor was to put the politics of the country right, and to show the advantages as well as the necessity of independence:

and until this was done, independence never could have succeeded. America at that time did not understand her own situation; and though the country was then full of writers, no one reached the mark; neither did I abate in my service, when hundreds were afterwards deserting her interest and thousands afraid to speak, for the first number of the "Crisis" was published in the blackest stage of affairs, six days before the taking the Hessians at Trenton. When this State [Pennsylvania] was distracted by parties on account of her Constitution, I endeavored in the most disinterested manner to bring it to a conclusion; and when Deane's impositions broke out, and threw the whole States into confusion, I readily took up the subject, for no one else understood it, and the country now sees that I was right. And if Mr. Jay thinks he derives any credit from his letter to Mr. Gerard, he will find himself deceived, and that the ingratitude of the composition will be his reproach, not mine.

Thomas Paine, from "Messrs. Deane, Jay and Gerard," September 14, 1779, in Van der Weyde, The Life and Works of Thomas Paine, *vol. 3, pp. 360–361.*

. . . About twelve Miles below the point their is a beautiful Situation as if by nature designed for a fortification (by every observation that has been taken lays a Quarter of a degree within the State of Virginia). Its Ellevation is Such that a Small Expence would Render it very Strong and of greater advantage than one four Miles up the Ohio. In Case you have one built a few years will prove the propriety of it. It would Amedeately become the key of the whole Trade of the Western Cuntrey and well situated for the Indian department in general. Besides Many Salutary effects it would Render during the War by Awing our Enemies the Chicasaws and the English posts on the Mississippie. . . .

George Rogers Clark, from a letter written at Louisville, Virginia Territory (Kentucky), to Thomas Jefferson, September 23, 1779, in Julian P. Boyd, ed., The Papers of Thomas Jefferson, *vol. 3, p. 88.*

Sir: My Sister informs me that she has received the Miniature picture you drew for her. I thank you for doing it and shall be glad to know the cost that I may pay it to you or your order. With esteem and regard I am, etc.

George Washington, a letter written at West Point, New York, October 15, 1779, to the artist Charles Willson Peale, in John C. Fitzpatrick, ed., The Writings of George Washington, *vol. 16, p. 468.*

We are now making large preparations in expectation of the arrival of Count de Estainge to carry on an expedition jointly against *New York*. Perhaps it may terminate against one at Rhode Island.

General Sullivan is on his return from the Indian Country. He has destroyed all their settlements on this side the Great Lakes. The savages are severely chastised for their former cruelties.

Nathanael Greene, from a letter written at West Point, New York, October 8, 1779, to William Greene, governor of Rhode Island, in Richard K. Showman, ed., The Papers of General Nathanael Greene, *vol. 4, p. 444.*

I received the Account of your Cruize and Engagement with the *Serapis*, which you did me the honour to send me from the Texel. . . . For some Days after the Arrival of your Express, scarce any thing was talked of at Paris and Versailles, but your cool Conduct and persevering Bravery during that terrible Conflict. You may believe, that the Impression on my Mind was not less strong than on that of others; but I do not chuse to say in a letter to yourself all I think on such an Occasion.

The Ministry are much dissatisfied with Captain Landais, and M. de Sartine has signified to me in writing that it is expected that I should send for him to Paris, and call him to Account for his Conduct. . . .

Benjamin Franklin, from a letter written at Passy, France, October 15, 1779, to John Paul Jones, in Albert Henry Smyth, ed., The Writings of Benjamin Franklin, *vol. 7, p. 395.*

Independence, it is agreed on all Hands, is the fix'd purpose of your Determination. Annihilation is preferable to a Reunion with Great Britain. To support this desirable End, you have enter'd into an alliance with France and Spain, to reduce the Power of this Country, and make Way for the Glory of America. What Effect this Connection will have on you, or this Kingdom, Time alone can discover; But be it rememberd, that France is perfidious, Spain insignificant, and Great Britain formidable. The united Fleets of the House of Bourbon, lately cover'd the Seas, and paraded off Plymouth. A Descent was threaten'd, and universally expected. The British Fleet was then in a distant Part of the Channel. . . . Soon after this, the two Fleets came in Sight of each other, (a Great Superiority in Number lying on the Side of the Enemy) and a bloody barrage was expected to follow. The british Fleet in the Evening,

form'd themselves into a Line of Battle and brought to, imagining that the combin'd Fleet, wou'd in the Morning begin the attack; but when that Period arriv'd, there was not an Enemy to be seen. . . .

John Randolph, from a letter written in London, to Thomas Jefferson, October 25, 1779, in Julian P. Boyd, ed., The Papers of Thomas Jefferson, *vol. 3, p. 117.*

My Lord, . . . as it is probable the very unexpected visit of the Court d'Estaing to this coast with so powerful a squadron and a considerable body of land troops, when known, would have excited some uneasiness for our safety, it is with very sincere pleasure I do myself the honour to inform you that we have seen the last of the French fleet this day depart we hope off the coast, [and] got both them and their American allies off our hands in a manner which we humbly hope our gracious Sovereign will not think unhandsome.

Maj. Gen. Augustine Prevost, from a letter written at Savannah, Georgia, November 1, 1779, to Lord George Germain, in K. G. Davies, ed., Documents of the American Revolution, *vol. 17, p. 241.*

About daybreak on the ninth, the united forces of France and America, consisting of upwards of four thousand French, and the Lord knows how many rebels, attempted to storm our lines [at Savannah]. . . . The count [D'Estaing], in person, began the attack with great vigor, but was soon thrown into confusion by the well-pointed fire from our batteries and redoubts. A choice body of grenadiers came on with such spirit to attack the old redoubt upon the Ebenezer road, that if Tawse, with a number of his men, had not thrown himself in very opportunely, it must have been carried; upwards of sixty men were lying dead in the ditch after the action. Poor Tawse fell bravely fighting for his country. The rebels could not be brought to the charge, and in their confusion are said to have fired upon their allies, and killed upwards of fifty of them. It is almost incredible the trifling loss we sustained; the only officer killed was poor Tawse, and there were not twenty privates killed and wounded. The enemy's loss was astonishing. I never saw such a dreadful scene, as several hundred lay dead in a space of a few yards, and the cries of many hundreds wounded was still more distressing to a feeling mind. . . . Two days ago the last of the French troops embarked; the rebels have been gone some time, and we are now in as much tranquility as we have been for any time these six months past. Mutual animosity and reviling have arisen to such a height between the French and rebels since they were defeated, that they were almost ready to cut one another's throats.

From a letter sent from Savannah, Georgia, Rivington Gazette, November 20, 1779, in Frank Moore, compiler, The Diary of the American Revolution, p. 400.

... in the afternoon one of the Serjts.... brought a very handsom patch Gound to my Quarters which he had taken from one Mrs. Thomas a Soldiers wife in the Regiment. which She had Stolen from a woman at Updikes Newtown in the State of Rhode Island. I took the Gound in order to Send it to the owner. and ordered all the Drums and fifes to parade and Drum her out of the Regt. with a paper pind to her back, with these words in Capital letters, /A THIEF/ thus She went off with Musick—

Col. Israel Angell, diary entry of December 1, 1779, while encamped at Fishkill, New York, in Angell, The Diary of Colonel Israel Angell, p. 99.

I told the Irish Gentleman [Mr. Linde], that Americans hated War: that Agriculture and Commerce were their Objects, and it would their Interest as much as that of the Dutch to keep Peace with all the World, untill their Country should be filled with Population which could not be in many Centuries. That War and the Spirit of Conquest was the most diametrically opposite to their Interests, as they would divert their Attention, Wealth, Industry, Activity &c. from a certain Source of Prosperity, and even Grandeur and Glory, to an uncertain one, nay to one that it is certain they could never make any Advantage of.... That it was amazing to me that a Writer so well informed as Reynale [Abbe Raynal] could ever give an Opinion that it was not for the Interest of the Powers of Europe, that America should be independant, when it was so easy to demonstrate that it was for the Interest of every one, except England. That they could loose nothing by it, but certainly would every one gain Something, many a great deal.

John Adams, from a diary entry while in El Ferrol del Caudillo, Spain, December 14, 1779, in L. H. Butterfield, ed., Diary and Autobiography of John Adams, p. 408.

The situation of the army with respect to supplies is beyond description alarming. It has been five or six weeks past on half allowance, and we have not more than three days bread at a third allowance on hand, nor any where within reach. When this is exhausted, we must depend on the precarious gleanings of the neighbouring country. Our magazines are absolutely empty everywhere, and our commissaries entirely destitute of money or credit to replenish them. We have never experienced a like extremity at any period of the war.... Unless some extraordinary and immediate exertions are made by the States ... there is every appearance that the army will infallibly disband in a fortnight....

George Washington, from a circular to the governors of the Middle States written at Morristown, New Jersey, December 16, 1779, in John C. Fitzpatrick, ed., The Writings of George Washington, vol. 17, pp. 273–274.

The inclosed letter from Governor Lee and intelligence (from the French Minister) accompanying it, gives reason to apprehend that the enemy meditate an invasion of this state.... It is our duty to provide against every event, and the Executive are accordingly engaged in concerting proper measures of defence. Among others we think to call an immediate force from the militia to defend the post at York, and to take a proper post on the South side of James river, but the expense, the difficulties which attend a general call of the militia into the field, the disgust it gives them more especially when the find no enemy in place, and the extreme rigor of the season, induce us to refer to the decision of the general assembly, whether we shall on the intelligence already received and now communicated to them, call a competent force of militia to oppose the numbers of the enemy spoken of; or whether we shall make ready all orders and prepare other circumstances, but omit actually issuing these orders till the enemy appear or we have further proof of their intentions? ...

Governor Thomas Jefferson, from a letter written in Council at Williamsburg to Benjamin Harrison, speaker of the Virginia House, December 23, 1779, in Julian P. Boyd, ed., The Papers of Thomas Jefferson, vol. 3, p. 241.

I have done what, perhaps, I shall be blamed for; but my pride as an American, and my feelings as a man, were not on this occasion to be resisted. The [naval] officers of the Confederacy were here without money, or the means of getting any. The idea of our officers being obliged to sneak, as they phrase it, from the company of French officers for fear of running in debt with them for a bottle of wine, or a bowl of punch, because not able to pay for their share of the reckoning, was too humiliating to be tolerable, and too destructive to that pride and opinion of independent equality which I wish to see influence all our officers. Besides, some of them wanted necessaries too much to be comfortable, or in this country, decent. In a word, I have drawn on the fund pointed out for the payment of part of my salary, for one hundred guineas in their favour, to be divided among them according to their respective ranks....

John Jay, from a letter written in St. Pierre, Martinique, December 25, 1779, to the president of the Continental Congress, in William Jay, The Life of John Jay, *vol. 1, p. 105.*

We went to bed ... but not before we had a fresh encounter with Antony [a servant], who had taken upon him (although I had before charged him not to concern himself with her ...) to abuse the negro woman as she had not made his bed, as he said, fit for him to lie in. I interfered and desired him to go to bed and not disturb the house. This rather inflamed him so that I took him by the arm to put him up stairs. He started from me, went out in the yard, said he would not be thus abused; he would not be insulted. I accordingly shut the door. After a considerable space of time, he came and requested I would let him in. I did so and spoke to him to this purpose, Antony, thy behavior is such that I cannot have thee about house, except thou wilt behave thyself in another manner....

Christopher Marshall, Philadelphia merchant and Quaker then in Lancaster, Pennsylvania, from diary entry of December 31, 1779, in Marshall, Extracts from the Diary of Christopher Marshall, *p. 233.*

7

Defeat and Treachery
1780

WINTER WOES

An augury of how events might develop for the American cause during 1780 occurred on the year's very first day. At West Point, about 100 men among the Massachusetts regiments forming part of the garrison mutinied. Mistakenly believing that their three-year terms of enlistment had expired, the men gathered together their equipment and belongings and left the fort, heading for their homes. Other troops followed and returned the mutineers to the fort; most received pardons and resumed their duties. The episode truly seemed to foreshadow the much more bitter news West Point would generate as the year proceeded.[1]

The Continental army troops with General Washington in winter quarters at Morristown, New Jersey, experienced severe deprivations. Most occupied log huts, but they lacked supplies and adequate food and clothing; some had no shoes. The exceptionally harsh weather, with deep snow and extreme cold, aggravated the effects of their malnutrition. Washington appealed to the neighboring states to supply food but to little avail. Living conditions at the camp worsened, and the soldiers began foraging and plundering in nearby communities in their quest for food. Their hunger overrode their officers' efforts to enforce discipline. In response, Washington reorganized his procurement system, dividing New Jersey into 11 districts required to provide food allotments, and sending out officers to collect the allotments under threat of force. The new tactics worked well enough that by the end of January the food shortage at the camp had ended. As spring approached, however, the food crisis returned.[2]

During the winter months, brutal skirmishes and plundering characterized the war effort in the North. For example, in February a British force under Lt. Col. Chapple Norton assaulted a patrol of Connecticut Continentals in Westchester County, New York. While Norton endured only 23 casualties, his men killed 14 of the Continentals, wounded 37, and took 76 prisoners. Similarly, as commander at New York City, General von Knyphausen sent raids into New Jersey. On one such raid in March, his troops entered the undefended town of

Gen. Sir Henry Clinton's army lays siege to Charleston. *(The Siege of Charleston, courtesy of Anne S. K. Brown Military Collection, Brown University Library)*

Hackensack, broke into and pillaged homes, and set fire to the courthouse and several houses.[3]

THE SIEGE OF CHARLESTON

Gen. Sir Henry Clinton, who left von Knyphausen in charge at New York, now acted on his decision that the time was ripe for conquering the South. He set Charleston, South Carolina, as his initial objective. Patriots had tenaciously held the city since the beginning of the war. The forts in the harbor that could protect the town's seaward approach of islands and channels had badly deteriorated, however, and Gen. Benjamin Lincoln had concentrated the troops under his command within the town itself. His comparatively small force—800 Continentals, some 380 remnants of Pulaski's Legion, and 2,000 militia from the Carolinas—appeared inadequate to oppose Clinton's armada, recommending withdrawal as the apt tactic. But Governor John Rutledge and local officials insisted that Lincoln remain and defend Charleston.[4]

Clinton's expedition seemed somewhat star-crossed from its beginning. His fleet of 90 transports and 14 warships set sail from New York harbor on December 26, 1779, in relatively mild weather but within two days experienced a violent storm that tossed the ships about—Clinton himself, who hated the sea, apparently endured relentless seasickness thereafter. As January ensued, rain, hail, snow, and other wintry weather plagued the voyage for many days—scattering the fleet, shattering masts, rending sails, and damaging stores. Near the end of January, the ships stood off of the Savannah River's mouth, well to the south of their destination. They entered the river and found harbor at Tybee Island, where the crews could recover and make needed repairs. Despite the rough passage, General Clinton remained determined to fulfill the vision he, his predecessors, and the British ministry clung to that the presumed majority loyalty of the South would secure ultimate victory over the rebels.[5]

Clinton sailed into North Edisto Inlet to land his expedition on Johns Island at the mouth of Charleston Harbor on February 11. His force of 8,500 British regulars and Loyalists, with the 5,000 sailors manning Admiral Arbuthnot's fleet of ships and their 650 cannons, presented Lincoln an overwhelming opponent. Clinton began slowly to tighten the noose. He occupied James Island and set up a post at Stono Ferry north of the town. At the same time, workmen, including 600 slaves requisitioned by Governor Rutledge, built earthworks and otherwise made improvements in Charleston's defenses. By late March troops had arrived overland from Savannah to reinforce Clinton's force, also now augmented by two Loyalist units, Lt. Col. Banastre Tarleton's British Legion and Capt. Patrick Ferguson's American Rangers. In addition, Arbuthnot had managed to cross the bar in Charleston Harbor and position his ships to cannonade the town's defenses. Clinton also sent troops across the Ashley River to occupy the peninsula leading to Charleston, severing Lincoln's main line of retreat—the final preparation for laying siege to the town.[6]

Clinton and Arbuthnot had quarreled over where to land the troops, the first of many disagreements between the two commanders of equal rank. At age 68, the often indecisive Arbuthnot lacked energy and responded slowly to implementing tactics urged by Clinton, sometimes failing entirely to follow through. Clinton also quarreled with Lord Cornwallis, who commanded the 33rd Regiment during the siege. Both men were, for opposed reasons, disappointed to learn that Clinton's resignation had been rejected; thus Clinton could not relinquish his command and Cornwallis could not inherit it, as he hoped to do. These rifts among the commanders probably delayed fulfillment of the siege but fell well short of jeopardizing its ultimate success.[7]

On April 1, the siege began. British sappers broke ground within 800 yards of Lincoln's fortifications to dig the first of a series of trenches that would move continually closer to the town. Gen. William Woodford led 750 Virginia Continentals through the British lines to reinforce Lincoln. But then Arbuthnot ran eight frigates and six supply transports past the ineffectual defenses at Fort Moultrie to anchor between James Island and the town, giving the British effective control of every approach. As the first of his siege trenches neared completion, Clinton pressed Lincoln to surrender. Lincoln refused. On April 13 the British began to bombard the town, igniting many fires and damaging many structures; the following day Tarleton's men surprised and overwhelmed American troops posted at Monck's Corner, gaining control of Lincoln's only remaining escape route. During the third week of April, Lord Rawdon arrived with still more reinforcements for Clinton, swelling his army to 10,000.

With the British trenches only 250 yards distant, Lincoln on April 19 called a council to consider surrender, but Lieutenant Governor Christopher Gadsden derailed the proposal by threatening a civilian uprising. Two days following, Lincoln nevertheless proposed a surrender to Clinton, who rejected the American commander's terms. A few days later, an American bayonet sortie at night proved futile against the British lines, and the siege trenches moved ever closer. At the end of the first week of May, the British landed troops on Sullivan's Island and captured Fort Moultrie and the 200-man garrison Lincoln had left there. The next day, Clinton again summoned Lincoln to surrender. Lincoln again refused.

During the night of May 9, the British pounded the town mercilessly with cannon fire, terrifying the residents, who petitioned Lincoln to surrender. On May 12, Lincoln accepted Clinton's terms and surrendered Charleston to the British. The successful siege cost few casualties on either side but netted Clinton 5,000 prisoners, nearly 400 artillery and 6,000 muskets, and huge quantities of ammunition. Charleston's fall was the Americans' greatest defeat of the Revolutionary War and left all of South Carolina open to British conquest.[8]

A tragedy three days following the American surrender compounded the death and destruction wrought by the British siege and Lincoln's resistance. The victorious troops had carelessly tossed captured American muskets into a wooden structure used for storing gunpowder. Somehow the gunpowder ignited—perhaps when one of the tossed muskets misfired—and the resulting explosion torched six nearby houses and killed 200 people, leaving many more wounded with agonizingly painful powder burns. Among the dead were British, German, and American soldiers as well as Charleston civilians.[9]

THE FRENCH ARMY ARRIVES

Near the end of April, the marquis de Lafayette, who had sailed for France in January 1779 aboard Capt. Pierre Landais's *Alliance,* arrived back in Boston. The marquis had spent more than a year helping to negotiate the conditions of French military assistance to the United States. He brought back for General Washington commissions as both a French lieutenant general and a vice admiral, which Lafayette hoped would profit the commander in his dealings with French commanders being sent to assist the American cause, including Jean de Vimeur, count de Rochambeau, who had been appointed commander of French forces in America. During the second week of July, the count arrived at Newport with a fleet of eight ships of the line bearing about 6,000 soldiers—the first French army unit of several that nation promised to provide. Once disembarked, Rochambeau discovered a town of nearly empty streets and no welcoming party until Gen. William Heath finally showed up representing Washington.

Unfortunately, the Continental army's debilitated state left Washington unprepared to plan any significant operations in conjunction with Rochambeau. Fearful that Rochambeau and other French commanders would discover the true circumstances of the American army and perhaps return in dismay to France, Washington stalled. When Washington and the count finally met in Hartford, Connecticut, during the third week of September to discuss joint endeavors, Rochambeau greatly admired Washington's dignity and bearing. Even so, Washington restricted his conversation to general remarks, pending restoration of his army's fighting capabilities. For many months, Rochambeau would wait impatiently with his troops in or near Newport.[10]

DISASTER AT CAMDEN

With Charleston secured, Clinton sent Lord Cornwallis with 2,500 troops in pursuit of Col. Abraham Buford's remnant of about 350 Continentals, the only remaining American force active in South Carolina. Under orders from Gen. Isaac Huger, Buford retreated toward Hillsboro, North Carolina. Although Cornwallis hastened up the Santee River, he failed to gain ground on Buford; and so he dispatched Tarleton and his cavalry to chase Buford down. Moving swiftly, Tarleton caught up with Buford at Waxhaws near the North Carolina border. Although Buford's force outnumbered Tarleton's 270 Loyalists and dragoons, Tarleton engaged Buford in transit and totally unprepared.

Buford withheld fire too long, and Tarleton's mounted troops slaughtered his men with bayonets and swords, killing 113 while taking only 19 casualties. Tarleton captured 203 prisoners, but Buford managed to escape on horseback. The gory victory generated the ironic term *Tarleton's Quarter* (meaning a take-no-prisoners approach to war) and earned its commander the nickname Bloody Tarleton, but it also eliminated the last organized Patriot resistance in South Carolina. Content with the outcome in South Carolina, Clinton left Cornwallis in charge of the southern campaign and returned to New York in early June.[11]

On June 13, without consulting Commander in Chief George Washington, the Continental Congress appointed Maj. Gen. Horatio Gates, "the hero of Saratoga" and a popular figure among the congressional delegates, as commander of the army in the Southern Department. Gates arrived at Coxe's Mill, North Carolina, in late July and assumed his command from the nominal commander Maj. Gen. Johann de Kalb. Gates immediately determined to move against the British at Camden, South Carolina, and began to march on July 27, two days after assuming command, directly toward his objective along a route that provided little food or other goods to sustain his already undernourished and poorly supplied army. As he advanced, Gates acquired reinforcements, including several hundred Virginia militia and about 2,000 well-supplied North Carolina militia led by former governor Richard Caswell.[12]

At Little Lynches Creek, about 15 miles from Camden, Gates encountered opposition from British troops led by Lord Rawdon. But Rawdon soon withdrew toward Camden, where the British concentrated their forces, totaling about 2,200 seasoned troops, under the command of Lord Cornwallis. Gates reached Camden in mid-August with a force of 4,100 men, a sizable number of them physically unfit for duty. During the night of August 15–16, Gates marched his army down the main road into Camden; at the same time, Cornwallis began to march out of Camden on the same road in search of Gates's force. The two armies encountered each other at about 2:30 A.M., skirmished briefly, and then

Johann de Kalb falls mortally wounded as British troops rout the Americans at the Battle of Camden. (The Battle of Camden—Death of De Kalb, *courtesy of Anne S. K. Brown Military Collection, Brown University Library*)

ceased firing to await the light of morning. A wide, sandy area strewn with pines and flanked on both sides by swamps composed their battle site.

Cornwallis's line consisted, on the right, of Royal Welsh Fusiliers, Volunteers of Ireland (Irish deserters from the American army), and North Carolina Loyalist militia and, on the left, of Highlanders under Lord Rawdon, backed by Tarleton's legion. Gates positioned militia on his left and Maryland and Delaware Continentals under de Kalb on his right. Gates himself remained hundreds of yards to the rear, offered a few initial comments, and then gave no further orders. When the British attacked, the American left—half of the line—collapsed immediately, with the North Carolina and Virginia militiamen throwing down their arms and fleeing. The well-seasoned Continentals of the right wing stood fast despite the left's flight but soon became overwhelmed by Rawdon's Highlanders; de Kalb also held firm but suffered several wounds. The British attacked against the Americans' front, flanks, and rear, and de Kalb fell mortally wounded from gunfire and saber thrusts. A few of the Maryland and Delaware Continentals managed to retreat, and the remnant of the American force fled northward, with Tarleton's cavalry at their heels.

A catastrophe for the American cause, the Battle of Camden ended with Gates's army effectively destroyed. Perhaps as many as 900 of his troops died in the battle; another 1,000 fell into British hands as prisoners. British losses included 68 dead and 350 wounded. The ragged remnant of Gates's army struggled toward Hillsboro. Only 700 of the army's original 4,100 men managed to reach safety there three days following the battle. Gates himself fled as soon as his army's left wing collapsed in the first moments of the battle. He commandeered a swift horse at Rugeley's Mill and feverishly raced off, reaching Charlotte, 60 miles distant from the Camden battlefield, by nightfall. Two days later, as the brave de Kalb died of his wounds, Gates arrived in Hillsboro. On the previous day, August 18, Tarleton fulfilled the British triumph with a surprise attack on Thomas Sumter's militia, which had supported Gates's Camden effort with raids on British and Loyalist outposts—Tarleton's legion killed 150 of Sumter's men and took 300 prisoners. Disgraced by his cowardice, Gates later retired to his Virginia farm.[13]

ARNOLD'S TREASON

The other hero of Saratoga fared differently. Although he survived the court-martial for his conduct in Philadelphia with a mere reprimand, Benedict Arnold continued to be disgruntled over his treatment. With his wife Peggy's blessing, he pursued the treasonous correspondence with Clinton's headquarters. Arnold demanded £10,000 from the British for his information and twice that amount if he provided a major American post and a large body of troops for their capture. Through his maneuvering toward this end, the desired opportunity presented itself when Arnold received command of the important Hudson River post of West Point in August.[14]

Arnold arranged a secret meeting with Clinton's adjutant general, Maj. John André, for September 21 at Haverstraw on the American-controlled western bank of the Hudson. Although instructed by Clinton not to cross American lines, to wear his uniform, and not to carry incriminating documents, André succumbed to the theatricality of the episode and donned a disguise. He sailed up the river aboard the sloop *Vulture* and parleyed with Arnold regarding the traitor's fee until dawn of September 22. Unable to return to his ship, André hid out at the home of Joshua Hett Smith, one of Arnold's liaisons, until nightfall. But when an American shore battery fired on the *Vulture,* the sloop's captain headed his ship downriver, stranding André. Persuaded by Arnold to travel overland, André left on horseback with Smith to return to British lines. Dressed in civilian clothes, he carried documents signed by Arnold and a list of Arnold's spies stuffed in his stocking. The two riders crossed the river and spent the night of September 23 at a farmhouse near British-held territory.

On the morning of September 24, Smith left André to travel on alone. As André neared Tarrytown, three American militiamen stopped him. Mistaking them for British partisans, André told them he was British, realized his mistake, and attempted to use a pass given him by Arnold. The militiamen searched him, discovered the documents, and turned him over to an officer, who took André and the documents to Lt. Col. John Jameson. Bewildered by the documents, Jameson sent them to General Washington, who was nearby, en route to West Point. Jameson also ordered that André be taken to West Point with a letter informing Arnold of his

This portrait of George Washington was painted by Charles Wilson Peale in 1780. *(Courtesy of Anne S. K. Brown Military Collection, Brown University Library)*

capture. Although this order was countermanded at the last moment, the letter continued on to West Point. Arnold received the letter as he ate breakfast on September 24. He quietly informed his wife of the letter's content, left the house, hastened to the river, and took a barge to the *Vulture.* His suspicions aroused by the documents received from Jameson, Washington arrived moments too late at West Point. Later in the day, he received a letter from Arnold that confirmed Arnold's treason.[15]

With his true identity soon revealed, André faced the prospect of summary execution under the rules of war because he had been caught behind enemy lines wearing a disguise and carrying incriminating documents. Nevertheless, Washington chose to convene a board of officers to examine the evidence. General Clinton and other associates and friends of André sent appeals, arguing that the adjutant was merely carrying out orders. The board rejected the appeals. Given the offer to exchange Arnold for André, Clinton refused. The board sentenced André to death by hanging. Accepting the judgment with resignation, André appealed to Washington to allow execution by firing squad as appropriate for a soldier, but Washington denied the appeal. On October 2 at Tappan, André confronted his death at the gallows with such great dignity and calmness that his American captors felt admiration and even affection for him. Their anger and outrage toward Arnold, however, seemed boundless.[16]

General Washington had been thunderstruck once he understood the purport of the letters found on André that Alexander Hamilton had delivered directly to him. He reacted initially with anguish, then with anxiety over the vulnerability of the fort at West Point. He sent word to Nathanael Greene and Anthony Wayne

Major John André is executed for spying. *(Courtesy of the National Archives and Records Administration)*

to rush reinforcements to the fort; receiving the order at 1:00 A.M. on September 26, Wayne quick marched his Pennsylvania troops for 16 miles to reach West Point by sunrise, much to Washington's relief. Henry Clinton never ordered an attack on West Point, and so the fort remained in Continental control. Although Arnold's scheme had foundered, Clinton fulfilled André's promise to Arnold, paying the traitor £6,000 for his services and £350 more as expenses; Arnold also received a British army commission as a provisional brigadier general with an annual salary of £650, much more than he had received as an American commander. Accepting her innocence, Washington sent Peggy Arnold and her baby back to Philadelphia. Arnold's foiled treason, sufficiently dismaying and outrageous in itself, also deprived Washington of one of his most able commanders.[17]

THE ROLE OF CONGRESS

The disgrace of both Gates and Arnold highlighted one of the major issues the Continental Congress dealt with throughout the year: the appointment of military commanders. As in previous years, Congress struggled to raise both troops and money to prosecute the war effort mandated by the delegates' control of the government. Their interference in the appointment of commanders, however, actually worked against military success. In fall 1778, without consulting Washington, Congress had appointed Maj. Gen. Benjamin Lincoln as commander of the Southern Department. In spring 1780, Lincoln presided over the catastrophic loss of Charleston, his army and its equipment, and South Carolina. In June 1780, again without consulting Washington, Congress appointed Maj. Gen. Horatio Gates to replace Lincoln. Gates rewarded the delegates' confidence with the disaster at Camden. Finally, in October 1780, the commander in chief secured from Congress the appointment of his own choice, Maj. Gen. Nathanael Greene, to command in the South. Perhaps the one earlier sign of Congress's evolving discernment relating to commanders was the delegates' January decision to expel Maj. Gen. Charles Lee from the military, but Lee's own vituperative letters compelled this outcome.[18]

Responding to Washington's appeals, the Continental Congress in early February requested that the states draft 35,000 men by April 1 to restore the Continental army and also provide $1.2 million each month to sustain the national treasury. But the states, grown weary of the ongoing war and either unwilling or unable to comply, largely ignored the request. Consequently, the treasury on which both troop recruitment and finances depended showed signs of crisis in March. In response, Congress determined to retire the severely depreciated Continental currency by setting the ratio of paper money to specie (coined money) at 40 to 1, allowing the states to pay their levies at one-fortieth of the money's face value. Prices of goods stood three times higher in 1780 than they did in 1779 and had leaped to nearly 100 times their levels of 1776. Congress also responded to other appeals from Washington, after long resistance, by voting in October to provide half-pay to Continental army officers for life. The decision helped boost morale among officers commissioned by Congress. In November, the Continental Congress renewed its request to the states for increased levies.[19]

THE BATTLE OF KING'S MOUNTAIN

Although overall the year's disasters generated broad discouragement among supporters of the American cause, at least two promising events occurred as its end approached. On October 7, Loyalist troops commanded by Maj. Patrick Ferguson assembled on the wooded eminence of King's Mountain, South Carolina, their commander intent on crushing the frontier rebel militia. Ferguson made the tactical error, however, of failing to secure the slopes approaching his position on the hill. About 1,000 rebel frontiersmen under command of Col. Isaac Shelby and William Campbell crept quietly up the slopes and attacked Ferguson from two directions. Ferguson ordered a bayonet charge, but the frontiersmen handily evaded the Loyalists and fired on them from cover with murderous effect. Forced back to their central encampment, the Loyalists suffered withering and concentrated volleys from the surrounding rebels. Ferguson fell dead from six shots, and his embattled men surrendered. Shelby and Campbell counted 28 dead and 64 wounded. But their men exacted a heavy toll among the Loyalists: 157 dead, 163 wounded, and 700 captured. The rebel victory liquidated the Loyalist support in the Carolinas that Cornwallis had counted on. Now fearful of attack on his rear, Cornwallis retreated to Winnsboro, South Carolina, to establish winter quarters.[20]

On the very same day that the rebel frontiersmen gained their important victory at King's Mountain, the Continental Congress appointed Nathanael Greene as commander of the Southern Department—the second promising event. Chagrined by the results of its earlier appointments, Congress on October 6 resolved that Commander in Chief Washington should appoint a commander to replace Gates. Washington recommended Greene, and Congress followed through. Greene arrived at Charlotte, North Carolina, where Gates had set up his headquarters, on December 2 and assumed command of the Southern Department the next day. Greene had wisely consulted with other commanders, especially Washington, about conditions in the South; had made an evaluation of foods, supplies, and troops the South could provide for his army; and had concluded that his best strategy against Cornwallis lay in dividing his own army into two units to move swiftly, to confuse Cornwallis, and to threaten attack while evading the British in an effort to weaken Cornwallis over time. Toward this latter end, he also encouraged Francis Marion and Thomas Sumter to continue their raids on British supply lines. Quickly discerning the enervated state of his army, Greene moved into winter quarters near Cheraw to retrain and refit his troops.[21]

CHRONICLE OF EVENTS

1780

January 1: Mutiny erupts among members of the Massachusetts regiments participating in the garrisoning of West Point. About 100 men leave for home with their equipment, but they are followed and brought back, most being pardoned and returned to duty.

January 2: Washington's troops at Morristown, many lacking huts or tents and blankets, endure severe weather, with record-breaking cold and two feet of snow on the ground. Surgeon James Thatcher observes that some of them "are actually barefoot and almost naked."

January 9: Washington unsuccessfully appeals to governments of states bordering New Jersey to provide food for the army, as his hungry men forage for food in communities near Morristown.

January 10: Congress has received a letter (composed in December) from Gen. Charles Lee concerning rumors of his permanent dismissal from service, a letter so offensive that the delegates decided to substantiate the rumor—then dismissed Lee. Lee had stayed at his estate in the Shenandoah Valley during his year's suspension. He now moves to Philadelphia but has no further role in the Revolutionary War.

January 14: Lord Stirling leads 2,500 men, moving by sled across ice and snow, from Elizabeth Point for a surprise attack against the British on Staten Island, but the British detect their movement, withdraw into their fortifications, and the attack fizzles. The Americans spend the night exposed to subzero temperatures. New Jersey civilians in the role of militia loot farms on the island, but Stirling comes away with only 17 prisoners and a small supply of food, tents, and arms, at a cost of six dead.

January 25: Retaliating for the attack on Staten Island, the British raid Newark, burning its academy, and Elizabeth, New Jersey, where they burn the courthouse and meetinghouse.

January 26: Gen. Benedict Arnold's court-martial on charges of financial speculation and malfeasance while commander at Philadelphia concludes, finding him guilty on two minor charges and dismissing two others—in effect, a vindication, as the only penalty is a reprimand from Washington. But Arnold expected a thorough acquittal and finds the judgment enraging.

January 27: Washington has reorganized the system of requisitions from New Jersey, dividing the state into 11 districts, requiring a food allotment from each, and dispatching officers to collect grains and cattle under threat of force—the system works, greatly improving the food supply at the Morristown encampment, as he informs the Continental Congress.

January 28: Settlers from North Carolina, which claims Tennessee as part of its western lands but can do little to protect settlers there while the British menace its coastline, establish Fort Nashborough (now Nashville) on the Tennessee River, naming it for North Carolina governor Abner Nash.

February 1: General Clinton's expedition arrives at Savannah en route to attack Charleston, where Lincoln has concentrated his army. Lincoln has a total force of less than 3,200 men; he vacillates between withdrawal and preparing for a siege, while under political pressure from Gov. Edward Rutledge, Lt. Gov. Christopher Gadsden, and Charleston officials to defend the city.

February 3: Lt. Chapple Norton leads a large British force from Fort Knyphausen (formerly Fort Washington) in an effort to engage Lt. Col. Joseph Thompson's five Connecticut companies (supported by Massachu-

Benjamin Lincoln was forced to surrender to General Clinton in 1780. *(From* The Pictorial Field Book of the Revolution, *2 vols., by B. J. Lossing. New York: Harper Brothers, 1851 and 1852.)*

setts troops) on roving patrol in Westchester County. Norton captures Thompson's outposts, and during the ensuing fight, the British surround the Americans, who retreat. Norton has 23 casualties, including five dead; but Thompson's toll is 14 dead, 37 wounded, and 76 taken prisoner.

February 9: The Continental Congress requests that the states provide 35,000 more men, raised by draft, for military service and contribute $1.2 million per month to the confederate treasury.

February 10: Clinton disembarks from Savannah and sails for Charleston.

February 11: Unopposed by Lincoln, General Clinton sails into North Edisto Inlet and disembarks his troops on Johns Island at the mouth of Charleston Harbor. His 8,500 British regulars and Loyalist units greatly outnumber Lincoln's Charleston garrison.

February 14: Clinton begins a series of strategic moves to box in Lincoln, establishing a base at Stono Ferry above Charleston, occupying James Island entirely, and building up his onshore supply base. Lincoln has strong defenses against a land assault, with a complex system of waterways making the approach hazardous; his fortifications are anchored between the Ashley and Cooper Rivers, protected by marshes, solid earthworks, and gun emplacements. Clinton waits for Admiral Arbuthnot's ships to enter the harbor and support the siege with heavy guns.

February 23: Lt. Col. Banastre Tarleton's British Legion of Loyalist heavy dragoons and mounted infantry surprises a small force of patriot South Carolina militia, kills 10, and takes four prisoner. The horses he captures replace his men's mounts, which died during the Clinton expedition's voyage south.

February 26: Col. William Washington's horse troops encounter Tarleton's British Legion along the banks of the Ashley River, pushing them back while taking several prisoners and then withdrawing to join other American forces near Monck's Corner.

February 29: At St. Petersburg, Russia, the Empress Catherine announces the formation of the League of Armed Neutrals comprised of Russia, Denmark, and Sweden but later to be joined by other European nations. Intending to keep commerce flowing unhindered, the Armed Neutrality evokes these principles in its treaty: free navigation, free passage of cargoes carried by neutral ships, a limited definition of blockades, and the legal disposition of prizes taken on the seas. France and the United States welcome the Armed Neutrality,

but Great Britain ignores it, and its effect on the Revolutionary War proves minimal.

March 1: The Pennsylvania assembly enacts an Act of Emancipation, introduced the previous November, which will gradually free the slaves within the state—the first emancipation law enacted in America. Since the war began, both slaves (mostly sent as substitutes for their masters) and freedmen have enlisted in the Continental army and fought in the North, but the southern states refuse to allow slaves to serve as troops in the South.

March 3: The arrival of 700 North Carolina Continentals, sent overland on a three-month winter march, would enhance Lincoln's Charleston garrison, but an equal number of North Carolina militiamen leave the city at the same time.

March 5: Governor Rutledge has requisitioned the services of 600 slaves to build more earthworks at Charleston, and work continues on the city's defenses, with its main defensive site a redoubt surmounted with stonework called The Citadel.

March 14: With a few ships and 1,400 troops, Bernardo de Gálvez attacks the 300-man British garrison at Mobile commanded by Elias Dunford. A relief column sent from Pensacola fails to reach Mobile in time to help Dunford, who, after two days of fighting, surrenders to Gálvez.

March 18: The Constitutional Congress sets the ratio of paper to specie (hard money) at 40 to 1 in order to retire the paper money in circulation by accepting it in payment of levies due from the states at only one-fortieth of its face value. The national treasury in fact has minuscule holdings of specie, and Continental dollars are declining in value toward worthlessness. Inflation has reached a wartime high.

March 19: Learning that the resignation he submitted in hopes of relinquishing command to Cornwallis and returning to England has been rejected, Clinton acknowledges that he must fulfill the campaign against Charleston. He orders more troops from Savannah to augment his force.

March 20: The small fleet purchased from Admiral d'Estaing that represents the American navy at Charleston has insufficient strength to combat Arbuthnot's fleet, so Commodore Whipple withdraws the ships up the Cooper River and sinks most of them in the channel to impede British navigation in the river. Arbuthnot forces a crossing of the bar in Charleston Harbor and moves his ships into position to support an attack.

March 22: General von Knyphausen leads 400 British and German troops from New York into New Jersey to raid an undefended Hackensack. His men break into and loot houses and then burn the courthouse and several homes.

March 25: Clinton's force at Charleston is swollen by the arrival of Tarleton's Legion and Ferguson's American Rangers, a Loyalist infantry unit.

March 27: Gálvez sails past Pensacola, the seat of British governance in West Florida, unable to attack.

March 28–29: During the night, Clinton's troops cross the Ashley River and position themselves across the peninsula leading to Charleston, sealing off Lincoln's main avenue of retreat but leaving him a slender exit route along the Cooper River and north to Biggin's Bridge.

April 1: Clinton's engineers break ground within 800 yards of Lincoln's Charleston fortifications and begin to dig a series of trenches for the siege operation as the Americans watch helplessly.

April 6: Fulfilling the requirement of Benedict Arnold's court-martial conviction, Commander in Chief George Washington sends Arnold an official letter of reprimand.

Having marched 500 miles in only 28 days, Gen. William Woodford leads 750 Virginia Continentals past the British and into Charleston to reinforce Lincoln's garrison.

April 8: Eight of Arbuthnot's frigates with six supply transports race past the defenses at Fort Moultrie, suffering six dead but minimal damage. They anchor between James Island and Charleston, giving the British control of nearly every approach to the city.

April 10: As his first parallel of siege trenches nears completion, Clinton sends Lincoln a request to surrender. Although he could still retreat up the Cooper River, Lincoln decides to remain in Charleston and rejects the request.

April 12: Tarleton and Ferguson begin moving their troops up the Cooper River to attack the only American troops remaining outside Charleston—near Monck's Corner—under command of Gen. Isaac Huger.

April 13: The British batteries on James Island bombard Charleston with red-hot shot that creates fires

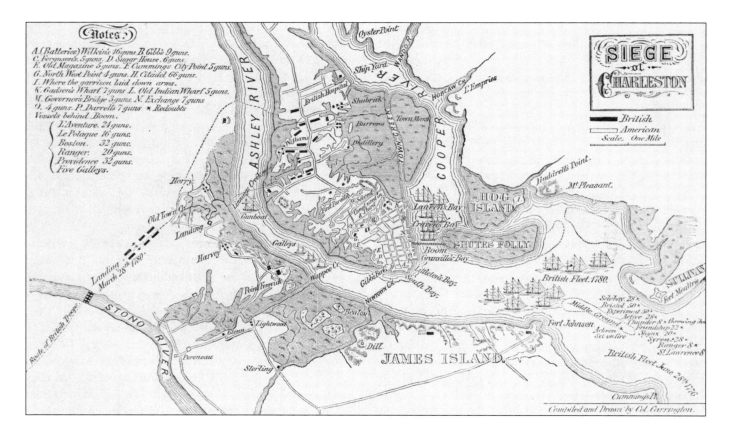

This map depicts the siege of Charleston. *(Courtesy of Anne S. K. Brown Military Collection, Brown University Library)*

and aerial bombs that damage buildings, but with little loss of life. Lincoln calls a council of war, rejects leaving the city, and asks his officers to consider the prospects a while longer.

April 14: Tarleton and Ferguson sweep down on Huger's men at Monck's Corner, taking them totally by surprise as Huger has not posted patrols or enough sentries. Tarleton captures 400 mounts for his dragoons and 42 wagonloads of supplies. Enduring only two casualties, the British kill 20 Americans and take 67 prisoners; among the dead is Maj. Pierre Vernier, commander of Pulaski's Legion. Huger and William Washington barely manage to escape into the swamps. The British now control Lincoln's only escape route.

April 17: Adm. Luc Urbain de Guichen's naval squadron engages a British squadron commanded by Adm. George Rodney off Martinique. British ineptitude allows the French to escape the inconclusive battle.

April 18: Lord Rawdon arrives at Charleston with more reinforcements, giving Clinton a total of nearly 10,000 troops on land and 5,000 seamen aboard ships in the harbor.

April 19: With Clinton's trenches within 250 yards of his Charleston fortifications, Lincoln calls another council of war to consider surrendering; but North Carolina Lieutenant Governor Christopher Gadsden insists that Lincoln remain and fight.

April 21: Accepting the futility of his position, Lincoln surmounts pressure from Gadsden and city officials, and proposes a surrender to Clinton, but Clinton rejects Lincoln's terms.

April 23–24: During the night, Lincoln sends a modest sortie against the British. Virginia and Carolina troops attack the first line of British works with their bayonets but are repulsed at the second line. Both sides suffer several deaths.

April 27: Clinton's men reach a flooded ditch fronting Lincoln's defenses; they use 200 workers at a time, digging round the clock, to press their trenches forward and man them with 1,200 troops.

April 28: Following a year's absence in France, the marquis de Lafayette returns to Boston. He bears French commissions of lieutenant general and vice admiral for Washington.

May 6: Tarleton's dragoons rout a ragtag American force trying to rally at Lenud's Ferry by the Santee River, killing or wounding 40 while incurring no losses, and sending Col. William Washington again into a hasty escape.

May 7: British troops land on Sullivan's Island in Charleston Harbor and capture the garrison of 200 left behind at Fort Moultrie when the Americans effectively abandoned the fort.

May 8: Clinton again summons Lincoln to surrender, but Lincoln holds out for better terms.

May 9: Monstrous nighttime artillery barrages from both sides terrify Charleston's citizens into petitioning Lincoln to surrender.

May 12: In the Americans' greatest defeat of the war, Lincoln accepts Clinton's terms and surrenders Charleston. Lincoln's troops march out with colors cased and lay down their arms. The terms of surrender allow militiamen to return to their homes on parole, but all regular Continentals become prisoners. Many revolutionary leaders, Governor Rutledge a prominent exception, are also to be held as prisoners, essentially ending their involvement in the Revolutionary War.

May 14: His regiment the only American force remaining at large in all of South Carolina, Abraham Buford is ordered to retreat toward Hillsboro to salvage at least a remnant patriot fighting presence in the state.

May 18: Lord Cornwallis marches out from Huger's Bridge in pursuit of Buford, hastening up the Santee River. Unable to gain on the fleeing Americans, he halts and assigns the task to Tarleton.

May 21: After sailing up Lake Champlain and marching undetected overland, a force of 400 Loyalists and 200 Indians commanded by Sir John Johnson attacks the settlements at Johnstown, New York, in reprisal for the depredations of Sullivan's expedition.

May 22: Holding half of his force at Johnstown, Johnson sends the rest to Caughnawaga. The Loyalists kill settlers and burn houses as they proceed, setting the Mohawk Valley aflame once more.

May 23: Johnson's troops reunite and continue their march in the Mohawk Valley, killing settlers and destroying any property not owned by a Loyalist; they reach Crown Point and withdraw.

May 25: Lacking adequate food and with their pay five months in arrears, Washington's troops at Morristown have grown restive. Two Connecticut regiments decide to go in search of food; acting brigade commander Col. R. J. Meigs tries to stop them, and a soldier hits him. The arrival of the Pennsylvania Line restores order, and the Connecticut dissidents return to their huts—a few arrested, but with no action taken against them.

May 26: The British frigate *Iris* captures the American ship *Aurora* one day out of Philadelphia and bound for Santa Cruz, off Cape Henlopen. The British send the *Aurora's* crew and passengers, among them the poet Philip Freneau, to New York to be imprisoned aboard four prison ships in the harbor—Freneau assigned to the *Scorpion.*

A force of British regulars and Indian auxiliaries from Michilimackinac attacks the Spanish fort at St. Louis (called San Luis de Ylinoises) and is repulsed by the Spanish defenders commanded by Capt. Fernando de Leyba.

May 29: Tarleton catches up with Buford's Virginia Continentals and mixed cavalry at Waxhaws Creek near the North Carolina border. When Tarleton demands his surrender under a flag of truce, Buford dithers and then decides to do battle. Tarleton's 17th Dragoons smash his lines with a cavalry charge. Those among Buford's force who are not casualties try to surrender, but Tarleton's men decimate them with swords and bayonets. American losses are 113 dead and 203 taken prisoner, most of them wounded, while Tarleton has only 19 casualties. Tarleton's victory ends organized American resistance in South Carolina.

June 2: Off Bermuda, the 30-gun American frigate *Trumbull* commanded by Capt. James Nicholson

Banaster Tarleton was a British officer. *(From* The Pictorial Field Book of the Revolution, *2 vols., by B. J. Lossing. New York: Harper Brothers, 1851 and 1852.)*

encounters the British privateer *Watt* commanded by John Coulthard. A fierce ship-to-ship battle ensues between the evenly matched ships, leaving both badly damaged and neither with the advantage. After two and a half hours, they break off and return to port. Nicholson has 18 dead and 21 wounded; Coulthard, 13 dead and 79 wounded.

June 2–9: An Irish peer, Lord George Gordon, has formed the Protestant Association to oppose introduction of a bill in Parliament that would remove political restrictions against Roman Catholics. Gordon's agitation on the issue incites large-scale riots, with mobs of more than 60,000 people rampaging in London's streets, pillaging and destroying Catholic homes and chapels and also public buildings. Throwing the government into temporary disarray, the mobs besiege Parliament, whose members must be rescued by the police. The army finally quells the Gordon Riots.

June 6: With reports of the critical state of Washington's army at Morristown, New Jersey, von Knyphausen decides on a show of strength to attract mutinous American troops or to disable Washington's fighting capacity; he lands 5,000 troops on the Jersey shore for an inland march.

June 7: Near Connecticut Farms, Continental infantrymen commanded by Col. Elias Dayton, along with local militia, make a stand against von Knyphausen's advance into New Jersey; their musket fire prevents him from crossing the Rahway River. Von Knyphausen's British and German troops burn several farms and then withdraw to dig in at De Hart's Point.

June 8: Gratified by the capture of Charleston, Gen. Sir Henry Clinton prepares to relinquish command of the southern campaign to Cornwallis and return to New York.

June 13: Neglecting to consult Washington, the Continental Congress appoints Horatio Gates commander of the army in the Southern Department. Delegates to Congress know nothing about Gates's military capabilities but have lowered their estimation of Washington.

June 20: At Ramsur's Mill, North Carolina, about 1,200 Patriot militiamen commanded by Col. Francis Locke launch a preemptive strike against about 1,300 Loyalists, many of them unarmed. The Loyalists have been assembled by Col. John Moore, who served with Cornwallis in South Carolina but has ignored Cornwallis's instructions to delay a Loyalist uprising. The two forces clash in chaotic, hand-to-hand skirmishing, with

Locke's militia routing Moore's men and sending them into flight, weakening Cornwallis's hopes for Loyalist support of his planned campaign in North Carolina.

June 21: Maj. Gen. Johann de Kalb arrives at Hillsboro, North Carolina, with a force of 1,400 of Smallwood's Marylanders and Gist's Delaware Continentals en route from Morristown to aid in defending the already lost Charleston. Local authorities ignore de Kalb's appeal for food and supplies for his weary and ill-nourished men.

June 23: Concerned by von Knyphausen's position on the Jersey shore and by a possible British move up the Hudson, Washington has stationed a strong force under Nathanael Greene near Springfield. General Clinton, returned from South Carolina, orders von Knyphausen to advance in hopes of drawing Washington's strength away from New York, and the two forces clash. Failing in a frontal assault on Greene, von Knyphausen is forced to withdraw to Staten Island. He destroys property in Springfield during the withdrawal, but New Jersey is again free of British troops.

July 10: A French fleet of eight ships of the line, two frigates, and two bomb vessels arrives off Newport carrying the count de Rochambeau and 6,000 troops. Another 2,000 troops, however, are left behind at Brest lacking transport and will never reach America.

July 11: Rochambeau and his officers come ashore at Newport and find no welcoming party. Gen. William Heath finally arrives as Washington's representative to take control.

July 12: Near Williamson's Plantation, South Carolina, about 350 Patriot militia led by a disorganized group of officers headed by Gen. Thomas Sumter attacks 400 Loyalists and dragoons commanded by Capt. Christian Houk, whose orders are to organize Loyalists and put down the Patriot militia. The Patriots' fire kills Houk and more than 30 of his men, wounding another 50, and sends the survivors into flight. The Patriots have one casualty.

July 13: A powerful British squadron commanded by Adm. Thomas Graves arrives off New York at Sandy Hook, too late to prevent Rochambeau's troops from landing at Newport.

July 25: Traveling from Virginia, Gen. Horatio Gates arrives at Coxe's Mill, North Carolina, to assume command of the Southern Department from de Kalb, who has held nominal command. Gates confirms de Kalb's command of the Delaware and Maryland troops he brought from New Jersey and the survivors of Armand's Legion and decides on attacking the British at Camden.

July 27: Gates begins to march toward Camden across well-foraged countryside that affords no support for his ill and undernourished troops.

July 30: A force led by Tennessee-region Indian fighter Col. Isaac Shelby surrounds a post of Loyalists near Cowpens, South Carolina, and wins their surrender without firing a shot.

August 1: His militia force now augmented to 600 men, Gen. Thomas Sumter assaults a fort at Rocky Mount manned by Loyalists as an outpost protecting the British army at Camden, but his efforts to burn out the defenders fail, and he withdraws.

August 3: Gates's army crosses the Pee Dee River at Mask's Ferry and is joined by a handful of Virginia militiamen who have eluded the British since the loss of Charleston. Francis Marion and his ragged band of 20 followers also join Gates; they ignore the derisive comments of Gates's regulars and return to South Carolina to scout.

August 5: Gen. Benedict Arnold has been maneuvering to secure a significant command with the intention of turning it over to the British. He now succeeds, winning appointment as commander at West Point.

Former governor Richard Caswell, with a force of 2,000 well-supplied North Carolina militia, joins Gates's army at Lynches Creek, South Carolina, for the march to Camden.

August 6: Sumter attacks the British outpost at Hanging Rock garrisoned by members of the British Legion and Loyalist regiments from North and South Carolina. Following a very successful initial assault, his men turn to repulse a flanking attack, collapsing the Loyalists' resistance. Sumter's men begin to loot the outpost's supplies. A force of Loyalist mounted infantry arrives and renews the battle; unable to rally his men from their looting, Sumter disengages and withdraws. Sumter's force suffers 12 dead and 51 wounded; the Loyalist outpost, 192 casualties.

August 11: A British force under Lord Rawdon opposes Gates's crossing of Little Lynches Creek, but a poorly executed American effort to flank the British fails, and Rawdon withdraws toward Camden, 15 miles distant. Still needing food, Gates can detour to Waxhaws, where supplies are available, or approach Camden to engage the British army.

August 13: Lord Cornwallis arrives at Camden to assume command from Lord Rawdon. Having summoned troops from outposts, the British garrison numbers about 2,200 seasoned troops, including regulars of the Royal Welch Fusiliers and the 33rd West Riding Regiment and Loyalists from Tarleton's British Legion. Cornwallis resolves to engage Gates in battle.

August 14: Some 700 Virginia militia swell Gates's army to about 4,100 men, but many are in poor condition. Thinking that his army numbers 7,000 men, Gates refuses to believe his aide Otho Williams's report that only half that number are fit for battle.

August 15: Now reinforced with 100 of Gates's Maryland Continentals and 300 North Carolina militia, Sumter attacks a British post at Wateree Ferry, capturing food, clothing, rum, and prisoners; later in the day he also seizes a British supply train moving toward Camden.

Lacking rum, Gates ill-advisedly issues a ration of molasses to his men that, mixed with their poor diet, creates severe gastric distress, leaving the majority severely debilitated.

August 16: During the night, Gates begins to march his men down the main road leading to Camden. At nearly the same time, Cornwallis's men march from Camden on the same road with the intention of locating Gates's army. At a wide, sandy area strewn with pines and hemmed in by bordering swamps, the two armies meet. Gates moves hundreds of yards to the rear, gives a few initial orders only, and plays no active role in the ensuing battle, letting Otho Williams, de Kalb, and a few other officers shoulder the burden of command. When the British attack, the militiamen on the American left panic, toss aside their arms, and flee to the rear. A fraction of the Maryland and Delaware troops manages to escape, fleeing northward with Tarleton's horsemen hard after them. The disaster leaves Gates's army decimated—only 700 of the original 4,100 reach the safety of Hillsboro three days later. British losses are 68 dead and 350 wounded.

August 18: At Fishing Creek, Tarleton and his men sweep down on Sumter's unguarded camp in a surprise attack, killing 150 and capturing 300 prisoners and the supplies Sumter has seized.

Isaac Shelby and Elijah Clarke battle Loyalists on the Encore River near Musgrove Mills, inflicting 63 deaths.

September 3: Off Newfoundland, the British capture the American brig *Mercury,* which is transporting Henry Laurens to the Netherlands. Laurens throws his papers overboard, but the British retrieve them (their contents will influence the British to declare war on

Johann de Kalb fought in the Battle of Camden. *(From* The Pictorial Field Book of the Revolution, *2 vols., by B. J. Lossing. New York: Harper Brothers, 1851 and 1852.)*

the Netherlands) and take Laurens to London as a prisoner of war.

September 15: Col. Elijah Clarke and Lt. Col. James McCall have recruited 400 men and lead them in attacking the Loyalist post at Augusta, Georgia. They surprise an outlying Indian camp, rousing the town's defenders; capture two fortified buildings; and begin a siege of the main stronghold, where Loyalists and Indians led by Col. Thomas Browne have assembled. The brief siege fails, and the Patriots withdraw with a sizable quantity of plunder.

September 20: General Washington meets formally with the count de Rochambeau at Hartford, Connecticut, to discuss plans.

September 21: Maj. Gen. Benedict Arnold meets secretly at Haverstraw, New York, with Maj. John André.

September 22: André is dismayed to learn the *Vulture* has sailed off, leaving him stranded ashore. He hides through the day in the home of Joshua Hett Smith.

September 23: Arnold urges André to forgo the river and escape overland through the disputed region north of New York City. André dons civilian clothes, hides in his boot documents Arnold wrote detailing West Point's weaknesses, mounts a horse, and sets off with Smith as his guide. They cross the river and spend the night in a farmhouse.

September 24: Hopeful that a pass in the name of John Anderson issued to him by Arnold will permit his safe transit through American lines, André sets off alone after daybreak. Three patriot militiamen stop him near Tarrytown, search him, discover the documents from Arnold, and send him to Lt. Col. John Jameson. Jameson sends the documents to Washington, who is nearby en route to West Point. Jameson orders that André be taken to West Point with a letter informing Arnold of his capture. Though the order is countermanded, the letter travels to West Point.

September 25: While at his breakfast table at West Point, Arnold, who is preparing for Washington's arrival later in the day, receives the warning letter. Arnold hastens to the river and rows his barge to the safety of a British sloop. His wife, Peggy, feigns hysteria to create a distraction. At the end of the day, Arnold sends Washington a letter confirming his treason. His identity now known, André remains a prisoner.

September 29: André is subject to execution under the rules of war, but Washington convenes a board of general officers at Tappan, New York, to review the evidence against the major. The board decides that André should be hanged at Tappan.

Benedict Arnold was a traitor to the Patriots' cause and became a brigadier in the British army. *(From* The Pictorial Field Book of the Revolution, *2 vols., by B. J. Lossing. New York: Harper Brothers, 1851 and 1852.)*

October 1: Western Patriots who have been gathering under such leaders as Isaac Shelby, John Sevier, Arthur Campbell, and William Campbell to protect their settlements from raids by Loyalists, wish to attack Loyalists led by Maj. Patrick Ferguson, and they ask General Gates to appoint Daniel Morgan as their commander for this effort. Since Morgan proves unavailable, they choose William Campbell as their temporary leader.

October 2: André endures his execution with a calmness and dignity that earn his American captors' admiration.

Aroused to return to active duty by the disastrous defeat at Camden, Daniel Morgan arrives at Gates's headquarters in Hillsboro, North Carolina, and receives appointment as commander of a special corps of light troops.

October 4: Although commissioned by Clinton essentially to consolidate British gains in South Carolina, Cornwallis, whose political strength in London allows him to communicate directly with the ministry instead of through Clinton, decides to move against American resistance in North Carolina. He sends Patrick Ferguson's Loyalist force toward King's Mountain to combat Patriot partisans, while he moves eastward toward Charlotte.

October 5: With illusions about Gates's performance at Saratoga dispelled and many congressmen embarrassed over his performance, the Continental Congress pursues an investigation into Gates's conduct during and after the Battle of Camden.

October 6: The Continental Congress formally requests Gen. George Washington to appoint a new commander of the Southern Department to replace Gates.

Pleased with Laurens's capture, British officials confine him in the Tower of London in harsh conditions that threaten his health.

October 7: Maj. Patrick Ferguson posts his Loyalists on King's Mountain, sends a message to Cornwallis requesting reinforcements, and prepares for battle. Ferguson blunders, however, in failing to secure the slopes of the hill and encamping at an open site atop the hill. The Patriot frontiersmen sneak up the slopes, and Isaac Shelby's men attack from one side as William Campbell's attack from the opposite. Conspicuous in his gaudy hunting shirt, Ferguson takes at least six bullets and falls dead. The remaining Loyalists surrender. The Patriots have 26 dead and 64 wounded to the

Tories 57 dead, 163 wounded, and almost 700 taken prisoner.

On Washington's recommendation, the Continental Congress appoints Nathanael Greene, currently in command at West Point, as commander of the Southern Department.

October 8: At Gilbert Town, South Carolina, the rebel militia victors of King's Mountain convene an ad hoc court to try some of their prisoners as war criminals, sentencing 12 Loyalists to be hanged on the spot. They turn hundreds of other prisoners over to the poorly organized governments of the Carolinas; most will escape but nevermore pose a military threat.

October 11: Loyalists and Indians led by Sir John Johnson and Joseph Brant capture Fort George at the southern tip of Lake George and then continue their raids on upper New York settlements.

October 13: The Continental Congress finally promotes Daniel Morgan to the rank of brigadier general. It was the earlier denial of this well-deserved promotion that led to his withdrawal from duty.

October 14: Learning of the defeat at King's Mountain and fearing that the victors will attack his rear, Cornwallis decides to retreat to Winnsboro, South Carolina, to establish winter quarters. The army's march begins, impeded by rains that render the roads muddy and the swamps impassable, while American militia harass the baggage train and fever and illness wrack Cornwallis and many of his men.

The Continental Congress approves a resolution thanking Gist, Smallwood, Porterfield, Armstrong, and Armand for their efforts at the Battle of Camden.

October 16: Maj. Gen. Alexander Leslie sails from New York with 2,500 men to reinforce Cornwallis, whose plan to capture North Carolina has Lord George Germain's approval.

With a large raiding party, Sir John Johnson besieges Middle Fort in the Schoharie Valley, New York, but, lacking artillery, cannot launch an effective attack. The fort's commander, Maj. Melancton Woolsey, nevertheless decides to surrender but is prevented from doing so by Timothy Murphy and other frontiersmen in the fort. Johnson withdraws to move up the Mohawk Valley.

October 17: Fires set by Johnson's men spread through the Schoharie Valley, destroying farms and crops that supplied grain to the Continental army.

October 19: Col. John Brown leads a foray from Stone Arabia against Sir John Johnson, who crushes his outnumbered foe and destroys Stone Arabia. But about 850 militia commanded by Gen. Robert Van Rensselaer catch up with Johnson near Klock's Field and do battle. Johnson's men hold against a flanking attack; they will withdraw the following morning.

October 20: At Washington's behest, Henry Lee chooses Sgt. Maj. John Champe to slip into New York City, abduct Arnold, and bring him back for punishment. Champe feigns desertion and passes through the British lines. He nearly succeeds in his mission, by his own account, but is foiled at the final moment, is forced to remain in the guise of a deserter, and later is shipped to Virginia under Arnold's command.

October 21: After many months of petitioning by Washington and many of his officers, the Continental Congress finally agrees to extend half-pay to Continental officers for life.

October 26: Col. Francis Marion continues his harassment of Cornwallis's rear and Tory supporters, moving out from Tearcoat Swamp to attack Loyalist troops under Col. Samuel Tynes and seizing prisoners, horses, and supplies. In the process, he earns his nickname—the Swamp Fox.

November 4: The Continental Congress requests higher war-support quotas from the states, which some are unwilling or unable to supply because of poor administrative apparatuses, British control, or a burdened citizenry.

November 9: Sent by Cornwallis to track down Thomas Sumter, now a brigadier general of the South Carolina militia, Major Wemyss and his mixed infantry and horsemen find Sumter's camp near Fish Dam Ford for a surprise attack, but Sumter's alert men repulse the attack and take Wemyss prisoner.

November 15: Marion attacks the British garrison at Georgetown, South Carolina, but Loyalist reinforcements arrive before Marion and thwart his efforts.

November 20: Cornwallis now sends Banastre Tarleton, with most of his British Legion and men from the 63rd Regiment, to find and quash Sumter, but Sumter learns of their approach from a deserter and forms his 450 troops at Blackstock's plantation on high ground, skirted by thick undergrowth. Splitting his force, Tarleton attacks without success and must withdraw. Although Sumter receives severe wounds, his force remains intact, with only three dead against Tarleton's nearly 50.

November 22: Maj. Benjamin Tallmadge, who crossed by boat to Long Island with 80 of his 2nd Continental Dragoons the night before, leads their attack

Francis Marion was also known as the Swamp Fox. *(From* The Pictorial Field Book of the Revolution, *2 vols., by B. J. Lossing. New York: Harper Brothers, 1851 and 1852.)*

on a British fortified house in Brookhaven; they subdue the garrison, capture 54 prisoners, and return safely to the American lines.

November 27: Nathanael Greene arrives at Hillsboro, North Carolina, on his journey south to assume command. En route, he has requested supplies and equipment from state governments but without success.

November 30: Henry (Light-Horse Harry) Lee receives promotion to lieutenant colonel, and his corps of three mounted infantry troops is augmented by three foot companies. The new Lee's Legion is made up of well-equipped and well-trained men, specially selected by officers from all units of the Continental army.

December 2: Nathanael Greene arrives at Gates's headquarters at Charlotte, North Carolina.

December 3: Greene assumes command of the Southern Department. Greene decides to utilize Sumter's and Marion's skills—he sends them messages urging their continued harassment of the British and their Loyalists allies. Greene also decides to pursue a daring strategy: dividing his army, giving Daniel Morgan command of one section, confusing the British with threats from two directions—if Cornwallis commits to pursuing one section, then the other can attack his

rear. Greene prepares to move his section of the army into quarters near Cheraw to be refit and trained; he assigns Edward Carrington to reconnoiter roads and river crossings to the north to prepare for rapid withdrawal toward North Carolina.

December 4: Col. William Washington, whose dragoons form part of Morgan's command, traps a group of 100 Loyalists commanded by Col. Henry Rugeley in a fortified barn at Rugeley's Mill. Washington has a fake cannon made with a log, wheels it into position, and calls on Rugeley to surrender. The ruse works.

December 16: Greene orders Morgan, with about 600 of Greene's effective force of 2,500, to cross the Catawba River, assemble North Carolina militia units headed by William Davidson, and conduct operations between the Broad and Pacolet Rivers. Greene leaves Morgan free to take the offensive if warranted but instructs him to attack the British rear or rejoin Greene if Cornwallis moves against Greene at Cheraw.

December 19: Greene begins to move his section of the army from Charlotte to Cheraw.

December 20: Impressed by the formation of the League of Armed Neutrality, Congress appoints Francis Dana of Massachusetts as envoy to Russia, sending him on what will be a fruitless mission.

Swayed by tacit Dutch support of the Americans and French and by the contents of papers found on Henry Laurens, Great Britain declares war on the Netherlands, freeing the Royal Navy to attack Dutch outposts and ships.

An expedition commanded by Benedict Arnold, now a brigadier general in the British army, sets out from Sandy Hook to sail to Virginia with the objective of seizing or destroying rebel property and supplies as a means of depriving Greene of supplies. Arnold's 1,600 troops include Lt. Col. John Simcoe's Loyalist Queen's Rangers.

December 26: Greene's army arrives at Cheraw to encamp at a site chosen by Kościuszko.

December 27: Sent out by Morgan, William Washington's dragoons, accompanied by mounted militia, successfully attack Loyalists at Williamson's Plantation and push on to capture Fort William. Considering the move a threat to his rear, Cornwallis dispatches Tarleton to crush Morgan.

December 30: Though now diminished by 400 troops, Arnold's expedition arrives at Hampton Roads and begins to move up the James River.

EYEWITNESS TESTIMONY

1780

Continuing in Elissebeth town 'till Near Sun rise / then crossed the River on the Ice / came to Staton Island & proceeded on towards the Enemies fort which was 5 miles / hear we manoeuver'd back & forth for two or 3 hours / then we took post on a hill half a mile from one of the forts where the Snow was about two feet deep / hear we dug the Snow off the Ground & built up fires and tarried all Night and very cold with a Number of our mens feet fros'd.

> *Ensign Jeremiah Greenman, whose Rhode Island unit was encamped with the army near Morristown, diary entry of January 15, 1780, in Greenman,* Diary of a Common Soldier in the American Revolution, 1775–1783, *p. 167.*

I have now the pleasure to inform Congress, that the situation of the Army for the present, is, and it has been for some days past, comfortable and easy on the score of provision. We were reduced at last to such extremity. . . . that I was obliged to call upon the Magistrates in every County in the State for specific quantities to be supplied in a limited number of days. I should be wanting in justice to their zeal and attachment and to that of the Inhabitants of the State in general, were I not to inform Congress, that they gave the earliest and most chearful attention to my requisitions, and exerted themselves for the Army's relief in a manner that did them the highest honor . . .

> *George Washington, from a letter written at Morristown, New Jersey, January 27, 1780, to the president of the Continental Congress, in John C. Fitzpatrick, ed.,* The Writings of George Washington, *vol. 17, pp. 449–450.*

It is possible you may have heard that in the course of the last summer an expedition was meditated by our Colo. Clarke against Detroit; that he had proceeded so far as to rendezvous a very large body of Indians (I believe four or five thousand) at Saint-Vincennes; but being disappointed in the number of whites he expected, and not chusing to rely principally on the Indians, was obliged to decline it. We have a tolerable prospect of reinforcing him this spring to the number which he thinks sufficient for the enterprize. We have informed him of this, and left to himself to decide between this object and that of giving rigorous chas-

tisement to those tribes of Indians whose eternal hostilities have proved them incapable of living on friendly terms with us. It is our opinion his inclination will lead him to the former. . . .

> *Governor Thomas Jefferson, from a letter written at Williamsburg, to George Washington, February 10, 1780, in Julian P. Boyd, ed.,* The Papers of Thomas Jefferson, *vol. 3, p. 291.*

This [North] ministry, and many of the minority, sacrifice their time in disputing on a question with which they have nothing to do, namely whether America shall be independent or not. Whereas the only question that can come under their determination is whether they will accede to it or not. They confound a military question with a political one, and undertake to supply by a vote what they lost by a battle. Say she shall not be independent, and it will signify as much as if they voted against a decree of fate, or say that she shall, and she will be no more independent than before. Questions which, when determined, cannot be executed, serve only to show the folly of dispute and the weakness of disputants.

> *Thomas Paine, from "The American Crisis VIII, Address to the People of England," March 1780, in Van der Weyde,* The Life and Works of Thomas Paine, *vol. 3, pp. 111–112.*

Should peace arrive after another Campaign or two, and afford us a little Leisure, I should be happy to see your Excellency in Europe, and to accompany you, if my Age and Strength would permit, in visiting some of its ancient and most famous Kingdoms. You would, on this side of the Sea, enjoy the great Reputation you have acquir'd, pure and free from those little Shades that the Jealousy and Envy of a Man's Countrymen and Contemporaries are ever endeavouring to cast over living Merit. Here you would know, and enjoy, what Posterity will say of Washington. . . .

> *Benjamin Franklin, from a letter written at Passy, France, March 5, 1780, to George Washington, in Albert Henry Smyth, ed.,* The Writings of Benjamin Franklin, *vol. 8, p. 28.*

Many reasons have occurred lately for declining the expedition against Detroit. Want of men, want of money, scarcity of provisions, are of themselves sufficient, but there are others more cogent which cannot be trusted to a letter. We therefore wish you to decline that object, and consider the taking post on the Mississipi and chastising the hostile Indians as the business of this summer.

There is reason to apprehend insurrection among some discontented inhabitants (Tories) on our South-Western frontier. I would have you give assistance on the shortest warning to that quarter, should you be applied to by the militia officers, to whom I write on the subject. Nothing can produce so dangerous a diversion of our force, as a circumstance of that kind if not crushed in it's infancy.

Governor Thomas Jefferson, from a letter written at Williamsburg, to George Rogers Clark, March 19, 1780, in Julian P. Boyd, ed., The Papers of Thomas Jefferson, *vol. 3, p. 317.*

Reinforcements are expected—General Hogan is within a few miles. *The Virginia troops are somewhere!—assistance from that sister state has been expected these eighteen months.* General Moultrie is forming a camp at Bacon Bridge.... General Williamson is encamped at Augusta—a thousand men are expected from this brigade. General Richardson and Colonel Carlen are raising the militia at and about Camden. At this moment [February 15] the escape of the Americans depends on further delay on the enemy's part: two or three weeks more will make this garrison strong. The inhabitants in general are in good spirits; competent judges say that Sir Henry Clinton will then have cause to repent his enterprise. This affords encouragement, but events in war are uncertain; and if we do not receive assistance, the next intelligence may be quite contrary.

From a letter sent from Charleston by Col. John Laurens, Maryland Journal, *March 21, 1780, in Frank Moore, compiler,* The Diary of the American Revolution, *pp. 410–411.*

... Among the various conjectures of alarm and distress which have arisen in the course of the revolution, it is with pain I affirm to you Sir, that no one can be singled out more truly critical than the present. Our army threatened with an immediate alternative of disbanding or living on free quarters; the public Treasury empty; public credit exhausted, nay the private credit of purchasing Agents employed, I am told, as far as it will bear, Congress complaining of the extortion of the people; the people of the improvidence of Congress, and the army of both; our affairs requiring the most mature and systematic measures, and the urgency of occasions admitting only of temporizing expedients and those expedients generating new difficulties. Congress from a defect of adequate Statesmen more likely to fall into wrong measures and of less weight to enforce right ones, recommending plans to the several states for execution and the states separately rejudging the expediency of such plans.... These are the outlines of the true picture of our public situation. I leave it to your imagination to fill them up....

James Madison, Virginia delegate to the Continental Congress, from a letter written in Philadelphia, to Thomas Jefferson, March 27, 1780, in Julian P. Boyd, The Papers of Thomas Jefferson, *vol. 3, p. 335.*

My sentiments concerning public affairs correspond too much with yours. The prospect my Dear Baron is gloomy and the storm thickens [sic]. Not to have the anxieties you express at the present juncture would be not to feel that zeal and interest in our cause, by which all your conduct shows you to be actuated. But I hope we shall extricate ourselves, and bring every thing to a prosperous issue. I have been so inured to difficulties in the course of this contest that I have learned to look upon them with more tranquility than formerly...

George Washington, from a letter written at Morristown, New Jersey, April 2, 1780, to Baron Friedrich von Steuben, in John C. Fitzpatrick, ed., The Writings of George Washington, *vol. 18, p. 204.*

The last accounts from America were of the 10th March, contained in two or three Boston newspapers, brought to Bilboa from Newbury. They give us reason, indeed, to expect that your namesake's fleet has been thoroughly dispersed, and his designs on South Carolina thereby defeated. I am anxious for confirmation of this intelligence; it would operate in Europe as much to our advantage ... as a victory. As long as you can maintain your importance, and appear neither to want friends or fear foes, you will enjoy respectability on this side of the water, and reap all the advantages resulting from it. By her power, justice, commerce, and consequence, America must expect to gain and keep friends. The equity of her cause is with many only a secondary consideration.

John Jay, from a letter written in Aranjuez, Spain, May 6, 1780, to New York governor George Clinton, in William Jay, The Life of John Jay, *vol. 1, p. 112.*

I am sorry an idea should prevail in France that if they should be unsuccessful this campaign we should make terms with England. Believe me no opinion can have less foundation. The disinterested exertions of France for us have not only made real impression on the leaders of the people, but are deeply felt by the people themselves, and the sentiment of making separate terms with England is so base that I verily believe no man in America would venture to express such a one. It is an unfortunate truth that we were left so long to struggle alone that our resources had become exhausted, and Great Britain has been so lucky as to encounter her adversaries as the surviving Horatius did the Curiatii, one after another, and not all together. . . . Yet I am thoroughly satisfied that the attachment of the people to the cause in which we are engaged and their hatred to Great Britain remain unshaken. Wherever the French and American troops have acted together the harmony has been real. . . . There has been no instance of the smallest bickering except between some French and American sailors at Boston, who had a fracas, such as eternally happens among people of that kind, and I believe one life was lost.

Governor Thomas Jefferson, from a letter written at Richmond, Virginia, to Philip Mazzei, diplomatic agent in Europe for Virginia, May 31, 1780, in Julian P. Boyd, ed., The Papers of Thomas Jefferson, *vol. 3, p. 405.*

To [the] Loan Office; received certificates for interest due Two Thousand Dollars, in cash Nineteen and a half Dollars and two shillings and six pence, as they complained they had no cash to pay off the interest due on the former certificates. Poor encouragement to us Whigs who had confided and trusted our all in the public funds! . . .

Christopher Marshall, merchant and Quaker then in Lancaster, Pennsylvania, diary entry of June 5, 1780, in Marshall, Extracts from the Diary of Christopher Marshall, *pp. 243–244.*

Afflicting as the loss of Charleston may be, yet if it universally rouse us from the slumber of twelve months past, and renew in us the spirit of former days, it will produce an advantage more important than its loss. America *is* what she *thinks* herself to be. Governed by sentiment, and acting her own mind, she becomes, as she pleases, the victor or the victim.

It is not the conquest of towns, nor the accidental capture of garrisons, that can reduce a country so extensive as this. The sufferings of one part can never be relieved by the exertions of another, and there is no situation the enemy can be placed in that does not afford to us the same advantages which he seeks himself. By dividing his force, he leaves every post attackable. It is a mode of war that carries with it a confession of weakness, and goes on the principle of distress rather than conquest.

Thomas Paine, from "The American Crisis IX," June 9, 1780, in Van der Weyde, The Life and Works of Thomas Paine, *vol. 3, pp. 117–118.*

Our intelligence from the Southward is most lamentably defective. Tho' Charlestown [Charleston, South Carolina] has now been in the hands of the enemy a month, we hear nothing of their movements which can be relied on. Rumours are that they are penetrating Northward. To remedy this defect I shall immediately establish a line of expresses from hence to the neighborhood of their army, and send thither a sensible judicious gentleman to give us information of their movements. This intelligence will I hope be conveyed to us at the rate of 120 miles in 24 hours. They set out to their stations tomorrow. . . .

Governor Thomas Jefferson, from a letter written at Richmond, Virginia, to George Washington, June 11, 1780, in Julian P. Boyd, ed., The Papers of Thomas Jefferson, *vol. 3, pp. 432–433.*

. . . Although they [British troops] observed great discipline and decorum in Elizabethtown, yet at the Connecticut Farms every step was marked with wanton cruelty and causeless devastation. . . .

Soon after their possessing themselves of the neighborhood, a soldier came to the [Caldwell] house, and putting his gun to the window of the room where this worthy woman was sitting, (with her children, and a maid with an infant in her arms, along side of her,) he shot her through the lungs dead on the spot. Soon after an officer with two Hessians came in, and ordered a hole dug and her body thrown in, and the house to be set on fire. At the earnest request of an officer of the new levies, and with some difficulty, the body was suffered to be carried to a small house in the neighborhood, and Mr. Caldwell's dwelling-house immediately set on fire, and every thing belonging to him consumed together. . . .

From an account of the June 6 attack on Elizabethtown, New Jersey, the Pennsylvania Packet, *June 13, 1780, in Frank Moore, compiler,* The Diary of the American Revolution, *pp. 426–427.*

With respect to Charles Town [Charleston, South Carolina], although I have received no Official advices of it on our part, the loss of it seems placed beyond doubt. . . . The Garrison, at least the part denominated Continental, are prisoners of War. This is a severe blow; but not such as will ruin us, if we exert ourselves virtuously and as we are able. Something like it seems to have been necessary, to rouse us from the . . . unaccountable state of security in which we were sunk. Heaven grant the blow may have this effect. If it should, the misfortune may prove a benefit and the means of saving us.

George Washington, from a letter written at Springfield, New Jersey, June 14, 1780, to Massachusetts official James Bowdoin, in John C. Fitzpatrick, ed., The Writings of George Washington, *vol. 19, p. 9.*

Whilst the troops were advancing to Connecticut Farms, the rebels fired out of the houses, agreeable to their usual practice, from which circumstance Mrs Caldwell had the misfortune to be shot by a random ball. What heightens the singularity of this lady's fate is, that upon inquiry, it appears beyond doubt that the shot was fired by the rebels themselves, as it entered the side of the house from their direction, and lodged in the wall nearest to the troops, when advancing. The manner in which the rebels aggravate this unfortunate affair in their publications, is of a piece with their uniform conduct—plausible, but fallacious; nor is it to be wondered at, if a rebellion which originated in falsehood, is prosecuted with deceit. The soldiery received with smiles one moment, and the following instant butchered (for in a military view it merits no other name) by a set of people, who, by their clothing and appointments, cannot be distinguished from the quiet inhabitants of the country, may well be supposed to be exasperated; nor need we be surprised at their using the torch to dwellings which they find hourly occupied by armed men. . . . Whatever may be the humane wishes of the com-

manders, human nature at times steps over the barrier of discipline. . . .

From a British officer's account of the Elizabethtown attack, Rivington's Gazette, *June 21, 1780, in Frank Moore, compiler,* The Diary of the American Revolution, *pp. 430–431.*

You will proceed with the riders provided for you, stationing one at every forty miles or thereabouts from hence to the vicinity of the British army in Carolina where you will continue yourself, observing their movements and when their importance requires it, communicating them to me. Instruct your riders to travel by night and day without regard to weather giving and taking waybills expressing the hour and minute of their delivering and receiving dispatches. . . . Important events also tho they should not be attended by any movement, which respects us, I would wish you to communicate. The state and resources of our friends, their force, the disposition of the people, the prospect of provisions, ammunition, arms, and other circumstances, the force and condition of the enemy, will also be proper articles of communication. . . .

Governor Thomas Jefferson, from a letter written at Richmond, Virginia, to James Monroe, June 16, 1780, in Julian P. Boyd, ed., The Papers of Thomas Jefferson, *vol. 3, p. 451.*

. . . My Dear Laurens, our countrymen have all the folly of the ass and all the passiveness of the sheep in their compositions. They are determined not to be free and they can neither be frightened, discouraged not persuaded to change their resolution. If we are saved France and Spain must save us. I have the most pigmy-feelings at the idea, and I almost wish to hide my disgrace in universal ruin. Don't think I rave; for the conduct of the states is enough most pitiful that can be imagined. . . .

Alexander Hamilton, from a letter written at Ramapo, New Jersey, June 30, 1780, to Lt. Col. John Laurens, in Harold C. Syrett, ed., The Papers of Alexander Hamilton, *vol. 2, pp. 347–348.*

I hasten to impart to you the happiness I feel at the welcome news of your arrival; and as well in the name of the American army as my own name to present you with an assurance of our warmest sentiments for allies who have so generously come to our aid. As a citizen of the United States and as a soldier in the cause of liberty,

I thankfully acknowledge this new mark of friendship from His Most Christian Majesty. . . .

George Washington, from a letter written at his Bergen County, New Jersey, headquarters, July 16, 1780, to Count de Rochambeau, in John C. Fitzpatrick, ed., The Writings of George Washington, *vol. 19, p. 185.*

Count de Rochambeau was a French general. *(From* The Pictorial Field Book of the Revolution, *2 vols., by B. J. Lossing. New York: Harper Brothers, 1851 and 1852.)*

State of North Carolina August 1780

500	Tents Compleat
2000	Barrels Flour
4000	do. Corn
250	do. Rice
50	Hogsheads Rum
10	Hogsheads Sugar
10	Barrels Coffee
10	Barrels Vinegar
1000	Bushels Salt
	Intrenching Tools
500	Spades
200	Grubbing Hoes
100	Common Hoes
200	Felling Axes

Gen. Horatio Gates, a list of required supplies sent to both the Continental Congress and Thomas Jefferson from Hillsborough, North Carolina, August 1780, in Julian P. Boyd, ed., The Papers of Thomas Jefferson, *vol. 3, p. 582.*

Gentlemen, the reduction of the whole province of South Carolina and the concurrence of all our accounts from the provinces in rebellion of the distress of the inhabitants and their anxious desire to return to the King's obedience, together with the reduced state of Mr Washington's force, the decay of the power of the Congress, and the total failure of their paper money, open a fair and flattering prospect of a speedy and happy termination of the American war. Your able and vigorous conduct in your respective commands leaves no room to apprehend anything will be wanting to accelerate this happy event that the exertion of great military talents can accomplish. . . .

Lord George Germain, from a letter written at Whitehall, London, August 3, 1780, to Gen. Sir Henry Clinton and Vice Adm. Marriot Arbuthnot, in K. G. Davies, ed., Documents of the American Revolution, *vol. 18, p. 131.*

You are to proceed to West point and take the command of that post and its dependencies, in which are included all from Fishkill to Kings Ferry. The Corps of Infantry and Cavalry advanced towards the Enemy's line on the East side of the River will [also] be under your orders and will take directions from you, and you will endeavor to obtain every intelligence of the Enemy's Motions. . . .

George Washington, from a letter written at Peekskill, New York, August 3, 1780, to Maj. Gen. Benedict Arnold, in John C. Fitzpatrick, ed., The Writings of George Washington, *vol. 19, p. 309.*

Clear and hott, this morning, the Brigade was Inspected by Baron Stuben [sic] my Regt. was the first for Inspection, and the Baron was Exceedingly pleasd with the mens array being in the best Order. Nothing Remarkable.

Col. Israel Angell, diary entry of August 10, 1780, while encamped in northern New Jersey, in Angell, The Diary of Colonel Israel Angell, *pp. 103–104.*

But was there ever an instance of a General running away as Gates has done from his whole army? and was there ever so precipitous a flight? One hundred and eighty miles in three days and a half. It does admirable credit to the activity of a man at his time of life. But it disgraces the General and the Soldiers. I always believed him to be very far short of a Hector, or an Ulysses. All the world I think will begin to agree with me.

But what will be done by Congress? ... If he is changed for God's sake overcome prejudice, and send Greene. You know my opinion of him. I stake my reputation on the events, give him but fair play.

Alexander Hamilton, from a letter written in Bergen County, New Jersey, September 6, 1780, to James Duane, New York delegate to the Continental Congress, in Harold C. Syrett, ed., The Papers of Alexander Hamilton, *vol. 2, p. 421.*

... A variety of disappointments with respect to the prospects of my private fortune previous to my acquaintance with your Excellency ... perplex'd my plan of life and expos'd me to inconveniences which had nearly destroyed me. In this situation had I not form'd a connection with you I should most certainly have retir'd from society with a resolution never to have enter'd on the stage again. I could never have prevail'd on myself to have taken an introduction to the Country or to have deriv'd any advantages or even to have remain'd in connection with one, by whom I felt myself injur'd but whose near relationship and situation in life put it in his power to serve me. In this situation you became acquainted with me and undertook the direction of my studies and believe me I feel that whatever I am at present in the opinion of others or whatever I may be in future has greatly arose from your friendship. My plan of life is now fix'd, has a certain object for its view. ...

James Monroe, from a letter written in Richmond, Virginia, to Thomas Jefferson, September 9, 1780, in Julian P. Boyd, ed., The Papers of Thomas Jefferson, *vol. 3, p. 622.*

The situation of America at this time is critical; the Government without finances; its paper credit sunk, and no expedients it can adopt capable of retrieving it; the resources of the country much diminished, by a five Years war, in which it has made efforts beyond its ability. Clinton with an army of ten thousand regular troops, aided by a considerable body of militia, ... in possession of one of our capital towns, and a large part of the State to which it belongs; the savages desolat-

ing the other frontier; a fleet superior to that of our allies. ... Lord Cornwallis with seven or eight thousand men in complete possession of two States, Georgia and South Carolina; a third, North Carolina, by recent misfortunes at his mercy, his force dayly increasing by an accession of adherents. ...

George Washington, from a letter written at his Bergen County, New Jersey, headquarters, September 12, 1780, to Comte de Guichen, commander of the French navy in the West Indies, in John C. Fitzpatrick, ed., The Writings of George Washington, *vol. 20, p. 40.*

This day the army was paraded & reviewed by his Excellency Genl. Washington and [a] Number of Indian Chifes after which sat on a Genl. Court Martial / Tryed a Serjeant for Desertion who was found Guilty & sentenced to be reduced & receive 100 Lashes on his naked back—

Ensign Jeremiah Greenman, diary entry of September 13, 1780, when the army was encamped at Steenrapie, New Jersey, in Greenman, Diary of a Common Soldier in the American Revolution, 1775–1783, *p. 181.*

... I can neither confirm, nor refute, the intelligence I sent your Excellency in my Letter of the 9th. Instant: as I have not since then, been able to Learn with any Certainty the real Designs of the Enemy. Good Spies are difficult to be had without Gold; There I have most Sensibly Felt, the Advantage Lord Cornwallis has Over me. A Special Express will set out instantly, the moment I am convinced of the Route the Enemy are taking. I am much Obliged to Your Excellency for Supplying Col. Kosciuszco with Money for His Journey. ...

Gen. Horatio Gates, from a letter written at Hillsborough, North Carolina, to Thomas Jefferson, September 14, 1780, in Julian P. Boyd, ed., The Papers of Thomas Jefferson, *vol. 3, p. 647.*

... the Gentlemen met again this day to Settle the dispute between Barron Stuben and Col [Moses] Hazen, but did not finish the business, went to dobbs ferry in the afternoon on our way back a merry Scean happened Genl Stark goining to water his hors at a place Call'd the Stole, mired him, and got him into the mud and mire. the Genl. Got out without aney damage Except bedaubing himself with mud, the adj. Genl. Allso mired his hors.

but he got out without difficulty. Genl. Stark drawd out by the Soldiers.

Col. Israel Angell, diary entry of September 21, 1780, while encamped at Tappan near West Point, in Angell, The Diary of Colonel Israel Angell, *p. 121.*

The events of coming within an enemy's post, and of changing my dress, which led to my present situation, were contrary to my own intentions, as they were to your orders; and the circuitous route which I took to return was imposed (perhaps unavoidably) without alternative upon me. I am perfectly tranquil in mind, and prepared for any fate to which an honest zeal for my king's service may have devoted me.

Major John André, from a letter written, with General Washington's permission, to Sir Henry Clinton, September 30, 1780, recorded in André, Major André's Journal, *p. 8.*

Buoy'd above the Terror of Death by the Consciousness of a Life devoted to honorable pursuits, and stained with no action that can give me Remorse, I trust the request I make to your Excellency at this serious period, and which is to soften my last moments, will not be rejected.

Sympathy towards a Soldier will surely induce your Excellency and a military Tribunal to adopt the mode of my death to the feelings of a man of honor.

Let me hope Sir, that if aught in my character impresses you with esteem towards me, if aught in my misfortunes marks me as the victim of policy, and not of resentment, I shall experience the Operation of these Feelings in your Breast by being informed that I am not to die on a Gibbet.

Major John André, a letter to General Washington, October 1, 1780, recorded in André, Major André's Journal, *p. 9.*

If you are not so fortunate in Spain, continue however the even Temper you have hitherto manifested. Spain owes us nothing; therefore, whatever Friendship she shows us in lending Money, or furnishing Cloathing, &c., tho' not equal to our Wants & Wishes, is however *tant de gagne.* Those, who have begun to assist us, are more likely to continue than to decline, and we are still so much obliged as their aids amount to. . . .

Benjamin Franklin, from a letter written at Passy, France, October 2, 1780, to John Jay, in Albert Henry Smyth, ed., The Writings of Benjamin Franklin, *vol. 8, pp. 143–144.*

This afternoon [September 30] the people of Philadelphia and vicinity made a demonstration somewhat unfavorable to the late commander at West Point. . . . The exhibition was as follows:—A stage raised on the body of a cart, on which was an effigy of General Arnold sitting; this was dressed in regimentals, had two faces, emblematical of his traitorous conduct, a mask in his left hand, and a letter in his right from Beelzebub, telling him that he had done all the mischief he could do, and now he must hang himself.

At the back of the general was a figure of the Devil, dressed in black robes, shaking a purse of money at the general's left ear, and in his right hand a pitchfork, ready to drive him into hell as the reward due for the many crimes which his thirst for gold had made him commit.

From the Pennsylvania Packet, *October 3, 1780, in Frank Moore, compiler,* The Diary of the American Revolution, *pp. 448–449.*

The true character of Arnold is that of a desperado. . . . [W]here either plunder or profit was the object, no danger deterred, no principle restrained him. In his person he was smart and active, somewhat diminutive, weak in his capacities and trifling in his conversation; and though gallant in the field, was defective in the talents necessary for command. . . . His march to Quebec gave him fame, and the plunder of Montreal put the first stamp to his public character. His behavior, at Danbury and Saratoga once more covered over his crimes, which again broke forth in the plunder of Philadelphia, under pretence of supplying the army. From this time, the true spring of his conduct being known, he became both disregarded and disesteemed, and this last instance of his treachery has proved the public judgment right.

. . . . .

But there is one reflection results from this black business that deserves notice, which is that it shows the declining power of the enemy. An attempt to bribe is a sacrifice of military fame, and a confession of inability to conquer; as a proud people they ought to be above it, and as soldiers to despise it; and however they may feel on the occasion, the world at large will despise them for it, and consider America superior to their arms.

Thomas Paine, in a postscript to "The Crisis Extraordinary, On the Subject of Taxation," October 4, 1780, in Van der Weyde, The Life and Works of Thomas Paine, *vol. 3, pp. 155–157.*

Andre was executed, he book'd both meek and
mild;
Around on the spectators most pleasantly he smiled;
It moved each eye to pity, and every heart there
bled,
And everyone wished him heles'd, and Arnold in
his stead.
He was a man of honor, in Britain he was born,
To die upon the gallows most highly he did scorn:
And now his life has reached its end, so young and
blooming still,
In Tappan's quiet countryside he sleeps upon the
hill.
A bumper to John Paulding! Now let your voices
sound,
Fill up your flowing glasses, and drink his health
around;
Also to those young gentlemen who bore him
company,
Success to North America, ye sons of liberty!

*From "The Ballad of Major André," sung to the tune
of "Bonny Boy," October 1780, in Frank Moore,
compiler,* The Diary of the American Revolution,
p. 455.

My Lord, conscious of the rectitude of my intentions (whatever constructions may have been put on
my conduct) and convinced of the benevolence and
goodness of your lordship, I am emboldened to request
your interest and intercession that I may be restored
to the favour of my most gracious Sovereign. In the
fullest confidence of his clemency I most cheerfully
cast myself at his feet, imploring his royal grace and
protection.

*Brig. Gen. Benedict Arnold, from a letter written in New
York, October 7, 1780, to Lord George Germain, in
K. G. Davies, ed.,* Documents of the American
Revolution, *vol. 18, p. 180.*

In no instance since the commencement of the War
has the interposition of Providence appeared more conspicuous than in the rescue of the Post and Garrison
of West point from Arnolds villainous perfidy.... Andre
has met his fate, and with that fortitude which was to be
expected from an accomplished man, and gallant Officer.
But I am mistaken if at *this time,* Arnold is undergoing
the torments of a mental Hell. He wants feeling! From
some traits of his character which have lately come to
my knowledge, he seems to have been so hackneyed in

villainy, and so lost to all sense of honor and shame that
while his faculties will enable him to continue his sordid
pursuits there will be no time for remorse.

*George Washington, from a letter written at Passaic Falls,
New York, October 13, 1780, to Lt. Col. John Laurens,
in John C. Fitzpatrick, ed.,* The Writings of George
Washington, *vol. 20, p. 173.*

. . . I have the pleasure to acquaint you that His Majesty was graciously pleased to express his satisfaction
in the demonstrations you have given of the sincerity
of your return to your allegiance and of your earnest
desire to atone for past errors by a zealous attachment
to his royal person and government in future, and His
Majesty has further been graciously pleased to command me to signify to Sir Henry Clinton his royal
approbation of the rank he has given you in the army
under his command and of his having appointed you
to raise a corps.

*Lord George Germain, from a letter written at Whitehall,
London, December 7, 1780, to Brig. Gen. Benedict
Arnold, in K. G. Davies, ed.,* Documents of the
American Revolution, *vol. 18, pp. 249–250.*

Marquis de Lafayette left France to support the Continental
army. (*From* The Pictorial Field Book of the Revolution, *2 vols.,
by B. J. Lossing. New York: Harper Brothers, 1851 and 1852.*)

316 The American Revolution

Dear Sir: I persuade myself you will embrace the oppertunity of the Marquis de la Fayette's visit to Philadelphia to give the picture of him the finishing touches. You may not have another oppertunity, and I wish its completion. I am, etc.

P.S. As I presume you must be done with my picture of the King of Prussia 'ere this, I should be glad to have it returned to me.

George Washington, from a letter written at New Windsor, New York, New York, December 12, 1780, to Charles Willson Peale, in John C. Fitzpatrick, ed., The Writings of George Washington, *vol. 20, p. 463.*

My wife rose early, having some things to do; made fire in my room; called her negro woman, which affronted her so that she behaved very saucy to her mistress. Hearing the noise in the kitchen I arose, went, found Madam very impertinent. This obliged me to give her sundry stripes with a cowskin, but as she promised to behave better in future I was pacified for the present.

Christopher Marshall, Philadelphia merchant and Quaker then in Lancaster, Pennsylvania, diary entry of December 23, 1780, in Marshall, Extracts from the Diary of Christopher Marshall, *p. 267.*

8

An Improbable Triumph
1781

MUTINY

The very first day of the year portended a potentially traumatic future for the Continental army. Unpaid for months, subjected to many weeks of inadequate food and shelter during a cold winter, regiments of the Pennsylvania Line in winter quarters with Gen. George Washington at Morristown, New Jersey, mutinied. The immediate catalyst for their mutiny arose from their belief that they had fulfilled their three-year terms of enlistment and had no obligation to continue in service. About half of the 2,500 Pennsylvania troops at Morristown mustered in full gear prepared to leave the encampment. Gen. Anthony Wayne unsuccessfully tried to dissuade them. Other officers intervened as the mutineers attempted to enlist more troops in their uprising; in the ensuing melee several officers and men received wounds. The mutineers marched off headed for Philadelphia to present their grievances to the Continental Congress.

General Wayne pursued the mutineers, and on January 2, he issued an order that committed him to pleading their case if they returned to their duties. The men disregarded the offer and marched on to spend their third day out at Princeton. Their sergeants organized as a board to conduct discussions with their officers and the delegates to the Continental Congress. On January 4, the marquis de Lafayette, Gen. Arthur St. Clair, and John Laurens visited their camp at Princeton, but the mutineers would not listen to their pleas. Informed of the mutiny, the British commander in chief, Gen. Sir Henry Clinton, sent an agent from New York to visit the mutineers and offer them pardons or money or both in an effort to reap advantage from the uprising.

On January 6, Joseph Reed arrived at Maidenhead near Princeton as Congress's representative to negotiate with the mutineers, and that evening, John Mason, guided by Loyalist James Ogden, arrived as Clinton's agent. Meeting with Mason and Ogden on January 7, the mutineers swiftly rejected Mason's offers, took him and Ogden into custody, and turned them over to Reed. That evening they met with Reed, who promised on behalf of Congress that the problems related to enlistments would be resolved and accepted the departure of any of the men whose original enlistment terms had been fulfilled. The mutineers

317

accepted Reed's proposals, and the entire Pennsylvania Line received furloughs until March as negotiations with Congress continued and each soldier's case underwent review. Thus the mutiny ended. On January 11, Mason and Ogden were hanged as spies.

American officials could conclude that, however distressing the episode, it at least indicated that the rebellious Pennsylvania troops had no intention of defecting to the enemy. And when members of the New Jersey Brigade followed the Pennsylvanians' lead later in the month, ignored their officers, and marched from camp at Pompton, New Jersey, a thoroughly disgusted Washington, along with Gen. Robert Howe, rode forth with 500 loyal troops to suppress the mutineers. The mutineers returned to their camp at Pompton, where Washington's and Howe's force surrounded them on January 26. The loyal troops brought out the ringleaders, of whom two were sentenced and shot on the spot, and the mutiny abruptly ended.[1]

THE BATTLE OF COWPENS

Cavalry clashes at the Battle of Cowpens. *(Courtesy of Anne S. K. Brown Military Collection, Brown University Library)*

As 1780 had drawn to a close, a contingent from the special corps of light infantry commanded by Brig. Gen. Daniel Morgan, who returned to service

following the Camden disaster, had defeated a Loyalist unit and captured Fort William, South Carolina. Viewing Morgan's initiative as a threat to his rear, Lord Cornwallis dispatched the redoubtable Lt. Col. Banastre Tarleton and his British Legion to neutralize Morgan's corps. In mid-January, aware of Tarleton's pursuit, Morgan paused near Thickety Creek to assess Tarleton's intentions and strength—about 1,100 troops. On January 16, Morgan encamped at Cowpens, a hilltop meadow used to graze cattle and his chosen site for engaging Tarleton. Morgan had 600 light infantry, including many Delaware and Maryland Continentals who had survived Camden; 200 riflemen from Virginia; and 500 militiamen from Georgia and the Carolinas. Realizing the militiamen's low tolerance for sustained battle, Morgan decided to emplace them as his two front lines with orders for each line to fire two volleys at the enemy and then withdraw uphill to entice Tarleton's legion, presumably reduced by the volleys, into attacking his Continentals.

The next day, January 17, Tarleton had his men on the march by 3:00 A.M., quickly learned of Morgan's position, and prepared to attack. Tarleton's dragoons led the assault, falling before the fire of Morgan's first line of militia, who then withdrew. Tarleton's infantry then attacked, only to be shot down by volleys from Morgan's second line of militia. With both lines of militia in retreat, Tarleton's badly cut-up force sensed a rout and raced ahead in pursuit—and toward Morgan's flanks. Morgan's cavalry and dragoons emerged from cover and overwhelmed Tarleton's cavalry. Precise firing from Morgan's Continentals shattered Tarleton's advancing troops as Morgan's dragoons pounded their flanks. The Continentals attacked with bayonets, and the presumed rout transformed into a surrender by Tarleton's troops and the flight of his remaining cavalry. After fighting one-on-one with the mounted Lt. Col. William Washington, Tarleton himself wheeled his horse and fled. Morgan had only 12 dead and 60 wounded, but Tarleton's force suffered 100 killed, 229 wounded, and 600 captured—in effect, the British Legion ceased to exist. Morgan's victory in the Battle of Cowpens boosted American spirits and halted the string of British triumphs in the South.[2]

NATHANAEL GREENE'S TACTICS

Following the loss of Tarleton's strike force at Cowpens, Cornwallis decided to pursue Morgan with his entire army, stripped of baggage, tents, and other supplies for swift movement. By the end of January he was trailing both Morgan and Greene, whose forces had reunited at the Catawba River and headed for North Carolina. Cornwallis crossed the river at Cowan's Ford, routed a North Carolina militia unit posted as guards, and hastened to Tarrant's Tavern, North Carolina. In early February, Green began to withdraw toward the Dan River through topography that required the crossing of several rivers in an effort to both evade and entice Cornwallis. He also appointed Otho Williams to command the light infantry and cavalry led by Morgan, whose crippling arthritis forced his retirement from service. Greene won the race to the Dan in mid-February, successfully getting his men across before Cornwallis arrived to find the river flooded and all boats safely on the Virginia side, where Greene could pause to resupply and refit his troops. Cornwallis began marching his men back to Hillsboro to rest and resupply his troops.[3]

This portrait of Nathanael Greene was painted by Charles Wilson Peale. *(Courtesy of Anne S. K. Brown Military Collection, Brown University Library)*

Greene sent troops under Lt. Col. Henry Lee and militia colonel Andrew Pickens back across the Dan River to harass Cornwallis. In the final week of February, Greene recrossed the river himself with his Continentals and began a march toward Hillsboro but with frequent diversions to confuse Cornwallis. In the meantime, Lee successfully attacked Loyalist units attempting to join Cornwallis and skirmished with advance units of the British army. In mid-March, with his army enhanced to more than 4,000 men by the arrival of Virginia and North Carolina militiamen, even though most of them lacked battle experience, Greene decided to engage Cornwallis's army at a site of his own choosing—the isolated Guilford Courthouse, surrounded by woods. Greene positioned his troops and waited.[4]

THE BATTLE OF GUILFORD COURTHOUSE

Cornwallis's army of 1,900 well-seasoned soldiers set out in the early morning and reached Guilford Courthouse on March 15. Although ignorant of the battlefield and greatly outnumbered, Cornwallis felt confident of his troops' superiority. Emerging from the woods, the British advance units discovered Greene's force arrayed much like Morgan's had been at King's Mountain, with militia posted in the two front lines—the first behind a log frence and the second behind the initial stand of trees—backed and flanked by Continentals, with Lee's and Lt. Col. William Washington's mounted troops guarding the flanks. An encounter erupted between Tarleton's men and Lee's and Washington's on Greene's flanks. Then the British center attacked the first line of militia, whose firing temporarily halted the advance, until the militiamen quickly retreated well to the rear.

The British troops reformed and simultaneously attacked the second line of militia and Greene's flanks. Firing and a bayonet charge by the Maryland Continentals stalled the British advance, but the flight of inexperienced Continentals opened Greene's center. Cornwallis directed his three artillery to fire into the very midst of the ensuing melee, and the British pushed forward. Lacking any reserve to stage a relief attack, Greene ordered a retreat. His troops withdrew in an orderly march to Troublesome Creek, while Cornwallis's occupied the battle site. Although triumphant, Cornwallis had attained a largely Pyrrhic victory—his casualties totaled a staggering 532. Greene suffered 78 dead and 183 wounded, with the consolation that his loss had severely depleted Cornwallis's force. Thus weakened, Cornwallis began a retreat toward Wilmington.[5]

Foreseeing an opportunity, Greene hoped to push the British out of the Carolinas, but his army suffered an immediate reduction to only 1,500 men as the militia departed following the battle at Guilford Courthouse. On April 24, as Cornwallis left Lord Rawdon in charge of British troops in the Carolinas and headed for Virginia, Greene encamped with 1,200 Continentals and 200 militia atop Hobkirk's Hill a few miles from Rawdon's position at Camden, South Carolina. While Greene's men ate, Rawdon surprised them and attacked with a force of 900 men from the Camden garrison. Hoping to envelop the narrow British advance, Greene ordered a downhill bayonet charge. Initially successful, the charge collapsed when the Maryland Continentals faltered. The British rushed forward, and the remaining Continentals broke and ran. William Washington's dragoons arrived in time to prevent disaster, allowing Greene to organize an orderly retreat. Although defeated, Greene again exacted a heavy toll, with Rawdon suffering 258 men dead, wounded, or missing. Greene's own losses numbered 19 dead, 115 wounded, and 136 missing. His campaign of attrition would continue.[6]

Although Lord Rawdon had about 8,000 troops in South Carolina, the majority defended outposts across the state. Lee and Francis Marion had subdued Fort Watson and taken its garrison of 114 men prisoner on April 15. They then continued to raid other outposts. On May 10, Rawdon sent orders to all the British garrisons to evacuate their posts, and he withdrew his own troops from Camden. Before Rawdon's orders could be received, militia general Thomas Sumter and his men captured the British post and garrison at Orangeburg, and Lee and Marion seized Fort Motte. Altogether 165 British troops and 70 Loyalist militiamen were taken prisoner. In addition, Lee conquered Fort Galphin, the headquarters of British deputy superintendent of Indian affairs George Galphin, and he confiscated a year's supply of trading goods sent from England.

As Rawdon withdrew from South Carolina, Greene cautiously followed him. During the fourth week of May, Greene reached the important British post at Ninety-Six, South Carolina, garrisoned by Loyalists, many of them New Yorkers led by Col. John Cruger. Lacking artillery, Greene began a siege of the post from trenches. But Cruger dispatched sorties that interrupted the trench digging, and several assaults by Greene's troops proved futile. In mid-June, Greene abandoned the siege as Rawdon approached the post with a force outnumbering his own.[7]

THE VIRGINIA FRONT

As Greene struggled in the Carolinas the war in Virginia heated up. Sent by Gen. Sir Henry Clinton, Benedict Arnold had arrived with a small force at Hampton Roads at the end of 1780. He immediately began moving up the James River to raid American posts. On January 3, Arnold's force easily captured Hood's Point. The following day, he arrived at Richmond, the new capital of Virginia, and dispatched a unit under Col. John Simcoe to destroy the iron foundry, gunpowder factory, and machine shops at nearby Westham. Arnold

Lieutenant Colonel Henry ("Light-Horse Harry") Lee poses on horseback. (*Courtesy of the National Archives and Records Administration*)

sent a letter to Governor Thomas Jefferson offering to spare Richmond from destruction if the governor let the British confiscate tobacco without interference. Jefferson rejected the offer. Arnold directed his men to pillage the town and torch its public buildings, official documents, and many houses.[8]

In late February, Gen. George Washington gave the marquis de Lafayette a new assignment: command of 1,200 New England light infantry and New Jersey Continentals to march to Virginia and attack Arnold. The count de Rochambeau agreed to send 1,200 of his troops by ship to join Lafayette's expedition in Virginia. In fact, after conferring in Newport with Washington on strategy, Rochambeau's troops formed part of a naval expedition, as the entire French fleet set sail under command of Capt. Charles-René-Dominique Destouches from Newport on March 8—bound for the Chesapeake Bay with the intent of aiding Lafayette, already encamped at Annapolis, by entrapping Arnold. Unfortunately, Adm. Marriot Arbuthnot roused himself, sped out of New York, and arrived in the bay before Destouches. The two fleets, each comprised of eight ships, confronted each other off the Chesapeake Capes on March 16. Although Destouches achieved a slight advantage in their engagement, he nevertheless withdrew to sail back to Newport, leaving Lafayette bereft of reinforcements and Arbuthnot in control of the bay. Concerned that Arbuthnot had reinforced Arnold, Lafayette withdrew from Annapolis to Head of Elk, then to Baltimore, to Alexandria, and, by the end of March, to Fredericksburg. At the same time, Maj. Gen. William Phillips, sent by Sir Henry Clinton with 2,000 men, arrived in Virginia to assume command from Arnold.[9]

On April 18, Arnold and his 2,500-man army broke camp at Portsmouth to continue making raids. Arnold's and Phillips's forces combined and, on April 24, attacked Petersburg. They finally drove off the 1,000 militia defenders, occupied the town, and burned tobacco stores and boats. Phillips marched to Chesterfield Courthouse, where his troops burned a barracks and a flour cache; Arnold attacked Osborne, burned a rebel supply fleet, and carted off 4,000 hogsheads of tobacco. Their combined forces also attacked Manchester before returning to Portsmouth. By the end of April, however, Lafayette held Richmond. In mid-May, Phillips died of typhoid fever at Petersburg, leaving Arnold again in command. A few days later, Cornwallis arrived in Petersburg with 1,500 troops and assumed command of the British forces in Virginia. He soon received reinforcements augmenting his army to 7,200 men. Arnold returned to New York.[10]

WAR IN THE NORTH

As the Revolutionary War raged in the South, in the northern states it appeared dormant. Besides defusing mutinies early in the year, the Continental army units with Commander in Chief George Washington remained inactive. Skirmishes with Loyalist troops occurred in New York and New Jersey, but these had negligible consequences for the overall war. Finally, during the third week of May, Washington and the count de Rochambeau met in Wethersfield, Connecticut, to discuss joint strategy. Both understood that control of the sea-lanes along the eastern coast remained crucial to an ultimate victory—the French navy must challenge British control of these lanes. Both commanders hoped that Louis, count de Barras, a new French naval commander recently arrived in Newport, might prove more cooperative than his predecessors, but their request that he help bottle up Cornwallis in Virginia fell on deaf ears—Barras wanted to attack Newfoundland instead. Washington and Rochambeau also knew that Adm. François de Grasse commanded the largest French fleet (20 ships of the line) yet sent to American waters—it had sailed from France in March—but de Grasse's destination was the West Indies. So the two commanders determined that their only recourse lay in probes against New York City, where Clinton's superior strength precluded a full-scale attack.[11]

In early June, having failed to persuade Cornwallis to move his army to the Delaware River area and join forces in attacking Washington and Rochambeau, Clinton received captured letters from Washington outlining the Wethersfield Plan for American-French probes against New York. The British commander suspected a subterfuge. A few days later, Rochambeau began to march his army from Newport to join Washington for the joint operation. The two forces united at Dobbs Ferry, but after reconnoitering New York, Washington and Rochambeau concluded that they lacked the capabilities in men and equipment needed to lay siege to the city. As they paused near New York in mid-August, Rochambeau received a letter from Admiral de Grasse, now granted authority to aid Washington and Rochambeau in any way they desired, informing him that de Grasse's fleet would set sail from Haiti bound for the Chesapeake Bay. The news provoked Washington's most momentous decision of the entire war.[12]

THE ADVANCE ON YORKTOWN

Perceiving that if de Grasse controlled the sea approaches while the American and French armies controlled the land approaches to Yorktown, Cornwallis could be trapped and defeated, Washington decided that the allied armies would immediately abandon their New York operation and hasten to Virginia. He sent orders to Lafayette to keep Cornwallis contained in Yorktown. (The British commander had selected the city as his base and occupied it in early August, along with Gloucester Point across the York River.) Washington also ordered Gen. William Heath to assume command of half of the Continental army and keep Clinton occupied and distracted in New York until it was too late for the British commander in chief to intervene in Virginia. On August 21, Washington's and Rochambeau's armies began to march south. They crossed the Hudson River, divided their armies into three columns, and pursued indirect routes to convince the British that New York City remained their objective. At the same time, de Barras, finally persuaded by Washington, sailed out of Newport to join de Grasse in the Chesapeake. Washington and Rochambeau paused in Chatham, New Jersey, to delude Clinton and then, as August ended, rode into Philadelphia and began the race to Virginia, while de Grasse disembarked troops at Jamestown to reinforce Lafayette.[13]

On September 5, at Chester, Pennsylvania, where the allied armies would embark by water for Head of Elk and on to Williamsburg, Washington learned that de Grasse's fleet had safely arrived in the Chesapeake Bay—electrifying news for the commander, who until this moment had no way of knowing that the French admiral would really follow through. Clinton now fully realized the allied armies' destination and also the peril Cornwallis faced, but the British commander in chief could mount no effective challenge. Both commanders had yet to learn that, on this same day, de Grasse moved his fleet out of its anchorage to engage a combined British fleet commanded by Admirals Thomas Graves and Samuel Hood. De Grasse's fleet not only outnumbered the combined British fleet but also greatly exceeded the firepower the British ships could muster. The enemies engaged at 4:00 P.M. and battled for two hours, until the badly damaged British fleet withdrew and de Grasse sailed back to the mouth of the bay. Graves and Hood decided to sail back to New York, leaving Cornwallis to his certain fate. A few days later De Barras arrived with his fleet, and the French had total control of the Chesapeake Bay.[14]

THE BATTLE OF EUTAW SPRINGS

As finality approached at Yorktown, the persistent Gen. Nathanael Greene launched into battle at Eutaw Springs, South Carolina. Lord Rawdon had departed for England, leaving Lt. Col. Alexander Stewart in command of an army of about 2,000 men that Greene discovered encamped on the Santee River. On September 8, with a force of equivalent size composed of Delaware, Maryland, and Virginia Continentals, Henry Lee's Legion, William Washington's mounted troops, partisans led by Marion and Pickens, and militiamen, Greene cautiously advanced on the British encampment, intent on a surprise attack. His advance units surprised and captured a British foraging party. Then they ambushed a scouting party of Loyalist South Carolina cavalry led by Maj. John Coffin; but Coffin escaped to warn Stewart of Greene's approach, providing time for Stewart to form his lines for battle.

Early in the battle, Greene's militiamen held firm and fired more than 17 rounds before Stewart's reserve infantry and cavalry broke their stance. Then the Maryland and Virginia Continentals moved into the center, attacked with bayonets, and pushed the British back into their camp. A victory for Greene appeared secure, but his troops paused to loot the British tents. William Washington and Lee attempted to rally the men and attacked a British unit com-

Smoke rises from the Battle of Eutaw Springs. *(Courtesy of Anne S. K. Brown Military Collection, Brown University Library)*

Marquis de Lafayette and General Washington confer at Yorktown. *(Courtesy of the National Archives and Records Administration)*

manded by Maj. John Marjoribanks in a thicket. Volleys from Marjoribank's troops felled the American dragoons and wounded Washington. Marjoribanks led his men in a dash for safety within a brick house, from which they decimated Greene's troops with musket and swivel-gun fire. The Americans fell back, using British troops as shields. Marjoribanks led a sortie against the Americans looting the camp and forced Greene's withdrawal. Near victory yet again defeated, Greene counted 500 casualties. Stewart's small army, however, suffered 693 dead (including the heroic Marjoribanks), wounded, or missing—the highest loss rate of any army during the war. Having won another Pyrrhic victory at the Battle of Eutaw Springs, the British retreated toward Charleston.[15]

THE SIEGE OF YORKTOWN

By mid-September, Washington's and Rochambeau's armies, joined by Lafayette's small force, assembled at Williamsburg to prepare for the siege of Yorktown—a total of 16,000 men against Cornwallis's 6,000. Washington and Rochambeau conferred with de Grasse aboard the admiral's flagship. They planned for de Grasse to control the sea approach while the armies encircled Yorktown, constructed trenches approaching Cornwallis's fortifications, and used siege guns unloaded from the French ships to bombard the town. The allied armies moved into position around the town on September 28. As the month ended, Cornwallis withdrew his men from his outer fortifications in order to conserve his strength while awaiting hoped-for rescue from the sea. The allies occupied the abandoned defensive positions, began to dig new trenches, and moved their artillery forward.[16]

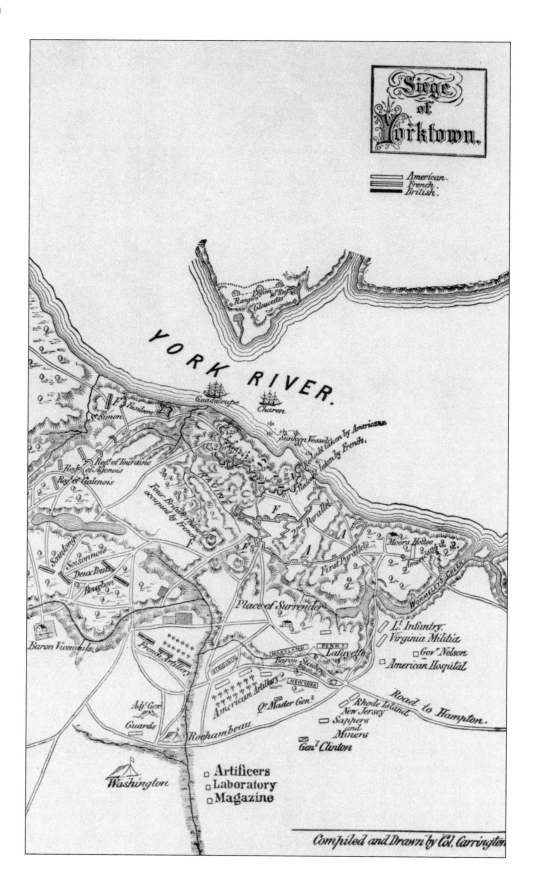

American and French forces lay siege to Cornwallis's army trapped in Yorktown. *(Siege of Yorktown, courtesy of Anne S. K. Brown Military Collection, Brown University Library)*

During the first week of October, about 1,500 allied troops set to work digging approach trenches at angles to the Yorktown fortifications, and the allied artillery began full-scale bombardments of the British lines. The enemies exchanged artillery fire. Casualties mounted from the artillery duels and the skirmishes that erupted outside the British redoubts or between British foraging parties and allied troops. As mid-October approached, the British artillery grew increasingly silent, and the allies' trenches approached within 300 yards of Cornwallis's main defenses. American and French troops each captured a British redoubt, allowing extension of the trenches to the river. Hoping to evacuate his army and march to the Delaware River, Cornwallis on October 16 sent his guard and light infantry units across the river to Gloucester by boat, intending that the remainder of his army would follow. But a violent storm prevented the boats from returning to transport the remaining troops. With escape now impossible, the guard and infantry units returned to Yorktown the following morning, and Cornwallis accepted the inevitable.

A British officer stood on a parapet and raised a white handkerchief; an American officer met him and led him to General Washington to request an armistice. Washington agreed to a two-hour cease-fire and demanded a written proposal from Cornwallis, who asked that his troops be paroled and returned to England. Washington insisted on unconditional surrender. By nightfall on October 17, Cornwallis conceded. With the allied troops assembled on October 19, the British troops marched out of Yorktown, threw down their arms, and watched sullenly as Gen. Charles O'Hara presented Lord Cornwallis's sword to Washington—Gen. Benjamin Lincoln stepped forth to accept it. Cornwallis himself remained in Yorktown, professing illness in order to avoid the humiliation of the surrender ceremony. His subdued troops piled their muskets in an open field. Although the French troops sported good uniforms, the American

The British surrender to General Washington at Yorktown. *(Courtesy of Anne S. K. Brown Military Collection, Brown University Library)*

victors—mostly ragged and many barefoot except for the fully uniformed blacks of the 1st Rhode Island—looked far more bedraggled than their foe, since the British and Hessian troops had donned new uniforms for the occasion. But melancholy marked the Britons' demeanor as one of their bands played "The World Turned Upside Down." Lafayette ordered his fifers and drummers to respond with "Yankee Doodle." The allies marched more than 7,000 prisoners away to prison camps. Lord Cornwallis and his main officers received paroles and returned to New York. After six and a half years of strife, the Revolutionary War had reached its climax. Carried by Washington's aide-de-camp Tench Tilghman, news of the surrender reached Philadelphia in the early morning of October 22. Euphoric celebration swept the city.[17]

A NEW GOVERNMENT

In January, the Continental Congress approved legislation establishing an office of foreign secretary as the first of several executive offices intended to rationalize government administration and end the inefficiency of administering by congressional committees. Political rivalries, however, prevented appointment of someone to fill the office. In February, the delegates approved a plan to establish other executive offices, including departments of finance, war, and marine affairs. They appointed the wealthy merchant and financial genius Robert Morris as secretary of the Department of Finance.[18]

On March 1, the Articles of Confederation were finally ratified—an event that had been pending since late 1777. Ratification confirmed a stronger union and a new government. The Confederation Congress assumed leadership of the new government. Despite these various developments, problems with finances, currency, and administration persisted. Robert Morris did not become secretary of finance until mid-May, after Congress finally accepted granting him total control of fiscal affairs, including the power to choose his subordinates. By the end of May, Morris had also secured Congress's approval of a plan to incorporate a national bank, but Congress delayed granting the bank's charter until the end of the year. A subsidy from France entrusted to Morris's administration eased the monetary crisis but not the devaluation of the Continental currency. And so, as the end of 1781 neared, the Confederation Congress remained in the uneasy position of begging the states for revenues. Continuing financial crisis threatened the durability of the ratified confederate union even as the war concluded.[19]

Of course, although totally subdued at Yorktown, the British still maintained more than 30,000 active troops in America and still controlled New York and all the other major American ports except Boston. After Yorktown, Washington tried to persuade de Grasse to help recapture Savannah and Charleston, but the French admiral rejected the appeal and sailed for the West Indies. Gen. Arthur St. Clair left Yorktown with a force of the Continental troops to reinforce Gen. Nathanael Greene's efforts in the Carolinas, and Washington led the remainder of the Continentals back to the Hudson River to keep watch on New York City. Rochambeau remained in Virginia with his army. Hostilities continued to be possible, but the final outcome appeared quite clear. News of Yorktown reached London in late November as a death knell. Burdened with heavy debts from the war and concerned over the threat from the combined French and Spanish fleets, Parliament concluded that Great Britain could not afford to continue the war.

The North ministry agreed, but George III remained adamant—time must pass for his acceptance of defeat.[20]

For the long-term outlook, the appointment of Morris as restorer of Continental finances proved efficacious. A masterful financier, Morris devoted himself to fulfillment of his herculean task; his past efforts had included, when he had deemed it vital, provision of his own funds and supplies to sustain the army. The most dedicated and capable aide that Morris engaged in his enterprise was Haym Salomon, a Jewish financier and broker who had arrived in New York from Europe only in 1772 and had remained in the city after the British occupation to serve as a spy for Washington. Arrested and imprisoned for spying, Salomon had managed to escape and flee to Philadelphia. Setting himself up in Philadelphia as a broker and commission agent, he became well known to Morris and his assistant, Gouverneur Morris, and supported them in placing French bills of credit and shoring up the Continental dollar. Salomon also frequently consulted with Robert Morris on conditions in the money market and how to obtain the most favorable terms; he enjoyed Morris's total trust. Salomon and Morris both became stockholders in the Bank of North America upon its founding. Another Philadelphia Jewish merchant, Isaac Moses, also became a shareholder and bought bills of credit to assist the national treasury. Jewish citizens as a whole—their numbers estimated to total only 1,500 to 2,500 in all the colonies—perceived the Revolution as their great opportunity to achieve equality and acceptance in American society; consequently, many also enlisted in the army, some becoming officers, including Major David S. Franks, who served as an aide to Benedict Arnold both in Philadelphia and at West Point but knew nothing of Arnold's treasonous behavior.[21]

CHRONICLE OF EVENTS

1781

January 1: Unpaid; plagued by cold, poor housing, and inadequate food; and convinced that their three-year enlistments are fulfilled and they have no obligation to serve until the war's end, some 2,500 regimental troops of the Pennsylvania Line mutiny at Morristown, New Jersey. The mutineers form with their full gear and move out of camp, heading for Philadelphia to present their grievances to the Continental Congress. They pause for the night at Bernardsville.

January 2: General Wayne attempts to regain control of the mutineers, but they ignore him.

January 3: The Pennsylvania mutineers enter Princeton and pause on the college campus. Their sergeants have formed a board to deal with their officers and Congress; Wayne stops at a tavern, where some of the sergeants stand guard. (Washington is too far distant to intervene.)

Arriving at Hood's Point, a fortified post on the James River near Jamestown, Benedict Arnold's force draws fire from the defenders, runs beyond the guns, and attacks with 130 troops led by Simcoe, only to find that the rebels have fled.

January 4: Lafayette, Arthur St. Clair, and John Laurens visit the mutineers' camp at Princeton but to no avail. Learning of the mutiny and hoping for an advantage, Sir Henry Clinton orders troops to prepare for a march into New Jersey and chooses agents to approach the mutineers.

Arnold's expedition readily captures Richmond, Virginia. Arnold sends a letter to Governor Thomas Jefferson with an offer to spare Richmond if his troops are allowed to seize tobacco; Jefferson rejects the offer, and Arnold's troops pillage the city. Afterward, most of his force withdraws to Portsmouth and begins to dig in.

January 6: Sent by the Continental Congress as their representative, Joseph Reed arrives with James Ogden in Maidenhead, New Jersey, and sends letters to General Wayne, still in the Princeton tavern and ostensibly under guard. Clinton's agent John Mason arrives to present Clinton's offer to the mutineers.

January 7: The Pennsylvania mutineers immediately reject Clinton's offer. Reed and Wayne, who had been allowed to travel to Maidenhead, determine to talk with the sergeants representing the mutineers, for

whom Wayne harbors some sympathy despite being appalled by their mutiny. Reed promises on behalf of Congress to provide redress and to allow all soldiers who have fulfilled the terms of their original enlistments to depart from the service.

January 8: The Pennsylvania mutineers accept the terms Reed has presented and agree to pursue final negotiations. The entire Pennsylvania Line receives a furlough, and the mutiny ends. During subsequent weeks, each mutineer's case will be examined individually, with many being discharged and many, ironically, reenlisting.

Col. Simcoe's Queen's Rangers entrap and rout a Patriot militia contingent under Colonel Dudley at Charles City Courthouse, Virginia; they kill 20, capture eight, and then rejoin Arnold.

January 10: The Continental Congress has relied initially on special committees and then on standing committees to conduct all the nation's political, diplomatic, and administrative affairs, with a resulting governmental crisis during 1780–81. Responding to this crisis, Congress now approves legislation to create the office of foreign secretary, the first of several projected executive offices.

January 11: Mason and Ogden are hanged as spies at Princeton.

Daniel Morgan was a general in the Continental army. *(From* The Pictorial Field Book of the Revolution, *2 vols., by B. J. Lossing. New York: Harper Brothers, 1851 and 1852.)*

January 14: Aware that Tarleton trails him, Daniel Morgan withdraws to Thickety Creek, South Carolina, to appraise Carleton's strength and intentions. Tarleton has 1,100 men, including most of his British Legion.

January 16: Morgan reaches the elevated meadow (well suited to his plans for battle) known as Cowpens. Morgan's force consists of 1,300 men. Accepting that the militiamen will not endure a long battle on open ground, Morgan devises an ingenious strategy. The militia will be stationed in two front ranks with orders to fire two accurate volleys and then hasten up the hill past his solidly ensconced and experienced Maryland and Delaware regulars. During the night, Morgan moves among the campfires making certain every militia unit fully understands its duty.

January 17: Reaching Cowpens and noting Morgan's stance, Tarleton attacks. Taken in by Morgan's tactics, Tarleton's men press forward and around Morgan's flank. Morgan's dragoons and cavalry emerge from hiding and attack the British cavalry from the rear. The Continentals finally rush forward with a bayonet attack that shatters the British troops' offensive and forces their surrender. Morgan leaves some men to assemble the captured supplies and booty and withdraws with his main force across the Broad River to encamp in the afternoon. Tarleton's force has suffered 100 dead, 229 wounded, and 600 taken prisoner, while Morgan's losses are only 12 killed and 60 wounded.

January 20: Members of the New Jersey Brigade posted at Pompton, New Jersey, have decided that their grievances are the same as those of the Pennsylvania mutineers. Ignoring their officers, they march out of camp headed for Chatham.

January 21: Disgusted with the mutineers, Washington sends 500 troops commanded by Gen. Robert Howe to suppress them.

January 22: Lt. Col. William Hull leads a Patriot force into Westchester County to raid Loyalists there, notably James De Lancey. They seize many cattle and horses and destroy area forage.

January 24: Lee and Marion join forces to attack Georgetown, South Carolina, but discover the British garrison secure in buildings throughout the coastal town and withdraw.

January 25: Without Tarleton's defeated British Legion, Lord Cornwallis decides to move his entire army in pursuit of Morgan. At Ramsur's Mill, South Carolina, he orders nearly all the army's food and baggage burnt so that his men, carrying minimal equip-ment and victuals, can become a rapidly mobile army to catch Morgan or to turn quickly and go after Greene.

January 26: Gen. Robert Howe's force, joined by Washington himself, surrounds the New Jersey mutineers at Pompton. The ringleaders are brought to the front, two are sentenced and shot on the spot, and the mutiny abruptly ends.

January 30: Greene's and Morgan's armies reunite at the Catawba River and retreat rapidly toward North Carolina, pursued by Cornwallis.

February 1: Hoping to cross the Catawba River quickly and advance on Morgan's flank, Cornwallis sends his men across at Cowan's Ford. Although many men and horses perish in the strong current, the British reach the far bank unopposed because 100 North Carolina militia under Gen. William Davidson stand guard at another branch of the river. Cornwallis suprises Davidson with an attack that scatters his men and costs his life. But Morgan has safely withdrawn.

After crossing with Cornwallis at Cowan's Ford, Tarleton hastens to Tarrant's Tavern, routs a band of militia there, presses on, and nearly encounters Greene.

The Continental Congress accepts a plan to create more executive offices, including secretaries for finance, war, and marine affairs.

February 3: A British fleet commanded by Adm. George Rodney captures St. Eustatius, West Indies, a Dutch trading port that has been a major supply point for the Americans. The British capture goods worth millions of pounds. Hoping to realize a large personal gain, Rodney sells some of the booty and ships the remainder to England—most of to be recaptured en route by the French.

North Carolina congressional delegate Thomas Burke, long a proponent of a weak central government, reverses himself by introducing a plan that would empower the Continental Congress to levy an import duty of 5 percent and thereby solve many of the government's financial problems. Rhode Island refuses to go along, thwarting the plan.

Greene sends parts of his army to feint Cornwallis out of following the Americans' primary route of march. Greene's goal is the Dan River, which marks the Virginia border. Crippled with arthritis, Morgan relinquishes his command to return home. Greene places Otho Williams in command of the light infantry and mounted troops, including Lee's Legion, that will screen his army during its northward march. Greene's tactics succeed.

February 6: As a halfway measure, the Continental Congress establishes a department of finance, with Robert Morris as superintendent. Morris assumes a large role in national affairs by addressing the economic crisis that is the Continental Congress's most acute problem.

February 10: Greene decides to make haste for the lower crossing of the Dan River, with Cornwallis closing in.

February 12: Capt. Eugenio Pourre commands a small Spanish force of militia and Indians in capturing Fort St. Joseph, a British outpost in what is now Michigan, whose garrison surrenders without resistance. Although Pourre holds the fort only one day before departing, Spain can later use the conquest as a basis for territorial claims.

February 14: Outdistancing Cornwallis, Greene reaches the Dan River and moves his men across to safety in Virginia, where he can resupply and refit his army to prepare to take the offensive. When Cornwallis arrives, the river is at flood stage, and all the boats are on the Virginia side.

February 18: His supplies depleted, Cornwallis marches his men toward Hillsboro. Greene sends Lee and Pickens back across the Dan River to harass the withdrawing British.

February 23: Greene recrosses the Dan River, returning to North Carolina with his troops rested. Although many of his militia have left because of expired enlistments, Greene maintains a solid core of Continentals and expects to receive fresh drafts of militiamen from North Carolina and Virginia. He begins to march toward Hillsboro but will veer often to confuse Cornwallis.

February 25: After several days of tag with Tarleton, Henry Lee learns that Col. John Pyles is leading 400 mounted Loyalists to join the British. He approaches Pyles on the same road, successfully pretends to be Tarleton (both legions wear green dragoon coats), and induces the Loyalists to draw aside and ground their weapons. Lee's men ride up with their sabers drawn and kill 90 of Pyles's men and wound most of the remainder, without enduring a single casualty.

Washington dispatches Lafayette in command of 1,200 New England light infantry and the New Jersey Continentals, assembled at Peekskill, to march south and engage Arnold in Virginia. Rochambeau agrees to send 1,200 French troops by sea to join Lafayette. Washington has also sent General von Steuben into Virginia to recruit militiamen, but von Steuben has little success.

March 1: Final ratification of the Articles of Confederation officially ends the Continental Congress, replacing it with a new government known as the Confederation Congress. When the news is announced at noon, Philadelphia celebrates with bells, cannonfire, and fireworks.

March 2: Lee's men skirmish with Tarleton's near Clapp's Mill, North Carolina.

March 3: Lafayette and his men arrive at Head of Elk, Maryland, and embark on boats for Annapolis, where the French troops are to meet them.

March 6: In an effort to catch Otho Williams's force, Cornwallis pushes forward, with Tarleton's horsemen and Col. James Webster's light infantry in the advance. Williams retreats across the Haw River at Wetzall's Mill and hastens to rejoin Greene, as American troops under Lee, William Washington, and Col. William Campbell skirmish with the British when they cross the river and then slip away.

Washington arrives in Newport, Rhode Island, to confer with Rochambeau on strategy. Although Rochambeau has prepared an expedition for Virginia, its departure has been delayed because some of Destouches's transport ships needed repairs.

March 8: The entire French fleet, with a sizable number of infantry aboard, sets sail from Newport. Adm. Marriot Arbuthnot vigorously pursues the French and arrives ahead of them in Chesapeake Bay, preventing their entrapment of Arnold.

March 9: A Spanish squadron of 35 ships carrying 7,000 soldiers commanded by Bernardo de Conde de Gálvez sails into Pensacola, Florida. Although the British garrison comprises exhausted troops, criminals, and deserters commanded by Brig. Gen. John Campbell, they mount a strong defense. Gálvez must begin a siege and cannonade to bring them into submission.

March 14: With his force augmented to 4,000 by militia reinforcements from Virginia and North Carolina, Greene resolves to do battle with Cornwallis. He chooses Guilford Courthouse, North Carolina, a site surrounded by woods, to make his stand, positioning his troops to await Cornwallis's arrival.

March 15: Starting out early, Cornwallis marches his troops the 12 miles remaining to Guilford Courthouse to do battle. Greene's tactics resemble Morgan's at King's Mountain. The British advance against the first line of Greene's militia, which unleashes a withering volley and then races to the rear. The British attack Greene's flanks and then his second militia line, which finally falls back. An inexperienced regiment of Americans breaks and runs, allowing the British to move within arm's length of Greene's defensive lines. The Americans fall back, and Greene orders a retreat to an earlier campsite on Troublesome Creek. Although he may claim victory, Cornwallis suffers terrible losses of 532 men, while Greene has 78 dead and 183 wounded. His losses force Cornwallis to retreat to Wilmington.

March 20: Not trusting Arnold, Clinton orders Maj. William Phillips to sail from Sandy Hook with 2,000 men and assume command from Arnold of the British forces in Virginia, but he sees the Carolinas as the main theater of war in the South.

March 26: Destouches returns to Newport. Concerned that Arbuthnot has reinforced Arnold, Lafayette leaves Annapolis for Head of Elk.

March 30: Phillips arrives in Portsmouth, Virginia, and assumes command from Arnold. After refitting his command in Baltimore, Lafayette marches on to Alexandria and Fredericksburg.

April 1: Although he now has only 1,500 troops (the militia departed after Guilford Courthouse), Greene decides to return to the offensive in South Carolina, where Lord Rawdon commands a total force of 8,000 men, most of them dispersed among 10 small outposts throughout the state that Greene can attack one at a time.

April 6: Washington orders Lafayette to occupy Richmond, Virginia, and hold it against any British offensive; but Lafayette's New England and New Jersey troops, fed up with marching and countermarching, begin to desert. Lafayette has one recaptured deserter hanged and stands down his men with an order that any not wanting to face the approaching danger may depart. The desertions cease.

April 7: Cornwallis and his depleted force arrive in Wilmington, North Carolina.

April 15: With their forces combined, Henry Lee and Francis Marion invade Fort Watson, South Carolina. They lack artillery, but Col. Hezekiah Maham builds a tall rectangle of logs harvested from the nearby woods and places a platform atop it; from here riflemen can fire over the fort's stockade walls. Defenseless before the so-called Maham Tower, the garrison of 114 surrenders.

April 18: With 2,500 men, Arnold leaves camp at Portsmouth, Virginia, to resume his raids.

April 24: Cornwallis heads for Virginia from Wilmington, leaving Rawdon to deal with Greene and the partisan forces in the Carolinas.

Their forces now combined, Arnold and Phillips attack Petersburg, Virginia, but are held at bay for most of the day by the town's 1,000 militia defenders commanded by Col. J. P. G. Muhlenberg. British artillery and a flanking movement force the militia's withdrawal. The British enter the town and burn boats and tobacco stores.

Greene has encamped with a force of 1,200 Continentals and 200 militia atop Hobkirk's Hill, South Carolina, a few miles from Rawdon's army posted at Camden. As the Americans eat, Rawdon launches a surprise attack with 900 men. At the critical moment the men of the elite 1st Maryland regiment waver, and Col. John Grumby orders them to withdraw and reform, allowing the British to plunge forward. The Continentals break and run. Greene organizes a retreat, and Rawdon withdraws to Camden. The British have won another costly "victory," with 258 killed, wounded, or missing. Greene's losses are 115 wounded, 19 killed, and 136 missing.

April 27: Phillips attacks Chesterfield Courthouse, Virginia, meets no resistance, and burns barracks and large flour stores. Arnold assaults the village of Osborne on the James River, discovering and burning a rebel supply fleet and seizing 4,000 hogsheads of tobacco.

April 29: Lafayette occupies Richmond, previously sacked by Arnold.

De Grasse's fleet thwarts British resistance and sails into the harbor of Front Royal, Martinique.

April 30: Frustrated by Lafayette's occupation of Richmond, Phillips and Arnold march back to Portsmouth, destroying more tobacco en route.

May 7: Protesting the declining economy, Philadelphians tar a dog, plaster it with worthless Continental bills, and parade it through the city's streets; merchants threaten to close their stores unless paid in gold or silver.

May 9: Gálvez's artillery cannonade blows up the Pensacola garrison's main powder magazine, convincing the British commander Brig. Gen. John Campbell that continued resistance is futile. He surrenders the town and his 1,600 men, effectively giving Spain control of East and West Florida.

May 10: Rawdon sends orders to other British garrisons throughout South Carolina to evacuate as he withdraws from Camden. Greene follows cautiously.

May 11: Before the garrison at Orangeburg can execute Rawdon's orders to evacuate, Thomas Sumter's men surround and capture the 15 British regulars and 70 militia at the post.

May 12: Marion and Lee besiege the fortified house that protects the British post at Fort Motte. Learning that Rawdon is approaching, the Americans hasten their efforts, firing flaming arrows into the mansion's shingle roof and forcing the surrender of its 150-man garrison.

May 13: At Petersburg, Gen. William Phillips dies of typhoid fever, leaving Arnold temporarily in command of British forces in Virginia.

May 14: Desperate to resolve its financial problems, Congress has acceded to Robert Morris's demands that he be given complete control of fiscal affairs, be empowered to choose all his subordinates, and be allowed to continue his private business on the side. Morris now formally accepts the post of superintendent of finance.

Loyalists attack the rebel outpost at Croton River, New York, and kill Col. Christopher Greene.

At Friday's Ferry, South Carolina, Lee entraps Loyalist troops led by Maj. Andrew Maxwell, notorious for his plundering, and promises to allow all "private property" to pass freely if the Loyalists surrender. Maxwell surrenders and drives toward promised parole in Charleston with two wagonloads of goods.

May 20: Lord Cornwallis, pursuing his own strategy rather than Sir Henry Clinton's, arrives in Petersburg with 1,500 troops to assume command of British forces in Virginia. Reinforcements will augment his force to 7,200 within a few days.

In Westerfield, Connecticut, for a strategic conference with Rochambeau, Washington sends Gen. Anthony Wayne orders to move south with 1,000 men to support Lafayette.

May 21: Henry Lee's force overwhelms the British garrison at Fort Galphin, headquarters of Britain's deputy superintendent of Indian affairs George Galphin. Lee confiscates the year's supply of trading goods—blankets, clothing, medicine, small, arms, ammunition, and other items—shipped from England.

May 21–22: Washington and Rochambeau confer on strategy. Washington has been hopeful that a new French naval commander, Paul-François, count de Barras, would prove more cooperative than previous French admirals, but that hope has proven futile. Consequently, the best strategy Washington and Rochambeau are able to devise entails probes against New York City.

In addition, the two commanders hope the American cause in Virginia may be aided by Admiral de Grasse, whose strong fleet lingers in the West Indies.

Gen. Nathanael Greene, with about 1,000 Maryland, Delaware, and Virginia Continentals, arrives at Ninety-Six, South Carolina, a major British post with strong fortifications manned by Loyalists, including many from New York under command of Col. John Cruger. Lacking artillery, Greene must lay siege, digging approaches with picks and shovels, but Cruger sends out swift sorties that disrupt the digging.

May 24: Cornwallis marches from Petersburg, crosses the James River, and encamps at Hanover Junction. Arnold leaves Virginia, headed for New York.

May 26: Congress accepts Robert Morris's plan to incorporate a national bank; a subsidy of 6 million livres from France, which Congress entrusts to Morris, alleviates the immediate money crisis.

Wayne leaves York, Pennsylvania, on his march to Virginia with a force assembled from Pennsylvania regiments that were reorganized following the mutiny. When some of his men express dissatisfaction over pay, Wayne has seven of them shot, quelling an incipient mutiny.

June 1: Dismayed over Cornwallis's shift out of the Carolinas and into Virginia, Clinton proposes that Cornwallis either move his army north to join with Clinton in the Delaware River region or withdraw by sea and return to New York for operations against Washington and Rochambeau. Cornwallis, who has Lord George Germain's ear, decides instead to build a strong presence in Virginia with naval support, and Clinton reluctantly acquiesces.

June 2: Admiral de Grasse seizes the British post of Tobago, West Indies, after a brief siege.

June 3: Letters from Washington outlining the allies' Wethersfield Plan are seized and delivered to Clinton, who suspects a ruse and reacts cautiously.

June 4: Hoping to capture the legislature and Governor Jefferson, Tarleton leads members of his British Legion and mounted troops from other regiments in a lightning strike on Charlottesville. But Capt. John Jouett of the Virginia militia races to bring a warning, and the legislators flee to Staunton. Tarleton sends a detachment of dragoons toward Monticello, where Jefferson entertains the speaker of the legislature, but Jouett arrives just in time to send Jefferson into flight on horseback moments before Tarleton's men arrive.

Following a brief skirmish, Tarleton enters Charlottesville and captures military supplies and tobacco stores.

June 5: After intermittent, unsuccessful attacks on the British fort at Augusta, Georgia, by various partisan forces since April, Lee now joins in a siege using the Maham Tower tactic; the garrison surrenders.

At Point of Forks, Virginia, where von Steuben has stashed many supplies for safety after hauling them across the Fluvanna River, Simcoe deploys his small force to feign an advance guard of the entire British army; von Steuben retreats and Simcoe crosses the river to seize the supplies.

June 9: Rochambeau marches his infantry from Newport to Providence en route to joining Washington near New York.

June 10: Wayne's force arrives in Virginia to reinforce Lafayette.

June 11: Although cognizance of the imperative need for French aid has convinced Congress to accede to French insistence on determining the terms of a peace settlement, the delegates decide to appoint a commission with instructions to insist on one term: recognition of American independence. Benjamin Franklin, John Jay, and Henry Laurens (still in the Tower of London) will be appointed to the commission to serve with John Adams. Thomas Jefferson also will be appointed but will decline to serve.

June 12: Lafayette positions his force at Mechunk Creek to prevent Cornwallis from moving against Charlottesville or Staunton.

June 15: Blocked by Lafayette, Cornwallis begins to move back to Richmond.

June 19: Unsuccessful in his efforts to take Ninety-Six, South Carolina, and heedful of Lord Rawdon's approach with a superior force, Greene abandons the siege.

June 20: Seeking a strong position that can be supplied from the sea, Cornwallis leaves Richmond and heads toward Williamsburg.

June 24: Washington encamps at Peekskill to await Rochambeau.

June 26: Col. Richard Butler and Col. William McPherson, trying to intercept Simcoe, encounter him about six miles from Williamsburg. Their fierce battle includes mounted hand-to-hand combat and forces the rebels to withdraw after suffering 31 casualties while inflicting 33.

June 29: Deciding its fort is indefensible, the British evacuate Ninety-Six.

July 3: Sent by Washington with 800 troops to attack British outposts in northern Manhattan or alternatively to join Armand-Louis, duke de Lauzun in attacking De Lancey's Loyalists in Morrisiana, Gen. Benjamin Lincoln meets only frustration at Fort Knyphausen, and Lauzun's cavalry arrives too late to implement the attack on the Loyalists.

July 6: Rochambeau joins Washington at Dobbs Ferry.

Near the Green Spring crossing of the James River, Cornwallis hides his main force of 7,000 in a woods with the intention of entrapping Lafayette. Wayne's small force of 500 skirmishes with the edge of the British army but does not surmise its strength. Lafayette arrives in late afternoon, reconnoiters, and realizes the truth but too late to warn Wayne. Cornwallis attacks Wayne, who chooses the desperate recourse of a full frontal counterattack against overwhelming odds. The assault halts the British, giving Lafayette a chance to withdraw Wayne's men into an orderly retreat. Wayne has 127 casualties, including 28 killed; Cornwallis, 75.

July 9: A force of Loyalists and Indians effects a surprise raid on Currytown, New York, killing several settlers and burning twelve buildings.

July 15: Ignoring the advice of Francis Marion, Henry Lee, and Col. Thomas Taylor, Thomas Sumter leads a poorly executed running battle with Lt. Col. Coates's British troops near Quinby's Bridge, South Carolina. The resulting unnecessary casualties outrage Taylor, who promises never again to serve with Sumter. Also disgusted, Lee and Marion depart the following day.

July 21: Rochambeau and Washington reconnoiter New York and decide they lack the manpower and equipment needed for the full-scale siege an attack would require.

August 5: After a period of indecision, Cornwallis chooses Yorktown as his base of operations in Virginia and occupies the city and Gloucester Point across the river—the point provides a means of supply and overland escape.

August 8: Capt. James Nicholson's *Trumbull* engages the British ship *Iris* in the Atlantic, but his crew of British deserters refuses to fight, forcing Nicholson's surrender.

August 13: With a powerful fleet carrying 3,000 troops and many siege cannons, Admiral de Grasse sets sail from Haiti for the Chesapeake Bay, with orders to aid Rochambeau and Washington but to return to the

West Indies by October 15, before the hurricane season begins.

August 14: Rochambeau receives a letter from de Grasse relaying the admiral's plan to sail to the Chesapeake. The letter generates Washington's pivotal decision: to abandon operations in New York and move the American and French armies immediately to Virginia. If they arrive in time, with de Grasse controlling the sea approaches, they can trap and overwhelm Cornwallis in Yorktown. Washington sends Lafayette orders to keep Cornwallis penned in Yorktown and orders Gen. William Heath to use half the Continental army to bottle up Clinton in New York.

August 21: Beginning their march south, Washington and Rochambeau cross the Hudson River, divide their forces into three columns, and pursue a roundabout path to convince Clinton that New York remains their objective. When they turn south, they must move rapidly so that Clinton does not reinforce Cornwallis by sea before they can march the 450 miles to Yorktown.

Reluctantly acceding to Washington's entreaties, Admiral de Barras prepares to sail from Newport to meet de Grasse.

August 26: After eluding Rodney's squadron in the West Indies, de Grasse arrives off the Virginia coast, taking control of the sea approaches to Yorktown for the time being, making contact with Lafayette, and planning the disembarkation of his troops.

August 28: To mislead Clinton, Washington and Rochambeau halt temporarily at Chatham, New Jersey.

August 30: Riding ahead of their armies, Washington and Rochambeau arrive in Philadelphia.

August 31: De Grasse begins to land his troops at Jamestown to reinforce Lafayette.

September 2: The French and American armies reach Philadelphia and pause long enough for the Continentals, all northern units, to demand a month's pay in hard money. Washington implores Robert Morris to provide the funds; Morris's only option is to use money loaned by Rochambeau to pay the men. Mollified, the Continentals march on with the French toward Head of Elk.

Sir Henry Clinton finally realizes that Yorktown is Washington's and Rochambeau's objective, but there is little he can do to assist Cornwallis.

September 5: At Chester, Pennsylvania, while traveling overland to meet Rochambeau, who proceeds by water to Head of Elk, Washington receives news from an express rider that de Grasse's fleet has safely arrived. Elated, the commander in chief hastens to join Rochambeau, shouting the news at him as he approaches the jetty at Head of Elk.

After sighting the sails of a British fleet, de Grasse sails out to do battle with the combined forces of admirals Graves and Hood. De Grasse's flagship *Ville de Paris,* probably the largest warship afloat, carries 110 guns; he also has 24 ships of the line with 64 to 80 guns each and six frigates. The British force is 19 ships of the line and seven frigates. The foes begin battle at 4:00 P.M., with the wind favoring the British but de Grasse's superiority in cannons proving decisive. Following a two-hour battle, the British withdraw with several badly damaged ships and sail for New York, leaving Cornwallis trapped in Yorktown without hope of rescue.

September 6: Advance units of the Continental army arrive at Head of Elk for transport by boat down the Chesapeake Bay to Williamsburg; other units ship out from Baltimore and Annapolis.

Benedict Arnold lands with an amphibious force of regulars and Loyalists at New London, Connecticut, where, joined by local Loyalists, they overwhelm the defenders and pillage the town. They also brutally kill several American officers who have surrendered. The cruelty of the raid seals forever the traitorous reputation of Arnold, who will soon leave for England.

September 8: Nathanael Greene hopes to surprise about 2,000 British troops encamped along the Santee River near Eutaw Springs, South Carolina, under command of Lt. Col. Alexander Stewart, who succeeded Lord Rawdon. The element of surprise is lost, however, when Maj. John Coffin, a Loyalist, rides into an ambush with his scouting unit but escapes to warn Stewart. In the ensuing battle, Greene's militia perform well, and Greene's Marylanders and Virginians push back an advance with a bayonet attack. Stewart's men seem on the verge of collapse when Greene's men pause to plunder the British tents. The British flee to safety in a brick house and fire on the advancing Americans. A sortie led by Maj. John Marjoribanks brings victory to the British, although at the cost of the major's life. Greene withdraws with about 500 casualties. But the British toll comprises 693 killed, wounded, or missing. Stewart retreats toward Charleston.

Rochambeau's troops reach Head of Elk and begin embarking on the Chesapeake for Williamsburg.

September 9: De Barras's fleet arrives at the mouth of Chesapeake Bay to join de Grasse, giving the French total control of the bay.

Washington detours to visit Mount Vernon, sleeping in his own home for the first time in six years.

September 13: Col. David Fanning leads a Loyalist force of about 1,000 on an all-night march and a daring raid on Hillsboro, North Carolina, capturing Gov. Thomas Burke, his council, and several Continental officers and men. As they march from Hillsboro in the afternoon, Continentals led by Gen. John Butler attack. Each side suffers about 100 casualties; the severely wounded Fanning remains on the field as his remaining force flees with their prisoners.

September 15: The troops assembled at Williamsburg, Virginia, march in military review before Washington and Rochambeau; the American officers visit Washington in a body. Some 16,000 men make up the allied force, with the American army organized into three divisions under command of Lafayette, Benjamin Lincoln, and von Steuben. Rochambeau's army includes four regiments that marched from Rhode Island and three regiments brought by de Grasse from the West Indies, as well as Lauzun's cavalry, 600 artillerymen, and 800 marines. In defense of Yorktown, Cornwallis has 6,000 troops, mostly British regulars and German mercenaries but also some marines and Loyalist militia. Cornwallis has posted part of his force across the river to secure landings at Gloucester Point.

September 17: Washington and Rochambeau meet with de Grasse aboard the *Ville de Paris.* Their plan entails de Grasse's controlling the sea approaches while the allied armies surround Yorktown, using the heavy siege cannons brought ashore from the French fleet to bombard the town. Allied engineers will dig trenches at angles approaching Yorktown's fortifications and move artillery successively closer. Seven redoubts and six artillery batteries connected by trenches encircling the town, with other batteries and redoubts in support, make up Yorktown's defenses. Trenches protect Gloucester.

September 23: Unable to devise a plan to relieve Yorktown, Clinton receives a letter from Cornwallis warning him to prepare "to hear the worst" if no aid is forthcoming.

September 28: At dawn, the allied armies move out from Williamsburg to establish positions surrounding Yorktown, with the British outposts withdrawing at their approach.

September 30: Believing that his only hope is relief by sea and hearing that Clinton intends to sail soon from New York with reinforcements, Cornwallis decides to conserve his strength and orders Yorktown's outer works abandoned during the night. As his men withdraw, allied troops scramble forward, occupy the abandoned sites, and begin their siege operation. Fierce skirmishing occurs as allied troops drive outlying British detachments back. Washington sends General de Choisy across the York River with Lauzun's cavalry to confine Tarleton's British Legion at Gloucester.

October 1: American batteries mounted in the outer works abandoned by the British at Yorktown pound the town; British cannons return the fire.

October 3: As de Choisy presses closer to the British trenches at Gloucester, Lauzun's troopers surprise a foraging party of Tarleton's dragoons, skirmish with them, and drive them back inside their fortifications. De Choisy positions his troops to prevent further British forays.

October 6: Washington ceremonially breaks ground for the first approach trench at Yorktown, and allied sappers begin digging 600 yards from the main British fortifications. Soon, 1,500 men with picks and shovels throw up a protective embankment, and as the digging progresses armed troops occupy the trench. French troops attack the outermost British redoubt to prevent sorties from interrupting the digging.

October 9: With more cannons now in place, the allies bombard Yorktown relentlessly. Washington fires the first shot from a new American battery, and a French battery of four 12-pounders plus howitzers and mortars pounds the British Fusiliers' Redoubt. The shelling can now reach Gloucester, and it drives away the two British frigates that still remain in the York River.

October 10: Continental dragoons led by Maj. Lemuel Trescott capture Fort Slongo, a Loyalist post near Treadwell's Neck, burn the blockhouse, and then withdraw across Long Island Sound.

The allied bombardment of Yorktown intensifies as still more cannons come on line and troops defend the trenches against British raids. The French fire red-hot shot that sets afire a British brig and two transports on the river.

October 11: The first allied approach trench at Yorktown now extends 1,000 yards. Work on a second trench begins at a different angle only 300 yards from Cornwallis's main works. By nightfall, it stretches 750 yards in length.

October 14: At Yorktown, during the night, American troops led by Alexander Hamilton and French troops commanded by Col. De Deux-Ponts overwhelm two British redoubts that prevent the allies from extending their trenches to the York River. Sappers quickly extend the trenches and incorporate the redoubts into the allied fortifications.

October 16: Cornwallis sends a sortie of 350 men against the second allied line of trenches that succeeds in overrunning the forward batteries and spiking the guns, but French grenadiers under Louis-Marie, viscount de Noailles, drive them back, and the guns are returned to service within a few hours.

October 17: At about 10:00 A.M. a British drummer mounts a parapet at Yorktown and beats the tune for a parley; then an officer appears holding a white handkerchief and moves forward with the drummer. An allied officer advances to meet them, sends the drummer back, ties the handkerchief over the British officer's eyes, and brings him to General Washington. The British officer requests an armistice and the appointment of commissioners to discuss surrender terms. Washington grants a two-hour cease-fire and demands that Cornwallis submit a written proposal. Cornwallis requests that his troops be paroled and returned to England. Washington demands unconditional surrender. By nightfall, Cornwallis accedes.

After belatedly preparing to sail to Cornwallis's rescue, Sir Henry Clinton will learn of the surrender and turn back.

October 19: Formed in double lines a mile long, with American troops to the right and French troops to the left, the allied forces wait at Yorktown. Astride his horse, Washington heads the American line, with Rochambeau opposite. After an hour, the British begin to march out of their fortifications with colors cased. Cornwallis pleads illness to avoid the ignominy of surrendering to the Americans. The British troops throw down their arms. Gen. Charles O'Hara presents Cornwallis's sword to Washington in token of surrender; Gen. Benjamin Lincoln, who was forced to surrender at Charleston, steps forward to accept it. At Gloucester, across the river, Tarleton surrenders to De Choisy. The allies receive more than 7,000 prisoners. Cornwallis and his principal officers receive paroles and transport to New York.

October 20: Robert Livingston assumes office as secretary of foreign affairs, and Robert Morris becomes secretary of finance. Although Congress created the for-

eign affairs office in January, the delegates were unable to select a secretary during the succeeding months.

October 22: At 3:00 A.M., Tench Tilgham, an aide-de-camp to Commander in Chief George Washington, rides into Philadelphia and immediately heads for the home of President Thomas McKean with news of the victory at Yorktown. The night watchman who guided Tilgham begins to cry the news in the city's streets, and euphoria spreads as residents awaken to learn of the American triumph. The city celebrates with cannon salutes and festivities. Because the national treasury lacks the money to pay Tilgham's expenses, individual congressmen each contribute a dollar to cover the costs of his journey from Yorktown.

October 24: Washington's official report on Cornwallis's surrender reaches Congress, and President McKean writes official and profuse congratulations to the commander in chief. Congress, officials of the Pennsylvania and Philadelphia governments, and French minister Luzerne attend a service at the Lutheran Church conducted by one of the chaplains of Congress.

October 30: Congress appoints Gen. Benjamin Lincoln secretary of war and also implores the states to provide $8 million immediately to pay the government's and the army's costs.

November 5: Disregarding Washington's pleas to remain at Yorktown and organize campaigns to recapture Savannah and Charleston, Admiral de Grasse sets sail for the West Indies. He has stayed beyond his original commitment, and he also has made a secret agreement with the Spanish to spend the winter in the Caribbean.

November 10: American troops fill in their siege trenches at Yorktown, and units of the army begin to disperse. General St. Clair leads one force of Continentals to the Carolinas to reinforce Greene's army. Washington and another force head for the Hudson River to watch over Clinton's army in New York City. Rochambeau and his French troops remain in Virginia.

November 18: The British garrison at Wilmington, North Carolina, evacuates the city.

November 20: French foreign minister Vergennes summons Benjamin Franklin to his Paris offices to give him the news of the victory at Yorktown.

November 25: The disheartening news of Cornwallis's surrender reaches London by packet boat from Paris, with a letter from Clinton arriving simultaneously in confirmation. Dismay settles upon the entire government. Although 30,000 British troops remain on duty in North America and in control of every major port but Boston, the will to continue the war is at low ebb, the huge debt incurred during the struggle approaches crisis levels, and the ministry harbors great anxiety over the combined French and Spanish fleets.

The French recapture St. Eustatius, West Indies, from the British.

December 1: Nathanael Greene's army pressures the main British force, temporarily commanded by Maj. John Doyle, near Dorchester, South Carolina, and Doyle retreats to hole up in Charleston.

December 6: Plagued by financial crisis, Congress sends a delegation to Rhode Island, the last holdout, to urge acceptance of the 5 percent national duty on imports that could resolve the crisis; but shortly after the delegation's departure, news arrives that Virginia has rescinded its previous approval, precluding any resolution.

December 20: A brief session of Parliament that included debate on the war in America comes to an end. Lord North tries to convey to George III the members' general conclusion that Great Britain cannot afford to continue the war, but the king remains obdurate. Lord George Germain tries to resign, but the king insists he stay or be replaced by someone willing to prosecute the war. With support for the war in both Parliament and the armed forces collapsing, however, the king's hand must in time be forced.

December 22: With his service to America completed, the marquis de Lafayette boards ship at Boston to return to France.

December 31: Congress reluctantly grants a charter to the national bank, the Bank of North America, acceding to the demands of Robert Morris and the bank's subscribers. At its founding, the bank has a capitalization of $400,000 as a money supply for the government.

Eyewitness Testimony

1781

No masts or sails these crowded ships adorn,
Dismal to view, neglected and forlorn!
Here, mighty ills oppress the imprison'd throng,
Dull were our slumbers, and our nights too long—
From morn to eve along the decks we lay
Scorch'd into fevers by the solar ray;
No friendly awning cast a welcome shade,
Once was it promis'd, and was never made;
No favors could these sons of death bestow,
'Twas endless cursing, and continual woe:
Immortal hatred doth their breasts engage,
And this lost empire swells their souls with rage.

. . . . .

But such a train of endless woes abound,
So many mischiefs in these hulks are found,
That on them all a poem to prolong
Would swell too high the horrors of my song—
Hunger and thirst to work our woe combine,
And moldy bread, and flesh of rotten swine,
The mangled carcase, and the batter'd brain,
The doctor's poison, and the captain's cane,
The soldier's musquet, and the steward's debt,
The evening shackle, and the noon-day threat.

Philip Freneau, from "The British Prison Ship,"
written 1780, not published until 1781, in Fred Lewis
Pattee, The Poems of Philip Freneau,
vol. 2, pp. 26 and 31.

At this distance, and under your present circumstances, it is impossible to recommend (if advice could reach you in time) any particular line of conduct, but only in general to observe, that such measures founded in justice, and a proper degree of generosity, as will have a tendency to conciliate or divide the Men, appear most likely to succeed. . . .

George Washington, from a letter written at New
Windsor, New York, New York, January 7, 1781, to
Brig. Gen. Anthony Wayne concerning the Pennsylvania
mutineers, in John C. Fitzpatrick, ed., The Writings of
George Washington, *vol. 21, p. 71.*

. . . General Wayne, with some other officers, determined to follow and keep with them [mutinous soldiers], at all events, though the general could not prevail on them to stop till they came to Princeton. They marched through the country with great regularity and good conduct. . . . While they continued at Princeton, a sergeant of the British army with one Ogden, an inhabitant of New Jersey, for a guide, came to them, and made proposals from General Clinton. These they rejected with so much honor and indignation, that they seized the messengers and delivered them to General Wayne, who put them under guard. Soon after this a Committee of the Council of Pennsylvania together with a Committee of Congress met the soldiery. Their grievances were redressed. . . . They marched from Princeton on Tuesday the ninth. On Wednesday the tenth, the two spies were tried, and executed next day. . . .

Upon the whole, this affair, which at first appeared so alarming, has only served to give a new proof of the inflexible honor of the soldiery, and their inviolable attachment to American liberty; and will teach General Clinton, that though he could bribe such a mean toad-eater as Arnold, it is not in his power to bribe an American soldier.

From an account of the Pennsylvania soldiers' mutiny,
New-Jersey Gazette, *January 17, 1781, in Frank*
Moore, compiler, The Diary of the American
Revolution, *pp. 479–480.*

You are to take command of the detachment, which has been ordered to march from this post against the mutineers of the Jersey line. . . . The object of your detachment is to compel the mutineers to unconditional submission. . . . The manner of executing this I leave to your discretion according to circumstances. If you succeed in compelling the revolted troops to surrender you will instantly execute a few of the most active and most incendiary leaders.

George Washington, from orders written at West Point,
New York, January 22, 1781, to Maj. Gen. Robert
Howe, in John C. Fitzpatrick, ed., The Writings of
George Washington, *vol. 21, p. 128.*

This morning [January 17], after a very severe action, General Morgan, with a detachment of the southern army, obtained a complete victory over Colonel Tarleton at the Cowpens, with eleven hundred and fifty men, the flower of Cornwallis's army. . . .

This is but the prelude to the era of 1781, the close of which, we hope, will prove memorable in the annals of history, as the happy period of peace, liberty, and independence to America.

From the New-Jersey Gazette, *February 21, 1781, in Frank Moore, compiler,* The Diary of the American Revolution, *pp. 482–483.*

This day [March1] will be memorable in the annals of America to the last posterity, for the final ratification in Congress of the articles of confederation and perpetual union between the States.

This great event, which will confound our enemies, fortify us against their arts of seduction, and frustrate their plans of division, was announced to the public at twelve o'clock, under the discharge of the artillery on the land and the cannon of the shipping in the Delaware. The bells were rung, and every manifestation of joy shown on this occasion. The *Ariel* frigate, commanded by the gallant Paul Jones, fired a *feu de joie,* and was beautifully decorated. . . .

. . . . .

Thus has the union, began by necessity, been indissolubly cemented. Thus America . . . is growing up in war into greatness and consequence among the nations. But Britain's boasted wealth and grandeur are crumbling to pieces, never to be again united. . . . [T]here will be a time when scarcely a monument of her former glory will remain. The fragments of her empire, and its history, will then be of little other use to mankind, but like a landmark to warn against the shoals and rocks on which her political navigators had ship-wrecked that infatuated nation.

From the Pennsylvania Packet, *March 3, 1781, in Frank Moore, compiler,* The Diary of the American Revolution, *pp. 486–487.*

I have been engaged in public affairs, and enjoyed public confidence . . . during the long term of fifty years, and honour sufficient to satisfy any reasonable ambition; and I have no other left but that of repose, which I hope the Congress will grant me, by sending some person to supply my place. At the same time, I beg they may be assured, that it is not any the least doubt of their success in the glorious cause, nor any disgust received in their service, that induces me to decline it, but purely and simply the reasons above mentioned. . . .

Benjamin Franklin, from a letter written at Passy, France, March 12, 1781, to president of the Congress Samuel Huntington, in Albert Henry Smyth, ed., The Writings of Benjamin Franklin, *vol. 8, p. 221.*

. . . This [lack of recruits and provisions], and ten thousand reasons which I could assign, prove the necessity of something more than recommendatory powers in Congress. If that body is not vested with a controuling power in matters of common concern, and for the great purposes of War, I do not scruple to give it, decidedly, as my opinion, that it will be impossible to prosecute it to any *good effect.* . . .

George Washington, from a letter written at New Windsor, New York, March 26, 1781, to Maj. Gen. John Armstrong, in John C. Fitzpatrick, ed., The Writings of George Washington, *vol. 21, p. 379.*

. . . I live in a Part of the Country remarkable for its Whigism, & Attachment to the Cause of Liberty; and it is with much Concern I find a general Opinion prevailing, that our Allies are spinning out the War, in order to weaken America, as well as Great Britain, and thereby leave Us, at the End of it, as dependent as possible upon themselves; however unjust this Opinion may be, it is natural enough to Planters & Farmers,

Lord Cornwallis was a British general. *(From* The Pictorial Field Book of the Revolution, *2 vols., by B. J. Lossing. New York: Harper Brothers, 1851 and 1852.)*

burdened with heavy Taxes, & frequently draged from their Familys upon military Duty. . . .

George Mason, from a letter written at Gunston-Hall, Virginia, April 3, 1781, to the Virginia delegates to Congress, in William T. Hutchinson and William M. E. Rachal, eds., The Papers of James Madison, *vol. 3, p. 54.*

. . . I have, however, the satisfaction of informing you that our military operations were uniformly successful and the victory at Guildford, although one of the bloodiest of this war, was very complete. The enemy gave themselves out for nine or ten and undoubtedly had seven thousand men in the field. . . . Our force was 1360 infantry rank and file, and about 200 cavalry. General Greene retreated the night of the action to the Ironworks on Troublesome Creek. . . .

Lord Cornwallis, from a letter written at Wilmington, North Carolina, April 10, 1781, to Gen. Sir Henry Clinton, in K. G. Davies, ed., Documents of the American Revolution, *vol. 20, p. 107.*

. . . Indeed the behavior and conversation of most here on the nature of the times gives me pain. Men in words assuming to be hearty Whigs, but in their behavior rank Tories and enemies of Independency, there being but a small number of the true, sincere hearted Whigs left here at present to mourn for the abomination of the times, and of such there is great need, as so great a number are engaged in monopolizing, gaming, drinking, dancing, swearing, idleness, &c.

Christopher Marshall, merchant and Quaker then in Lancaster, Pennsylvania, from diary entry of April 12, 1781, in Marshall, Extracts from the Diary of Christopher Marshall, *p. 272.*

I am thoroughly perswaded that you acted from your best judgment; and believe, that your desire to preserve my property, and rescue the buildings from impending danger, were your governing motives. But to go on board their Vessels; carry them refreshments; commune with a parcel of plundering Scoundrels, and request a favor by asking the surrender of my Negroes, was exceedingly ill-judged, and 'tis to be feared, will be unhappy in its consequences, as it will be a precedent for others, and may become a subject of animadversion.

George Washington, from a letter written at New Windsor, New York, April 30, 1781, to Lund Washington concerning a British raid at Mount Vernon, in John C. Fitzpatrick, ed., The Writings of George Washington, *vol. 22, p. 15.*

I find no reason to flatter ourselves that we have much to expect either from the ability or inclination of Spain. Her government is far from being so rich as is vulgarly imagined. The mines of South America of late years have been less liberal of their profits; and for fear of accidents, but a small part of their product since the war has been imported into Europe. The extreme indolence of the Spaniards and their neglect of agriculture, manufactures and trade make them tributary to their more industrious neighbours who drain them of their precious metals as fast as they arrive.

Alexander Hamilton, from a letter written at De Peyster's Point, New York, April 30, 1781, to Robert Morris, in Harold C. Syrett, ed., The Papers of Alexander Hamilton, *vol. 2, p. 615.*

The Congress is finally bankrupt! Last Saturday a large body of the inhabitants with paper dollars in their hats by way of cockades, paraded the streets of Philadelphia, carrying colors flying, with a DOG TARRED, and instead of the usual appendage and ornament of feathers, his back was covered with the Congress' paper dollars. This example of disaffection   . . . was directly followed by the jailer, who refused accepting the bills in purchase of a glass of rum, and afterwards by the traders of the city, who shut up their shops, declining to sell any more goods but for gold or silver. It was declared also by the popular voice, that if the opposition to Great Britain was not in future carried on by solid money instead of paper bills, all further resistance to the mother country were vain, and must be given up.

From Rivington's Gazette, *May 12, 1781, in Frank Moore, compiler,* The Diary of the American Revolution, *pp. 504–505.*

The English are in a fair way of gaining still more Enemies; they play a desperate Game. Fortune may favour them, as it sometimes does a drunken Dicer: But by their Tyranny in the East, they have at length roused the Powers there against them, and I do not know that they have in the West a single Friend. If they lose their India Commerce (which is one of their present great Supports), and one Battle at Sea, their Credit is gone, and their Power follows. Thus Empires, by Pride, Folly, and Extravagance, ruin themselves like Individuals. . . .

Benjamin Franklin, from a letter written at Passy, France, May 14, 1781, to marquis de Lafayette, in Albert Henry Smyth, ed., The Writings of Benjamin Franklin, *vol. 8, p. 251.*

The retrograde progress of our arms in this country, you have seen in your newspapers, if they dare tell you the truth. This precious commodity is not to be had in the government paper which is printed here, for a fell licenser hangs over the press, and will suffer nothing to pass but what is palatable; that is, in plain terms, what is false. Our victories have been dearly bought, for the rebels seem to grow stronger by every defeat, like Antaeus.... I wish our ministry could send us a Hercules to conquer these obstinate Americans, whose aversion to the cause of Britain grows stronger every day.

   ...An officer told Lord Cornwallis not long ago, that he believed if he had destroyed all the men in North America, we should have enough to do to conquer the women. I am heartily tired of this country, and wish myself at home.

From a letter written May 20, 1781 by a British soldier at Charleston, South Carolina, to a friend in London, reproduced in the Pennsylvania Packet, *December 11, 1781, in Frank Moore, compiler,* The Diary of the American Revolution, *pp. 506–507.*

A day or two ago I requested Colo. Harrison to apply to you for a pair of Pincers to fasten the wire of my teeth. I hope you furnished him with them. I now wish you would send me one of your scrapers, as my teeth stand in need of cleaning, and I have little prospect of being in Philadelpa, soon....

George Washington, from a letter written at New Windsor, New York, May 29, 1781, to Dr. John Baker, in John C. Fitzpatrick, ed., The Writings of George Washington, *vol. 22, p. 129.*

The rapidity of your movements through a country so thinly inhabited and so little cultivated is justly matter of astonishment to all Europe as well as to the rebels in America; and although they appear to make every possible exertion to oppose your progress and conduct their enterprises in Carolina with more spirit than they have shown in any other part of America, His Majesty has such confidence in your lordship's great military talents that he entertains no doubt of your fulfilling his utmost expectations in the course of the campaign....

Lord George Germain, from a letter written at Whitehall, London, June 4, 1781, to Lord Cornwallis, in K. G. Davies, ed., Documents of the American Revolution, *vol. 20, p. 151.*

Our march towards Kingsbridge depends on a number of circumstances—We are at present destitute of every necessary but provisions—The Qr. Master's department cannot furnish horses to move a single Brigade; besides this, our present numbers will not justify our taking a critical position—Connecticut, 'tis universally said, for two years past has done nothing at all—Her supplies have been trifling—her promises great—and her exertions a Puff. Of this our present weakness in men is a shameful proof....

Samuel Blachley Webb, from a letter written at Peekskill, New York, June 27, 1781, to his brother Joseph Webb, in Worthington Chauncey Ford, ed., Correspondence and Journals of Samuel Blachley Webb, *vol. 2, p. 345.*

This day all the officers that are present on the Island assembled, to commemorate the 4th. July it being the anniversary of Independancy and drank the 13 following 1st. United States of America may they ever be free Independant & Suvering [sovereign], 2nd. the King of France / 3d. The King of Spain, 4th. the United States of Holland / 5th. The Continental Congress / 6th. Genl. Washington / 7th our American ambassador in Europe / 8th. The French Ambassador in America / 9th. The French Adml. And Navy in America. 10th. Genl. DeRochambeau & the French Army in America / 11th. The American Arms / 12th. A Speedy Releasement to the Allied Prisoners, 13th what we gained by our arms may we support by our Virtue—and spent the remainder of the Day in Jollety & Mirth under a Flagg which had the Figure of his Excellency Genl. Washington on it.

Lieutenant Jeremiah Greenman, then being held prisoner at Gravesend, Long Island (he had been captured by a troop of Loyalists while commanding a guard unit at Pines Bridge on the Croton River in Westchester County), diary entry of July 4, 1781, in Greenman, Diary of a Common Soldier in the American Revolution, 1775–1783, *p. 212.*

No description can give you an adequate idea of the barbarity with which the Enemy have conducted the war in the Southern States. Every outrage which humanity could suffer has been committed by them. Desolation rather than conquest seems to have been their object. They have acted more like desperate bands of Robbers or Buccaneers than like a nation making war for dominion. Negroes, Horses, Tobacco &c not the standards and arms of their antagonists are the trophies which display their success. Rapes, murders & the whole catalogue of individual cruelties . . . characterize . . . their usurped Jurisdiction. . . .

> *James Madison, from a letter written in Philadelphia, July 7, 1781, to Philip Mazzei, diplomat for Virginia to court of Tuscany, in William T. Hutchinson and William M. E. Rachal, eds.,* The Papers of James Madison, *vol. 3, p. 180.*

The present, then, is the critical day for America. Dissensions, languor in our councils or conduct, would revive the hopes of Britain, and might be an irreparable injury to the Americans and their latest posterity. Union and vigor through the present campaign, may lay a stable foundation of liberty and happiness to these States. Having expended already so much blood and treasure in their glorious cause, it should be a first principle in the mind of every free citizen, that the only way to reap the fruits of all, and to make a safe and honorable peace, is to conduct the remainder of the war with vigor. This, and this alone, will make it short. . . . A good army in the field, and well provided, is absolutely necessary to give the finishing stroke to the establishment of America's invaluable rights. One signal defeat of the British will have more effect on the negotiations at Vienna, than all the eloquence of the most accomplished plenipotentiaries.

> *From the* Pennsylvania Packet, *July 14, 1781, in Frank Moore, compiler,* The Diary of the American Revolution, *p. 515.*

I have just received your friendly Letter . . . announcing your Appointment to the Superintendent of our Finances. This gave me great Pleasure, as, from your Intelligence, Integrity, and Abilities, there is reason to hope every Advantage . . . You are wise in estimating beforehand, as the principal Advantage you can expect, the consciousness of having done Service to your Country; for the Business you have undertaken is of so complex a Nature . . . and the Publick is often niggardly, even of its Thanks, while you are sure of being censured by malevolent Criticks and Bugwriters, who will abuse you while you are serving them, and wound your Character in nameless Pamphlets; thereby resembling those little dirty stinking insects, that attack us only in the dark, disturb our Repose, molesting and

wounding us, while our Sweat and Blood are contributing to their Subsistence. . . .

> *Benjamin Franklin, from a letter written at Passy, France, July 26, 1781, to Robert Morris, in Albert Henry Smyth, ed.,* The Writings of Benjamin Franklin, *vol. 8, p. 288.*

. . . The action of Camden was much more bloody according to the numbers engagd than that of Guilford on both sides. The enemy had more than one third of their whole force engagd either killed, or wounded; and we had not less than a quarter. Depend upon it our actions have been bloody and severe according to the force engagd; and we should have had Lord Rawden and his whole command prisoners in the three Minutes, if Col [John] Gunby had not orderd his Regiment to retire; the greater part of which were advancing rapidly at the time they were orderd off. I was almost frantick with vexation at the disappointment. Fortune has not been much our friend. . . .

> *Nathanael Greene, from a letter written at High Hills of the Santee, South Carolina, August 6, 1781, to Joseph Reed, president of the Pennsylvania Council, in Dennis M. Conrad, ed.,* The Papers of General Nathanael Greene, *vol. 9, p. 135.*

See!—dread *Seraphis* flames again—
And art thou, Jones, among the slain,
　　And sunk to Neptune's caves below—
He lives—though crowds around him fall,
Still he, unhurt survives them all;
　　Almost alone he fights the foe.

And can thy ship these strokes sustain?
Behold thy brave companions slain,
　　All clasp'd in ocean's dark embrace.
"Strike or be sunk!"—the Briton cries—
"Sink, if you can!"—the chief replies,
　　Fierce lightnings blazing in his face.

> *Philip Freneau, from "On the Memorable Victory," August 8, 1781, in Fred Lewis Pattee,* The Poems of Philip Freneau, *vol. 2, p. 78.*

But my dear Marquis, I am distressed beyond expression, to know what is become of the Count de Grasse, and for fear the English Fleet, by occupying the Chesapeake . . . should frustrate all our flattering prospects in that quarter. I am not a little solicitous for the Count de Barras. . . . Of many contingencies we will hope for the most propitious events.

Should the retreat of Lord Cornwallis by water, be cut off by the arrival of either of the French Fleets, I am persuaded you will do all in your power to prevent his escape by land. May that great felicity be reserved for you!

You See, how critically important the present Moment is: for my own part I am determined still to persist, with unremitting ardour in my present Plan, unless some inevitable and insuperable obstacles are thrown in our way.

George Washington, from a letter written at Philadelphia, September 2, 1781, to marquis de Lafayette, in John C. Fitzpatrick, ed., The Writings of George Washington, *vol. 23, p. 77.*

The measures which are now pursuing, are big with great events; the Peace and Independence of this Country, and the general tranquility of Europe will, it is more than probable, result from our Compleat success; disgrace to ourselves, Triumph to the Enemy, and probable Ruin to the American Cause, will follow our disappointment. The first is certain, if the powerful Fleet, now in Chesapeak Bay . . . can remain to the close of the regular Operation, which, from various unforeseen causes, may be protracted beyond our present expectation. The second is much to be apprehended, if from the fear of loosing the Aid of the Fleet, the operations by Land are precipitated faster than a necessary prudence and regard to the lives of Men, will warrant; the first may be slow, but sure; the second must be bloody and precarious.

George Washington, from a letter at Williamsburg, September 17, 1781, to count de Grasse, in John C. Fitzpatrick, ed., The Writings of George Washington, *vol. 23, p. 123.*

Since I wrote you before we have had a most bloody battle and obtained a complete victory over the enemy, and have driven them near to the gates of Charles Town. We took five hundred prisoners and killed & wounded a greater number. We also took near a thousand stand of arms, . . . and had it not been for one of those incidents to which military operations are subject and against which there is no guarding, we should have taken the whole British army, notwithstanding our numbers were much inferior to theirs. The gallantry of the officers and the bravery of the troops would do

honor even to the arms of his Prussian Majesty [Frederick the Great].

Nathanael Greene, from a letter written at High Hills of the Santee, South Carolina, September 17, 1781, to Baron Friedrich von Steuben, in Dennis M. Conrad, ed., The Papers of General Nathanael Greene, *vol. 9, p. 360.*

Where you are I know not, but if you are where I wish you, it is with the General [Washington] in Virginia; the prospect is so bright and the glory so great that I want you to be there to share in them. . . . [T]o take a General [Cornwallis] who has been the terrour of the South and oblige his Army to pile their Arms, will be a rich feast even for the eyes of a prince. . . . Never was there a more inviting object to glory. The General is a most fortunate Man, and may success and laurels attend him. Our force has been so small that nothing capital could be effected, and our operations have been conducted under every disadvantage that could embarrass either a General or an Army. We have done all we could, and if the public and our friends are not satisfied we cannot help it. . . .

Nathanael Greene, from a letter written at High Hills of the Santee, South Carolina, September 29, 1781, to Gen. Henry Knox, in Daniel M. Conrad, ed., The Papers of Nathanael Greene, *vol. 9, pp. 411–412.*

. . . My uneasiness at not hearing from you is abated by the sweet prospect of soon taking you in my arms. Your father [Maj. Gen. Philip Schuyler] will tell you the news. Tomorrow Cornwallis and his army are ours. In two days after I shall in all probability set out for Albany, and I hope to embrace you in three weeks from this time. Conceive my love by your own feelings, how delightful this prospect is to me. Only in your heart and in my own can any image be found of my happiness upon the occasion. . . .

Adieu My Charming beloved wife, I kiss you a thousand times, Adieu, My love

Alexander Hamilton, from a letter written at Yorktown, October 18, 1781, to Elizabeth Hamilton, in Harold C. Syrett, ed., The Papers of Alexander Hamilton, *vol. 2, p. 683.*

. . . The Neglect of funding the public Debt, has introduced a Practice of issuing Loan Office Certificates. This I have absolutely forbidden, nor will I ever consent to it. Such Accumulation of Debt, while it distresses the Public, and destroys its Credit, by no means relieves the unfortunate Individual who is a public Creditor. For if Revenue is not provided, increasing the Certificates would only lessen their Value. This would be such a Fraud, as would stamp our national Character with indelible Marks of Infamy, and render us the Reproach and Contempt of all Mankind. It is high Time to relieve ourselves from the Infamy we have already sustained, and to rescue and restore the national Credit. This can only be done by solid Revenue. . . .

Robert Morris, from a Circular to the Governors of the States issued at Philadelphia, October 19, 1781, in E. James Ferguson, ed., The Papers of Robert Morris, *vol. 3, p. 87.*

Sir: I have the Honor to inform Congress, that a Reduction of the British Army under the Command of Lord Cornwallis, is most happily effected. The unremitting Ardor which actuated every Officer and Soldier in the combined Army on this Occasion, has principally led to this Important Event, at an earlier period than my most sanguine Hopes had induced me to expect.

The singular Spirit of Emulation, which animated the whole Army from the first Commencement of our Operations, has filled my Mind with the highest pleasure and Satisfaction, and had given me the happiest presages of Success.

George Washington, from a letter written near Yorktown, Virginia, October 19, 1781, to the president of Congress, in John C. Fitzpatrick, ed., The Writings of George Washington, *vol. 23, p. 241.*

Sir, I have the mortification to inform your Excellency that I have been forced to give up the posts of York and Gloucester and to surrender the troops under my command by capitulation on the 19th instant as prisoners of war to the combined forces of America and France.

I never saw this post in a very favourable light . . . nothing but the hopes of relief would have induced me to attempt its defence, for I would either have endeavoured to escape to New York by rapid marches from the Gloucester side immediately on the arrival of General Washington's troops at Williamsburgh, or I would notwithstanding the disparity of numbers have attacked them in the open field. . . . But being assured by your Excellency's letters that every possible means would be tried by the navy and army to relieve us, I could not think myself at liberty to venture on either of those desperate attempts. . . .

Lord Cornwallis, from a letter written at Yorktown, Virginia, October 20, 1781, to Gen. Sir Henry Clinton, in K. G. Davies, ed., Documents of the American Revolution, *vol. 20, p. 244.*

BE IT REMEMBERED That on the 17th day of October, 1781, Lieut. General Charles Earl Cornwallis, with above 5000 British troops surrendered themselves prisoners of war to his excellency Gen. George Washington, commander in chief of the allied forces of France and America,

LAUS DEO!—

From the Freeman's Journal, *October 24, 1781, quoted in Fred Lewis Pattee,* The Poems of Philip Freneau, *vol. 2, p. 93.*

I return you my fervent congratulations on the glorious success of the combined arms at York & Glocester. We [Congress] have had from the Commander in chief an official report of the fact with a copy of the capitulation. . . . If these severe doses of ill fortune do not cool the phrenzy and relax the pride of Britain, it would seem as if Heaven had in reality abandoned her to her folly & her fate. . . . A fair trial has then been made of the strength: and what is the result? They have lost another army, another colony, another island, and another fleet of her trade. . . .

James Madison, from a letter written in Philadelphia, October 30, 1781, to Edmund Pendleton, presiding justice of the Virginia supreme court of appeals, in William T. Hutchinson and William M. E. Rachal, eds., The Papers of James Madison, *vol. 3, p. 296.*

The Surrender of his Lordship [Cornwallis] was celebrated here on Wednesday last—an Entertainment was provided in the open field for all the Officers of the Army—where we made use of 120 gallons of Madeira with a Quantam Sufficit of Spirit &c. A more Sociable time I never experienc'd—every one was happy—many *perfectly* so—indeed the whole week has been but one continued Hurra—from Right to Left.

Capt. S. W. Williams, from a letter written at Peekskill, New York, November 2, 1781, to Samuel Blachley Webb, in Worthington Chauncey Ford, ed., Correspondence and Journals of Samuel Blachley Webb, *vol. 2, pp. 372–373.*

Such horrid deeds your spotted soul defame
We grieve to think your shape and ours the same!
Enjoy what comfort in this life you can,
The form you have, not feelings of a man;
Haste to the rocks, thou curse to human kind,
There thou may'st wolves and brother tygers find;
Eternal exile be your righteous doom

And gnash your dragon's teeth in some sequester'd
    gloom;
Such be the end of each relentless foe
Who feels no pity for another's woe;
So may they fall—even you, though much too late,
Shall curse the day you languished to be great;
Haste from the torments of the present life,
Quick, let the halter end thee or the knife;
So may destruction rush with speedy wing,
Low as yourself, to drag your cruel king;
His head torn off, his hands, his feet, and all,
Deep in the dust may Dragon's image fall;
His stump alone escape the vengeful steel,
Sav'd but to grace the gibbet or the wheel.

*Philip Freneau, from "On the Fall of General
Earl Cornwallis," November 7, 1781, in Fred Lewis
Pattee,* The Poems of Philip Freneau, *vol. 2,
pp. 99–100.*

Never was a plan more wisely concerted, or more happily and vigorously executed, than the present. The wisdom, perseverance, and military talents of our illustrious commander, shone with superior luster on this occasion, and if possible, must increase the love and veneration of his countrymen. The well-concerted and animated support of the Count de Grasse, was essentially conducive to the completion of this glorious event, and deserves the warmest thanks of his own country, and the grateful plaudits of every American.

. . . An army, thus cemented by affection, created by a union of interests and the intercourse of good offices, and animated by an attachment to the rights of mankind, could not fail of triumphing over a body of troops, enlisted under the banners of despotism, and led on by the hope of plunder; who, made insolent by partial victories, gave loose to the greatest licentiousness and brutality that ever disgraced a disciplined corps. The expiring groans of thousands, who in vain begged Cornwallis for protection, and whom he inhumanely starved, have ascended to the throne of Almighty justice, and must bring down vengeance on his guilty head. It is sincerely to be wished, for the sake of humanity, that his lordship had made a more obstinate defence, that the allied army, obliged to storm his works, might have offered up him and his troops as a sacrifice to the violated rights of humanity!

A commentary on the victory at Yorktown, Virginia, the
New-York Journal, *November 12, 1781,
in Frank Moore, compiler,* The Diary of
the American Revolution, *p. 542.*

I am thus far myself on my Way to the Northward; I shall remain but a few Days here, and Shall proceed to Philadelphia, where I shall attempt to stimulate Congress to the best Improvement of our late Success [Yorktown], by takg. the most vigorous and effectual Measures, to be ready for an early and decisive Campaign the next Year. My greatest Fear is, that Congress viewing this stroke in too important a point of Light, may think our Work too nearly closed, and will fall into a State of Langour and Relaxation; to prevent this Error I shall employ every Means in my Power, and if unhappily we sink into that fatal Mistake, no part of the Blame shall be mine.

*George Washington, from a letter written at
Mount Vernon, Virginia, November 16, 1781, to Maj.
Gen. Nathanael Greene, in John C. Fitzpatrick, ed.,*
The Writings of George Washington,
vol. 23, p. 347.

Under all these circumstances I thought it would have been wanton and inhuman to the last degree, to sacrifice the lives of this small body of gallant soldiers who had ever behaved with so much fidelity and courage, by exposing them to an assault, which, from the numbers and precautions of the enemy, could not fail to succeed. I therefore proposed to capitulate.

I sincerely lament that better terms of capitulation could not be obtained, but I have neglected nothing to alleviate the misfortunes and distress of both officers and soldiers. . . . The treatment in general that we have received from the enemy since our surrender, has been perfectly good and proper, but the kindness and attention that has been shown us by the French officers in particular, their delicate sensibility of our situation, their generous and pressing offers of money both public and private to any amount, has really gone beyond what I can possibly describe, and will, I hope, make an impression on the breast of every British officer whenever the fortune of war should put any of them into our power.

*From a letter written by Lord Cornwallis to Sir Henry
Clinton on October 20, 1781,* Rivington's Gazette,
November 24, 1781, in Frank Moore, compiler, The
Diary of the American Revolution, *pp. 549–550.*

The picture I have already given of this Country will not be pleasing to you. Truth bids me add that it will admit of a higher coloring. But what else could be expected from us? A Revolution, a War, the Dissolution of Government, the creating of it anew, Cruelty, Rapine and Devastation in the midst of our very Bowels, these Sir are Circumstances by no means favorable to finance. The wonder then is that we have done so much, that we have borne so much, and the candid World will add that we have dared so much. . . .

Robert Morris, from a letter written in Philadelphia, November 27, 1781, to Benjamin Franklin, in E. James Ferguson, ed., The Papers of Robert Morris, *vol. 3, p. 268.*

The natural strength of this country [South Carolina] in point of numbers, appears to me to consist much more in blacks, than the whites. Could they be incorporated, and employed for it's defence, it would afford you double security. That they would make good Soldiers I have not the least doubt and I am pursuaded the State has it not in its power to give sufficient reinforcements without incorporating them, either to secure the country, if the Enemy mean to act vigorously upon an offensive plan, or furnish a force to dispossess them of Charlestown, should it be defensive.

Nathanael Greene, from a letter written at Round O, South Carolina, December 9, 1781, to John Rutledge, governor of South Carolina, in Dennis M. Conrad, ed., The Papers of General Nathanael Greene, *vol. 10, p. 22.*

9

An Unpromising Outcome
1782–1783

WAITING FOR THE END

After Yorktown, achieving the final success of the American cause no longer depended on fighting but on waiting. Pressured by the French foreign minister, the count de Vergennes, to let France decide the terms of a peace settlement—and conceding the need for French military and financial support—the Confederation Congress in summer 1781 had appointed members of a commission to negotiate peace, insisting on only one condition: recognition of American independence. The delegates chose John Adams, Benjamin Franklin, John Jay, Henry Laurens (imprisoned in London), and Thomas Jefferson to serve on the commission, but Jefferson declined. With the commission in place, political maneuvering would displace military maneuvering at the heart of the revolutionary drama.[1]

Before any peace settlement could be negotiated, however, George III had to be convinced that Great Britain had lost the war. Resolute in his determination to continue prosecuting the war, the king actually prepared a statement of abdication in January 1782—he would give up the throne before admitting defeat. The North ministry managed to persuade the king that his abdication would only compound the crisis. In February, the king finally yet reluctantly accepted the resignation of Lord George Germain as secretary of state for the colonies. In early March, the House of Commons approved a resolution stating that anyone who tried to pursue the war in America was an enemy of the king and the nation and another resolution enabling the king to make peace. About two weeks later, Lord North resigned, and George III asked the marquess of Rockingham, leader of the opposition, to form a new government. Lord Shelburne became secretary of state for American affairs in charge of conducting peace negotiations.[2]

The Rockingham ministry appointed Richard Oswald to negotiate with the American peace commissioners. He arrived in Paris in mid-April to find Benjamin Franklin as the lone commissioner: Adams had lingered in Holland to negotiate a loan; Jay was in Spain on a fruitless mission to persuade the government to support American peace claims. By this time, it had become evident that France's main purpose was to support Spain's claims in the Americas and that Spain, which had never recognized American independence, intended to discourage American claims while trying to secure Spanish control of the Floridas and the Mississippi Valley. Consequently, Franklin recognized that he must proceed cautiously. Disgruntled with the Spanish, Jay arrived in Paris in late June to aid Franklin's efforts.[3]

Rockingham died on the first day of July. Succeeding him as prime minister, Shelburne set in motion a more determined course toward negotiating a peace settlement. In September, Jay learned that Vergennes had sent his secretary to England to hold separate talks with the Shelburne ministry, concluded that the French would advocate Spanish interests, and urged Franklin to propose that the Rockingham ministry authorize Richard Oswald to negotiate with the "United States" instead of the 13 colonies—tacit recognition of American independence. To undermine the French-American alliance, the Shelburne ministry agreed.

In October, having succeeded in negotiating a treaty of commerce and friendship with the Dutch, Adams arrived in Paris. He supported Jay's argument persuading Franklin to pursue peace negotiations without informing the French. In early November the American commissioners, now joined by Henry Laurens, concluded a revised set of articles for peace with the British. And at the end of November, the American and British commissioners signed a provisional treaty that, once formally approved by the two governments, terminated hostilities and established the conditions for a postwar settlement. In mid-December, Franklin informed Vergennes of this separate provisional peace treaty. The news outraged Vergennes, but Franklin managed to placate him and even to arrange the grant of another loan.[4]

A DISCONTENTED ARMY

On the first day of April, Commander in Chief George Washington established a new headquarters for the Continental army at Newburgh, New York. Although some units of the army remained on duty in the Carolinas and along the Hudson River, the majority of the Continental troops assembled at the headquarters. Washington desired to maintain the army intact until the end of hostilities proved certain. But the government's lack of funding continued to severely limit the provision of pay and supplies for the army, and the officers and their men began to complain. Their complaints had some positive results, as the states began to furnish adequate food and clothing in May.

Unfortunately, money for pay remained unavailable. Disgruntled over lack of pay and concerned that the Confederation Congress would never prove effective, a group of officers wrote a letter to Washington proposing that the commander in chief seize control of the government and be proclaimed king. Dismayed and horrified by the proposal, Washington responded with a letter summarily rejecting the scheme and abjuring the officers to abandon any further consideration of pursuing it. The scheme disintegrated.[5]

In contrast to the disaffected officers' behavior, Deborah Sampson offered commitment and enthusiastic service. Dressed in a man's clothing that she made, Sampson had enlisted in the Continental army in October 1778 using the name Robert Shirtliffe. During her three years of service, she suffered two woundings: a sword cut on the side of her head and a bullet in her shoulder. Finally stricken with camp fever, Sampson received treatment from a Doctor Birney, who discovered her secret but chose to send her to his own house in Philadelphia rather than expose her fraud. There Birney's niece helped minister to Sampson and fell in love with "him." Following Sampson's recovery, Birney sent her to General Washington, who in October 1783 awarded her an honorable discharge and, supposedly, some funds to pay the expenses she would incur in searching for a place to live. Records indicate that at least a few other women followed Sampson's example.[6]

FINAL COMBAT

Although the Continental army fought no further battles, some isolated engagements occurred in scattered areas. During June in the region of Upper Sandusky, Ohio, Col. William Crawford led his men in attacking Indian villages and skirmishing with Butler's Rangers and Indian warriors, until British troops and artillery appeared and sent Crawford's men into panicked retreat. In August at Blue Licks on the Licking River in Kentucky, Indians and Loyalists led by the notorious Simon Girty ambushed frontiersmen, including Daniel Boone, who were pursuing Girty and his men for raiding frontier outposts. Seventy men were killed or captured in the ambush. During the same month, Gen. Mordecai Gist detached a small force from Gen. Nathanael Greene's army near Charleston for raids on British foraging parties and on ships in the Combahee River. In the last land engagement of the war involving British and American troops, one of Gist's units led by Col. John Laurens (son of Henry) walked into a British ambush that left Laurens and another American soldier dead.[7]

During the second week of May, Sir Guy Carleton arrived in New York City to assume command from Gen. Sir Henry Clinton and to fulfill his orders: provide protection to any Loyalists who might wish to leave the United States and prepare to withdraw from all the British posts in the United States while also

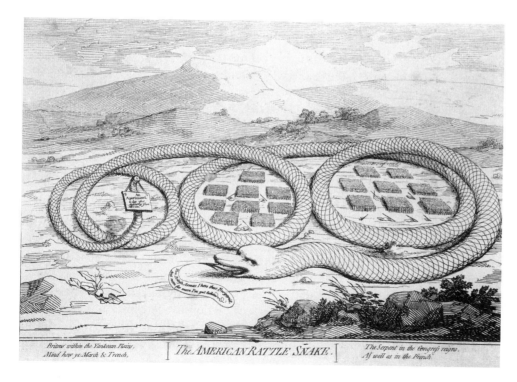

This cartoon depicts the American rattlesnake. *(Library of Congress)*

avoiding offensive combat so that British troops could be deployed elsewhere against the French and Spanish. In late June, the count de Rochambeau left Virginia with his army, marching toward Boston. During the second week of July, at Savannah, the British loaded the occupying army, 4,000 Georgia Loyalists, and 5,000 slaves onto ships and evacuated the town. In December, the British garrison at Charleston evacuated, while at Boston, the French army commanded by Rochambeau disembarked by ship for the West Indies. For the British, the West Indies afforded a ray of hope, since on the seas there in April a British fleet commanded by Adm. George Rodney devastated Adm. Count de Grasse's fleet, captured the count, and dispersed his surviving warships in a victory that ameliorated the government's concerns about the threat from the French navy following Yorktown.[8]

THE CONFEDERATION CONGRESS

As the year began, the new national bank, finally chartered by the Confederation Congress, began operations in Philadelphia, thus alleviating the government's financial difficulties to some extent. Restoring the national treasury, however, remained a problem. Robert Morris complained that in 1782 no money had been forthcoming from any of the states except New Jersey, which provided less than 1 percent of the levy assessed. Although $4 million was due from the states on July 1, they submitted only $50,000. The financial shortfall, of course, threatened the continuing existence not only of the Continental army and the government but also of the Confederation itself. The Congress had proposed to the states an impost of 5 percent on manufactured goods as a means of raising revenues, but that proposal had to be accepted by all 13 states under stipulations of the Articles of Confederation, and Rhode Island and Georgia withheld their concurrence, and then Virginia repealed its approval, dooming the proposal. On the verge of final victory, the union itself stood imperiled.[9]

As 1783 began, an army initiative underscored the financial crisis and the Congress's ineffectualness. Three officers brought a petition to Congress in Philadelphia on behalf of the Continental army officers. The officers were concerned because, although Congress had approved giving officers half-pay for life, no action had been taken, and funds to fulfill the policy appeared unlikely to be collected. The officers requested in their petition that Congress provide their back pay in full before they became discharged from service and their promised half-pay in a lump-sum payment. While Congress mulled this petition, political supporters of a strong central government began to cultivate an alliance with the army to further their purposes.[10]

During early March, the so-called Newburgh Addresses, apparently written by Maj. John Armstrong, circulated among Continental army officers, many of whom had lost patience with Congress. The addresses advocated holding an unauthorized meeting of officers to discuss their grievances with Congress; notifying Congress that unless the delegates quickly redressed these grievances, the officers would refuse to disband the army when peace came; and taking the stance that in case hostilities resumed, the officers would withdraw to "some unsettled country" and leave Congress without an army. Such proposals clearly implied the threat of a full-scale mutiny.

Washington bids farewell to his officers. *(Courtesy of the National Archives and Records Administration)*

Commander in Chief George Washington learned of the Newburgh Addresses and responded forcefully. Appalled by the content of the addresses, Washington informed the Congress of the unrest among his officers and issued a general order calling for a meeting on March 15 of officers representing every regiment. His commanding presence and integrity prevailed as he admonished the officers to voice their condemnation of "the Man who wishes . . . to overturn the liberties of our Country. . . ." The officers, many moved to tears by Washington's speech, voted to reject the Newburgh propositions and reaffirm their loyalty to the nation. Washington's masterful handling of the "conspiracy" preserved the army and its role and also saved the Congress from great humiliation.[11]

The financial crisis and its impact on army morale nevertheless continued. Congress declared the war officially ended in April, and in late May, noncommissioned officers and enlisted men received furloughs and left Newburgh for home. But they left without the final pay owed them. Congress issued promissory notes equaling three months' pay, but without providing for a method of redeeming them. In June, the sergeants of a furloughed Pennsylvania regiment posted in Lancaster, Pennsylvania, sent Congress a letter asserting their demands and implying a threat to march on Philadelphia. By mid-June, 80 of the men arrived in the city and began residence in an abandoned barracks; another 300 to 400 angry soldiers appeared with fixed bayonets and surrounded the statehouse as Congress met inside. Unnerved by the soldiers' presence, the delegates voted to adjourn to Princeton. The soldiers ceased their demonstrations and disbanded. Congress met in Princeton but rarely with a quorum until November, when the delegates adjourned to reconvene in Annapolis.[12]

From the spring until the end of the year, Continental soldiers, singly or in groups, straggled homeward. No hero's greeting awaited them. On the contrary, their countrymen welcomed them back with indifference, ingratitude, and even

Washington resigns his commission at Annapolis. *(Courtesy of the National Archives and Records Administration)*

outright hostility. Many Americans considered the Continental army as having enlisted society's dregs and fostered corruption. And the public overwhelmingly regarded the Revolutionary War not as a conflict won by regular troops but as "a people's war"—that is, military service had simply been both voluntary and everyone's duty and the struggle to attain liberty had comprised its own reward. Disillusioned by such attitudes, and in many cases destitute or disabled and unfit for work, the veterans also mostly returned to badly degenerated farms or vocations, wasted away by years of neglect, inflation, and heavy taxes; some rightly complained that supporters of the losing side often faired better economically than themselves. Perhaps the most egregious evocation of the nation's ingratitude occurred when the Congress in 1783 denied officers pensions, reneging on its promise of 1780 that the officers would receive half pensions for life. Now they would get only commutation certificates equivalent to five years of full pay, and these proved essentially worthless in the veterans' time of greatest need, since Congress would have no funds to redeem the certificates until 1790. Not until the turn of the 19th century would the Patriot soldiers of the American Revolution begin to receive public recognition, thanks, and praise for their sacrifice; not until 1818 would their government provide these heroes—many of them already dead and thus cheated of any benefit from such compensation—with well-deserved pensions.[13]

THE FINAL ACT

In January 1783, the government of Great Britain signed preliminary articles that ended hostilities with France and Spain, and on February 4, King George III proclaimed an end to hostilities with the United States. On March 12, official word finally arrived in the United States that a provisional peace treaty had been signed in Paris at the end of November, and on April 15, Congress ratified the provisional treaty. Commissioners meeting in Paris signed the formal treaty on September 3. By its terms, Great Britain officially recognized the independence of the United States; the 31st and the 45th parallels, the Atlantic Ocean, and the Mississippi River formed the boundaries of the United States; Americans received the right to fish off the Newfoundland and Nova Scotia banks; each nation promised to honor legal debts; no penalties would be imposed on any citizens for their actions during the war; hostilities ceased, and British troops would evacuate all posts in the United States; navigation on the Mississippi River would be free to all nations; and all territories conquered by either nation during the war would be restored. Because of its difficulties in convening a quorum of its members after leaving Philadelphia, the Confederation Congress remained unable to ratify the peace treaty until January 13, 1784, with only nine states represented in the voting.[14]

General Washington issued his final general order on October 18, reviewing the course of the war, extolling the achievement of independence, and bidding farewell to his troops. On November 25, the British garrison in New York City—the mother country's last remaining post in the United States—evacuated the city along with 7,000 Loyalists. (Altogether, nearly 100,000 Loyalists left after the war's end, some for Canada and others for Great Britain, which set up a commission to compensate the Loyalists for property losses incurred during the war. Those transported included some 20,000 blacks, destined for Britain, Nova Scotia, Jamaica, Florida, or Sierra Leone in Africa; a corps of black drummers who had served with Baron von Riedesel went to Germany.) On December 4, in New York City, Washington met at the Fraunces Tavern with those officers who had been closest to him during the war to bid them farewell. Finally, on December 23, Washington appeared before the Confederation Congress convened in Annapolis. He presented an emotion-laden speech, submitted his commission as commander in chief to president of Congress Thomas Mifflin, left the hall, and set out for Mount Vernon. Washington had fulfilled his duty. Thanks to the resolute commander in chief, the eight-year struggle of the glorious American cause ended nobly.[15]

CHRONICLE OF EVENTS

1782

January 7: The new national bank opens for business in Philadelphia, temporarily alleviating some of Congress's financial crisis, but the national treasury still has no funds.

February 11: George III finally accepts Lord George Germain's resignation as secretary of state and creates him Viscount Sackville in reward for his services during the war.

March 4: The House of Commons passes a resolution declaring that anyone attempting to prolong the war in America is an enemy of the nation and the king.

March 20: With his control of the House of Commons in steady decline over many weeks, Lord North must resign or face the humiliation of a formal vote of no confidence. The king accepts his decision to resign, which North announces in the House, obliging George III to invite the opposition to form a new government when his efforts to create a coalition fail.

March 22: Granted the condition that Great Britain will recognize the independence of the United States, the marquess of Rockingham agrees to form a new government. Lord Shelburne becomes secretary of state in charge of American affairs with the mandate to conduct peace negotiations.

April 1: Washington establishes the Continental army's headquarters at Newburgh, New York, assembling there all of his forces except those maintaining surveillance of the upper Hudson River and the troops serving with Greene in the Carolinas. With virtually no money available for pay or supplies, both officers and men begin to voice disgruntlement.

April 4: The Rockingham government appoints Sir Guy Carleton commander in chief of British forces in North America with instructions to avoid any offensive actions, to prepare for withdrawal from all bases within the United States, and to protect any Loyalists who may want to leave for a British territory. British troops evacuated from the United States can serve in the West Indies and the Mediterranean to protect British bases against attack by France or Spain.

April 12: Richard Oswald, appointed by the Rockingham ministry to negotiate with the American peace commissioners, arrives in Paris, but only Benjamin Franklin is available for talks, as John Adams remains in Holland negotiating a loan, John Jay serves futilely at the Spanish court, and Henry Laurens remains in British custody (soon to be released). Franklin faces a serious challenge. France evidences minimal concern for the interests of the United States while supporting Spain's territorial claims. These include control of the Floridas and the Mississippi Valley and limitations on expansion by the United States, whose independence Spain has never recognized. Also, despite official American policy of insisting only on recognition of independence while leaving other peace terms to France's discretion, the United States wishes to secure fishing rights off Newfoundland and free navigation on the Mississippi River. Thus, Franklin must proceed with caution.

In the West Indies, Adm. George Rodney's fleet inflicts a crushing blow on the French navy, capturing Admiral de Grasse and his *Ville de Paris* and dispersing the remainder of de Grasse's fleet—a victory that alleviates British anxieties about the French threat.

April 19: At The Hague, the government of the Netherlands officially recognizes the independence of the United States and receives John Adams as American ambassador.

May 9: Sir Guy Carleton arrives in New York City to assume command of British forces.

May 22: Although the states have greatly improved supplies to the army at Newburgh, money for pay is still lacking, and some officers believe Congress can never solve the problems it confronts. A small group of officers decides that a monarchy is needed and proposes to General Washington through a letter from Col. Lewis Nicola that he seize control of the government and be declared king. Profoundly horrified, Washington summarily rejects the proposal.

June 4: With no effort to throw his foe off track, Col. William Crawford leads his troops in the Upper Sandusky region of Ohio in attacks on Indian villages. In an engagement with Indians and Butler's Rangers, he holds the advantage until British reinforcements arrive and his men panic and retreat in disarray. Crawford and several of his officers are captured and tortured to death.

June 23: Following his unsuccessful efforts in Madrid advocating American claims, John Jay arrives in Paris convinced that Spain represents nearly as great a threat to the United States as Great Britain.

Rochambeau begins to march his army from Virginia to Boston.

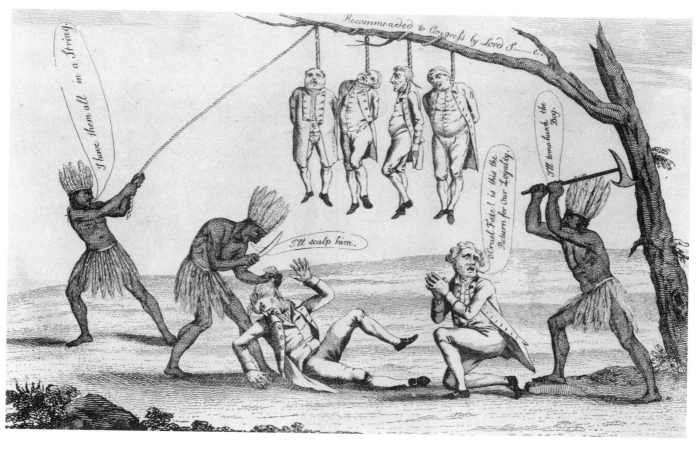

"The Savages Let Loose," a British cartoon, depicts the imagined fate of Loyalists left behind following the peace and the British evacuation. *(Library of Congress)*

July 1: Rockingham dies, and Lord Shelburne becomes prime minister, still hopeful of being able to avoid recognizing American independence.

July 11: After boarding nearly 4,000 Georgia Loyalists and 5,000 slaves on their ships to sail off with them, the British evacuate Savannah.

July 20: Having worked on a design since July 1776, the Congress adopts the Great Seal of the United States. One side of the seal bears an eagle triumphant, its opposed talons bearing an olive branch and arrows, a shield covering its breast, and its beak holding a banner with the motto *E Pluribus Unum* ("One from many"). The reverse side bears a pyramid surmounted by the all-seeing "Eye of Providence" in a triangle emanating rays—a symbol taken from Freemasonry—and two mottoes: *Annuit Coeptis* ("He [God] favors our undertakings") and *Novus Ordo Seclorum* ("A new age now begins," derived from Virgil's *Eclogues*).

July 23: John Jay and Benjamin Franklin confer in Paris on a strategy for renewed discussions with the British.

August 7: General Washington institutes the Badge of Military Merit, popularly known as the Purple Heart.

August 19: A band of American frontiersmen, including Daniel Boone, pursues Simon Girty, who has been leading a force of Indians and Loyalists in raids on frontier outposts in Kentucky. At Blue Licks on the Licking River, the pursuing frontiersmen blunder into an ambush, and Girty's men quickly kill or capture 70 of them.

August 27: With a detachment of light infantry and cavalry from Greene's army, Gen. Mordecai Gist searches for British foraging parties and shipping along the Combahee River in South Carolina. Some of his men commanded by Col. John Laurens march into an ambush prepared by a superior British force. In this final land engagement of the war between organized British and

American forces, the British troops kill Laurens and one other American and then withdraw without losses.

September 9: Discovering that Vergennes has sent his secretary, Rayneval, to England for separate talks with the British, John Jay correctly surmises that the French will press for Spanish interests ahead of American interests. He urges Franklin to open a new initiative with Oswald and Shelburne. Franklin proposes that Great Britain authorize Oswald to negotiate with the United States instead of with the thirteen colonies—a tacit recognition of American independence that would circumvent French maneuvering.

September 19: Seeing the move as an inexpensive means of rending the French-American alliance, the Shelburne ministry revises Oswald's instructions to allow him to negotiate with the "13 United States."

October 1: Franklin and Jay begin the first formal peace negotiations with Oswald in Paris, determined to strike their own deal with the British in disregard of the French.

October 5: Oswald, Franklin, and Jay reach agreement on a draft of peace terms that include new boundaries for the United States, evacuation of British troops from American bases, American access to the Newfoundland fishing banks, and free trade and navigation on the Mississippi River.

October 8: At The Hague, John Adams signs a treaty of friendships and commerce with representatives of the Netherlands.

October 26: John Adams arrives in Paris to join Franklin and Jay in the final negotiations with Great Britain.

November 1: Adams supports Jay's argument that their peace commission should proceed with negotiations without informing the French, and Franklin concurs.

November 5: Franklin, Jay, and Adams, now joined by Henry Laurens, reach agreement with the British on slightly revised terms for peace that will become the basis for the final treaty.

November 30: The American and British peace commissioners sign a provisional treaty in Paris which, pending approval of their respective governments, ends hostilities and establishes the conditions of the postwar settlement. In effect, the American commissioners have concluded a separate peace in disregard of the wishes of France and Spain.

December 5: John Singleton Copley's portrait of Elkanah Watson, sponsor of American agricultural fairs,

includes the Stars and Stripes flying above a ship in the background—the first depiction of the United States flag to be displayed in England.

December 14: The British garrison at Charleston, South Carolina, evacuates the city.

December 17: Franklin informs Vergennes about the provisional treaty with the British. Initially outraged, the French foreign minister can do little to alter the outcome. Franklin handles Vergennes so deftly that the foreign minister is soon placated, and the French government approves a new loan of 6 million livres to the United States.

December 24: The French army boards ships at Boston and sets sail for the West Indies.

1783

January 6: On behalf of the Continental army, Gen. Alexander McDougall, Col. John Brooks, and Col. Matthias Ogden present a petition to Congress requesting full settlement of back pay before being discharged and conversion of the promised half-pay for life into a lump-sum payment, including a specific means of payment. Advocates of a strong central government regard the army officers as a possible means of securing revision of the Articles of Confederation and therefore cultivate an alliance with the army, which remains a potent force.

January 20: In London, representatives of the British government sign preliminary articles ending hostilities with France and Spain.

February 4: King George III formally proclaims the end of hostilities with the United States.

March 8: Secretary of Finance Robert Morris declares that, under the Articles of Confederation, the Congress has implied powers to devise the means of paying the national debt, so that if the states refuse to pay, Congress will directly levy taxes and import duties—an implicit ultimatum that Morris lacks political power to fulfill.

March 10: Two unsigned documents (actually written by Horatio Gates's aide-de-camp, Maj. John Armstrong, Jr.) known as the Newburgh Addresses circulate among officers of the Continental army at Newburgh, New York. The Newburgh Addresses suggest that the army may be on the verge of mutiny.

In the Atlantic, en route to Philadelphia with hard currency for Congress, John Barry's ship *Alliance* and his companion ship *Lauzun* are overtaken by three British warships. A French man-of-war scares off two of the British ships, while the *Alliance* battles with the *Sybille* for three-quarters of an hour before breaking off and continuing its voyage.

March 11: Shocked by the Newburgh Addresses, Washington issues a general order for a meeting of officers and sends word of the unrest to Congress.

March 15: In addressing his officers, assembled at Newburgh, Washington asserts that their distrust of Congress is both unfounded and dishonorable, that they should remain calm and set an example for posterity, and that acting rashly might destroy all for which they had fought. Persuaded of the rightness of their commander's view, the officers vote to repudiate the Newburgh Addresses and to affirm their loyalty to the United States. Congress subsequently approves changing the half-pay policy to a promise of full pay for five years provided in the form of federal securities.

April 11: Congress officially proclaims the Revolutionary War at an end.

April 15: Congress ratifies the provisional peace treaty previously signed by the commissioners in Paris.

May 26: The noncommissioned officers and enlisted men to the Continental army receive furloughs and begin to depart from Newburgh for home without money or final pay, but they are permitted to keep their muskets for personal use. Congress issues them promissory notes for the equivalent of three-months' pay, but with no specific date or method of redemption indicated. A final settlement, usually in the form of land grants, will take decades to complete. The soldiers' discharges become effective on the official signing of the peace treaty. Washington retains command of a small contingent of three-year enlistees until the British have evacuated New York City.

May 30: Publisher Benjamin Towne's *Pennsylvania Evening Post,* the first daily newspaper in the United States, begins publication in Philadelphia.

June 13: Congress receives a threatening letter from the sergeants of a furloughed Pennsylvania regiment posted near Lancaster stating their demands for pay and hinting at a possible march on Philadelphia. Secretary at War Benjamin Lincoln manages to placate the soldiers temporarily.

June 14: Learning that 80 men of the 3rd Pennsylvania Regiment are approaching Philadelphia, Congress asks John Dickinson, president of the Supreme Council of Pennsylvania, to provide troops to protect the government. Dickinson refuses. The soldiers arrive in the city and take up residence in an abandoned barracks.

June 15: As Congress conducts an emergency session in the state house, 300–400 angry soldiers with fixed bayonets surround the building. The anxious congressmen adjourn at mid-afternoon, and the soldiers grant them passage through their lines with no show of violence.

June 17: Congress approves adjourning to Princeton to evade the mutinous Pennsylvania soldiers and to be closer to Washington's remaining force, which might provide protection. The soldiers in Philadelphia disband without further demonstration. Reconvened in Princeton, congressmen indulge themselves in remonstrances over their humiliating experience.

July: The Shelburne ministry creates a commission to settle damage claims of American Loyalists, whose property in many of the states was seized at great loss. More than 4,000 claims will be submitted, and the commission will award more than £3.3 million in compensation.

August: Rejecting an invitation to return to Philadelphia, Congress approves moving to Annapolis in the fall.

September 3: The formal treaties of Paris and Versailles are signed in Paris, bringing the war to its end. The formal terms nearly replicate those of the provisional and preliminary agreements signed months earlier.

October 18: At Newburgh, Commander in Chief George Washington issues his final general orders, bidding farewell to all his troops everywhere, reviewing the war and the army's steadfastness, extolling the winning of independence, urging conciliation toward the national government, and charging his officers to support a strong federal government.

November 4: Having lacked a quorum during most of its stay in Princeton, Congress adjourns.

November 25: The British garrison in New York City, the last remaining garrison in the United States, evacuates the city, taking along nearly 7,000 Loyalists.

November 26: Congress convenes in Annapolis.

December 4: At the Fraunces Tavern in New York City, a group of officers closest to Washington during the war gathers to say goodbye to their commander. At the gathering's conclusion, Washington tearfully embraces each officer and leaves for his journey to Annapolis.

December 23: Washington appears before the Congress in Annapolis and delivers a highly emotional speech in preparation for resigning his commission as commander in chief. At the end of his speech, Washington withdraws the resignation document from his pocket, hands it to President Thomas Mifflin, and exits to begin his journey homeward to Mount Vernon.

EYEWITNESS TESTIMONY

1782

The fatal issue of the Virginia expedition and the loss of so fine a body of men as were made prisoners at York Town must of necessity occasion an alternation in the mode of prosecuting the war in North America, for no more regiments or corps can be sent from this country.... With that force it is expected the posts and districts which are now in His Majesty's possession may be maintained, and such detachments may occasionally be spared for such joint operations with the navy against the ports and towns upon the seacoasts of the revolted provinces ... to prevent them from acting offensively against us.

Lord George Germain, from a letter written at Whitehall, London, January 2, 1782, to Gen. Sir Henry Clinton, in K. G. Davies, ed., Documents of the American Revolution, *vol. 21, p. 27.*

And now Sir let me congratulate you on the Establishment of the Bank of the United States or according to the Stile of it the national Bank of America which opens and does Business this Day. I expect to derive great Advantage from it, and that the Commerce of this Country will lie under great Obligations to an Institution long wanted among us. Several of the shares are yet in the Hands of the Public so that if you chuse to become interested or any of your Friends it can be done without Difficulty.

Robert Morris, from a letter written in Philadelphia, January 7, 1782, to Benjamin Franklin, in E. James Ferguson, ed., The Papers of Robert Morris, *vol. 3, p. 503.*

Mr. Laurens, being now at Liberty, perhaps may soon come hither, and be ready to join us, if there should be any Negociations for Peace. In England they are mad for a separate one with us, that they may more effectually take Revenge on France & Spain. I have had several Overtures hinted to me lately from different Quarters, but I am deaf. The Thing is impossible. We can never agree to desert our first & our faithful Friend on any Consideration whatever. We should become infamous by such abominable Baseness....

Benjamin Franklin, from a letter written at Passy, France, January 19, 1782, to John Jay, in Albert Henry Smyth, The Writings of Benjamin Franklin, *vol. 8, pp. 366–367.*

It is from the same Conviction which you feel of the advantages which must result to our Country from an early and vigorous Campaign, that I have spent Money and Stretched my Credit to the utmost Extent which I dare, in Order that you might take the Field at an early Hour and in a respectable Manner.... But if they [the states] do grant me those Sums, I pledge myself to support you fully in all your Views, and you shall then have the Pleasure of seeing your brave Troops as regularly paid as they are now fed, and ... you will be enabled to accomplish those Plans for the Defence and Salvation of our Country which lie nearest your Heart....

Robert Morris, from a letter written in Philadelphia, January 26, 1782, to George Washington, in E. James Ferguson, ed., The Papers of Robert Morris, *vol. 4, p. 119.*

France is generous: but we are languid. It is true it is better to be under obligations to France than Subject to the tyranny of Great Britain. But I cannot help thinking ourselves but half free when we owe it to another and not to ourselves. Much has been done for us. I wish we had done more. And what adds to my mortification is I see little prospect of more vigor in our councils or union in our measures than there has been. Congress wants power, and the States subordination. Upon the present constitution of the first and the general temper prevailing among the last, little is to be expected but imbecility and indecision....

Nathanael Greene, from a letter written at Pon Pon, South Carolina, February 1, 1782, to Dr. Benjamin Rush, in Dennis M. Conrad, ed., The Papers of General Nathanael Greene, *vol. 10, p. 299.*

The union of America is the foundation-stone of her independence; the rock on which it is built; and is something so sacred in her constitution, that we ought to watch every word we speak, and every thought we think, that we injure it not, even by mistake. When a multitude, extended, or rather scattered, over a continent in the manner we were, mutually agree to form on common centre whereon the whole shall move to accomplish a particular purpose, all parts must act together and alike, or act not at all, and a stoppage in any one is a stoppage of the whole, at least for a time.

Thomas Paine, from "The American Crisis X, To the People of America," March 5, 1782, in Van der Weyde, The Life and Works of Thomas Paine, *vol. 3, pp. 186–187.*

You will see by the English papers which I send to Mr. Secretary [Robert R.] Livingston, that the sense of the nation is now fully against the continuance of the American war. The petitions of the cities of London and Bristol were unanimous against it; Lord North mustered all his force, yet had a majority against him of nineteen. It is said there were but two who voted with him that are not placemen or pensioners, and that even these, in their private conversations, condemn the prosecution of the war, and lay it all upon the king's obstinacy. We must not, however, be lulled by the appearances. . . .

Benjamin Franklin, from a letter written at Passy, France, March 7, 1782, to Robert Morris, in Albert Henry Smyth, ed., The Writings of Benjamin Franklin, *vol. 8, p. 396.*

By late advices from Europe and from the declarations of the British Ministers themselves, it appears, that they have done with all thoughts of an excursive War, and that they mean to send small if any further reinforcements to America. It may be also tolerably plainly seen, that they do not mean to hold all their present posts, and that New York will be occupied in preference to any other. Hence, and from other indications, I am induced to believe that an evacuation of the southern States will take place. Should this happen, we must concentre our force as the enemy do theirs: You will therefore, upon the appearance of such an event, immediately make preparations for the march of the Army under your command to the Northward. . . .

George Washington, from a letter written at Philadelphia, March 18, 1782, to Maj. Gen. Nathanael Greene, in John C. Fitzpatrick, ed., The Writings of George Washington, *vol. 24, pp. 73–74.*

The General has the pleasure to inform the army that there is a large and general assortment of Clothing on the way from Philadelphia for this army. He has also the satisfaction to assure the army that the moment Returns arrive at the Northward . . . not less than two or three months pay will be forwarded. It is with no small pains the General has heard some little uneasiness has prevailed among the troops for want of pay and cloathing, and from the irregular supplies of provisions. He hopes the troops are persuaded . . . that their sufferings result from unavoidable difficulties, convinced of this he flatters himself that they will bear up under their sufferings with that degree of patience and mag-

nanimity which has so remarkably distinguished them heretofore.

Nathanael Greene, from orders issued at Bacons Bridge, South Carolina, April 2, 1782, in Dennis M. Conrad, ed., The Papers of General Nathanael Greene, *vol. 10, p. 573.*

In short, we have nothing to do but to go on with vigor and determination. The enemy is yet in our country. They hold New York, Charleston, and Savannah, and the very being in those places is an offence, and a part of offensive war, and until they can be driven from them, or captured in them, it would be folly in us to listen to an idle tale. I take it for granted that the British ministry are sinking under the impossibility of carrying on the war. Let them then come to a fair and open peace with France, Spain, Holland and America, in the manner they ought to do; but until then, we can have nothing to say to them.

Thomas Paine, conclusion of "The American Crisis XI, On the Present State of News," May 22, 1782, in Van der Weyde, The Life and Works of Thomas Paine, *vol. 3, p. 210.*

Yesterday the Count du Nord was at the Academy of Sciences, when sundry Experiments were exhibited for his Entertainment; among them, one by M. Lavoisier, to show that the strongest Fire we yet know, is made in a Charcoal blown upon with dephlogisticated air. In a Heat so produced, he melted Platina presently, the Fire being much more powerful than that of the strongest burning mirror. . . .

Benjamin Franklin, from a letter written at Passy, France, June 7, 1782, to Joseph Priestley, in Albert Henry Smyth, ed., The Writings of Benjamin Franklin, *vol. 8, p. 453.*

Continuing Incampt Near opposited West Point, we are informed by an officer from the S[o]uthward that a Conspiracy had been in adjutation by the Sergeants of the Army under Command of Genl. Greene—they was to indevoar to have the armey surprised & make Prisoner of Genl. Greene & all the Officers, but by a Sergeants wife it was brought to Light / the head was immediately shot & in two days after a Nother hung, & Some More confined whose fate was not yet known.

Lieutenant Jeremiah Greenman, diary entry of June 10, 1782, in Greenman, Diary of a Common Soldier in the American Revolution, 1775–1783, *p. 252.*

... I pant for retirement and am perswaded that an end of our warfare is not to be obtained but by vigorous exertions; the Subjugation of America so far at least as to hold it in a dependt. State is of too much importance to Great Britain to yield the palm to us whilst her resources exist, or our inactivity, want of System, or dependence upon other powers or upon one another prevail. I can truely say that the first wish of my Soul is to return speedily into the bosom of that Country which gave me birth and in the sweet enjoyment of demestick pleasures and the Company of a few friends to end my days in quiet when I shall be call'd from this Stage....

George Washington, from a letter written at Newburgh, New York, June 15, 1782, to Virginia businessman Archibald Cary, in John C. Fitzpatrick, ed., The Writings of George Washington, *vol. 24, pp. 347–348.*

With evil omens from the harbor sails
   The ill-fated barque that worthless Arnold
     bears,—
God of the southern winds, call up the gales,
   And whistle in rude fury round his ears.
With horrid waves insult his vessel's sides,
   And may the east wind on a leeward shore
Her cables part while she in tumult rides,
   And shatter into shivers every oar.

Philip Freneau, from "Arnold's Departure," July 10, 1782, in Fred Lewis Pattee, The Poems of Philip Freneau, *vol. 2, p. 103.*

As to the people [of New York], in the early periods of the war, near one half of them were avowedly more attached to Great Britain than to their liberty; but the energy of the government has subdued all opposition. The state by different means has been purged of a large part of its malcontents; but there still remains I dare say a third whose secret wishes are on the side of the enemy; the remainder sigh for peace, murmur at taxes, clamour at their rulers.... [I]f the Legislature can be brought to adopt a wise plan for its finances, we may put the people in better humour.... The people of this state as far as my observation goes, have as much firmness in their make and as much submissiveness to government as those of any part of the Union.

Alexander Hamilton, from a letter written in Albany, New York, August 13, 1782, to Robert Morris, in Harold C. Syrett, ed., The Papers of Alexander Hamilton, *vol. 3, pp. 141–142.*

Alexander Hamilton served in Congress from 1782 to 1783. *(From* The Pictorial Field Book of the Revolution, *2 vols., by B. J. Lossing. New York: Harper Brothers 1851 and 1852.)*

They [Britain] have now had seven years of war, and are no further on the continent than when they began. The superstitious and populous parts will therefore conclude that *it is not to be,* and the rational part of them will think they have tried an unsuccessful and expensive project long enough, and by these two joining issue in the same eventful opinion, the obstinate part among them will be beaten out; unless, consistent with their former sagacity, they should get over the matter by an act of Parliament, *"to bind TIME in all cases whatsoever,"* or declare him a rebel.

Thomas Paine, from a letter to George Washington, September 7, 1782, in Van der Weyde, The Life and Works of Thomas Paine, *vol. 4, p. 214.*

... Hence it became our duty to take one side or the other; and no man is to be blamed for preferring the one which his reason recommended as the most just and virtuous.

Several of our countrymen indeed left, and took arms against us, not from any such principles, but from the most dishonourable of human motives. Their conduct has been of a piece with their inducements, for they have far outstripped savages in perfidy and cruelty. Against these men every American must set his face and steel his heart. There are others of them, though not many, who,

I believe, opposed us because they thought they could not conscientiously go with us. To such of these as have behaved with humanity, I wish every species of prosperity that may consist with the good of my country.

John Jay, from a letter written in Paris, September 17, 1782, to Peter Van Schaack, exiled Loyalist and lawyer, in William Jay, The Life of John Jay, *vol. 1, pp. 161–162.*

. . . The measures and the policy of the enemy are at present in great perplexity and embarrassment—but I have my fears whether their necessities (which are the only operative motive with them) are yet arrived to that point which must drive them unavoidably into what they will esteem disagreeable and dishonorable terms of peace—such, for instance, as an absolute, unequivocal admission of American Independence, upon the terms on which she can alone accept it.

For this reason, added to the obstinacy of the King—and the probable consonant principles of some of his principal ministers, I have not so full a confidence in the success of the present negotiation for peace as some gentlemen entertain.

Should events prove my jealousies to be ill founded, I shall make myself happy under the mistake—consoling myself with the idea of having erred on the safest side, and enjoying with as much satisfaction as any of my countrymen the pleasing issue of our severe contest.

George Washington, from a letter written at Verplank's Point, New York, September 18, 1782, responding to Thomas Paine's letter proposing to send him 50 copies of "The Crisis," in John C. Fitzpatrick, ed., The Writings of George Washington, *vol. 25, p. 176.*

After a foreigner from any part of Europe is arrived, and become a citizen, let him devoutly listen to the voice of our great parent. . . . ". . . If thou wilt work, I have bread for thee; if thou wilt be honest, sober, and industrious, I have greater rewards to confer on thee—ease and independence. I will give thee fields to feed and clothe thee; a comfortable fireside to sit by . . . ; and a decent bed to repose on. I shall endow thee beside with the immunities of a freeman. If thou wilt carefully educate thy children, teach them gratitude to God, and reverence to that government, that philanthropic government, which has collected here so many men and made them happy. . . ."

J. Hector St. Jean de Crevecoeur, from Letters from an American Farmer, *first published in London in 1782, pp. 67–68.*

In September the Light Infantry were embodied in Five Battallions, makeing about Twelve Hundred Men and the command given to Me . . . and I flatter's myself the Field of Glory was full in view—but the prospect seems vanished—Campaign is nearly pass'd without our seeing the Enemy—they do not think it prudent to quit their strongholds, nor will the Finances of these United States furnish Money for Horses to drag our Artillery, or Forage to subsist them.—I hope devoutly the War is nearly over, & the next time I enter the lists of an Army, of Republican States, I wish I may be a Corporal. . . .

Samuel Blachley Webb, from a letter written in camp near the Croton River, New York, October 8, 1782, to his half brother Joseph Barrell, in Worthington Chauncey Ford, ed., Correspondence and Journals of Samuel Blachley Webb, *vol. 2, p. 427.*

You will perhaps learn before this reaches you that I have been appointed a member of Congress. I expect to go to Philadelphia in the ensuing month, where I shall be happy to correspond with you with our ancient confidence and I shall entreat you not to confine your observations to military subjects but to take in the whole scope of national concerns. I am sure your ideas will be useful to me and to the public.

I feel the deepest affliction at the news we have just received of the loss of our dear and [inesti]mable friend [John] Laurens. His career of virtue is at an end. How strangely are human affairs conducted, that so many excellent qualities could not ensure a more happy fate? . . . I feel the loss of a friend I truly and most tenderly loved, and one of a very small number.

Alexander Hamilton, from a letter written in Albany, New York, October 12, 1782, to Nathanael Greene, in Harold C. Syrett, ed., The Papers of Alexander Hamilton, *vol. 3, pp. 183–184.*

But a thousand pleadings, even from your lordship, can have no effect. Honor, interest, and every sensation of the heart, would plead against you. We are a people who think not as you think; and what is equally true, you cannot feel as we feel. The situations of the two countries are exceedingly different. Ours has been the seat of war; yours has seen nothing of it. The most wanton destruction has been committed in our sight; the most insolent barbarity has been acted on our feelings. We can look round and see the remains of burnt and destroyed houses, once the fair fruit of hard industry, and now the striking monuments of British brutality. We walk over the dead whom we loved, in every part of America, and remember by whom they fell. There is scarcely a village but brings to life some melancholy thought, and reminds us of what we have suffered, and of those we have lost by the inhumanity of Britain. A thousand images arise to us, which, from situation, you cannot see, and are accompanied by as many ideas which you cannot know; and therefore your supposed system of reasoning would apply to nothing, and all your expectations die of themselves.

Thomas Paine, from "The American Crisis XII, To the Earl of Shelburne," October 29, 1782, in Van der Weyde, The Life and Works of Thomas Paine, *vol. 3, pp. 223–224.*

We have no certainty of what the British Cabinet design.... My own opinion of the matter is, that the unwillingness of the King, and his present Prime Minister Lord Shelburne to acknowledge the independency, of this Country, is such as to induce them to trust to the Chapter of accidents (altho by so doing they hazard all) rather than swallow this bitter pill. The Negociations are going on, but very limpingly, this Winter will, no doubt, bring them to a conclusion; but whether they will terminate in a peace or protraction of the War, is beyond my ken.

George Washington, from a letter written at Newburgh, New York, November 14, 1782, to George Augustine Washington, in John C. Fitzpatrick, ed., The Writings of George Washington, *vol. 25, p. 343.*

Nothing has been agreed in the preliminaries contrary to the interests of France; and no peace is to take place between us and England, till you have concluded yours. Your observation is, however, apparently just, that, in not consulting you before they were signed, we have been guilty of neglecting a point of *bienseance.* But, as this was not from want of respect for the King, whom we all love and honour, we hope it will be excused, and that the great work, which has hitherto been so happily conducted, is so nearly brought to perfection, and is so glorious to his reign, will not be ruined by a single indiscretion of ours. And certainly the whole edifice sinks to the ground immediately, if you refuse on that account to give us any further assistance.

Benjamin Franklin, from a letter written at Passy, France, December 17, 1782, to count de Vergennes, in Albert Henry Smyth, ed., The Writings of Benjamin Franklin, *vol. 8, pp. 642–643.*

1783

The Army, as usual, are without Pay; and a great part of the Soldiery without Shirts; and tho' the patience of them is equally thread bear, the States seem perfectly indifferent to their cries. In a word, if one was to hazard for them an opinion, upon this subject, it would be, that the Army had contracted such a habit of encountering distress and difficulties, and of living without money, that it would be impolitic and injurious to introduce other customs in it! ...

George Washington, from a letter written at Newburgh, New York, January 10, 1783, to Maj. Gen. John Armstrong, in John C. Fitzpatrick, ed., The Writings of George Washington, *vol. 26, pp. 26–27.*

The deputies of the army are still here, urging the objects of their mission. Congress are thoroughly impressed with the justice of them, and are disposed to do every thing which depends on them. But what can a Virginia Delegate say to them, whose constituents declare that they are unable to make the necessary contributions, and unwilling to establish funds for obtaining them elsewhere? The valuation of lands is still under consideration.

James Madison, from a letter written in Philadelphia, January 22, 1783, to Edmund Randolph, in William T. Hutchinson and William M. E. Rachal, eds., The Papers of James Madison, *vol. 6, pp. 55–56.*

... I am commanded by the King to signify to you His Majesty's pleasure that you proceed in the several arrangements necessary for withdrawing the troops, provisions, stores, and British artillery from all the posts under your command to which the seventh article of the provisional articles of peace with the United States of America hath reference. But you are not actually to commence the evacuation until the King's farther pleasure be known, except with respect to the artillery, stores, and heavy baggage intended for the West Indies, which you may cause to be embarked ready to be transported to whatever places may want them.

Thomas Townshend, secretary of state for Home Department, from a letter written at Whitehall, London, February 16, 1783, to Gen. Sir Guy Carleton, in K. G. Davies, ed., Documents of the American Revolution, *vol. 21, p. 156.*

A letter of the 24. Decr. From Dr. Franklin ...says that uncertainties were arising from the unsettled state of

minds in England & incloses a letter from Ct. de Vergennes observing that difficulties had arisen from the
very facilities yielded on the part of France. . . .

Franklin's correspondence on this occasion denotes a
vigor of intellect, which is astonishing at his age. A letter
to the British Minister on the case of the Tories in particular is remarkable for strength of reasoning, of sentiment
& of expression. He concludes his letter to Congs. with
observing that he is now entering on his 78th year, 50
of wh[ich] have been spent in public Service; and . . . his
prayer is that he may be permitted to retire from public
life. Mr. Adams has also transmitted a resignation.

*James Madison, from a letter written in Philadelphia,
March 12, 1783, to Edmund Randolph, in William
T. Hutchinson and William M. E. Rachal, eds.,* The
Papers of James Madison, *vol. 6, pp. 340–341.*

. . . And let me conjure you . . . to express your utmost
horror and detestation of the Man who wishes . . . to
overturn the liberties of our Country, and who wick-
edly attempts to open the flood Gates of Civil discord, and deluge our rising Empire in Blood. By thus
determining, and thus acting, you . . . will give one
more distinguished proof of unexampled patriotism
and patient virtue, rising superior to the pressure of
the most complicated sufferings; And you will, by the
dignity of your Conduct, afford occasion for Posterity
to say, when speaking of the glorious example you have
exhibited to Mankind, "had this day been wanting, the
World had never seen the last stage of perfection to
which human nature is capable of attaining."

*George Washington, from a letter to his officers
responding to the Newburgh Addresses, March 15, 1783,
in John C. Fitzpatrick, ed.,* The Writings of George
Washington, *vol. 26, p. 227.*

Let us now forgive and forget. Let each Country seek
its Advancement in its own internal Advantages of Arts
and Agriculture, not in retarding or preventing the
Prosperity of the other. America will, with God's blessing, become a great and happy Country; and England,
if she has at length gained Wisdom, will have gained
something more valuable, and more essential to her
Prosperity, than all she has lost; and will still be a great
and respectable Nation. . . .

*Benjamin Franklin, from a letter written at Passy, France,
March 17, 1783, to Jonathan Shipley, Anglican bishop
and Whig politician, in Albert Henry Smyth, ed.,* The
Writings of Benjamin Franklin, *vol. 9, p. 23.*

No Man in the United States is, or can be more
deeply impressed with the necessity of a reform in
our present Confederation than myself. No Man
perhaps has felt the bad effects of it more sensibly;
for the defects thereof, and want of Powers in Congress, may justly be ascribed the prolongation of the
War, and consequently the expenses occasioned by it.
More than half the perplexities I have experienced
in the course of my command, and almost the whole
of the difficulties and distress of the Army, have their
origin here. . . .

*George Washington, from a letter written at Newburgh,
New York, March 31, 1783, to Alexander Hamilton, in
John C. Fitzpatrick, ed.,* The Writings of
George Washington, *vol. 26,
pp. 277.*

Upon this great occasion [peace proclamation], sir, I am
to offer my strongest assurances that during the short
period of my command here I shall be ready and earnest to cultivate that spirit of perfect goodwill which,
between the United States of America and the King
of Great Britain and the subjects and citizens of both
countries, will I trust always remain.

*Gen. Sir Guy Carleton, conclusion of a letter
written in New York City, April 6, 1783, to
Gen. George Washington, in K. G. Davies, ed.,*
Documents of the American Revolution,
vol. 21, p. 160.

"The times that tried men's souls," are over—and the
greatest and completest revolution the world ever knew,
gloriously and happily accomplished.

. . . . .

It was the cause of America that made me an author.
The force with which it struck my mind, and the
dangerous condition the country appeared to me in,
by courting an impossible and an unnatural reconciliation with those who were determined to reduce her,
instead of striking out into the only line that could
cement and save her, A DECLARATION OF INDEPEN-
DENCE, made it impossible for me, feeling as I did,
to be silent: and if, in the course of more than seven
years, I have rendered her any service, I have likewise
added something to the reputation of literature, by
freely and disinterestedly employing it in the great

cause of mankind, and showing that there may be genius without prostitution.

Thomas Paine, from "The American Crisis XIII, Thoughts on the Peace, and the Probable Advantages Thereof," April 19, 1783, in Van der Weyde, The Life and Works of Thomas Paine, *vol. 3, pp. 237 and 246–247.*

But we, sad outcasts from our native reign,
Driven from these shores, a poor deluded train,
In distant wilds, conducted by despair,
Seek, vainly seek, a hiding place from care!
Even now yon' tribes, the foremost of the band,
Croud to the ships and cover all the strand:
Forc'd from their friends, their country, and their
        God,
I see the unhappy miscreants leave the sod!
Matrons and men walk sorrowing side by side
And virgin grief, and poverty, and pride,
All, all with aching hearts prepare to sail
And late repentance that has no avail!
While yet I stand on this forbidden ground
I hear the death-bell of destruction sound,
And threat'ning hosts with vengence on their brow
Cry, "Where are Britain's base adherents now?"

Philip Freneau, from "A New-York Tory's Epistle," May 7, 1783, in Fred Lewis Pattee, The Poems of Philip Freneau, *vol. 2, pp. 221–222.*

I thank you for the sentiments you express in my favor. You will have seen that contrary to [my] every private Interest and Sentiment I have agreed to a longer Continuance in Office. . . . [N]othing but a View of the public Necessities should have induced me still longer to bear up under the Burthen. Not because I regard the Calumnies I meet with for altho they excite my Feelings they shall not influence my Conduct but because I do not think those Measures are pursued which are calculated for the Happiness of this Country and I do not wish to participate in any others.

There are many Persons in the Southern States who think the Measures of Congress and of their Servants are directed to the particular good of Pennsylvania and more who pretend to think so. It is a little History of human Weakness and I might say Meanness, the manner in which Antipathies have

been imbibed and propagated with respect to my Department. . . .

Robert Morris, from a letter written in Philadelphia, May 16, 1783, to Nathanael Greene, in Elizabeth M. Nuxoll and Mary A. Gallagher, eds., The Papers of Robert Morris, *vol. 8, pp. 75–76.*

It is proper I should inform Your Excellency that Congress have lately removed to this place. I cannot enter into a detail of the causes; but I imagine they will shortly be published for the information of the United States. You will have heard of a mutiny among the soldiers stationed in the barracks of Philadelphia, and of their having surrounded the state house where Congress was sitting. Fortunately no mischief insued. There was an insolent message sent to the Council. It was at once determined that should any propositions be made to Congress they would not take them into consideration whatever extremities might ensue, while they were surrounded by an armed force.

Alexander Hamilton, from a letter written in Princeton, New Jersey, June 29, 1783, to George Clinton, governor of New York, in Harold C. Syrett, ed., The Papers of Alexander Hamilton, *vol. 3, p. 407.*

. . . It appeared evident, that his [Vergenne's] plan of a treaty for America was far from being such as America would have preferred; and as we disapproved of his model, we thought it imprudent to give him an opportunity of moulding our treaty by it. Whether the minister was influenced by what he really thought best for us, or by what he really thought would be best for France, is a question which, however easy or difficult to decide, is not very important to the point under consideration. Whatever his motives may have been, certain it is that they were such as opposed our system; and as in private life it is deemed imprudent to admit opponents to full confidence, especially respecting the very matters in competition, so in public affairs the like caution seems equally proper.

John Jay, from a letter written at Passy, France, July 19, 1783, to Robert R. Livingston, New York delegate to Congress, in William Jay, The Life of John Jay, *vol. 1, pp. 175–176.*

I ought not, however, to conceal from you, that one of my Colleagues [John Adams] is of a very different Opinion from me in these Matters. He thinks the French Minister one of the greatest Enemies of our Country, that he would have straitned our Boundaries, to prevent the Growth of our People; contracted our Fishery, to obstruct the Increase of our Seamen; and retained the Royalists among us, to keep us divided; . . . that to think of Gratitude to France is the greatest of Follies, and that to be influenc'd by it would ruin us. He makes no Secret of his having these Opinions, expresses them publicly. . . .

. . . I am persuaded, however, that he means for his Country is always an honest Man, often a wise one, but sometimes, and in some things, absolutely out of his senses.

Benjamin Franklin, from a letter written at Passy, France, July 22, 1783, to Robert R. Livingston, secretary of the United States Department of Foreign Affairs, in Albert Henry Smyth, ed., The Writings of Benjamin Franklin, *vol. IX, pp. 61–62.*

My present Call for Taxes has also been anticipated by a Slanderous Report that I have Speculated on this very Paper which I urge the Redemption of. Most solemnly I declare that I have never been concerned, directly or indirectly in any such Speculation. If there be a Man in the World who knows any Instance to disprove what I say let him step forth with the Accusations. No sir, the Object is in nowise a personal one to me, I only Advocate the Interest and Reputation of America. . . . [L]et it be remembered, that the Country which will not support faithful Servants, can never be faithfully served. Guilt and Desperation will ever pant for Scenes of Tumult and Disorder, Office will ever excite Envy and Malevolence delight in Slanderous Tales. . . .

Robert Morris, from a circular to the governors of the states issued at Philadelphia, July 28, 1783, in Elizabeth M. Nuxoll and Mary A. Gallagher, eds., The Papers of Robert Morris, *vol. 8, pp. 350–351.*

Permit me through you to recall the attention of Congress to the Interest of the gallant Officers and brave Men who served in the Squadron I had the Honor to command in Europe. It is now four Years since the Services were performed which did so much honor to themselves and to the Flag of America, yet they have not in all that Time received any gratification either in respect of Wages, Bounties, Prize money, or the losses which many of them sustained when the Bonhomme Richard sunk. . . .

John Paul Jones, from a letter written in Philadelphia, October 13, 1783, to Robert Morris, in Elizabeth M. Nuxoll and Mary A. Gallagher, eds., The Papers of Robert Morris, *vol. 8, pp. 617–618.*

. . . To the various branches of the Army the General takes this last and solemn opportunity of professing his inviolable attachment and friendship. He wishes more than bare professions were in his power, that he were really able to be useful to them all in future life. . . . [B]eing now to conclude these his last public Orders . . . and to bid final adieu to the Armies he has so long had the honor to Command, he can only again offer in their behalf his recommendations to their grateful country, and his prayers to the God of Armies. May ample justice be done them here, and may the choicest of heaven's favours, both here and hereafter, attend those who, under the devine auspices, have secured innumerable blessings for others; with these wishes, and this benediction, the Commander in Chief is about to retire from Service. The Curtain of separetion will soon be drawn, and the military scene to him will be closed for ever.

George Washington, from his farewell orders, written near Princeton, New Jersey, November 2, 1783, in John C. Fitzpatrick, ed., The Writings of George Washington, *vol. 27, p. 227.*

This Evening we are informed by two British officers (on their way to Canada) that the Definitive Treaty had arrived at New York / Continuing in Garrison waiting anxiously for Order to leave this post, our men in Miserable Condition / Some of Then [them] not a shoe or a Stocking to their feet and the climate at this place much severer, than in the Estern States—Continuing at Saratoga / no thing of consequence happin'd till 5th Decr. When we r[e]cieved orders for Discharging our men. & the officers permission to return home which order had laid in the post office at Albany sine 18th of Novr.

Lieutenant Jeremiah Greenman, then stationed at Saratoga, New York, diary entry covering the period November 8–December 5, 1783; with receipt of the discharge orders, he first saw to his men's departure—he described them as "naked"—and then himself left for home on December 25, in Greenman, Diary of a Common Soldier in the American Revolution, 1775–1783, *p. 270.*

We think of nothing here at present but of Flying; the Balloons engross all Conversation. Messrs. Charles and Robert made a Trip last Monday thro' the Air to a Place farther distant than Dover is from Calais; and could have gone much farther if there had been more

Wind and Daylight. They have perfect Command of the Machine, descending and rising again at pleasure. The Progress made in the Management of it has been rapid, yet I fear it will hardly become a common Carriage in my time. . . .

Benjamin Franklin, from a letter written at Passy, France, December 6, 1783, to Henry Laurens, in Albert Henry Smyth, ed., The Writings of Benjamin Franklin, *vol. 9, p. 123.*

3

    He comes!—the Genius of these lands—
        Fame's thousand tongues his worth confess,
    Who conquer'd with his suffering bands,
        And grew immortal by distress:
        Thus calms succeed the stormy blast,
        And valour is repaid at last.

4

    O Washington!—thrice glorious name,
        What due rewards can man decree—
    Empires are far below thy aim,
        And scepters have no charms for thee;
        Virtue alone has thy regard,
        And she must be thy great reward.

O say, thou great, exalted name!
        What Muse can boast of equal lays,
Thy worth disdains all vulgar fame,
        Transcends the noblest poet's praise,
Art soars, unequal to the flight,
        And genius sickens at the height.

Philip Freneau, from "Verses," December 10, 1783, in Fred Lewis Pattee, The Poems of Philip Freneau, *vol. 2, pp. 225–226 and 229.*

I consider it an indispensable duty to close this last solemn act of my Official life, by commending the Interests of our dearest Country to the protection of Almighty God, and those who have the superintendence of them, to his holy keeping.

Having now finished the work assigned me, I retire from the great theatre of Action; and bidding an Affectionate farewell to this August body under whose orders I have so long acted, I here offer my Commission, and take my leave of all the employment of public life.

George Washington, from his final address to Congress delivered in Annapolis, December 23, 1783, in John C. Fitzpatrick, ed., The Writings of George Washington, *vol. 27, p. 285.*

APPENDIX A
Documents

1. The Stamp Act, passed by Parliament on March 22, 1765
2. Resolutions of the Stamp Act Congress, October 19, 1765
3. John Dickinson's *Letters from a Farmer in Pennsylvania to the Inhabitants of the British Colonies,* 1768
4. The Quartering Act, June 2, 1774
5. Declaration and Resolves of the Continental Congress, October 14, 1774
6. Continental Association adopted by the Continental Congress, October 20, 1774
7. "Yankee Doodle," 1776
8. Excerpt from Thomas Paine's *Common Sense,* January 9, 1776
9. The Declaration of Independence, July 4, 1776
10. The Articles of Confederation, adopted November 1777, in effect 1781

1. THE STAMP ACT, PASSED BY PARLIAMENT ON MARCH 22, 1765

An act for granting and applying certain stamp duties, and other duties, in the British colonies and plantations in America, toward further defraying the expenses of defending, protecting, and securing the same; and for amending such parts of the several acts of Parliament relating to the trade and revenues of the said colonies and plantations, as direct the manner of determining and recovering the penalties and forfeitures therein mentioned.

Whereas, by an act made in the last session of Parliament, several duties were granted, continued, and appropriated toward defraying the expenses of defending, protecting, and securing the British colonies and plantations in America: *And whereas* it is just and necessary that provision be made for raising a further revenue within Your Majesty's dominions in America toward defraying the said expenses: We, Your Majesty's most dutiful and loyal subjects, the Commons of Great Britain in Parliament assembled, have therefore resolved to give and grant unto Your Majesty the several rates and duties hereinafter mentioned; and do most humbly beseech Your Majesty that it may be enacted, and be it enacted by the King's most excellent majesty, by and with the advice and consent of the Lords spiritual and temporal, and Commons, in this present Parliament assembled, and by the authority of the same, that from and after November, 1765, there shall be raised, levied, collected, and paid unto His Majesty, His Heirs, and Successors, throughout the colonies and plantations in America which now are, or hereafter may be, under the dominion of His Majesty, His Heirs, and Successors.

For every skin or piece of vellum or parchment, or sheet or piece of paper, on which shall be engrossed, written, or printed any declaration, plea, replication, rejoinder, demurrer, or other pleading, or any copy thereof, in any court of law within the British colonies and plantations in America, a stamp duty of 3*d*.

For every skin . . . on which shall be engrossed, written, or printed any special bail and appearance upon such bail in any such court, a stamp duty of 2*s*.

For every skin . . . on which shall be engrossed, written, or printed any petition, bill, answer, claim, plea, replication, rejoinder, demurrer, or other pleading in any Court of Chancery or Equity within the said colonies and plantations, a stamp duty of 1*s*. 6*d*.

For every skin . . . on which shall be engrossed, written or printed any license, appointment, or admission of any counselor, solicitor, attorney, advocate, or proctor to practice in any court, or of any notary within the said colonies and plantations, a stamp duty of £10.

For every skin . . . on which shall be engrossed, written, or printed any note or bill of lading which shall be signed for any kind of goods, wares, or merchandise to be exported from, or any cocket or clearance granted from within, the said colonies and plantations, a stamp duty of 4*d*.

For every skin . . . on which shall be engrossed, written, or printed letters of mart, or commission for private ships of war, within the said colonies and plantations, a stamp duty of 20*s*.

For every skin . . . on which shall be engrossed, written, or printed any grant, appointment, or admission of or to any public beneficial office or employment, for the space of one year, or any lesser time, of or above the value of £20 per annum sterling money, in salary, fees, and perquisites, within the said colonies and plantations (except commissions and appointments of officers of the Army, Navy, Ordnance, or Militia, of judges, and of justices of the peace), a stamp duty of 10*s*.

For every skin . . . on which any grant of any liberty, privilege, or franchise, under the seal of any of the said colonies or plantations, or under the seal or sign manual of any governor, proprietor, or public officer alone, or in conjunction with any other person or persons, or with any council, or any council and assembly, or any exemplification of the same, shall be engrossed, written, or printed, within the said colonies and plantations, a stamp duty of £6.

For every skin . . . on which shall be engrossed, written, or printed any license for retailing of spirituous liquors, to be granted to any person who shall take out the same, within the said colonies and plantations, a stamp duty of 20*s*. . . .

For every skin . . . on which shall be engrossed, written, or printed any probate of a will, letters of administration, or of guardianship for any estate above the value of £20 sterling money, within the British colonies and plantations upon the continent of America, the islands belonging thereto, and the Bermuda and Bahama islands, a stamp duty of 5*s*. . . .

For every skin . . . on which shall be engrossed, written, or printed any such order or warrant for surveying or setting out any quantity of land above 200 and not exceeding 320 acres, and in proportion for every such order or warrant for surveying or setting out every other 320 acres, within the said colonies and plantations, a stamp duty of 1s. 6d. . . .

For every skin . . . on which shall be engrossed, written, or printed any grant, appointment, or admission of or to any public beneficial office or employment, not hereinbefore charged, above the value of £20 per annum sterling money in salary, fees, and perquisites, or any exemplification of the same, within the British colonies and plantations upon the continent of America, the islands belonging thereto, and the Bermuda and Bahama islands (except commissions of officers of the Army, Navy, Ordnance, or Militia, and of justices of the peace), a stamp duty of £4. . . .

For every skin . . . on which shall be engrossed, written, or printed any register, entry, or enrollment of any grant, deed, or other instrument whatsoever hereinbefore charged, within the said colonies and plantations, a stamp duty of 3d. . . .

And for and upon every pack of playing cards, and all dice, which shall be sold or used within the said colonies and plantations, the several stamp duties following. . . .

And for and upon every paper, commonly called a pamphlet, and upon every newspaper containing public news, intelligence, or occurrences, which shall be printed, dispersed, and made public within any of the said colonies and plantations, and for and upon such advertisements as are hereinafter mentioned, the respective duties following (that is to say):

For every such pamphlet and paper contained in half a sheet, or any lesser piece of paper which shall be so printed, a stamp duty of one halfpenny for every printed copy thereof.

For every such pamphlet and paper (being larger than half a sheet, and not exceeding one whole sheet) which shall be so printed, a stamp duty of one penny for every copy printed thereof.

For every pamphlet and paper being larger than one whole sheet, and not exceeding six sheets in octavo, or in a lesser page, or not exceeding twelve sheets in quarto, or twenty sheets in folio which shall be so printed, a duty after the rate of 1s. For every sheet of any kind of paper which shall be contained in one printed copy thereof.

For every advertisement to be contained in any gazette, newspaper, or other paper, or any pamphlet which shall be so printed, a duty of 2s.

For every almanac or calendar for any one particular year, or for any time less than a year, which shall be written or printed on one side only of any one sheet, skin, or piece of paper, parchment, or vellum, within the said colonies and plantations, a stamp duty of 2d.

For every other almanac or calendar for any one particular year, which shall be written or printed within the said colonies and plantations, a stamp duty of 4d.

And for every almanac or calendar, written or printed within the said colonies and plantations, to serve for several years, duties to the same amount respectively shall be paid for every such year.

For every skin . . . on which any instrument, proceeding, or other matter or thing aforesaid shall be engrossed, written, or printed, within the said colonies and plantations, in any other than the English language, a stamp duty of double the amount of the respective duties before charged thereon.

And there shall also be paid in the said colonies and plantations, a duty of 6d. For every 20s., in any sum not exceeding £50 sterling money, which shall be given, paid, contracted, or agreed for, with or in relation to any clerk or apprentice, which shall be put or placed to or with any master or mistress to learn any profession, trade, or employment.

And also a duty of 1s. For every 20s. In any sum exceeding £50, which shall be given, paid, contracted, or agreed for, with or in relation to any such clerk apprentice. . . .

And be it further enacted by the authority aforesaid that every deed, instrument, note, memorandum, letter, or other monument or writing between the captain or master or owner of any ship or vessel and any merchant, trader, or other person, in respect to the freight or conveyance of any money, goods, wares, merchandise, or effects, laden or to be laden on board of any such ship or vessel, shall be deemed and adjudged to be a charter party within the meaning of this act.

And be it further enacted by the authority aforesaid that the said several duties shall be under the management of the commissioners, for the time being, of the duties charged on stamped vellum, parchment, and paper in Great Britain; and the said commissioners are hereby empowered and required to employ such officers under them, for that purpose, as they shall think proper; and to use such stamps and marks to denote the stamp duties hereby charged as they shall think fit; and to repair, renew, or alter the same, from time to time, as there shall be occasion; and to do all other acts, matters, and things necessary to be done for putting this act in execution with relation to the duties hereby charged. . . .

And every commissioner and other officer, before he proceeds to the execution of any part of this act, shall take an oath in the words, or to the effect following (that is to say):

I . . . do swear that I will faithfully execute the trust reposed in me, pursuant to an act of Parliament made in the fifth year of the reign of His Majesty King George the Third, for granting certain stamp duties, and other duties, in the British colonies and plantations in America, without fraud or concealment; and will from time to time true account make of my doing therein, and deliver the same to such person or persons as His Majesty, His Heirs, or Successors shall appoint to receive such account; and will take no fee, reward, or profit for the execution or performance of the said trust, or the business relating thereto, from any person or persons, other than such as shall be allowed by His Majesty, His Heirs, and Successors, or by some other person or persons under him or them to that purpose authorized. . . .

And be it further enacted by the authority aforesaid that, if any person or persons shall sign . . . in any of the said colonies or plantations, or in any other part of His Majesty's dominions, any matter or thing for which the vellum, parchment, or paper is hereby charged to pay any duty, before the same shall be marked or stamped with the marks or stamps to be provided as aforesaid, or upon which there shall not be some stamp or mark resembling the same; or shall sign . . . any matter or thing upon any vellum, parchment, or paper that shall be marked or stamped for any lower duty than the duty by this act made payable in respect thereof; every such person so offending shall, for every such offense, forfeit the sum of £10. . . .

And be it further enacted by the authority aforesaid that if any person shall forge, counterfeit, erase, or alter any such certificate, every such person so offending shall be guilty of felony, and shall suffer death as in cases of felony without the benefit of clergy. . . .

And be it further enacted by the authority aforesaid that all the monies which shall arise by the several rates and duties hereby granted (except the necessary charges of raising, collecting, recovering, answering, paying, and accounting for the same, and the necessary charges from time to time incurred in relation to this act and the execution thereof) shall be paid into the receipt of His Majesty's Exchequer, and shall be entered separate and apart from all other monies, and shall be there to be, from time to time, disposed of by Parliament, toward further defraying the necessary expenses of defending, protecting, and securing the said colonies and plantations. . . .

And be it hereby further enacted and declared that all the powers and authorities by this act granted to the commissioners for managing the duties upon stamped vellum, parchment, and paper shall and may be fully and effectually carried into execution by any three or more of the said commissioners; anything heretofore contained to the contrary notwithstanding.

And be it further enacted by the authority aforesaid that all forfeitures and penalties incurred after the 29th day of September, 1765, for offenses committed against an act passed in the fourth year of the reign of His present Majesty, entitled "An act for granting certain duties in the British colonies and plantations in America . . ." and for offenses committed against any other act or acts of Parliament relating to the trade or revenues of the said colonies or plantations, shall and may be prosecuted, sued for, and recovered in any court of record, or in any Court of Admiralty, in the respective colony or plantation where the offense shall be committed, or in any Court of Vice-Admiralty appointed or to be appointed, and which shall have jurisdiction within such colony, plantation, or place . . . at the election of the informer or prosecutor. . . .

And be it further enacted by the authority aforesaid that all the offenses which are by this act made felony, and shall be committed within any part of His Majesty's dominions, shall and may be heard, tried, and determined before any court of law within the respective kingdom, territory, colony, or plantation where the offense shall be committed, in such and the same manner as all other felonies can or may be heard, tried, and determined in such court.

2. RESOLUTIONS OF THE STAMP ACT CONGRESS, OCTOBER 19, 1765

The members of this congress, sincerely devoted, with the warmest sentiments of affection and duty to his majesty's person and government, inviolably attached to the present happy establishment of the protestant succession, and with minds deeply impressed by a sense of the present and impending misfortunes of the British colonies on this continent, having considered as maturely as time would permit, the circumstances of said colonies, esteem it our indispensable duty to make the following declarations, of our humble opinions, respecting the most essential rights and liberties of the colonists, and of the grievances under which they labor, by reason of several late acts of parliament.

I. Resolved, That his Majesty's Subjects in these colonies owe the same Allegiance to the Crown of Great Britain, that is owing from his Subjects born within the Realm, and all due Subordination to that august Body the Parliament of Great Britain.

II. That his Majesty's liege Subjects in these Colonies, are entitled to all the inherent Rights and Liberties of his natural born subjects within the Kingdom of Great Britain.

III. That it is inseparably essential to the Freedom of a People, and the undoubted Right of Englishmen, that no Tax be imposed upon them, but with their own Consent, given personally, or by their Representatives.

IV. That the People of these Colonies are not, and from their local Circumstances, cannot be represented in the House of Commons in Great Britain.

V. That the only Representatives of the People of these Colonies, are the Persons chosen therein by themselves; and that no Taxes ever have been, or can be, constitutionally imposed on them but by their respective Legislatures.

VI. That all Supplies to the Crown being free Gifts of the People, it is unreasonable, and inconsistent with the Principles and Spirit of the British Constitution, for the People of Great Britain to grant to his Majesty the Property of the Colonies.

VII. That trials by jury are the inherent and invaluable right of every British Subject in these Colonies.

VIII. That the late Act of Parliament, intitled, "An Act for granting certain Stamp Duties, and other Duties, in the British Colonies and Plantations in America," &c., by imposing Taxes on the Inhabitants of these Colonies, and the said Act, and several other Acts, by extending the Jurisdiction of the Courts of Admiralty beyond its ancient Limits, have a Tendency to subvert the Rights and Liberties of the Colonists.

IX. That the Duties imposed by several Acts of Parliament, from the peculiar Circumstances of these Colonies, will be extremely burthensome and grievous, and, from the Scarcity of Specie, the Payment of them absolutely impracticable.

X. That the profits of the Trade of these Colonies, ultimately center in Great Britain, to pay for the Manufactures which they are obliged to take from thence, they eventually contribute very largely to all Supplies granted there to the Crown.

XI. That the Restrictions imposed by several late Acts of Parliament, on the Trade of these Colonies, will render them unable to purchase the Manufactures of Great Britain.

XII. That the Increase, Prosperity and Happiness of these Colonies depend on the full and free Enjoyment of their Rights and Liberties, and an Intercourse with Great Britain, mutually affectionate and advantageous.

XIII. That it is the Right of the British Subjects in these Colonies, to petition the King, or either House of Parliament.

Lastly. That it is the indispensable Duty of these Colonies to the best of Sovereigns, to the Mother-country and themselves, to endeavor, by a loyal and dutiful Address to his Majesty and humble Applications to both Houses of Parliament, to procure the Repeal of the Act for granting certain Stamp Duties, of all Clauses of any other Act of parliament, whereby the Jurisdiction of the Admiralty is extended, as aforesaid, and of other Acts for Restriction of American Commerce.

3. JOHN DICKINSON'S *LETTERS FROM A FARMER IN PENNSYLVANIA TO THE INHABITANTS OF THE BRITISH COLONIES*, 1768

LETTER XII

My Dear COUNTRYMEN,

Some states have lost their liberty by *particular accidents:* But this calamity is generally owing to the *decay of virtue.* A people is travelling fast to destruction, when *individuals* consider *their* interests as distinct from *those of the public.* Such notions are fatal to their country, and to themselves. Yet how many are there, so *weak* and *sordid* as to *think* they perform *all the offices of life,* if they earnestly endeavor to increase their own *wealth, power,* and *credit,* without the least regard for the society, under the protection of which they live; who, if they can make an *immediate profit to themselves,* by lending their assistance to those, whose projects plainly tend to the injury of their country, rejoice in their *dexterity,* and believe themselves entitled to the character of *able politicians.* Miserable men! Of whom it is hard to say, whether they ought to be most the objects of *pity* or *contempt:* But whose opinions are certainly as *detestable,* as their practices are *destructive.*

Tho' I always reflect, with high pleasure, on the integrity and understanding of my countrymen, which, joined with a pure and humble devotion to the great and gracious author of every blessing they enjoy, will, I hope, ensure to them, and their posterity. All temporal and eternal happiness; yet when I consider, that in every age and country there have been bad men, my heart, at this threatening period, is so full of apprehension, as not to permit me to believe, but that there may be some on this continent, *against whom you ought to be upon your guard*—Men, who either hold or expect to hold certain advantages, by setting examples of servility to their countrymen. Men, who trained to the employment, or self taught by a natural versatility of genius, serve as decoys for drawing the innocent and unaware into snares. It is not to be doubted but that such men will diligently bestir themselves on this and every occasion, to spread the infection of their meanness as far as they can. On the plans *they* have adopted, this is *their* course. *This* is the method to recommend themselves to their *patrons*.

From *them* we shall learn, how *pleasant* and *profitable* a thing it is, to be for our SUBMISSIVE behavior *well spoken* of at *St. James* or *St. Stephen's*; at *Guildhall*, or the *Royal Exchange*. Specious fallacies will be drest up with all the arts of delusion, to persuade one colony *to distinguish herself from another*, by unbecoming condescension, *which will serve the ambitious purposes of great men* at home, and therefore will be thought by them *to entitle their assistants in obtaining them* to considerable rewards.

Our fears will be excited. Our hopes will be awakened. It will be insinuated to us, with a plausible affection of *wisdom* and *concern*, how *prudent* it is to please the *powerful*—how *dangerous* to provoke them—and then comes in the perpetual incantation that freezes up every generous purpose of the soul in cold, inactive expectation—"that if there is any request to be made, compliance will obtain a favorable attention."

Our *vigilance* and our *union* are *success* and *safety*. Our *negligence* and our *division* are *distress* and *death*. They are *worse*—they are *shame* and *slavery*. Let us equally shun the benumbing stillness of *overweening sloath*, and the feverish activity of that *ill informed zeal*, which busies itself in maintaining *little, mean*, and *narrow* opinions. Let us, with a truly wise *generosity* and *charity*, banish and discourage all *illiberal distinctions*, which may arise from differences in *situation*, forms of *government*, or modes of *religion*. Let us consider ourselves as MEN—FREEMEN—CHRISTIAN FREEMEN—*separate from the rest of the world, and firmly bound together by the same rights, interests* and *dangers*. Let *these* keep our attention inflexibly fixed on the GREAT OBJECTS, which we must CONTINUALLY REGARD, in order to *preserve those rights, to promote those interests,* and to *avert those dangers.*

Let these *truths* be indelibly impressed on our minds—*that we cannot be* HAPPY, *without being* FREE—that we cannot be free, *without being secure in our property*—that *we* cannot be secure in our property, *if without our consent, others may, as by right, take it away*—that *taxes imposed on us by parliament,* do thus take it away—that *duties laid for the sole purpose of raising money, are taxes*—that *attempts* to lay such duties *should be instantly and firmly opposed*—that this opposition can never be effectual, *unless it is the united effort of these provinces*—that therefore BENEVOLENCE *of temper towards each other,* and UNANIMITY *of councils* are essential to the welfare of the whole—and lastly, that for this reason, every man amongst us, who in any manner would encourage either *dissension, diffidence,* or *indifference* between these colonies, is an enemy to *himself,* and to *his country.*

The belief of these truths, I verily think, my countrymen, is indispensably necessary to your happiness. I beseech you, therefore, "teach them diligently unto your children, and talk of them when you sit in your houses, and when you walk by the way, and when you lie down, and when you rise up." What have these colonies to *ask,* while they continue free? Or what have they to *dread,* but insidious attempts to subvert their freedom? *Their prosperity* does not depend on *ministerial favors doled* out to *particular* provinces. *They* form *one* political body, of which *each colony* is a *member. Their happiness* is founded on *their constitution;* and is to be promoted, by preserving that constitution in unabated vigor, *throughout every part.* A spot, a speck of decay, however small the limb on which it appears, and however remote it may seem from the vitals, should be alarming. We have *all the rights* requisite for our prosperity. The *legal authority* of *Great-Britain* may indeed lay hard restrictions upon us; but, like the spear of *Telephus,* it will cure as well as wound. Her unkindness will instruct and compel us, after some time, to discover, in our *industry* or *frugality,* surprising remedies—*if our rights continue unviolated:* For as long as the *products* of our *labor,* and the *rewards* of our *care,* can properly be called *our own,* so long it will be worth our while to be *industrious* and *frugal.* But if when we plow—sow—reap—gather—and thresh—we find that we plow—sow—reap—gather—and thresh *for others,* whose PLEASURE is to be the SOLE LIMITATION *how* much they shall *take,* and *how much* they shall *leave,* WHY should we repeat the unprofitable toil? *Horses* and *oxen* are content with *that portion of the fruits of their work,* which their *owners* assign them, in order to keep them strong enough to raise successive crops; but even *these beasts* will not submit to draw for their *masters,* until they are *subdued* by *whips* and *goads.*

Let us take care of our *rights,* and we *therein* take care of *our prosperity.* "SLAVERY IS EVER PRECEDED BY SLEEP." *Individuals* may be *dependent* on ministers, if they please. STATES SHOULD SCORN IT;—and if *you* are not wanting *to yourselves,* you will have a *proper regard* paid *you* by *those,* to whom if you are not *respectable,* you will be *contemptible.* But—if *we have already forgot* the *reasons* that urged us, with unexampled unanimity, to exert ourselves two years ago—if *our zeal* for the public good is *worn out* before the *homespun cloaths,* which it has caused us to have made—if *our resolutions* are *so faint,* as by our present conduct to *condemn* our own late *successful* example—if *we are not affected* by any reverence for the memory of our ancestors, who transmitted to us that freedom in which they had been blest—if *we are not animated* by any regard for posterity, to whom, by the most sacred obligations, we are bound to deliver down the invaluable inheritance—THEN, indeed, any *minister*—or any *tool* of a minister—or any *lower instrument of administration,* if lower there be, is a *personage* whom it may be dangerous to offend.

I shall be extremely sorry, if any man mistakes my meaning in anything I have said. Officers employed by the crown, are, while according to the laws they conduct themselves, entitled to legal obedience, and sincere respect. These it is a duty to render them; and these no good or prudent person will withhold. But when these officers, thro' rashness or design, desire to enlarge their authority beyond its due limits, and expect improper concessions to be made to them, from regard for the employments they bear, their attempts should be courageously and constantly opposed. To suffer our ideas to be confounded by *names* on such occasions, would certainly be an *inexcusable weakness,* and probably an *irremediable error.*

We have reason to believe, that several of his Majesty's present ministers are good men, and friends to our country; and it seems not unlikely, that by a particular concurrence of events, we have been treated a little more severely than they wished we should be. *They* might think it prudent to stem a torrent. But what is the difference to *us,* whether arbitrary acts take their rise from ministers, or are permitted by them? Ought any point to be allowed to a good minister, that should be denied to a bad one? The mortality of ministers, is a very frail mortality. A____ may succeed a *Shelburne*—A____ may succeed a *Cornway.*

We find a new kind of minister lately spoken of at home—"THE MINISTER OF THE HOUSE OF COMMONS." The term seems to have peculiar propriety when referred to these colonies, *with a different meaning annexed to it,* from that in which it is taken there. By the word "minister" we may understand not only a *servant of the crown,* but a *man of influence* among the commons, who regard themselves as having a share in the *sovereignty* over us. The "minister of the house" may in a point respecting the colonies, be so strong, that the minister of the crown *in the house, if he is a distinct person, may not choose, even where his sentiments are favorable to us, to come to a pitched battle upon our account. For tho' I have the highest opinion of the deference of the house for the King's minister, yet he may be so good natured, as not to put it to the test, except it be for the mere and immediate profit of his master or himself.*

But whatever kind of minister he is, that attempts to innovate *a single iota* in the privileges of these colonies, him I hope you will *undauntedly oppose;* and that you will never suffer yourselves to be either *cheated* or *frightened* into any *unworthy obsequiousness.* On such emergencies you may surely, without presumption, believe, that ALMIGHTY GOD himself will look down upon your righteous contest with gracious approbation. You will be a *"band of brothers,"* cemented by the dearest ties,—and strengthened with inconceivable supplies of force and constancy, by that sympathetic ardor, which animates good men, confederated in a good cause. Your *honor* and *welfare* will be, as they now are, most intimately concerned; and besides—*you are assigned by divine providence,* in the appointed order of things, the *protectors of unborn ages,* whose *fate* depends upon your *virtue.* Whether *they* shall arise the *generous* and *indisputable heirs* of the noblest patrimonies, or the *dastardly* and *hereditary drudges* of imperious task-masters, YOU MUST DETERMINE.

To discharge this double duty to *yourselves,* and to your *posterity,* you have nothing to do, but to call forth into use the *good sense* and *spirit* of which you are possessed. You have nothing to do, but to conduct your affairs *peaceably—prudently—firmly—jointly.* By *these means* you will support the character of *freemen,* without losing that of *faithful subjects*—a good character in any government—one of the best under a *British* government—You will *prove,* that *Americans* have that true MAGNANIMITY of soul, that can resent injuries, without falling into rage; and that tho' your devotion to *Great-Britain* is the most affectionate, yet you can make PROPER DISTINCTIONS, and know what you owe *to yourselves,* as well as to her—You will, at the same time that you advance your *interests,* advance your *reputation*—You will convince the world of the *justice of your demands,* and the *purity of your intentions.*—While all mankind must, with unceasing applause, confess, that YOU indeed DESERVE liberty, who *so well understand* it, so *passionately love* it, so *temperately enjoy* it, and so *wisely, bravely,* and *virtuously assert, maintain,* and *defend* it.

"Certe ego libertatem, quae mihi a parente meo tradita est, experiar: Verum id frustra an ob rem faciam, in vestra manu situm est, quirites."

For my part I am resolved to contend for the liberty delivered down to me by my ancestors; but whether I shall do it effectually or not, depends on you, my countrymen.

"How little soever one is able to write, yet when the liberties of one's country are threatened, it is still more difficult to be silent."

A FARMER

Is there not the strongest probability, that if the universal sense of these colonies is immediately expressed by RESOLVES of the assemblies, in support of their rights, by INSTRUCTIONS to their agents on the subject, and by PETITIONS to the crown and parliament for redress, these measures will have the same success now, that they had in the time of the *Stamp-Act.* D.

FINIS

4. THE QUARTERING ACT, JUNE 2, 1774

Whereas doubts have been entertained whether troops can be quartered otherwise than in barracks, in case barracks have been provided sufficient for the quartering of all the officers and soldiers within any town, township, city, district, or place within His Majesty's dominions in North America; and *whereas* it may frequently happen from the situation of such barracks that, if troops should be quartered therein they would not be stationed where their presence may be necessary and required: *be it therefore enacted* by the King's Most Excellent Majesty, by and with the advice and consent of the Lords . . . and Commons, in this present Parliament assembled . . . that, in such

cases, it shall and may be lawful for the persons who now are, or may be hereafter, authorized by law, in any of the provinces within His Majesty's dominions in North America, and they are hereby respectively authorized, empowered, and directed, on the requisition of the officer who, for the time being, has command of His Majesty's forces in North America, to cause any officers or soldiers in His Majesty's service to be quartered and billeted in such manner as is now directed by law where no barracks are provided by the colonies.

2. *And be it further enacted* by the authority aforesaid that, if it shall happen at any time that any officers or soldiers in His Majesty's service shall remain within any of the said colonies without quarters for the space of twenty-four hours after such quarters shall have been demanded, it shall and may be lawful for the governor of the province to order and direct such and so many uninhabited houses, outhouses, barns, or other buildings as he shall think necessary to be taken (making a reasonable allowance for the same) and make fit for the reception of such officers and soldiers, and to put and quarter such officers and soldiers therein for such time as he shall think proper.

3. *And be it further enacted* by the authority aforesaid that this act, and everything herein contained, shall continue and be in force in all His Majesty's dominions in North America, until March 24, 1776.

5. DECLARATION AND RESOLVES OF THE CONTINENTAL CONGRESS, OCTOBER 14, 1774

Whereas, since the close of the last war, the British parliament, claiming a power of right to bind the people of America by statutes in all cases whatsoever, has in some acts expressly imposed taxes on them, and in others, under various pretenses but in fact for the purpose of raising a revenue, has imposed rates and duties payable in these colonies; established a Board of Commissioners with unconstitutional powers; and extended the jurisdiction of Courts of Admiralty, not only for collecting the said duties but for the trial of causes merely arising within the body of a county.

And whereas, in consequence of other statutes, judges, who before held only estates at will in their offices, have been made dependent on the Crown alone for their salaries, and standing armies kept in times of peace. *And whereas* it has lately been resolved in Parliament that, by force of a statute made in the thirty-fifth year of the reign of King Henry the Eighth, colonists may be transported to England and tried there upon accusations for treasons, and misprisions, or concealment of treasons committed in the colonies; and by a late statute, such trials have been directed in cases therein mentioned.

And whereas, in the last session of Parliament, three statutes were made; one, entitled "An act to discontinue, in such manner and for such time as are therein mentioned, the landing and discharging, lading, or shipping of goods, wares, and merchandise at the town, and within the harbor of Boston, in the province of Massachusetts Bay, in North America"; another, entitled "An act for the better regulating the government of the province of Massachusetts Bay in New England"; and another, entitled "An act for the impartial administration of justice in the cases of persons questioned for any act done by them in the execution of the law, or for the suppression of riots and tumults in the province of the Massachusetts Bay in New England"; and another was then made, "for making more effectual provisions for the government of the province of Quebec, etc."; all which statutes are impolitic, unjust, and cruel, as well as unconstitutional, and most dangerous and destructive of American rights.

And whereas, assemblies have been frequently dissolve, contrary to the rights of the people, when they attempted to deliberate grievances; and their dutiful, humble, loyal, and reasonable petitions to the Crown for redress have been repeatedly treated with contempt by His Majesty's ministers of state:

The good people of the several colonies of New Hampshire; Massachusetts Bay; Rhode Island and Providence Plantations; Connecticut; New York; New Jersey; Pennsylvania; Newcastle, Kent, and Sussex on Delaware; Maryland; Virginia; North Carolina; and South Carolina, justly alarmed at these arbitrary proceedings of Parliament and administration, have severally elected, constituted, and appointed deputies to meet and sit in General Congress in the city of Philadelphia in order to obtain such establishment as that their religion, laws, and liberties may not be subverted:

Whereupon the deputies so appointed being now assembled, in a full and free representation of these colonies, taking into their most serious consideration the best means of attaining the ends aforesaid, do, in the first place, as Englishmen, their ancestors in like cases have usually done, for affecting and vindicating their rights and liberties, declare,

That the inhabitants of the English colonies in North America, by the immutable laws of nature, the principles of the English constitution, and the several charters or compacts, have the following rights:

Resolved:

1. That they are entitled to life, liberty, and property, and they have never ceded to any sovereign power whatever a right to dispose of either without their consent.

2. That our ancestors, who first settled these colonies, were at the time of their emigration from the mother country entitled to all the rights, liberties, and immunities of free and natural-born subjects, within the Realm of England.

3. That by such emigration they by no means forfeited, surrendered, or lost any of those rights, but that they were, and their descendants now are, entitled to the exercise and enjoyment of all such of them as their local and other circumstances enable them to exercise and enjoy.

4. That the foundation of English liberty, and of all free government, is a right in the people to participate in their legislative council; and as English colonists are not represented, and from their local and other circumstances cannot properly be represented in the British Parliament, they are entitled to a free and exclusive power of legislation in their several provincial legislatures, where their right of representation can alone be preserved, in all cases of taxation and internal polity, subject only to the negative of their sovereign, in such manner as has been heretofore used and accustomed. But, from the necessity of the case and a regard to the mutual interest of both countries, we cheerfully consent to the operation of such acts of the British Parliament as are bona fide, restrained to the regulation of our external commerce, for the purpose of securing the commercial advantage of the whole empire to the mother country, and the commercial benefits of its respective members; excluding every idea of taxation, internal or external, for raising a revenue on the subjects in America without their consent.

5. That the respective colonies are entitled to the common law of England, and more especially to the great and inestimable privilege of being tried by their peers of the vicinage according to the course of that law.

6. That they are entitled to the benefit of such English statutes as existed at the time of their colonization; and which they have, by experience, respectively found to be applicable to their several local and other circumstances.

7. That these, His Majesty's colonies, are likewise entitled to all immunities and privileges granted and confirmed to them by royal charters, or secured by their several codes of provincial laws.

8. That they have a right peaceably to assemble, consider of their grievances, and petition the King; and that all prosecutions, prohibitory proclamations, and commitments for the same are illegal.

9. That the keeping of a standing army in these colonies, in times of peace, without the consent of the legislature of that colony in which such army is kept is against law.

10. It is indispensably necessary to good government, and rendered essential by the English constitution, that the constituent branches of the legislature be independent of each other; that, therefore, the exercise of legislative power in several colonies, by a council appointed during pleasure by the Crown, is unconstitutional, dangerous, and destructive to the freedom of American legislation.

All and each of which the aforesaid deputies, in behalf of themselves and their constituents, do claim, demand, and insist on as their indubitable rights and liberties; which cannot be legally taken from them, altered or abridged by any power whatever, without their own consent, by their representatives in their several provincial legislatures.

In the course of our inquiry, we find many infringements and violations of the foregoing rights, which, from an ardent desire that harmony and mutual intercourse of affection and interest may be restored, we pass over for the present, and proceed to state such acts and measures as have been adopted since the last war, which demonstrate a system formed to enslave America.

Resolved, that the following acts of Parliament are infringements and violations of the rights of the colonists; and that the repeal of them is essentially necessary in order to restore harmony between Great Britain and the American colonies, viz.:

The several acts. . . . which impose duties for the purpose of raising a revenue in America, extend the powers of the Admiralty Courts beyond their ancient limits, deprive the American subject of trial by jury, authorize

the judge's certificate to indemnify the prosecutor from damages that he might otherwise be liable to, requiring oppressive security from a claimant of ships and goods seized, before he shall be allowed to defend his property, and are subversive of American rights.

Also [the act] entitled "An act for the better securing His Majesty's dockyards, magazines, ships, ammunition, and stores," which declares a new offense in America, and deprives the American subject of a constitutional trial by jury of the vicinage, by authorizing the trial of any person, charged with the committing any offense described in the said act, out of the Realm, to be indicted and tried for the same in any shire or county within the Realm.

Also the three acts passed in the last session of Parliament for stopping the port and blocking up the harbor of Boston, for altering the charter and government of Massachusetts Bay, and that which is entitled "An act for the better administration of justice, etc."

Also the act passed the same session for establishing the Roman Catholic religion in the province of Quebec, abolishing the equitable system of English laws, and erecting a tyranny there to the great danger, from so total a dissimilarity of religion, law, and government of the neighboring British colonies, by the assistance of whose blood and treasure the said country was conquered from France.

Also the act passed the same session for the better providing suitable quarters for officers and soldiers in His Majesty's service in North America.

Also, that the keeping a standing army in several of these colonies, in time of peace, without the consent of the legislature of that colony in which the army is kept, is against law.

To these grievous acts and measures Americans cannot submit, but in hopes that their fellow subjects in Great Britain will, on a revision of them, restore us to that state in which both countries found happiness and prosperity, we have for the present only resolved to pursue the following peaceable measures:

1. To enter into nonimportation, nonconsumption, and nonexportation agreement or association.

2. To prepare an address to the people of Great Britain and a memorial to the inhabitants of British America.

3. To prepare a loyal address to His Majesty, agreeable to resolutions already entered into.

6. CONTINENTAL ASSOCIATION ADOPTED BY THE CONTINENTAL CONGRESS, OCTOBER 20, 1774

We, His Majesty's most loyal subjects, the delegates of the several colonies of New Hampshire, Massachusetts Bay, Rhode Island, Connecticut, New York, New Jersey, Pennsylvania, the three lower counties of Newcastle, Kent, and Sussex on Delaware, Maryland, Virginia, North Carolina, and South Carolina, deputed to represent them in a Continental Congress, held in the city of Philadelphia, on the 5th day of September, 1774, avowing our allegiance to His Majesty, our affection and regard for our fellow subjects in Great Britain and elsewhere, affected with the deepest anxiety and most alarming apprehensions at those grievances and distresses, with which His Majesty's American subjects are oppressed; and having taken under our most serious deliberation the state of the whole continent, find that the present unhappy situation of our affairs is occasioned by a ruinous system of colony administration, adopted by the British Ministry about the year 1763, evidently calculated for enslaving these colonies and with them, the British empire.

In prosecution of which system, various acts of Parliament have been passed for raising a revenue in America; for depriving the American subjects, in many instances, of the constitutional trial by jury; exposing their lives to danger by directing a new and illegal trial beyond the seas for crimes alleged to have been committed in America. And in prosecution of the same system, several late, cruel, and oppressive acts have been passed respecting the town of Boston and the Massachusetts Bay, and also an act for extending the province of Quebec, so as to border on the western frontiers of these colonies, establishing an arbitrary government therein, and discouraging the settlement of British subjects in that wide-extended country; thus, by the influence of civil principles and ancient prejudices to dispose the inhabitants to act with hostility against the free Protestant colonies, whenever a wicked Ministry shall choose to direct them.

To obtain redress of these grievances which threaten destruction to the lives, liberty, and property of His Majesty's subjects in North America, we are of opinion that a nonimportation, nonconsumption, and nonexportation agreement, faithfully adhered to, will prove the most speedy, effectual, and peaceable measure. And, therefore, we do, for ourselves and the inhabitants of the several colonies whom we represent, firmly agree and associate, under the sacred ties of virtue, and love of our country, as follows:

1. That from and after the 1st day of December next, we will not import into British America from Great Britain or Ireland any goods, wares, or merchandise whatsoever, or from any other place, any such goods, wares, or merchandise, as shall have been exported from Great Britain or Ireland. Nor will we, after that day, import any East India tea from any part of the world; nor any molasses, syrups, paneles, coffee, or pimento from the British plantations or from Dominica; nor wines from Madeira or the Western Islands; nor foreign indigo.

2. We will neither import nor purchase any slave imported after the 1st day of December next; after which time, we will wholly discontinue the slave trade and will neither be concerned in it ourselves, nor will we hire our vessels, nor sell our commodities or manufactures to those who are concerned in it.

3. As a nonconsumption agreement, strictly adhered to, will be an effectual security for the observation of the nonimportation, we, as above, solemnly agree and associate that from this day we will not purchase or use any tea imported on account of the East India Company, or any on which a duty has been or shall be paid. And from and after the 1st day of March next, we will not purchase or use any East India tea whatever; nor will we, nor shall any person for or under us, purchase or use any of those goods, wares, or merchandise we have agreed not to import, which we shall know or have cause to suspect, were imported after the 1st day of December, except such as come under the rules and directions of the 10th Article hereafter mentioned.

4. The earnest desire we have not to injure our fellow subjects in Great Britain, Ireland, or the West Indies induces us to suspend a nonexportation [agreement] until the 10th day of September, 1775; at which time, if the said acts and parts of acts of the British Parliament hereinafter mentioned are not repealed, we will not directly or indirectly export any merchandise or commodity whatsoever to Great Britain, Ireland, or the West Indies, except rice to Europe.

5. Such as are merchants and use the British and Irish trade will give orders, as soon as possible, to their factors, agents, and correspondents in Great Britain

and Ireland not to ship any goods to them, on any pretense whatsoever, as they cannot be received in America; and if any merchant residing in Great Britain or Ireland shall directly or indirectly ship any goods, wares, or merchandise for America in order to break the said nonimportation agreement or in any manner contravene the same, on such unworthy conduct being well attested, it ought to be made public; and, on the same being so done, we will not, from thenceforth, have any commercial connection with such merchant.

6. That such as are owners of vessels will give positive orders to their captains or masters not to receive on board their vessels any goods prohibited by the said nonimportation agreement, on pain of immediate dismission from their service.

7. We will use our utmost endeavors to improve the breed of sheep and increase their number to the greatest extent; and to that end, we will kill them as seldom as may be, especially those of the most profitable kind; nor will we export any to the West Indies or elsewhere; and those of us who are or may become overstocked with, or can conveniently spare any, sheep will dispose of them to our neighbors, especially to the poorer sort, on moderate terms.

8. We will, in our several stations, encourage frugality, economy, and industry, and promote agriculture, arts, and the manufactures of this country, especially that of wool; and will discountenance and discourage every species of extravagance and dissipation, especially all horse racing, and all kinds of gaming, cockfighting, exhibitions of shows, plays, and other expensive diversions and entertainments. And on the death of any relation or friend, none of us, or any of our families, will do into any further mourning dress than a black crape or ribbon on the arm or hat for gentlemen, and a black ribbon and necklace for ladies, and we will discontinue the giving of gloves and scarves at funerals.

9. Such as are vendors of goods or merchandise will not take advantage of the scarcity of goods that may be occasioned by this association, but will sell the same at the rates we have been respectively accustomed to do for twelve months last past. And if any vendor of goods or merchandise shall sell such goods on higher terms, or shall, in any manner or by any device whatsoever, violate or depart from this agreement, no person ought nor will any of us deal with any such person, or his or her factor or agent, at any time thereafter, for any commodity whatever.

10. In case any merchant, trader, or other person shall import any goods or merchandise after the 1st day of December and before the 1st day of February next, the same ought forthwith, at the election of the owner, to be either reshipped or delivered up to the committee of the country or town wherein they shall be imported, to be stored at the risk of the importer until the nonimportation agreement shall cease or be sold under the direction of the committee aforesaid. And in the last-mentioned case, the owner or owners of such goods shall be reimbursed out of the sales the first cost and charges, the profit, if any, to be applied toward relieving and employing such poor inhabitants of the town of Boston as are immediate sufferers by the Boston port bill; and a particular account of all goods so returned, stored, or sold to be inserted in the public papers. And if any goods or merchandise shall be imported after the said 1st day of February, the same ought forthwith to be sent back again, without breaking any of the packages thereof.

11. That a committee be chosen in every county, city, and town by those who are qualified to vote for representatives in the legislature, whose business it shall be attentively to observe the conduct of all persons touching this association. And when it shall be made to appear, to the satisfaction of a majority of any such committee, that any person within the limits of their appointment has violated this association, that such majority do forthwith cause the truth of the case to be published in the gazette; to the end that all such foes to the rights of British America may be publicly known and universally condemned as the enemies of American liberty; and thenceforth we respectively will break off all dealings with him or her.

12. That the Committee of Correspondence, in the respective colonies, do frequently inspect the entries of their custom houses, and inform each other, from time to time, of the true state thereof, and of every other material circumstance that may occur relative to this association.

13. That all manufactures of this country be sold at reasonable prices, so that no undue advantage be taken of a future scarcity of goods.

14. And we do further agree and resolve that we will have no trade, commerce, dealings, or intercourse

whatsoever with any colony or province in North America which shall not accede to, or which shall hereafter violate, this association, but will hold them as unworthy of the rights of freemen and as inimical to the liberties of their country.

And we do solemnly bind ourselves and our constituents, under the ties aforesaid, to adhere to this association until such parts of the several acts of Parliament passed since the close of the last war, as impose or continue duties on tea, wine, molasses, syrups, paneles, coffee, sugar, pimento, indigo, foreign paper, glass, and painters' colors imported into America, and extend the powers of the Admiralty Courts beyond their ancient limits, deprive the American subject of trial by jury, authorize the judge's certificate to indemnify the prosecutor from damages, that he might otherwise be liable to form a trial by his peers, require oppressive security from a claimant of ships or goods seized, before he shall be allowed to defend his property, are repealed.

And until that part of the act of the 12th of George III entitled "An act for the better securing His Majesty's dockyards, magazines, ships, ammunition, and stores," by which any persons charged with committing any of the offenses therein described, in America, may be tried in any shire or county within the Realm, is repealed; and until the four acts, passed the last session of Parliament, viz.: that for stopping the port and blocking up the harbor of Boston; that for altering the charter and government of the Massachusetts Bay; that which is entitled "An act for the better administration of justice, etc."; and that "for extending the limits of Quebec, etc.," are repealed. And we recommend it to the provincial conventions, and to the committees in the respective colonies, to establish such further regulations as they may think proper, for carrying into execution this association.

The foregoing association being determined upon by the Congress, was ordered to be subscribed by the several members thereof; and thereupon, we have hereunto set our respective names accordingly.

7. "YANKEE DOODLE," 1776

This tune antedated the American Revolution and was brought to America by British soldiers during the French and Indian War. British soldiers substituted the "Yankee Doodle" words to mock and deride the American soldiers—*Yankee* was a British nickname of contempt for New Englanders, and *doodle* meant "fool"

or "half-wit." The American soldiers, in turn, following the Battle of Bunker Hill, added their own words and transformed the song into a battle march. It was produced in many different broadside versions, some verses of which are incorporated here.

Father and I went down to camp
Along with Captain Gooding,
And there we saw the men and boys
As thick as hasty pudding.
    Yankee Doodle keep it up,
    Yankee Doodle Dandy,
    Mind the music and the step,
    And with the girls be handy.

And there we see a thousand men,
As rich as "Squire David;
And what they wasted every day,
I wish it could be saved.

There was Captain Washington
And gentlefolks about him,
They say he's grown so tarnal proud,
He will not ride without 'em.

He got him on his meeting clothes,
Upon a slapping stallion,
He set the world along in rows,
In hundreds and in millions.

Then I saw a swamping gun
As large as logs of maple
Upon a deuced little cart,
A load for father's cattle.

Every time they shot it off
It took a horn of powder
And made a noise like father's gun
Only a nation louder.

There I saw a wooden keg
With heads made out of leather;
They knocked upon it with some sticks
To call the folks together.

Then they'd fife away like fun
And play on cornstalk fiddles,
And some had ribbons red as blood
All bound around their middles.

I can't tell you all I saw—
They kept up such a smother.
I took my hat off, made a bow,
And scampered home to mother.

8. EXCERPT FROM THOMAS PAINE'S COMMON SENSE, JANUARY 9, 1776

Some writers have so confounded society with government, as to leave little or no distinction between them; whereas they are not only different, but have different origins. Society is produced by our wants and government by our wickedness; the former promotes our happiness *positively* by uniting our affections, the latter *negatively* by restraining our vices. The one encourages intercourse, the other creates distinctions. The first is a patron, the last a punisher.

Society in every state is a blessing, but government, even in its best state, is but a necessary evil; in its worst state an intolerable one; for when we suffer, or are exposed to the same miseries *by a government,* which we might expect in a country *without government,* our calamity is heightened by reflecting that we furnish the means by which we suffer. Government, like dress, is the badge of lost innocence; the palaces of kings are built upon the ruins of the bowers of paradise. . . .

. . . . .

Absolute governments, (though the disgrace of human nature) have this advantage with them, they are simple; if the people suffer, they know the head from which their suffering springs; know likewise the remedy; and are not bewildered by a variety of causes and cures. But the Constitution of England is so exceedingly complex, that the nation may suffer for years together without being able to discover in which part the fault lies; some will say in one and some in another, and every political physician will advise a different medicine.

I know it is difficult to get over local or longstanding prejudices, yet if we will suffer ourselves to examine the component parts of the English Constitution, we shall find them to be base remains of two ancient tyrannies, compounded with some new Republican materials.

First.—The remains of monarchical tyranny in the person of the king.

Secondly.—The remains of aristocratical tyranny in the persons of the peers.

Thirdly.—The new Republican materials, in the persons of the Commons, on whose virtue depends the freedom of England.

The two first, by being hereditary, are indendent of the people; wherefore in a *constitutional sense* they contribute nothing towards the freedom of the State.

To say that the Constitution of England is a union of three powers, reciprocally *checking* each other, is farcical; either the words have no meaning, or they are flat contradictions.

To say that the Commons is a check upon the king, presupposes two things.

First.—That the king is not to be trusted without being looked after; or in other words, that a thirst for absolute power is the natural disease of monarchy.

Secondly.—That the Commons, by being appointed for that purpose, are either wiser or more worthy of confidence than the crown.

But as the same constitution gives the Commons a power to check the king by withholding the supplies, gives afterwards the king the power to check the Commons, by empowering him to reject their other bills; it again supposes that the king is wiser than those whom it has already supposed to be wiser than him. A mere absurdity!

There is something exceedingly ridiculous in the composition of monarchy; it first excludes a man from the means of information, yet it empowers him to act in cases where the highest judgment is required. The state of a king shuts him from the world, yet the business of a king requires him to know it thoroughly; wherefore the different parts, by unnaturally opposing and destroying each other, prove the whole character to be absurd and useless.

. . . . .

To the evil of monarchy we have added that of hereditary succession; and as the first is a degradation and lessening of ourselves, so the second, claimed as a matter of right, is an insult and imposition on posterity. For all men being originally equals, no one by birth could have a right to set up his own family in perpetual preference to all others for ever, and though himself might deserve some decent degree of honors of his contemporaries, yet his descendants might be far too unworthy to inherit them. One of the strongest natural proofs of the folly of hereditary right in kings, is that nature disapproves it, otherwise she would not so frequently turn it into ridicule, by giving mankind an *ass for a lion.*

Secondly, as no man at first could possess any other public honors than were bestowed upon him, so the givers of those honors could have no power to give away the right of posterity, and though they might say "We choose for our head," they could not without manifest injustice to their children say "that your children and your children's children shall reign over ours forever." Because such an unwise, unjust, unnatural compact might (perhaps) in the next succession put them under the government of a rogue or a fool. Most wise men in their private sentiments have ever treated hereditary right with contempt; yet it is one of those evils which when once established is not easily removed; many submit from fear, others from superstition, and the more powerful part shares with the king the plunder of the rest.

. . . . .

THOUGHTS ON THE PRESENT STATE OF AMERICAN AFFAIRS

In the following pages I offer nothing more than simple facts, plain arguments, and common sense: and have no other preliminaries to settle with the reader, than that he will divest himself of prejudice and prepossessions, and suffer his reason and his feelings to determine for themselves: that he will put on, or rather that he will not put off, the true character of a man, and generously enlarge his views beyond the present day.

Volumes have been written on the subject of the struggle between England and America. Men of all ranks have embarked in the controversy, from different motives, and with various designs; but all have been ineffectual, and the period of debate is closed. Arms as the last resource decide the contest; the appeal was the choice of the king, and the continent has accepted the challenge.

. . . . .

The sun never shone on a cause of greater worth. 'Tis not the affair of a city, a country, a province, or a kingdom but of a continent—of at least one eighth part of the habitable globe. 'Tis not the concern of a day, a year, or an age; posterity are virtually involved in the contest, and will be more or less affected even to the end of time, by the proceedings now. Now is the seed-time of continental union, faith and honor. The least fracture now will be like a name engraved with the point of a pin on the tender rind of a young oak; the wound would enlarge with the tree, and posterity read it in full grown characters.

By referring the matter from argument to arms, a new era for politics is struck—a new method of thinking has arisen. All plans, proposals, &c. prior to the nineteenth of April, *i.e.* to the commencement of hostilities, are like the almanacs of the last year; which proper then, are superceded and useless now. Whatever was advanced by the advocates on either side of the question then, terminated in one and the same point, viz. A union with Great Britain; the only difference between the parties was the method of effecting it; the one proposing force, the other friendship; but it has so far happened that the first has failed, and the second has withdrawn her influence.

As much has been said of the advantages of reconciliation, which, like an agreeable dream, has passed away and left us as we were, it is but right that we should examine the contrary side of the argument, and inquire into some of the many material injuries which these colonies sustain, and always will sustain, by being connected with and dependant on Great Britain. To examine that connection and dependance, on the principles of nature and common sense, to see what we have to trust to, if separated, and what we are to expect if dependant.

I have heard it asserted by some, that as America has flourished under her former connection with Great Britain, the same connection is necessary towards her future happiness, and will always have the same effect. Nothing can be more fallacious than this kind of argument. We may as well assert that because a child has thrived upon milk, that it is never to have meat, or that the first twenty years of our lives is to become a precedent for the next twenty. But even this is admitting more than is true; for I answer roundly, that America would have flourished as much, and probably much more, had no European power taken any notice of her. The commerce by which she hath enriched herself are the necessaries of life, and will always have a market while eating is the custom of Europe.

But she has protected us, say some. That she hath engrossed us is true, and defended the continent at our expense as well as her own, is admitted; and she would have defended Turkey from the same motive, *viz.* for the sake of trade and dominion.

Alas! we have been long led away by ancient prejudices and made large sacrifices to superstition. We have boasted the protection of Great Britain, without considering, that her motive was *interest* not *attachment;* and that she did not protect us from *our enemies* on *our account;* but from *her enemies* on *her own account,* from those who had no quarrel with us on any *other account,* and who will always be our enemies on the *same account.* Let Britain waive her pretensions to the continent, or the continent throw off the dependance, and we should be at peace with France and Spain, were they at war with Britain. The miseries of Hanover's last war ought to warn us against connections.

. . . . .

But Britain is the parent country, say some. Then the more shame upon her conduct. Even brutes do not devour their young, nor savages make war upon their families; wherefore, the assertion, if true, turns to her reproach; but it happens not to be true, or only partly so, and the phrase *parent* or *mother country* hath been jesuitically adopted by the king and his parasites, with low papistical design of gaining an unfair bias on the credulous weakness of our minds. Europe, and not England, is the parent country of America. This new world hath been the asylum for the persecuted lovers of civil and religious liberty from *every part* of Europe. Hither have they fled, not from the tender embraces of the mother, but from the cruelty of the monster; and it is so far true of England, that the same tyranny which drove the first emigrants from home, pursues their descendants still.

. . . . .

Much hath been said of the united strength of Britain and the colonies, that in conjunction they might bid defiance to the world. But this is mere presumption; the fate of war is undertain, neither do the expressions mean any thing; for this continent would never suffer itself to be drained of inhabitants, to support the British arms in either Asia, Africa or Europe.

Besides, what have we to do with setting the world at defiance? Our plan is commerce, and that, well attended to, will secure us the peace and friendship of all Europe; because it is the interest of all Europe to have America a free port. Her trade will always be a protection, and her barrenness of gold and silver secure her from invaders.

I challenge the warmest advocate for reconciliation to show a single advantage that this continent can reap by being connected with Great Britain. I repeat the challenge; not a single advantage is derived. Our corn will fetch its price in any market in Europe, and our imported goods must be paid for buy them where we will.

But the injuries and disadvantages which we sustain by that connection, are without number; and our duty to mankind at large, as well as to ourselves, instruct us to renounce the alliance: because, any submission to, or dependence on, Great Britain, tends directly to involve this continent in European wars and quarrels, and set us at variance with nations who would otherwise seek our friendship, and against whom we have neither anger nor complaint. As Europe is our market for trade, we ought to form no partial connection with any part of it. It is the true interest of America to steer clear of European contentions, which she never can do, while, by her dependence on Britain, she is made the makeweight in the scale of British politics.

Europe is too thickly planted with kingdoms to be long at peace, and whenever a war breaks out between England and any foreign power, the trade of America goes to ruin, *because of her connection with Britain.* The next war may not turn out like the last, and should it not, the advocates for reconciliation now will be wishing for separation then, because neutrality in that case would be a safer convoy than a man of war. Everything that is right or reasonable pleads for separation. The blood of the slain, the weeping voice of nature cries, 'TIS TIME TO PART. Even the distance at which the Almighty hath placed England and America is a strong and natural proof that the authority of the one over the other, was never the design of heaven. The time likewise at which the continent was discovered, adds weight to the argument, and the manner in which it was peopled, increases the force of it. The Reformation was preceded by the discovery of America: As if the Almighty graciously meant to open a sanctuary to the persecuted in future years, when home should afford neither friendship nor safety.

The authority of Great Britain over this continent, is a form of government, which sooner or later must have an end. And a serious mind can draw no true pleasure by looking forward, under the painful and positive conviction that what he calls "the present constitution" is merely temporary. As parents, we can have no joy, knowing that this government is not sufficiently lasting to insure any thing which we may bequeath to posterity. And by a plain method of argument, as we are running the next generation into debt, we ought to do the work of it, otherwise we use them meanly and pitifully. In order to discover the line of our duty rightly, we should take our children in our hand, and fix our station a few years farther into life; that eminence will present a prospect which a few present fears and prejudices conceal from our sight.

Though I would carefully avoid giving unnecessary offence, yet I am inclined to believe, that all those who espouse the doctrine of reconciliation, may be included within the following descriptions.

Interested men, who are not to be trusted, weak men who *cannot* see, prejudiced men who will not see, and a certain set of moderate men who think better of the European world than it deserves; and this last class, by an ill-judged deliberation, will be the cause of more calamities to this continent than all the other three.

It is the good fortune of many to live distant from the scene of present sorrow; the evil is not sufficiently brought to their doors to make them feel the precariousness with which all American property is possessed. But let our imaginations transport us a few moments to Boston; that seat of wretchedness will teach us wisdom, and instruct us for ever to renounce a power in whom we can have no trust. The inhabitants of that unfortunate city who but a few months ago were in ease and affluence, have now no other alternative than to stay and starve, or turn out to beg. Endangered by the fire of their friends if they continue within the city, and plundered by the soldiery if they leave it, in their present situation they are prisoners without the hope of redemption, and in a general attack for their relief they would be exposed to the fury of both armies.

Men of passive tempers look somewhat lightly over the offences of Great Britain, and, still hoping for the best, are apt to call out, *Come, come, we shall be friends again for all this.* But examine the passions and feelings of mankind: bring the doctrine of reconciliation to the touchstone of nature, and then tell me whether you can hereafter love, honor, and faithfully serve the power that hath carried fire and sword into your land? If you cannot do all these, then are you only deceiving yourselves, and by your delay bringing ruin upon posterity. Your future connection with Britain, whom you can neither love nor honor, will be forced and unnatural, and being formed only on the plan of present convenience, will in a little time fall into a relapse more wretched than the first. But if you say, you can still pass the violations over, then I ask, hath your house been burnt? Hath your property been destroyed before your face? Are your wife and children destitute of a bed to lie on, or bread to live on? Have you lost a parent or a child by their hands, and yourself the ruined and wretched survivor? If you have not, then are you not a judge of those who have. But if you have, and can still shake hands with the murderers, then are you unworthy the name of husband, father, friend, or lover, and whatever may be your rank or title in life, you have the heart of a coward, and the spirit of a sycophant.

This is not inflaming or exaggerating matters, but trying them by those feelings and affections which nature justifies, and without which we should be incapable of discharging the social duties of life, or enjoying the felicities of it. I mean not to exhibit horror for the purpose of provoking revenge, but to awaken us from fatal and unmanly slumbers, that we may pursue determinately some fixed object. 'Tis not in the power of Britain or of Europe to conquer America, if she doth not conquer herself by delay and timidity. The present winter is worth an age if rightly employed, but if lost or neglected the whole continent will partake of the misfortune; and there is no punishment which that man doth not deserve, be he who, or what, or where he will, that may be the means of sacrificing a season so precious and useful.

'Tis repugnant to reason, to the universal order of things, to all examples from former ages, to suppose that this continent can long remain subject to any external power. The most sanguine in Britain doth not think so. The utmost stretch of human wisdom cannot, at this time, compass a plan, short of separation, which can promise the continent even a year's security. Reconciliation is *now* a fallacious dream. Nature has deserted the connection, and art cannot supply her place. For, as Milton wisely expresses, "never can true reconcilement grow where wounds of deadly hate have pierced so deep."

. . . . .

I am not induced by motives of pride, party or resentment to espouse the doctrine of separation and independence; I am clearly, positively, and conscientiously persuaded that it is the true interest of this continent to be so; that everything short of *that* is mere patchwork, that it can afford no lasting felicity,—that it is leaving the sword to our children, and shrinking back at a time when a little more, a little further, would have rendered this continent the glory of the earth.

As Britain hath not manifested the least inclination towards a compromise, we may be assured that no terms can be obtained worthy the acceptance of the continent, or any ways equale to the expence of blood and treasure we have been already put to.

The object contended for, ought always to bear proportion to the expense. The removal of North, or the whole detestable junto, is a matter unworthy the millions we have expended. A temporary stoppage of trade was an inconvenience, which would have sufficiently balanced the repeal of all acts complained of, had such repeals been obtained; but if the whole continent must take up arms, if every man must be a soldier, 'tis scarcely worth our while to fight against a contemptible ministry only. Dearly, dearly do we pay for the repeal of the acts, if that is all we fight for; for, in a just estimation 'tis as great a folly to pay a Bunker Hill price for law as for land. As I have always considered the independency of this continent, as an event which sooner or later must arrive, so from the late rapid progress of the continent to maturity, the event cannot be far off. Wherefore, on the breaking out of hostilities, it was not worth the while to have disputed a matter which time would have finally redressed, unless we meant to be in earnest: otherwise it is like wasting an estate on a suit at law, to regulate the trespasses of a tenant whose lease is just expiring. No man was a warmer wisher for a reconciliation than myself, before the fatal nineteenth of April, 1775, but the moment the event of that day was made known, I rejected the hardened, sullen-tempered Pharaoh of England for ever; and disdain the wretch, that with the pretended title of FATHER OF HIS PEOPLE can unfeelingly hear of their slaughter, and composedly sleep with their blood upon his soul.

But admitting that matters were now made up, what would be the event? I answer, the ruin of the continent. And that for several reasons.

First. The powers of governing still remaining in the hands of the king, he will have a negative over the whole legislation of this continent. And as he hath shown himself such an inveterate enemy to liberty, and discovered such a thirst for arbitrary power, is he, or is he not, a proper person to say to these colonies, *You shall make no laws but what I please!?* And is there any inhabitant of America so ignorant as not to know, that according to what is called the *present Constitution,* this continent can make no laws but what the king gives leave to; and is there any man so unwise as not to see, that (considering what has happened) he will suffer no laws to be made here but such as suits *his* purpose? We may be as effectually enslaved by the want of laws in America, as by submitting to laws made for us in England. After matters are made up (as it is called) can there be any doubt, but the whole power of the crown will be exerted to keep this continent as low and humble as possible? Instead of going forward we shall go backward, or be perpetually quarrelling, or ridiculously petitioning. We are already greater than the king wishes us to be, and will he not hereafter endeavor to make us less? To bring the matter to one point, Is the power who is jealous of our prosperity, a proper power to govern us? Whoever says *No,* to this question, is an independent for independency means no more than this, whether we shall make our own laws, or, whether the king, the greatest enemy this continent hath, or can have, shall tell us *there shall be no laws but such as I like.*

But the king, you will say, has a negative in England; the people there can make no laws without his consent. In point of right and good order, it is something very ridiculous that a youth of twenty-one (which hath often happened) shall say to several millions of people older and wiser than himself, "I forbid this or that act of yours to be law." But in this place I decline this sort of reply, though I will never cease to expose the absurdity of it, and only answer that England being the king's residence, and America not so, makes quite another case. The king's negative here is ten times more dangerous and fatal than it can be in England; for there he will scarcely refuse his consent to a bill putting England into as strong a state of defense as possible, and in America he would never suffer such a bill to be passed.

America is only a secondary object in the system of British politics. England consults the good of this country no further than it answers her own purpose. Wherefore, her own interest leads her to suppress the growth of ours in every case which doth not promote her advantage, or in the least interferes with it. A pretty state we should soon be in under such a second hand government, considering what has happened! Men do not change from enemies to friends by the alteration of a name: And in order to show that reconciliation now is a dangerous doctrine, I affirm, *that it would be policy in the king at this time to repeal the acts, for the sake of reinstating himself in the government of the provinces;* In order that HE MAY ACCOMPLISH BY CRAFT AND SUBTLETY, IN THE LONG RUN, WHAT HE CANNOT DO BY FORCE AND VIOLENCE IN THE SHORT ONE. Reconciliation and ruin are nearly related.

Secondly. That as even the best terms which we can expect to obtain can amount to no more than a temporary expedient, or a kind of government by guardianship, which can last no longer than till the colonies come of age, so the general face and state of things in the interim will be unsettled and unpromising. Emigrants of property will not choose to come to a country whose form of government hangs but by a thread, and who is every day tottering on the brink of commotion and disturbance; and numbers of the present inhabitants would lay hold of the interval to dispose of their effects, and quit the continent.

But the most powerful of all arguments is, that nothing but independence, *i.e.* a continental form of government, can keep the peace of the continent and preserve it inviolate from civil wars. I dread the event of a reconciliation with Britain now, as it is more than probable that it will be followed by a revolt some where or other, the consequences of which may be far more fatal than all the malice of Britain.

. . . . .

But where, say some, is the king of America? I'll tell you, friend, he reigns above, and doth not make havoc of mankind like the royal brute of Great Britain. Yet that we may not appear to be defective even in earthly honors, let a day be solemnly set apart for proclaiming the charter; let it be brought forth placed on the divine law, the Word of God; let a crown be placed thereon, by which the world may know, that so far as we approve of monarchy, that in America the law is king. For as in absolute governments the king is law, so in free countries the law ought to be king; and there ought to be no other. But lest any ill use should afterwards arise, let the crown at the conclusion of the ceremony be demolished, and scattered among the people whose right it is.

A government of our own is our natural right: and when a man seriously reflects on the precariousness of human affairs, he will become convinced, that it is infinitely wiser and safer, to form a Constitution of our own in a cool deliberate manner, while we have

it in our power, than to trust such an interesting to time and chance. If we omit it now, some Massanello may hereafter arise, who, laying hold of popular disquietudes, may collect together the desperate and the discontented, and by assuming to themselves the powers of government, finally sweep away the liberties of the continent like a deluge. Should the government of America return again into the hands of Britain, the tottering situation of things will be a temptation for some desperate adventurer to try his fortune; and in such a case, what relief can Britain give? Ere she could hear the news, the fatal business might be done; and ourselves suffering like the wretched Britons under the oppression of the conqueror. Ye that oppose independance now, ye know not what ye do: ye are opening a door to eternal tyranny, by keeping vacant the seat of government. There are thousands and tens of thousands, who would think it glorious to expel from the continent, that barbarous and hellish power, which hath stirred up the indians and negroes to destroy us; the cruelty hath a double guilt, it is dealing brutally by us, and treacherously by them.

To talk of friendship with those in whom our reason forbids us to have faith, and our affections wounded through a thousand pores instruct us to detest, is madness and folly. Every day wears out the little remains of kindred between us and them; and can there be any reason to hope, that as the relationship expires, the affection will increase, or that we shall agree better when we have ten times more and greater concerns to quarrel over than ever?

Ye that tell us of harmony and reconciliation, can ye restore to us the time that is past? Can ye give to prostitution its former innocence? Neither can ye reconcile Britain and America. The last cord now is broken, the people of England are presenting addresses against us. There are injuries which nature cannot forgive; she would cease to be nature if she did. As well can the lover forgive the ravisher of his mistress, as the continent forgive the murders of Britain. The Almighty hath implanted in us these inextinguishable feelings for good and wise purposes. They are the guardians of his image in our hearts. They distinguish us from the herd of common animals. The social compact would dissolve, and justice be extirpated from the earth, or have only a casual existence were we callous to the touches of affection. The robber and the murderer would often escape unpunished, did not the injuries which our tempers sustain, provoke us into justice.

O! Ye that love mankind! Ye that dare oppose not only the tyranny but the tyrant, stand forth! Every spot of the old world is overrun with oppression. Freedom hath been hunted round the globe. Asia and Africa have long expelled her. Europe regards her like a stranger, and England hath given her warning to depart. O! Receive the fugitive, and prepare in time an asylum for mankind.

. . . . .

TO CONCLUDE, however strange it may appear to some, or however unwilling they may be to think so, matters not, but many strong and striking reasons may be given to show, that nothing can settle our affairs so expeditiously as an open and determined DECLARATION FOR INDEPENDENCE. Some of which are,

First—It is the custom of nations, when any two are at war, for some other powers, not engaged in the quarrel, to step in as mediators, and bring about the preliminaries of a peace: But while America calls herself the subject of Great Britain, no power, however well disposed she may be, can offer her mediation. Wherefore, in our present state we may quarrel on for ever.

Secondly—It is unreasonable to suppose, that France or Spain will give us any kind of assistance, if we mean only to make use of that assistance for the purpose of repairing the breach, and strengthening the connection between Britain and America; because, those powers would be sufferers by the consequences.

Thirdly—While we profess ourselves the subjects of Britain, we must, in the eyes of foreign nations, be considered as Rebels. The precedent is somewhat dangerous to their peace, for men to be in arms under the name of subjects: we, on the spot, can solve the paradox; but to unite resistance and subjection, requires an idea much too refined for common understanding.

Fourthly—Were a manifesto to be published, and despatched to foreign courts, setting forth the miseries we have endured, and the peaceful methods which we have ineffectually used for redress; declaring at the same time, that not being able any longer to live happily or safely under the cruel disposition of the British court, we had been driven to the necessity of breaking off all connections with her; at the same time, assuring all such courts of our peaceable disposition towards them, and of our desire of entering into trade with them: such a memorial would produce more good effects to this continent, than if a ship were freighted with petitions to Britain.

Under our present denomination of British subjects, we can neither be received nor heard abroad: the custom of all courts is against us, and will be so, until by an independence we take rank with other nations.

These proceedings may at first seem strange and difficult, but like all other steps which we have already passed over, will in a little time become familiar and agreeable: and until an independence is declared, the continent will feel itself like a man who continues putting off some unpleasant business from day to day, yet knows it must be done, hates to set about it, wishes it over, and is continually haunted with the thoughts of its necessity.

9. THE DECLARATION OF INDEPENDENCE, JULY 4, 1776

When, in the course of human events, it becomes necessary for one people to dissolve the political bands which have connected them to another, and to assume, among the powers of the earth, the separate and equal station to which the laws of nature and of nature's God entitle them, a decent respect to the opinions of mankind requires that they should declare the causes which impel them to the separation.

We hold these truths to be self-evident, that all men are created equal, that they are endowed by their Creator with certain unalienable rights, that among these are life, liberty, and the pursuit of happiness. That, to secure these rights, governments are instituted among men, deriving their just powers from the consent of the governed. That, whenever any form of government becomes destructive of these ends, it is the right of the people to alter or to abolish it, and to institute new government, laying its foundation on such principles, and organizing its powers in such form, as to them shall seem most likely to effect their safety and happiness.

Prudence, indeed, will dictate that governments long established should not be changed for light or transient causes; and, accordingly, all experience has shown, that mankind are more disposed to suffer, while evils are sufferable, than to right themselves by abolishing the forms to which they are accustomed.

But, when a long train of abuses and usurpations, pursuing invariably the same object, evinces a design to reduce them under absolute despotism, it is their right, it is their duty, to throw off such government, and to provide new guards for their future security. Such has been the patient suffering of these colonies; and such is now the necessity which constrains them to alter their former systems of government. The history of the present King of Great Britain is a history of repeated injuries and usurpations, all having in direct object the establishment of an absolute tyranny over these states. To prove this, let the facts be submitted to a candid world.

He has refused his assent to laws the most wholesome and necessary for the public good.

He has forbidden his governors to pass laws of immediate and pressing importance, unless suspended in their operation till his assent should be obtained; and when so suspended, he has utterly neglected to attend to them.

He has refused to pass laws for the accommodation of large districts of people, unless those people would relinquish the right to representation in the legislature; a right estimable to them and formidable to tyrants only.

He has called together legislative bodies at places unusual, uncomfortable, and distant from the depository of their public records, for the sole purpose of fatiguing them into compliance with his measures.

He has dissolved representative houses repeatedly, for opposing, with manly firmness, his invasions on the rights of the people.

He has refused for a long time, after such dissolutions, to cause others to be elected; whereby the legislative powers, incapable of annihilation, have returned to the people at large for their exercise; the state remaining in the meantime exposed to all dangers of invasion from without, and convulsions within.

He has endeavored to prevent the population of these states; for that purpose obstructing the laws for naturalization of foreigners; refusing to pass others to encourage their migrations hither, and raising the conditions of new appropriations of lands.

He has obstructed the administration of justice, by refusing his assent to laws for establishing judiciary powers.

He has made judges dependent on his will alone, for the tenure of their offices, and the amount and payment of their salaries.

He has erected a multitude of new offices, and sent hither swarms of officers to harass our people, and eat out their substance.

He has kept among us, in times of peace, standing armies, without the consent of our legislatures.

He has affected to render the military independent of and superior to the civil power.

He has combined with others to subject us to a jurisdiction foreign to our constitution, and unacknowledged by our laws; giving his assent to their acts of pretended legislation:

For quartering large bodies of armed troops among us;

For protecting them, by a mock trial, from punishment for any murders which they should commit on the inhabitants of these states;

For cutting off our trade with all parts of the world;

For imposing taxes on us without our consent;

For depriving us, in many cases, of the benefits of trial by jury;

For transporting us beyond seas to be tried for pretended offenses;

For abolishing the free system of English laws in a neighboring province, establishing therein an arbitrary government, and enlarging its boundaries, so as to render it at once an example and fit instrument for introducing the same absolute rule into these colonies;

For taking away our charters, abolishing our most valuable laws, and altering fundamentally the forms of our governments;

For suspending our own legislatures, and declaring themselves invested with power to legislate for us in all cases whatsoever.

He has abdicated government here, by declaring us out of his protection, and waging war against us.

He has plundered our seas, ravaged our coasts, burnt our towns, and destroyed the lives of our people.

He is at this time transporting large armies of foreign mercenaries to complete the works of death, desolation, and tyranny, already begun with circumstances of cruelty and perfidy scarcely paralleled in the most barbarous ages, and totally unworthy the head of a civilized nation.

He has constrained our fellow citizens, taken captive on the high seas, to bear arms against their country, to become the executioners of their friends and brethren, or to fall themselves by their hands.

He has excited domestic insurrections amongst us, and has endeavored to bring on the inhabitants of our frontiers, the merciless Indian savages, whose known rule of warfare is an undistinguished destruction of all ages, sexes, and conditions.

In every stage of these oppressions, we have petitioned for redress, in the most humble terms. Our repeated petitions have been answered only by repeated injury. A prince, whose character is thus marked by every act which may define a tyrant, is unfit to be the ruler of a free people.

Nor have we been wanting in attentions to our British brethren. We have warned them from time to time of attempts by their legislature to extend unwarrantable jurisdiction over us. We have reminded them of the circumstances of our emigration and settlement here. We have appealed to their native justice and magnanimity, and we have conjured them by the ties of our common kindred, to disavow these usurpations, which would inevitably interrupt our connections and correspondence. They too have been deaf to the voice of justice and of consanguinity. We must, therefore, acquiesce in the necessity, which denounces our separation, and hold them, as we hold the rest of mankind, enemies in war, in peace friends.

We, therefore, the representatives of the United States of America, in General Congress assembled, appealing to the Supreme Judge of the world for the rectitude of our intentions, do, in the name, and by authority of the good people of these colonies, solemnly publish and declare, that these United Colonies are, and of right ought to be free and independent states; that they are absolved from all allegiance to the British Crown, and that all political connection between them and the state of Great Britain is and ought to be totally dissolved; and that, as free and independent states, they have full power to levy war, conclude peace, contract alliances, establish commerce, and to do all other acts and things which independent states may of right do. And for the support of this declaration, with a firm reliance on the protection of Divine Providence, we mutually pledge to each other our lives, our fortunes, and our sacred honor.

10. The Articles of Confederation, Adopted November 1777, in Effect 1781

Articles of Confederation and Perpetual Union Between the States of New Hampshire, Massachusetts Bay, Rhode Island and Providence Plantations, Connecticut, New York, New Jersey, Pennsylvania, Delaware, Maryland, Virginia, North Carolina, South Carolina, and Georgia.

Article I.

The style of this confederacy shall be "The United States of America."

Article II.

Each state retains its sovereignty, freedom, and independence, and every power, jurisdiction, and right which is not by this confederation expressly delegated to the United States in Congress assembled.

Article III.

The said states hereby severally enter into a firm league of friendship with each other, for their common defense, the security of their liberties, and their mutual and general welfare, binding themselves to assist each other against all force offered to, or attacks made upon them, or any of them, on account of religion, sovereignty, trade, or any other pretense whatever.

Article IV.

The better to secure and perpetuate mutual friendship and intercourse among the people of the different states in this union, the free inhabitants of each of these states, paupers, vagabonds, and fugitives from justice excepted, shall be entitled to all privileges and immunities of free citizens in the several states; and the people of each state shall have free ingress and regress to and from any other state and shall enjoy therein all the privileges of trade and commerce, subject to the same duties, impositions, and restrictions as the inhabitants thereof respectively, provided that such restrictions shall not extend so far as to prevent the removal of property imported into any state, to any other state of which the owner is an inhabitant; provided also that no imposition, duties, or restriction shall be laid by any state on the property of the United States, or either of them.

If any person guilty of or charged with treason, felony, or other high misdemeanor in any state shall flee from justice, and be found in any of the United States, he shall, upon demand of the governor or executive power of the state from which he fled, be delivered up and removed to the state having jurisdiction of his offense.

Full faith and credit shall be given in each of these states to the records, acts, and judicial proceedings of the courts and magistrates of every other state.

Article V.

For the more convenient management of the general interests of the United States, delegates shall be annually appointed in such manner as the legislature of each state shall direct, to meet in Congress on the first Monday in November, in every year, with a power reserved to each state to recall its delegates, or any of them, at any time within the year and to send others in their stead for the remainder of the year.

No state shall be represented in Congress by less than two nor more than seven members; and no person shall be capable of being a delegate for more than three years in any term of six years; nor shall any person, being a delegate, be capable of holding any office under the United States for which he, or another for his benefit, receives any salary, fees, or emolument of any kind.

Each state shall maintain its own delegates in a meeting of the states and while they act as members of the Committee of the States.

In determining questions in the United States in Congress assembled, each state shall have one vote.

Freedom of speech and debate in Congress shall not be impeached or questioned in any court or place out of Congress, and the members of Congress shall be protected in their persons from arrests and imprisonments during the time of their going to and from, and attendance on, Congress, except for treason, felony, or breach of the peace.

Article VI.

No state, without the consent of the United States in Congress assembled, shall send any embassy to, or receive any embassy from, or enter into any conference, agreement, alliance, or treaty with any king, prince, or state; nor shall any person holding any office of profit or trust under the United States, or any of them, accept of any present, emolument, office, or title of any kind whatever from any king, prince, or foreign state; nor shall the United States in Congress assembled, or any of them, grant any title of nobility.

No two or more states shall enter into any treaty, confederation, or alliance whatever between them without the consent of the United States in Congress assembled, specifying accurately the purposes for which the same is to be entered into and how long it shall continue.

No state shall lay any imposts or duties which may interfere with any stipulations in treaties entered into by the United States in Congress assembled with

any king, prince, or state, in pursuance of any treaties already proposed by Congress, to the courts of France and Spain.

No vessels of war shall be kept up in time of peace by any state except such number as shall be deemed necessary by the United States in Congress assembled for the defense of such state or its trade; nor shall any body of forces be kept up by any state in time of peace except such number only as in the judgment of the United States in Congress assembled shall be deemed requisite to garrison the forts necessary for the defense of such state; but every state shall always keep up a well-regulated and disciplined militia, sufficiently armed and accoutered, and shall provide and constantly have ready for use, in public stores, a due number of field pieces and tents and a proper quantity of arms, ammunition, and camp equipage.

No state shall engage in any war without the consent of the United States in Congress assembled unless such state be actually invaded by enemies, or shall have received certain advice of a resolution being formed by some nation of Indians to invade such state, and the danger is so imminent as not to admit of a delay till the United States in Congress assembled can be consulted; nor shall any state grant commissions to any ships or vessels of war, nor letters of marque or reprisal, except it be after a declaration of war by the United States in Congress assembled, and then only against the kingdom or state and the subjects thereof against which war has been so declared and under such regulations as shall be established by the United States in Congress assembled, unless such state be infested by pirates, in which case vessels of war may be fitted out for that occasion and kept so long as the danger shall continue or until the United States in Congress assembled shall determine otherwise.

Article VII.

When land forces are raised by any state for the common defense, all officers of or under the rank of colonel shall be appointed by the legislature of each state respectively, by whom such forces shall be raised, or in such manner as such state shall direct, and all vacancies shall be filled up by the state which first made the appointment.

Article VIII.

All charges of war and all other expenses that shall be incurred for the common defense or general welfare, and allowed by the United States in Congress assembled, shall be defrayed out of a common treasury, which shall be supplied by the several states in proportion to the value of all land within each state, granted to or surveyed for any person, as such land the buildings and improvements thereon shall be estimated according to such mode as the United States in Congress assembled shall from time to time direct and appoint. The taxes for paying that proportion shall be laid and levied by the authority and direction of the legislatures of the several states within the time agreed upon by the United States in Congress assembled.

Article IX.

The United States in Congress assembled shall have the sole and exclusive right and power of determining on peace and war, except in the cases mentioned in the sixth article—of sending and receiving ambassadors—entering into treaties and alliances, provided that no treaty of commerce shall be made whereby the legislative power of the respective states shall be restrained from imposing such imports and duties on foreigners as their own people are subjected to or from prohibiting the exportation or importation of any species of goods or commodities whatsoever—of establishing rules for deciding in all cases what captures on land or water shall be legal, and in what manner prizes taken by land or naval forces in the service of the United States shall be divided or appropriated—of granting letters of marque and reprisal in times of peace—appointing courts for the trial of piracies and felonies committed on the high seas and establishing courts for receiving and determining finally appeals in all cases of captures, provided that no member of Congress shall be appointed a judge of any of the said courts.

The United States in Congress assembled shall also be the last resort on appeal in all disputes and difference now subsisting or that hereafter may arise between two or more states concerning boundary, jurisdiction, or any other cause whatever, which authority shall always be exercised in the manner following: Whenever the legislative or executive authority or lawful agent of any state in controversy with another shall present a petition to Congress stating the matter in question and praying for a hearing, notice thereof shall be given by order of Congress to the legislative or executive authority of the other state in controversy, and a day assigned for the appearance of the parties by their lawful agents, who shall then be directed to appoint, by joint consent, commissioners or judges to constitute a court for hearing and determining the matter in question. But if they cannot agree, Congress shall name three persons out of each of the United States, and from the list of such persons each party shall alternately strike out one, the petitioners beginning, until the number shall be reduced to thirteen. And from that number not less than seven nor more than nine names, as Congress shall direct, shall in the presence of Congress be drawn out by lot, and the persons whose names shall be drawn, or any five of them, shall be commissioners or judges to hear and finally determine the controversy, so always as a major part of the judges who shall hear the cause shall agree in the determination. . . .

If either party shall neglect to attend at the day appointed, without showing reasons, which Congress shall judge sufficient, or being present shall refuse to strike, the Congress shall proceed to nominate three persons out of each state, and the secretary of Congress shall strike in behalf of such party absent or refusing. . . . The judgment and sentence of the court to be appointed, in the manner before prescribed, shall be final and conclusive. . . . If any of the parties shall refuse to submit to the authority of such court, or to appear or defend their claim or cause, the court shall nevertheless proceed to pronounce sentence or judgment, which shall in like manner be final and decisive, the judgment or sentence and other proceedings being in either case transmitted to Congress and lodged among the acts of Congress for the security of the parties concerned. Provided that every commissioner, before he sits in judgment, shall take an oath to be administered by one of the supreme or superior court of the state where the cause shall be tried, "well and truly to hear and determine the matter in question, according to the best of his judgment, without favor, affection, or hope of reward": provided, also, that no state shall be deprived of territory for the benefit of the United States.

All controversies concerning the private right of soil claimed under different grants of two or more states, whose jurisdictions as they may respect such lands, and the states which passed such grants are adjusted, the said grants or either of them being at the same time claimed to have originated antecedent to such settlement of jurisdiction shall, on the petition of either party to the Congress of the United States, be finally determined as near as may be in the same manner as is before prescribed for deciding disputes respecting territorial jurisdiction between different states.

The United States in Congress assembled shall also have sole and exclusive right and power of regulating the alloy and value of coin struck by their own authority or by that of the respective states—fixing the standard of weights and measures throughout the United States—regulating the trade and managing all affairs with the Indians not members of any of the states, provided that the legislative right of any state within its own limits be not infringed or violated—establishing or regulating post offices from one state to another, throughout all the United States, and exacting such postage on the papers passing through the same as may be requisite to defray the expenses of the said office—appointing all officers of the land forces in the service of the United States excepting regimental officers—appointing all the officers of the naval forces, and commissioning all officers whatever in the service of the United States—making rules for the government and regulation of the said land and naval forces, and directing their operations.

The United States in Congress assembled shall have authority to appoint a committee, to sit in the recess of Congress, to be denominated "A Committee of the States," and to consist of one delegate from each state; and to appoint such other committees and civil officers as may be necessary for managing the general affairs of the United States under their direction—to appoint one of their number to preside, provided that no person be allowed to serve in the office of President more than one year in any term of three years; to ascertain the necessary sums of money to be raised for the service of the United States, and to appropriate and apply the same for defraying the public expenses—to borrow money or emit bills on the credit of the United States, transmitting every half-year to the respective states an account of the sums of money so borrowed or emitted—to build and equip a navy—to agree upon the number of land forces, and to make requisitions from each state for its quota, in proportion to the number of white inhabitants in such state, which requisition shall be binding. . . .

Thereupon the legislature of each state shall appoint the regimental officers, raise the men and clothe, arm, and equip them in a soldier-like manner, at the expense of the United States; and the officers and men so clothed, armed, and equipped shall march to the place appointed and within the time agreed on by the United States in Congress assembled. But if the United States in Congress assembled shall, on consideration of circumstances, judge proper that any state should not raise men or should raise a smaller number than its quota and that any other state should raise a greater number of men than the quota thereof, such extra number shall be raised, officered, clothed, armed, and equipped in the same manner as the quota of such state, unless the legislature of such state shall judge that such extra number cannot be safely spared out of the same, in which case they shall raise, officer, clothe, arm, and equip as many of such extra number as they judge can be safely spared. And the officers and men so clothed, armed, and equipped shall march to the place appointed and within the time agreed on by the United States in Congress assembled.

The United States in Congress assembled shall never engage in a war, nor grant letters of marque and reprisal in time of peace, nor enter into any treaties or alliances, nor coin money, nor regulate the value thereof, nor ascertain the sums and expenses necessary for the defense and welfare of the United States, or any of them, nor emit bills, nor borrow money on the credit of the United States, nor appropriate money, nor agree upon the number of vessels of war to be built or purchased or the number of land or sea forces to be raised, nor appoint a commander in chief of the Army or Navy, unless nine states assent to the same; nor shall a question on any other point, except for adjourning from day to day, be determined unless by the votes of a majority of the United States in Congress assembled.

The Congress of the United States shall have power to adjourn to any time within the year, and to any place within the United States, so that no period of adjournment be for longer duration than the space of six months, and shall publish the journal of their proceedings monthly, except such parts thereof relating to treaties, alliances, or military operations as in their judgment require secrecy; and the yeas and nays of the delegates of each state on any question shall be entered on the journal when it is desired by any delegate; and the delegates of a state, or any of them, at his or their request, shall be furnished with a transcript of the said journal, except such parts as are above excepted, to lay before the legislatures of the several states.

Article X.

The Committee of the States, or any nine of them, shall be authorized to execute, in the recess of Congress, such of the powers of Congress as the United States in Congress assembled, by the consent of nine states, shall from time to time think expedient to vest with them; provided that no power be delegated to the said committee, for the exercise of which, by the Articles of Confederation, the voice of nine states in the Congress of the United States assembled is requisite.

Article XI.

Canada acceding to this Confederation, and joining in the measures of the United States, shall be admitted into and entitled to all the advantages of this union; but no other colony shall be admitted into the same unless such admission be agreed to by nine states.

Article XII.

All bills of credit emitted, moneys borrowed, and debts contracted by or under the authority of Congress, before the assembling of the United States, in pursuance of the present Confederation, shall be deemed and considered as a charge against the United States, for payment and satisfaction whereof the said United States and the public faith are hereby solemnly pledged.

Article XIII.

Every state shall abide by the determinations of the United States in Congress assembled on all questions which by this Confederation are submitted to them.

And the Articles of this Confederation shall be inviolably observed by every state, and the union shall be perpetual; nor shall any alteration at any time hereafter be made in any of them; unless such alteration be agreed to in a Congress of the United States and be afterward confirmed by the legislature of every state.

And whereas it has pleased the Great Governor of the world to incline the hearts of the legislatures we respectively represent in Congress to approve of, and to authorize us to ratify the said Articles of Confederation and Perpetual Union. Know ye that we the undersigned delegates, by virtue of the power and authority to us given for that purpose, do by these presents, in the name and in behalf of our respective constituents, fully and entirely ratify and confirm each and every of the said Articles of Confederation and Perpetual Union and all and singular the matters and things therein contained. And we do further solemnly plight and engage the faith of our respective constituents that they shall abide by the determinations of the United States in Congress assembled on all questions which by the said Confederation are submitted to them. And that the articles thereof shall be inviolably observed by the states we respectively represent and that the union shall be perpetual. In witness whereof we have hereunto set our hands in Congress.

APPENDIX B
Biographies of Major Personalities

Adams, Abigail (1744–1818) *wife of John Adams*
Born in Weymouth, Massachusetts, she had a limited formal education but was well read and knowledgeable. She and John Adams, a lawyer practicing in Braintree (now Quincy) and Boston, met in 1758 and married in 1764. They had five children, including John Quincy. In 1774, John left for Philadelphia to serve in the Continental Congress, remaining there for 10 years through the Revolutionary War. During their separation, Abigail managed the family's farm and business and wrote prolific letters to her husband that greatly influenced his views on political and social issues. Following the Revolutionary War, she accompanied John to Europe, where he served as American emissary in France, Great Britain, and Holland. After John's election to the vice presidency and then to the presidency, she lived alternatively in the seat of government and Massachusetts. She was the first wife of a president to live in the official residence in Washington but only for a few months before his leaving office in 1800, when they returned to Massachusetts. She continued managing the family's affairs and writing letters to family members and friends. Her letters comprise a record of invaluable commentary on the Revolutionary War and early republic periods.

Adams, John (1735–1826) *statesman, member of Continental Congress, diplomat, president*
Born in Braintree (now Quincy), Massachusetts, Adams graduated from Harvard in 1755 and then taught in Worcester. He studied law and was admitted to the bar in Boston in 1758. He married Abigail Smith (*see* Adams, Abigail) in 1764. In 1765, he emerged as a leader of American opposition to British policies and allied himself with other prominent patriots. In his writings, he advocated views that eventually led him to support independence. Elected a delegate to the first Continental Congress in 1774, he drafted a declara-

tion of rights and moved increasingly toward advocating independence. During the Second Continental Congress, he formed close ties with delegates from the southern colonies, was appointed in June 1776 to the committee that drafted the Declaration of Independence, and proved instrumental in securing the declaration's approval. He left Congress in late 1776, returned the following February, left again in November 1777, and then accepted appointment as a diplomat. He sailed for France with his 10-year-old son, John Quincy, as his clerk in February 1778 to join the American commission to that nation. Adams returned to Massachusetts in 1779, drafted the constitution adopted by the state convention, and then returned again to France. Adams, Benjamin Franklin, and John Jay negotiated the 1783 Treaty of Paris that ended the revolution. In 1785, Adams was appointed minister to Great Britain. In 1789, he was selected as the United States's first vice president, and in 1796, he was elected the second president but served only one term, losing to Thomas Jefferson in the 1800 election. Adams returned to Braintree and devoted himself to study and writing. He and Jefferson both died on July 4, 1826, the 50th anniversary of the Declaration of Independence that they had both helped to draft.

Adams, Samuel (1722–1803) *firebrand revolutionary, delegate to the Continental Congress*
Born in Boston, where his father was a prosperous merchant and brewer, Adams attended Harvard but failed in business and career pursuits, spending most of his life in debt. But he proved a masterful propagandist and political organizer and was the primary leader of the Patriot opposition in Massachusetts during the 10 years leading to the revolution. Adams was the driving force of the opposition to the Stamp Act and the Townshend Acts in Boston, where he helped to organize the Sons of Liberty. He was a relentless advocate

of the rights of the colonists in the ongoing controversies over British taxes and oppression, leading the fight against paying the duty on tea that eventuated in the Boston Tea Party. He was selected as a delegate to the First and Second Continental Congresses, but his influence rapidly declined after 1775. He held varied public offices in Massachusetts, was elected governor in 1793, and died in Boston.

Alexander, William (Lord Stirling) (1726–1783) *major general in the Continental army*

Born in New York to an affluent merchant family, Alexander was of aristocratic background and was socially ambitious but somewhat dissolute. He lived in Great Britain from 1756 until 1761, unsuccessfully claimed the lapsed title of the earl of Stirling, but would designate himself Lord Stirling for the remainder of his life. Returned to America, he squandered his fortune and disdained the revolutionary movement, but in 1774, he declared himself a Patriot and received command of the New Jersey militia. Alexander's troops joined the Continental army in New York in 1776, and Washington appointed him brigadier general. Although his force fought well during the Battle of Long Island, they were surrounded, and Alexander was captured. Exchanged a few months later, he again was given command of a brigade. His command served at Trenton and throughout the New Jersey campaign. He became a major general in February 1777 and commanded major segments of the army at Brandywine, Germantown, and Monmouth. Alexander served as commander in chief during Washington's absences to confer with Congress and also presided at Charles Lee's court-martial. His health began to fail in 1782, and he died of severe gout in January 1783.

Allen, Ethan (1738–1789) *major general of Vermont militia, brevet colonel in the Continental army*

Allen was born in Litchfield, Connecticut, but his life centered in Vermont, then known as the New Hampshire Grants, an area in dispute between New Hampshire and New York. Allen formed a vigilante militia called the Green Mountain Boys that by 1774 effectively ruled the area. Following news of Lexington and Concord, Allen led his men in a successful surprise attack on Fort Ticonderoga on May 10, 1776. He secured the Continental Congress's approval to have the Green Mountain Boys subsumed into the Continental army, but he was then voted out of command. Allen joined Gen. Philip Schuyler's army. Captured at Montreal, he was detained in an English prison and then exchanged in May 1778. He received a commission as brevet colonel in the Continental army but returned to Vermont, where he regained his influence and accepted a commission as major general in the militia. Allen worked hard to gain Vermont's recognition as a separate state, failed to secure Congress's approval, and unsuccessfully plotted to turn Vermont over to British control. His subsequent focus was on business and writing.

André, John (1751–1780) *British army major, spy*

André came to America in 1774, was captured at St. John's in November 1775, spent a year in captivity, and after his exchange joined the British army occupying Philadelphia. There he became a friend of Peggy Shippen, who soon after married Benedict Arnold. Following the British withdrawal to New York, André became Sir Henry Clinton's aide-de-camp. He learned of the treasonous correspondence between Arnold and the British command in the spring of 1780 and assumed major responsibility for dealing with Arnold. After Arnold became commander at West Point, André arranged a meeting. Defying orders by disguising himself, he sailed up the Hudson, landed on the American side, and met with Arnold but returned too late to reboard his ship. Arnold persuaded him to return to British lines overland, carrying documents from Arnold. Militia stopped André, and Arnold managed to escape. Found behind American lines in disguise and bearing incriminating documents, André was sentenced to execution as a spy. He was hanged at Tappan.

Arbuthnot, Marriot (1711–1794) *British admiral*

Arbuthnot rose slowly in the navy to the rank of captain in 1747. Appointed commissioner at Halifax in 1775, he served until being recalled to Britain and promoted in 1778. In spring 1779, he replaced James Gambier as commander in America. Tactless and incompetent, Arbuthnot failed to coordinate efforts with Sir Henry Clinton, hesitated to respond to Admiral d'Estaing's threat to Rhode Island, and, in 1780, allowed a French expeditionary force to land at Newport. In March 1781, he engaged the French in an inclusive but punishing battle off the Virginia capes, following which he was recalled to Britain. Although promoted, he never served again with the Admiralty.

Arnold, Benedict (1741–1801) *general in the Continental army, traitor*

Arnold was born in Connecticut, where he became a prosperous merchant. Following news of Lexington and Concord, Arnold marched with his militia company to join the American forces at Cambridge. He participated in capturing Fort Ticonderoga and attacking St. John's, and in September 1775, he led an expedition to attack Quebec, where he was severely wounded. Arnold was appointed brigadier general, thwarted a British invasion of Valcour Island, and assumed an assignment in Rhode Island. Enraged when, in February 1777, five officers junior to him were promoted to major general, Arnold submitted his resignation, but Washington persuaded him to stay on and join the army in the North to confront Burgoyne's invasion. Arnold's leadership and heroism in the Second Battle of Saratoga, where he was again wounded, were crucial to American victory. Appointed military commander of Philadelphia in 1778, Arnold there met and married Margaret (Peggy) Shippen. But in May 1779, he offered to divulge military information to the British and began a yearlong treasonous correspondence with the British command. Following a clandestine meeting with British spy Major John André in September 1780, André was captured by American troops but Arnold managed to escape to British lines. Commissioned a brigadier in the British army, he led raids in Virginia and Connecticut. He and Peggy then moved to England, where Arnold suffered public and private contempt for his treason. Arnold sought a livelihood in privateering and business, lived briefly in Canada, and died encumbered with debts in London.

Arnold, Margaret (Peggy Shippen) (1760–1804) *wife of Benedict Arnold*

Born and raised in Philadelphia, Peggy was a local belle and the daughter of Pennsylvania's chief justice. After the British occupied Philadelphia, Peggy received much attention from British officers, including then Captain John André, and made known her Loyalist leanings and social ambitions. She was only 18 when she married Arnold, whose first wife had died while he was on his expedition to Canada. Peggy apparently knew of and approved Arnold's dealings with André. She moved with Arnold to England, then to New Brunswick, and back to England as his fortunes waned. Arnold's death in 1801 left her encumbered with huge debts and a large family. She courageously accepted her duty, sup-porting even Arnold's children by his first marriage and managing to pay off the debts. Admired for her dignity and strength of character, she died of cancer when only 44.

Attucks, Crispus (ca. 1723–1770) *martyr of the Boston Massacre*

Apparently born near Framingham, Massachusetts, of mixed African and Indian parentage, Attucks fled slavery in 1750 and became a free sailor. Living in Boston under the name Michael Johnson, Attucks, who was large and more than six feet tall, assumed leadership of a mob confronting British soldiers at the Customs House on the night of March 5, 1770. Armed with a club, he stood at the front of the mob berating the soldiers, deflected a soldier's rifle, and struck at the soldier. The troops opened fire, and Attucks fell instantly dead. Boston Patriots staged an elaborate funeral for Attucks and the three others who died in the massacre. During the trial of British troops involved in the massacre, defense lawyer John Adams cited Attucks's provocation as a cause of the shooting, while prosecuting lawyers touted Attucks's heroism.

Barras, Louis (count de Barras) (unknown–ca. 1800) *French admiral*

Barras had risen to squadron leader in the French navy by 1778 and became naval lieutenant general in 1782. After Admiral Ternay's death, he received command of part of the French fleet in American waters under Admiral d'Estaing. In command at Newport in 1781, Barras received a request from Washington and Rochambeau to assist the movement of troops and supplies southward to entrap Cornwallis in Virginia, but he wished instead to sail for an attack on Newfoundland. Finally persuaded, he sailed to join de Grasse's fleet in the Chesapeake. Barras brought the artillery that proved instrumental in the siege of Yorktown. Following Yorktown, Barras sailed with de Grasse to engage the British, and in 1782, he captured Montserrat. Ill health forced his retirement in 1783.

Barry, John (1745–1803) *captain in the Continental navy*

An Irishman, Barry immigrated to Philadelphia in 1760. In 1776, the Continental Congress commissioned him captain of the 16-gun brig *Lexington*. After capturing the British tender *Edward* off Cape Charles, Virginia, he received command of the 32-gun

Effingham in October 1776, but he spent the winter of 1776–77 on land as commander of a Pennsylvania militia unit. Forced to abandon the *Effingham* to the British, who burned the ship when they occupied Philadelphia, Barry harassed British shipping on the Delaware. In September 1778, Barry assumed command of the frigate *Raleigh* and sailed for Boston. While on patrol, his ship was forced aground after a long battle. Subsequently commanding the *Alliance,* Barry captured several British ships scattered by a mid-Atlantic storm. Barry's ship carried Lafayette on his return to France. In January 1783, he engaged the *Sybille* in one of the last sea battles of the revolution. In 1794, when Congress organized a new navy for defense against Algerian pirates, Barry was appointed senior captain and commander of the *United States,* which he also commanded during the 1798–1801 naval struggle with France. Barry is known as the Father of the American Navy.

Boudinot, Elias (1740–1821) *statesman, member of the Continental Congress*
Boudinot was born in Philadelphia but spent most of his life in New Jersey, where he was a prominent member of the bar, an early Patriot, and an ardent foe of Royal Governor William Franklin. Boudinot served on the New Jersey committee of correspondence in 1774 and supported the colony's approval of the Continental Congress. In 1775, he was a delegate to the New Jersey Provincial Congress. He formed close ties with Washington, and in 1777, he was appointed commissary of prisoners with a rank equivalent to colonel and was also elected to the Continental Congress. In 1782, Boudinot was elected to a one-year term as president of the Congress, making him chief executive under terms of the Articles of Confederation, while also serving as secretary of foreign affairs. At the end of his term as president, Boudinot asked not to be reelected, but he was returned to Congress after adoption of the Constitution. In 1795, he became superintendent of the mint.

Brant, Joseph (Thayendanega) (1742–1807) *Indian leader, warrior*
A Mohawk, Brant was born in Ohio and named Thayendanegea; thereafter, he lived with his parents at Canajoharie Castle in New York's Mohawk Valley. After his father died, his mother married an Indian whom the white settlers called Brant, giving him his Anglicized name. Brant's sister Molly married the British superintendent of Indian affairs, Sir William Johnson, and at age 13, Brant served with Johnson at the Battle of Lake George in 1755. Johnson then sent Brant to school in Lebanon, Connecticut. In 1763, Brant served as interpreter for a missionary and then joined the Iroquois who fought with the British to put down Pontiac's Rebellion. In 1765, he married an Oneida chief's daughter. Brant converted to Anglicanism and helped translate the Book of Common Prayer and other religious texts into the Mohawk language. In 1774, Brant became secretary to Guy Johnson, Sir William's successor; he endeavored to persuade the Six Nations to support the British. In 1775, he was commissioned captain, sent to England, and presented at court. Benjamin West painted him with Guy Johnson in a double portrait. Brant returned to America, fought at The Cedars and with St. Leger's expedition, led the ambush at Oriskany in 1777, and then joined the Johnsons and Walter Butler in the Border Wars. He was a participant in the so-called Cherry Valley Massacre. George III appointed him colonel of Indians. As the Revolution's end approached, Brant endeavored to secure peace on the frontier. Subsequently, he bought land in Ontario with funds given him by the king, became a leader of the Mohawk there, and helped set up the Old Mohawk Church.

Burgoyne, John (1722–1792) *British general, member of Parliament, playwright*
Burgoyne entered the army in 1740; he won the favor of the king, who awarded him several lucrative posts and promoted him to major general. Burgoyne served in Parliament, supporting the government's policies in the years leading up to the revolution. In April 1775, he was sent to Boston, where he wrote bombastic proclamations to the colonists. He returned to England in 1776 and proposed a campaign to split apart the northern colonies that included recapturing Fort Ticonderoga and marching on Albany. He returned to America, launched the campaign in June 1777, succeeded in retaking Fort Ticonderoga, but met defeat in battles at Saratoga, Freeman's Farm, and Bemis Heights that forced his surrender to Gen. Horatio Gates—the greatest defeat the British suffered during the Revolutionary War. Burgoyne, known as Gentleman Johnny, returned to Britain, where he dabbled in politics and wrote plays.

Byron, John (1723–1786) *British admiral*
Byron made his first voyage as a midshipman in 1740, experiencing shipwreck off the coast of Chile that his grandson George Gordon, Lord Byron, made use of in his poem *Don Juan*. During 1764–66, he explored the South Seas, earning the nickname Foul-weather Jack. He was governor of Newfoundland from 1769 until 1772. Byron became a rear admiral in 1775 and a vice admiral in 1778. He replaced Admiral Lord Howe in the summer of 1778, with the assignment of hunting down and engaging Admiral d'Estaing's fleet. In July 1779, he did battle with d'Estaing in the West Indies and would have suffered defeat but for d'Estaing's unexpected withdrawal. Thereafter, Byron asked to be recalled on the grounds of poor health, and he returned to Britain in October 1779. At the time of his death, he was commander of one of three operating squadrons of the British navy.

Campbell, William (1745–1781) *Virginia militia officer*
Campbell's family emigrated from Argyll, Scotland, and settled in Virginia's Holston Valley. He married Patrick Henry's sister Elizabeth. A captain in the Virginia militia, Campbell fought against the Cherokee and served in Lord Dunmore's War of 1774. In December 1774, he became a captain in Patrick Henry's 1st Virginia Regiment and helped to expel Governor Dunmore from Virginia. Campbell resigned his commission in fall 1776, then fought on the frontier, and served as honorary commissioner in negotiations with the Cherokee. He became a colonel in the state militia and served in the House of Burgesses. Persuaded by Isaac Shelby to join the Western force set up to fight Tory troops led by Patrick Ferguson, Campbell was a leader of the militiamen in the defeat of Ferguson at King's Mountain, South Carolina, in October 1780. Promoted to brigadier general, he and some of his troops joined Nathanael Greene for the Battle of Guilford Courthouse in March 1781 and then helped reinforce Lafayette in Virginia. Campbell became ill and died in August 1781.

Carleton, Guy (1724–1808) *British general-governor of Canada*
Born into an Irish Protestant family, Carleton joined the British army in 1742 and became a lieutenant colonel in 1757. He served at Louisbourg in July 1758; he was appointed colonel and quartermaster general for Gen. James Wolfe at the end of 1758. He fought with Wolfe at Quebec in 1759, receiving a wound; participated in the siege of Belle Isle in 1761; and fought at Port Andro, again being wounded. Promoted to full colonel in 1762, he served at the siege of Havana and once more was wounded. In April 1766, he became lieutenant governor of Canada, and in 1767, he succeeded to the governorship. Carleton returned to England in 1770 and was appointed colonel of the 47th Foot Regiment and later major general. He supported the Quebec Act in Parliament in 1774. Returning to Canada at the end of 1774, Carleton was appointed governor of Quebec in January 1775 and, later that year, commander of British forces in Canada. Carleton successfully defended Canada against Arnold's expedition, pursued the defeated Americans into New York, and earned a knighthood. Carleton supported Burgoyne's expedition but sought to be recalled to England. Still in Canada in 1777, he was promoted to lieutenant general. In 1778, he was appointed governor of Charlemont, Ireland, for life. In early 1782, Carleton was appointed commander in chief in America and governor of New York. In New York City, he aided the peace process, then evacuated the city in November 1783, and returned to England. Carleton again became governor of Quebec in 1786, serving until 1796 except for a hiatus during 1791–93. Carleton survived a shipwreck while returning to England in 1796 and spent his remaining years in retirement.

Clark, George Rogers (1752–1818) *American general*
Clark was born in Charlottesville, Virginia, worked as a surveyor, and served as a militia captain in 1774 in Lord Dunsmore's War. Commissioned a major in the Virginia militia in 1776, Clark organized a force of frontiersmen to invade the British-led Illinois territory, which was inhabited largely by French settlers and served as a staging areas for Indian raids, organized by the British army at Detroit. Clark and his men set out from the falls of the Ohio in late June 1777 and captured Kaskaskia without firing a shot. They moved on to take Prairie de Rocher, Cahokia, and finally Vincennes, which the British recaptured. Largely in control of the West, Clark remained unable to mount an offensive against the British at Detroit. Following his war exploits, Clark's life was marked by failure, debt, and poor health. He died forgotten.

Clinton, George (1739–1812) *governor of New York, general in the Continental army, vice president*
Born in Little Britain, New York, Clinton served as a subaltern during the British capture of Fort Frontenac in 1757. During 1758, he was a privateer but then studied law and began a law career. In 1768, he became a member of the New York assembly, rivaling Philip Schuyler as a leader of those favoring revolution. Clinton was elected to the Second Continental Congress in 1775 but, because of Washington's assigning him to command defenses at Hudson Highlands, was absent when Congress approved the Declaration of Independence. Appointed a brigadier general in the state militia, he received the same rank in the Continental army in March 1777, but his defense of New York against Sir Henry Clinton's army proved ineffectual. He acknowledged his military inadequacies and was elected governor of New York in April 1777. A popular governor, Clinton was reelected five times. Clinton opposed ratification of the Constitution. He refused to run for reelection in 1795, but, as an ally of Aaron Burr and the Livingstons, he again became governor in 1800. Becoming vice president in 1804 and 1808, Clinton served with Presidents Jefferson and Madison; he died in office.

Clinton, Henry (1738–1795) *British general*
The son of Adm. George Clinton, he was raised in New York, where his father served as governor in 1741–51. The Clintons returned to Britain, and Henry became a lieutenant in the Coldstream Guards; in 1758 he was promoted to lieutenant colonel in the Grenadier Guards. During the Seven Years' War, he served as aide-de-camp to Prince Ferdinand of Brunswick. In 1772, Clinton became a major general and also a member of Parliament. In 1775, he sailed with Generals Howe and Burgoyne for Boston, where he served in the Battle of Bunker Hill and became a lieutenant general, second in command to General Howe, who sent Clinton on the Charleston expedition of 1776. Clinton returned to the North and served in the Battle of Long Island. Desiring to be rid of him, Howe then sent Clinton to capture Newport. Clinton returned to England, received a knighthood, and, in July 1777, returned to New York City, whose defense Howe awarded to him. In October 1777, he captured Hudson Highlands, and in May 1778, he succeeded Howe as commander in chief. Clinton's tactics in New Jersey failed, and he fell back to New York, but in 1779, he took Stony Point

and Verplanck's Point and made raids on Connecticut. In 1780, he led the successful expedition against Charleston and then returned to New York. Carleton succeeded him in 1782. In 1783, Clinton published his *Narrative of the Campaign of 1781 in North America.* He lost his seat in Parliament in 1784 but gained reelection in 1790. Promoted to full general in 1793, he became governor of Gibraltar in 1794 and died there at the end of 1795.

Corbin, Margaret (1751–1800) *Patriot*
Born in Pennsylvania and orphaned at age four as the result of an Indian attack, Corbin in 1772 married John Corbin, a Virginian who enlisted in the Pennsylvania artillery. In November 1776, John was killed while manning his cannon during the Battle of Fort Washington; Margaret stepped forward and took his place. Although severely wounded and captured along with the garrison, she was evacuated to Philadelphia and there recovered. In 1779, Congress awarded Captain Molly, as she was called, half-pay for life in recognition of her bravery. She died in Westchester County and is now buried at West Point.

Cornwallis, Charles (1738–1805) *British general*
Born in London the son of the first earl Cornwallis and educated at Eton, Cornwallis became an ensign in the Grenadier Guards at age 18. Early in the Seven Years' War, he was called to active duty with Prince Ferdinand of Brunswick while attending military school at Turin. In 1759, he returned to Britain as a captain in the 85th Regiment. In 1760, Cornwallis became a member of Parliament and also lieutenant colonel and commander of the 12th Regiment. After his father's death in 1762, he became Earl Cornwallis, entering the House of Lords as a Whig. He subsequently held varied posts, including aide-de-camp to George III, and was promoted to major general in 1775. Cornwallis arrived in New York in 1776 and served in the battles of Long Island, Kip's Bay, Fort Washington, and Fort Lee. Defeated at Princeton in January 1777, he left for a sojourn in England and then returned to America in June 1777. Cornwallis served in the New Jersey campaign and was prominent in the Battle of Brandywine and the occupation of Philadelphia. He returned to England in January 1778, was made lieutenant general, and in the summer, returned again to America to serve as second in command under Henry Clinton. He sailed for England in December 1778 because his wife was

dying but returned to America a year later. In 1780, he served with Clinton in the Charleston expedition and then became commander of British forces in the South. Cornwallis won at Camden but depleted his army in pursuing Nathanael Greene and had to withdraw to Yorktown, Virginia. Besieged there by the French from the sea and the Americans on land, Cornwallis was forced to surrender in October 1781. In 1786, he became governor general of India, proved an able administrator, and defeated Tippoo Sultan. Cornwallis returned to England in 1793, became governor-general of Ireland in 1797, and in 1805 returned to India, where he died.

Deane, Silas (1737–1789) *member of the Continental Congress, diplomat*
Deane was born in Groton, Connecticut. He graduated from Yale in 1758 and began a law practice in Wetherfield in 1762. Deane led opposition to the Townshend Acts in the Connecticut General Assembly in 1772 and served as secretary of the Committee of Correspondence in 1773. He served in both Continental Congresses, and in 1776, Congress sent him to France as a secret agent to negotiate with the French government—the first United States diplomat. In Paris, he secured eight shiploads of arms and supplies and recruited several officers for the Continental army, but then Deane began to advocate reconciliation with Great Britain, generating suspicion in Congress; that body sent Benjamin Franklin and Arthur Lee to assume negotiations with the French. In 1778, Deane returned to America charged with disloyalty and embezzlement. Attacked in Congress, Deane wrote letters denouncing the war that were printed in a New York Tory newspaper, and he fled as an exile to London, where, in 1789, he published a defense of his actions. He died aboard a ship returning to America; he was later interred in Deal, England.

d'Estaing, count Jean-Baptiste-Charles-Henri-Hector-Théodat (1729–1794) *French admiral*
Born in Auvergne, he became colonel of a regiment at 16 and brigadier at 26. D'Estaing went to the West Indies in 1757, was captured by the British in 1759 while serving in India, and, in 1760, violated parole through combat against the British, who again captured him and briefly imprisoned him at Portsmouth. In 1763, he became a lieutenant general; in 1777, a vice admiral in the French navy. In 1778, he received command of the French fleet sent to support the Americans, but he failed in efforts to dislodge the British from New York and Newport, defaulted on a Franco-American plan to attack Halifax and Newfoundland, and sailed for the West Indies. There, he withdrew from battle with a fleet under Adm. John Byron and returned to the American coast, participating in the disastrous failure to recapture Savannah. In 1780, d'Estaing returned to France. In 1783, he was organizing a fleet at Cádiz for service in the West Indies when the Revolutionary War ended. Elected to the Assembly of Notables in 1787, chosen commandant of the National Guard in 1789, and appointed admiral in 1792 by the National Assembly, d'Estaing remained loyal to the king and was tried and executed in 1794.

Dickinson, John (1732–1808) *lawyer, writer, government official*
Dickinson was born in Talbot County, Maryland; he studied law in Philadelphia and at the Middle Temple in London (1753–57) and began to practice law in Philadelphia in 1757. He was a member of the Assembly of Lower Counties (Delaware) in 1760 and served as Philadelphia's representative in the Pennsylvania legislature in 1762–64 and 1770–76. In 1765, the legislature sent him as a delegate to the Stamp Act Congress, whose declaration requesting repeal of the Stamp Act he drafted. In 1768, Dickinson wrote his responses to the Townshend Acts in the popular *Letters from a Farmer in Pennsylvania,* disputing Britain's right to tax the colonies and supporting nonimportation of goods from Britain. In 1774, he was chairman of the Committee of Correspondence and elected a delegate to the first Continental Congress. In 1776–77 and 1779–80, he represented Delaware in the congress. Dickinson advocated reconciliation and peace and therefore voted against adoption of the Declaration of Independence, but when war came, he supported the Patriot cause as a colonel in Philadelphia's 1st Battalion and as a drafter of the Articles of Confederation. Dickinson served as president of the Supreme Executive Council of Delaware in 1781, as president of the Supreme Council of Pennsylvania in 1782–85, as president of the Annapolis Convention in 1786, and as a Delaware delegate to the Constitutional Convention in 1787. He advocated adoption of the Constitution in a series of letters signed *Fabius.* In 1783, he helped found Dickinson College, named in his honor. He died in Wilmington.

Dunmore, John Murray, earl of (1732–1809) *royal colonial governor*

Of Scottish royal birth as a Stuart descendant, Dunmore inherited his title in 1756 and was selected a peer with a seat in the House of Lords in 1761. He then moved to London and steeped himself in the city's political and social life. The king appointed him royal governor of New York in 1770. He assumed the post in October 1770 but left before completing a year when promoted to the governorship of Virginia, then considered the best post in the colonies by British officialdom. He moved his family into the governor's mansion in Williamsburg and began a promising tenure. Soon, however, anti-British dissidence supporting the Massachusetts rebels and led by Patrick Henry generated a fractiousness that prodded Dunmore to dissolve the House of Burgesses. As tensions mounted, Dunmore led a militia force against the Shawnee, who were under the leadership of Cornstalk in what is now West Virginia, winning a decisive victory at Point Pleasant; the subsequent settlement ended what has since been known as Lord Dunmore's War. Returned to Williamsburg, Dunmore confronted mounting rebellion following Henry's famed "give me liberty or give me death" speech. On June 1, 1775, after the outbreak of war, Dunmore fled with his family to the safety of HMS *Fowey* in harbor at Norfolk, Virginia. He declared martial law and attempted, with minimal resources at hand, to suppress the rebellion. He offered freedom to black slaves who would join the British forces, thus only further antagonizing white Virginians. Dunmore raised a force, partially comprised of blacks, but his forays against the Patriot forces proved abortive. In January 1776, Dunmore ordered a small British fleet to bombard Norfolk, but this attack and a sally toward the Chesapeake Bay foundered, and he withdrew the fleet, which carried away many Loyalists. Dunmore removed to New York and then sailed for England. In 1787, he became governor of the Bahamas, serving in that post until 1796.

Duportail, Louis (1743–1802) *major general in the Continental army*

Born in Pithiviers, France, to an aristocratic family (his father was a king's councillor), he entered the school of engineering at Mezières as a lieutenant in 1762, graduating in 1765. In 1773, he was promoted to captain. In response to Benjamin Franklin's request for trained military engineers to aid the Continental army, the French ministry chose Duportail as one of four to send to America. He reported for duty with the Continental army on February 13, 1777, became a colonel of engineering, and in November was promoted to brigadier general and chief of engineers. Duportail served in the Philadelphia campaign, had charge of fortifying the forts on the Delaware River, remained with Washington at Valley Forge through the winter, and participated in the Monmouth campaign. In June 1778, Washington sent him to strengthen Philadelphia's defenses. In 1779, Duportail became commandant of the Corps of Engineers and Sappers and Miners and served in the Hudson Highlands. In March 1780, he was assigned to Benjamin Lincoln's command, arriving at Charleston too late to assist. Duportail was taken prisoner on May 12, 1780, but was exchanged in October in time to join Washington for the siege of Yorktown. He was promoted to major general in November 1781. Duportail resigned in October 1783 and returned to France, accepting the post of brigadier general of infantry. In November 1790, he began a one-year stint as minister and secretary of state for war. In January 1792, he was promoted to lieutenant general with command of the Moulins region but was prevented from assuming his duties because he supported Lafayette, then under political suspicion. Duportail was accused of political disloyalty, went into hiding for two years, and then escaped to America, settling on a small farm near Philadelphia. The charge of disloyalty was dropped in June 1797. Duportail died aboard ship while returning to France and was buried at sea.

Franklin, Benjamin (1706–1790) *printer, writer, inventor, scientist, statesman*

Born in Boston, Franklin had little formal schooling, worked in his father's tallow shop, and became an apprentice printer with his brother James. In 1723, he fled to Philadelphia, having only a copper shilling and a Dutch dollar on his arrival. By 1730, he was sole owner of a printing business and the *Pennsylvania Gazette*. In 1732, he established a circulating library and began publishing *Poor Richard's Almanac*, which he continued editing until 1757. In 1743, the Junto debating society he had founded in 1727 became the American Philosophical Society. Franklin was the main leader in founding Philadelphia's first fire company, an academy, and the University of Pennsylvania (1747). By 1748, he had a large enough fortune to leave his printing business in control of his partner and pursue his interest in science. In 1751, Franklin published *Experiments and*

Observations on Electricity, which established his scientific reputation in Europe; the same year, he was elected to the Pennsylvania assembly, serving through 1763. In 1753, the British ministry appointed him deputy postmaster general of the colonies, a post he held until 1774. He attended the Albany Convention in 1754, submitting a proposal that served as a precedent for formation of the American union. Franklin served as agent of the Pennsylvania assembly in London in 1757–62 and again in 1764–75, while also representing Georgia and Massachusetts. During his second sojourn, he voiced American dissent over British policies and, in 1766, spoke against the Stamp Act in the House of Commons. Returning to America in 1775, he was immediately chosen a delegate to the Continental Congress; he helped draft the Declaration of Independence. In 1776, Congress sent Franklin to Paris to obtain supplies for the army, raise loans, and negotiate a treaty of alliance. He served in Paris as American minister plenipotentiary during the years 1778–85 and was a member of the commission that drafted the 1783 Treaty of Paris ending the Revolutionary War. Franklin returned to Philadelphia in fall 1785. He was elected president of the Supreme Executive Council of Pennsylvania, a post he held for three years. In 1787, he became president of the Pennsylvania Society for Promoting the Abolition of Slavery and also represented Pennsylvania as a delegate to the Constitutional Convention. He advocated unanimous adoption of the Constitution. Franklin received honorary degrees from Harvard, Yale, Oxford, William and Mary, and St. Andrews. He never completed his *Autobiography,* begun while he was an agent in London.

Freneau, Philip (1752–1832) *poet, journalist*
A member of a Huguenot family and born in New York, Freneau in 1768 entered Princeton (then known as the College of New Jersey), where his classmate friends included Hugh Henry Brackenridge and James Madison. Shortly after graduating in 1771, he and Brackenridge collaborated on writing a patriotic poem entitled "The Rising Glory of America." Freneau worked for a brief period as a teacher but then chose to focus on writing poetry and studying theology. A series of poems satirizing the British published in 1775 confirmed his role as a literary Patriot. In February 1776, Freneau sailed to the West Indies; he worked as a secretary at Santa Cruz in the Virgin Islands and visited other islands in the Caribbean. During a return voyage

to the United States in July 1778, the British captured him; upon his release, Freneau went to Philadelphia. He joined the New Jersey militia and started publishing a newspaper entitled *The American Independence.* As the Revolutionary War proceeded, Freneau wrote poems, practiced journalism, and spent time at sea aboard merchant and privateer ships. In May 1780, the British captured him aboard the privateer *Aurora* and confined him in one of the notorious prison ships in New York harbor, causing a serious decline in his general health—they released him in 1781. Following the war, Freneau continued his occupations of poet, sailor, and journalist. In 1786, Freneau's first complete volume of poems was published in Philadelphia. An ally of Thomas Jefferson, Freneau in 1791 became editor of the *National Gazette,* an anti-Federalist newspaper published in Philadelphia that attacked George Washington, Alexander Hamilton, and other Federalists. Freneau moved to Mount Pleasant, a farm near Freehold, New Jersey, in 1794; this home burned down in 1818, and he moved his family into a small farmhouse nearer to town. In 1815, he collected his later poems together to be published in two volumes. Freneau's last published poem (treating the Battle of Monmouth) appeared in a Trenton newspaper in 1827. Impoverished and nearly forgotten, Freneau died at the age of 80 as a result of being trapped in a blizzard. His work gained renewed attention in the early 20th century, and he is now often referred to as the "Father of American Poetry."

Gage, Thomas (1721–1787) *British general*
Born in Firle, England, Gage was educated at Westminster School; commissioned as an ensign in 1740, he became captain and aide-de-camp to Lord Albemarle in 1743. In 1745, he fought at the battles of Fontenoy and Culloden, and in 1747–48, he served in the Low Countries campaign. Gage became a member of the 44th Foot Regiment, rising to lieutenant colonel rank in 1751. Gage's regiment was sent to America at the outbreak of the French and Indian War to serve under Gen. Edward Braddock and was involved in Braddock's disastrous Pennsylvania campaign of 1755, during which Gage became acquainted with George Washington. In 1758, Gage suffered minor wounds at Ticonderoga, received promotion to brigadier general, and was married. In 1759, he became commandant at Albany and participated in the British conquest of Canada. Following the French surrender in 1760, Gage became governor of Montreal

and a region including Crown Point and extending to Lake Ontario. In 1761, he became a major general; in 1763, he was named commander in chief of British forces in America, headquartered in New York City. Gage visited Boston and strengthened its garrison as conflict surfaced there. He and his family returned to Britain in 1773, but in 1774, he was made both commander in chief in America and royal governor of Massachusetts, serving in both roles through the battles at Lexington, Concord, and Bunker Hill and then returning to England to suffer the disfavor of the North ministry. After struggling to attain a livelihood, he was appointed to the staff at Amherst in 1781, and, in 1782, he was promoted to full general.

Gálvez, Bernardo de (1746–1786) *Spanish soldier, government official*

Gálvez attended military school at Ávila; served with the Spanish army in Portugal, Algiers, and New Spain; and arrived in New Orleans with the rank of colonel, becoming governor of Louisiana and Florida in 1777. He had British privateers seized, supported the efforts of American agent Oliver Pollock to obtain supplies for the American army, and pursued other policies to weaken the British. After Spain entered the war in support of America, Gálvez seized Natchez, Baton Rouge, and other British outposts on the Mississippi River. He captured Mobile in 1780 and Pensacola in 1781, gaining control of western Florida, which resulted in Britain's ceding control of East and West Florida and the mouth of the Mississippi to Spain under terms of the Treaty of Paris. Gálvez served in Spain in 1783–84 as an adviser on policies for the Florida and Louisiana territories, was promoted to major general and awarded Castilian noble titles, and was appointed captain general of the Floridas and Louisiana. In 1785, he became viceroy of New Spain, but the following year, he died in Mexico of a severe fever.

Gambier, James (1723–1789) *British admiral*

Gambier became a lieutenant in the British navy in 1743; he served at Louisbourg in 1758 and in the West Indies in 1759. During the years 1770–73, he was commander in chief of naval operations in America. In January 1778, Gambier was promoted to rear admiral, becoming second in command under Admiral Lord Howe and later under Adm. John Byron and serving as temporary commander in chief during their absences. In 1779, he returned to England; he became vice admi-

ral in 1780. In 1783–84, Gambier served as commander in chief in Jamaica but gave up the post because of poor health.

Gates, Horatio (1728–1806) *major general in Continental army*

Gates was born in England, joined the British army while young, and served in America during the French and Indian War, participating in Gen. Edward Braddock's unsuccessful march on Fort Duquesne in 1755 and also fighting in Martinique. In 1765, he retired from the army at half-pay with the rank of major, and in 1772, with George Washington's help, he settled in Virginia on a farm. In June 1775, Gates joined the Continental army with the rank of brigadier general to serve as Washington's adjutant general. In May 1776, he was promoted to major general with orders to serve in the Northern Department under Gen. Philip Schuyler, but at the end of the year, he rejoined Washington for the New Jersey campaign. In spring 1777, the Continental Congress appointed Gates commander at Ticonderoga, ostensibly in anticipation of his succeeding Schuyler. When Congress reneged on making him Schuyler's successor, Gates traveled to Philadelphia to protest to its members. In August 1777, following the fall of Ticonderoga, Washington appointed Gates as Schuyler's successor in command of the Northern Department, the role he filled during General Burgoyne's defeat, so Congress acknowledged him as the Hero of Saratoga. An effort to have him appointed commander in chief in place of Washington led Congress to appoint Gates president of the Board of War created in October 1777. Tangentially implicated in the Conway Cabal effort to discredit Washington, Gates later re-created his working relationship with Washington. In April 1778, he resumed command of the Northern Department and thereafter commanded the Eastern Department in Boston. In July 1780, without consulting Washington, the Continental Congress appointed Gates commander of the Southern Department. But after his disastrous loss and flight from the battlefield at Camden, Nathanael Greene replaced him. Gates retired to his farm and for two years sought a congressional inquiry to clear his name, succeeding in time to return to the army at Newburgh in 1782 for the final year of the war. He retired again to his farm; his wife died in 1784, and in 1786, he remarried. In 1790, Gates set free his slaves and moved to New York City. In 1800–01, he served in the New York legislature.

George III (1738–1820) *king of Great Britain*
Ascending to the throne in 1760, George III worked to diminish Whig power and succeeded in ending the ministry of William Pitt. He also secured his terms for the 1763 Treaty of Paris ending the Seven Years' War. His struggle with Parliament culminated in 1770 with installation of Lord North's ministry, whose policies, encouraged by the king, resulted in the Revolutionary War and the eventual loss of the British colonies. In March 1782, the king finally allowed North to resign and authorized peace negotiations. After conclusion of the Treaty of Paris in 1783, George III appointed William Pitt the younger as prime minister in December 1783. In fall 1788, an affliction rendered the king mad, but he recovered. With the advent of the French Revolution, his public popularity revived. In 1811, he became permanently incapacitated, and the Prince of Wales assumed the role of regent.

Germain, George Sackville, Lord (1716–1785) *British soldier, government minister*
Germain was the son of the first duke of Dorset, lord lieutenant of Ireland under George II. He attended Westminster School and was awarded an M.A. degree by Trinity College, Dublin, in 1734. In 1737, he became a captain in the 7th Horse Regiment of the Irish Establishment and, in 1740, lieutenant colonel of the 28th Foot Regiment. He entered Parliament in 1741. As commander of his regiment, he fought in the Low Countries and was wounded at the Battle of Fontenoy in May 1745. In 1746, he became commander of the 20th Foot Regiment, and in 1749, of the 12th Dragoons. In 1750, he returned to the 7th Horse Regiment as commander. In 1751–56, Germain served as his father's secretary in Ireland, and in 1755, he became a major general. He was second in command to the duke of Marlborough under Prince Ferdinand and assumed command upon the duke's death in September 1758. Germain's misconduct at the 1759 Battle of Minden led to his court-martial and the judgment in 1760 that he was unfit for military service. In 1770, he assumed the name Germain through an inheritance from Lady Betty Germain. In November 1775, Germain became secretary of state for the colonies as well as lord commissioner of trade and plantations, placing him in control of British forces in America during the Revolutionary War. As the war proceeded, Germain had numerous conflicts with Generals Howe, Carleton, and Clinton but favored Generals Burgoyne

and Cornwallis. Germain resigned in February 1782. He was elevated to the peerage as Viscount Sackville, and in 1783, he retired to his country home in Sussex in declining health.

Glover, John (1732–1797) *general in the Continental army*
Born in Salem, Massachusetts, but raised from an early age in Marblehead, Glover became an affluent fisherman, shipowner, and merchant who was active in the local militia. Commissioned a colonel by the Provincial Congress in April 1775, he raised the 21st Massachusetts Regiment, known as the Marblehead Mariners, comprised of fishermen and seafarers from Marblehead with expertise in handling small craft in any kind of weather. The Mariners demonstrated their value in evacuating Washington's troops from Long Island in August 1776. Then, on Christmas Day 1776, they transported Washington and his troops across the Delaware River for the victory at Trenton, where they also prevented the Hessians' escape and rowed the army and 900 prisoners back across the river to safety. The Mariners dissolved at the end of their enlistment period, but Glover became a brigadier general in June 1777. Ill health forced his retirement in 1782; he was breveted as a major general in 1783. Glover was a member of the Massachusetts convention that ratified the Constitution.

Grant, James (1720–1806) *British general*
In fall 1744, Grant entered military service as captain in the 1st Battalion of the Royal Scots and served at the battles of Fontenoy and Culloden. He became a major in the 77th Highlanders in February 1757. On September 21, 1758, he led his 800-man unit into defeat at Fort Duquesne and was taken as prisoner to Montreal. Promoted to lieutenant colonel in 1760, he was successful in an expedition against the Cherokee in 1761. In 1763, he became British governor of the Floridas, a post he held until illness forced his return to Britain in 1771. In 1772, he assumed command of the 40th Foot Regiment in Ireland. Grant became a member of Parliament in 1773. In December 1775, he was appointed a colonel in the 55th Foot Regiment, and he came to America with the rank of brigadier general, serving on Long Island. He succeeded Cornwallis as commander in New Jersey, holding this post when Washington successfully attacked Trenton and Princeton. Grant served at the battles of Brandywine

and Germantown. His efforts in 1778 to trap Lafayette at Barren Hill and to protect General Clinton's rear at Monmouth proved unsuccessful, and in December 1778, he was sent with a detachment of Clinton's army to capture St. Lucia in the West Indies. He then served as commander in the West Indies, returning to England in the summer of 1779. Grant was promoted to lieutenant general in 1782 and to full general in 1796. He served in Parliament in 1787, 1790, 1796, and 1801.

Grasse, François-Joseph-Pau (count de Grasse, marquis de Grasse-Tilly) (1722–1788)
French admiral

Born into an aristocratic family, de Grasse entered the naval school at Toulon at age 11 and the next year became a page to the grand master of the Knights of St. John at Malta. He served in the French navy during the War of Jenkins' Ear in 1740. In May 1747, the British captured him in battle, and he spent three months in prison. In following years, his naval career took him to India, the West Indies, Morocco, and around the Mediterranean. In 1774, he commanded a marine brigade at Saint-Malo, and in 1775, he commanded a ship at Saint-Domingue (Haiti). De Grasse became a commodore in 1778 and commanded a force at the Battle of Ushant. Serving under Admiral d'Estaing in America, he commanded a squadron in battle at Granada and served at Savannah. He briefly commanded the French fleet in the West Indies. In ill health, de Grasse returned to France in October 1780, but in March 1781, he became rear admiral and sailed for the West Indies. His fleet served a major role in securing the victory at Yorktown. In November 1781, he sailed again at the West Indies. In February 1782, he captured St. Kitts, but in April, he suffered defeat and capture. Sent to London, he held discussions with Lord Shelburne that resulted in his role as intermediary during the preliminary peace negotiations. A tribunal in May 1784 exonerated de Grasse for his losses in the West Indies.

Greene, Nathanael (1742–1786) *major general in the Continental army*

Born in Warwick, Rhode Island, to Quaker parents, he worked in his father's iron foundry in Potowomut and, in 1770, assumed management of the family's iron foundry in Coventry. Greene served in the Rhode Island general assembly in 1770–72 and again in 1775. In 1773, he was barred from the Quaker meetinghouse because he attended a military parade. In October 1774,

he helped organize the Kentish Guards as a militia unit, but a defective knee prevented his serving as an officer. In May 1775, Greene became a brigadier general of three Rhode Island militia units, which he led to Long Island for service in the Continental army, becoming the army's youngest brigadier general. He served at the siege of Boston. Promoted to major general, he was given command of the army in New Jersey; he suffered a defeat at Fort Washington but succeeded well at Trenton. General Washington sent him to confer with the Continental Congress and then to join Gen. Henry Knox in reconnoitering the Hudson Highlands. In fall 1777, he served well in the battles of Brandywine and Germantown. In February 1778, he reluctantly accepted the post of quartermaster general, returned to combat at Monmouth and Newport during the summer, and then resumed the quartermaster general's duties. He brought improvements in providing supplies and transportation for the army but in 1780 was criticized by a former rival, Thomas Mifflin, and resigned his post. Greene served as president of the board that judged Maj. John André and then replaced Benedict Arnold as commander in the Hudson Highlands. In October 1780, General Washington appointed Greene commander of the Southern Department; he directed an effective strategy against Lord Cornwallis, limiting British control in South Carolina to Charleston. In 1783, Greene returned to Rhode Island, but his finances were depleted, and he sold his properties there, becoming a resident of Georgia in 1785 as owner of a Loyalist's former property near Savannah, given to Greene by the state.

Hale, Nathan (1755–1776) *American soldier, spy*

Born in Coventry, Connecticut, Hale graduated from Yale in 1773 and taught school in East Hadden and then in New London. In July 1775, he was commissioned a lieutenant in the 7th Connecticut Militia, and in January 1776, he became a captain in the 19th Regiment of the Continental army. He participated in the siege of Boston and then in April went to New York City, serving in the Battle of Long Island and with Washington on the retreat from Brooklyn. Thomas Knowlton chose Hale as commander of a company of his rangers, and Hale volunteered when Washington asked for a rangers' captain to obtain intelligence before the Battle of Harlem Heights. Disguised as a Dutch schoolteacher, Hale traveled to Long Island and garnered information on the British army's positions, but while returning to American lines on September 21, he was captured. Taken to Gen. William Howe's headquarters, Hale was found to be carrying incriminating documents. Because he was not in uniform, he was condemned to hang the next day. Hale died with composure, his final words reportedly being, "I only regret that I have but one life to lose for my country."

Hamilton, Alexander (1757–1804) *officer in the Continental army, statesman*
Hamilton was born in Nevis, British West Indies, to a Scottish merchant and his Huguenot mistress, who died in 1768 estranged from his father, leaving Hamilton effectively an orphan. Having been tutored by his mother and a Presbyterian minister in St. Croix, Hamilton spoke fluent French and went to work as a clerk in St. Croix. In 1772, funded by his aunts, he traveled to New York and enrolled in King's College (now Columbia University). Hamilton wrote a series of pamphlets opposing British policies. He formed a volunteer artillery company in 1775, and, in March 1776, he was commissioned a captain in the Provincial Company of the New York Artillery, with whom he served during the battles of Long Island, Harlem Heights, Trenton, and Princeton. In March 1777, Hamilton was promoted to lieutenant colonel and appointed secretary and aide-de-camp to Washington, a post he held for nearly four-and-a-half years; Washington trusted him and had high regard for his counsel on military and political affairs. In December 1780, Hamilton married Elizabeth Schuyler, member of a powerful New York family. Hamilton left Washington's service in July 1781 to command a battalion under Lafayette, serving at Yorktown; he left the military in December 1783. Hamilton served in Congress in 1782–83 and then practiced law in New York. His efforts at the Annapolis Convention in 1786 helped bring about the Constitutional Convention of 1787, where he was a delegate from New York and an advocate for a strong central government. Hamilton joined with John Jay and James Madison in writing *The Federalist* and securing New York's ratification of the Constitution. Hamilton served as the first secretary of the treasury from 1789 until 1795 and was a powerful member of Washington's cabinet and a supporter of Federalism. He resigned in January 1795 to return to his New York law practice but continued as an adviser to Washington and helped to write his Farewell Address of 1796. In 1798, Hamilton was commissioned a brigadier general and made inspector general of the army as war with France threatened. His political maneuvering alienated President John Adams and contributed to Adams's defeat for reelection in 1800, when Thomas Jefferson and Aaron Burr tied as finalists. Although opposed to his views, Hamilton helped secure the presidency for Jefferson. In 1804, he helped to derail the movement to elect Burr governor of New York. The ensuing enmity between them led to their duel at Weehawken Heights on July 11, 1804, during which Burr wounded Hamilton, who died the following day.

Hamilton, Henry (unknown–1796) *British officer*
Hamilton served in the West Indies and at the battles of Louisbourg and Quebec during the French and Indian War. From 1775 to 1779, he was lieutenant governor of Canada and commandant at Detroit, where he had only a few regulars from the 8th Regiment but augmented them with Indians and renegades, including the infamous Simon Girty. In June 1777, he received orders to undertake raids on American frontier settlements. He attacked Wheeling, but then his Indian recruits joined the Burgoyne expedition, leaving Hamilton unable to pursue ongoing raids until early 1778. George Rogers Clark's expedition thwarted these efforts and compelled Hamilton to march on Vincennes. Clark captured Hamilton in February 1779; he was held at Williamsburg, Virginia, for several months and then paroled and sent to New York. Americans nicknamed Hamilton "The Hair Buyer," although no proof exists that he paid Indians to obtain settlers' scalps. Hamilton served as governor of Quebec (1784–85), of Bermuda (1790–94), and then of Dominica.

Hancock, John (1737–1793) *merchant, Patriot, statesman*
Hancock was born in Braintree (now Quincy), Massachusetts, orphaned as a youngster, and adopted by his uncle Thomas Hancock, Boston's wealthiest merchant. He graduated from Boston Latin School and Harvard (1754). In 1763, he became a partner in Thomas Hancock and Company, and in 1764, he inherited the firm. A Patriot supporter, Hancock evaded the Stamp Act duties by smuggling. In 1768, British authorities seized his ship *Liberty* and its cargo of Madeira for unpaid duties, raising Hancock to prominence as a tax resister and securing his election in 1769 to the Massachusetts General Court, in which he served until 1774. In 1770, Hancock headed the town committee that investigated the Boston Massacre. He served as treasurer of Harvard in 1773 and as president of the Provincial Congress in

1774–75. When General Gage sent troops to arrest him and Samuel Adams, they escaped to Lexington. Hancock became a delegate to the Continental Congress and served as president from May 1775 until October 1777; as president, he was first to sign the Declaration of Independence. He resigned and returned to Boston. In 1778, as a brigadier general, he commanded Massachusetts troops at Newport. Hancock became the first nonroyal governor of Massachusetts on September 1, 1780, serving until 1785, when he resigned to assume the presidency of Congress but was prevented from doing so by ill health. Reelected governor in 1787 and in subsequent elections, he served until his death. In 1788, he was president of the Massachusetts Convention that ratified the Constitution.

Hanson, John (1721–1783) *American statesman*
Hanson was born in Mulberry Grove, Maryland. A staunch Patriot and early advocate of independence, he served in the Maryland House of Delegates from 1757 until 1773 and on the committee that drafted instructions for the colony's delegates to the Stamp Act Congress (1765). In 1769, Hanson signed Maryland's nonimportation agreement targeting the Townshend Acts. In 1774, he supported the Association of Maryland that sanctioned armed resistance against Britain. Hanson was treasurer of Frederick County in 1775 and helped raise troops and weapons for the Continental army. He became a delegate to the Continental Congress in June 1780; laboring to secure ratification of the Articles of Confederation, he convinced authorities in Virginia and other states to give up claims to western lands. In November 1781, Hanson was elected the first president of the Confederation Congress; when his one-year term ended, he retired from public service.

Hays, Mary Ludwig (Molly Pitcher) (ca. 1754–1832) *legendary American heroine*
The most likely candidate among several women for the epithet Molly Pitcher, Hays was a domestic servant and resident of Carlisle, Pennsylvania. When her husband, a barber named John Hays, enlisted as a gunner in a Pennsylvania regiment in 1775, Mary traveled with him. Apparently by 1778 she was established as a camp follower who provided washing, cooking, and nursing for the troops. At the Battle of Monmouth on June 28, 1778, she was carrying water to the front lines (thus, the nickname "Molly Pitcher") when her husband collapsed by his gun from a wound or exhaus-

tion. Legend says she took his place, loading the cannon throughout the remainder of the battle. Following the war, the Hayses returned to Carlisle, where Mary worked as a cleaning woman. After John died, Mary wed John McCauley. In 1822, the Pennsylvania legislature approved paying Mary $40 and an annuity "for her services during the revolutionary war." Her contemporaries described Mary as uncouth, tobacco-chewing, and foulmouthed but also warmhearted and generous.

Heath, William (1737–1814) *general in the Continental army*
Heath was born in Roxbury, Massachusetts. Selected as a delegate to the Massachusetts General Court in 1761 and in 1771, he served until the assembly was dissolved in 1774. Heath joined the Ancient and Honorable Artillery Company of Boston in 1765. In 1774–75, he served as a member of the Committee of Safety and of the Massachusetts Provincial Congress, which appointed him brigadier general in February 1775. The first American general on the scene following the battles of Lexington and Concord, he deployed troops to begin the siege of Boston. Heath organized troops at Cambridge before the Battle of Bunker Hill, and in June 1775, he was appointed brigadier general to serve with Washington. In March 1776, he led the first detachment of Continental troops to New York and there became second in command to General Putnam. In November, he received command of the troops defending the Highland Heights. His failure in leading an attack on Fort Independence in January 1777 earned censure and denial of any future field commands by Washington. Heath succeeded Artemas Ward as commander of the Eastern Department. In June 1779, he was given command of the troops on the east side of the lower Hudson River and, except for three months in Providence to arrange the arrival of Rochambeau and his troops, served in this post for the remainder of the war. In July 1783, Heath returned to Roxbury. In 1788, he was a delegate to the Massachusetts Convention that ratified the Constitution. He served in the state senate in 1791–92 and as a member of the probate court in Norfolk in 1792. Heath was elected lieutenant governor in 1806 but declined to serve.

Heister, Leopold Phillip von (1701–1777) *commander in chief of Hessian mercenary troops*
Von Heister commanded the first contingent of German mercenaries (7,800 men) brought to America,

sailing from Spithead in May 1776 along with 1,000 British regulars. They arrived in Halifax following General Howe's departure and sailed on to debark on Staten Island in July. Von Heister led the center of the British forces in the Battle of Long Island and personally accepted Lord Stirling's surrender. He commanded the German troops at the Battle of White Plains in October 1776, but the American victory at Trenton in December 1776 and his conflicts with Howe led to his being recalled and replaced by Baron Wilhelm von Knyphausen in 1777.

Henry, Patrick (1736–1799) *statesman, Patriot orator*
Born in Hanover County, Virginia, to a Scottish immigrant father, Henry became a store clerk at age 15 and the next year opened a store in partnership with his brother. When he was 18, he married and began to farm but returned to storekeeping after a disastrous fire. Deeply in debt, he obtained a law license and entered into a successful law practice in 1760. In 1765, Henry became a member of the House of Burgesses, where he championed dissent and adoption of the Virginia Resolves as a response to the Stamp Act. The resolves and Henry's oratory secured his repute throughout the colonies. When Lord Dunmore dissolved the House of Burgesses, Henry led meetings of the delegates at the Raleigh Tavern; he delivered a speech in March 1775 containing his famed declaration, "Give me liberty or give me death." He served in both the First and Second Continental Congresses but opposed complete independence. Political opponents prevented his assuming command after his appointment as colonel of the first regiment formed in Virginia. In May 1776, Henry helped draft the Virginia constitution, and he served as the first governor in 1776–79, authorizing George Rogers Clark's expedition. Succeeded by his ally Thomas Jefferson, Henry retired to Henry County southwest of Richmond. His support in 1781 of a faction seeking an investigation of Jefferson's conduct as governor created lifelong enmity between the former allies. Henry served as governor again in 1784–86. As a delegate to the Virginia Convention in 1788, he advocated states rights in opposing ratification of the Constitution but helped secure adoption of the Bill of Rights. In 1795, Henry declined Washington's offer of the positions of secretary of state and chief justice but praised the president publicly. In 1799, Washington persuaded Henry to switch parties and campaign for a seat in the Virginia House of Delegates as a Federalist;

he defeated John Randolph for the seat but died before he could be sworn in.

Herkimer, Nicholas (1728–1777) *militia general*
Born to German immigrants in the Mohawk Valley near present-day Herkimer, New York, he served in the French and Indian War as a militia lieutenant and commander of Fort Herkimer. He later headed the Tyron County Patriots' committee of safety. In 1776, he became brigadier general of the New York militia assigned to thwart Indian and Tory attacks. His conference with Joseph Brant in July 1777 failed to secure the neutrality of the Mohawk. In August 1777, he led a march to relieve Fort Stanwix from attack by St. Leger's troops, but on August 6, his force was ambushed by Tories and Indians at Oriskany. Although the battle prevented St. Leger's joining Burgoyne, Herkimer received severe wounds. He bled to death 10 days later after a French surgeon amputated his leg.

Hopkins, Esek (1718–1802) *commander of the Continental navy*
Born on a farm near Providence, Rhode Island, Hopkins went to sea in 1738 and succeeded as a captain and, during the French and Indian War, as a privateer, retiring to the family farm in 1772. In October 1775, he became a brigadier general and was appointed commander of the state militia. His brother Stephen, the leading political figure in Rhode Island and a delegate to the Continental Congress and member of its Marine Committee, apparently maneuvered Esek's appointment in December 1775 as the first commander in chief of the newly created navy. Esek's son John was appointed captain. Hopkins had difficulties recruiting crews and equipping the few available ships. Assigned in February 1776, the formidable task of clearing the Chesapeake Bay and the coasts of Carolina and Rhode Island, Hopkins instead sailed to the West Indies; he captured Nassau in March. While returning, he encountered the HMS *Glasgow* but failed to capture it despite his superior force. Congress responded by investigating Hopkins and censuring him for insubordination. In March 1777, Congress suspended Hopkins from command and, in January 1778, dismissed him. From 1779 to 1786, Hopkins served in the Rhode Island General Assembly, and in 1783, he was collector of imposts. He also served as trustee of Brown University from 1782 until 1802.

Howe, Richard (1726–1799) *British admiral*
Born in London, Howe entered a naval career at age 14 on an around-the-world voyage with Adm. George Anson; Howe's ship suffered damages rounding Cape Horn and was forced to return to England. In 1742, Howe served in the West Indies and received promotion to lieutenant. He captained the *Dunkirk* in American waters during the French and Indian War. He inherited an Irish title of viscount following his elder brother's death at Ticonderoga in 1758. In 1762, he served in Parliament and, in 1763 and 1765, on the Admiralty Board. He was also treasurer of the navy from 1765 to 1770. In December 1775, Howe was promoted to vice admiral, and in February 1776, he was appointed commander of the navy in America, where his brother William commanded British military forces. The Howe brothers held a mandate to negotiate a peace, but they failed to do so. Howe provided naval support during the New York campaign, but, displeased with inadequate support (in his view) from the ministry and with the Carlisle peace commission having arrived in 1778, he resigned, staying on long enough, however, to defend New York and Newport (August 1778). Replaced by Admiral Byron, he returned to Britain and refused to serve again while Lord Sandwich headed the admiralty. In 1782, with Sandwich's retirement and installation of the Rockingham ministry, he accepted command of the navy in the English Channel and successfully relieved the British garrison at Gibraltar. For most of 1783 and from then until August 1788, Howe was first lord of the Admiralty. He again received command of the navy in the English Channel after the outbreak of war with France in 1793 and served well. In 1797, Howe was sent to Spithead to end a naval mutiny. He received the United Kingdom title of viscount in 1782 and became baron and earl in 1788.

Howe, Robert (1732–1786) *major general in the Continental army*
Howe was born in Bladen County, North Carolina, and educated in Europe. He attained great wealth as owner of a rice plantation. He served as justice of the peace for Bladen County in 1756 and for Brunswick County in 1764. During 1764–75, he was a member of the North Carolina assembly. In 1766–67 and 1769–73, he was militia commander of Fort Johnson. Appointed a colonel, Howe served in Governor Tryon's expedition against the Regulators. In 1774, he was a delegate to the Colonial Congress convened in New Bern. He also served on the North Carolina Committee of Correspondence, and he helped to recruit and train militiamen. When the Revolution began, he was commissioned a colonel in the 2nd North Carolina Regiment. In January 1776, Howe participated in the actions that forced Lord Dunsmore out of Virginia, earning appointment as brigadier general in the Continental army. Promoted to major general in fall 1777, he received command of the Southern Department, but he was removed from command after his disastrous expedition against the British at St. Augustine and was replaced by Benjamin Lincoln in September 1778, although retaining command in Georgia. After the British captured Savannah in December, Howe was recalled to the North and court-martialed. Exonerated of fault at Savannah, Howe was given charge of Benedict Arnold's court-martial for misconduct as commander at Philadelphia. In February 1780, Washington placed him in command of West Point and outposts in the Hudson Highlands—a command that passed to Arnold in August. In September, he served on the board of officers that recommended that Maj. John André be hanged. In January 1781, Howe commanded the troops who quelled the mutiny of Pennsylvania and New Jersey soldiers. In 1783, he commanded the force that dispersed the demonstrating furloughed soldiers who had forced Congress out of Philadelphia; then he returned to his rice plantation. In 1785, the Congress appointed him to aid boundary negotiations with the Indians. Elected in 1786 to serve in the North Carolina legislature, Howe died before he could assume the post.

Howe, William (1729–1814) *British general*
Educated at Eton, Howe became a cornet in the duke of Cumberland's Light Dragoons in 1746 and was promoted to lieutenant in 1746. In 1750, he joined the 20th Foot Regiment and was promoted to captain. In 1756, he became a major in the 58th Foot Regiment; he had attained lieutenant colonel rank by the end of 1759. During the French and Indian War, Howe led his regiment at Louisbourg, gained fame for his leadership on the Plains of Abraham during the Battle of Quebec, and participated in capturing Montreal in 1760. In 1761, he fought at Belle Isle, and in 1762, he was involved in capturing Havana. When his brother George was killed at Ticonderoga in 1758, Howe succeeded him as member of Parliament representing Nottingham, a post he held until 1780. In Parliament, he opposed repressive policies in America. Howe became colonel of the 46th Foot Regiment in Ireland in 1764 and governor of the

Isle of Wight in 1768. He was promoted to major general in 1772 and ordered to America in February 1775, arriving in time to be involved in the Battle of Bunker Hill; in October 1775, he assumed command of British troops at Boston. Howe replaced Gen. Thomas Gage as commander in chief of British forces in America in April 1776. He evacuated Boston, moved his forces to New York, and achieved victory in the Battle of Long Island. In summer and fall 1777, Howe launched campaigns in Pennsylvania and New Jersey, attaining victory at Brandywine and capturing Philadelphia. Considering government support inadequate, Howe resigned; replaced by Gen. Henry Clinton, he sailed for Britain in May 1778. In May 1779, Parliament began a formal inquiry into Howe's and his brother Adm. Richard Howe's conduct in America that ended inconclusively in June. He was appointed lieutenant general of the ordnance in 1782 and promoted to full general in 1793. After Richard's death in 1799, he inherited the Irish title of viscount. Ill health forced his resignation as general of ordnance in 1803. He suffered a painful illness for 11 years leading to his death.

Jefferson, Thomas (1743–1826) *statesman, diplomat, president*
Born in Albemarle County, Virginia, Jefferson was related to the prominent Randolph family through his mother, Jane Randolph. His father, a surveyor who drafted the first accurate map of Virginia, served in the House of Burgesses; at his death in 1757, he left Jefferson 2,750 acres of land. Jefferson graduated from the College of William and Mary in 1762 and was licensed to practice law in 1767, a career he pursued for seven years. Elected to the House of Burgesses in 1769, he served until his election to the Continental Congress in 1775. He attacked the Crown and established his revolutionary credentials in his *Summary View of the Rights of America* of 1774. Absent from Congress from December 1775 until May 1776, Jefferson was appointed to the committee to draft a Declaration of Independence on his return and became the primary writer of the document. Reelected to the Continental Congress and also offered the post of commissioner to France, Jefferson chose instead to return to Virginia. Elected to the Virginia House of Delegates in October 1776, he was appointed to serve on a five-man board to revise the state's laws which, in June 1778, proposed 126 bills, with 100 achieving approval to secure Jefferson's goals of abolishing primogeniture, entail, and an estab-

lished church. Jefferson succeeded Patrick Henry as governor in June 1779 but proved an inept wartime leader. He barely escaped capture when the British invaded Virginia in 1781, forcing the government to flee Richmond. Jefferson retreated to Monticello, effectively relinquishing the governorship; the legislature replaced him with Thomas Nelson, Jr., and ordered an investigation of his conduct. Although in December the investigating committee judged that Jefferson had done nothing deserving censure, he stood diminished in public esteem. He spent 1781–83 composing *Notes on the State of Virginia*. His wife died in September 1782, and he was appointed a peace commissioner in November but never joined the other commissioners in France. He was elected to Congress in June 1783. Jefferson drafted a bill in March 1784 that served as precedent for the Northwest Ordinance of 1787 and provided for banning slavery in the western territories after 1800. In August 1784, he joined John Adams and Benjamin Franklin in Paris to negotiate commerce treaties with France, and in 1785, he succeeded Franklin as minister to France while also negotiating a commerce treaty with Prussia. Returned to America in fall 1789, Jefferson accepted appointment as President Washington's secretary of state, serving from March 1790 until December 1793. In 1796, Jefferson was elected vice president and, in 1800, president, after a tie vote left the selection to the House of Representatives. He was the first president to be inaugurated in Washington, D.C., the seat of government from 1800. As president, Jefferson secured the Louisiana Purchase and launched the Lewis and Clark Expedition. Reelected in 1804, he left the presidency in 1809 to return to Monticello for the remainder of his life. Jefferson was president of the American Philosophical Society (1797–1815) and primary founder of the University of Virginia (1819) and architect of its original buildings. Financial ruin caused by the Embargo of 1807 (his own policy) forced him to sell his library of 10,000 volumes to the government in 1815. By 1819, he was again in financial straits. Both he and John Adams, with whom Jefferson had a lengthy correspondence, died on the 50th anniversary of the signing of the Declaration of Independence.

Jones, John Paul (1747–1792) *Continental navy commander*
Born John Paul (he added the Jones in 1773) in Kirkcudbrightshire, Scotland, Jones became apprenticed at age 12 to a Whitehaven shipowner, whose later

bankruptcy led Jones to join the crew of a slave ship. At age 19, he was first mate on the slaver *Two Friends* that traded between Jamaica and the Guinea coast. He left this trade and booked passage on a ship to England of which he assumed command when the captain and first mate died of fever; the grateful owners rewarded him with 10 percent of the cargo and command of their merchantship *John* out of Dumfries. Jones captained the ship on two voyages to the West Indies in 1769–70. On the second voyage, he flogged the ship's carpenter for dereliction; the man died two weeks later from the wounds, and Jones was arrested for murder when he returned to Scotland. Cleared of the charge, he became master in 1773 of the *Betsey* out of London. In Tobago, he killed the leader of a mutiny by his crew and, to avoid a trial, sailed secretly to America, where he assumed the name Jones. Unemployed when the Revolution began, Jones traveled to Philadelphia and was hired to help outfit the *Alfred,* the first ship the Continental Congress purchased for the Continental navy. In December 1775, through the efforts of two congressmen he had befriended, Jones was commissioned as first lieutenant on the *Alfred.* In 1776, he received command of the *Providence.* His success resulted in the rank of captain and command of a small fleet to harass British shipping. In June 1777, he received command of the *Ranger.* Sent to France to assume command of the *Indien,* Jones discovered that the ship was being given to France, and in 1778, he sailed the *Ranger* for a series of coastal raids on Scotland that earned him hero status in France. Awarded command of the French ship *Duras,* Jones renamed it *Bonhomme Richard* in honor of Benjamin Franklin, who had helped him in France. He set sail in August 1779 and the next month defeated the *Serapis* in a renowned battle. In December 1780, Jones sailed for America where, in 1781, Congress gave him command of *America,* the navy's largest ship, but when its construction was completed, the ship was given to France. Following decommissioning of the navy, Jones returned to France as an American agent to claim the prize money for the ships he had captured during the war. Louis XVI made him a chevalier. On his final visit to America in 1787, the Continental Congress awarded him a gold medal, the only one presented to a Continental navy officer. In 1788, at Catherine the Great's request, Jones served in the Russian navy against the Turks but found the duty in the Black Sea unrewarding, and in September 1789, he returned to Paris.

Kalb, Johann (Baron de Kalb) (1721–1780)
general in the Continental army

Born to a peasant family named Kalb in Huttendorf, Bavaria, he left home at 16 and in his early 20s emerged as Jean de Kalb, a lieutenant in a French infantry unit. De Kalb served throughout the War of the Austrian Succession (1740–48) and the Seven Years' War, becoming a major at its onset in 1756. In 1764, he married an heiress, and in 1765, he retired from the military. In the early months of 1768, he traveled in America as a secret agent for the French foreign minister. De Kalb returned to military service in 1774 following Louis XVI's accession to the throne, and in November 1776, he became a brigadier general. Recruited by Silas Deane in Paris, he left for America in April 1777 with the marquis de Lafayette. Both men demanded that the Continental Congress grant them the rank of major general. De Kalb, who portrayed himself as baron de Kalb, responded to Congress's initial indifference by preparing to return to France, but in September 1777, Congress relented and gave him the desired rank. He spent the winter at Valley Forge with Washington's army. In April 1780, he was assigned to relieve Charleston; arriving too late, he took command of the American forces remaining in North Carolina, until the Continental Congress appointed Horatio Gates as commander of the Southern Department. De Kalb served under Gates, who ignored his counsel, and, on August 16, 1780, fought bravely at the Battle of Camden, holding fast as Gates and the militia fled the field. Severely wounded during the battle, he died three days later.

Knox, Henry (1750–1806) *general in the Continental army*

Knox was born in Boston, where he owned a bookstore and served with the militia at the time the Revolution began. A self-taught soldier, huge (300 pounds) but energetic, and a good manager, Knox formed a close and enduring relationship with Washington, who appointed him commander of artillery following the Battle of Bunker Hill, where Knox served as a volunteer. In winter 1775, Knox supervised transporting 60 captured heavy artillery from Fort Ticonderoga by sled 300 miles to Boston to support the siege of the city, forcing the British to evacuate. Knox's artillery served on Long Island and at Trenton. Promoted to brigadier general after the Battle of Trenton, Knox served as commander of the Continental artillery throughout the New Jersey campaign and at Brandywine, Germantown, and Monmouth. He also commanded the artillery at Yorktown, and after Cornwallis's surrender, he took command at West Point. Knox became a major general in 1782 and succeeded Washington as commander in chief in 1783. He became secretary of war under the Articles of Confederation and the first secretary of war under the Constitution by Washington's appointment, serving until his retirement in 1794. A chicken bone lodged in his intestines caused his death.

Knyphausen, Wilhelm von (1716–1800) *German commander with the British army*
Von Knyphausen began service in the Prussian army in the mid-1730s and was a lieutenant general in 1776, when he sailed to America in command of 4,000 mercenaries from Hesse-Kassel to serve with the British. He participated in battles in the New York and New Jersey campaigns and replaced Gen. Leopold von Heister as senior German officer after the debacle at Trenton. He commanded half of Howe's army at the Battle of Brandywine and was in charge of escorting baggage for the march from Philadelphia to New York. In 1779, during Sir Henry Clinton's absence to lead the campaign at Charleston, von Knyphausen held command of British forces in New York and made several moderately successful assaults in New Jersey. His health began to fail in 1781, and he assumed a diminished role following Clinton's return. In 1782, he returned to Europe and retired but later served as military governor of Kassel.

Kościuszko, Tadeusz (1746–1817) *Polish patriot, volunteer in the Continental army*
Born in a part of Poland that belonged to the Grand Duchy of Lithuania, Kościuszko was orphaned as a boy but attended the Polish royal military school and the French army school of engineering and artillery. He came to America in 1776, and the Continental Congress granted him a commission as colonel of engineers to serve with the Continental army. Assigned to the command of Gen. Horatio Gates, he planned the entrenchments at Saratoga that assisted the American victory there against Gen. John Burgoyne. Kościuszko also planned the defenses at West Point. Then, in 1780, he set out to join Gates in the Southern Department, arriving after Gates's humiliating defeat at Camden; he stayed on to serve with Gates's successor, Gen. Nathanael Greene. Kościuszko served Greene both as an engineer and as a commander of cavalry. In 1783,

he was appointed brigadier general; he returned to Europe in 1784. A staunch supporter of Polish independence, Kościuszko led the abortive campaign against the 1792 Russian invasion, after which he moved to Paris. Captured by the Russians during another Polish uprising in 1794, he came to the United States following his release. The American government awarded him a lump-sum payment and land in Ohio in appreciation of his services during the Revolution. Kościuszko returned to Europe in 1798.

Lafayette, marquis de (Marie-Joseph du Motier) (1757–1834) *French volunteer, general in the Continental army*
Born to a wealthy and aristocratic family but orphaned at an early age, Lafayette married at age 16 and entered military service as a teenager. Inexperienced as a soldier but inspired by the romance of helping the Americans achieve freedom, Lafayette came to America in 1777 with his mentor, Johann de Kalb, and a guarantee of their appointment as major generals from Silas Deane. Congress reluctantly awarded the commissions but gave no command to the 19-year-old Lafayette, but Washington immediately befriended Lafayette and promoted his career. Lafayette served on Washington's staff as a volunteer at Brandywine, where he was wounded. In late 1777, the Continental Congress appointed him to a division of Virginia light infantry. He commanded reasonably well at Monmouth, and he led two brigades at the unsuccessful French-American effort at Newport. When the likelihood of official French support of the American Revolution increased, Lafayette returned to France to advocate sending a major expedition to America. Lafayette returned to America in April 1780, but despite his hopes of serving as a liaison, the French commander Rochambeau rebuffed him. Washington gave Lafayette command of an army in Virginia assigned to halt British depredations; though successful in forestalling British movements, he achieved no major victory. Lafayette pinned down Cornwallis's army at Yorktown while Washington and Rochambeau moved their forces from New York to Yorktown in 1781, and he commanded one of the three American divisions during the siege. Two months after Cornwallis's surrender, Lafayette returned to France, where his revolutionary activities had mixed results. He served in several assemblies, and in 1792, he commanded a French army until a radical faction

condemned him and forced him into flight. After several years as a prisoner of the Austrians and Prussians, he was freed by Napoleon. Lafayette rejected an offer to be American governor of Louisiana but accepted a grant of money and extensive lands from the United States government. A hero to the American public, he returned to America in 1824 for a yearlong triumphal tour and numerous accolades as a symbol of French support for the American Revolution.

Laurens, Henry (1724–1792) *Patriot, member of Congress, diplomat*
Born in Charleston, Laurens lived for several years in England but nevertheless became a staunch Patriot in the early 1770s. A wealthy merchant, he served on the Charleston Committee of Safety. Chosen a delegate to the Second Continental Congress in 1777, he became president of the South Carolina assembly in 1778 but resigned because of involvement in the controversy over Silas Deane, to whom he was implacably opposed. Laurens served as president of the Continental Congress from November 1777 until December 1778. In 1779, Congress chose him to be an emissary to the Netherlands, and he set sail in 1780 to negotiate a treaty and a large loan with the Dutch, but the British captured his ship and imprisoned him in severely harsh conditions in the Tower of London. Although ill and suffering, he rejected British offers of pardon in exchange for his cooperation. He was released in 1782 to be exchanged for Cornwallis. Congress had selected him as one of the peace commissioners while he was still imprisoned, and he joined the commission shortly before the treaty was signed. In 1782–83, Laurens served as unofficial ambassador to Great Britain. He returned to the United States, retired from politics, and worked toward restoring his lost fortunes in South Carolina.

Lee, Arthur (1740–1792) *American representative in Europe during the Revolution*
Born in Virginia, Lee studied medicine in Edinburgh, practiced in Virginia for two years, and returned to Great Britain in 1766 to study law. During the late 1760s, he attained public notice through a series of letters published in Virginia and London. In 1770, Massachusetts appointed him as the colony's representative in London. He worked with Beaumarchais in 1775 in creating the dummy corporation Roderigue Hortalez et Cie to supply arms to the American revo-lutionaries. Appointed to join Benjamin Franklin and Silas Deane as an agent in Paris, Lee, who had become suspicious of other American agents in Europe, soon fell out totally with Deane. The ensuing controversy soured his relationship with Franklin. Lee undertook missions to Spain and Berlin and then returned to America in 1780. He served in the Virginia House of Delegates. Elected to Congress in 1782, he was ineffectual as a member because of his rancor and cynicism, and he left Congress in 1784.

Lee, Charles (1731–1782) *general in the Continental army*
Lee was born in Britain to a military family and joined his father's regiment in 1747. He came to North America in 1755 with Braddock's expedition and served through most of the French and Indian War. Lee returned to England in 1761, served under Burgoyne in Portugal, and then retired on half-pay as a lieutenant colonel. He went to Poland in 1765 and intermittently served the Polish Crown as a mercenary until 1770. In 1775 he moved to America and bought an estate in the territory that is now West Virginia. After the Revolution began, he petitioned the Continental Congress for a commission in the Continental army and was appointed major general. Although his service in the New York campaign was undistinguished, he received command of the Southern Department in 1776 and successfully directed the defense of Charleston against a British invasion. During the New Jersey campaign, he failed to comply with Washington's request for support, perhaps in hopes Washington would fail. (Lee was next in line to be commander in chief.) Lee wrote letters to politicians revealing his envy of and contempt for Washington. Captured at Basking Ridge in December 1776 by a British raiding party and imprisoned at New York, Lee proposed to General Howe a tactic for defeating the Americans by sundering the Middle Colonies (this treason remained unknown until the mid-1800s). Lee was exchanged in time to command part of the army at Monmouth, where his failure to provide Washington crucial support and his subsequent bitter complaints resulted in charges of disobedience and misbehavior. Found guilty by the court-martial and suspended from command for a year, Lee wrote a letter to the Continental Congress when his suspension ended that was so offensive that Congress dismissed him from service. He retired to his estate in the Shenandoah Valley.

Lee, Henry (Light–Horse Harry) (1756–1818) *Continental army officer, state official*
Born into a prominent Virginia family, Lee was preparing to leave for England to study law when the Revolution began. He was appointed a captain of Virginia cavalry. While serving with Washington's army in the North in spring 1777, he attracted the commander in chief's attention and received command of a special elite force of dragoons and infantry known as Lee's Legion, which became one of the outstanding units of the Continental army. In August 1779, the legion won an important victory at Paulus Hook, New York, that earned Lee the thanks of Congress and one of the few medals awarded during the war. In November 1779, Lee was promoted to lieutenant colonel. Sent by Washington in 1780 to join Greene in the southern campaign, Lee and his legion participated in nearly every important action in the South during the next two years. The legion functioned both as the core of the American cavalry and as partisan raiders on British outposts in the Carolinas, often joining with Francis Marion's or Andrew Pickens's forces. Lee was instrumental in saving Greene's army at the Battle of Eutaw Springs in 1781. Lee withdrew from active command after the victory at Yorktown. In subsequent years, Lee served in varied political offices, including governor of Virginia, but he suffered from bouts of depression and financial reverses. He also fathered Robert E. Lee. Lee's *Memoirs of the War in the Southern Department of the United States* is considered one of the best accounts of the Revolutionary War by a participant.

Lincoln, Benjamin (1733–1810) *general in the Continental army*
A native of Massachusetts and brigadier in the colony's militia when the revolution began, Lincoln had responsibility for militiamen at Boston and later at New York. Despite holding no prior commission in the Continental army, he received promotion to major general in February 1777, to the outrage of many junior officers, including Benedict Arnold. Sent to New England in August 1777, he persuaded the Vermont militia to attack Baum's Hessians at Bennington and thereafter commanded the Bemis Heights defenses at Saratoga, where he suffered a severe wound that left him invalided for several months. The Continental Congress appointed him commander of the Southern Department in September 1778 without first consulting Washington. Lincoln arrived too late to prevent the British capture of Savannah and then allowed most of his army to be pinned down in Charleston, which he was forced to surrender to General Clinton in 1780 in a major defeat. Taken prisoner, Lincoln was paroled at the end of the year, and in 1781, he received command of the army as it marched south to Yorktown, where he commanded one of the three divisions during the siege. A few weeks later, Congress appointed him the nation's first secretary at war. He held the post until the war ended in 1783 and then returned to Massachusetts. He held several state offices and, in 1787, commanded the troops sent to quell Shays's Rebellion.

Lord Stirling *See* **Alexander, William.**

Madison, James (1751–1836) *statesman, president*
A Virginia native, Madison graduated from the College of New Jersey (now Princeton) in 1771. In 1775, he joined his local committee of safety, and in 1776, he was elected to the Virginia Convention. Madison helped to draft the Virginia constitution, and he served in the first state assembly but failed of reelection and then served on the governor's council. He was elected a delegate to the Congress in 1779, serving for three years; he was instrumental in formulating American diplomacy, creating a compromise among the states over contentious western land claims that threatened the union, and negotiating the formula for counting slaves for determining political representation. Madison gained wide renown for his contributions to *The Federalist,* in which he presented arguments in support of ratifying the Constitution. He served as secretary of state in the Jefferson administration. Madison was elected president in 1809 and served two terms, disrupted by the War of 1812. He retired to private life in 1817.

Marion, Francis (The Swamp Fox) (ca. 1732–1795) *South Carolina militia officer*
Marion gained initial repute as an Indian fighter with the South Carolina militia. When the Revolution began, he was serving as a delegate to the provincial congress and a militia captain. In 1776, as a major he played a vital role in defending Charleston and then took command of a full regiment of the militia. An accident that broke his ankle forced his evacuation from Charleston before it fell to the British in 1780. With no organized American army in the state, Marion adopted irregular tactics. He and his men lived in the swamps, frequently changed locales, made

partisan raids on British outposts, and avoided British forces through stealth and speed. Marion well served Nathanael Greene during the 1781 campaign. He also joined with Henry Lee and William Washington in fielding an effective, mobile strike force, but his efforts with Thomas Sumter proved unsuccessful. His crowning achievement was helping to save the American army from a severe defeat at the Battle of Eutaw Springs in September 1781. Following the war, Marion served in various state offices.

Martin, Josiah (1737–1786) *royal governor of North Carolina*
Martin served in the British army for 12 years, sold his lieutenant colonelcy in 1769, and in 1771, became governor of North Carolina. As revolutionary fervor rose, the colony's judicial system collapsed, and by 1773, Martin was forced to operate the criminal courts by royal prerogative. In 1774, the rebels convened an extralegal provincial assembly. Convinced that Loyalists comprised a solid majority in North Carolina, Martin believed he could resist the Patriot militia. In July 1775, however, he was forced to take refuge aboard a British ship. In New York, he petitioned to lead a British army to North Carolina, expecting a Loyalist uprising in support, but his 1776 expedition to retake Charleston failed. Martin's hopes suffered further with the Loyalists' defeat at Moore's Creek Bridge. Martin served as a volunteer in Cornwallis's successful 1780 expedition to retake Charleston and the Carolinas. He returned to England in spring 1781.

Monroe, James (1758–1831) *officer in the Continental army, statesman, president*
A Virginia native, Monroe was a student at the College of William and Mary when the Revolution began. He joined the Virginia Line of the Continental army and served as a junior officer in most of the early battles of the war. During the Battle of Trenton in December 1776, he was wounded on a city street. Promoted to major, he became aide-de-camp to Lord Stirling. Monroe fought at Brandywine, Germantown, and Monmouth and then resigned his commission. He began to study law with Thomas Jefferson in 1780. After the war, Monroe was elected a delegate to the Congress, where he took an Antifederalist position. He served as senator from Virginia, governor, and envoy to France. Appointed secretary of state in 1811 by Madison, Monroe later became secretary of war.

Elected president in 1816, Monroe served two terms and authored the famed Monroe Doctrine.

Montgomery, Richard (1738–1775) *general in the Continental army*
A native of Ireland, Montgomery joined the British army as an ensign. He fought in North America in 1757–60 during the French and Indian War and thereafter served in the West Indies. He spent 10 years in England and then, in 1772, sold his commission and moved to New York to be a farmer. When the Revolution began, he accepted a commission as a brigadier general in the Continental army and was sent on the 1775 expedition against Quebec as Phillip Schuyler's second in command. Montgomery assumed command when Schuyler fell ill. Although his men were poorly trained and equipped, he captured St. John's en route to Quebec. Montgomery was fatally wounded while leading the unsuccessful assault at Quebec.

Morgan, Daniel (1736–1802) *general in the Continental army*
Born in New Jersey, Morgan left home to live in the Shenandoah Valley as a teenager. In 1755, he served as a teamster with Braddock's expedition. A 1756 encounter with a British officer earned him 500 lashes, with enduring scars he referred to during the Revolution. In subsequent years, Morgan fought in the Indian wars when not farming. Commissioned in June 1775 to raise a company of Virginia riflemen, he soon gained fame as these marksmen's leader. Morgan's rifle company marched to Boston to join Washington, who assigned them to Arnold's expedition against Canada. Morgan was in the vanguard during the assault at Quebec; he took charge when Arnold was wounded but was captured and held at Quebec until being paroled in 1776. Commissioned a colonel, he raised a corps of 500 riflemen that joined Gates's army and played a crucial role in the battles at Saratoga resulting in Burgoyne's defeat. Morgan and his men wintered with Washington at Valley Forge and then served with Washington until the summer of 1779, when Morgan resigned over disgruntlement at being passed over for promotion, although he professed the reason was ill health. He returned to farming in Virginia, but news of the disastrous American defeat at Camden, North Carolina, in 1780 nudged him to return to service. The Continental Congress finally promoted him to brigadier general, and Greene placed him in charge of his light infantry.

Morgan achieved a stunning victory over Carleton at the Battle of Cowpens in January 1781. Again pleading ill health, Morgan returned home, serving the army again briefly in Virginia. Following the war, he farmed and speculated in land, commanded troops sent to quell the Whiskey Rebellion in 1793, and served in Congress.

Morris, Gouverneur (1752–1816) *statesman, diplomat*

Born into the aristocratic Morris-Gouverneur families of New York, Morris attended King's College (now Columbia University), becoming a lawyer before he turned 20. A stern foe of democracy, he nevertheless supported the principles underlying the Revolution. Morris served in the New York Provincial Congress in 1776 and 1777 and helped to draft the state's constitution. Elected to the Continental Congress in 1778, he was active in financial and diplomatic issues, but entanglement in New York's state politics cost him reelection, and he moved to Philadelphia. A series of articles on finances published in 1780 earned him appointment by Robert Morris (no relation) as assistant to the superintendent of finance. Although a fall from his carriage necessitated amputating his leg, he continued to aid Robert Morris in managing the national finances until 1785. Morris supported the Constitution and a strong central government. After serving with distinction as a diplomat during the 1790s in England and then in France during the Reign of Terror, Morris returned to New York and rebuilt his fortune.

Morris, Robert (1734–1806) *merchant, congressional delegate, finance superintendent*

Born in Liverpool, England, Morris emigrated to Maryland at age 13 with his father. He later moved to Philadelphia and worked in a countinghouse. As the Revolution loomed, he was a partner in Willing, Morris & Co., the major mercantile firm in the thirteen colonies with control over a sizable share of the colonies' commerce. A delegate to the First Continental Congress and active in Pennsylvania revolutionary politics during 1775, Morris gained reelection to the Congress in 1776; he signed the Declaration of Independence. Morris served on the Secret Committee, becoming involved in the Silas Deane controversy. Still prospering as a merchant, Morris committed much of his personal fortune to the Revolutionary cause and his abilities to managing Congress's unsound finances. He also

donated funds and supplies to Washington's army at critical junctures. Morris left the Congress in 1778 but was recalled in 1781 to serve as the first superintendent of the department of finance (later secretary of finance) following upon the near collapse of the government's finances. Confronting unchecked inflation, a worthless Continental dollar, and no government income, Morris labored to effect solvency for the national government. He gained approval of the charter for the first national bank and manipulated foreign loans to secure America's credit worthiness. Failing to convince the states to support a national system of finance controlled by the central government, he resigned in 1784. Declining the post of secretary of the treasury in George Washington's first presidential term, Morris served in the Senate. Largely due to failed land speculations, Morris's financial fortunes collapsed in his later years; imprisoned for debt, he died in total penury—a grim irony for the man known as the "Financier of the American Revolution."

Moultrie, William (1730–1805) *general in the Continental army*

Born in Great Britain, Moultrie moved as a boy to Charleston, South Carolina, with his father. During the 1760s, he served as a militia leader in the Indian wars. He was commissioned a colonel at the outbreak of the Revolution; he was also twice elected to the Continental Congress but declined to serve. Moultrie gained fame in 1776 for his defense of Fort Sullivan in Charleston Harbor, preventing Admiral Parker's fleet from taking control of the harbor and thereby thwarting the British attempt to capture the city. (Fort Sullivan was renamed in Moultrie's honor.) Promoted to brigadier general, he led his troops to protect Prevost after the British captured Savannah. In 1779, he was victorious at Beaufort, South Carolina, but in 1780, he was captured when British forces under Clinton took control of Charleston, whose defenses had been allowed to deteriorate since 1776. Although exchanged in 1782 and promoted to major general, Moultrie had no further role in the war. Following the war, he served two terms as governor of South Carolina.

North, Lord (Frederick North) (1732–1792) *British prime minister during the American Revolution*

Born in London, the son of a nobleman, North was educated at Eton and Oxford. At age 22, he was elected to Parliament. In 1759, North became lord of the treasury, and he moved upward in the official ranks during the following decade to become prime minister in March 1770. Forming a close association with George III, he worked assiduously to uphold the king's majority and policies in Parliament. North was responsible for many of the policies and acts leading to the American Revolution, including the Boston Port Bill of 1774. Doubting his own capabilities, North repeatedly tried to resign, but the king demanded he stay on. North recognized the futility of continuing the war against the Americans following Cornwallis's surrender at Yorktown in 1781, but the king insisted that he remain in office and continue to push the war effort. Losing support in Parliament, North resigned in March 1782. He returned briefly to power in 1783 in a coalition government and continued his involvement in politics through the succeeding years despite going blind in 1789.

Paine, Thomas (1737–1809) *writer, soldier*
Paine was born in England and trained as a corsetmaker. At Benjamin Franklin's urging, he came to America in 1774. During the winter of 1775–76, he published an anonymous pamphlet entitled *Common Sense* that advocated independence in eloquent but simple language; it quickly sold tens of thousands of copies, helping to tilt public sentiment toward separation from Great Britain. In 1776, Paine joined the Continental army, serving as an aide to Nathanael Greene. After the American defeats in New York, he wrote a series of essays called *The Crisis* to inspire patriotic ardor. Appointed by the Continental Congress as secretary of the committee overseeing foreign affairs, Paine became embroiled in the Silas Deane controversy and was forced to resign. After the war, New York awarded him a confiscated Loyalist estate and a cash bonus. In 1787, he returned to England and began to write *The Rights of Man*. In 1791, he moved to Paris and was elected to the revolutionary French assembly, but after a change of regimes, he was imprisoned in December 1793. In prison, Paine wrote *The Age of Reason*. Following his release in November 1794, he was readmitted to the National Convention. In September 1802, Paine returned to the United States to live out his life forgotten and poor.

Peale, Charles Willson (1741–1827) *painter, militia officer*
Son of an English emigrant gentleman and born in Maryland, Peale became an apprentice saddlemaker in Annapolis following his father's death in 1750. Aspiring to be an artist, he traded a saddle to John Hesselius, then a local portraitist, for some lessons. Besieged by creditors, Peale fled to Boston in the mid-1760s, leaving his wife behind. In Boston, he studied briefly with John Singleton Copley. Returning to Maryland, Peale received funds raised by local supporters to pursue his studies in England. For three years, Peale studied with expatriate Benjamin West in London, polishing his techniques in portraiture. Returned to Maryland, Peale launched a career that earned him status as the most accomplished portraitist in the middle colonies. In 1772, he painted a portrait of George Washington—the first of seven he would do from life. Peale had joined the Sons of Liberty in 1765; his outspoken criticisms of the Crown lost him commissions among wealthy Loyalists, and in 1776, he moved to Philadelphia to produce portraits of American leaders. Peale joined the militia, becoming a captain; he crossed the Delaware River with Washington as a participant in the attacks on Trenton and Princeton, New Jersey. Recognizing his shortcomings as a soldier, Peale left the service, but all the while continuing his portrait work. Ultimately, he produced more than 250 portraits of leading Revolutionary figures. Peale served in the Pennsylvania legislature in 1779, having charge of the state's confiscated Loyalist properties. Continuing his painting career after the war, Peale also became interested in natural history, and in 1786, he established the Peale Museum, the first science museum in the nation. Peale fathered 17 children by three wives and named many of them for artists and also trained several, including his daughters, as artists. Two of the children, Raphaelle and Rembrandt, especially the latter, had distinguished careers in art.

Pitcher, Molly *See* **Corbin, Margaret and Hays, Mary Ludwig.**

Prevost, Augustine (1723–1786) *British general*
Prevost was born in Switzerland. He joined the British army in 1756, served under Wolfe during the Seven Years' War, and suffered severe wounds at the Battle of Quebec. When the Revolutionary War began, Prevost was a colonel commanding British forces in East Florida. He participated in the capture of Savannah in 1778 and then assumed command of all British forces in the South. He achieved several important victories against American forces that included thwarting the American effort to retake Savannah. He had secured

British control of Georgia by the end of 1779, when he returned to England.

Pulaski, Kazimierz (1747–1779) *general in the Continental army*

Pulaski was born into a noble family in Poland and fought with his father's troops against the Russians. When the First Partition of Poland occurred, he fled to Turkey and served in that nation's army. Pulaski traveled to Paris, where he met Benjamin Franklin, who advised him to go to America and provided him with a recommendation to the Continental Congress. He arrived in America in 1777 and served as a volunteer aide to Washington at the Battle of Brandywine. Adhering to Washington's suggestion, the Continental Congress commissioned Pulaski as brigadier general and commander of the newly authorized cavalry. He fought ineffectually at Germantown and then wintered with the Continental army at Valley Forge. Overconfident of his own abilities and quarrelsome, he bickered with his subordinate officers, although he spoke no English, and brought charges against his second in command for a perceived slight. Resigning in 1778 as cavalry commander, he received permission to raise his own "elite" corps and recruited men among British deserters and prisoners. The Pulaski Legion actually imperiled American efforts and proved ineffectual. Finally stationed in the South, Pulaski led the legion in a foolhardy cavalry charge at Savannah in late 1779, was wounded in the groin, and died two days later aboard an American ship following surgery.

Putnam, Israel (1718–1790) *major general in the Continental army*

Putnam was born in Massachusetts but spent most of his life farming in Connecticut. In 1755, he joined Rogers's Rangers to fight in the French and Indian War, rising to the rank of lieutenant colonel of militia. In 1758, he was captured by Indians, who were preparing to burn him at the stake when a French officer intervened. Putnam was exchanged and sailed on a mission against Havana, but the mission shipwrecked off Cuba, with Putnam among the few survivors. As the Revolution approached, he was a successful farmer and tavernkeeper and member of the Sons of Liberty. Following the battles at Lexington and Concord, he hastened to Boston and was made colonel of a Connecticut regiment and brigadier of the Connecticut militia. Putnam fought courageously as one of two commanders of Bunker Hill, after which the Continental Congress appointed him as major general in the Continental army. Washington placed him in command of troops at Long Island, where his ineptitude proved largely responsible for the American defeat. He was seldom thereafter entrusted with any vital task, although he remained a field commander during the New Jersey campaign. Placed in charge of American defenses in the Hudson Highlands, he allowed Clinton to seize two strategic forts. Putnam suffered a paralytic stroke in 1779 that forced him out of active service, and he thereafter functioned as a recruiter.

Randolph, Peyton (1721–1775) *president of Continental Congress*

A member of the wealthy and powerful Randolph family of Virginia, Peyton Randolph was the grandson of William and Mary Randolph, whose other descendants included Thomas Jefferson and Henry Lee. He received a large estate of lands and wealth from his father Sir John Randolph of Tazewell. Randolph attended William and Mary College and received legal training at the Middle Temple in London, England. In 1745, he established a legal practice in Williamsburg; in 1748, he became king's attorney for Virginia. In 1764, Randolph became a delegate in the House of Burgesses, retaining his seat for 10 years. Chosen chairman of the committee of correspondence, Randolph also served as president of the provincial conventions in 1774 and 1775. Sent as a delegate to the Continental Congress in 1774, he was elected its first president. Illness caused him to resign in October 1774; reelected in the spring of 1775, he again resigned because of illness. He died of a stroke in October 1775 in Philadelphia.

Reed, Joseph (1741–1785) *delegate to Continental Congress, aide to George Washington*

Son of a wealthy merchant, Reed was born in Trenton, New Jersey, to an Irish immigrant family. He attended the Academy of Philadelphia and graduated from the College of New Jersey (later Princeton) in 1757. After reading law with Richard Stockton (later a delegate to the Continental Congress), Reed was admitted to the bar in 1762; he then traveled to London to study at the Middle Temple. Reed established a law practice in Philadelphia in 1770. He served on the Philadelphia Committee of Correspondence in 1774 and as president of the Pennsylvania provincial congress in 1775. Committed to American independence and a lieutenant colonel in the Pennsylvania militia, Reed became George Washington's military secretary. In late 1775, he left active duty to supervise his law practice, but he returned to duty in spring 1776 as a colonel and adjutant general of the army, becoming Washington's chief staff officer. Reed's advice to vacate New York and Fort Washington went unheeded, and he also engendered Washington's suspicions because of a letter the commander intercepted sent to Reed by Charles Lee that denounced Washington. Still he retained Washington's confidence and was helpful to the success of the attacks on Trenton and Princeton. Reed resigned his commission in late January 1777 but continued intermittently as a volunteer aide to Washington. In 1778, Reed became a delegate to the Continental Congress from Pennsylvania. After one term, he left to serve as head of the Pennsylvania Supreme Executive Council, holding the post until 1781. Reed publicly revealed the Carlisle Commission's efforts to bribe him, helping to derail its mission. Falsely accused of disloyalty by Arthur Lee, Reed returned to his law practice following the war.

Revere, Paul (1735–1818) *silversmith, Patriot*
Born in Boston, Revere learned silversmithing from his father. Following service as an officer in the French and Indian War, he returned to Boston and established a silversmith trade, becoming locally renowned for his skills with both silver and copper engraving. An early Patriot and leader of the Sons of Liberty, he promoted popular resistance to the Stamp Act and the Boston Massacre through his widely disseminated engravings. In 1773, Revere helped plan and carry out the Boston Tea Party. He served as a courier among rebel organizations, his most famous exploit being the ride of April 18–19, 1775, to Lexington and Concord to warn John Hancock, Samuel Adams, and other Patriots of the British march to confiscate Patriot arms. Revere served the war effort by manufacturing gunpowder and making engravings for the Continental Congress and other official entities. He served briefly as a lieutenant colonel of militia and played a leading role in the disastrous 1779 Massachusetts expedition to Maine. Following the war, Revere returned to his silversmithing and other businesses.

Riedesel, Baron Friedrich von (1738–1800) *German mercenary officer*
A native of Hesse, Riedesel served in the Seven Years' War and rose to the rank of colonel. He was serving with the duke of Brunswick when appointed to lead the first contingent of Brunswickers to America during the Revolution. He arrived in Quebec in summer 1776 with about 2,300 men. Riedesel commanded the German soldiers in the expedition of Burgoyne, who to his own loss ignored Riedesel's counsel on such matters as sending Baum against Bennington. Riedesel fought with distinction at both of the Saratoga battles; following Burgoyne's surrender, he was held by the Americans and exchanged in 1780. He served as commander on Long Island and then returned to Canada as an adviser in 1781. He and his family returned to Europe in 1783. His wife, Frederica, wrote a memoir of their experiences in America.

Rochambeau, count de (Jean-Baptiste-Donatien de Vimeur) (1725–1807) *French general*
An aristocrat by birth, Rochambeau joined the French army during the War of the Austrian Succession, rising to colonel and aide-de-camp to the Duke of Orleans by 1747. He served with distinction in the Seven Years' War, was wounded in 1760, received promotion to brigadier, and in 1765 became inspector of cavalry. In 1780, Rochambeau was promoted to lieutenant and given command of the French expeditionary force sent to America. He arrived in Newport with about 6,000 troops in July 1780 to find the Continental army so depleted that no joint effort could be launched, but the skillful and diplomatic Rochambeau formed a solid working relationship with Washington. In 1781, they devised a plan to attack upper Manhattan to draw Clinton out of New York, but the French fleet's arrival in the Chesapeake switched their effort instead to a march on Yorktown, where they laid siege to the city. After Cornwallis's surrender, Rochambeau stayed on in Virginia, returning to France in 1783. He held command of armies in France but was arrested during the Reign of Terror and narrowly escaped being executed.

Rush, Benjamin (1746–1813) *physician, delegate to Continental Congress, surgeon general*
Although born near Philadelphia, Rush was educated in Maryland following his father's death in 1754. In 1760, he graduated from the College of New Jersey (now Princeton) and then studied medicine privately in Philadelphia. Rush went to the University of Edinburgh in 1766 to pursue his medical studies and graduated in 1768. Thereafter, he studied medicine in

London and returned to Philadelphia, where he began a private practice and also served as professor of chemistry at the College of Philadelphia. Among the most prominent and accomplished physicians in the colonies and a political aspirant, Rush included among his friends and acquaintances Thomas Jefferson, Benjamin Franklin, John Adams, and Thomas Paine. In 1776, he married Julia Stockton, the daughter of Richard Stockton, a New Jersey delegate to the Continental Congress. Wholeheartedly embracing the independence movement, Rush earned the Pennsylvania convention's election as delegate to the Continental Congress in mid-1776—in time to sign the Declaration of Independence. Serving only one official term in the Congress, he became surgeon general in April 1777. Thereafter, Rush became involved in varied political intrigues, including attacks on William Shippen, chief physician for the Continental army, whom he accused of maladministration. George Washington referred the charges to the Continental Congress, which found in Shippen's favor. Rush resigned his military post and became involved in the Conway Cabal effort to replace Washington. When this effort failed, Rush returned to private practice and teaching. After the Revolutionary War, he helped found the first American medical college, at the University of Pennsylvania. Rush gained stature as the leading medical educator in the United States and was among the founders of an antislavery society, a free Philadelphia medical dispensary, and Dickinson College. Rush was appointed head of the U.S. Mint in 1797. He died of typhus at age 67.

Salomon, Haym (1740–1785) *financier, American secret agent*
Born in Lissa (Leszno), Poland, a polyglot but with little formal education, Salomon probably arrived in America in 1772 and began a brokerage and mercantile enterprise. Remaining in New York following American evacuation of the city in 1776, he served as a secret agent, providing George Washington with information on the strengths and positions of British troops. Arrested for espionage in September 1776, Salomon obtained release into the custody of Leopold Phillip von Heister, who employed him as an interpreter. But Salomon continued as an American agent, resulting in his arrest in August 1778 and a death sentence. By means of bribes, Salomon gained release from prison and fled to Philadelphia. Unsuccessful in his efforts to obtain a post from the Continental

Congress, Salomon set up a financial brokerage firm. Subsequently, Congress employed him frequently to conduct official financial transactions, and he served as the main broker for the bills of exchange used to sustain the government's imperiled solvency. After the French forces arrived in 1779, Salomon effectively became treasurer for count de Rochambeau and other French commanders. Salomon also personally provided money advances to congressional delegates and American officers. His most important role, however, came in his support of Robert Morris's policies; in this effort, Salomon frequently provided hard currency in exchange for essentially worthless congressional paper. With the war ended, Salomon bought a house in New York in 1784, apparently intending to return to the city, but he died before he could make the move. Salomon left an apparently sizable estate of more than $350,000, but mostly in government currency and debt certificates, which depreciated nearly to worthlessness; a final 1789 evaluation of the estate revealed that he had in fact died insolvent, with debts exceeding his assets. His family's efforts to secure due recompense from the Congress, stretching into the mid-19th century, eventuated in failure.

Schuyler, Philip (1733–1804) *major general in the Continental army*
Born to wealth and influence as a member of the well-established New York Dutch Schuyler–Van Renssalaer–Van Cortlandt families, Schuyler possessed a keen interest in military affairs and served as a captain during the French and Indian War, evidencing major abilities as an organizer of supplies and an administrator. He resigned his commission in 1757 but served as a private supplier to the British army. He rejoined the army in 1758 as a major, still operating in supplies. After the war, he inherited large tracts of land in northern New York and assumed his role among the gentry. Although an early Patriot, Schuyler disliked the radical element within the Sons of Liberty. He served as commissioner in the dispute over Vermont's status, alienating many New Englanders by favoring New York and by his perceived imperiousness. In 1775, for political reasons, the Continental Congress appointed him one of the first major generals of the Continental army. Placed in charge of the Canada expedition, he prepared slowly and irritated New England troops. Stricken by gout, he was replaced as leader of the expedition by Richard Montgomery. Schuyler made matters worse through a

dispute with Congress but continued to hold command of the Northern Department during Burgoyne's expedition. After Fort Ticonderoga fell, Congress appointed Horatio Gates to replace Schuyler. In 1779, Schuyler resigned his generalship, but he continued as an adviser to Washington and as an administrator. He also served as a delegate to the Continental Congress. In later life, Schuyler became a United States senator from New York.

Sherman, Roger (1721–1793) *statesman*
Born on a farm in Massachusetts, Sherman moved to New Milford, Connecticut, and amassed large land holdings and considerable wealth there. Hardworking and well respected, he was elected to the Continental Congress in 1774 and served until 1781 and also in 1783–84. Sherman served on the committee that drafted the Declaration of Independence, the Ways and Means Committee, the Board of War and Ordnance, the Treasury Board, the Committee for Indian Affairs, and the committee that drafted the Articles of Confederation. In 1784, he returned to Connecticut to serve as judge of the superior court and mayor of New Haven. Chosen a delegate in 1787 to the Constitutional Convention, he introduced the concept of dual representation in the federal government (the Connecticut Compromise). Elected to the House of Representatives, Sherman helped draft the Judiciary Act of 1789 establishing the federal court system. He was later appointed a United States senator from Connecticut and served in this position until his death. Sherman was the only person to sign all four great documents of the Revolution: the Articles of Association, the Declaration of Independence, the Articles of Confederation, and the Constitution.

Shippen, Peggy *See* **Arnold, Margaret.**

Stark, John (1728–1822) *general in the New Hampshire militia and the Continental army*
Born in New Hampshire and raised in its frontier region, Stark was kidnapped by Indians when a child and ransomed back to his parents. He served as a captain in Rogers's Rangers during the French and Indian War. When the Revolution erupted, Stark recruited a regiment and marched to join the militia forces surrounding Boston. He and his men served admirably at the Battle of Bunker Hill. In 1776, Stark was commissioned a colonel in the Continental army; his ser-

vice at Trenton and Princeton was exceptional. Piqued at not being promoted to general, Stark resigned and returned to New Hampshire, assuming command of the state militia with the proviso that he would not be responsible to accept orders from the Continental Congress or officers of the Continental army. During Burgoyne's expedition in 1777, Stark refused Benjamin Lincoln's orders to join the American army across the Hudson River, but when Burgoyne detached Baum's German troops to foray toward Bennington, Stark saw his opportunity, leading his men skillfully in an envelopment and near-annihilation of Baum's force. Following Burgoyne's surrender, Congress rewarded Stark with a commission as brigadier general. After the war, Stark retired from public life.

Steuben, Baron Friedrich Wilhelm von (1730–1794) *general in the Continental army*
Born at Magdeburg, Prussia, von Steuben was a veteran of the War of the Austrian Succession and the Seven Years' War, when he served as an aide to Frederick the Great. He had fallen on hard times as a half-pay captain when he met Benjamin Franklin in Paris. Nonetheless, he professed to be a lieutenant general when the Continental Congress accepted him as a volunteer, at Franklin's suggestion, and Washington appointed him acting inspector general of the Continental army in 1777. During the winter of 1777–78 at Valley Forge, von Steuben organized and trained the army, wrote the first American army manual of drill and regulations, and distracted the troops from their miseries by parading in his Prussian uniform and cursing them incomprehensibly (he spoke no English and little French). Subsequently, von Steuben continued to serve Washington as a one-man general staff, helping to reorganize the army's structure, creating a system to reduce waste, and acting as a liaison with Congress. In fall 1780, he joined American forces in Virginia under Lafayette, but his role in the final campaign of the war was modest. Von Steuben was discharged from the army in 1784. He became an American citizen and retired in New York.

Sullivan, John (1740–1795) *major general in the Continental army*
A New Hampshire native and a practicing lawyer, Sullivan became an early and fervid patriot, helping to lead a raid to seize gunpowder before the Battle of Lexington. In 1774, he served in the first Continental

Congress, and in 1775, he was commissioned a brigadier general in the Continental army. In 1776, he led an ineffectual relief effort toward Canada. Promoted to major general, he had command of the army at Long Island under Washington; he was captured by the British and soon exchanged. Rejoining Washington's command, he served well at Trenton, during the New Jersey campaign, and at Brandywine and Germantown. Sullivan created political difficulties for himself through quarrels with the Continental Congress, and he may have been involved with the Conway Cabal, but Washington continued to regard him with favor. Sullivan lost most of his command in the disastrous joint attack with the French on Newport, Rhode Island, in 1778, and another disaster on Staten Island instigated a congressional inquiry. In 1779, Washington sent Sullivan to subdue the Iroquois; during the late summer, he laid waste most of the Indian villages in upper New York. He resigned his commission after this expedition. In 1780, Sullivan again served in Congress, and subsequently he filled varied offices in New Hampshire. In 1789, Washington appointed Sullivan as a judge of the U.S. district court of New Hampshire.

Tarleton, Banastre (1754–1833) *British officer*
Born in Liverpool, the son of a wealthy merchant, Tarleton graduated from Oxford and in 1775, joined the army as a colonel. Shipped to America, he participated in the unsuccessful attack on Charleston in 1776. Service in New York earned him promotion, and by 1778, he was a lieutenant colonel and created the British Legion of green-clad light infantry and dragoons, made up largely of Loyalists. He and the legion were sent with General Clinton's expedition to South Carolina in 1779. He lost all of his horses on the voyage and replaced them by defeating American cavalry and seizing their horses. Carleton scored clear-cut victories at Monck's Corner and Lenud's Ferry, and he established his reputation for ruthlessness at Waxhaws in May 1779, when his men destroyed the remnants of the American forces and killed many prisoners after the surrender, giving rise to the ironic term *Tarleton's Quarter.* Invariably successful, Tarleton's British Legion became Cornwallis's primary mobile strike force, but the Battle of Cowpens saw it nearly destroyed. Although his reputation declined because of this defeat, Tarleton regrouped and scored successes against Greene and on raids in Virginia. Tarleton commanded the troops holding the landings at Gloucester during the siege

of Yorktown; after the surrender, he received a parole and returned to England. In 1790, Tarleton entered Parliament and also returned to active duty. Promoted to major general in 1794, he served in varied posts until being promoted to full general in 1812. Created a baronet in 1815, Tarleton was knighted in 1820.

Trumbull, John (1756–1843) *painter, Continental army officer*
Son of Jonathan Trumbull (the elder), governor of Connecticut, Trumbull lost sight in one eye while a boy. Although his father discouraged Trumbull's early interest in painting and in studying with John Singleton Copley, Trumbull nevertheless taught himself in art; he graduated from Harvard in 1773. Trumbull served as an adjutant to General Joseph Spencer when still a teenager; then in July 1775, he became aide-de-camp to George Washington for a brief period, leaving that post to serve in the field. In 1776, he became deputy adjutant to Horatio Gates with the rank of colonel. After campaigning with Gates through early 1777, Trumbull transferred to Benedict Arnold's command. In spring 1777, Trumbull resigned to pursue art studies in Boston. He returned to military duty for the 1778 campaign at Newport, Rhode Island. In 1780, Trumbull traveled to France and then to London to become a pupil of expatriate Benjamin West. British authorities arrested him for treason in November 1780, releasing him a month later. Trumbull fled to Holland. He returned to England in late 1783; there he began producing heroic scale canvases depicting events of the American Revolution. In 1787, Trumbull sojourned in Paris; in 1789, he returned home, settling in Philadelphia, where he produced portraits of the Revolutionary leaders. Becoming private secretary to John Jay in 1793 took him back to Europe; he returned to the United States in 1804. Trumbull's 200-plus paintings of Revolutionary War events and leaders continue to be the best known of all depictions of their subjects.

Ward, Artemas (1727–1800) *major general in the Continental army*
Born in Shrewsbury, Massachusetts, and a graduate of Harvard, Ward was politically active and served in the colony's legislature. During the French and Indian War, he was a lieutenant colonel in the Massachusetts militia, and in 1774, he was appointed brigadier and its commander in chief. Although in bed ill when the battles occurred at Lexington and Concord, Ward rushed to

Boston and assumed command of the militia laying siege to the British but contributed little. When the Continental Congress adopted the Continental army, Ward was appointed major general and second in command, but he resented being passed over by the appointment of Washington as commander in chief. Ward resigned his commission after the British left Boston in 1776. From 1777 to 1779, he was president of the Massachusetts Council, and from 1780 to 1782, he served in Congress. Later he was elected to the U.S. House of Representatives.

Warren, Mercy Otis (1728–1814) *poet, dramatist, historian*
Daughter of a prominent politician and sister of rebel leader James Otis, Warren, who was born in Cape Cod, pursued the serious education that colonial American society denied to most women, whose presumed role in life was to become wife, housekeeper, and child rearer. Accessing her uncle Jonathan Russell's library, she became knowledgeable in history, politics, and literature. In 1754, she married James Warren; they had five children. As the march to revolution progressed, Warren maintained a large correspondence with many leading Patriots, including her close friend Abigail Adams, and also wrote propaganda. More politically astute than her husband and many other Patriots, Warren remained close to her brother James, among Boston's leading radicals until he became highly erratic and finally insane following a severe blow to his head during a brawl. She wrote three fictional works in the years leading up to the Revolution, most notably *The Group,* published in January 1775. Warren's major writing achievement was *History of the Rise, Progress and Termination of the American Revolution,* published in 1805. An anti-Federalist, her views on the Revolution inspired a vitriolic dispute with longtime friend John Adams that lasted for five years.

Washington, George (1732–1799) *commander in chief of the Continental army, first United States president*
Born the second son of a wealthy Virginia planter, Washington had little formal education. After his father's death when he was 11, he lived in the shadow of his elder brother, Lawrence, inheritor of Mount Vernon and most of the family wealth, and spent most of his time at another family estate near Fredericksburg. Washington became a surveyor at age 16. Sometime after Lawrence's death in 1752, he inherited the family

estate and slaves. He was involved in local military affairs, and the royal governor sent him in 1753 on a mission to the French in the Ohio Valley. In 1754, Washington became a lieutenant colonel of militia and led an expedition into the northwest; he fought in the opening skirmish of the French and Indian War and met defeat at Fort Necessity. In 1755, he served as Braddock's aide-de-camp and as commander of the Virginia militia. In 1759, Washington resigned his commission and married a rich widow, Martha Custis, thereby becoming one of the wealthiest men in the colonies. They settled at Mount Vernon, with Washington assuming the role of influential planter. Washington served in the House of Burgesses, becoming an early supporter of the colonists' rights. Chosen as a representative of Virginia in both the First and Second Continental Congress, Washington was selected by his fellow members as commander in chief of the Continental army in June 1775. Lacking military genius, Washington lost numerous battles and seldom won clear victories; but he succeeded over the long term through his tenacity as a commander, political agility, capable administering, and adamantine determination. His major victory occurred with the surprise attack on Trenton on Christmas Day 1776. In 1781, he made the fortunate gamble that the French fleet would bottle up Cornwallis and marched his army along with Rochambeau's French army south to achieve the final victory at Yorktown. During the following two years until the British withdrew, Washington ably managed the American army's disaffected and unpaid troops. With the British gone, he resigned and returned to Mount Vernon. But in 1787, he served as presiding officer of the convention to revise the Articles of Confederation and forcefully advocated creating a strong central government. Following ratification of the Constitution, Washington was elected the first president of the United States and then reelected in 1792. Declining a third term, he delivered his Farewell Address in September 1796 and then retired to Mount Vernon.

Wayne, Anthony (1745–1796) *general in the Continental army*
Wayne was born in Pennsylvania and worked as a tanner. A member of the Pennsylvania legislature in 1774–75, he was appointed colonel of the 4th Pennsylvania Battalion in January 1776. Wayne led his troops in the battle at Trois-Rivières and afterward held command at Ticonderoga. Promoted to brigadier gen-

eral in February 1777, he commanded in the field at Brandywine and Germantown. Surprised by the British at Paoli, he lost many of his troops. Wayne planned and carried out the successful night attack to recapture Stony Point, New York, on July 16, 1779, and he thereafter continued serving in New York through 1780. In January 1781, he helped to resolve the mutiny of the Pennsylvania Line and then moved his troops south to join Lafayette in Virginia. Isolated and confronting Cornwallis's entire army at the Battle of Green Spring (July 6, 1781), he ordered his small force to charge, startling the enemy and allowing most of his men to escape to safety. At the war's end, he was breveted as a major general. Unsuccessful as a farmer in the postwar years, Wayne won election to Congress in 1791 but was denied his seat because of irregular residence. In 1792, Wayne was appointed major general and commander of an army sent to quell the Indians in the Old Northwest. He conducted a skillful campaign that culminated in a decisive victory at the Battle of Fallen Timbers in August 1794.

Wheatley, Phillis (ca. 1753–1784) *poet*

Brought to America from Africa as a slave in 1761 at age seven, according to her master John Wheatley of Boston, Wheatley attained the astonishing feat of learning English in only 16 months. She had already had several poems published in *The London Magazine* when her first collection, *Poems on Various Subjects, Religious and Moral,* gained publication in London in 1773. In 1771, Wheatley had traveled to London, where she met the Lord Mayor of London, the earl of Dartmouth, and the Countess of Huntington. In 1773, she returned to Boston to attend to her ailing mistress, Susannah Wheatley; she was granted freedom in fall 1773, six months before Mrs. Wheatley's death. The Wheatleys' daughter Mary had assumed responsibility for Phillis's education, which inspired her interest in the Bible, poet John Milton, and poet Alexander Pope; she also learned enough Latin to read some classics in that language—evidence that she was likely far more learned than most of her white contemporaries. Wheatley attained considerable status in society in both Boston and London. George Washington received her in 1776. In 1778, Wheatley married John Peters, a freeman, with whom she had three children, who all died young. Planning a second volume of poems, she died in poverty at age 31.

Wooster, David (1711–1777) *Continental army general*

Born in Stratford, Connecticut, Wooster graduated from Yale University but pursued the profession of mason. He gained extensive military experience during the colonial wars preceding the Revolution, serving as captain of a sloop, a militia officer, a commissioned officer of a British regiment, and a colonel in a Connecticut militia. The Connecticut legislature commissioned Wooster as a major general in command of six state regiments when the Revolution began in 1775, and in June of that year, the Continental Congress appointed him as a brigadier general in the Continental army, which he viewed as a demotion. Wooster disputed Philip Schuyler's order that he serve in the invasion of Canada led by Benedict Arnold. At Quebec, however, he succeeded to command following the death of Richard Montgomery; but he was soon replaced by John Thomas, who then also died, with command again reverting to Wooster. Ineffective as a commander, Wooster was recalled by the Continental Congress. He resumed his militia rank in Connecticut. Mortally wounded during the British raid on Danbury (April 27, 1777), he died five days later.

APPENDIX C
Maps

1. Benedict Arnold's Route, September 19, 1775–November 15, 1775
2. The Attack on Quebec, November 1775–May 1776
3. Battle of Bennington, August 16, 1777
4. Battle of Brandywine, September 11, 1777
5. First Battle of Saratoga, September 19, 1777
6. Battle of Germantown, October 4, 1777
7. Second Battle of Saratoga (Bemis Heights), October 7, 1777
8. Battle of Monmouth, June 28, 1778
9. Battle of Camden, August 16, 1780
10. Battle of King's Mountain, October 7, 1780
11. Battle of Cowpens, January 17, 1781
12. Battle of Guilford Courthouse, March 15, 1781
13. Battle of Eutaw Springs, September 8, 1781

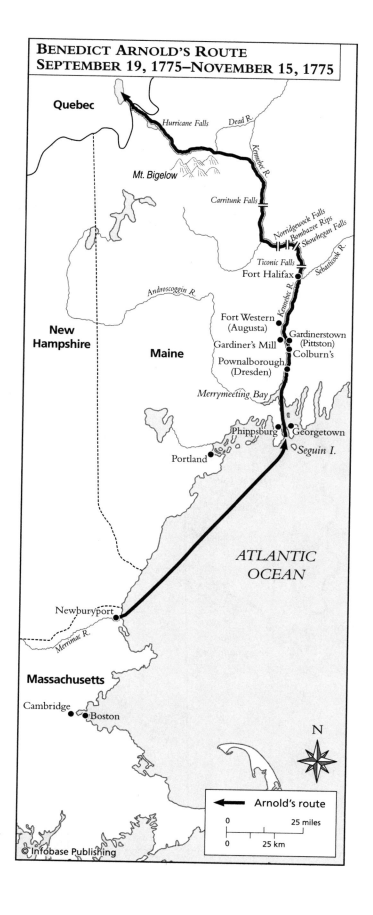

BENEDICT ARNOLD'S ROUTE
SEPTEMBER 19, 1775–NOVEMBER 15, 1775

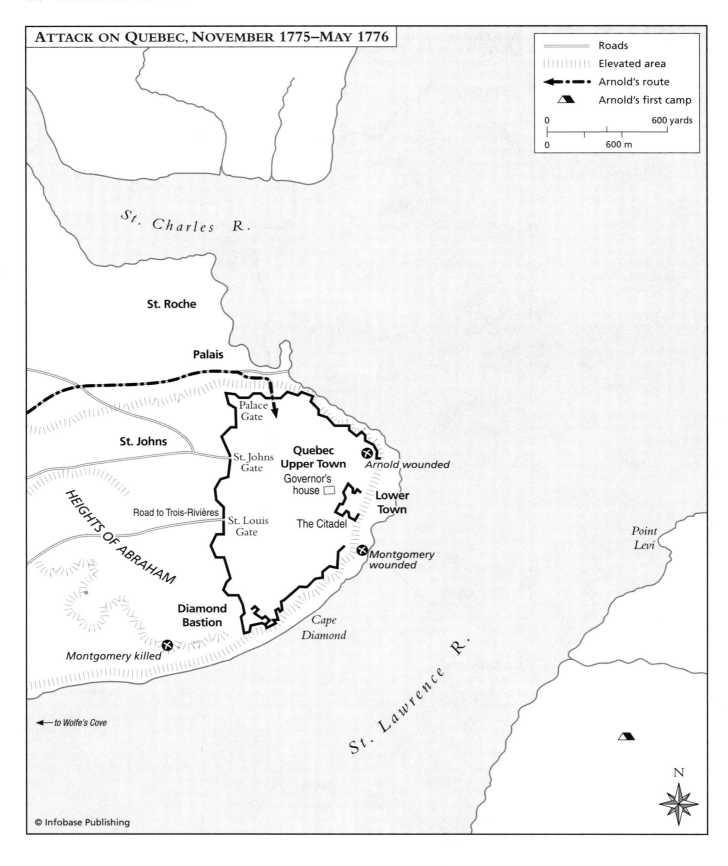

ATTACK ON QUEBEC, NOVEMBER 1775–MAY 1776

Roads

Elevated area

Arnold's route

Arnold's first camp

| 0 | | 600 yards |
| 0 | | 600 m |

St. Charles R.

St. Roche

Palais

Palace Gate

St. Johns

St. Johns Gate

Quebec Upper Town

Governor's house

Lower Town

Road to Trois-Rivières

St. Louis Gate

The Citadel

Arnold wounded

Montgomery wounded

HEIGHTS OF ABRAHAM

Diamond Bastion

Montgomery killed

Cape Diamond

St. Lawrence R.

Point Levi

to Wolfe's Cove

N

© Infobase Publishing

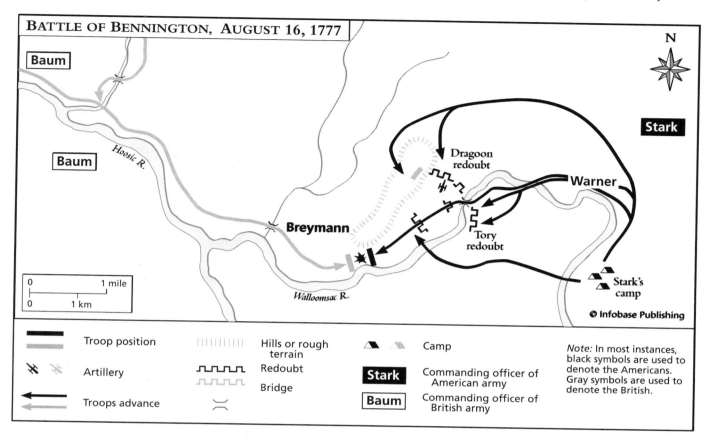

BATTLE OF BENNINGTON, AUGUST 16, 1777

N

Baum

Baum

Hoosic R.

Breymann

Walloomsac R.

Dragoon redoubt

Tory redoubt

Stark

Warner

Stark's camp

© Infobase Publishing

0   1 mile
0   1 km

	Troop position		Hills or rough terrain		Camp

Troop position — Hills or rough terrain — Camp

Artillery — Redoubt

Troops advance — Bridge

Stark Commanding officer of American army

Baum Commanding officer of British army

Note: In most instances, black symbols are used to denote the Americans. Gray symbols are used to denote the British.

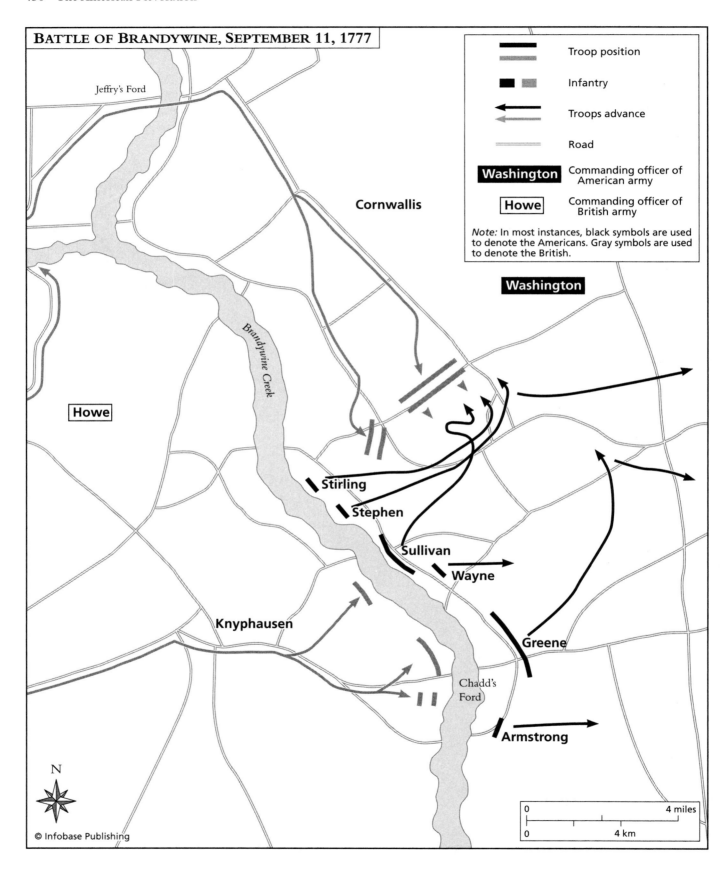

BATTLE OF BRANDYWINE, SEPTEMBER 11, 1777

Jeffry's Ford

Cornwallis

Brandywine Creek

Howe

Washington

	Troop position
	Infantry
	Troops advance
	Road
Washington	Commanding officer of American army
Howe	Commanding officer of British army

Note: In most instances, black symbols are used to denote the Americans. Gray symbols are used to denote the British.

Washington

Stirling

Stephen

Sullivan

Wayne

Knyphausen

Greene

Chadd's Ford

Armstrong

N

0   4 miles

0   4 km

© Infobase Publishing

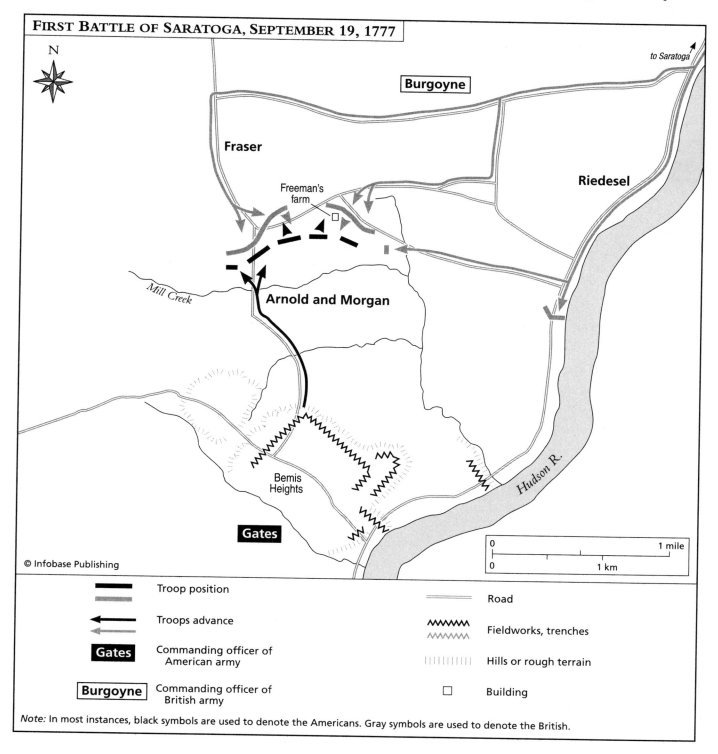

FIRST BATTLE OF SARATOGA, SEPTEMBER 19, 1777

N

to Saratoga

Burgoyne

Fraser

Riedesel

Freeman's farm

Mill Creek

Arnold and Morgan

Hudson R.

Bemis Heights

Gates

© Infobase Publishing

0   1 mile
0   1 km

Troop position

Road

Troops advance

Fieldworks, trenches

Gates   Commanding officer of American army

Hills or rough terrain

Burgoyne   Commanding officer of British army

Building

Note: In most instances, black symbols are used to denote the Americans. Gray symbols are used to denote the British.

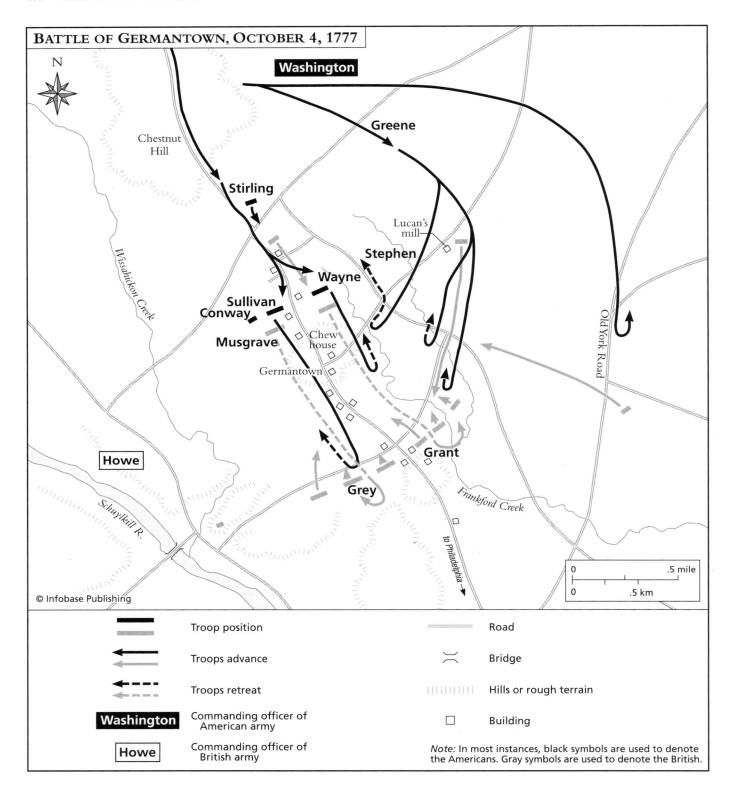

BATTLE OF GERMANTOWN, OCTOBER 4, 1777

N

Washington

Chestnut
Hill

Greene

Stirling

Wissahickon Creek

Lucan's
mill

Stephen

Wayne

Sullivan
Conway

Chew
house

Musgrave

Germantown

Old York Road

Howe

Grant

Frankford Creek

Schuylkill R.

Grey

to Philadelphia

0   .5 mile

0   .5 km

© Infobase Publishing

	Troop position		Road
	Troops advance	)(	Bridge
	Troops retreat	|||||||	Hills or rough terrain
Washington	Commanding officer of American army	☐	Building
Howe	Commanding officer of British army		*Note:* In most instances, black symbols are used to denote the Americans. Gray symbols are used to denote the British.

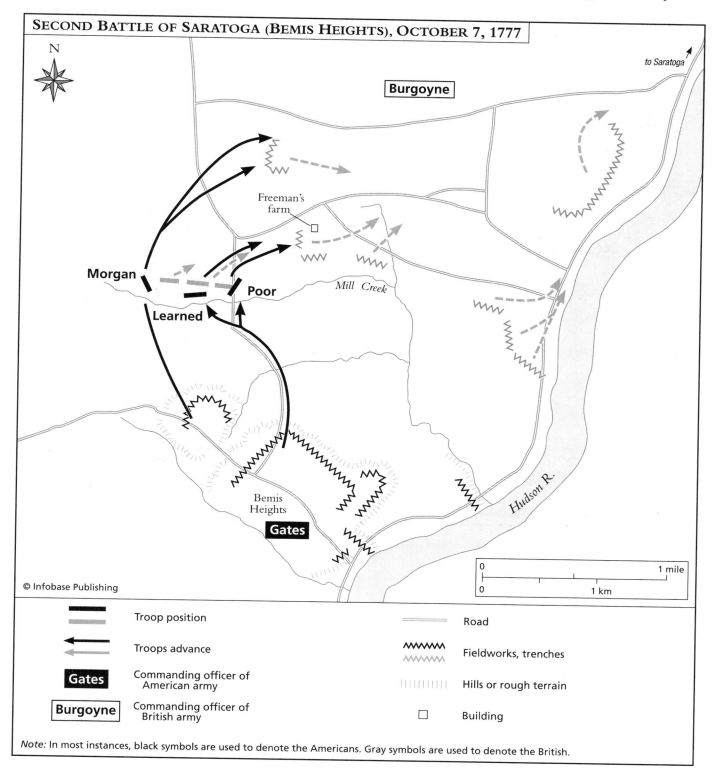

SECOND BATTLE OF SARATOGA (BEMIS HEIGHTS), OCTOBER 7, 1777

N

Burgoyne

to Saratoga

Freeman's farm

Morgan

Poor

Learned

Mill Creek

Bemis Heights

Gates

Hudson R.

© Infobase Publishing

| 0 | 1 mile |
| 0 | 1 km |

Troop position

Troops advance

Gates — Commanding officer of American army

Burgoyne — Commanding officer of British army

Road

Fieldworks, trenches

Hills or rough terrain

Building

Note: In most instances, black symbols are used to denote the Americans. Gray symbols are used to denote the British.

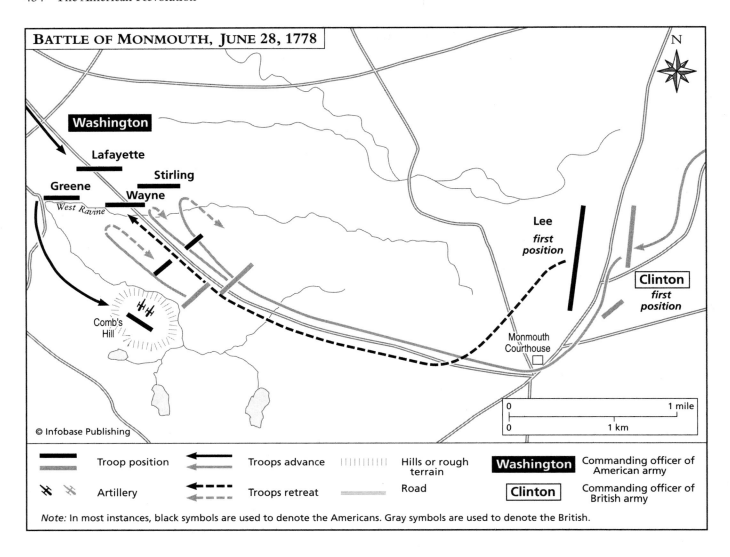

BATTLE OF MONMOUTH, JUNE 28, 1778

N

Washington

Lafayette

Stirling

Greene

Wayne

West Ravine

Comb's Hill

Lee
first position

Clinton
first position

Monmouth Courthouse

© Infobase Publishing

| 0 | | 1 mile |
| 0 | | 1 km |

| | Troop position | | Troops advance | |||||||||||| Hills or rough terrain | **Washington** | Commanding officer of American army |
| | Artillery | | Troops retreat | | Road | Clinton | Commanding officer of British army |

Note: In most instances, black symbols are used to denote the Americans. Gray symbols are used to denote the British.

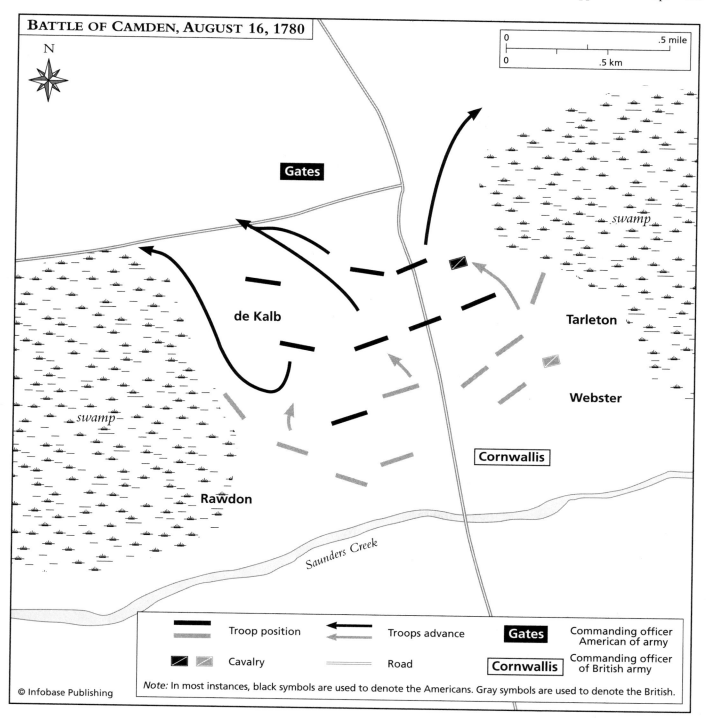

BATTLE OF CAMDEN, AUGUST 16, 1780

N

0 ——————————— .5 mile

0 ——————————— .5 km

Gates

swamp

de Kalb

Tarleton

Webster

swamp

Cornwallis

Rawdon

Saunders Creek

—— Troop position	← Troops advance	**Gates** Commanding officer American of army
◼ ◪ Cavalry	== Road	**Cornwallis** Commanding officer of British army

Note: In most instances, black symbols are used to denote the Americans. Gray symbols are used to denote the British.

© Infobase Publishing

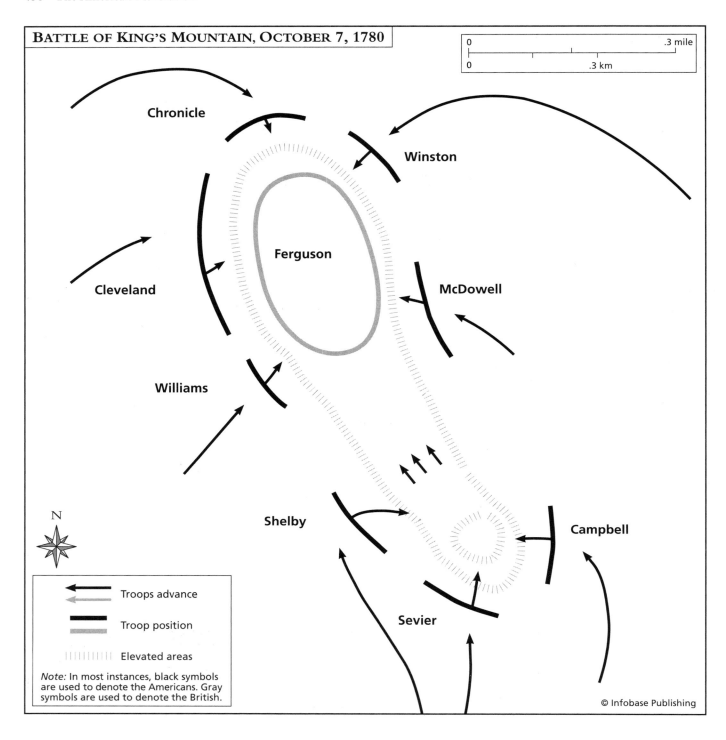

BATTLE OF KING'S MOUNTAIN, OCTOBER 7, 1780

0   .3 mile

0   .3 km

Chronicle

Winston

Ferguson

Cleveland

McDowell

Williams

Shelby

Campbell

N

Sevier

→ Troops advance

━━ Troop position

||||||||| Elevated areas

Note: In most instances, black symbols are used to denote the Americans. Gray symbols are used to denote the British.

© Infobase Publishing

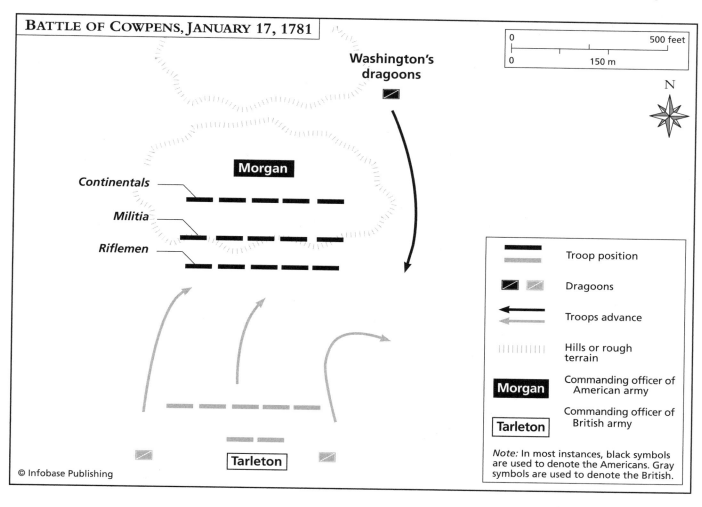

BATTLE OF COWPENS, JANUARY 17, 1781

Washington's dragoons

Morgan

Continentals

Militia

Riflemen

Tarleton

| 0 | | 500 feet |
| 0 | 150 m | |

N

	Troop position
	Dragoons
← ←	Troops advance
‖‖‖‖‖	Hills or rough terrain
Morgan	Commanding officer of American army
Tarleton	Commanding officer of British army

Note: In most instances, black symbols are used to denote the Americans. Gray symbols are used to denote the British.

© Infobase Publishing

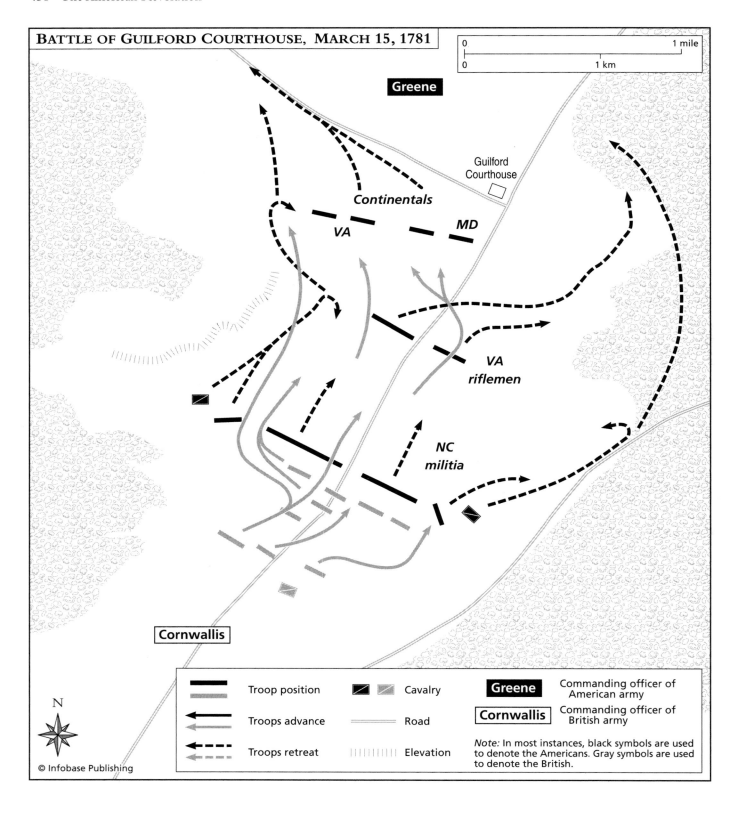

BATTLE OF GUILFORD COURTHOUSE, MARCH 15, 1781

Greene

Guilford
Courthouse

Continentals

VA   *MD*

*VA
riflemen*

*NC
militia*

Cornwallis

	Troop position		Cavalry	**Greene**	Commanding officer of American army
	Troops advance		Road	**Cornwallis**	Commanding officer of British army
	Troops retreat		Elevation		

0   1 mile
0   1 km

N

© Infobase Publishing

Note: In most instances, black symbols are used to denote the Americans. Gray symbols are used to denote the British.

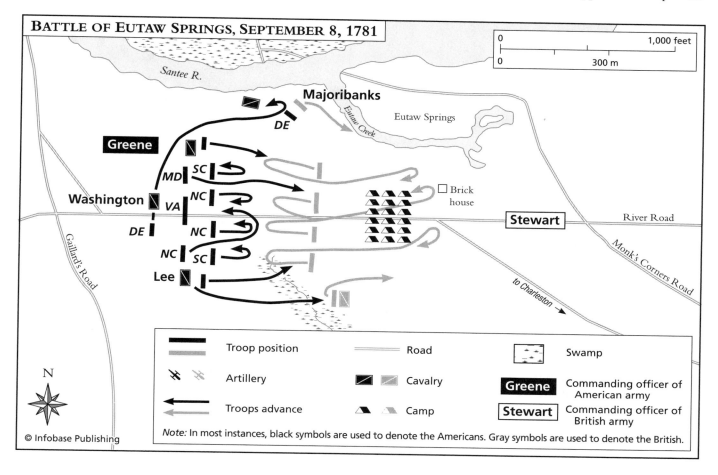

BATTLE OF EUTAW SPRINGS, SEPTEMBER 8, 1781

Santee R.

0 _____ 1,000 feet

0 _____ 300 m

Majoribanks

Eutaw Springs

DE

Eutaw Creek

Greene

MD   SC

Washington   VA   NC

Brick house

DE   NC

Stewart   River Road

NC   SC

to Charleston →

Monk's Corners Road

Lee

Gaillard's Road

N

| | Troop position | | Road | | Swamp |

| | Artillery | | Cavalry | | Greene — Commanding officer of American army |

| | Troops advance | | Camp | | Stewart — Commanding officer of British army |

Note: In most instances, black symbols are used to denote the Americans. Gray symbols are used to denote the British.

© Infobase Publishing

NOTES

1. PRELUDE TO REVOLT: 1756–1774

1. A. J. Langguth, *Patriots: The Men Who Started the American Revolution* (New York: Touchstone, 1989), pp. 296–298.
2. Fred Anderson, *Crucible of War* (New York: Alfred A. Knopf, 2000), p. 506.
3. Anderson, pp. 177–178, 211–216, 225–231, 298–304.
4. Anderson, pp. 185–202, 240–286, 325–344, 391–410, *passim.*
5. Anderson, pp. 505–510, 566, 593; Bruce Lancaster, *The American Revolution* (Boston: Houghton Mifflin, 1971), pp. 37–38.
6. Anderson, pp. 742–746; Dorothy Denneen Volo and James M. Volo, *Daily Life during the American Revolution* (Westport, Conn.: Greenwood Press, 2003), pp. *xiii–xv.*
7. Robert Middlekauff, *The Glorious Cause,* revised and expanded edition (New York: Oxford University Press, 2005), pp. 58–60.
8. Middlekauff, pp. 60–67; Anderson, pp. 574–580.
9. John Richard Alden, *The American Revolution* (New York: Harper & Row, 1954), pp. 5–6; Page Smith, *A New Age Now Begins,* Vol. I (New York: Penguin Books, 1976), pp. 189–199, 225–235; Middlekauff, pp. 74–123, *passim.*
10. Smith, Vol. I, pp. 219–224, 235, 243–249; Middlekauff, pp. 87, 128–129.
11. Smith, Vol. I, pp. 272–276; Middlekauff, pp. 166, 169, 186, 213–215.
12. Middlekauff, pp. 160–162.
13. Langguth, pp. 94–100; Smith, pp. 274–276, 281–286.
14. L. Edward Purcell and David F. Burg, *The World Almanac of the American Revolution* (New York: World Almanac, 1992), p. 15.
15. Lancaster, pp. 63–64; Smith, Vol. I, pp. 331–363.
16. Smith, Vol. I, pp. 293–299.
17. Middlekauff, pp. 219–220; Purcell and Burg, p. 19.
18. Smith, Vol. I, pp. 373–379.
19. T. H. Breen, *The Marketplace of Revolution* (New York: Oxford University Press, 2004), pp. 301–302; Smith, Vol. I, pp. 373–384.
20. Breen, p. 302; Smith, pp. 384–388.
21. Breen, pp. 302–304; Middlekauff, pp. 235–256, *passim.*
22. Smith, Vol. I, pp. 417–418, 430–444; Purcell and Burg, pp. 24–26.
23. Smith, Vol. I, pp. 442–444; Purcell and Burg, pp. 26–27.
24. Volo and Volo, p. 19.
25. Lancaster, p. 18; Middlekauff, pp. 122–124.
26. Smith, Vol. I, pp. 72–73, 675–676.
27. Richard McLanathan, *The American Tradition in the Arts* (New York: Harcourt, Brace & World, 1968), pp. 86–96.
28. Samuel M. Green, *American Art* (New York: Ronald Press, 1966), pp. 149–151.
29. Green, pp. 32–33.
30. Randall Huff, *The Revolutionary War Era, American Popular Culture through History Series* (Westport, Conn.: Greenwood Press, 2004), pp. 161–169.

2. SHOTS HEARD ROUND THE WORLD: 1775

1. Robert Middlekauff, *The Glorious Cause,* revised and expanded edition (New York: Oxford University Press, 2005), pp. 266–272; L. Edward Purcell and David F. Burg, *The World Almanac of the American Revolution* (New York: World Almanac, 1992), pp. 32–37.
2. Middlekauff, pp. 272–273; Purcell and Burg, p. 37.
3. Christopher Ward, *The War of the Revolution,* Vol. I (New York: Macmillan, 1952), pp. 33–37.

4. Mark Mayo Boatner, III, *Encyclopedia of the American Revolution* (New York: David McKay, 1974), pp. 623–625; Ward, pp. 37–39.

5. Boatner, pp. 628–629; Ward, pp. 40–51.

6. Boatner, pp. 629–631.

7. A. J. Langguth, *Patriots: The Men Who Started the American Revolution* (New York: Touchstone, 1988), p. 252.

8. Middlekauff, pp. 282–283; Ward, pp. 63–69.

9. Page Smith, *A New Age Now Begins*, Vol. I (New York: Penguin Books, 1976), pp. 543–548; Purcell and Burg, pp. 43–46, *passim.*

10. Boatner, pp. 120–129; Langguth, pp. 271–286; Gail Buckley, *American Patriots* (New York: Random House, 2001), p. 11.

11. David McCullough, *1776* (New York: Simon & Schuster, 2005), pp. 41–44; Ward, vol. 1, pp. 101–105; Buckley, p. 14.

12. Smith, Vol. I, pp. 558–563; Purcell and Burg, pp. 50–52.

13. Smith, Vol. I, pp. 594–595.

14. Smith, Vol. I, pp. 595–605; Middlekauff, pp. 309–311; Ward, vol. 1, pp. 144–162.

15. Ward, Vol. 1, pp. 183–195; Smith, Vol. I, pp. 614–617.

16. Middlekauff, pp. 318–321; Purcell and Burg, pp. 54–55, 62, 64.

17. Buckley, pp. 15–16; Elizabeth A. Fenn, *Pox Americana* (New York: Hill and Wang, 2001), pp. 49–51.

18. McCullough, pp. 61–62; Fenn, pp. 49–51; Smith, Vol. II, pp. 883–884, 1,696–1,697.

3. DECLARING INDEPENDENCE: 1776

1. L. Edward Purcell and David F. Burg, *The World Almanac of the American Revolution* (New York: World Almanac, 1992), p. 68.

2. Don Higginbotham, *The War of American Independence* (Boston: Northeastern University Press, 1983), pp. 135–137.

3. Purcell and Burg, p. 68; Page Smith, *A New Age Now Begins*, Vol. I (New York: Penguin Books, 1976), pp. 648–649.

4. Smith, Vol. I, pp. 649–655.

5. Christopher Ward, *The War of the Revolution*, Vol. I (New York: Macmillan, 1952), p. 196; Purcell and Burg, p. 79.

6. Ward, vol. 1, pp. 196–197.

7. Mark Mayo Boatner, III, *Encyclopedia of the American Revolution* (New York: David McKay, 1974), pp. 177–178.

8. Ward, Vol. 1, pp. 200–201; Boatner, pp. 178–179.

9. Robert Middlekauff, *The Glorious Cause*, revised and expanded edition (New York: Oxford University Press, 2005), pp. 323–326.

10. Purcell and Burg, pp. 72–73.

11. Smith, Vol. I, pp. 686–693, 699–702; Middlekauff, p. 325.

12. Smith, Vol. I, pp. 702–707; Middlekauff, pp. 327–328.

13. Middlekauff, pp. 338–339; A. J. Langguth, *Patriots: The Men Who Started the American Revolution* (New York: Touchstone, 1988), pp. 357–360.

14. Gail Buckley, *American Patriots* (New York: Random House, 2001), pp. 19–20, 22; Benjamin Quarles, "The Revolutionary War as a Black Declaration of Independence," in Ira Berlin and Ronald Hoffman, eds., *Slavery and Freedom* (Charlottesville: University Press of Virginia, 1983), pp. 283–285.

15. Higginbotham, pp. 152–154.

16. Higginbotham, pp. 154–159; Ward, pp. 211–227.

17. Langguth, pp. 384–385; Middlekauff, pp. 353–354.

18. Higginbotham, pp. 159–160; Middlekauff, pp. 355–356.

19. Langguth, pp. 397–398; Boatner, pp. 490–491; Smith, Vol. I, pp. 772–773.

20. David McCullough, *1776* (New York: Simon & Schuster, 2005), pp. 229–232; Smith, pp. 781–784.

21. Smith, Vol. I, pp. 785–789; Purcell and Burg, p. 105.

22. Smith, Vol. I, pp. 791–798; Langguth, pp. 399–401; David Hackett Fischer, *Washington's Crossing* (New York: Oxford University Press, 2004), pp. 121–129.

23. Fischer, pp. 131–137; Smith, pp. 804–809, 811.

24. Higginbotham, pp. 165–166; Fischer, pp. 201–203.

25. Fischer, pp. 206–220, 223–231, 234–235.

26. McCullough, pp. 404–405; Langguth, pp. 431–433.

27. Middlekauff, pp. 408–410; Purcell and Burg, pp. 102, 103, 105, 109.

28. Purcell and Burg, pp. 87, 103, 105.

4. VICTORIES AND LOSSES: 1777

1. David Hackett Fischer, *Washington's Crossing* (New York: Oxford University Press, 2004), pp. 290–291, 295–296.

2. Fischer, pp. 296–301, 305–307, 324–338; Christopher Ward, *The War of the Revolution,* Vol. I (New York: Macmillan, 1952), pp. 312–316.

3. Page Smith, *A New Age Now Begins,* Vol. II (New York: Penguin Books, 1976), pp. 875–876.

4. Robert Middlekauff, *The Glorious Cause,* revised and expanded edition (New York: Oxford University Press, 2005), pp. 371, 377; Mark Mayo Boatner, III, *Encyclopedia of the American Revolution* (New York: David McKay, 1974), pp. 100–101, 1,126.

5. Carol Berkin, *Revolutionary Mothers* (New York: Alfred A. Knopf, 2005), pp. 21–22; Joan R. Gundersen, *To Be Useful to the World* (New York: Twayne Publishers, 1996), p. 150.

6. Gundersen, pp. 149–150; Linda R. Kerber, *Women of the Republic* (Chapel Hill: University of North Carolina Press, 1980), pp. 42–43.

7. Kerber, pp. 55–61; Berkin, pp. 50–66, 67–91; Dorothy Denneen Volo and James M. Volo, *Daily Life during the American Revolution* (Westport, Conn.: Greenwood Press, 2003), p. 241.

8. Don Higginbotham, *The War of American Independence* (Boston: Northeastern University Press, 1983), p. 188.

9. Ward, vol. 1, pp. 407–410, 417–420.

10. Ward, pp. 421–431.

11. Higginbotham, pp. 182–183; Ward, pp. 328–329.

12. Ward, vol. 1, pp. 334–343, 348–353; L. Edward Purcell and David F. Burg, *The World Almanac of the American Revolution* (New York: World Almanac, 1992), p. 142.

13. Middlekauff, pp. 391–401; Smith, Vol. II, pp. 963–969; Boatner, pp. 828–829, 426–429.

14. Smith, Vol. II, pp. 908–911, 913–914.

15. A. J. Langguth, *Patriots: The Men Who Started the American Revolution* (New York: Touchstone, 1989), pp. 442–445; Purcell and Burg, pp. 142–143. .

16. Smith, Vol. II, p. 931.

17. Langguth, pp. 445–457; Richard M. Ketchum, *Saratoga* (New York: Henry Holt, 1997), pp. 390–425.

18. Higginbotham, p. 187; Smith, pp. 978–982.

19. Smith, Vol. II, pp. 983–987.

20. Higginbotham, pp. 187–188.

21. Boatner, p. 259; Purcell and Burg, pp. 118, 124–125.

22. Smith, Vol. I, pp. 844–846; Boatner, p. 43.

23. Middlekauff, pp. 409–410.

5. FROM VALLEY FORGE TO VINCENNES: 1778

1. A. J. Langguth, *Patriots: The Men Who Started the American Revolution* (New York: Touchstone, 1988), pp. 460–464; Mark Mayo Boatner, III, *Encyclopedia of the American Revolution* (New York: David McKay, 1974), pp. 278–281.

2. Robert Middlekauff, *The Glorious Cause,* revised and expanded edition (New York: Oxford University Press, 2005), pp. 419–422; Page Smith, *A New Age Now Begins,* Vol. II (New York: Penguin Books, 1976), pp. 1,026–1,027.

3. Boatner, p. 455; Dorothy Denneen Volo and James M. Volo, *Daily Life during the American Revolution* (Westport, Conn.: Greenwood Press, 2003), pp. 170–171.

4. Christopher Ward, *The War of the Revolution,* Vol. II (New York: Macmillan, 1952), pp. 549–550.

5. Randall Huff, *The Revolutionary War Era* (Westport, Conn.: Greenwood Press, 2004), pp. 161–162.

6. Smith, Vol. II, pp. 1,008–1,018.

7. L. Edward Purcell and David F. Burg, *The World Almanac of the American Revolution* (New York: World Almanac, 1992), pp. 161–162; Smith, pp. 1,061–1,063.

8. Middlekauff, pp. 413–414; Smith, pp. 1,065–1,068.

9. Smith, Vol. II, pp. 1,069–1,074; Boatner, pp. 844–845.

10. Smith, Vol. II, p. 1,257; Boatner, p. 918.

11. Middlekauff, pp. 416, 426–429.

12. Middlekauff, pp. 427–429.

13. Don Higginbotham, *The War of American Independence* (Boston: Northeastern University Press, 1983), pp. 246–247; Ward, pp. 579–585; Boatner, pp. 710–711.

14. Higginbotham, p. 322; Smith, pp. 1,190–1,196.

15. Smith, Vol. II, pp. 1,196–1,211.

16. Purcell and Burg, p. 164.

17. Colin G. Calloway, *The American Revolution in Indian Country* (New York: Cambridge University Press, 1995), p. 123; Purcell and Burg, p. 186.

18. Smith, Vol. II, pp. 1,156–1,158.

19. Middlekauff, pp. 410, 413–414.

20. Middlekauff, pp. 415–416, 438–439; Higginbotham, p. 245; Purcell and Burg, p. 182.

21. Middlekauff, pp. 436–438; Ward, pp. 586–593.

22. Higginbotham, p. 250; Boatner, p. 965.

23. Boatner, pp. 179–180, 611–612, 636; Smith, pp. 942–943; Langguth, pp. 491–494; Smith, pp. 1,143–1,144.

24. Smith, Vol. II, pp. 1,027–1,029.
25. Purcell and Burg, p. 171; Smith, p. 1,304; Boatner, pp. 1,033–1,034.

6. A GREAT SEA BATTLE: 1779

1. Claude Van Tyne, *The Loyalists in the American Revolution* (New York: Burt Franklin, 1970), p. 85; Robert McCluer Calhoon, *The Loyalists in Revolutionary America, 1760–1781* (New York: Harcourt Brace Jovanovich, 1973), pp. 39, 370–371; Page Smith, *A New Age Now Begins,* Vol. II (New York: Penguin Books, 1976), pp. 1,342–1,343; Christopher Ward, *The War of the Revolution,* Vol. II (New York: Macmillan, 1952), pp. 596–597.
2. Ward, Vol. II, pp. 598–600; Gail Buckley, *American Patriots* (New York: Random House, 2001), p. 26.
3. Ward, Vol. II, pp. 600–602.
4. Smith, Vol. II, 1,353–1,358.
5. Don Higginbotham, *The War of American Independence* (Boston: Northeastern University Press, 1983), pp. 354–355; Smith, Vol. II, pp. 1,310–1,311.
6. Ward, Vol. II, p. 684.
7. Smith, Vol. II, pp. 1,319–1,322; Ward, Vol. II, pp. 684–687.
8. Ward, Vol. II, p. 867.
9. Benjamin Quarles, "The Revolutionary War as a Black Declaration of Independence," in Ira Berlin and Ronald Hoffman, eds., *Slavery and Freedom in the Age of the American Revolution* (Charlottesville: University Press of Virginia, 1983), p. 291; Sylvia R. Frey, *Water from the Rock* (Princeton, N.J.: Princeton University Press, 1991), pp. 108, 113–114.
10. Buckley, pp. 24–25; Smith, Vol. II, pp. 1,804–1,806.
11. Ward, Vol. II, pp. 688–694.
12. Higginbotham, pp. 322–323.
13. Higginbotham, pp. 324–325; Smith, pp. 1,202–1,211.
14. Ward, Vol. II, pp. 638–641.
15. Ward, pp. 642–643.
16. Ward, pp. 643–645; Colin G. Calloway, *The American Revolution in Indian Country* (New York: Cambridge University Press, 1999), pp. 51–53.
17. Calloway, pp. 15–19, 23–25.
18. Calloway, pp. 26–29, 31–33, 36–37.
19. Calloway, pp. 46–56, 58–60, 62–64.
20. Higginbotham, pp. 341–342; Smith, pp. 1,273–1,275.
21. Smith, Vol. II, pp. 1,275–1,281.
22. L. Edward Purcell and David F. Burg, *The World Almanac of the American Revolution* (New York: World Almanac, 1992), p. 196.
23. Purcell and Burg, pp. 196–197.
24. Smith, Vol. II, pp. 1,147–1,149, 1,519; Purcell and Burg, pp. 203, 219, 225.
25. Joan R. Gundersen, *To Be Useful to the World* (New York: Twayne Publishers, 1996), pp. 162–163; Carol Berkin, *Revolutionary Mothers* (New York: Alfred A. Knopf, 2005), pp. 43–49.
26. A. J. Langguth, *Patriots: The Men Who Started the American Revolution* (New York: Touchstone, 1988), p. 494; Smith, Vol. II, pp. 1,556–1,559.
27. Smith, Vol. II, pp. 1,557, 1,560–1,563; Purcell and Burg, p. 227.

7. DEFEAT AND TREACHERY: 1780

1. L. Edward Purcell and David F. Burg, *The World Almanac of the American Revolution* (New York: World Almanac, 1992), p. 230.
2. Page Smith, *A New Age Now Begins,* Vol. II (New York: Penguin Books, 1976), pp. 1,513–1,516; Christopher Ward, *The War of the Revolution,* Vol. II (New York: Macmillan, 1952), pp. 611–615.
3. Ward, Vol. II, pp. 620–623.
4. Walter Edgar, *Partisans and Redcoats* (New York: William Morrow, 2001), p. 49.
5. Robert Middlekauff, *The Glorious Cause,* revised and expanded edition (New York: Oxford University Press, 2005), pp. 444–446.
6. Edgar, pp. 49–50; Robert McCluer Calhoon, *The Loyalists in Revolutionary America, 1760–1781* (New York: Harcourt Brace Jovanich, 1973), pp. 491–492.
7. Middlekauff, p. 446.
8. Edgar, pp. 50–51; Middlekauff, pp. 449–455.
9. Middlekauff, p. 455.
10. Mark Bayo Boatner, III, *Encyclopedia of the American Revolution* (New York: David McKay, 1974), p. 939; Don Higginbotham, *The War of American Independence* (Boston: Northeastern University Press, 1983), pp. 379–380.
11. Higginbotham, p. 361; Smith, Vol. II, pp. 1,394–1,396.
12. Higginbotham, pp. 357–358; Middlekauff, pp. 459–460.
13. Ward, Vol. II, pp. 724–730; Higginbotham, pp. 359–360.
14. Smith, Vol. II, pp. 1,558–1,566.

15. Smith, pp. 1,572–1,587.
16. Boatner, pp. 41–42; Langguth, pp. 506–509.
17. Smith, Vol. II, pp. 1,584–1,588; Langguth, pp. 502, 509.
18. Middlekauff, p. 469; Boatner, p. 607.
19. Higginbotham, p. 402; Langguth, p. 518; Purcell and Burg, pp. 233, 235, 255.
20. Ward, Vol. II, pp. 727–747.
21. Ward, pp. 748–749; Smith, pp. 1,435, 1,444–1,446.

8. AN IMPROBABLE TRIUMPH: 1781

1. Don Higginbotham, *The War of American Independence* (Boston: Northeastern University Press, 1983), pp. 403–405; Page Smith, *A New Age Now Begins,* Vol. II (New York: Penguin Books, 1976), pp. 1,605–1,623.
2. Christopher Ward, *The War of the Revolution,* Vol. II (New York: Macmillan, 1952), pp. 755–762.
3. Ward, Vol. II, pp. 764–766; Higginbotham, pp. 367–369.
4. Smith, Vol. II, pp. 1,470–1,477; Ward, pp. 778–783.
5. Ward, Vol. II, pp. 784–793.
6. Ward, pp. 798–807.
7. Higginbotham, pp. 372–373; Robert Middlekauff, *The Glorious Cause,* revised and expanded edition (New York: Oxford University Press, 2005), pp. 496–497.
8. Ward, Vol. II, pp. 866–869.
9. Ward, Vol. II, pp. 870–871.
10. Mark Bayo Boatner, III, *Encyclopedia of the American Revolution* (New York: David McKay, 1974), pp. 1,149–1,152.
11. Ward, Vol. II, pp. 879–880; Higginbotham, p. 380; Boatner, pp. 1,194–1,195; L. Edward Purcell and David F. Burg, *The World Almanac of the American Revolution* (New York: World Almanac, 1992), p. 277.
12. Ward, Vol. II, pp. 880–882; Higginbotham, p. 380.
13. Ward, Vol. II, pp. 882–884.
14. Ward, Vol. II, pp. 884–885; Smith, pp. 1,668, 1,675–1,687.
15. Smith, Vol. II, pp. 1,688–1,691; Ward, pp. 823–834.
16. Smith, Vol. II, pp. 1,693–1,696.
17. Smith, Vol. II, pp. 1,697–1,710; A. J. Langguth, *Patriots: The Men Who Started the American Revolution* (New York: Touchstone, 1989), pp. 533–541; Gail Buckley, *American Patriots* (New York: Random House, 2001), pp. 33–34.
18. Smith, Vol. II, pp. 1,538.

19. Smith, Vol. II, p. 1,539; Boatner, pp. 743–744.
20. Ward, Vol. II, p. 895; Smith, Vol. II, pp. 1,717–1,719; Middlekauff, p. 590; Langguth, pp. 542–544.
21. Samuel Rezneck, *Unrecognized Patriots* (Westport, Conn.: Greenwood Press, 1975), pp. 15, 27–29, 69–71, 81–97.

9. AN UNPROMISING OUTCOME: 1782–1783

1. Page Smith, *A New Age Now Begins,* Vol. II (New York: Penguin Books, 1976), pp. 1,728–1,731; Robert Middlekauff, *The Glorious Cause,* revised and expanded edition (New York: Oxford University Press, 2005), pp. 591–592.
2. Middlekauff, p. 591; Don Higginbotham, *The War of American Independence* (Boston: Northeastern University Press, 1983), p. 422.
3. Higginbotham, pp. 423–425; Smith, pp. 1,725–1,728.
4. Smith, Vol. II, pp. 1,731–1,739.
5. Middlekauff, pp. 603–604.
6. Smith, Vol. II, p. 1,812; Dorothy Denneen Volo and James M. Volo, *Daily Life during the American Revolution* (Westport, Conn.: Greenwood Press, 2003), p. 249.
7. Smith, Vol. II, pp. 1,221–1,226, 1,229–1,230; Mark Bayo Boatner, III, *Encyclopedia of the American Revolution* (New York: David McKay, 1974), pp. 436, 601.
8. Middlekauff, p. 558; Boatner, pp. 183, 939; Claude H. Van Tyne, *The Loyalists in the American Revolution* (New York: Burt Franklin, 1970), pp. 288–289; L. Edward Purcell and David F. Burg, *The World Almanac of the American Revolution* (New York: World Almanac, 1992), pp. 298–299.
9. Smith, Vol. II, pp. 1,762–1,763.
10. Smith, Vol. II, pp. 1,764–1,765; A. J. Langguth, *Patriots: The Men Who Started the American Revolution* (New York: Touchstone, 1988), pp. 557–558.
11. Langguth, pp. 558–559; Higginbotham, pp. 409–411; Smith, Vol. II, pp. 1,768–1,772.
12. Langguth, p. 550; Smith, Vol. II, pp. 1,777–1,780.
13. John Resch, *Suffering Soldiers* (Amherst: University of Massachusetts Press, 1999), pp. 1–4.
14. Middlekauff, pp. 593–595; Purcell and Burg, pp. 303, 304, 305–306.
15. Smith, Vol. II, pp. 1,758–1,761, 1,784, 1,788–1,792; Sylvia R. Frey, *Water from the Rock* (Princeton, N.J.: Princeton University Press, 1991), pp. 193–199.

BIBLIOGRAPHY

Adams, John. *Diary and Autobiography of John Adams.* Edited by L. H. Butterfield. Vol. 2. Cambridge, Mass.: Belknap Press of Harvard University, 1961.

Adams, Samuel. *The Writings of Samuel Adams.* Edited by Harry Alonzo Cushing. Vol. 3. New York: G. P. Putnam's Sons, 1907.

Alden, John Richard. *The American Revolution.* New York: Harper & Row, 1954.

Anderson, Fred. *Crucible of War: The Seven Years' War and the Fate of Empire in British North America, 1754–1766.* New York: Alfred A. Knopf, 2000.

André, John. *Major André's Journal: Operations of the British Army under Lieutenant Generals Sir William Howe and Sir Henry Clinton.* Reprint. New York: Arno Press, 1968.

Angell, Israel. *Diary of Colonel Israel Angell.* Edited by Edward Field. Reprint. New York: Arno Press, 1971.

Bailyn, Bernard, ed. *Pamphlets of the American Revolution, 1750–1776.* 2 vols. Cambridge, Mass.: Belknap Press of Harvard University, 1965.

Bakeless, John Edwin. *Turncoats, Traitors, and Heroes.* New York: Da Capo Press, 1998.

Ballagh, James Curtis, ed. *The Letters of Richard Henry Lee.* 2 vols. New York: Macmillan, 1911–1914.

Berkin, Carol. *Revolutionary Mothers: Women in the Struggle for American Independence.* New York: Alfred A. Knopf, 2005.

Berlin, Ira, and Ronald Hoffman, eds. *Slavery and Freedom in the Age of the American Revolution.* Charlottesville: University Press of Virginia, 1983.

Blakeley, Phyllis, and John N. Grant. *Eleven Exiles: Accounts of Loyalists of the American Revolution.* Toronto: Dunburn Press, 1982.

Blumenthal, Walter Hart. *Women Camp Followers of the Revolution.* Salem, N.H.: Ayer, 1992.

Boatner, Mark Mayo, III. *Encyclopedia of the American Revolution*. New York: David McKay, 1974.

Bobrick, Benson. *Angel in the Whirlwind: The Triumph of the American Revolution*. New York: Simon & Schuster, 1997.

Bradley, Patricia. *Slavery, Propaganda, and the American Revolution*. Jackson: University Press of Mississippi, 1998.

Breen, T. H. *The Marketplace of Ideas: How Consumer Politics Shaped American Independence*. New York: Oxford University Press, 2004.

Brumwell, Stephen. *Redcoats: The British Soldier and War in the Americas, 1755– 1763*. New York: Cambridge University Press, 2002.

Buckley, Gail. *American Patriots: The Story of Blacks in the Military from the Revolution to Desert Storm*. New York: Random House, 2001.

Burke, Edmund. *Selected Writings and Speeches on America*. Edited by Thomas H. D. Mahoney. Indianapolis: Bobbs-Merrill, 1964.

Burnett, Edmund C., ed. *Letters of Members of the Continental Congress*. 8 vols. Washington, D.C.: Carnegie Institution of Washington, 1921–1936.

Butterfield, L. H., ed. *Adams Family Correspondence*. Vols. 1–2. Cambridge, Mass.: Belknap Press of Harvard University, 1963.

Calhoon, Robert M. *The Loyalists in Revolutionary America, 1760–1783*. New York: Harcourt Brace Jovanovich, 1973.

Calloway, Colin G. *The American Revolution in Indian Country: Crisis and Diversity in Native American Communities*. New York: Cambridge University Press, 1999.

Clinton, Henry. *The American Rebellion: Sir Henry Clinton's Narrative of His Campaigns, 1775–1782*. Edited by William B. Wilcox. New Haven, Conn.: Yale University Press, 1954.

Commager, Henry Steele, and Richard B. Morris, eds. *The Spirit of 'Seventy-Six: The Story of the American Revolution as Told by Participants*. 2 vols. Indianapolis: Bobbs-Merrill, 1958.

Davies, K. G., ed. *Documents of the American Revolution, 1770–1783*. Vols. 9, 11, 14, 15, 17, 18, and 21. Dublin: Irish University Press, 1975–1981.

Dickinson, H. T. *Britain and the American Revolution*. London and New York: Longman, 1998.

Dickinson, John. *The Political Writings of John Dickinson, 1764–1774*. Edited by Paul Leicester Ford. Reprint. New York: Da Capo Press, 1970.

Edgar, Walter. *Partisans and Redcoats: The Southern Conflict That Turned the Tide of the American Revolution.* New York: William Morrow, 2001.

Fenn, Elizabeth A. *Pox Americana: The Great Smallpox Epidemic of 1775–82.* New York: Hill & Wang, 2001.

Ferling, John E. *A Leap in the Dark: The Struggle to Create the American Republic.* New York and Oxford: Oxford University Press, 2003.

———. *Setting the World Ablaze: Washington, Adams, Jefferson, and the American Revolution.* New York and Oxford: Oxford University Press, 2000.

Finkelman, Paul. *Slavery, Revolutionary America, and the New Nation.* New York and London: Garland Publishing, 1989.

Fischer, David Hackett. *Washington's Crossing.* New York: Oxford University Press, 2004.

Franklin, Benjamin. *The Papers of Benjamin Franklin.* Edited by Leonard W. Labaree, et al. Vols. 6–28. New Haven, Conn., and London: Yale University Press, 1963.

———. *The Writings of Benjamin Franklin.* Edited by Albert Henry Smyth. Vols. 7–9. New York: Macmillan, 1907.

Freneau, Philip. *The Poems of Philip Freneau: Poet of the American Revolution.* Edited by Fred Lewis Pattee. 2 vols. New York: Russell & Russell, 1963.

Frey, Sylvia R. *Water from the Rock: Black Resistance in a Revolutionary Age.* Princeton, N.J.: Princeton University Press, 1992.

George III. *The Correspondence of King George the Third, from 1760 to December 1783.* Edited by Sir John Fortescue. 6 vols. London: Macmillan, 1927–1928.

Gilman, Arthur, ed. *Theatrum Majorum. The Cambridge of 1776: Wherein is Set Forth an Account of the Town, and of the Events it Witnessed: With Which is Incorporated the Diary of Dorothy Dudley.* 1876. Reprint, Fort Washington, N.Y., and London: Kennikat Press, 1970.

Granger, Bruce I. *Political Satire in the American Revolution, 1763–1783.* Ithaca, N.Y.: Cornell University Press, 1960.

Green, Samuel. *American Art: A Historical Survey.* New York: Ronald Press, 1966.

Greene, Nathanael. *The Papers of General Nathanael Greene.* Edited by Dennis M. Conrad, et al. Vols. 2–11. Chapel Hill: University of North Carolina Press, 1997.

Greenman, Jeremiah. *Diary of a Common Soldier in the American Revolution, 1775–1783: An Annotated Edition of the Military Journal of Jeremiah Greenman.* Edited by Robert C. Bray and Paul E. Bushnell. DeKalb: Northern Illinois University Press, 1978.

Gundersen, Joan R. *To Be Useful to the World: Women in Revolutionary America, 1740–1790.* New York: Twayne Publishers, 1996.

Hamilton, Alexander. *The Papers of Alexander Hamilton.* Edited by Harold C. Syrett. Vols. 1–3. New York: Columbia University Press, 1961.

Henry, John Joseph. *Account of Arnold's Campaign against Quebec.* Reprint, New York: Arno Press, 1968.

Higginbotham, Don. *The War of American Independence: Military Attitudes, Policies, and Practice, 1763–1789.* Boston: Northeastern University Press, 1983.

Holmes, Richard. *Redcoat: The British Soldier in the Age of Horse and Musket.* New York: W. W. Norton, 2002.

Huff, Randall. *The Revolutionary War Era, American Popular Culture through History Series.* Westport, Conn.: Greenwood Press, 2004.

Idzerda, Stanley J., ed. *France and the American War for Independence.* New York: Scott Limited Editions, 1976.

Jay, William. *The Life of John Jay, with Selections from His Correspondence and Miscellaneous Papers.* Vol. 1. New York: J. & J. Harper, 1833.

Jefferson, Thomas. *The Papers of Thomas Jefferson.* Edited by Julian P. Boyd. Vols. 1–3. Princeton, N.J.: Princeton University Press, 1950.

Kerber, Linda K. *Women of the Republic: Intellect and Ideology in Revolutionary America.* Chapel Hill: University of North Carolina Press, 1980.

Ketchum, Richard M. *Divided Loyalties: How the American Revolution Came to New York.* New York: Holt, 2002.

———. *Saratoga: Turning Point of America's Revolutionary War.* New York: Henry Holt, 1997.

Lafayette, Marquis de. *Memoirs, Correspondence and Manuscripts of General Lafayette.* Vol. 1. New York: Saunders and Oley, 1837.

Lancaster, Bruce. *The American Revolution.* Boston: Houghton Mifflin, 1971.

Langguth, A. J. *Patriots: The Men Who Started the American Revolution.* New York: Simon & Schuster, 1988.

Laurens, Henry. *The Papers of Henry Laurens.* Edited by David R. Chesnutt and C. James Taylor. Vols. 12–13. Columbia: University of South Carolina Press, 1990.

Lee, Henry. *The Revolutionary War Memoirs of General Henry Lee.* New York: Da Capo Press, 1998.

Lender, Mark E., and James Kirby Martin, eds. *Citizen Soldier: The Revolutionary War Journal of Joseph Bloomfield.* Newark: New Jersey Historical Society, 1982.

Macleod, Duncan. *Slavery, Race, and the American Revolution.* New York and Cambridge: Cambridge University Press, 1974.

Madison, James. *The Papers of James Madison.* Edited by William T. Hutchinson and William M. E. Rachals. Vols. 2–3. Chicago: University of Chicago Press, 1963.

Marshall, Christopher. *Extracts from the Diary of Christopher Marshall, 1774–1781.* Edited by William Duane. Reprint, New York: Arno Press, 1969.

McClanathan, Richard. *The American Tradition in the Arts.* New York: Harcourt, Brace & World, 1968.

McCullough, David. *1776.* New York: Simon & Schuster, 2005.

Middlekauf, Robert. *The Glorious Cause: The American Revolution, 1763–1789.* Revised and expanded edition. New York and Oxford: Oxford University Press, 2005.

Moore, Frank, compiler. *The Diary of the American Revolution, 1763–1789.* Edited by John Anthony Scott. Reprint, New York: Washington Square Press, 1967.

Morgan, Edmund S. *The Birth of the Republic.* Chicago: University of Chicago Press, 1967.

———. *The Challenge of the American Revolution.* New York: W. W. Norton, 1976.

Morgan, Edmund S., and Helen M. Morgan. *The Stamp Act Crisis: Prologue to Revolution.* Chapel Hill: University of North Carolina Press, 1953.

Morris, Richard B. *The American Revolution Reconsidered.* New York: Harper & Row, 1967.

———. *The Peacemakers: The Great Powers and American Independence.* New York: Harper & Row, 1965.

Morris, Robert. *The Papers of Robert Morris, 1781–1784.* Edited by E. James Ferguson. Vols. 3–4. Pittsburgh, Pa.: University of Pittsburgh Press, 1977.

Morton, Joseph C. *The American Revolution.* Westport, Conn.: Greenwood Press, 2003.

Nash, Gary B. *The Urban Crucible: Social Change, Political Consciousness, and the Origins of the American Revolution.* Cambridge, Mass.: Harvard University Press, 1979.

Neimeyer, Charles P. *America Goes to War: A Social History of the Continental Army.* New York: New York University Press, 1996.

Norton, Mary Beth. *Liberty's Daughters: The Revolutionary Experience of American Women, 1750–1800.* Boston and Toronto: Little, Brown, 1980.

Ostrander, Gilman Marston. *Republic of Letters: The American Intellectual Community, 1776–1865.* Madison, Wis.: Madison House, 1999.

Pestana, Carla Gardinia, and Sharon V. Salinger, eds. *Inequality in Early America.* Hanover, N.H.: University Press of New England, 1999.

Purcell, L. Edward. *Who Was Who in the American Revolution.* New York: Facts On File, 1993.

Purcell, L. Edward, and David F. Burg. *World Almanac of the American Revolution.* New York: World Almanac, 1992.

Rankin, Hugh F. *Narratives of the American Revolution as Told by a Young Sailor, a Home-Sick Surgeon, a French Volunteer, and a German General's Wife.* Chicago: Lakeside Press, 1976.

Raphael, Ray. *A People's History of the American Revolution: How Common People Shaped the Fight for Independence.* New York: New Press, 2001.

Reich, Jerome R. *British Friends of the American Revolution.* Armonk, N.Y.: M. E. Sharpe, 1997.

Reiss, Oscar. *Medicine and the American Revolution: How Diseases and Their Treatments Affected the Colonial Army.* Jefferson, N.C.: McFarland, 1998.

Resch, John. *Suffering Soldiers: Revolutionary War Veterans, Moral Sentiment and Political Culture in the Early Republic.* Amherst: University of Massachusetts Press, 1999.

Rezneck, Samuel. *Unrecognized Patriots: The Jews in the American Revolution.* Westport, Conn.: Greenwood Press, 1975.

Robinson, William H. *Phillis Wheatley and Her Writings.* New York and London: Garland Publishing, 1984.

Robson, Eric. *The American Revolution in its Political and Military Aspects, 1763–1783*. Hamden, Conn.: Archon Books, 1965.

Royster, Charles. *A Revolutionary People at War: The Continental Army and American Character, 1775–1783*. Chapel Hill: University of North Carolina Press, 1979.

Rush, Benjamin. *Letters of Benjamin Rush*. Edited by L. H. Butterfield. 2 vols. Princeton, N.J.: Princeton University Press, 1951.

St. Jean de Crevecoeur, J. Hector. *Letters from an American Farmer*. Edited by Warren Barton Blake. New York: E. P. Dutton, 1926.

Senter, Isaac. *The Journal of Isaac Senter, on a Secret Expedition against Quebec*. Reprint, New York: Arno Press, 1969.

Shy, John W. *The American Revolution*. Northbrook, Ill.: AHM Publishing, 1973.

Silverman, Kenneth. *A Cultural History of the American Revolution: Painting, Music, Literature, and Theatre in the Colonies and the United States from the Treaty of Paris to the Inauguration of George Washington, 1763–1789*. New York: T. Y. Crowell, 1976.

Smith, Page. *A New Age Now Begins: A People's History of the American Revolution*. 2 vols. New York: Penguin Books, 1976.

Smith, Paul H. *Loyalists and Redcoats: A Study in British Revolutionary Policy*. Chapel Hill: University of North Carolina Press, 1964.

Syrett, David. *The Royal Navy in European Waters during the American Revolution*. Columbia: University of South Carolina Press, 1998.

Tucker, Robert W. *The Fall of the First British Empire: Origins of the War of American Independence*. Baltimore: Johns Hopkins University Press, 1982.

Van der Weyde, William M. *The Life and Works of Thomas Paine*. Patriots edition, vols. 2–4. New Rochelle, N.Y.: Thomas Paine National Historical Association, 1925.

Van Doren, Mark, ed. *Travels of William Bartram*. New York: Dover Publications, 1928.

Van Tyne, Claude Halstead. *The Loyalists in the American Revolution*. Gansevoort, N.Y.: Corner House Historical Publications, 1999.

Volo, Dorothy Denneen, and James M. Volo. *Daily Life during the American Revolution*. Westport, Conn.: Greenwood Press, 2003.

Ward, Christopher. *The War of the Revolution,* 2 vols. New York: Macmillan, 1952.

Washington, George. *The Writings of George Washington from the Original Manuscript Sources, 1745–1799.* Edited by John C. Fitzpatrick. Vols. 2–25. Washington, D.C.: U.S. Government Printing Office, 1931.

Webb, Samuel Blachley. *Correspondence and Journals of Samuel Blachley Webb.* Edited by Worthington Chauncey Ford. Vol. 2. 1893. Reprint, New York: Arno Press, 1969.

INDEX

Locators in *italics* indicate illustrations. Locators in **boldface** indicate main entries/topics and biographies. Locators followed by *m* indicate maps. Locators followed by *c* indicate chronology entries.